The Rise and Fall of the Third Reich: The History and Legacy of Nazi Germany under Adolf Hitler

By Charles River Editors

Nazis in Munich's St. Mary's Square during the Beer Hall Putsch

About Charles River Editors

Charles River Editors provides superior editing and original writing services across the digital publishing industry, with the expertise to create digital content for publishers across a vast range of subject matter. In addition to providing original digital content for third party publishers, we also republish civilization's greatest literary works, bringing them to new generations of readers via ebooks.

Sign up here to receive updates about free books as we publish them, and visit Our Kindle Author Page to browse today's free promotions and our most recently published Kindle titles.

Introduction

Members of the Nazi Party during the Beer Hall Putsch

"You can see that what motivates us is neither self-conceit or self-interest, but only a burning desire to join the battle in this grave eleventh hour for our German Fatherland ... One last thing I can tell you. Either the German revolution begins tonight or we will all be dead by dawn!" - Hitler

"I cannot remember in my entire life such a change in the attitude of a crowd in a few minutes, almost a few seconds ... Hitler had turned them inside out, as one turns a glove inside out, with a few sentences. It had almost something of hocus-pocus, or magic about it." - Dr. Karl Alexander von Mueller

It is often claimed that Adolf Hitler rose to power in Germany through democratic means, and while that is a stretch, it is true that he managed to become an absolute dictator as Chancellor of Germany in the 1930s through a mixture of politics and intimidation. Ironically, he had set such a course only because of the failure of an outright coup attempt known as the Beer Hall Putsch about a decade earlier.

At the close of World War I, Hitler was an impoverished young artist who scrapped by through selling souvenir paintings, but within a few years, his powerful oratory brought him to the forefront of the Nazi party in Munich and helped make the party much more popular. A smattering of followers in the hundreds quickly became a party of thousands, with paramilitary forces like the SA backing them, and at the head of it all was a man whose fiery orations denounced Jews, communists and other "traitors" for bringing upon the German nation the Treaty of Versailles, which had led to hyperinflation and a wrecked economy.

During the first few years of the decade, the government in Munich had actually supported the fledgling Nazi party as a counterweight against the communists, which had attempted a coup years earlier, but it would nearly come back to haunt the authorities on November 8, 1923, when Hitler and his forces attempted to start a revolution and take over the city. Backed by men like Rudolf Hess, Hermann Goering, and Ernst Röhm, Hitler and the Nazis came perilously close to succeeding, and they may have been undone only because of the SA's refusal to initiate violence against German police and Army members.

By the following day, the police and Army put down the putsch, which climaxed with a short firefight in which the man standing next to Hitler was killed by a shot through the lungs, a bullet that came close to striking the future Fuhrer in the torso. However, despite being the instigator and being arrested in its aftermath as a traitor, the political atmosphere not only saved Hitler from a potential death sentence but practically made him a sympathetic figure. He would end up serving less than a year in prison (during which he dictated *Mein Kampf* to Hess), and as soon as he was released he went back to working with the Nazis, now convinced that the path to power lay through peaceful means.

The early 1930s were a tumultuous period for German politics, even in comparison to the ongoing transition to the modern era that caused various forms of chaos throughout the rest of the world. In the United States, reliance on the outdated gold standard and an absurdly parsimonious monetary policy helped bring about the Great Depression. Meanwhile, the Empire of Japan began its ultimately fatal adventurism with the invasion of Manchuria, alienating the rest of the world with the atrocities it committed. Around the same time, Gandhi began his drive for the peaceful independence of India through nonviolent protests against the British.

It was in Germany, however, that the strongest seeds of future tragedy were sown. The struggling Weimar Republic had become a breeding ground for extremist politics, including two opposed and powerful authoritarian entities: the right-wing National Socialists and the left-wing KPD Communist Party. As the 1930s dawned, these two totalitarian groups held one another in a temporary stalemate, enabling the fragile ghost of democracy to continue a largely illusory survival for a few more years.

That stalemate was broken in dramatic fashion on a bitterly cold night in late February 1933, and it was the Nazis who emerged decisively as the victors. A single act of arson against the famous Reichstag building proved to be the catalyst that propelled Adolf Hitler to victory in the elections of March 1933, which set the German nation irrevocably on the path towards World War II. That war would plunge much of the planet into an existential battle that ultimately cost an estimated 60 million lives.

Given its importance, the burning of the Reichstag has been viewed as a turning point in history, but the mystery over who was actually responsible still lingers. Officially, a German court convicted and executed a Dutch Communist, Marinus van der Lubbe, and the Nazis would rail against the fire as a Communist plot in the ensuing weeks. Van der Lubbe claimed at trial that he acted alone, and many Communists accused the Nazis of conducting the fire as a false flag operation, but in any case, in the wake of the fire, Communists across Germany were purged, allowing Hitler and the Nazis to strengthen their hold on political power.

Like other totalitarian regimes, the leader of the Nazis kept an iron grip on power in part by making sure nobody else could attain too much of it, leading to purges of high-ranking officials in the Nazi party. Of these purges, the most notorious was the Night of the Long Knives, a purge in the summer of 1934 that came about when Hitler ordered the surprise executions of several dozen leaders of the SA. This fanatically National Socialist paramilitary organization had been a key instrument in overthrowing democratic government in Germany and raising Hitler to dictatorial power in the first place. However, the SA was an arm of the Nazi phenomenon which had socialist leanings and which was the private army of Ernst Röhm, which was enough for Hitler to consider the organization dangerous. Röhm was a challenger to the Fuhrer's position with his mushrooming SA ranks, which were more loyal to him than to the nominal head of Nazi Germany.

Though the SA as a whole survived Hitler's purge, its star was eclipsed by the rise of the newly favored Schutzstaffel (SS), which was instrumental in implementing the Night of the Long Knives. Additionally, the SA's senior leadership was decimated, leading to a loss of cohesion and focus. Even its overall commander, Ernst Röhm, fell victim to Hitler's violence, and Hitler himself later spoke words which summed up the calculated ruthlessness he used to deal with his enemies, both domestic and foreign: "The victor will not be asked afterwards whether he told the truth or not. When starting and waging war it is not right that matters, but victory. Close your hearts to pity. Act brutally."

Several other factions were also involved. The German Army, or Reichswehr, was theoretically limited to a total of 100,000 men by the treaties ending World War I, but the German military was one of the major keys to power. Röhm dreamed of subsuming it totally into the SA, a nightmare from the point of view of the highly conservative and aristocratic officer corps. A man who championed the cause of the Reichswehr and kept it free of subordination to the SA could likely win its loyalty for years to come regardless of his own political and cultural agenda, which Hitler managed to accomplish with the purge.

"My good friends," the mustached, bony man with thick eyebrows and large, strong teeth somewhat reminiscent of those of a horse, shouted to the crowds from the second-floor window of his house at 10 Downing Street, "this is the second time in our history, that there has come back to Downing Street from Germany peace with honor. I believe it is peace for our time." (McDonough, 1998, 70).

The man addressing the crowd, British Prime Minister Neville Chamberlain, had just returned from the heart of Nazi Germany following negotiations with Adolf Hitler, and the crowd gathered outside the English leader's house on September 30, 1938 greeted these ringing words with grateful cheers. The piece of paper Chamberlain flourished exultantly seemed to offer permanent amity and goodwill between democratic Britain and totalitarian Germany. In it, Britain agreed to allow Hitler's Third Reich to absorb the Sudeten regions of Czechoslovakia without interference from either England or France, and since high percentages of ethnic Germans – often more than 50% locally – inhabited these regions, Hitler's demand for this territory seemed somewhat reasonable to Chamberlain and his supporters. With Germany resurgent and rearmed after the disasters inflicted on it by the Treaty of Versailles following World War I, the pact – known as the Munich Agreement – held out hope of a quick end to German ambitions and the return of stable, normal international relations across Europe.

Of course, the Munich agreement is now notorious because its promise proved barren within a very short period of time. Chamberlain's actions either failed to avert or actually hastened the very cataclysm he wished to avoid at all costs. The "Munich Agreement" of 1938 effectively signed away Czechoslovakia's independence to Hitler's hungry new Third Reich, and within two years, most of the world found itself plunged into a conflict which made a charnelhouse of Europe and left somewhere between 60-80 million people dead globally.

Many people hailed Chamberlain's "success" at defusing Nazi aggression by handing over Czechoslovakia tamely to Hitler's control, but others remained dubious. Édouard Daladier, the French prime minister, "later told Amery that he turned up his coat collar to protect his face from rotten eggs when he arrived in Paris." (Gilbert, 1963, 179-180). A Foreign Office man, Orme Sargent, was disgusted, and he later said bitterly, "For all the fun and cheers, you might think they were celebrating a major victory over an enemy instead of merely the betrayal of a minor ally." (Gilbert, 1963, 180). Winston Churchill, the deal's most famous critic, bitterly remarked, "England has been offered a choice between war and shame. She has chosen shame, and will get war."

Munich is widely reviled today and is held up as the epitome of appeasement, but historians still debate its effects on the Second World War, as well as Neville Chamberlain's character and motivations. Some believe the attempted appeasement of Nazi Germany hastened, or even caused, the mayhem occupying the next seven years. Others believe that the pact merely failed to alter war's inevitable arrival in either direction. Historians and authors alternately interpret Chamberlain as a bumbling, arrogant fool, a strong-willed statesman who simply miscalculated the nature of Hitler and Nazi Germany, or even a man with dictatorial ambitions surreptitiously inserting himself into the Fuhrer's orbit and prevented from further damaging democracy only by his fall and death from bowel cancer. Another possible interpretation, with considerable documentary support, asserts Chamberlain wished to enlist Germany's aid against the state most Europeans perceived as the true threat of the era, the Soviet Union.

Europe's attempts to appease him, most notably at Munich in 1938, failed, as Nazi Germany swallowed up Austria and Czechoslovakia by 1939. Italy was on the march as well, invading Albania in April of 1939. The straw that broke the camel's back, however, was Germany's invasion of Poland on September 1 of that year. Two days later, France and Great Britain declared war on Germany, and World War II had begun in earnest.

Of course, as most people now know, the invasion of Poland was merely the preface to the Nazi blitzkrieg of most of Western Europe, which would include Denmark, Belgium, and France by the summer of 1940. The resistance put up by these countries is often portrayed as weak, and the narrative is that the British stood alone in 1940 against the Nazi onslaught, defending the British Isles during the Battle of Britain and preventing a potential German invasion.

At the beginning of 1941, it was unclear whether the Allies would be able to remain in the war for much longer. British Prime Minister Winston Churchill had already immortalized the men of the Royal Air Force with one of the West's most famous war-time quotes, but the potential of a German invasion of Britain still loomed. With the comfort of hindsight, historians now suggest that the picture was actually more complex than that, but the Battle of Britain, fought throughout the summer and early autumn of 1940, was unquestionably epic in scope. The largest air campaign in history at the time, the vaunted Nazi Luftwaffe sought to smash the Royal Air Force, but thankfully, the RAF stood toe to toe with the Luftwaffe and ensured Hitler's planned invasion was permanently put on hold. The Allied victory in the Battle of Britain inflicted a psychological and physical defeat on the Luftwaffe and Nazi regime at large, and as the last standing bastion of democracy in Europe, Britain would provide the toehold for the June 1944 invasion of Europe that liberated the continent. For those reasons alone, the Battle of Britain was one of the decisive turning points of history's deadliest conflict.

In the warm predawn darkness of June 22, 1941, 3 million men waited along a front hundreds of miles long, stretching from the Baltic coast of Poland to the Balkans. Ahead of them in the darkness lay the Soviet Union, its border guarded by millions of Red Army troops echeloned deep throughout the huge spaces of Russia. This massive gathering of Wehrmacht soldiers from Adolf Hitler's Third Reich and his allied states – notably Hungary and Romania – stood poised to carry out Operation Barbarossa, Hitler's surprise attack against the country of his putative ally, Soviet dictator Joseph Stalin.

Though Germany was technically Russia's ally, Stalin had no delusions that they were friends. Instead, he used this time to build up his forces for what he saw as an inevitable invasion. First, on the heels of the German invasion of Poland in September 1939, Stalin had his troops invade and reclaim the land Russia had lost in World War I. Next he turned his attention to Finland, which was only 100 miles from the newly named Leningrad. He initially tried to negotiate with the Finnish government for some sort of treaty of mutual support. When this failed he simply invaded. While the giant Russian army ultimately won, the fact that little Finland held them off for three months demonstrated how poorly organized the bigger force was.

Stalin knew that if he could delay an invasion through the summer of 1941, he would be safe for another year, but Hitler began to plan to invade Russia by May of 1941. Since military secrets are typically the hardest to keep, Stalin soon began to hear rumors of the invasion, but even when Winston Churchill contacted him in April of 1941 warning him that German troops seemed to be massing on Russia's border, Stalin remained dubious. Stalin felt even more secure in his position when the Germans failed to invade the following May.

What Stalin did not realize was that Hitler had simply overstretched himself in Yugoslavia and only planned to delay the invasion by a few weeks. Hitler aimed to destroy Stalin's Communist regime, but he also hoped to gain access to resources in Russia, particularly oil. Throughout the first half of 1941, Germany dug in to safeguard against an Allied invasion of Western Europe as it began to mobilize millions of troops to invade the Soviet Union. Stalin even refused to believe the report of a German defector who claimed that the troops were massing on the Soviet border at that very moment.

The Soviets were so caught by surprise at the start of the attack that the Germans were able to push several hundred miles into Russia across a front that stretched dozens of miles long, reaching the major cities of Leningrad and Sevastopol in just three months. The first major Russian city in their path was Minsk, which fell in only six days. In order to make clear his determination to win at all costs, Stalin had the three men in charge of the troops defending Minsk executed for their failure to hold their position. This move, along with unspeakable atrocities by the German soldiers against the people of Minsk, solidified the Soviet will. In the future, Russian soldiers would fight to the death rather than surrender, and in July, Stalin exhorted the nation, "It is time to finish retreating. Not one step back! Such should now be our main slogan. ... Henceforth the solid law of discipline for each commander, Red Army soldier, and commissar should be the requirement — not a single step back without order from higher command."

As the beginning the start of the fighting on the Eastern Front, the deadliest part of history's deadliest war, Operation Barbarossa would turn out to be arguably the most fateful choice of World War II., but if it wasn't, that distinction may very well go to another decision made in the second half of 1941.

The United States began 1942 determined to avenge Pearl Harbor, but the Allies, now including the Soviet Union by necessity, did not agree on the war strategy. In 1941, both the Germans and British moved armies into North Africa, where Italy had already tried and failed to reach the Suez Canal. The British sought American help in North Africa, where British General Bernard Montgomery was fighting the legendary "Desert Fox," General Erwin Rommel. At the same time, Stalin was desperate for Allied action on the European continent that could free up the pressure on the besieged Soviets.

President Roosevelt had a consequential decision to make, and he eventually decided to land American forces on North Africa to assist the British against Rommel, much to Stalin's chagrin. While the Americans and British could merely harass the Germans with air power and naval forces in the Atlantic, Stalin's Red Army had to take Hitler's best shots in Russia throughout 1942. But the Red Army's tenuous hold continued to cripple the Nazi war machine while buying the other Allies precious time.

As it turned out, Roosevelt's decision to first fight in North Africa would make an Allied invasion of the European continent possible in 1943. As Rommel pushed east, he now had to worry about American forces to his west. The Allies eventually gained the upper hand across North Africa after the battle at El Alamein near the end of 1942 that all but forced the Germans to quit the theater without achieving their objectives.

With the Axis forced out of North Africa, the Allies had freed up its North African forces for an invasion of Western Europe. Moreover, with North Africa as a potential staging around for that invasion, the Germans had to prepare for the possibility of the Allies invading not only from Britain but also from North Africa. The Allies would make that decision in early 1943.

Entering 1943, the Allies looked to press their advantage in the Pacific and Western Europe. The United States was firmly pushing the Japanese back across the Pacific, while the Americans and British plotted a major invasion somewhere in Western Europe to relieve the pressure on the Soviets. By the time the Allies conducted that invasion, the Soviets had lifted the siege of Stalingrad. The Allies were now firmly winning the war.

Even before the British and Americans were able to make major strategic decisions in 1943, a massive German surrender at Stalingrad in February marked the beginning of the end for Hitler's armies in Russia. From that point forward, the Red Army started to steadily push the Nazis backward toward Germany. Yet it would still take the Red Army almost an entire two years to push the Germans all the way out of Russia.

In July, just a few months after the surrender at Stalingrad, the Allies conducted what at the time was the largest amphibious invasion in history, coordinating the landing of two whole armies on Sicily, over a front more than 100 miles long. Within weeks of the beginning of the Allied campaign in Italy, Italy's government wasted no time negotiating peace with the Allies and quickly quit the war.

Though Italy was no longer fighting for the Axis, German forces continued to occupy and control Italy in 1943. The Germans attempted to resist the Allies' invasion on Sicily but were badly outmanned and outgunned, leading to a German evacuation of the island within a month. The Allies would land on the mainland of Italy in September and continue to campaign against the Germans there.

With Allied forces firmly established in Italy, the British and Americans began to plot a much more massive invasion to liberate Western Europe from the Nazis. In December 1943, President Roosevelt appointed General Dwight Eisenhower Supreme Allied Commander for the upcoming invasion, with General Montgomery as the top British commander coordinating with Eisenhower.

During the first half of 1944, the Americans and British began a massive buildup of men and resources in England, while the military leaders devised an enormous and complex amphibious invasion of Western Europe. Though the Allies used misinformation to try deceiving the Germans, the sensible place for an invasion was just across the narrow English Channel. The Germans had built coastal fortifications throughout France to protect against just such an invasion, requiring the Allies to use an elaborate battle plan that would include naval and air bombardment, paratroopers, and even inflatable tanks that would be able to fire on fortifications from the coastline, all while landing nearly 150,000 men across nearly 70 miles of French beaches. The Allies would then use their beachhead to create an artificial dock, eventually planning to land nearly 1 million men in France.

In June 1944, the Allies waited for the right weather to stage the largest, most complex invasion in military history. On June 6, 1944, General Eisenhower, who had already written a letter apologizing for the failure of the invasion and was carrying it in his coat, commenced the D-Day invasion.

From the very beginning of June 6, 1944, events were not going as the Allies had planned. Though the weather was good enough to carry out the amphibious invasion, low cloud-cover caused the Allies' planes to mostly miss German fortifications on their bombing runs. Furthermore, the plan called for tens of thousands of paratroopers to land directly behind German lines, but bad visibility caused many of them to be dropped out of place. And basically none of the operations on the integral Omaha Beach went according to plan. Allied leaders would have likely been astounded to hear that victory in Europe would be achieved in 11 months.

Despite the problems, by nightfall the Allies had managed to accomplish their objectives in every landing point, at the cost of about 10,000 casualties. Throughout the summer, Allied forces advanced east along a wide front, liberating vast swaths of France and Western Europe. On August 25, 1944, the Allies finally liberated Paris.

While the British, Canadians and Americans pushed east, the Red Army pushed west. During their nearly three year stay in Russia, the Germans had completely burned and destroyed thousands of Russian villages and murdered millions of Russian citizens. The Red Army was seeking revenge by the end of 1944.

Facing imminent defeat, Hitler ordered one last desperate offensive against the Allies in December 1944 in the Ardennes, where the Nazis had surprised the French 4 years earlier. Known as the Battle of the Bulge, the Nazis bent but could not break the Allies' advancing lines. Realizing that the Germans were nearing their end, the Allies in the west and the Soviets in the east began the race to Berlin.

After resisting the German attack during the Battle of the Bulge, the Allied armies began advancing, and with that, the race to Berlin was truly on. While much has been written of the Battle of the Bulge, Okinawa, Midway, Stalingrad, and many other conflicts of the Second World War, the Battle for Berlin has remained in the shadows for many historians. Its importance in toppling Hitler cannot be denied, despite the fact that some thought its strategic value unnecessary to the war itself. The capture of the city and the red Soviet banner hanging victorious over the Reichstag is one of history's most famous (an ominous) images. In the weeks it took for the Battle of Berlin to be fought, an American president passed away, a British Prime Minister had to make concessions he did not desire, a Russian leader fought his way into Western Europe to stay, and a German one took his own life. The battle's implications would be felt for the next 50 years.

In April 1945, the Allies were within sight of the German capital of Berlin, but Hitler refused to acknowledge the collapsed state of the German military effort even at this desperate stage, and he confined himself to his Berlin bunker where he met for prolonged periods only with those that professed eternal loyalty, even to the point of death. In his last weeks, Hitler continued to blame the incompetence of military officers for Germany's apparent failings, and he even blamed the German people themselves for a lack of spirit and strength. As their leader dwelled in a state of self-pity, without remorse or mercy but near suicide, the people of Berlin were simply left to await their fate as Russians advanced from the east and the other Allies advanced from the west.

Most Berliners had given up hope of a win, and few cared for anything but relief from their circumstances, but Berliners did have a deep fear of which of the victor nations would arrive in Berlin first. The Soviets, closing in from hard fought battles in the east, had lost millions of men in the war already, and with an invasion force 2.5 million strong, they longed for revenge and a chance to right the wrongs of not only this war but the last. Even for Berliners too exhausted to be saddened by a German loss, "liberation" by the Soviets was unthinkable. At the same time, though most believed it would not happen, the Americans and British suddenly appeared to shift priorities regarding the need to take the actual capital city. Since it was "no longer a military objective", according to Eisenhower, it would be left for the Soviet armies to arrive in Berlin first, bringing to fruition many Germans' worst fears.

The battle would technically begin on April 16, 1945, and though it ended in a matter of weeks, it produced some of the war's most climactic events and had profound implications on the immediate future. In the wake of the war, the European continent was devastated, leaving the Soviet Union and the United States as uncontested superpowers. This ushered in over 45 years of the Cold War, and a political alignment of Western democracies against the Communist Soviet bloc that literally split Berlin in two.

The Rise and Fall of the Third Reich: The History and Legacy of Nazi Germany under Adolf Hitler chronicles the rise and fall of the Nazi regime. Along with pictures of important people, places, and events, you will learn about Nazi Germany like never before.

The End of World War I

Pictures of Canadian soldiers fighting at Valenciennes in November 1918

"At eleven o'clock this morning came to an end the cruellest and most terrible War that has ever scourged mankind. I hope we may say that thus, this fateful morning, came to an end all wars." – David Lloyd George, November 11th, 1918

By early November 1918, the Allies were steadily pushing the Germans back across the Western Front. The Americans and French moved forward in the Meuse-Argonne area, the British and ANZAC troops pressed forward around the St Quentin Canal, the Army Group Flanders in the North advanced, and the British, Australian and Canadian troops continued from Cambrai. In the wake of their relatively bloodless victory at Cambrai, British and ANZAC troops resupplied and then broke through the German lines where they had attempted to rally at Naves and Thun-Saint-Martin, but the Allies held up again around Le Cateau, where the Germans had once again turned a river into a natural defensive bulwark by fortifying the eastern bank of the Selle River and dominating its approaches with guns and machineguns. The British commander, General Henry Rawlinson, had to determine how his troops would negotiate the river itself, then the fortified railway embankment on the eastern bank, and finally storm the heavily defended ridge beyond, which could rake the entire approach with heavy fire. While Field Marshal Haig advanced with his troops 5 miles eastwards towards the Selle to outflank the German positions at le Cateau, General Rawlinson paused for almost a week so that his heavy artillery could come up and commence bombarding the German defensive positions.

By this point, despite tens of thousands of Allied casualties suffered while securing the Selle and le Cateau, the German army was virtually spent as a fighting force. Hundreds of thousands of German soldiers were dead, incapacitated or captured, many of them irreplaceable veterans. Germany simply could not field more soldiers than were being lost, even by calling up age classes which had been considered ineligible for mobilization at the start of the war, or fudging the numbers by forcing sick or wounded men to take up arms. Additionally, the Royal Navy blockade ensured that Germany was virtually bereft of supplies, so the rations received by soldiers on the front were increasingly insufficient to meet their needs or absent altogether. There was also a dearth of ammunition and medical supplies, not to mention machineguns and light and heavy artillery pieces, of which the Allies had captured hundreds in their lightning advance.

At 11:00 a.m. on the 11th day of the 11th month, the "war to end all wars" finally came to an end. The Armistice brought about the cessation of all offensive activities in Europe, and the points detailed in the text of the armistice itself were mainly decided by Marshal Foch. Though based upon Woodrow Wilson's Fourteen Points, what they meant in brief was a complete and utter defeat for Germany. All military hostilities were to cease immediately within six hours, and Germany would withdraw all remaining troops from France, Luxembourg, Belgium and Alsace-Lorraine within two weeks. The Germans would also be obliged to pull back from their positions in Turkey, Romania and Austro-Hungary and resume the 1914 border line. Likewise, they would have to withdraw all forces on the Western front to the Rhine and submit to Allied occupation of a buffer zone. The German navy would also be confined to port, and all its submarines surrendered to the Allies, along with 5,000 artillery pieces, 25,000 machine guns, 3,000 mortars, 1,700 airplanes, 5,000 train locomotives and 150,000 train cars.

A painting depicting the signing of the Armistice in a carriage of Foch's private train, CIWL #2419

Foch (second from right in the front) at the signing of the Armistice

As the terms suggest, there was no sympathy for the Germans, either in the armistice terms or in those of the peace that followed. Likewise, public opinion (and that of the troops who had fought so hard and for so long) was strongly in favor of making examples out of the Germans. Millions had died, France and Belgium had been devastated, and Russia had been plunged into bloody revolution, and it was firmly believed that the Germans had been responsible for all of it and thus deserved everything they got. Accordingly, the Allies kept firing upon the German positions right until the very last possible second before the armistice came into effect. Carting spare ammunition back to the artillery depots seemed like an unnecessary task when it could simply be fired at the Germans, particularly in case they decided not to honor the terms of the agreement. In fact, Allied artillery was responsible for over 10,000 casualties on November 11th alone, with what was likely the final shot of the war being fired by Battery 4 of the U.S. Navy's Railway Guns at 10:57:30.

What followed World War I in the shell-shocked vacuum of a war-ravaged Germany is well-known, and the merits of meting out such a ruthless punishment on the losers, and the resentment and hatred this fostered within the German population, has been debated at length. That said, it is difficult not to sympathize with the decision-makers who forced the terms of surrender down the Kaiser's throat after seeing millions of their young men march off to fight and die against what they saw as unrepentant German aggression. The peace process was always bound to be an emotional issue, particularly for the French and Belgians at the table who had seen huge swaths of their countries turned into barren, shell-blasted wastelands by four years of warfare.

Still, some of the veterans at the time presumed the Great War would not be the "war to end all wars." Indeed, Foch himself prophetically asserted, "This is not a peace. It is an armistice for 20 years."

The Nazi Party After the War

Defeat in World War I left Germany reeling with shame, injured pride, and deep resentment, as well as racked by economic woes. The nation had been filled with discontent and problems even before the conflict began, including an extremely poisonous and widespread anti-Semitism which flourished because the Jews were defenseless and thus formed a group upon whom the miserable and destitute could take out their frustrations with impunity.

As a result, the combination of military and economic collapse at the end of the war left Germany subject to widespread economic pain and violent social conflict, the kind of conditions that lead to revolutions much like the one that had swept up Russia in 1917. "Fear and hatred ruled the day in Germany at the end of the First World War. Gun battles, assassinations, riots, massacres and civil unrest denied Germans the stability in which a new democratic order could flourish." (Evans, 2005, 100). Indeed, the communist Spartacists attempted a bloody revolution until they were crushed by the paramilitary right-wing Freikorps, which rose as a counter to the then very real threat of communist totalitarianism, and a general fear of the communist menace remained even after the Spartacists were broken decisively. Ironically that would allow for the formation of other paramilitary forces like the SA that Hitler would end up utilizing in his rise to power.

The problems were further exacerbated by the transition from class-based traditional society to modern culture, with its rationalism, emphasis on individual freedom, and intellectually penetrating doubts about the long-settled cultural status quo and its frequently illogical taboos and prejudices. Issues such as hair styles, modes of dress, and the role of women grew to overwhelming threats to civilization itself in the fevered imaginations of socially conservative elements, who were often those most paradoxically ready to embrace radical authoritarian politics.

The varied factions occupied a strange common ground in one regard: their frenzied anti-Semitism. A demonic, utterly destructive, inhuman Jew was seen behind every phenomenon that was hated, feared, or suspected, even those of diametrically opposed character. Germany's collective imagination deemed the Jews to be simultaneously architects of capitalist tyranny over the workers and communist incendiaries seeking to rouse Bolshevik hordes to slit the throats of entrepreneurs and good, honest, hard-working Germans. Every Jew who had ever lived or who was then living was viewed not as a regular person but as a bizarrely fanatical, devilish saboteur dedicated to destroying all society, culture, art, and hope on the earth. World War I had been lost, it was asserted, not because the Germans had been overwhelmed by force of numbers but because the Jews had stabbed the Imperial army in the back. This myth was vigorously fostered by the army's top generals, who wished to divert blame for the defeat from themselves.

The fear, despair, and deprivation of the German people quickly coalesced into action, usually anti-democratic and marked by outbursts of violence. The era "brought with it a 'new wind' in politics throughout Germany [...] The wind blew from the trenches, from the schools, from the universities [...] Fanned by it, a large number of political and political-military groups developed in postwar Germany [...] the new groups [...] opposed all existing political groups, institutions, and doctrines, and were to a considerable extent mutually competitive and destructive." (Gordon, 1972, 3).

Thus, a number of right-wing organizations quickly emerged in the years following Germany's surrender. One of the earliest of these was the Stahlhelm, or "Steel Helmets," a paramilitary veterans' organization which was both highly revolutionary and, in many ways, conservative. The Sturmabteilung (SA), which formed later, shared many of the Stahlhelm's goals but frequently espoused a working-class, brutally socialist agenda that the Steel Helmets found contemptible.

Political parties also flourished in the postwar years. The Social Democrats and the Center Party were the most rational of these, and they largely sought to create a stable republic amid the era's ongoing chaos and economic shocks. Dedicated to a peaceful and law-abiding cultural and political outlook, however, they found it difficult to rein in the other parties and factions, which had no such scruples. The German communist party, or KDP, remained a force even after the Spartacists, though its star was on the wane and it never mustered enough Reichstag seats to counter the other parties' agendas.

Looming behind all the other factions and parties was the Reichswehr, the German Army. Though nominally reduced to an active strength of 100,000 men by the treaties that ended World War I, millions of ex-soldiers still identified closely with it and thought of themselves as military men first and foremost, giving it tremendous power. Led by a "fiercely monarchist and ultra-conservative officer corps" (Evans, 2005, 102), the Army was also the main wielder of legally sanctioned armed force in Germany, making it an ally worth cultivating by any politician or demagogue seeking real, lasting power.

The soldiery also represented an excellent recruiting pool for any right-wing faction or leader who claimed the restoration of Germany's strength and glory as a primary objective: "[L]ife for the majority was an aimless, day-to-day affair, since the war had alienated the soldiers from everything that gives meaning to a civilian existence. In many cases their whole lives had been disrupted by the war [...] Baffled by the unfamiliar problems of earning a living in the civilian world, they yearned in their drab idleness after the heroic bustle that for so long had given direction and meaning to their lives and an outlet to their hunger for action." (Fest, 29).

Throughout all of this, the overarching problem for the Weimar Republic was the economy. The interplay of three factors – war reparations, taxes, and inflation – created a deadly puzzle from which the government ultimately proved unable to extract itself in time. War reparations demanded large amounts of money, but raising taxes infuriated all levels of society to the point of a real threat to oust the current government. The combination dealt a serious blow to the tenuous efforts at recovery made by the prostrate German economy.

Initially, the government's solution was to print vast quantities of money, which removed the need to raise taxes but also led to runaway hyperinflation. A moderate level of inflation would have been constructive, providing the growing capital needed for a modern economy to diversify, create new industries, and generate high-paying jobs, but the inflation rose far beyond this optimal level. That said, the policies did result in a rapid re-industrialization of Germany, which would prove highly useful to Hitler and the Nazi Party in the 1930s, even as one economic catastrophe after another came during the 1920s."Even the most diehard reactionary might eventually have learned to tolerate the Republic if it had provided a reasonable level of economic stability and a decent, solid income for its citizens. But from the start it was beset by economic failures of a dimension unprecedented in German history." (Evans, 2005, 125).

The inflationary process snowballed in a bizarre and unstoppable manner in late 1922 and into 1923, the year the Beer Hall Putsch took place in November. The Germans fell behind on coal shipments to France, which formed a part of their reparations to that country, and as a result, the French and Belgians invaded and seized the Ruhr district in early 1923. The loss of this coal and industrial district was a crippling blow to the already collapsing Germany economy, and extreme hyperinflation resulted. In mid-1922, $1 was worth 1,000 marks, but by the start of 1923, it was worth 4.2 trillion marks.

Naturally, the consequences for ordinary people were devastating. Considering the rise in inflation, it is perhaps astonishing that mayhem and serious attempts at revolution did not occur sooner. "The German correspondent of the British Daily Mail reported on 29 July 1923: "In the shops the prices are typewritten and posted hourly. For instance, a gramophone at 10 a.m. was 5,000,000 marks but at 3 p.m. it was 12,000,000 marks. A copy of the Daily Mail purchased on the street yesterday cost 35,000 marks but today it cost 60,000 marks." (Evans, 2005, 127).

The terror of the ordinary German, confronted by their own utter helplessness in a situation that must have appeared surreal and nightmarish to those trapped within it, was profound. The inflation struck at the most basic and inescapable need of everyone: the ability to eat. "The most dramatic and serious effects were on the price of food. A woman sitting down in a cafe might order a cup of coffee for 5,000 marks and be asked to give the waiter 8,000 for it when she got up to pay an hour later. A kilo of rye bread, that staple of the German daily diet, cost 163 marks on 3 January 1923 […] and 233 billion marks [...]on 19 November. At the height of the hyperinflation, over 90 per cent of the expenditure of an average family went on food." (Evans, 2005, 127).

After the First World War, Georges Clemenceau had wanted to destroy Germany's strength permanently with crippling reparations. Woodrow Wilson, showing far more statesmanship, took the position that exacting no reparations was a preferable course, which might allow a recovering country where democracy could take hold. The French and British, however, overruled this wise counsel and proceeded with their plan, and the French seizure of the Ruhr in 1923 precipitated the worst of the hyperinflation, creating utter desperation in the German population. Workers streamed into the farmland during the summer, attempting to seize crops from the fields, which the equally desperate farmers defended lethally, resulting in shootouts in the German countryside.

Clemenceau

In 1924, the American government once again showed a level head by negotiating the Dawes Plan, the brainchild of Nobel prize winner Charles G. Dawes. In broad strokes, this plan ended the French occupation of the Ruhr, giving the Germans back an industrial region critical for their economy, and it set up a staggered payment plan for the reparations which the Germans could actually meet without complete impoverishment. The United States also made massive loans to the German government in an effort to bolster its economy and give it the means necessary to pay the reparations without inflating its currency.

However, the damage caused by the British and French policies had been done. The economic recovery was slow and tentative, despite the Americans' best efforts, and fury, fear, resentment, hate, and humiliation filled the hearts of millions of Germans. Huge paramilitary organizations dedicated to exacting what amounted to a national revenge sprang up and attracted more and more followers every time the economic recovery faltered even slightly.

Perhaps most crucially, a man with a cookie-duster mustache and dreams of a Thousand-Year Reich, the extermination of Jews, and the rise of Germany as a dominant military power became a known political figure in the desperate days of 1923. At the moment when Germany was writhing in the fatal grip of hyperinflation and facing the real prospect of mass starvation in late 1923, and when the relief offered by the Dawes Plan still lay unseen several months in the future, this man emerged to challenge the world powers and issue the call for Germany's renewal. That man was Adolf Hitler, and the event which permanently catapulted him into the national and international political arena was the Beer Hall Putsch.

After his years as a pauper in Vienna, where he was frequently reduced to sleeping on park benches or in doorways after his mother died and her small pension ceased to be paid, Hitler moved to Munich, and he would return there after fighting in World War I. Thus, Munich was the place where his first experiment with revolutionary Nazi politics, the Beer Hall Putsch, would occur.

Hitler as a soldier in World War I

Hitler's choice of Munich as his base of operations for the new, political phase of his life was inspired. The Bavarian city had become a bastion of extreme right-wing politics and various fascist movements, some of which were illegal in the rest of Germany, and these discontented elements formed a ready-made audience for the tirades which the young former corporal would soon unleash upon them.

Before the war, Hitler worked as an artist, displaying moderate talent in drawing or painting architectural subjects, and in Vienna, he painted famous buildings and sold these as souvenirs to visitors or to people proud of the landmarks of their city. He carried out precisely the same program in Munich, focusing on the most well-known subjects and only rarely introducing human figures into his pictures. Those days ended once Hitler joined the German army during World War I, and he was emotionally devastated when it lost. The fact of Germany's defeat, combined with his inability to accept that Germans could be defeated by any foreigner in a straight fight, unhinged him even more, and he convinced himself that "12,000 Jewish scoundrels" had somehow decided the fate of millions of armed and disciplined men fighting hundreds of miles away.

Meanwhile, the Munich he returned to was torn by factions and subject to an unsuccessful uprising by Communists, which was short-lived but had profound repercussions. The ill-armed "Red Army" was made up of a rabble of untrained workers, and its sole triumph was in executing 10 hostages, including a university professor whose only "crime" was to sneer at a communist poster in public. In response, 35,000 members of the right-wing paramilitary Freikorps, made up principally of veterans with combat training and experience, attacked and took Munich. In a wild hunt for communists and communist sympathizers, the Freikorps members in their gray jackets, riding pants, and polished jackboots slaughtered some 600 Munich residents, many of whom had nothing whatsoever to do with the "Red Army."

In the process, Munich experienced a backlash against communism which saw it become one of Germany's most right-wing cities. Many other factions were also present, but the Bavarian capital became the metropolis where fascist extremists were most common and most openly tolerated. The local government, which sought to rebuild some type of civic order after these disturbances, undertook a vigorous program of propagandizing the Bavarian soldiery with a distinctly right wing nationalist agenda, further reinforcing Hitler's already fanatical beliefs. "Where Prussia had failed, Bavaria could show the way. The whole language of politics in Munich after the overthrow of the Communist regime was permeated by nationalist slogans, antisemitic phrases, reactionary keywords that almost invited the rabid expression of counter-revolutionary sentiment." (Evans, 2005, 184).

Though Hitler's beliefs were already in full accord with this program, the indoctrination sessions – carried out by groups known as Enlightenment Commandos – likely demonstrated to him that Germany's military men thought much as he did. Clearly grasping the importance of the Army in the nation's power structure (despite the nominal limitations imposed on it by the Allies), Hitler's discovery that his own agenda was mostly mirrored in the hearts of both rank and file soldiers and the officer corps could only have bolstered his self-confidence and belief that he could make himself into a transformational figure in Germany's history. Hitler was soon employed in an Enlightenment Commando himself, which gave him the chance to express his opinions and give the world the first glimpse of his forceful, repetitive rhetorical style, filled with fire and passion rather than the tedious lectures given by most of his contemporaries. In September 1919, he received a fateful assignment when he was sent to the meeting of a small, secretive party that met in Munich beer cellars. This party was then called the German Workers' Party, or DAP, but it would soon be called the NSDAP, adding "National Socialist" to its title. Of course, it would become notorious down the road as the Nazi Party.

In 1919, however, the group was tiny and relatively powerless, and its meetings rarely attracted more than three dozen people in addition to its founders, Anton Drexler (a machine fitter) and

Karl Harrer (a sports reporter). Hitler made an impression on his first visit by rising to challenge one of the speakers who called for Bavaria to secede from Germany. Infuriated because he believed passionately in a united Germany, Hitler battered his opponent with a ferocious torrent of words that deeply impressed his handful of listeners. Drexler intercepted the pale-faced corporal at the end of the evening and asked him to come back to attend more DAP meetings.

Anton Drexler, 2. Vorsitzender der D.A.P.

Drexler

A few days later, Hitler was given a DAP membership card that made him Member 555 of the small group. This prompted him to attend several more meetings, and finally, he decided to take a hand personally in addressing the DAP membership, which he did at what was then an exceptionally large gathering of 111 listeners on October 19th, 1919. Predictably, the meeting occurred in a beer cellar called the Haufbrau Cellar. In a moment that was destined to resonate across Munich and ultimately result in tens of millions of deaths, "Hitler rose to address his first public meeting [...] In a bitter stream of words the dammed-up emotions, the lonely man's suffocated feelings of hatred and impotence, burst out [...] hallucinatory images and accusations came pouring out; abandoning restraint, he talked till he was sweating and exhausted. 'I spoke for thirty minutes,' he writes [...] Jubilantly he made the overwhelming, liberating discovery. 'I could make a good speech!'" (Fest, 1995, 27-28).

A copy of Hitler's membership card in the DAP

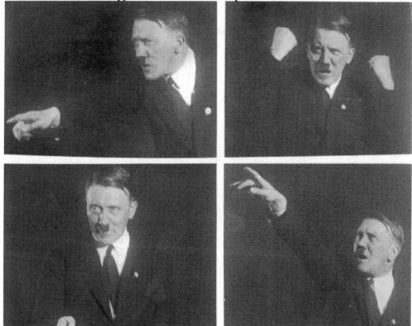

Hitler posing for the camera in the 1920s

Hitler was not the only person impressed with his speaking abilities; his rants were typically directed with frenzied persistence at Jews, a theme he seemingly never got tired of discussing, and his words clearly resonated among many fellow Germans. People began to attend these beer cellar speeches specifically to hear Hitler, and many of these people were excited and impressed enough by Hitler's speeches and his ideas to join the DAP. With that, the party's numbers began to mushroom as the corporal from the Enlightenment Commando grew ever more vigorous and bold, encouraged by the enthusiasm with which he was received. The former artistic drifter who had once slept in parks and eaten discarded food was becoming popular and savoring the hint of power that comes with popularity.

Moreover, many soldiers and former soldiers began to attend the DAP meetings and join its ranks, attracted by Hitler's steely vision of a Germany renewed in strength, "purity," and military power. They proved quite willing to shift the blame for their defeat in the war onto "treacherous" Jews and communists, two groups who soon became completely melded in the minds of Hitler's listeners. Hitler gave them the simultaneous release of disclaiming all responsibility for their own defeat and a renewed sense of pride, and many adored him for this.

Hitler also drew the notice of Ernst Röhm, the future leader of the SA, and Röhm directed yet more men to the meetings. A year later, by October of 1920, the DAP's membership had exploded from around 190 when Hitler first joined to over 5,000 members, and its growth continued rapidly thereafter, almost entirely thanks to Hitler himself. The emergent Nazi Party and Hitler were practically indistinguishable.

Ernst Röhm

The frenzied corporal soon came to the attention of the Munich government and business community, who greeted his appearance on the scene with overall approval. By December 21st, 1921, the newspapers declared that Hitler was now the leader of the NSDAP, having supplanted its founders, and this coincided with the authorities being terrified of a resurgence of communism among the restless, miserable workers. As such, Hitler was viewed as a stabilizing influence who controlled the rabble and channeled their energies in an approved direction. "The Munich Chief of Police, Pöhner, when asked whether he was aware of the existence of rightist political murder groups, gave the famous reply, 'Yes, but there aren't enough of them yet!' His subordinate, High Bailiff Frick, asserted, 'We held our protective hand over Herr Hitler and the National Socialist Party [because] we saw in it the seed of a renewal of Germany, because we were convinced from the beginning that the movement was the one suited to bring the workers back into the nationalist camp.'" (Fest, 1995, 31).

Holding magnetic sway over ordinary Germans, expressing the hopes and fears of the Army, and viewed as a solid bulwark against Communism by the Bavarian political, police, and military leadership, Hitler was able to continue expanding the Nazi Party and his own authority. He and his followers also began to develop a new social and cultural vision which did not fit readily – or at all – into the existing categories. Every other organized political system defined humanity in terms of class, whether social, economic, or a mix of both, and even the communists, for all their radicalism, did not reject this age-old form of human categorization. They simply disagreed over which class should be in command. The Nazis, however, took a new direction, one with a superficial gloss of science (which was actually false) and which enabled their message to appeal to all classes of Germans simultaneously. "[The Nazis] specifically and violently rejected the notion of class [...] They believed that the meaningful differences were to be made in terms of national differences, or, as they expressed it, in terms of 'race.' The categories as they saw them were, roughly: corrupt and debauched races, like the Jews and gypsies [...]; less valuable, but harmless races; and Nordic races, like the Germans." (Gordon, 1972, 20). If anything, the phrase "National Socialist" was largely a throwback that had no meaning to the actuality of the party, which was simultaneously socialist, capitalist, and authoritarian in economic terms (depending on which sector was involved). A more accurate label would have been "National Racist," for it was this theme that energized Hitler and his audiences alike and was the founding principle of the Third Reich.

Hitler's rhetorical techniques were simple but effective. His manner was fiery, powerfully emotional, fierce, and loud, designed to trigger the emotions of his listeners. This it did with overwhelming success, according to many surviving accounts from those who heard him speak during this period. The Nazi Party's head also believed that simple themes and endless repetition were needed to drive the message home and keep the ordinary men focused on the overall purpose of casting off the "foreign and Jewish yoke" and returning Germany to its former glory. Hitler summed up his opinion of his listeners with characteristically scornful candor: "The receptivity of the great masses is very limited, their intelligence is small, but their power of forgetting is enormous. In consequence, all effective propaganda must be limited to a very few points and must harp on these in slogans until the last member of the public understands what you want him to understand by your slogan." (Welch, 2002, 11).

Hitler also recruited and worked with a number of men who came to occupy important posts in the government of the Third Reich and/or assist with his ascent to dictatorial power. These included the coarse, brawling head of the SA, Ernst Röhm, who would be killed during Hitler's purge of the SA on the "Night of the Long Knives." Perhaps the most notorious was the wily and power-hungry former air ace, Hermann Goering, who would also lead the Luftwaffe in World War II. During this time, Hitler also recruited Rudolf Hess, the famous Deputy Fuhrer who ended up flying on a secret mission to Britain in 1941 in an effort to secure peace with the English, as well as Ernst Hanfstaengl, a businessmen whose fluency in English made him chief liaison between the Nazi party and the foreign press until his exile in 1933.

Goering

Hess

Two other notable figures were recruited by Hitler at this time. One was a Livonian German named Max Erwin von Scheubner-Richter, a man capable of concocting detailed plans of action for various projects. He laid out the details of the Beer Hall Putsch and was killed by a gunshot during it, possibly absorbing a shot which might otherwise have struck Hitler in the torso. The other was Erich Ludendorff, a World War I German infantry general. A bizarre eccentric who worshiped the ancient Norse divinity Odin and thought Christianity as worthy of destruction as Judaism, Ludendorff endorsed the Nazi Party due to its frenzied nationalism and took part in the Beer Hall Putsch.

Von Scheubner-Richter

Ludendorff

Röhm's SA, the famous "brownshirts" and "stormtroopers" who proved instrumental in Hitler's rise to power in 1933-34, was founded in direct response to the growing success of the Nazi Party with Hitler at the helm. Once it had become a recognized movement with a notable street presence, the NSDAP required some sort of "muscle" to prevent its members from being mauled by the numerous violent, unscrupulous factions also jockeying for ascendancy in the Bavarian city. Comprised of heavily armed roughnecks and discontented, impoverished men hoping to achieve a measure of success when Germany's economic disasters denied them the ordinary opportunities for a viable life, the brownshirts were far from a tame, obedient appendage of the Nazi Party, though they brawled enthusiastically with its opponents. "Founded in August 1921, the SA was meant to serve as a protection squad for Nazi meetings and leaders. Its effective commander, the ex-Reichswehr officer Ernst Röhm, had larger ambitions, hoping to mold the SA into the core of a revolutionary army aimed at overthrowing the Weimar Republic." (Brown, 2009, 60).

The other leaders of the Nazi party made one feeble attempt in 1921 to oust Hitler from his position of command over the NSDAP. While the energetic demagogue was in Berlin working to extend the party's influence nationally, Drexler and several others attempted to put him in his place and return control of the organization to themselves. However, when Hitler got wind of this effort almost immediately he returned to Munich in a fury and quashed the halfhearted "rebellion" through the simple technique of threatening to resign entirely from the Party. Since almost all of its membership was there because he was, and practically all its financial backing was explicitly offered because Hitler was in the NSDAP and could mobilize and control the workers with his thunderous oratory, accepting his resignation would have represented immediate and permanent political suicide. The Nazi Party without Hitler would have collapsed back into a powerless band of a few dozen malcontents droning futilely in beer cellars, and the hordes of followers and massive funding from the powerful would have followed the budding Fuhrer wherever he chose to go next. The other leaders had no choice but to capitulate immediately.

Hitler continued to build the NSDAP during 1922 and into 1923, attracting more members, gaining it national recognition, and reinforcing the brutal SA, which comprised its street-fighting arm. He also took note of the coup mounted by Mussolini's fascist supporters in late 1922, which elevated his Italian counterpart to the position of Duce in the nation south of the Alps. He kept an even keener lookout for an opportunity to emulate the Italian dictator and take over Germany with a coup of his own, and the hyperinflation of the next year appeared to offer him exactly what he yearned for: a chance to create a Third Reich based not on class but race and nationalism, with himself at its head as undisputed ruler.

1923

As hyperinflation burgeoned throughout Germany in 1923, Hitler and his inner circle had their metaphorical noses to the wind, smelling the opportunity for a bold coup. Despair, hopelessness, and panic provide fine tinder for a revolution, and the Nazi plotters believed that fortune was favoring them in this regard. At around this time, the government took feeble measures in an effort to curb the NSDAP, which only served to increase its fighting spirit and defiance and bring the inevitable confrontation closer.

January 1923 was a tumultuous month in German politics, both locally in Bavaria and throughout the whole country. The entire nation was on edge as prices continued to balloon alarmingly, and just two days after the New Year on January 3rd, the Bavarian government "discussed the National Socialist Party, [and] its members all agreed that the fledgling political organization was a very real menace to law and order and to the existing state. At the same time, in the way of men from time immemorial, they decided to do nothing about this menace, apparently hoping that it would abate or disappear." (Gordon, 1972, 185).

The Bavarian government, of course, had tacitly fostered the rise of Hitler's Nazi Party in order to keep a lid on the communist menace, but they were now fearful of the very organization they had partly funded and sheltered during its formative years. Their vacillating opposition was only one of many factors that brought matters to a head, but it compelled the Nazis into taking action sooner than might otherwise have been the case.

At the same time, the French, ham-handedly seeking the arrears on their war reparations, invaded the Ruhr district in this month and caused rage across Germany, as well as launching the most damaging phase of hyperinflation yet. Munich's residents were particularly livid over the French action, and nearly every political party from all portions of the spectrum began to project a mood of patriotic, martial defiance. Foreign oppression was not a mere conspiracy theory; it was objectively occurring and sending the economy hurtling toward a collapse.

In response, a bunch of extravagant national events were organized by the government. February 14th was declared to be a mourning day for the whole country, which would draw vast crowds into the streets to express their woe over Germany's defeat and subsequent suffering, and January 18th saw jingoistic mass celebrations of the Reich's founding, which were pointedly imperialistic, authoritarian, and anti-democratic in character. January 22nd was a busy day in the Munich beer halls, as the Crown Prince and various other luminaries gave rousing speeches that drew ovations from the populace and led to demonstrations, though these were mostly peaceful (other than a handful of incidental brawls and beatings).

Crown Prince Rupprecht

The NSDAP leadership took note of all these activities and decided to hold a Party Day, which was scheduled to occur on January 27th, 1923. The celebrations, which were a small-scale echo of the mass SA marches of 1933 and the later parades recorded in Leni Reifenstahl's *The Triumph of the Will*, included 12 separate rallies, mass marches, and a ceremony to formally dedicate the NSDAP's swastika banners, which, significantly, bore the three colors of the old flag of the German empire: red (the field), white (the circle at the field's center), and black (the swastika emblem itself).

On January 25th, government representatives approached Hitler and informed him that the government would not allow the Party Day to occur. Munich's officials, and the Weimar Republic's central government in Berlin, dreaded that the event would signal the start of a putsch, or coup attempt, by Hitler and his SA thugs. "Hitler reacted predictably and violently [...] He stressed the patriotism of his party [and] said that he had carefully held his men, particularly the Storm Troops, in check. Now he would give them their heads and see how the authorities liked the result. He would hold his dedication of standards (Fahnenweihe) in any case. The government could call up police and soldiers. They could shoot if they so wished. He would place himself in the front ranks." (Gordon, 1972, 187).

Having torn off the Nazi mask, the government was dismayed at what it found beneath. Eventually, it was decided to stand firm against Hitler and enforce the ban on the NSDAP Party Day celebrations. Tens of thousands of soldiers and police were mobilized in anticipation of rioting and a possible attempt at a putsch to seize power, even though many of the government leaders were dubious of their own enforcers' loyalty if actual conflict erupted. However, Hitler adroitly managed to arrive at a solution that both kept the government from interfering and appeased his followers as well; he approached the government representatives humbly, and stated that although it was too late to call off all the demonstrations and marches, he would make them much shorter and less numerous than had initially been planned. The government, eager to avoid combat in the streets, agreed to this seeming compromise.

On January 27th, the Party Day celebrations went ahead largely as originally planned. By the time they realized that they had been hoodwinked, it was too late for the government to act unless they wanted to unleash armed force on their own citizenry, which they were understandably reluctant to do. On the other hand, the feared coup did not materialize. The Nazi celebrations were predictably bombastic, but astonishingly peaceful. Hitler was not yet ready to make his move.

At this juncture, with the NSDAP in the public eye thanks to its Party Day, Röhm gathered a windfall of additional power for Hitler. In February, the short, stout, violent SA leader managed to convince no less than four right-wing Bavarian paramilitary groups to join the Nazi Party, forming what was called the Arbeitsgemeinschaft der Vaterlaendischen Kampfverbaende, or "Association of Patriotic Combat Leagues." Hitler's available armed manpower immediately skyrocketed to around 15,000 men, essentially putting him at the head of a private army. The Association of Patriotic Combat Leagues was headed by Christian Roth (general management), Hermann Kriebel (military leadership) and Wilhem Weiss (publicity), as well as Röhm. Formed on February 4th, just a week after the Nazis' Party Day show of strength, the Association flexed its muscle on May 1st when it demanded the government shut down a parade of communists taking place through Munich. The Munich Council initially declined to comply, but when the communist parade appeared to be in danger of becoming so large that a pitched battle between it and the Association was likely, the Council forced the "Reds" to hold seven much smaller parades instead, marking a partial victory for Hitler's new combat league.

With 15,000 armed men at his back and Röhm urging him to become dictator and reverse the nation's shameful surrender to the Allied powers, Hitler no longer saw any need to moderate his already rabid polemics. He began to speak in apocalyptic terms, thunderously denouncing German "traitors" – which essentially encompassed anyone who did not support the NSDAP and the Army – and speaking in increasingly alarming language about his future plans. Hitler's backing continued to swell, and by autumn of 1923, a horde of 55,000 supporters was at his beck and call. In short order, there was open talk of marching on Berlin and overthrowing the elected government.

The three main factions planning the putsch were Hitler's NSDAP (strengthened by the brownshirts and the Association of Patriotic Combat Leagues), the Freikorps, and the monarchists under von Kahr. The factions were loose allies, since all wanted to see the elected government in Berlin brought down and replaced with some species of authoritarianism. Von Seeckt provided a pithily sarcastic summary of the relationship the trio of revolutionary factions shared in 1923: "On one point there was unanimity; in no circumstances would any of the three leave action to its rivals. As the chief of the Army, General von Seeckt, commented at the time, each of the three groups was determined not to appear at all 'if the performance turned out to be a comedy', but to appear in the third act 'if it turned out to be a drama.'" (Fest, 1995, 35).

After the May 1st events, there was a brief time of relative quiet, which extended through May and June and through the first weeks of July. However, on July 14th, the Nazis held a large rally and then attempted to march into the center of the city, which was off-limits to political demonstrations of all stripes. The police attacked the SA men with rubber truncheons and, after a short but vicious brawl, forced them to retreat outside the hermetic circle of Munich's central precincts. This was the last major demonstration until autumn, but tensions continued to mount rapidly through later July and all through August.

On September 2nd, 1923, an ominous new development occurred when the various right-wing paramilitary organizations loyal to Hitler were combined into the Deutscher Kampfbund, or German Combat League. The occasion which witnessed its foundation was the celebration in Nuremberg of the German Empire's 1870 victory over the French at Sedan. The anniversary no doubt seemed highly relevant at the time, given that French armies were holding the Ruhr and strangling German industry, and the German Combat League's mission statement was quite clear and straightforward: "The objectives of the new Kampfbund were openly stated: overthrow of the Republic and the tearing up of the Treaty of Versailles." (Shirer, 2011, 71).

Hitler was made the leader of this League on September 24th, 1923 (though he was the de facto commander of the organization from the beginning and played a major role in its emergence), and he was only the German Combat League leader for three days before he began open, highly aggressive opposition to the government. The Nazi Party's activity, which had subsided to a low simmer during July and August, suddenly picked up again in the form of colossal gatherings, all of them with a highly threatening tone. Hitler set up no less than 14 simultaneous political rallies on September 27th, 1923. "Once again the government faced the menace of mass demonstrations of the National Socialists and their allies in an atmosphere of the utmost tension. It was the call for the fourteen rallies that set in motion the chain of events that led to the clash at the Feldherrnhalle on 9 November, but, in view of the determination of the Kampfbund to seize power, it is almost certain that had this match not set the trail of powder afire another would have been struck." (Gordon, 1972, 214)..

Events now began to take on a momentum of their own. The ordinary Nazis, the SA men of Röhm and Goering, and the fighters of the German Combat League were all overwhelmingly impatient to carry off a coup, topple the government, and install a new National Socialist state based on a dictatorial leader and racial politics. Hitler had stirred his followers to the point where, rather than directing them, he was now forced to come out with a plan for a putsch before he was ready, simply because he could not hold them back any longer. The paramilitaries were weary of demonstrating and chanting while taking no concrete action, and Hitler's rivals were beginning to size up their chances for a putsch of their own, which would likely cause many of the Fuhrer's supporters to abandon him and take up arms on behalf of those willing to act rather than merely rant.

Matters would come to a head in early November.

The Beer Hall Putsch

The local government recognized that Hitler and his NSDAP cronies were moving rapidly towards organizing a putsch, and in response they gave Gustav von Kahr sweeping yet also curiously limited powers to deal with the threat. Von Kahr himself was a curious figure, mixing hungry ambition almost on a par with Hitler's with a strange, bumbling incompetence that was all his own. Indeed, he was chosen in part because he was believed to be too ineffective to organize a putsch of his own despite the broad emergency powers he was granted.

Von Kahr

While that assessment was keenly accurate, von Kahr was also too ineffective to head off Hitler's incipient putsch and instead wasted time and resources. "Kahr never ceased to be a bureaucrat. He believed that action consisted of drawing up memoranda and proclamations, and his sense of his own infallibility kept him from seeing that he often mouthed empty phrases […] There is much truth in Röhm's bitter gibe that Kahr was the man of 'eternal preparations' […] Unfortunately, Kahr's characterization of Dr. Schweyer as 'the man with ten thumbs' also applies remarkably well to Kahr himself." (Gordon, 1972, 218).

Von Kahr's appointment as de facto temporary dictator of Bavaria delayed the inevitable Nazi strike slightly, but the pressures were too great to contain for long. Von Kahr carried out haphazard deportations of Jews from Bavaria in an effort to appease the NSDAP, but that only managed to infuriate all parties. The Nazis were outraged by the obvious pose and low numbers of Jews expelled, which were so paltry as to make von Kahr's motives glaringly transparent, while other groups, including the Catholic Church (a powerful influence in Bavaria), were equally disgusted by the petty tyranny of these anti-Semitic gestures.

In terms of the economy, von Kahr was well-intentioned and wanted to assist the people, but he had absolutely no knowledge of how to do so. In fairness, he was also severely limited in what he could do because of the general ruin of the German economy. Bavaria did not exist in isolation, and it is now believed by historians that even had von Kahr been far more competent in economics than was actually the case, he would have been powerless to change the course of the hyperinflation and various other major factors affecting Munich's and Bavaria's population.

Moreover, the elevation of von Kahr to this commanding position drew the wrath not only of the Nazis but of the Weimar Republic's central government. The Bavarians attempted to explain that they had appointed von Kahr to his post in order to deal with Hitler, but the central government refused to listen to these explanations. Instead, the Reichstag appointed a counter-dictator of their own choosing, Dr. Otto Gessler, to take command in Bavaria and oust von Kahr. Gessler was unable to dislodge von Kahr from his position, but the struggle between the Bavarian and German governments provided Hitler with the opportunity he had been waiting for, as both were distracted from monitoring his activities or interfering with the Nazis' preparations for a putsch because of their incompetent attempts to sabotage one another. Von Kahr and Gessler were busy trying to convince the local Army commanders, who wanted no part of this preposterous quarrel, to quash the other "dictator" and give them full command of Bavaria.

Gessler

Von Kahr's energies were stretched even thinner with his attempts to deal with the French. The French general de Metz was endeavoring to cause violence and insurrection in the areas of Germany under his control in order to destabilize and weaken the nation he loathed and feared, and while von Kahr vowed to take on this opponent, he had no men to do so and was forced to rely on what he called "intellectual resistance," which amounted to little more than wishing the French ill. "[T]his struggle was more in the nature of a flea attacking a giant. It is doubtful if the giant even knew it was being attacked." (Gordon, 1972, 234).

At this moment, Alfred Rosenberg, one of Hitler's lieutenants, came up with a plan to take over the local government bloodlessly on November 4th, 1923, and after this, the Nazis believed it would be an easy step to seeing "Bavarian fists setting things right in Berlin" (Hanser, 1971, 310). Von Kahr, the Crown Prince Rupprecht, and several leading military men were to review a parade on Memorial Day, November 4th, and a battalion of SA was to appear in this march. Rosenberg's plan was to have the SA men arrive early, which would not arouse suspicion since they were supposed to take part in the parade in any case, and they could seize Von Kahr and the other officials. At that point, Hitler could approach them and use his rhetoric – in a highly respectful manner – to convince them to lend their support to his plan for toppling the corrupt current government in Berlin and restore Germany's fortunes despite the best efforts of communists, Jews, and traitors.

This plan, half well-conceived plot and half product of lunatic optimism, was actually launched, but it did not reach a successful conclusion. In fact, its targets were never aware that it existed at all. On the morning of November 4th, 1923, the SA men arrived early, as planned, and though the military units chosen to appear in the parade were indeed absent, the SA detachment was heavily outnumbered by an unexpected battalion of armed police that surrounded the putative hostages in a dense cordon. The SA, baffled and unwilling to actually spill the blood of the police, took no action, and the November 4th putsch fizzled out.

Undeterred by that setback, Hitler was determined to have his putsch anyway. Probably canny enough to predict that the hyperinflation would eventually cease and the revolutionary mood would wane, he also wanted to strike while von Kahr was still distracted by the French, the Weimar government, and various other factions. The Beer Hall Putsch was originally planned to occur on the weekend of November 10th to 11th, dates chosen by Hitler due to the fact that "[t]he preferred time for staging a coup is the weekend, when the apparatus of government slows down to a standstill. Offices and bureaus are deserted. Officials whose hands usually grip the levers of power are away. The police and military establishments go slack. One's own people, on the other hand, are unfettered by shop and factory and can more readily assemble to devote themselves to the business at hand, such as marching, shooting, and occupying buildings." (Hanser, 1971, 314).

As fate would have it, Hitler was compelled to move the date of the putsch up by two days because of an action taken by Gustav von Kahr. The future Fuhrer believed that his ability to become the master of all Germany depended on his acting first before any other faction managed to organize a putsch or otherwise draw nationalist support decisively towards itself and away from him. However, an invitation from von Kahr was forwarded to Hitler, an unusual step since there was growing tension between the government's temporary dictator and the ambitious NSDAP leader. This invitation asked Hitler to appear at a speech where von Kahr would describe his plans for the future of Bavaria. Hitler took immediate alarm at this and decided to move the date of his putsch up so that it would occur on von Kahr's speaking date because "suspicion was growing into certainty that [von Kahr] was maneuvering toward his own coup […] The meeting and speech, whatever their announced purpose, might well be the occasion for proclaiming Bavaria's final break with Berlin, the restoration of the Wittelsbach monarchy, and Kahr's public anointment as the true Messiah of the nationalist cause." (Hanser, 1971, 315).

Thus, Hitler and his top men were left with little time to organize their coup, even less than they had originally thought. Their plan was slapdash in parts, but an effort was made to cover all eventualities as best as could be contrived with the time and resources available. Whatever else may be said of them, the early Nazis were energetic men of action, bold, confident, highly aggressive, and, in the case of many of their leaders, fairly intelligent. Men who had endured the trenches of World War I, poison gas and tank attacks, and fighting with communist revolutionaries were unlikely to sit out the putsch at home out of fear of the police, even if it might have been in their own best interests to do so. As such, bands of SA men, Combat League members, and other Nazi "muscle" were ordered to assemble and be ready for action on November 8th. This did not arouse suspicions because the NSDAP continually mustered its members in a similar fashion for demonstrations, marches, or simply to keep them in form and ready to respond to political emergencies.

This time, however, sealed orders were given to commanders with strict commands not to open them until late on November 8th. Pursuant to these orders, groups were chosen to take key installations not only in Munich but also in a number of other Bavarian towns, including Wurzburg, Nuremberg, Augsburg, Ingolstadt, and Regensburg. The targets to be occupied included communications centers (the radio stations, telegraph offices, and telephone companies), political centers (police stations, town halls, the meeting-places of rival organizations), and crucial infrastructure (the railway stations and utilities). Leading political figures were to be arrested and confined until further notice.

The main action, of course, was to transpire in Munich, and preparations here were correspondingly intensive. The intention was to involve the Army, or Reichswehr, in the putsch, though a secondary plan to seize the Infantry School and other key points was formulated in case the Army proved intransigent. It would be necessary to move large numbers of men quickly, so the NSDAP's existing fleet of vehicles was augmented with a number of rental trucks and taxis. Nazi Party members with private automobiles, delivery trucks, and the like also volunteered their vehicles for the night of the putsch, though most probably believed this was only to support major rallies and speeches.

In the meantime, Röhm came up with a simple ruse to gain more weapons without alarming the authorities. He requested rifles and pistols for a "night exercise," but he asked for no bullets. His request was readily granted and the arms were supplied, and nobody paid heed because he did not request ammunition at the same time.

Hitler committed himself to giving a speech in Freising on the evening of November 8th, 1923, thus creating the illusion that he would be absent from Munich proper when the putsch was set to occur. The Nazis also forged documents, allegedly from local Reichswehr commanders, calling for the overthrow of the Berlin government. This kept the Army and the Weimar government glaring suspiciously at each other and distracted them from keeping track of Hitler and the Nazis.

Von Kahr's speech – in which Hitler feared his rival would declare Bavaria's independence and put himself forward as the nationalist leader – was scheduled to occur at a beer hall named the Bürgerbräukeller. It had been chosen due to its huge indoor space, which could seat 3,000 comfortably at wooden tables where huge quantities of beer, sauerkraut, meat, and salted potatoes were usually consumed by the convivial Bavarians. Von Kahr was speaking in Nazi territory at the Bürgerbräukeller Cellar, which had been used by Hitler constantly over the previous years. It had, in fact, been chosen because it was the only large beer hall in Munich not in use for a different meeting, rally, or speech that night, indicating the political ferment of the Bavarian metropolis. Though some risk was anticipated, "authorities […] initially planned to place a company of Landespolizei in the building. The final decision was that this would make it look as though Kahr were afraid of the citizens […] and the police troops – forty-five men – were therefore tucked out of sight […] at least a quarter of a mile from the beer hall." (Gordon, 1972, 281-282).

Picture of a Nazi meeting at the Bürgerbräukeller in 1923

The speech was set for 8:30 p.m., so Hitler set 8:00 p.m. as the moment to begin the famous Beer Hall Putsch. Hitler began mustering his forces, and a strange, almost electrical, sense of excitement was present in the Munich streets, making the people uneasy. Munich was a city of many demonstrations, riots, and political brawls which began with truncheons and fists and ended with lethal gunfire, but November 8th felt different even to the hardened political activists of Munich. Hitler summed up the night's plans when he dropped in unexpectedly at fellow Nazi leader Alfred Rosenberg's house in the late morning. "'Rosenberg,' said the Fuhrer, 'tonight is the night. Kahr is giving an official speech in the Bürgerbräukeller, and we'll catch them all together. Do you want to come?' Rosenberg's answer was 'Of course!'" (Hanser, 1971, 316).

The total forces at Hitler's disposal in Munich on the fateful day numbered around 4,000 men in total. These included 1,500 men of the SA Regiment München, 3 battalions of the Bund Oberland (undersized at approximately 2,000 men), and a handful of other units, most of them platoon or company sized (including a single machine gun detachment). Von Kahr's government, though it did not yet know it was under threat, had some 1,800 police, including the famous Blue Police and Green Police, plus 800 regular army men at its disposal, backed by a squadron of 12 armored cars, several Motor Transport battalions, and a battery of artillery. In all, they totaled 2,600 men.

Though a fair number of Hitler's SA had combat experience, there were also many men among them who were experienced brawlers but by no means regular soldiers. This difference in troop quality – an amalgam of training, discipline, morale, initiative, tactical knowledge, and weapon skill – ultimately decided the outcome of the Beer Hall Putsch, but the Nazis didn't figure that would be the case beforehand. Though they were aware of the differences between their forces and von Kahr's forces, Hitler hoped to swing the Army over to his side and was only secondarily planning to depend solely on the armed strength of his SA units.

While von Kahr and his supporting speakers polished their speeches for the evening, the Nazis were busy mobilizing by using multiple communications channels. Most of the men were still not told what was afoot, but they were disciplined enough to prepare punctually anyway. The alert was sent out through every means available, including telephone calls, runners, and even notes slipped under the doors of those who were out working on that Thursday. "All over the city, hundreds of […] S.A. men were taking off their work clothes and putting on uniforms […] then hastening to designated assembly points. "Uniform" mean field-gray windbreaker with swastika brassard, field-gray ski cap, and revolver belt. For some the word came over the telephone with a curt 'Auf Gehts!' – 'This is it' – which was enough." (Hanser, 1971, 317).

Once mustered, most of the SA men realized something unusual was going on when they were issued rifles and ammunition. This was clearly no ordinary rally, nor was it a street brawl to break up marching communists or the like, where the rubber truncheon and the fist were the weapons of choice. Nevertheless, after some confusion, they obeyed their officers and began marching towards their objectives, even if they were ignorant of what those goals were.

Members of the Nazi Party during the putsch

While the SA men moved purposefully through the evening streets, a bright red Benz automobile pulled up at the Bürgerbräukeller beer hall, where von Kahr was beginning his speech in his usual lifeless style. Outside, Hitler and several top NSDAP officials stepped out of the red car and approached the leader of the small handful of police who were present for crowd control. The police greeted him in a relaxed fashion since he had received an invitation to attend the speech and his appearance on the scene was therefore expected to attend.

Hitler glanced around the packed street, where large numbers of people who had not been able to cram into the beer hall were waiting for news of whether or not von Kahr was declaring something unusual, such as Bavarian independence. He then remarked to the constables that the crowd was intolerable and suggested they should clear the throng before some kind of disorder occurred. The police complied, thereby neatly clearing the street for Nazi action and removing themselves from the vicinity of the beer hall entrance at the same time. No sooner was the street cleared than a series of trucks rolled up, disgorging heavily armed SA men. Some of the trucks parked in such a way as to block the street, and the men in them wore steel military helmets, rather than the usual soft SA caps. These were members of Hitler's personal bodyguard, the "Stosstrupp Hitler." Goering led a detachment with submachine guns, and another group carried a heavy tripod-mounted military machine-gun.

As the armed and helmeted SA riflemen charged into the beer hall, the few police still present put up their hands rather than be shot down. A few, recognizing Hitler, actually pulled swastika brassards from their pockets, attached them to their sleeves, and defected immediately. The heavy machine-gun team set up their weapon squarely in the entrance to the cavernous room where von Kahr was giving his speech and barked orders at the crowd, which began to panic and surge this way and that almost immediately amid curses, questions, and women's screams. Goering and his men pushed into the room to take up positions around the walls, from where they could kill anyone who attempted resistance or even mow down the crowd if it turned into an angry mob.

Hitler attempted to reach the podium but was blocked by a mass of milling, terrified humanity. Goering and several other men hastened to his side but were unable to force a way through the mass of swaying, shoving bodies. Finally, Hitler climbed up on a chair and fired a shot into the ceiling with his pistol, which had the effect of producing instant quiet. "'The national revolution has broken out!' Hitler shouted [...] 'The Bavarian government and the Reich government are deposed. The barracks of the Reichswehr and the state police have been occupied. Reichswehr and State Police are advancing under the banners of the swastika.'" (Hanser, 1971, 320).

In the meantime, a second machine-gun had been set up to cover the first, though this was not visible from the hall's interior and gave the lie to Hitler's later claim that the machine-gun was purely for show and would not have been fired into the crowd. Hitler then proceeded up onto the podium, where von Kahr, along with his chief backers General Otto von Lossow and Colonel von Seisser, were standing. Pistol in hand, looking as though he were "insane or drunk" according to some witnesses, Hitler "invited" his three chief prisoners to join him in a private room off the main hall. He also ordered beer to be brought, which he drank copiously before proceeding.

Von Lossow

Once in the room, Hitler asked the men's forgiveness, claiming he was only acting for Germany's sake, and as he smiled, he told them his pistol contained four bullets. Three were for von Kahr, von Lossow, and von Seisser if they proved to be "traitors," and the last was for Hitler himself if the putsch failed. Despite these threats, Hitler was unable to persuade the three men to assist him, and he was forced to return to the main hall alone 15 minutes later.

The crowd became angry at the sight of Hitler alone, and it appeared that fighting might break out. However, while he had failed to win the approval of von Kahr and his two main supporters for his plan to overthrow the government of Germany, the Nazi leader had one more card to play. He mounted the podium and began to speak, and as eyewitness Karl-Alexander von Muller reported, "He began quietly, without any pathos. The enterprise was not directed against Kahr […] Kahr had his full trust and shall be regent in Bavaria. At the same time, however, a new government must be formed: Ludendorff, Lossow, Seisser, and himself. I cannot remember in my entire life such a change in the attitude of a crowd in a few minutes, almost a few seconds.

[…] Hitler had turned them inside out, as one turns a glove inside out, with a few sentences. It had almost something of hocus-pocus, or magic about it. Loud approval roared forth." (Gordon, 1972, 288).

Cheer after thunderous cheer greeted Hitler's words, which spoke of overthrowing the corrupt current government and creating a "free" Germany in its stead. Hitler then returned to the room where von Kahr, von Lossow, and von Seisser were being held prisoner, accompanied this time by Ludendorff in his Imperial Army dress uniform. Swayed both by their fellow veteran's words and the fact that they sensed which way the wind was blowing, the three men finally agreed to support Hitler publicly. With that, Hitler, von Kahr, and the others returned to the beer hall, where they clasped hands symbolically to crashing ovations and bellowed cheers from the audience. The three prisoners made brief speeches approving of Hitler's plans.

At this point, however, a potentially crucial event occurred. The Nazis had successfully seized several key points, including the police headquarters, but there was trouble between SA men and Army regulars at the Engineer Kaserne. Hitler abandoned the Bürgerbräukeller beer hall and went to settle this dispute, leaving Ludendorff in command, but having no idea what he was supposed to do, he allowed von Kahr, von Lossow, and von Seisser to simply walk away from the Bürgerbräukeller. They left quietly and then fled into the darkness.

Six important hostages were taken from among the beer hall audience by Rudolf Hess, and the remainder of the thousands were allowed to depart, buzzing with happy excitement and anticipating the renewal of Germany in general and Bavaria in particular under the new nationalist government of Adolf Hitler.

Röhm, meanwhile, had been busy attempting to secure the "crucial points" the Nazis planned to seize as part of the overall putsch. The SA men who had been mobilized spent much of the evening at beer halls, drinking, eating, and listening to political speeches and band music, but Röhm soon sent some of them to fetch 3,000 additional rifles from a monastery cellar in St. Annaplatz, and dispatched others to seize key points, government buildings, and infrastructure. One historian noted the main problem the Nazi leaders faced when he wrote that "some of these ventures were successful, others were dismal failures. All were characterized by the reluctance of everyone concerned to initiate a bloody struggle." (Gordon, 1972, 292).

Two of the most important places in the city, the engineer barracks and the infantry barracks, eluded capture by the Nazis. Small detachments of regular soldiers at each of these installations managed to defeat larger numbers of SA, though again, this was due to the profound reluctance of the SA men to fire upon or even pummel the Army men who resisted them. A band of regular soldiers turned back the SA unit sent to the infantry barracks, and at the engineer barracks, an even more humiliating reverse awaited the Sturmabteilung. There, the captain on duty, Oskar Cantzler, lured the whole SA unit into the drill hall, and his tiny force of soldiers then swung the doors closed and locked them, taking the whole SA unit captive. Again, this resulted partly because of the Nazis' unwillingness to shoot their way free and kill Army men, whom they desperately wanted as allies and respected as fellow Germans.

As a result, as the night of November 8 went on, things were not going well for the Beer Hall Putsch. Von Kahr, von Lossow, and von Seisser, whose support Hitler had counted on, had escaped and were never recaptured by the Nazis during the putsch, and the SA had failed to take most of their objectives and had met with catastrophic rebuffs at two of the most important. Still, matters looked a little brighter to Hitler after he returned to the Bürgerbräukeller beer hall, as "an entire Reichswehr unit, about 1,000 strong and fully armed, came marching smartly up to the Bürgerbräukeller with a band playing and swastika banners flying – the first formation of the

German Regular Army to march openly under the flag of National Socialism. These were elite troops [...] Their leader was Lieutenant Gerhard Rossbach, a notorious swashbuckler and freebooter [...] he had convinced [his men] that the true way of soldierly honor was to break their oath of allegiance to the Republic and, instead, march against it." (Hanser, 1971, 328-329).

At the same time, a Nazi fifth columnist inside the police, Dr. Wilhelm Frick, had managed to prevent any police action against the putsch on the night of November 8th and into the early morning hours of November 9th. This wily individual "used his influence to prevent the Landespolizei duty officer from launching an immediate attack against the Putschists" (Gordon, 1972, 303), then spent hours fielding calls from alarmed police posts and reassuring them that all was well and that no action was required.

Frick

The Beer Hall Putsch had opened with a confused patchwork of successes and failures for Hitler and his fellow plotters, but the police, acting on their own initiative despite the reassurances of Dr. Frick, sent heavily armed men to the communication centers. When the SA arrived, they found these points already held against them and once again declined to initiate bloodshed.

Though this gave the government the nominal ability to coordinate a response rapidly with telecommunications, bungling was not confined to the Nazis on the night of the Beer Hall Putsch. "Kahr ordered that no telephone or telegraph traffic be allowed with points outside [Munich] except messages of the Reichswehr [...] He himself then attempted to send messages out through other channels, which were delayed by his own men for hours. Once again he was the man with ten thumbs." (Gordon, 1972, 307).

Though Kahr was acting in his usual fashion, von Lossow was proving much more capable. Having escaped from the Bürgerbräukeller beer hall after Hitler had left for a time, the general had made his way through the night to the 19th Infantry Barracks, where he was planning a surprise of his own for Hitler and the other members of the putsch. Around midnight, when the Nazis were feeling extraordinarily optimistic about their revolt, General von Lossow reached the

19th Infantry Barracks, which was garrisoned with soldiers loyal to him, and upon his arrival, he was greeted by his second in command, Jakob von Danner. "'Excellency,' said von Danner to his chief, 'that was surely all bluff?' Danner was commander of the local garrison; he could muster two divisions of regular troops and was to be reckoned with […] He and his fellow officers were against the Putsch, and offered Lossow a way out of his commitment at the Bürgerbräukeller. Lossow promptly agreed that it had all been bluff – 'putting on an act' – and began taking steps to suppress the insurgency he had publicly pledged to support." (Hanser, 1971, 333).

At this time, General von Lossow sent out word to activate various military units to crush the putsch, just as Hitler and Ludendorff had relaxed and stopped attempting to seize serious objectives. Ludendorff thought that von Lossow would keep his word as an officer and a gentleman, even though it had been coerced under duress, and Hitler thought the common soldiers would support him regardless of what their commanders decided. Thus, both men did nothing further that evening and allowed the initiative to slip out of their fingers and pass into the hands of their opponents.

During the night, Hitler, the Nazis, and the SA sat idle, sleeping occasionally as cold rain began during the early morning hours. While they frittered away the time, army units were converging on Munich from multiple directions despite the foul weather. The police were on alert but confused, uncertain of where the army's loyalties lay and who was now in command of Munich and Bavaria. Meanwhile, General von Lossow, the bungler von Kahr, and von Seisser gathered at the 19th Infantry Barracks and devised a plan to retake the city from Hitler.

Von Lossow favored an immediate, violent counterattack, showing signs of rage at his humiliation, but the other two men talked him into a less precipitous approach. The Nazis were known to be holding two buildings as their main centers of operation: the Wehrkreiskommando and the Bürgerbräukeller beer hall. According to the plan, the Army and police together would attack the former, while the latter would be taken by the police alone. The "Munich triumvirate" also received a message from the Reichswehr commander in Berlin, von Seeckt, who made clear that if von Kahr, von Lossow, and von Seisser did not deal with Hitler promptly, they would be considered traitors as well by the central government.

The first bad news reached the Nazi leaders at 5:00 a.m. on the 9th when a Colonel Leupold – an Army man who sympathized with the putsch – arrived to warn Hitler and Ludendorrf that von Lossow, on whom they pinned so many hopes, had turned against them and intended to crush their rebellion. He also cautioned the two leaders that the 7th Reichswehr Division was available to assist in the crushing, and that it showed no signs of being sympathetic to their scheme or disloyal to the official government. Hitler still believed that "propaganda" would carry the day, and Ludendorrf thought the Army would still end up supporting the putsch, but the two leaders and most of their followers decamped from their advance position at the Wehrkreiskommando and returned to the Bürgerbräukeller beer hall. The luckless Röhm was left to hold the Wehrkreiskommando as a forward post for the putsch, assisted by a detachment of SA men.

At approximately 6:00 a.m., a convoy of SA trucks arrived from Landshut to reinforce the putsch, bearing 150 armed men under the command of Paul Goebel. Goebel, a canny fellow, remarked with some alarm that the city appeared totally normal, which suggested that Hitler's putsch had either failed or was on its last legs. Though he pushed ahead to reinforce his fellow Nazis regardless, his assessment was not far off.

Breakfast was served to the increasingly anxious SA men at the Bürgerbräukeller beer hall, consisting of cheese and bread with strong black coffee, and the morale of these men was lowered further as the beer hall's telephones began to ring, reminding them of family ties. As one historian put it, "worried women [inquired] about husbands and sons who had gone off in uniform the evening before and had not come back. What was happening to them? When would they be back? Nobody could answer, because nobody knew. There were no announcements from the leadership, no orders from unit commanders." (Hanser, 1971, 341). The SA men expected to be paid, however, so a band was sent to a nearby print shop to steal freshly printed money. Some 14 quadrillion marks were confiscated, which, at the current hyperinflation exchange rate, was worth around $14,000 at the time. Each of the 1,500 men at the Bürgerbräukeller was given 2 trillion marks, or $2, and the rest of the money was retained as a sort of war chest by the Nazi leaders.

Hitler and Ludendorff now realized how desperate their situation was, but they couldn't think of a way to rectify it. They spent several hours in fruitless debate while their followers grew more anxious and the police tore down Nazi posters all over the city and put up their own posters declaring Ludendorff a "Prussian" and a "traitor." Ironically, less venom was directed at Hitler, whom the Bavarians had come to respect as a kind of honorary Bavarian nationalist. Some of the Nazi officials eventually suggested retreat, which finally pushed Ludendorff into action. Drawing himself up, he uttered two words that heralded the start of the final action of the Beer Hall Putsch: "We march!"

The idea was to march boldly into the city in the hopes that the citizens, who had been so enthusiastic at the Bürgerbräukeller the night before, would turn out en masse to support it. This would hopefully intimidate the Bavarian government and the local army units into yielding to the putsch or persuade them that it was popular and therefore the right thing to do, thereby converting them to the cause. One historian described the scene: "It was a thoroughly German response to a difficult situation [...] 'The sight of a marching column,' in the words of the [SA] leader Franz Pfeffer von Salomon, 'makes the deepest possible impression on a German and speaks to his heart a more convincing and compelling language than writing or talk of logic can ever do.'" (Hanser, 1971, 349).

However, with little overall organization, the SA men took several hours to assemble into a marching column in the open space in front of the beer hall. The day was cloudy, windy, and extremely cold, and moist snow fell periodically to soak the men's uniforms and render them thoroughly miserable. Goering, as loud and bloodthirsty as ever, originally placed the hostages taken the night before and a random selection of Jews he and his thugs had pounced on during the night into the column as well, with the intention of killing them if the police or Army fired on the column. This was too much even for Hitler, however, who ordered the prisoners out of the column and back into the beer hall, where a few men were left to guard them.

Heavily armed, wearing proper uniforms and steel helmets, and exhibiting near-military discipline, the SA bodyguards of the Stosstrupp Hitler and the 6th SA Company led the procession, just behind Hitler, Ludendorff, and several other Nazi functionaries. At almost precisely the same time, Reichswehr units moved forward towards the Wehrkreiskommando, where Röhm and his detachment were still on guard. A tense standoff ensued, with neither side willing to back down or initiate bloodshed. In fact, the situation would only be resolved after the main SA march failed.

Meanwhile, Hitler's column marched to the Ludwig Bridge across the River Isar. This bridge of four arches was held by a diminutive state police, or "Lapo," detachment under Georg Hofler. Hofler defied Hitler, but his vastly outnumbered men were afraid to fire. The SA men swarmed forward and took them prisoner at bayonet-point, after which the Nazis disarmed the police. A few officers were punched and kicked, but all were soon released, as the SA had other matters to attend to.

After that, the putsch column marched into the open square known as the Marienplatz, and from there, they took several streets to the Franz Josef Platz, changing direction several times to avoid direct confrontation with police patrols. Hitler's hopes of a successful "propaganda march" almost appeared justified; throngs of Munich residents turned out despite the bad weather and sang patriotic hymns to salute the passing SA men. A vast crowd began to follow the Nazis, which must have greatly bolstered Hitler's confidence.

However, the march came to an abrupt end at the Odeonsplatz, named for a nearby concert hall. A small band of police riflemen under Captain Rudolf Schraut barred the path of the SA column, which continued a slow advance and shouted for the police to get out of the way. The column menaced the police with a thicket of bayonets in the attack position, but while Schraut was a radical and a fascist, he believed in the sanctity of orders from duly constituted authority. He and his policemen held their ground, though they were reluctant to fire because of the large number of civilians accompanying the SA.

Bundesarchiv, Bild 119-1426
Foto: o.Ang. | 9. November 1923

A picture of people crowding the Odeonsplatz square in Munich on November 9

At this moment, a second, larger detachment of Lapo riflemen commanded by Lieutenant Michael Freiherr (knight) von Godin rushed into the Odeonsplatz from a side street. The Lieutenant charged directly into the Nazi column despite the forest of bayonets and pistols that he and his men were menaced with, and the Lapo men, though greatly outnumbered, began battering the SA troops furiously with their truncheons and rifle-butts. At that moment, as Godin later recalled, "Suddenly a Hitler man who stood one step half left of me fired a pistol at my head. The shot went by my head and killed Sergeant Hollweg behind me. For a fraction of a second, my company stood frozen. Then, before I could give an order, my people opened fire, with the effect of a salvo. At the same time the Hitler people commenced firing and for twenty or thirty seconds a regular firefight developed." (Gordon, 1972, 361).

Mowed down at close range by concentrated rifle fire, the SA men did not stand firm for long.

16 of them died within a minute or two of the battle's start, and many more were wounded, while four policemen were killed in the exchange. Goering was shot in the groin but nevertheless managed to flee and disappear into the crowd, and in the initial shooting, a bullet struck Max Erwin von Scheubner-Richter, who was walking arm in arm with Hitler. The bullet, which would otherwise have struck Hitler in the torso, penetrated both of Scheubner-Richter's lungs and stopped at his ribs on the side toward Hitler. Scheubner-Richter is reported to have died instantly, probably from hydrostatic shock as the heavy bullet's shockwaves damaged his heart and possibly his brain, but since their arms were linked, Scheubner-Richter dragged Hitler to the ground as he fell and thus out of the line of fire. That said, it is also possible that Hitler dropped flat, since he was an experienced soldier and such an action would have made sense in a sudden gun-battle.

In the midst of the fighting, the SA men quickly turned tail and fled, and Hitler joined them. Though he was later accused of cowardice by some of his enemies, the truth is that the day was already lost and his forces were in rapid retreat. Short of immediate suicide, there was no point in Hitler remaining alone to be shot by the enraged policemen. Ludendorrf, on the other hand, continued to walk forward alone, passing through the front ranks of the police unhindered. He was easily recognized and as one of Bavaria's heroes was unlikely to be gunned down unless it was by accident. Several police tackled him after he had passed through their front line and arrested him, at which point he began to act with childish petulance, as if the Lapo men had wronged him greatly by putting an end to his coup.

Back at the Wehrkreiskommando, the news of Ludendorrf's capture and the effective end of the putsch sapped Röhm's resolve to fight rather than surrender. Earlier, he left his strongpoint to negotiate with the Army officers, who demanded his surrender, and he had initially refused. While he was absent, his men fired on some Army engineers, killing one and wounding another, which prompted a flurry of machine gun fire that left two SA men dead. After that, the SA men began to surrender in bunches, and Röhm eventually agreed to give up when he heard Ludendorrf was a prisoner. In fact, Ludendorrf even sent him a written message urging him to surrender to prevent further deaths. Röhm himself was placed under arrest, while his men were disarmed and then allowed to simply leave and return to their homes.

The Beer Hall Putsch was over.

After the Beer Hall Putsch

A picture of the defendants: Pernet, Weber, Frick, Kiebel, Ludendorff, Hitler, Bruckner, Röhm, and Wagner

Nothing illustrates more clearly that Hitler's plans were in almost perfect accord with the secret hopes, fears, and wishes of his fellow countrymen than the fact that his defeat during the Beer Hall Putsch, which theoretically should have destroyed him utterly as a failed traitor, ultimately metamorphosed into a kind of victory under the actual circumstances.

Hitler went briefly into hiding at the house of the Hanfstaengl family, where he contemplated suicide, but his hosts dissuaded him from this step (if he was actually serious about it in the first place). He was arrested two days after the putsch, was confined in the fortress of Landsberg, and was brought to trial on February 24th, 1924, a little over three months after his abortive coup attempt.

Thomas Springer's picture of Landsberg

In theory, Hitler's putsch was a capital crime of treason for which he should have been liable for the death penalty. Furthermore, four policemen had died during the brief skirmish that ended the putsch, making the possible charges even more serious. However, the men putting Hitler on trial had been partly responsible for his rise and his actions, and they sympathized deeply with his cause. The trial therefore took a remarkable turn. "The course of the ensuing trial […] was determined by the tacit agreement of all those taking part not to 'touch upon the "essence" of those events', so that the hearing was reduced to a farce in which Hitler unexpectedly ceased to be the accused and became the accuser." (Fest, 1995, 36).

Thus, the courtroom became yet another beer hall where Hitler could give impassioned patriotic speeches to a rapt audience. He covered for his men by placing all blame for the Beer Hall Putsch on himself, and indeed, those who were tried alongside him received even lighter sentences and, in the case of Ludendorff, an acquittal. Hitler concluded the trial with a thunderous, triumphant declaration: "I nourish the proud hope that one day the hour will come when these rough companies will grow to battalions, the battalions to regiments, the regiments to divisions, that the old cockade will be taken from the mud, that the old flags will wave again [...] For it is not you, gentlemen, who pass judgement on us. That judgement is spoken by the eternal court of history. [...] that court will not ask us: Did you commit high treason, or did you not? The court will judge us […] as Germans who wanted only the good of their own people and Fatherland, who wanted to fight and die. Pronounce us guilty a thousand times over: the goddess of the eternal court of history will smile [...] for she acquits us." (Fest, 1995, 37).

The court nearly acquitted him outright before finally handing down a sentence of five years in prison with the likelihood of being granted release on probation after just six months. Sentenced on April 1st, 1924, he was released from prison slightly more than eight months later on December 20th, 1924. By then, he had dictated his voluminous *Mein Kampf* to Rudolf Hess while enjoying a large, comfortable cell with numerous amenities and frequent visitors.

Hitler began strengthening the NSDAP immediately upon his release, and furthermore he had learned a new approach to politics which would cause him to shun open putsches from that point forward. Due to the failure of the putsch, Hitler now saw "the starting point for a struggle for power in entirely new conditions and by new methods. Of decisive importance in this struggle was Hitler's realization that force was not the way to capture the modern state apparatus, that power could be seized only on the basis of the Constitution itself." (Fest, 1995, 38).

In time, he would be successful, but Hitler's shift from overt attempts to seize power by violence to covert seizure of the system via pseudo-legal means was not popular with all of his supporters. The SA and Röhm looked askance at what they perceived as this abandonment of a pure revolutionary focus on violence and a turn to the "vile" process of voting. The fact that Hitler eventually created a dictatorial state through clever electioneering and keen exploitation of legal loopholes made no difference to these men, for whom anti-democratic sentiment was a matter of principle. "There was, moreover, widespread unease in both the party organization and the Hitler Youth about the 'embourgeoisement' of the Nazi movement, a process symbolized above all by the NSDAP's participation in electoral politics. The NSDAP had always been oriented strongly against electoral politics, which were understood to be the most corrupt in a system of corrupt practices. The formative experience of the movement—the failed Munich Putsch—symbolized this orientation, and there continued to be many in the party, especially among the SA leadership, who preferred, on both practical and moral grounds, to seize power by force." (Brown, 2009, 60-61).

Hitler was a pragmatic revolutionary who learned from the Beer Hall Putsch that the source of power was immaterial as long as it was effective at moving him towards his goals. He was willing to don the cloaks of legality and democracy, temporarily at least, if that pretense would bring him closer to the center of power, which it ultimately did. Röhm preferred form over substance, and he believed erroneously that Hitler was "going soft" because he ceased attempts at a violent overthrow of Germany' government. Fatally wrong in this assessment, Röhm subsequently paid the ultimate price for thinking Hitler had become decadent and weak a decade later, when his dark hints at a "Second Revolution" prompted the Fuhrer to kill him and a thousand other leading SA men on the Night of the Long Knives. Hitler, as Röhm and Germany as a whole would come to learn, had not "gone soft" because he chose a legalistic route to achieving power. This was, after all, the man who "one of his own closest followers, repentant in a death cell at Nuremberg, could only liken [...] to a cataclysm of nature. 'Around his name,' wrote Dr. Hans Frank, who was Hitler's Governor-General of Poland, 'is the reek of millions of corpses, of ruins, starvation, despair, decay, and horror.'" (Hanser, 1971, 16).

Gustav von Kahr also learned what sort of man Hitler was, because the Fuhrer would not forgive or forget the role he played in the putsch. A particularly horrible death was reserved for him on the Night of the Long Knives some 11 years later. Driven to the edge of the Dachauer Moos swamp by a squad of SS men, von Kahr was hacked to death with axes and his mangled corpse was flung contemptuously into the stagnant water, perhaps qualifying him as the last of the putsch's direct casualties.

The Beer Hall Putsch appeared to its contemporaries to be a trivial, even risible, matter. Its apparent failure to produce any result and its ignominious end, with its chief author jailed like any common hoodlum disturbing the peace, led to its dismissal by practically all the political cognoscenti of early 1920s Germany. Filled with pride and misplaced self-assurance, these individuals were inclined to mockery rather than concern, to the extent that the putsch "was […] blindly misjudged when it happened, and misinterpreted for years thereafter. By many it was classed with the comic-opera riots of the previous century caused by Lola Montez, the Irish mistress of the Bavarian king, who stirred up the Munich citizenry […] with an unwelcome passion for social reform." (Hanser, 1971, 17).

In reality, the putsch was one of the first events that brought about the dark avalanche of Nazism upon which Hitler rode to power in one of Europe's most powerful nations. What marked it as distinct from the other political brawls that surrounded and preceded it was the individual at its heart. Hitler was remarkable for his colossal energy, drive, political acumen, conviction, and concentrated malice.

Two results of the putsch ended up having far-reaching consequences that altered the fate of Europe. The incident's first crucial effect was that it brought Hitler to widespread public notice, and the fact that he was the subject of considerable scorn among many people, and that his political movement attracted derision, was immaterial. Hitler had come to the attention of a large section of the population of the Weimar Republic. One of the vital, almost alchemical, elements to success – whether in the political, entrepreneurial, literary, or any other major sphere of human endeavor – is to become visible, and Hitler had forever risen above the anonymity that cloaks most people's lives. P.T. Barnum's axiom that "I don't care what the newspapers say about me as long as they spell my name right" applied to Hitler, whose later words and actions would henceforth gain a far-flung audience merely due to the fact they came from him.

The second effect was to impress on Hitler's warped but extremely keen mind that a revolution by force was impractical and doomed to failure. The true method of gaining power was to insinuate himself into the power structure, then find the flaws in the legal system – the inevitable loopholes left by human mortality's limitations – in order to exploit them boldly and powerfully. The Beer Hall Putsch was a moment of learning for Hitler if not an outright epiphany. It showed him clearly how he could use the potent force of his personality and intellect to achieve sole dominion over the German state by legal means, or at least by methods that were shielded from effective resistance by adopting a color of legality. To this day, people often point out that Hitler accrued power democratically, and while this is actually stretching the truth, the fact that he worked his way up through political means until the burning of the Reichstag is certainly accurate.

Most political agitators would have given up after such a failure, or they may have continued to make similar attempts until they were either imprisoned for a long period or killed during one of their dangerous coup efforts. Hitler, however, took the lesson to heart, with profoundly fateful consequences for almost everybody on the planet during the 1940s. Only later would Heiden, one of the pioneer chroniclers of Hitler's rise, write of him, "As a human figure, lamentable; as a political mind, one of the most tremendous phenomena in all history." (Hanser, 1971, 17). A man without rank, position, fame, or money, he succeeded in becoming the absolute master of an empire which is believed to have encompassed more than 400 million people at its height. All of this was thanks to an understanding gained via the Beer Hall Putsch.

The Weimar Republic's Missteps

In times of crisis, elections were held much more frequently than in more stable periods, but this feature of the Weimar Republic also helped ensure that any economic or political instability would be exacerbated by shifts in the governing bodies, which came at times when continuity would've been generally beneficial for keeping problems from spiraling out of control. Multiple elections occurred in close proximity to the date of the Reichstag fire, and both at the time and since, many ordinary people and historians have noted the convenient timing of the conflagration.

Unlike the U.S. Congress but similar to various European governmental councils, seats in the Reichstag were awarded on a proportional basis. For example, if a party won 20% of the vote, then it would also control 20% of the seats. This meant that at the time of the Reichstag fire, no political party held a majority. The strongest party, in numerical terms, consisted of the Social Democrats, a liberalizing force that mainly sought to increase the strength of democracy in the former German Empire. The Nazis represented a powerful bloc as well, but the number of seats they held increased when the economy faltered and decreased when a whiff of prosperity was in the air. The KDP Communists held a smaller but still significant portion of the Reichstag seats.

As might be expected, the Nazi Party and the KDP frequently worked at cross purposes, and relatively civilized feuds within the Reichstag's walls, where the leaders of the respective groups often addressed one another in highly formal and civil terms, were frequently mirrored by brutal outbreaks of violence in the streets. Once Goering became president of the Reichstag and overall leader of German police, the current of hooliganism grew stronger, sweeping Germany towards the precipice of dictatorship: "Simultaneously, the number of violent incidents and acts of anti-Semitism began to multiply significantly. The [SA and SS] began to attack the trade union and Communist offices along with the homes of their leaders but with the agreements in place with the police the common situation was that the Communists/Jews/Trade Unionists would get a kicking from the Nazis and then be arrested and thrown in prison for breaches of the peace." (Addington, 2014, Chapter 13).

The Nazis and KPD each represented, to the eyes of the people, a glimmer of hope and a way of extracting themselves from the labyrinth of poverty and humiliation the Allies had thrust them into. Though the 85 year old President Paul von Hindenburg, head of the Weimar Republic, was becoming vague at times, his Chancellor, Heinrich Brüning, clearly understood the source of Germany's woes and how these might deliver the nation into the hands of the Communists or Nazis. "During the summer the scholarly Chancellor had pondered long hours over the desperate plight of Germany. [...] To cope with the depression he had decreed lower wages and salaries as well as lower prices [...] The 'Hunger Chancellor' he had been called by both the Nazis and the Communists. Yet he thought he saw a way out that in the end would re-establish a stable, free, prosperous Germany. He would try to negotiate with the Allies a cancellation of reparations." (Shirer, 2011, 157).

Hindenburg

Brüning

Since the Allies had failed to disarm themselves as they had bound themselves by treaty to do, Brüning also wished to rearm the German nation. Indeed, he began a secret program for a modest military expansion, which he hoped would restore Germany to equality with the other nations rather than continue to be Europe's whipping boy. This program, of course, had a very different fate; rather than being the security force that reestablished the dignity of a free people as Brüning envisioned, it would ultimately form the nucleus of Hitler's genocidal Reichswehr.

Brüning's plan actually went even farther, as he contemplated means by which the rising power of the Nazis could be decisively and legally quashed. His solution was to create a new constitutional monarchy with strictly limited powers in Germany, but when he proposed this to Hindenburg, it was shot down forcefully by the Weimar Republic's president, not because it was too conservative but because the idea of a legally limited monarchy was too liberal for the former Imperial soldier: "When Brüning explained to [Hindenburg] that the Social Democrats and the trade unions, which [...] had given some encouragement to his plan if only because it might afford the last desperate chance of stopping Hitler, would not stand for the return of [...] Wilhelm II [...] and that moreover if the monarchy were restored it must be a constitutional and democratic one on the lines of the British model, the grizzly old Field Marshal was so outraged he summarily dismissed his Chancellor from his presence. A week later he recalled him to inform him that he would not stand for re-election." (Shirer, 2011, 158).

The next Chancellor to be appointed by Hindenburg was Franz von Papen, who practically handed Hitler the means to establish a dictatorship due to his own mistaken belief that he could easily control the man Hindenburg had dismissed contemptuously as "the Bohemian corporal." Von Papen did not last long in office, but he made the cardinal error of legalizing the SA, or Sturmabteilung, the infamous Brownshirts who served as the muscle enforcing Hitler's will on the streets. He did this in the erroneous belief that it would appease the Nazis.

Von Papen

Von Papen was almost immediately forced to resign, largely through the machinations of Hitler and allies like Goering. Economic troubles compelled the people to favor right-wing solutions, and in the disastrous days of the early 1930s, Hitler's anti-Semitism was an attractive feature to many German voters. The Jews formed an identifiable and useful scapegoat against whom to direct the rage, frustration, fear, and misery that ordinary Germans had experienced for nearly half a generation: "Germans felt the effects almost immediately. By December 1929, 1.5 million workers were unemployed. A month later, that number jumped to 2.5 million, and it kept climbing. Once again, the Nazis took advantage of a crisis by blaming everything on the Communists and the Jews. In the September 1930 election, the Nazis were expected to win 50 seats in Germany's parliament. To the surprise of many, they went from 12 seats to 107 seats." (Goldstein, 2012, 243).

Hitler's rise to power was boosted by the desperation of the Germans to extract themselves from a situation which seemingly showed no sign of a positive resolution, and his ability to appear as the champion against the forces causing Germany's troubles made him all the more popular. Since the Allies were out of reach, the helpless, vastly outnumbered Jews made an ideal substitute for the Nazis' purposes. "Hitler and other Nazis were now poised to destroy the Weimar Republic and 'restore' Germany and the 'Aryan race' to greatness by ending so-called Jewish racial domination and eliminating the Communist threat." (Goldstein, 2012, 243).

Although the Social Democrats were the overall majority party in Germany at the time, they suffered a massive disadvantage against Hitler's Nazis because they were dedicated to democratic government and were less apt to use systematic violence and intimidation to achieve their aims. The Nazis had no such scruples, and they constantly used beatings, arson, threats, and outright murder to disrupt opposing political movements, particularly around election times. The Communists were not averse to dirtying their hands with slaughter in the name of international revolution either, but they were much weaker than the Nazis. They had played their hand early in attempting a coup in 1919, seeking to prompt an armed worker's revolution that would create a Soviet-style tyranny in Germany, but they were quickly crushed by the brutal Freikorps, a right-wing paramilitary organization comprised of many World War I veterans. As such, the Freikorps possessed formidable combat skills the Communists could not match.

The Freikorps continued to seek out and kill Communists or suspected Communists during the following decade, greatly reducing the power of the party in Germany. Though still something of a force to be reckoned with, by 1933, the KDP (German Communist Party) simply did not have the manpower to go toe-to-toe with the Nazis and hope to survive, either in the German Parliament or the rough and tumble of the streets. The Freikorps would eventually be purged by Hitler, with most of its leaders executed and its rank and file absorbed first into the SA and then into the SS, but in the meantime, it rendered a considerable service to the future Fuhrer.

Elections held in November 1932 reduced the Nazis' seats in the parliament to around a third, with the deficit being claimed by the Communists, and the next elections were slated for March 6, 1933, exactly one week after the burning of the Reichstag occurred. Hitler and Goering were in need of a crisis both to generate a reason for passing dictatorial emergency powers, and to prevent the Nazis from losing further ground to the hated communists in the Reichstag.

Meanwhile, in late 1932 and early 1933, the German government "was preparing a massive job-creation programme to relieve unemployment through the state provision of public works (Evans, 2005, 308)." The Nazis had a firm grasp of the fact that it was economic disaster that made their extreme agenda seem appealing to the people at large. Their window of opportunity was shrinking, and they had only a few months left before their power would likely begin to wane. The Nazi Party and Hitler understood this instinctively.

At this moment, President Hindenburg made an utterly fatal error for the future of Germany, Europe, and the world. To the half-senile Field Marshal, "it seemed more urgent than ever at this point to tame the Nazis by bringing them into government (Evans, 2005, 310)," and this in turn "led to a plan to put Hitler in as Chancellor, with a majority of conservative cabinet colleagues to keep him in check." (ibid). In brief, the scheme concocted by the President and his ministers was to keep the Nazis from achieving power by giving them some power, buttressed by a naïve faith that the tut-tutting of a handful of aged politicians would suffice to rein in a man with approximately 400,000 SA brownshirts and 100,000 SS men at his disposal. Thus, with a surreal misjudgment, Hindenburg placed the few Nazis admitted into the highest ranks of government in precisely those positions best suited to the establishment of a dictatorship and police state: "Only two major offices of state went to the Nazis, but both of them were key positions on which Hitler had insisted as a condition of the deal: the Ministry of the Interior, occupied by Wilhelm Frick, and the Reich Chancellery itself, occupied by Hitler. Hermann Goring was appointed Reich Minister Without Portfolio and Acting Prussian Minister of the Interior, which gave him direct control over the police in the greater part of Germany. The Nazis could thus manipulate the whole domestic law-and-order situation to their advantage." (Evans, 2005, 312).

Hitler had played his hand brilliantly, exploiting circumstances, popular conspiracy theories, desperation, and the doddering incapacity of Germany's highest civilian leader to position himself in an extremely advantageous situation. The Nazis sensed that victory was within their grasp. For a few weeks, the real possibility existed that their power would melt away as economic programs finally helped Germany out of its long depression and into a newer, more democratic future, but Hitler managed to maneuver himself into the Chancellorship at essentially the last moment. Had Hindenburg chosen a different man as Chancellor and the job-creation program gained some breathing room to pick up momentum, there exists a very real possibility that there never would have been a Third Reich, a Final Solution, or World War II.

The Nazis had every reason to celebrate their stroke of good fortune at the 11th hour, and the victorious National Socialists marked the occasion in a fashion which expressed their own fierce satisfaction with the outcome and also served as a propaganda demonstration to showcase their strength, energy, and high degree of organization. "That Hitler's appointment as Reich Chancellor was no ordinary change of government became immediately clear, as Goebbels organized a torchlit parade of brownshirts, Steel Helmets and SS men through Berlin, beginning at seven in the evening on 30 January 1933 and going on well past midnight." (Evans, 2005, 315).

Still, at this point, Hitler still remained a functionary in the democratically elected government of the Weimar Republic, so a final touch was needed to grant him the powers which would transform a powerful but constitutionally limited Chancellor into the Fuhrer who would seek to establish a "Thousand Year Reich" on the ashes of the old European system. A high-profile incident was needed to give the pretext for Hitler to grant himself emergency powers and complete the metamorphosis from rabble-rousing former corporal to dictator.

Whether it occurred by accident or design, the burning of the Reichstag building on the night of February 27, 1933 provided Hitler with the necessary excuse.

The Reichstag in August 1932

The Burning of the Reichstag

The night of February 27 was an ideal one from the standpoint of an arsonist preparing to set fire to one of Germany's most important government buildings. The air temperature hovered around 20 degrees Fahrenheit, several degrees below the average February low for the region, ensuring that less people than usual were out and about. The presence of snow on the ground was also somewhat unusual, since snow often melts rather quickly in the mild climates of central Europe.

Other factors also favored the incendiary or incendiaries, regardless of whether the attack was carried out by a lone wolf, Nazi agents, or Communist revolutionaries. The late hour and the upcoming elections ensured that the structure was uncharacteristically abandoned, reducing the number of potential witnesses, meddlers, and casualties. "There was an election on and the Reichstag was not in session; many deputies were away campaigning, and the work of the building's staff slowed down after 9:00. Between the rounds of the lighting man at 8:45 and the Reichstag mailman at 8:50 or 8:55, and the first inspection of the night watchman at 10:00, no one would be moving about inside the building. For this hour or so the Reichstag would be quiet, and, presumably—apart from the porter at the north entrance—empty." (Hett, 2014, 10).

Of course, the absence of other persons ensured that once spotted, any activity in and around the building would be immediately deemed suspicious, especially by policemen. In fact, just such an individual was present at the time the fire was lit: Karl Buwert, who had been assigned to keep a lonely vigil over much of the Reichstag's perimeter. Though he likely expected a quiet, tedious period of sentinel duty, a very different situation ultimately emerged.

The darkness of that bitterly cold late winter night obscured both the policeman's view and that of later historians seeking to determine exactly who was seen on the premises of the Reichstag when it burned. Chief Constable Buwert's eventful evening began at approximately 9:10 p.m.

when Hans Floter, a theology student, approached him in a state of great excitement and announced that he had heard a window breaking and had seen a man with a torch on a second story balcony preparing to enter the building. Floter then left for home while the Chief Constable investigated, and almost immediately, a second figure hurried towards him through the gloom. This proved to be a young newspaper typesetter named Werner Thaler, who reported a broken window on another area of the facade and the sighting of two men with torches entering through this opening.

Buwert and Thaler investigated together, plainly seeing the broken window the young man had mentioned. There was already a glow of light inside, and the typesetter later claimed to have seen two torches inside, likely indicating a pair of arsonists at a minimum. Buwert fired his pistol in the general direction of the torches, prompting their carrier or carriers to move deeper into the building to avoid his bullets.

Picture of the window through which the alleged arsonist broke in

Fire engines began arriving on the scene, and at this point, Thaler felt his presence was superfluous and left. However, "as he crossed the Platz der Republik he 'turned around one more time and noticed that the cupola of the Reichstag was brightly lit.' That could only mean a much larger fire in the plenary chamber at the center of the building. 'I ran back to the firemen and told them that the interior of the building was also burning.'" (Hett, 2014, 15 – 16).

Thaler was not the only individual to note the ominous glare of rising light emerging from the iron and glass cupola that capped the Plenary Chamber. The Reichstag was one of the city's larger buildings, and many lines of sight to it existed thanks to its isolated placement on the Platz der Republik. This was no minor fire but an all-out blaze that threatened to gut the Reichstag's whole interior. Though the stone shell would remain largely intact save where intense heat might crack a few stone blocks, the curtains, chairs, paneling, and carpets inside were all highly inflammable, as were the large numbers of documents stored on the site.

Two of the main actors in the whole political tragedy, Paul von Hindenburg and Franz von Papen, were very close by, sharing a leisurely meal at the "Herrenklub" ("Gentlemen's' Club"), which commanded a view of the Reichstag. Von Papen reported, "Suddenly we noticed a red glow through the windows and heard sounds of shouting in the street. One of the servants came hurrying up to me and whispered: 'The Reichstag is on fire!' which I repeated to the President. He got up and from the window we could see the dome of the Reichstag looking as though it were illuminated by searchlights. Every now and again a burst of flame and a swirl of smoke blurred the outline." (Shirer, 2011, 196).

The brilliant illumination of the fire in the Plenary Chamber shining through the glass windows of the cupola was visible even further away. Hermann Goering's valet, Robert Kropp, was sipping mint tea in his employer's apartment while Goering was absent, working late on Unter dem Linden at the police offices (a fact that might have had an ominous significance). The valet's relaxing evening alone was not destined to last, however, for "the telephone rang, and when he answered it Adermann, the night porter at the presidential palace, was on the other end. He was excited and shouted: 'You must tell the minister at once! The Reichstag is on fire!'" (Mosley, 195).

After telephoning Goering (who had already received a report from the police), Kropp "slipped on his coat and went out and across to the Reichstag, from the dome of which he could now see, as he approached, flames licking." (Mosley, 195). Therefore, three separate accounts from widely separated individuals show that fire and smoke were already visible in the Plenary Chamber's cupola within a few minutes of the initial alarm being raised. This is an important question when trying to determine whether chemical accelerants such as gasoline were used to hasten the spread of the fire.

The Plenary Chamber clearly blazed up rapidly, almost suddenly, at about the same time the windows were broken and Buwert fired his pistol at an unknown prowler or prowlers inside the Reichstag. Though accelerants seem the most likely cause, a similar effect of a sudden, large fire in an enclosed space could theoretically result from flashover. Flashover occurs when the substances in a closed room reach their ignition temperature at the same time that the air is filled thickly with flammable gasses emitted from heated objects. When this threshold is reached, the entire room ignites suddenly, vastly increasing the size of the fire in an instant. Sometimes, the effect is even explosive, in which case the phenomenon is known as a "smoke explosion." Such an event can be lethal to anyone in the room, and it could potentially explain how the Plenary Chamber fire metamorphosed from a dim glow into a bright inferno that resembled "searchlights" shining out of the dome, with flames massive enough to lick out of the windows 246 feet above the chamber floor in a matter of a few minutes.

That said, one salient fact renders a flashover implausible. Without large quantities of accelerants to hasten the process, a long burn would be needed to set up the proper conditions for such an event to occur. The Plenary Chamber was a large space ,and considerable time would be needed for the surfaces to heat to the point of combustion and the huge gulf of air it contained to acquire a thick enough burden of flammable gasses to catch fire. There was insufficient time for a modest fire to expand to the point of flashover between 8:45 p.m. (when the lighting man came through the building) or the mail deliveries by the parliamentary building's mailman at 8:55 and the observed blaze at 9:15-9:20 p.m. Given that the use of accelerants was almost certainly needed to create such a daunting fire so quickly, and the conditions of the alleged lone arsonist's capture, it seems quite likely that several men were involved in the arson that night.

Police, firemen, and officials all quickly converged on the ominously burning Reichstag, where a desperate battle was soon underway to extinguish the colossal fire. Among the people who put in an appearance were Goering and Hitler himself. According to later accounts by Goering's valet Robert Kropp, Goering made an effort to reach his office in order to rescue his Gobelin tapestries, but he was driven back by fierce flames, his face blackened by soot and streaked with tears, the latter caused either by smoke irritation or sorrow at the destruction of the former air ace's favorite textile art.

Conversely, Hitler was in an exultant mood. As Goering emerged from the building and went to meet the Chancellor, "his faithful valet [...] was astonished to see the look of triumph, almost of pleasure, on Hitler's face. 'This is a beacon from heaven!' Hitler shouted, above the crackle of the flames." (Mosley, 196). Whether the fire was a serendipitous accident of timing or a deliberate act arranged at his instigation, Hitler clearly grasped what an opportunity the conflagration presented in the political arena. In the course of putting out the fire, a convenient culprit was also discovered wandering through the Reichstag's labyrinthine interior, and he promptly arrested by the swarms of police who had converged on the scene. This individual was Marinus van der Lubbe, a young man with Communist affiliations and Dutch origins who spoke very bad German. The arsonist was found shirtless, having used his upper garments as kindling for the fire he had no hesitation in admitting he had set, and he was carrying a box of matches. The police photographed him later holding this box, though by this time they had supplied him with a shirt and jacket to replace those he had incinerated in the depths of the Reichstag.

Van der Lubbe

No deaths or injuries resulted from the Reichstag fire, which occurred at a time when the building was empty save for the arsonist or arsonists. The solid stone construction eliminated the risk of collapse on the firemen and policemen who came to the scene, and they were careful enough to avoid any fatalities from direct fire exposure or smoke inhalation.

Slightly more than two hours after it began, the Reichstag fire was extinguished around 11:30 p.m., but by then, it had reduced practically the whole interior of the building to a charred shambles, destroying wood paneling, curtains, seats, lecterns, all manner of furniture, artworks, carpets, and reams of irreplaceable government documents and records. The fire went out due to a mix of intense efforts on the part of Berlin's firefighters and the fact that it had exhausted most of its potential fuel sources. The huge government building had been gutted, and it continued to send wisps of smoke upward into the icy air for days afterward.

A picture of ruins within the Reichstag

As the last smoldering ashes of the heaped wood and cloth inside cooled, however, a fire of a different kind had been lit in the hearts of the Nazi leadership. Feigning outrage against a Communist takeover plot of which there is scant to no evidence, the Nazis immediately began to exploit the Reichstag fire as a pretext for granting Hitler sweeping, unconstitutional powers, and for removing the Communists from the political scene as much as possible.

The Nazi Response to the Reichstag Fire

"I'm convinced he was responsible for the burning of the Reichstag, but I can't prove it." – Adolf Hitler in reference to Communist Party chairman Ernst Togler

The National Socialist party's response to the Reichstag fire was quick and forceful, in part because the Nazis and the police (who were now under the supervision of Goering) appeared to be readying their organizations for some kind of trouble. Goering was out of his home working with police officials when the Reichstag fire occurred, even though it was relatively late in the evening, but this was not the only indication that the Nazis were prepared for some sort of triggering event to offer them a pretext for arresting large numbers of their political rivals. The Gestapo was a newly formed organization in 1933, created as a secret police at the same time Hitler ascended to the Chancellorship on January 30, and the commander of this sinister new enforcement group was Rudolf Diels, a slippery figure who managed to avoid prosecution after World War II despite being neck deep in Nazi police state activities. In fact, the resourceful Diels, whose facial scars and icy, cynical gaze gave him the appearance of a villain from a Cold War spy thriller, actually wormed his way successfully into the postwar government of Lower Saxony.

Diels

Those days were remote in 1933, however. At that time, Diels made remarkable (and incriminating) preparations on the afternoon of January 27th, 1933, just a few hours before the fire at the Reichstag broke out. Making good use of early technology for coordinating his plan, the Gestapo leader "sent out an order by radio to all police stations in Prussia. 'Communists,' said Diels, were 'said to be planning attacks on police patrols and the members of national organizations' […] [and] 'suitable countermeasures' against the Communist threat were to be taken 'immediately.' Above all, 'in necessary cases' Communist functionaries were to be taken into 'protective custody.' By shortly after six that evening, all Prussian police stations had received Diels's order. Hours before fire consumed the Reichstag, the police were ready." (Hett, 2014, 39).

Both Diels and Goering had drawn up extensive arrest lists of influential Communists and others who were vocally opposed to the Nazis' rising fortunes, and these lists were up to date and ready for action when the flames shone through the darkness from the Reichstag's glass-paneled cupola. It is even possible that Goering was out of his house that fateful evening putting the finishing touches to them and making certain that no crucial names had been omitted among those who were destined to experience the horrors of Nazi "protective custody."

After his abortive attempt to rescue his Gobelin tapestries from the fire, Goering soon accosted Diels, who had also put in an appearance on the scene of the conflagration in record time. Most of the chief Nazi leaders of the day were at the Reichstag within minutes of the alarm being sounded, which made coordination of their ensuing actions remarkably quick and easy. Franz von Papen later provided a vivid account of the words Goering shouted at the Gestapo leader, for he had worked himself into a lather of rage and indignation by this time: "This is the beginning of the Communist revolution! We must not wait a minute. We will show no mercy. Every Communist official must be shot, where he is found. Every Communist deputy must this very night be strung up." (Shirer, 2011, 196).

A quick death from a bullet or noose would likely have been a kindness compared to the actual fate of many of those on Diels' lists. The first arrests began almost immediately, though they were not to achieve their full momentum until early the next afternoon, when Hitler's position as dictator was firmly established by legal decree of the President and Reichstag of the Weimar Republic. Hitler seized the opportunity presented to him with both hands. Loudly and forcefully trumpeting his version of events – that the Reichstag fire was a signal for a Communist revolution which, curiously, showed no signs whatsoever of developing in reality – the Chancellor appeared before the gathered officials of the Weimar Republic at 11 a.m. on the morning of February 28 while the ashes of the Reichstag interior were still hot. Hitler was bearing a decree from the 1920s, originally drafted during an anti-communist panic, and an authoritarian fanatic, Ludwig Grauert (a man in the employ of Hermann Goering), had added extra material to it in the form of a second clause which made the powers it granted to the Chancellor even more sweeping and arbitrary. If it was approved and signed by President Hindenburg, it would more or less give Hitler almost unlimited power. Incredibly, Hindenburg's cabinet, frightened by the Reichstag fire and the bogeyman of Communist revolution, accepted the document and presented it to the President, though Franz von Papen expressed dismay at the idea and urged his colleagues to reject the proposal out of hand. Hindenburg showed remarkably little hesitation before signing the decree, propelling Hitler to the position of absolute dictatorship he was to occupy until he took poison along with Eva Braun in the fire-streaked darkness of Berlin a dozen years later in order to avoid capture and torture at the hands of the victorious Soviets.

The decree, which has gone down in history as the "Reichstag Fire Decree," suspended most of the democratic guarantees and rights in the Weimar Republic. "Thus restrictions on personal liberty, on the right of free expression of opinion, including freedom of the press, on the right of assembly and association, and violations of the privacy of postal, telegraphic and telephonic communications, and warrants for house-searches, orders for confiscations as well as restrictions on property rights are permissible beyond the legal limits otherwise prescribed." (Evans, 2005, 336).

This remarkable document went on to give Hitler the power to assume absolute power over any of Germany's states where such a measure was deemed "necessary," and it gave the Chancellor and those he delegated the power to inflict death penalties for the appallingly broad, vague crime of "disturbing the peace." This decree was to remain in effect "until further notice," which in practice meant forever, or at least until shells, bombs, and bullets broke the strength of the "Thousand-Year Reich." Hindenburg's signature was the suicide note of the Weimar Republic, and it marked the President's personal obeisance to the man he had very recently scorned as the "Bohemian corporal." A single signature put an end to the democratic experiment in Germany and ushered in 12 years of terror, murder, war, and one of the most brutal dictatorships in history.

Naturally, Hitler wasted no time in utilizing his freshly acquired totalitarian powers. The arrests that Diels and Goering had already begun now attained the color of authority and legality, and the SA joined with the police in a sweeping purge of the German population. The flails of legalized Nazi aggression winnowed the political field, removing the best candidates of opposing parties and leaving only the compliant Nazi party members in the legislature: "Some four thousand Communist officials and a great many Social Democrat and liberal leaders were arrested, including members of the Reichstag […] Truckloads of storm troopers roared through the streets all over Germany, breaking into homes, rounding up victims and carting them off to S.A. barracks, where they were tortured and beaten. [...] the Social Democrat newspapers and many liberal journals were suspended and the meetings of the democratic parties either banned or broken up." (Shirer, 2011, 198 -199).

Notably, although the official Nazi party line was the that Reichstag fire was caused by Communists as a signal for a Soviet-style revolution, the Social Democrats were arrested and tormented with equal zeal by the police and SA. The agenda of silencing all potential political opponents, including those who were in favor of democracy and did not even think of using extralegal force to attain their goals, became nakedly apparent less than 24 hours after Chief Constable Buwert fired his pistol at unknown prowlers in the Reichstag. The Nazis' preeminence in the elections of March 6th, 1933 had been assured in one bold, unscrupulous stroke.

Oppression of the Jews began almost immediately as well. The populace had been propagandized into blaming the Jews for Germany's defeat in World War I, shifting blame rather than accepting that Germans, like all other humans, had limitations despite their courage and intelligence and could be overwhelmed by a numerous, determined adversary. The Jews also made a convenient scapegoat for the subsequent financial miseries that racked Germany during the postwar years.

Ironically, it was the very helplessness of the Jews that made them a prime choice for targeting because of their "undue power" over the fate of Germany. Accused of being so powerful as to be able to bring down a formidable military power through practically invisible means, the Jews were somehow also so powerless that they could fall ready victims to the anger of the mob. The reality, of course, is that the Jews were a "safe" target for the people to take out their frustrations on. Representing less than 1% of the population, they did not have the numbers to resist hordes of Germans baying for their blood, and even before the rise of the Nazis, the government tacitly colluded with the anti-Semites by failing to properly protect its own Jewish citizens.

Hitler may indeed have convinced himself of the bizarre conspiracy theories about World War I, thus justifying denial of the unpalatable truth that the despised Allies had simply outfought the German army and defeated it. Whatever the case of his personal beliefs, the Jews made a convenient conduit for the fear and aggression of the German people, which might otherwise have been directed against the SA thugs running rampant over civil liberties. Regardless, beatings, rapes, and killings of Jews became norms that the authorities winked at, and on April 1, 1933, just a little over a month after the Reichstag fire, Hitler began a boycott of Jewish businesses intended to deprive his chosen victims of what little economic power they actually had. Jackbooted SA roughnecks posted signs in shop windows or loitered menacingly at the entrances to deter people from entering and buying from the proprietors. The measure was mostly a failure, but it served as an ominous warning of worse events to ensue.

One aspect of Hitler's rise to power which is frequently overlooked by modern historians was the massive program of disarmament and gun control which the Nazis instituted, confiscating private firearms in order to ensure their rule was undisputed. A far-flung campaign of search and seizure was started, with anyone found in possession of a gun classified as a "Communist" even though most of those afflicted in this manner were law-abiding Social Democrats. "The Nazis succeeded in creating a 'Communist gun owner' bogeyman to justify extensive searches and seizures conducted by the police to confiscate firearms and arrest their owners. To carry out these measures, some 5,000 auxiliary police composed of SA, SS, and Stahlhelm members were enrolled in Berlin alone." (Halbrook). Of course, the three Nazi organizations that backed Hitler – the SA, SS, and Steel Helmets – were not only permitted to keep their weapons but were armed with pistols and steel-shafted clubs by the government in cases where the men did not already possess such arms. Anyone who did not belong to these organizations, however, was apt to be arrested and placed in the concentration camps Hitler already found necessary to contain the hordes of undesirables he and his cronies alone seemed to be able to detect in the German population.

Given the robust tradition of shooting clubs in Germany, which stretched back as far as the "crossbow leagues" of the medieval era, the arrests that followed Hitler's strict gun control measures were extensive and occurred all across Germany. Though most of those arrested were later released, perhaps somewhat worse for wear, this measure did have the effect of removing armed male citizens not directly affiliated with the Nazi party from circulation at precisely the moment when popular resistance to the Fuhrer's takeover might have been effective. After all, these measures came before the Nazi state had truly consolidated its grip on Germany and acquired tanks and aircraft.

A second decree passed on March 24, 18 days after the Nazis won 44% of the seats in the Reichstag, completed the transition of Germany from the democratic experiment of the Weimar Republic to the personal fief of Adolf Hitler: "The Enabling Law – the popular name for the euphemistically-worded Law to Remove the Distress of the People and State – […] was the last nail in Weimar Republic's coffin […] Passed by the Reichstag, which then dissolved itself, the act provided that the cabinet could decree laws without consulting the Reichstag or the president. The chancellor – Hitler – was empowered to draft the laws, which could deviate from the Constitution." (Holbrook, 2013).

The burning of the Reichstag, whether it was a deliberate "false flag" operation or a random act of individual arson, was adroitly used as a springboard to absolute power by Hitler and his close clique of followers. The wily Fuhrer might have achieved supreme command over Germany by other means, but this is by no means certain. By having arrest lists prepared and the police, SA, and SS standing by even prior to the actual arson, the Nazis were positioned to severely disrupt the other major political parties on the eve of a crucial election.

Furthermore, the Reichstag fire created an atmosphere of paranoia and panic in which Hitler found it possible to force the passage of two decrees which gave him absolute authority over every level of German government and the life and death of every German citizen. The "Reichstag Fire Decree" of February 28 and the Law to Remove the Distress of the People and State of March 24 effectively abolished the law except as a manifestation of Hitler's will. Under the deeply flawed Weimar Republic constitution, this abolition was actually legal, which, along with the massive arrest program directed at non-Nazi gun owners during March 1933, served to utterly deflate any organized resistance to the Nazis' smooth and successful coup d'etat.

Van der Lubbe was clearly guilty of at least some minor acts of arson in the Reichstag, but it remains difficult to imagine that he could have created such an unstoppable whirlwind of fire without any chemical accelerants whatsoever and no tools beyond a box of large matches and his own shirt as kindling, all within the space of perhaps 10-15 minutes. The volatility of an ordinary shirt is not high, and it is certainly insufficient to trigger a flashover in a huge wood-paneled council chamber in just a matter of a few minutes. Furthermore, the Dutch arsonist clearly relied more on enthusiasm and chance than a careful methodology or knowledge of fires, which makes his chances of such a massive success that much smaller.

Still, van der Lubbe was a Communist of sorts, and therefore he was potentially useful to the Nazi hierarchy as a propaganda weapon. Considering that van der Lubbe's personality, insofar as it has come down to the present day in records, bears every stamp of an irrational, drama-seeking crank, one might perhaps suppose that he chose to be a Communist more because it was "shocking" and dramatic than through any conviction or true understanding of Communist principles.

Despite the fact that the Dutchman was an ideal "patsy" for the Nazis' power grab, it is possible that he was drugged during his trial to eliminate any chance that he would say anything that would disturb the Nazis' theory of a far-flung Communist plot. Surviving photos of van der Lubbe from his trial show him standing with his head slumped forward on his chest, eyes closed, and mouth hanging. Written accounts confirm that this was his demeanor throughout the trial except on two occasions when he appeared slightly more alert and managed to provide semi-coherent statements in contrast to his typical vague rambling: "On all but two of the trial's fifty-seven days van der Lubbe appeared with his head bent down over his chest, often drooling or with his nose running so that his police attendants had continually to wipe his face. He spoke in monosyllables or not at all [...] He repeatedly answered 'yes' and then 'no' to the same question. At best he answered questions only after a long pause. Sometimes he did not answer at all. Sometimes he giggled." (Hett, 2014, 127).

There is additional reason to believe that this grotesque farce involved use of drugs because of the precise correspondence of the Dutch mason's behavior to a person heavily dosed with the most frequently utilized sedative in Germany at the time. As one historian explained, "van der Lubbe's appearance and behavior during the trial were consistent with the symptoms of excessive ingestion of potassium bromide, which, in its trade application Cabromal, was one of the most common sedatives at the time. Potassium bromide, which tastes like salt, can easily be slipped into food; symptoms of its abuse include mental slowness, loss of memory, apathy, a constantly running nose, and a slumped body posture." (Hett, 2014, 150).

Since van der Lubbe, unlike the other prisoners, admitted to setting a fire in the Reichstag, his guilt was never really in question. However, despite his evident sedation, he always refused to implicate anyone else in his arson plot and insisted that he alone had been the author of it. This insistence probably stemmed not only from a powerful desire to lay claim to the distinction of being the lone wolf who had gutted the mighty Reichstag, but also to the fact that van der Lubbe probably did not know anyone else to blame. He could not supply the names of Communist supporters of his actions because he simply did not know them. This refusal to blame a wider Communist plot drove the Nazis wild and caused the trial to drag on endlessly as they hoped for a breakthrough confession that would support their version of events. Finally, even van der Lubbe said that being executed would be preferable to continuing the endless, pointless trial, and the judges obliged him by sentencing him to death by the guillotine. Several of the judges experienced poor health as a result of the trial's stresses, and one of them died shortly after the trial concluded.

There is no doubt that the burning of the Reichstag was exceedingly convenient for the Nazi party and Hitler. The police and SA were mobilized earlier the same day in preparation for a sweeping series of arrests both of Communists and Social Democrat leaders, which is a highly incriminating circumstance. After all, if Marinus van der Lubbe was the only arsonist involved, Diels and Goering could not have known he was about to strike.

Furthermore, the burning occurred immediately before an election, with just enough time left to give the Nazis the necessary interval to capture most of their main adversaries. Hitler then adroitly transferred all power to himself and made his will superior to the Weimar Republic constitution, even while technically leaving it in place to give his reign the color of legal legitimacy, with the Reichstag Fire Decree and the Enabling Law. The SA sprang into action, imprisoning Communists, Social Democrats, and non-Nazi firearms owners in droves with fierce energy and a high degree of coordination.

Given the preparations and the aftermath, there is plenty to suggest that the arson at the Reichstag did not take the Nazis by surprise. Instead, they seemed fully prepared to exploit every opportunity it offered them in great detail. While this evidence is purely circumstantial, some physical evidence is also compelling in establishing a group of SA saboteurs as the chief arsonists in the Reichstag, including the short length of time available for van der Lubbe's burning shirt to start a massive fire. According to some estimates, the amount of time required for van der Lubbe to reach the Plenary Chamber after breaking in would have left a mere 150 seconds between the ignition of his shirt and the vast pyre that was sending tongues of flame out of the 246 foot high cupola. There is insufficient time for a flashover or smoke explosion to occur even with the most generous estimates of van der Lubbe's arson skills.

Furthermore, van der Lubbe did not bring accelerants with him and could not have carried them in sufficient amounts to produce the observed conflagration. He could have brought them in during multiple trips into the interior, but there was simply no time for this to happen. At the same time, several experienced firemen on the scene testified to seeing burn trails indicating that gasoline or another accelerant had been poured along the floor: "One of the supporting judges […] took up the matter of the gasoline on the carpet. The trail ran from one door to the other, said [the fireman named] Gempp; a few stretches of carpet along the trail were "completely burned out." Gempp had bent down to smell the carpet, and believed that it had been gasoline or benzene [Benzin oder Benzol], [...] Lateit also testified to seeing a fire on a runner that led from the lobby into the plenary chamber, and described another fire running in a line against the wall, which at first he took for floor lighting." (Hett, 2014, 135 to 136). Such claims are consistent with the size, power, and rapidity of the fire, and they also rule out van der Lubbe as the sole arsonist.

In the end, regardless of whether it was van der Lubbe, Karl Ernst and his stormtroopers, or some other party who set the main fire in the Reichstag, there is a certain symbolic appropriateness that Hitler was almost literally anointed upon the ashes of democracy. The Reichstag was the heart of the Weimar Republic's attempt at representative government and bore the inscription "The German People" above its main entrance. Hitler's ascent to power came over the scorched wreck of the building representing political freedom and the people themselves.

Nazi Paramilitary Organizations

Nazism was an elusive beast from its inception. Its precepts included a general emphasis on "military virtues" and obsession with purity (which included loathing of sexual freedom in general and homosexuality in particular), an irrational, fanatical hatred of Jews as the scapegoat for all of the nation's problems, and a determination to make Germany strong and powerful again. This, combined with an eagerness to use violence to achieve its aims quickly and effectively, marked out the most visible features of a system that actually contained many incongruous and even contradictory elements: "The common denominator of Nazi appeal was as remote as the smile of the Cheshire Cat. In its negative form, it was a promise to make things different, in its positive form, a promise to make things better. […] This was the homogeneity of common disaffection." (Schoenbaum, 1967, 2).

This is exemplified strikingly by differing causes for anti-Semitism among different factions. Right-leaning Nazis felt that the Jews were Communist saboteurs seeking to destroy the business strength of German industry, while left-leaning Nazis believed the Jews were capitalist plotters seeking to crush German socialism in the name of an international conspiracy of moneyed interests. Both of these viewpoints could not be true at the same time (and neither was); yet the Nazi party managed to accommodate both within its overall culture.

Several major paramilitary organizations arose in Germany following World War I, but the most important were the Sturmabteilung (SA), the Schutzstaffel (SS), and the Stahlhelm (Steel Helmets). Though others existed, they eventually faded or were dissolved without incident when Hitler came to power.

The Steel Helmets was a veterans' organization which initially opposed the Nazis despite espousing a similar anti-Semitic, anti-communist agenda and openly working towards creating a dictatorship in Germany to sweep away what they perceived as the weakness and decadence of liberal democracy. This group received considerable financial aid from the Italian fascist dictator Benito Mussolini, who "sometimes privately termed National Socialism a 'parody of Fascism.' Though he had maintained unofficial contacts with Hitler for several years, the political group he had most subsidized in Germany had been the right-wing Stahlhelm." (Payne, 1995, 231).

The Steel Helmets eventually reached a membership of more than 500,000 men on the eve of Hitler's takeover March 1933, which is amazing considering that the organization had begun with a mere eight members at its inception: "The Stahlhelm formed during the height of the 1918 November Revolution when Imperial Army captain Franz Seldte and seven other returning veterans met in the basement of Seldte's small factory in Magdeburg. The Stahlhelm evolved into an influential political force despite contending with internal divisions and external competitors envious of the combat league's growing national organization." (Jones, 2014, 198).

The Steel Helmets would play a role in supporting its fellow fascists in the suppression of the Social Democrats and communists in the wake of the Reichstag fire, and it eventually had to grudgingly acknowledge the primacy of Hitler over the whole fascist movement in Germany, much as its sponsor Mussolini did around the same time. The organization first became a third paramilitary arm of the Nazi party alongside the SA and SS, but it was subsequently incorporated into the SA from 1934-1935 and eventually ceased to have any independent existence at all.

The SS, also known as the blackshirts, began in 1920 as a special detachment of the SA that provided guards for Nazi party meetings. However, when Heinrich Himmler became the leader of the SS in 1925, he began to develop it as an independent paramilitary organization loyal to Hitler and infused with his exact vision of Nazism. Members were carefully selected for their willingness to give Hitler their total loyalty and embrace his particular brand of Nazi ideology. The SS grew rapidly in numbers and power, to the point that it was also the most formidable of the three major organizations, with a strongly martial and almost ascetic streak (in contrast to the Steel Helmets and the hooligans who made up much of the SA). The SS were Hitler's "warrior monks" and attracted far more self-controlled, competent individuals than either of the other two organizations could muster.

Hitler and Himmler inspecting the SS in 1938

The SA was a sprawling "combat league" that did the heavy lifting in bringing Hitler to power, despite the falling-out which ensued shortly thereafter. Its leader was Ernst Röhm, a slightly overweight man with a mustache who was rumored to be homosexual. Röhm was a committed Nazi, but he leaned more towards the socialist vision, unlike Hitler's elitist and nationalist vision. At the time of the Reichstag fire, however, the SA appeared to be the main branch of Nazism, and it shouldered much of the initial work of suppression following the promulgation of the Reichstag Fire Decree. Its men were also quite possibly the arsonists who set the blaze alongside the incompetent pyromaniac Marinus van der Lubbe.

Hitler and Röhm inspecting the SA at Nuremberg in 1933

The SA was brash, loud, and violent, but it lacked the focus and keen edge of competence that marks an actual military organization. Ultimately, it was not an instrument that could confront the rest of Europe and nearly fight it to a standstill, a role that was reserved for the professional soldiers of the Wehrmacht and the fanatical elite of the Waffen SS. Instead, it was largely a gang of unemployed and underemployed men attempting to right their fortunes through the only means that seemed left to them: organized violence. As one historian put it, the SA "was largely dominated now by the type of man who was an extremist only till he got what he wanted, the man whose trauma [...] was not [...] war [...] but unemployment which led to loss of social status and individual self-respect. [...] He did not want to change the world by revolution, but merely to obtain for himself a place in it [...] Konrad Heiden coined the unforgettable phrase 'SA class' for those classes [who] were content to make claims upon the state — desperadoes in search of a pension." (Fest, 1995, 166).

Ironically, Röhm, a man with many idiosyncrasies that helped bring about his own downfall, appeared to view those who had never been in the military as being almost as subhuman and pernicious as he thought the Jews were. He loathed the majority of Germans who had never fought and considered them as parasites and traitors rather than simply a different manifestation of the culture which also produced the soldiers of the Heer. The SA commander also summed up his own personality in a strange but pithy manner: "Ernst Röhm once declared that he always took the opposite view." (Fest, 1995, 154). And yet, the men of the SA had no larger goals for themselves other than a measure of security, money, and personal power, so they naturally mirrored their leader's ideology at moments when an ideological stance became necessary. Röhm was consumed by many of the same hatreds as Hitler, including hatred of Jews, democracy, and communism, but he had no particular goal in mind other wishing for a perpetual revolution spiced with occasional combat and ample helpings of soldierly camaraderie. It is difficult to conceive of Röhm being able to put together a nation-state, even one as rickety as Hitler's Third Reich.

Nevertheless, a temporary alliance at least was in the best interest of all the right-wing German factions as 1932 drew to a close. The National Socialists held an important voting bloc in the Reichstag, but the Social Democrats still controlled a plurality of seats and the economy was beginning to show signs of improvement, meaning that the Nazis were likely to lose ground in the March 1933 elections. At this juncture, however, the appointment of Hitler as Chancellor and the burning of the Reichstag opened up a remarkable opportunity for the right-wing factions, and the other political parties played into their hands with a new approach to propaganda, though this was only the beginning of the stroke of good fortune that propelled the National Socialists toward a dictatorship: "All over Germany, electors were confronted with violent images of giant workers smashing their opponents to pieces, kicking them aside, yanking them out of parliament, or looming over frock-coated and top-hatted politicians who were almost universally portrayed as insignificant and quarrelsome pygmies. Rampant masculinity was sweeping aside the squabbling, ineffective and feminized political factions. Whatever the intention, the subliminal message was that it was time for parliamentary politics to come to an end." (Evans, 2005, 268).

Though often at odds with one another, the three largest right wing "combat leagues" found a brief moment of solidarity during these events, which should have sent a warning to the established Weimar government that something was amiss. The savage, gloating mood of their celebrations, as reported by eyewitnesses, also gave strong hints of the death and destruction which were to follow: "20,000 brownshirts followed one another like waves in the sea, their faces shone with enthusiasm in the light of the torches. 'For our Leader, our Reich Chancellor Adolf Hitler, a threefold Hail!' They sang 'The Republic is shit' ... Next to us a little boy 3 years of age raised his tiny hand again and again: 'Hail Hitler, Hail Hitler-man!' 'Death to the Jews' was also sometimes called out and they sang of the blood of the Jews which would squirt from their knives." (Evans, 2005, 289).

After the burning of the Reichstag, the Nazis predictably gained ground in the March 5th, 1933 elections which followed almost immediately. Surprisingly, they did not win a full majority, but they did achieve a plurality. While the SA terrorized the opposition, looted, killed, raped, and arrested, Hitler continued his program of "legally" transferring power to himself. On March 24th, 1933, the Enabling Act – whose rather ironic actual name was the Law to Remedy the Distress of People and Reich – was passed by the Reichstag, giving the Chancellor the ability to pass laws without the approval of the Reichstag. This legislation made Hitler's word law.

The laws that passed were explicitly stated as being able to deviate from the constitution or alter it, and two factors helped make this outcome possible. The first was that the vote, which was held at the Kroll Opera House, was attended by large numbers of heavily armed SA brownshirts and SS blackshirts, who made no secret of their violent intent should the desired outcome not be forthcoming: "Wild chants greeted us: 'We want the Enabling Law!' Young lads with the swastika on their chests looked us cheekily up and down, virtually barring the way for us. They quite made us run the gauntlet, and shouted insults at us like 'Centrist pig', 'Marxist sow'. In the Kroll Opera it was swarming with armed SA and SS [...] The debating chamber was decorated with swastikas […] SA and SS men placed themselves by the exits and along the walls behind us in a half-circle. Their attitude did not bode well for us." (Evans, 2005, 327).

To top off this confection of badgering and raw intimidation, the Center Party, controlled by the Catholic Church, had come to a secret agreement with Hitler. The SA and SS presence alone would likely have been sufficient to coerce the desired result, but Hitler had decided to "make assurance doubly sure" by winning the support of the Catholic Church for his dictatorship with what the novelist Robert Crichton pithily called "the bribe of fear:" "Following the general trend of political Catholicism in interwar Europe, it had come to support the principles of authoritarianism and dictatorship out of fear of Bolshevism [...] Now, under stronger clerical influence than ever before, and led by a Catholic priest, Prelate Ludwig Kaas, the party was reassured in two days of discussions with Hitler that the rights of the Church would not be affected by the Enabling Act." (Evans, 2005, 326).

The vote for the Enabling Act was 444 in favor and 94 against. Several Social Democrat Reichstag representatives had been arrested on their way to the vote, reducing the number of unfavorable votes, while a number of others had already left Germany, fearing the consequences of the Act. Even had they been present, however, the outcome would have been the same.

Hitler's winning political strategy, apart from the use of conscienceless brutality and swift, violent application of force in whatever quantity was needed to overwhelm the opposition, was ultimately an adherence to legal procedures which gave all his actions the color of legitimate authority. At this point, he actually may have been able to summon his brownshirts, blackshirts, and Steel Helmets to depose and kill Paul von Hindenburg outright and subsequently declare himself dictator, but he chose a course in which bold, vigorous manipulation of the law sequentially granted him all the powers and attributes of a dictator while appearing to remain within the legal framework of the Weimar Republic's Constitution. That constitution, in fact, nominally remained in force until the fall of the Third Reich in 1945.

The Night of the Long Knives

In a matter of months, Hitler quickly assumed his powers in sequential fashion, rather than all at once. The sequence was rapid enough to keep his opponents off balance, and it was clearly of dubious legality, but it maintained an outward appearance of order that alleviated the fears of conservative elements such as the business community and the army General Staff, as well as middle-class Germans clinging to comforting illusions in an age of tumult. Of course, those who didn't support this rise to power were dealt with savagely by the stormtroopers and the Gestapo, sent to concentration camps, beaten to death while "resisting arrest," or arrested in the middle of the night to be tortured and executed in some secret police basement.

The impetuous Ernst Röhm and his rowdy brownshirts, however, threatened to upset Hitler's gradual progression. "It was precisely Ernst Röhm's lack of understanding of this concept of the gradual revolution carried out under the cloak of legality that led to his death and that of his followers. Naturally, Hitler's brutal action against Röhm lifted for one moment the carefully constructed backdrop and revealed what was going on offstage, where he and the rest of the leading actors of the 'legal revolution' were disclosed, without any disguise, in their unconditional determination to gain power." (Fest, 1995, 48).

The SA's presence vastly multiplied the effect of Goering's police in carrying out a nationwide series of arrests, beatings, and murders to secure Hitler's position atop the ruins of democratic government. The group continued to suppress elements which also opposed Hitler, such as champions of liberal democracy or communist sympathizers, and they carried out the Fuhrer's program of gradually introducing various oppressions against the Jews, whom they loathed with a bitter, irrational passion.

However, as time passed, the SA came to represent a hazard to the Third Reich with their ungovernable restlessness and personal allegiance to Röhm. In part, their importance and influence in the events of 1933 made Hitler worry about his own ability to control the group, and the Fuhrer attempted to keep the SA occupied with various kinds of busy-work, ranging from the horrific (such as torturing prisoners at early concentration camps, where the guards were under even less control than they were during the Holocaust) to the almost humorously mundane (such as parading around with collection boxes to gather a few extra marks for the Reich treasury or going to church on Sundays in their finest kit).

At the same time, many members of the SA were not content to be mere police in Hitler's new order. Many desired a higher social status, and some used the threat of force to become minor officials or business partners in lucrative enterprises. This problem was particularly rife away from the seat of authority; despite the existence of telecommunications, physical distance from the capital still had a much more notable effect in attenuating central command and control in the 1930s.

This petty self-aggrandizement might have been tolerated, but Röhm set about making himself inconvenient to Hitler almost from the day of the Fuhrer's ascension to supreme power in the new "Thousand-Year Reich." "With an unmistakably threatening undertone he declared, referring to the many mass proclamations of the victory of the national revolt, that he 'preferred to make revolutions rather than celebrate them' […] Deeply offended, he accused Hitler of being nothing but 'a civilian, an "artist", a dreamer'. From the summer of 1933 onwards he […] organized huge parades all over the Reich, voicing his discontent in numerous critical utterances." (Fest, 1995, 167-168).

Puffed up with his own self-importance, Röhm apparently did not appreciate that he was dealing with incredibly dangerous men. Himmler, a quiet, unassuming psychopath with a deceptively weak chin and thick glasses, was one of the individuals Röhm underestimated. Himmler, a strange mixture of serial killer and visionary, saw immense potential in the SS and set about honing it into an elite instrument of both political murder and battlefield excellence. Though theoretically still a branch of the SA, Himmler soon detached the SS from the brownshirts in all but name and made a truly formidable instrument out of them, unlike the loudmouthed but ultimately low quality ranks of the SA.

Hitler wanted to build a new order and thus had concrete objectives he hoped to achieve, but Röhm desired an ongoing state of revolution, and he was a loose cannon with a horde of utterly amoral followers. Röhm's avowed goal was the toppling of all governments, and this idea could hardly have been pleasing to Hitler, busy as he was building a new totalitarian government

That said, Röhm's complaints may have merely been examples of simple grumbling due to feeling useless. After all, for someone who had been in the thick of the action in 1933, it wouldn't be surprising if Röhm felt that Hitler was not giving him anything to do worthy of his mettle. It is even possible that his posturing was a strange cry for attention from the Fuhrer, and while he definitely got Hitler's attention, it was not in the manner he wished. Dictators have rarely survived and prospered by being hesitant to deal with potential threats, and Hitler was driven by his keenly-honed survival instinct to respond decisively to Röhm's vague but persistent bellowing about a second revolution.

Another highly important factor in Hitler's eventual opposition to the SA's continued existence was their effect on people the Fuhrer needed as props for his regime. Though he was master of life and death over every German citizen and literally commanded every resource of the state, Hitler was still human, and he needed powerful backers in order to maintain his position and carry out his plans. One major faction the SA threatened to alienate from the Third Reich's cause were the owners of big businesses and other major capitalists. These men gave tremendous financial and material backing to the Nazis, and Hitler was exceedingly weary of offending them, whatever his private opinion of them might have been. The SA's constant talk of a "Second Revolution" and its sporadic but strident calls for all businesses to be nationalized in the name of a socialist worker's state did go unnoticed. In fact, it engendered great alarm among the wealthy, including industrialists, investors, and successful entrepreneurs.

Of course, most of the SA members were merely fixated on short-term goals like obtaining a government paycheck and perhaps indulging their sadistic impulses and enjoying an unfamiliar sense of empowerment through occasional fights, beatings, arson, or murders. Some were likely harmless individuals who simply joined out of economic desperation and then kept their heads down while collecting their pay and staying out of trouble as much as possible. A much stronger revolutionary spirit was present in some, however, and particularly in the leadership, including Ernst Röhm.

The industrialists' fears of a communist fifth column within the SA, while considerably overblown, did have some basis in reality. Most SA members were working class people, unlike the middle and professional class SS, and a large number were former communists or perhaps cryptocommunists lurking within a dictatorial organization which made them feel comfortable in the absence of Soviet despotism. As one historian noted, "According to Diels's subordinate Gisevius, at least a third of the post-1933 SA was made up of former Communists for whom "the popular phrase ... was 'Beefsteak Nazis'—Brown on the outside, red inside.'" A leading functionary in the KPD's Red Sport organization gave a figure of 20 percent. The SA itself gave a figure of 55 percent. Internal SA memoranda, the surviving files of the Gestapo, and reports from the KPD [...] all contain evidence of a significant Communist presence in the SA." (Brown, 2009, 138-139).

If the SA's "Beefsteak Nazis" were distasteful and alarming to the business community, they were abhorred with equal intensity by the officer corps of the regular army. Deeply conservative, with large numbers of noblemen serving in their ranks, the army men turned up their noses at the plebeian boorishness of the SA, its avid enjoyment of beer halls, and its coarse approach to violence.

There was also a much deeper, politically founded objection to the SA beyond any repulsion caused by class. The Army, like any faction, wished to maintain its own existence and keep the power that it already possessed, as well as looking for opportunities to expand it. The SA represented an explicit threat to the Army's continued existence as an independent entity, and the brownshirts repeatedly called for the Army to be dissolved into its ranks. "Röhm was a particular enemy of the Reichswehr, and, because of his plans for amalgamating the Reichswehr and the SA into a National Socialist militia, antagonized the generals, who were jealous of their privileges. 'The grey rock,' he would say, 'must be submerged by the brown flood.'" (Fest, 1995, 168).

The "grey rock," of course, was the Reichswehr, which got its name from the distinctive "field gray" uniforms. The "brown flood" were the brownshirts of the SA, who eventually came to number between 3 million and 5.5 million. Winning over the Army, of course, would be a major advantage to Hitler in keeping his newfound power, and any action clipping the SA's wings tended to make a favorable impression on the influential officer corps. "The Army, for its part, regarded the SA as 'brown scum,' and was eager to cooperate with Hitler." (Littlejohn, 1990, 6).

Hitler, Goering, Joseph Goebbels, and Rudolph Hess all took part in planning the purge

June 30, 1934, the Night of the Long Knives, marked the start of a brief, violent, and highly effective purge of the SA's top ranks planned by the Nazi leadership and conducted through the SS and Himmler. By the end of this ruthless surgical strike, Ernst Röhm would be a bullet-riddled corpse and hundreds of others would be dead. Known by the codename of "Operation Kolibri" ("Operation Hummingbird"), the Night of the Long Knives is also called the Röhm Putsch in recognition of its chief victim. The plot took some time to develop, however, and it emerged out of the interplay of various factions and forces.

Hitler secured the backing of the Army in the first months after his accession to the Chancellorship by surreptitiously beginning rearmament, and he took further major steps in late July 1933 when "the Chancellor promulgated a new Army Law, abolishing the jurisdiction of the civil courts over the military and doing away with the elected representation of the rank and file, thus restoring to the officer corps its ancient military prerogatives. A good many generals and admirals began to see the Nazi revolution in a different and more favorable light." (Shirer, 2011,

201).

At the same time, Hitler apparently held back somewhat from immediately condemning Röhm, despite the SA leader's increasingly belligerent rhetoric. The coming of the cooler months at the end of 1933 seemed to have temporarily cooled the anger of the various faction leaders as well. Hitler appointed Röhm to his cabinet on December 1, 1933, an expansive gesture even though the bellicose Röhm was ill-suited to a political role that did not immediately involve the use of clubs, pistols, or dynamite. Nonetheless, on New Year's Day, 1934, the Nazi papers published an extremely warm and informal holiday greeting from the Fuhrer to Röhm.

Hitler was seemingly ready to reconcile with Röhm and the SA at this point, but events developing among the powerful factions would eventually force his hand. During 1933 and into the start of 1934, Goering and Himmler made an alliance out of necessity; Himmler was developing the SS into an effectively independent force and also moved to take over the Gestapo. Due to his quiet, calm personality, he was scarcely noticed for a long time by his colleagues, but he worked constantly to develop his control over the SS and hone it into a highly disciplined, coldly loyal fighting force utterly unlike the loutish SA. In the process, the SS threatened to grow more influential than Goering's political police, who were typically at the center of power in a police state such as the Third Reich. One historian explained, "By the autumn, his efforts began to bear fruit, as one state after another offered him the command of their political police. It was a slow, patient process, a nibbling and gnawing rather than grabbing and gobbling, but by March 1934 Himmler had achieved the remarkable feat of commanding every single political police force in the Reich, with the exception of Prussia." (Read, 2004, 347).

The remaining puzzle piece, Prussia, was Goering's private domain. In order to keep the Gestapo out of the hands of his rival, Wilhelm Frick (the Reich Minister of the Interior), Goering cut a deal with Himmler, enlisting the bespectacled psychopath's aid in exchange for officially making him Inspector of the Gestapo. This made Himmler the second in command of the sinister police force and left Goering as its head. Reinhard Heydrich, the notorious "Blond Beast" who once shot a full-length mirror in which he himself was reflected in a spasm of disgust over rumors of Jewish blood in his background, was also brought into the senior command structure.

Frick

Heydrich

    Goering's immediate objective was to keep Frick's hands off the Gestapo, which was a potent tool of political influence, but he had his sights set on much bigger goal, and enlisting Himmler was part of the former air ace's plan to encompass the destruction of the SA in general and Röhm in particular. Like Hitler, Goering viewed Röhm as a powerful threat to his own position and the stable Nazi state he hoped to help build and thrive in. As one historian pointed out, "it also meant that Göring could harness his nationwide secret police network and the SS to the dangerous task he was about to undertake: a deadly assault against Ernst Röhm and the SA. Göring had never liked Himmler, despising his priggish punctiliousness, but his SS was the only weapon capable of decapitating the SA without the risk of civil war; giving him the Gestapo was a necessary quid pro quo to ensure his support." (Read, 2004, 349).

    Goering had several reasons for taking this risky step. One was that he believed, rightly or wrongly, that Röhm intended to kill him along with Germany's capitalists when and if the SA leader brought about the "Second Revolution" that was seemingly always on his lips. Another was that he clearly understood Röhm's ambition to dissolve the German Army into the ranks of the SA, a step which outraged Goering's sense of propriety, as he was himself a decorated veteran of World War I. It also outraged his sense of greed and will to power, since he wanted the Reichswehr restored to full strength and himself placed at its head, something that would be impossible were it consumed by the upstart SA.

Goering and Himmler, having finally reached an accord in March 1934 and a pact to destroy Röhm, set about generating reams of falsified evidence indicating that Röhm intended to depose and execute Hitler. It is conceivable that Röhm had vague notions in this direction anyway, though he was later to vehemently deny it, but there was actually no concrete proof of such an intention. Himmler and Goering were not men to be stopped by a mere lack of evidence, however, and they soon had their forgers busily generating the necessary supporting documentation, complete with faked Röhm signatures.

This pair of schemers were not the only persons sharpening their metaphorical knives for Röhm's neck either. The Army was growing progressively more alarmed and infuriated as Röhm expressed more and more loudly and persistently that he would soon eliminate the Reichswehr by melding it into the SA. Röhm showed the cardinal weakness in a despotic leader of talking too much before he was prepared to actually put any of his schemes into action, giving his enemies ample time to ready their own counterstrike and, as the event proved, execute it with extreme prejudice. In fact, it is quite possible that Röhm's talk was nothing but bluster which he would never have acted on, but all that mattered was that his enemies thought it was true.

Moreover, Röhm took certain actions that also increased the alarm and aggression of the men seeking to work his ruin. The SA was supposed to be armed only with clubs, pistols, brass knuckles, and similar weapons, which were useful mainly for lethal political brawls and for mauling ordinary citizens on whom the wrath of the authorities had fallen. However, Röhm and his lieutenants began to stockpile rifles, heavy machine guns, and other military grade weapons. It was actually illegal for the SA to possess these armaments, so the acquisitions were carried out in a furtive manner intended to maintain strict secrecy. Nothing escaped the vigilance of the Gestapo, however, and Himmler, Goering, and the Army chiefs were soon apprised of this militarization of the SA. They did not dare to openly protest, but their resolve to see Röhm arrested and executed was further steeled and given additional urgency.

It was the Army that ultimately forced Hitler's hand, supported by Goering's bold forgeries. As the summer of 1934 began, Vice Chancellor Papen recovered a slight measure of backbone and indirectly confronted Hitler. He made a speech condemning the current state of affairs at Marburg on June 17, 1934, which infuriated the Fuhrer so much that he publicly called Papen a "pygmy." However, in a last flicker of his old fighting spirit, the elderly President, Paul von Hindenburg, called Hitler's bluff. The Fuhrer "was aware of reports that the President was so displeased with the situation that he was considering declaring martial law and handing over power to the Army. In order to size up the seriousness of this danger [...] he flew to Neudeck on the following day, June 21, to see Hindenburg. [...] He was met by General von Blomberg [who] brusquely informed Hitler [...] that unless the present state of tension in Germany was brought quickly to an end the President would declare martial law and turn over the control of the State to the Army." (Shirer 222).

Hindenburg saw Hitler briefly and fully confirmed this statement. It was likely this incident that compelled Hitler to seize the title of President (along with that of Chancellor) once Hindenburg died at the age of 86 on August 2 of that year. For the moment, however, he was unexpectedly backed into a corner, because the Army the destruction of the SA's leadership, the execution of Ernst Röhm, and that Hitler take steps to render the combat league harmless while reaffirming the independent power of the Reichswehr.

Hitler was still dubious enough to consult with his leading men, Goering and Himmler, who were no doubt filled with surprise and delight at this turn of events. With that, the two schemers presented their heaps of forged documents, which seemed to implicate Röhm in a coup attempt. Hitler's mood of doubt dissolved into white-hot rage against the SA chieftain and his followers. His anger was probably fueled by his sense of helplessness to resist the Army's demands as well.

At a secret meeting with Army representatives, the Fuhrer agreed to quash the SA. Hitler devised a simple but effective plan to corral the leading members of the SA and place them where he wanted them. Since Ernst Röhm was taking the waters at the famous spa town of Bad Wiessee, the Fuhrer proposed that he should meet there with all of the leading lights of the SA to discuss the situation and work out a solution to any difficulties. Bad Wiessee is a spa town located on the shore of Lake Tegernsee. Clustered along the shore of the narrow, blue-green lake, the town is backed by forested heights which are part of the northern Alps. Many of the trees are conifers, but the deciduous trees were also in full leaf in late June. The town is noted for its peaceful mood, sulfur spring, and excellent views. Röhm and his followers readily assented, and the date for the meeting was set for June 30th.

Hitler kept his appointment with Röhm to meet in Bad Wiessee on June 30, 1934, but the meeting was on very different terms than the SA chief expected. On the evening of June 29, 1934, Röhm and his accompanying lieutenants retired to a number of rooms rented at the Hanslbauer Hotel, a white-walled, multi-story lodging in Bad Wiessee that is still operational today (though it has been renamed as the Hotel Lederer am See). The men had indulged in an evening of good food and abundant liquor, and they soon fell into a sound sleep. In fact, Röhm felt so confident and relaxed that he left his bodyguard of armed SA men behind in Munich, many miles away and too far away to help. Only the SA chief's leading officers were present, including "Edmund Heines, the S.A. Obergruppenfuehrer of Silesia, a convicted murderer, a notorious homosexual with a girlish face on the brawny body of a piano mover, [who] was in bed with a young man." (Shirer, 2011, 224).

While the men slept and digested what was for some their last meal and final goblet of wine, a Junkers JU-52 "Iron Annie" aircraft landed at Munich airfield at 4:00 a.m. This airplane disgorged Adolf Hitler himself, Viktor Lutze (the future SA head), the press leader Otto Dietrich, the propagandist Goebbels, and a squad of grim-faced adjutants. Local Nazi party officials were waiting on the airfield to greet the Fuhrer of the Third Reich and take his orders, whatever they might be. The Fuhrer's first words upon arrival were to express a certain regret at the violence about to erupt at his command, for he remarked to several officers among the delegation meeting him, "This is the blackest day of my life. But I shall go to Bad Wiessee and pass severe judgment. Tell that to General Adam." (Read, 2004, 368). Hitler then ordered a car and drove to the Bavarian Interior Ministry, where he would soon order the day's first arrests.

Lutze

August Schneidhuber and Wilhelm Schmid, the local SA leaders, were summarily ordered to appear before the Fuhrer at the Interior Ministry, and when they arrived, Hitler met them with a shouting tirade in which he denounced them as traitors and promised their speedy execution. Rushing at the men, he furiously tore the rank insignia off their uniforms, after which they were dragged away by lurking SS men and flung into Stadelheim Prison. SS and police squads were sent scurrying in all directions to arrest other local SA functionaries and likewise remand them to Stadelheim.

Stadelheim Prison

The sun was coming up on a beautiful June morning when a shoal of black automobiles sped out of Munich along the road towards Bad Wiessee. These carried a furious Hitler, his small entourage, a band of heavily armed SS men, and a squad of Bavarian police detectives. The original plan had been to wait for the SS Leibstandarte and its leader, the infamous Sepp Dietrich, before moving on Röhm himself. However, Hitler was too enraged to wait, and he sped off with the men he was able to gather quickly.

Dietrich

Röhm was awakened at 6:30 in the morning when the door to his hotel room crashed open. Blinking sleepily in the light filtering through the neat hotel curtains, the SA commander saw Hitler standing at his bedside holding a drawn pistol. Nonplussed, Röhm greeted his former friend and leader with a muttered "Heil, mein Fuhrer!" In response, "his Fuhrer yelled that he was a traitor and was under arrest. Leaving two detectives to watch Röhm, Hitler moved on to bang on the doors of the other SA leaders […] and repeated the process. […] Edmund Heines […] was found in bed with a fair-haired young man, to the great disgust of Hitler and Goebbels, who later described the scene as 'revolting – almost nauseating.'" (Read, 2004, 369).

Heines

Heines resisted weakly and refused to get out of bed when ordered to do so. Hitler gave him five minutes to rouse himself or be shot on the spot, and when Heines was still in bed at the end of that period, the Fuhrer shouted for his SS men. Bursting into the room, the black-uniformed riflemen seized both Heines and his 18-year-old lover and dragged them roughly out onto the neat hotel grounds. There, both men were shot to death on the hotel lawn.

In a contrasting act of mercy, Erich Kempka, Hitler's driver, recalled a different though equally remarkable moment from the Night of the Long Knives: "Röhm's doctor comes out of a room and to our surprise he has his wife with him. I hear Lutze putting in a good word for him with Hitler. Then Hitler walks up to him, greets him, shakes hand with his wife and asks them to leave the hotel, it isn't a pleasant place for them to stay in that day." (Kempka, 2010, 48).

However, the rest of the SA men were herded temporarily into the hotel laundry room while police detectives were sent into the town to hire a vehicle in which to transport them to Stadelheim Prison. While waiting, Röhm sat under guard, saying nothing and looking sad and dejected, though the SS allowed the hotel staff to bring the fallen SA leader a cup of coffee. The police soon rented a bus from a local business, which proved to be a somewhat shabby vehicle but operational nevertheless, and the prisoners were hustled into it. With that, the cavalcade set out for Munich.

On the way, the convoy met a truck roaring along the road, and it happened to be filled with Röhm's SA bodyguards. These men had evidently been alerted by the arrests in Munich that all was not well and were coming to the rescue of their chief. However, the presence of Hitler appears to have overawed them, for they meekly returned to the city when ordered to do so by the Fuhrer even though they likely had enough firepower to wipe out Hitler and his small platoon of SS and detectives if they wanted to free their leaders from the bus.

Back in Munich, arrests continued. The SS staked out the railway stations and seized arriving SA dignitaries who thought they were on their way to a conference at Bad Wiessee, and by the end of the day, Hitler and his small SS detachment had bagged over 200 SA leaders, all of whom were locked away in the Stadelheim Prison.

At Hitler's instruction, Theodor Eicke and two SS officers were sent to Stadelheim Prison, and this grim trio entered Röhm's cell, where the SA leader sat and defiantly glared at them. As they had been directed by Hitler, the blackshirts placed one of Himmler's fake incriminating documents on the table, and beside it, a pistol containing one bullet. They then withdrew from the room and waited, listening for the sound of a shot. Hitler had thought himself merciful to give Röhm the "dignity" of taking his own life, but the only sound from within was obstinate silence. Accordingly, after waiting for 10 minutes, Eicke and his two henchmen drew their pistols and reentered the cell.

Whatever his many faults undoubtedly were – stupidity, arrogance, imprudence, and a coarse appetite for violence – Ernst Röhm was a brave and defiant figure in his last moments of life. He first declared, "If I am to be killed, let Adolf do it himself." According to a police lieutenant at the scene, "then Roehm stood at attention—he was stripped to the waist—with his face full of contempt" to await his death. The SS men raised their pistols and pumped a fusillade of bullets into the SA leader's boldly presented chest. Röhm, mortally wounded, toppled to the floor, gasped "Mein Fuhrer! Mein Fuhrer!" and died.

Although the purge of the SA is the best remembered part of the Night of the Long Knives, many other men died between 6:00 a.m. on June 30 and the end of July 2, 1934. As soon as the arrests had been completed at Bad Wiessee, Hitler called Goering on the telephone and gave him the code word "Kolibri" ("Hummingbird"), which launched the main phase of the purge that swept across Germany during those brutal three days. Goering carried out the attacks on the SA with venomous glee. He had always been a man capable of carrying an extreme grudge, and he now had the opportunity to avenge himself on those who had threatened and insulted him. "In Berlin, squads of Göring's special police roared out of their Lichterfelde barracks in trucks and on motorcycles to surround and take possession of the city's SA headquarters. Once they were in position, Göring joined them to march into the building at their head and supervise the arrests personally." (Read, 2004, 369).

Meanwhile, arrest and execution lists were sent throughout the country to local SS and Gestapo offices, and the purge got underway. Men were seized, flung into trucks, and taken to cells, forests, or other locations and shot to death. Some were killed with a flurry of blows from pickaxes. Vice Chancellor Papen was placed under house arrest for his own safety, but his luckless secretary, Herbert von Bose, was shot and killed by the SS when he sought to halt the ransacking of Papen's office.

As this was going on, a festively murderous mood took hold at Goering's headquarters as he, Heydrich, Himmler, and others worked on the execution lists. As Hans Gesevius described it, "Things suddenly begin to get very noisy in there. Police major Jakobi rushes out of the room in great haste with his helmet on and the chinstrap under his red face. Göring's hoarse voice booms out after him, 'Shoot them down. Take a whole company … shoot them down … shoot … just shoot them down … shoot!'" (Read, 2004, 370).

150 prisoners were shot at the police barracks in response to this tirade, while Karl Ernst, the SA man likely involved in burning down the Reichstag, was seized on his honeymoon road trip near Bremen. The SS men who pulled his car over smashed him on the head to render him unconscious and shot his new wife and his chauffeur, but both survived the ordeal. Ironically, Ernst evidently believed he was the victim of a Röhm plot; in the moments before he was executed, he defiantly bellowed "Heil Hitler!" at his executioners.

Many of those executed had no idea why they had been arrested and were now being lined up against a wall to be shot. One of the SA leaders Hitler had arrested when he arrived in Munich, August Schneidhuber, summed up both the confusion of the victims and the surprising courage many of them showed when he called out to the firing squad, "Gentlemen, I don't know what this is all about, but shoot straight." (Shirer, 2011, 225).

Finally, on July 2, 1934, Hitler and Goering agreed it was best to call an end to the killing. The order went out to stop arrests and executions, and by and large, this command was obeyed, though a few personal killings under official color occurred for a day or two afterward. Anywhere from around 300 to as many as 1,000 were dead, and thousands more SA men were in concentration camps being run by the SS or Gestapo. Hitler would actually forget to order the release of these prisoners, some of whom spent several years in the camps before being set free, but in any event, the Night of the Long Knives had successfully achieved its aim of destroying the SA leadership and thus rendering the "combat league" directionless and cowed.

Historians are still divided as to whether Röhm and SA threat was merely a figment of Hitler's fevered imagination fed by Goering's and Himmler's forgeries and impelled by the Army's determination to see the Sturmabteilung commanders liquidated, or whether Röhm was actually a genuine threat to the Fuhrer. On one hand, Röhm showed no signs of intending Hitler any harm at the Wiessee meeting, since he had dispensed with even his ordinary security detail. On the other hand, the SA chief was full of hubris and might have thought himself too powerful for Hitler to attack. Furthermore, the acquisition of heavy machine guns and other illegal weapons, accompanied by aggressive rhetoric about a Second Revolution, is somewhat damning.

One thing is certain, however; Hitler ended the Night of the Long Knives with his power strengthened, while Ernst Röhm died with pistol bullets puncturing their way through his heart and lungs in a squalid jail cell. Thus, in terms of the Fuhrer's perspective, the Night of the Long Knives cannot be classified as a mistake. At the very least, it had a neutral political outcome for Hitler, and at best, it headed off either an Army coup or a Second Revolution led by Röhm and his lieutenants. It was also an act of utterly cold-blooded murder of a man who had been a personal friend of the Fuhrer for decades, and of hundreds of other men who may well have been innocent of the charges against them. Regardless, the purge was carried out with almost no sign of remorse whatsoever, showing the true measure of Hitler in several ways.

The bulk of the SA survived the Night of the Long Knives, which was principally aimed at killing its leaders and certain obnoxious or dangerous individuals rather than a wholesale extermination of the organization. Even if the higher casualty figure of around 1,000 dead is accepted, it was a tiny number compared to the group's overall strength, which was in the millions. Nevertheless, the action had the desired effect. The working class SA members – perhaps accustomed to bowing to authority and accepting whatever misery fate inflicted on them thanks to their background, regardless of their outward swagger and braggadocio – accepted the results meekly and more or less quietly gave in to Hitler's arrangements.

The SA was not disbanded, but it was reorganized. Most notably, it gained a new Obergruppenführer in Viktor Lutze, a former postal worker and policeman who was a far cry from Ernst Röhm. A middle-class individual, Lutze enjoyed spending time with his wife and two daughters, playing ping-pong, and driving his car, which would prove fatal for him when he crashed while negotiating a sharp bend near Potsdam at excessive speed.

Lutze was unlikely to cause trouble for Hitler and appears to have been dedicated to simply doing his job. Charged by Hitler with the reorganization of the SA, including a directive noting that "SA men should be leaders, not ludicrous apes," Lutze oversaw a number of actions. The SS, which was already independent in fact, was formally split off from the SA and became a fully autonomous organization. The SA's air, motor, and skirmisher branches were detached and reassigned to completely different organizations.

The SA's focus shifted, but it continued to exist and perform various functions within the Third Reich. As World War II approached, it grew massively again as it was used to train men for the Wehrmacht without officially making them part of the Army, which would have been a dangerous signal to send to the rest of the world. Thus, what had once been a horde of revolutionary hooligans and stormtroopers became a professional training organization dedicated to instilling new recruits with discipline, weapons drill, and Nazi ideology. As one writer noted, the SA became "a sort of paramilitary sports club providing both physical and martial training […] The role of the SA as a preparatory school for the armed forces was established […] in January 1939 with the creation of the SA Wehrmannschaften." (Littlejohn, 1990, 7).

In the intervening years, the SA also served various other purposes. It provided a disciplined environment where energetic, aggressive young men could have their energies directed towards supporting the Third Reich rather than making trouble for the regime. It appeared in mass rallies, parades, and films as a unified, jack-booted colossus goose-stepping in unison and sending up thunderous salutes in response to the words of the Fuhrer, providing the German people and the world with an imposing vision of Nazi unity and power. It also furnished muscle for day-to-day intimidation of political dissidents and various assaults directed against Jews.

Indeed, one of its most notable actions following the Night of the Long Knives was Kristallnacht. This sudden outburst of anti-Semitic violence was triggered in 1938 when a young Jew named Herschel Feibel Grynszpan shot the diplomat Ernst vom Rath to death in Paris in revenge for the deportation of his family from Hamburg to Poland along with 12,000 other Jewish citizens of the Reich. At Hitler's command, the SA exacted a terrible vengeance on the Jews remaining in Germany, which served as a stark warning of worse horrors to follow: "Police officers watched as Nazi storm troopers looted thousands of Jewish homes and businesses, set fire to more than 300 synagogues in Greater Germany (Germany and Austria), and killed about 90 Jews. The government also shipped approximately 30,000 Jewish men to concentration camps. This pogrom was called Kristallnacht ('the night of broken glass')." (Goldstein, 2012, 249). The United States of America was one of the only nations in the world to make any protest over this outbreak of thuggery by withdrawing its embassy to signal its disapproval. Hitler simply believed that the Americans were under the thumb of Jewish financiers and not actually outraged over the Germans' trampling of human rights.

With the attention to detail characteristic of only the most cunning sadists, the Third Reich even punished Jews for the damage caused to city infrastructure in the process of attacking them. These penalties involved everything from vast fines to confiscations whose sole purpose was to lower the Jews' quality of life, cause difficulties for them, and inflict misery: "By the end of 1938, Jews in Germany had been fined one billion marks for the damage done to them on the night of the pogrom. In addition, they could no longer own or even drive a car; attend theaters, movie houses, concert halls, or events at sports arenas; or use public parks and swimming pools. The Gestapo, the German secret police, even went door to door confiscating radios." (Goldstein, 2012, 250).

With full control of the German state and his power consolidated, Hitler would subsequently focus outward, and in a matter of a few years, Austria, Czechoslovakia, and Poland would fall like dominoes as World War II. Less than 22 years later after the Armistice that ended World War I, another armistice would be signed in the same railway carriage used in November 1918. This time, it would bring about the end of hostilities in France after the Germans were victorious. A memorial building housing the carriage had been erected in 1927, and Hitler would symbolically use it for the surrender of France in 1940. American journalist William Shirer wrote of Hitler's reaction to the sight of the memorial and the carriage: "Through my glasses I saw the Führer stop, glance at the [Alsace-Lorraine] monument.... Then he read the inscription on the great granite block in the center of the clearing: 'Here on the eleventh of November 1918 succumbed the criminal pride of the German empire...vanquished by the free peoples which it tried to enslave.' I look for the expression on Hitler's face. I am but fifty yards from him and see him through my glasses as though he were directly in front of me. I have seen that face many times at the great moments of his life. But today! It is afire with scorn, anger, hate, revenge, triumph. He steps off the monument and contrives to make even this gesture a masterpiece of contempt. He glances back at it contemptuous, angry...Suddenly, as though his face were not giving quite complete expression to his feelings, he throws his whole body into harmony with his mood. He swiftly snaps his hands on his hips, arches his shoulders, plants his feet wide apart. It is a magnificent gesture of defiance, of burning contempt..."

After that Armistice was signed, the building was destroyed and the carriage was brought back to Berlin. It would take almost 5 more years for the Nazis to be decisively defeated, and as the Allies pushed towards Berlin at the end of World War II, the SS put the carriage to the torch.

Kristallnacht

In the intervening years, the SA also served various other purposes. It provided a disciplined environment where energetic, aggressive young men could have their energies directed towards supporting the Third Reich rather than making trouble for the regime. It appeared in mass rallies, parades, and films as a unified, jack-booted colossus goose-stepping in unison and sending up thunderous salutes in response to the words of the Fuhrer, providing the German people and the world with an imposing vision of Nazi unity and power. It also furnished muscle for day-to-day intimidation of political dissidents and various assaults directed against Jews.

Given the hindsight of the Holocaust and Kristallnacht, some often wonder about the continued presence of Jews in Hitler's Germany. With the increasing escalation of Hitler's anti-Jewish rhetoric, these people question why any Jews would have chosen to stay. Of course, it's necessary to understand both the context of the times and the way Jews were treated in other parts of the world. Even if Jews had been welcomed in other places in Europe at the time, there was the question of what would happen to their possessions, businesses, and relationships. Furthermore, there were obstacles to physically leaving Germany for average citizens as well.

In the 1930s, the Jewish population of Germany was quite small, comprising less than 1% of the population, and many of those Jews were not outwardly practicing their religion. Nevertheless, Hitler's new definitions of Jewishness targeted ethnicity, not simply religion, meaning that even those who had converted to other religions or married outside of the Jewish faith were potential targets of persecution.

In fact, Jews weren't experiencing much hospitality in Germany or Europe before Hitler's rise to power. In *Roots of Hate: Anti-Semitism in Europe Before the Holocaust*, William Brustein, a Jewish historian and author, focused on the existence of anti-Semitism throughout Europe and specifically compared generalized European anti-Semitism with Germany. In his studies, based upon the American Jewish Year Book (which catalogues notable events both positive and negative regarding the Jews by country[1]), he found that while all European countries had a record of anti-Semitic incidents, both the incidence and the level of violence involved in the acts were higher in Germany. The only place with a higher incidence of violent anti-Semitism was Romania.

As for when and why anti-Semitism became so common throughout Europe, Brustein marked 1870 as a key year in the rise of anti-Semitic activity in Europe. This can be explained, in part, by several historical changes. Among them, Brustein lists Russia's violent pogroms against the Jews, the success of political parties in several European states with outspoken anti-Jewish platforms, and the Dreyfus Affair.[2] This wave of anti-Semitic feeling was strengthened after World War I in the face of a collapsed economy and fear of the spread of Bolshevism in the wake of Russia's revolution in 1917.[3]

As early as 1850, Germany was influenced by at least two prominent thinkers who were outspoken anti-Semites, Paul de LaGarde and Julius Langbehn. Both thinkers "explicitly demanded a Fuhrer who would embody and compel unity and expunge all domestic conflicts"[4] in German region that had many. For both men, the world they knew had been destroyed by evil and "the villain was usually the Jew, who more and more frequently came to be depicted as the very incarnation of modernity".[5]

It was de LaGarde who first used the terms that Hitler so often employed - trichinae and bacilli - to describe the Jewish "vermin" who needed to be expelled from finance, journalism, and business. He wrote of the "Talmudic discipline" which had allowed the Jews to become a powerful influence in all cultures in which they dwelled, and he condemned German Christianity for its softness on them. Indeed, de LaGarde believed Christianity had to be condemned since it had refused to rid itself of its Jewish legacy, and he ultimately argued that the "twin agents of dissension"- liberals and Jews - had to be destroyed for Germany to live again.

---

[1] William I. Brustein, Roots of Hate: Anti-Semitism in Europe before the Holocaust (Cambridge, England: Cambridge University Press, 2003), 8, https://www.questia.com/read/107191654.
[2] Ibid., 6..
[3] Ibid., 7.
[4] Stern, Fritz. The Politics of Cultural Despair: A Study in the Rise of Germanic Ideology. Berkeley: University of California Press, 1961, p. xiii.
[5] Ibid., xix.

Paul de LaGarde

Julius Langbehn, a ne'er do well who would nonetheless capture the imagination of many German youth dissatisfied with Germany's political progress, explained his take on the Jews in the late 1880's: "The modern Jew has no religion, no character, no home, no children. He is a piece of humanity that had become sour…The aspiration of present-day Jews for spiritual and material domination evokes a simple phrase: Germany for the Germans. A Jew can no more become German than a plum can turn into an apple…"[6]

---

[6] Ibid., 141.

Julius Langbehn

In the years before 1938, the Jews had been systematically moved to the borders of cultural and political life in Germany, and some of the first overt acts of anti-Semitism consisted of random attacks on Jews following the Reichstag elections of 1933. This was followed by the Nazi party's effort to harass and eliminate Jewish lawyers and department stores (which were seen as detracting from German small businesses) from public life. In demonstrating against Jewish businesses, physical attacks occurred, but they remained rare; instead, Nazi supporters would block store entrances, place placards on store windows, and, in most cases, force the store to close temporarily by pressuring customers not to enter.[7]

As the *Judenpolitick*, or use of an anti-Semitic platform to help unite the German *volk*, continued to develop, the Nazis linked the Jew's lack of fitness to participate in economic life as lawyers and business owners with an inability and lack of right to vote. More organized boycotts came about as the Nazis successfully used the slogan "The Jews are our misfortune" to convince Germany's citizens that the root of all of their problems was the Jews living amongst them. By expelling the Jews from public life and punishing them for the "ills" they had brought on their Aryan neighbors, Germans could begin to restore greatness to their civilization.[8]

Much has been written about Germans who broke the boycott instituted by Hermann Goering on April 1st of 1933, but as Peter Longerich, professor of German History at the University of

---

[7] Longerich, Peter. Holocaust: The Nazi Persecution and Murder of the Jews. New York: Oxford University Press, 2010, p. 33.
[8] Ibid, 34-36.

London points out, those stories of bravery and disobedience were largely isolated to a few. Indeed, "the majority of the population evidently acted just as the regime had expected them to. On that day most people avoided going to Jewish shops. The boycott therefore largely achieved its aims."[9]

In the weeks that followed, Jews were removed by law from a large proportion of civil service positions, restricted from practicing in the medical and dental professions, and dismissed from their work in the arts. After that, there weren't many new restrictions and laws passed for a period of two years, but it was during this very period that discriminations against the Jews in the existing areas became status quo and a way of life unquestioned by most Germans and in some cases by the Jews themselves. Bringing the Jews to a state of "social death," a term used by sociologists and political scientists to describe slaves and others who find themselves of no account in a society, would allow actions against them that would have otherwise been unthinkable among polite society.

In the accounts of Kristallnacht that involved humiliating treatment of the elderly, women, children, World War I veterans, and others, some explanation for the apathy of the majority of non-Jewish Germans came about because of the next phase of discrimination: the passage of the Nuremberg Laws in 1935. Longerich credits the implementation of these laws as "one further step [after the segregation of Jews from public administration] towards the complete segregation of the Jewish minority from the German population."[10] The Nuremberg Laws had three major parts: to eliminate "racial miscegenation" between Jews and non-Jews; "to prevent 'marriages detrimental to the German people'"[11]; a separate citizenship law for Jews restricting full citizenship to 'those nationals of German or related blood who demonstrate by their behavior that they are willing and suitable to serve the German people and the Reich faithfully"[12]; and further restrictions on Jewish participation in economic life (restrictions that would result in close to 70% of businesses owned by Jews to be out of their control by 1938).[13]

Longerich also referred to the overt acts of violence and vandalism against Jews during this period as "a trial run for what was eventually to be the legally sanctioned isolation of the Jews".[14] He noted the importance of the Nuremberg Laws' passage "without notable resistance from the population" as important to meeting "conditions for continuing the persecution of the Jews" in Germany.[15] In other words, the apathy of the German people would be required for such actions to move forward.

As the Nazi party desired, the number of Jews who left Germany in response to the persecution increased in the years leading up to Kristallnacht. Emigration by the year has been estimated as follows:

1933: 37,000
1934: 23,000
1935: 21,000
1936: 25,000

By the last quarter of 1937, the number of Jews emigrating from Germany began to decline because it became more difficult to find countries that would accept them. Meanwhile, for Jews

---

[9] Ibid., 37.
[10] Ibid., 52.
[11] Ibid., 57.
[12] Ibid., 60.
[13] Ibid.
[14] Ibid., 54.
[15] Ibid. 61.

who stayed, whether by choice or by force, the gates continued to close on normal participation in German life in the areas of education, public accommodations, and entertainment. Jews began to develop their own subculture in response, one that showcased Jewish talent and creativity as and provided a place where Jews could gather in the continued hope that Nazi leadership and its pursuit of their demise would "blow over" and life would return to normal. Longerich argues that by the creation of these very alternatives, Jews helped consign themselves to their own elimination, in that "it made it easier for the NS state to record and control the Jews...[and that] the extensive attempts to achieve Jewish self organization [led to]further intensification of persecution".[16]

In his book *Nazi Terror: The Gestapo, Jews, and Ordinary Germans*, Eric Johnson attempts to clarify the issue of how "ordinary Germans" participated or merely observed apathetically as persecution of the Jews moved forward in Germany and its territories. In the year leading up to Kristallnacht, Johnson observed that there had been a significant stepping up of Jewish persecution and harassment in Germany, and once the Olympics of 1936 ended and Hitler no longer felt the pressure to put the best face on Nazi society internationally, Goering and others were given freer rein to do as they would with the Jews and their property. Even before Kristallnacht signaled the end of "any semblance of moderation in the Nazi's treatment of the Jews," new laws issued in 1937 and early 1938 forced Jews to sell their property and businesses for well below market value, prevented Jewish doctors, lawyers and other skilled workers from treating Aryans, segregated more of public life with the forced distinction of Jews in public accommodations and identification, and even required new parents to choose from a list of approved Jewish names for their children in order that they be identified as Jews.[17]

Within this atmosphere, cities such as Berlin that had once been considered havens for the Jews became dangerous places for them during Kristallnacht. One Jewish Berliner recalled, "On the 10th I had to go to work. As I went out of the house, I saw all the stores were smashed and Nazi storm troopers in their brown uniforms. Police stood around and didn't do anything. Berlin had always been a liberal city. Berliners as a whole have been tolerant to the Jews. Suddenly all that changed. Berliners turned out to be no different than anyone else."[18]

A study conducted on Jewish memoirs revealed that close to 40% of Jews living in Nazi Germany had not given up hope of staying until after the violence of the pogroms of 1938 and 1939. For the Jews of the city of Krefeld, where the Jews arrested on Kristallnacht were ultimately sent to Dachau prison camp, the November pogrom became a "turning point...even those that previously did not want to think about emigrating recognized that after their legal and economic elimination they were also threatened by their physical annihilation."[19]

By this time, however, emigration for Jews was harder than simply deciding to leave. Many countries erected walls to immigration as mass emigrations of the Jews took place, and it became harder to obtain a passport that would allow a Jew to return to Germany, a requirement for entrance into some countries. Furthermore, many Jews could ill afford the round trip tickets they would be required to purchase (despite having no intention of returning to Germany), and even those who could afford it found that the German bureaucracy made it practically impossible to exit the country. For those few who did manage to find a country of destination, secure exit

---

[16] Longerich, 89.
[17] Johnson, Eric. Nazi Terror: The Gestapo, Jews, and Ordinary Germans, New York: Basic Books, 2000, p. 116-117.
[18] Bard, 17.
[19] Johnson, 120.

visas, and pay for passage, their material possessions and remaining cash were stripped as they left the country, leaving them "beggars".[20]

Even before the November pogrom, the bombing of Guernica and the Anschluss had inspired many around the world to work for the rescue of Jews, especially children, and the Evian Conference was a meeting proposed by the United States to determine what to do with the increasing numbers of Jews who managed to emigrate from Germany in the months that preceded Kristallnacht. An invitation was issued to major European countries and the nations of the Americas to attend a meeting in which, it was promised, "no country would be expected or asked to receive a greater number of emigrants than is permitted by its existing legislation."[21] Instead, many nations, whether under pressure from the Nazis or fearing their inability to care and provide for the Jewish immigrants that looked to soon be arriving from all over the world, began to pass even more restrictions on Jewish immigration. By the beginning of the conference in July of 1938, the unintentional consequence of the meeting had been a virtual lock-out of Jews from the attendees' borders.[22] Of the participants, only the Dominican Republic determined to allow Jews entrance, and only 645 Jews ended up there.[23]

The 1930s witnessed several years of discrimination and outright persecution that the Jews had endured, but 1938 was a departure point for more stringent and open violence. Longerich has proposed that a "third wave of anti-Semitism of the Nazi era" took place when German Jews were "faced with dwindling opportunities for emigration [and] a series of radical steps characterized the transition to the third phase. The National Socialist *Judenpolitick* , which had been introduced late in 1937 and more intensely since spring 1938, definitively implemented the November pogrom, the complete isolation, and the deprivation of rights and expulsion of those Jews still living in Germany [which] became the goal. "[24]

Before late 1938, the German government had preferred a systematic and legislative approach to isolating and harassing the Jews instead of particular "individual actions", which they tended to condemn as disorderly and beneath the German people. Now, with the Jews stripped of their political, economic, and cultural influence as a result of German policy in recent years, "the German Jews had been publicly taken hostage, and the various threats of extermination voiced by leading representatives of the regime over the coming weeks and months made it clear that the lives of the hostages could be placed at their mercy once again into a far greater extent than before…the regime no longer only controlled the professional careers of Jewish Germans, their possessions, and their everyday behavior; it had now elevated itself to become master over life and death."[25]

Similarly, one form of anti-Semitism came in the form of the "Law Regarding the Legal Status of Jewish Communities," which put synagogues under Nazi administrative control and removed their power to tax members of the congregation. Jews were forced to give an account of any property valued over 5,000 marks and identify their shops as belonging to Jews. The requirements for passports to be marked with a "J", boycotting of Jewish businesses, and even deportations to concentration camps were taking place by the summer of 1938. [26]

---

[20] Kaplan, Marion A. Between Dignity and Despair: Jewish Life in Nazi Germany. New York: Oxford University Press, 1998, 129-131.
[21] Nicholas, p. 149-150.
[22] Ibid., 151.
[23] Bard, 175.
[24] Longerich, p. 95-96.
[25] Ibid., 97.
[26] Kaplan, Marion A. Between Dignity and Despair: Jewish Life in Nazi Germany. New York: Oxford University

In the early days of June 1938, Goebbels promoted a new and far more drastic policy for Berlin: "I am really going all the way. Without any sentimentality. The watchword is not law, but harassment. The Jews must leave Berlin. The police will help to achieve it."[27] Most historians see the June Operation in Berlin, which featured direct physical attacks, the burning of buildings, and public humiliation of Jews as a staged practice for the November action.

Goebbels

On November 7, 1938 a young Polish Jew by the name of Herschel Grynszpan entered the German embassy in France under the pretense of seeking a visa and delivering an important document. Having just missed the ambassador, Count Johannes von Welczeck, who had gone on a walk, he was instead ushered into the office of Ernst vom Rath. When vom Rath turned and asked to see the document, Grynszpan opened fire, firing 5 shots and hitting vom Rath with two bullets in the stomach. Grynszpan did not resist arrest and stated calmly, 'I do not regret it. I did it to avenge my parents who are miserable in Germany."[28]

Press, 1998. 119-20.

[27] Ibid., 103.

[28] Gerald Schwab, The Day the Holocaust Began: The Odyssey of Herschel Grynszpan (New York: Praeger, 1990), 3, https://www.questia.com/read/27216298

Ernst vom Rath

Herschel Grynszpan

Only a little over a week earlier, on October 27 and 28th, Germany had forced the movement of over 17,000 Polish Jews from Germany, including Grynszpan's parents and sister, and when Poland refused to receive the refugees, the families were left without a country, exposed to the elements, and without food. Though Jews with criminal records and male Jews had been arrested and/or deported for months, author Marion Kaplan notes that this was the first time Jews were subject to deportation "without regard for age or sex".[29] When Grynszpan was captured, he was carrying a postcard from her sister Berta that read, "You undoubtedly heard of our great misfortune. I will describe to you what happened. On Thursday evening rumors circulated that all Polish Jews had been expelled from a city. But we didn't believe it. On Thursday evening at 9 o'clock a 'Sipo' [Sicherheitspolizei or Security Police] came to us and informed us that we had to go to Police Headquarters and bring along our passports. As we were, we went together to Police Headquarters, accompanied by the 'Sipo.' ...We were not told what it was all about, but we saw that everything was finished for us. Each of us had an extradition order pressed into his hand, and one had to leave Germany before the 29th [Saturday]. They didn't permit us to return home anymore. I asked to be allowed to go home to get at least a few things. I went, accompanied by a 'Sipo,' and packed the necessary clothes in a suitcase. And that is all I saved. We don't have a

---

[29] Kaplan, Marion A. Between Dignity and Despair: Jewish Life in Nazi Germany. New York: Oxford University Press, 1998., 121.

'Pfennig'. More next time. Best regards and kisses from all of us. – Berta.[30]

A picture of Polish Jews being deported

Grynszpan also carried a picture postcard featuring his likeness with the following confessional on the back: "With God's help, my dear parents, I could not do otherwise, may God forgive me, the heart bleeds when I hear of your tragedy and that of the 12,000 Jews. I must protest so that the whole world hears my protest and that I will do. Forgive me. —Hermann"[31]

After being shot, Ernst vom Rath was aided and transported to a nearby hospital, while Grynszpan awaited arrest and underwent an interrogation. In the questioning that took place following the shooting, Grynszpan stated that he had planned to kill a member of the German embassy soon after receiving the postcard from his sister on behalf of the Jews being persecuted in Germany. His testimony was so direct in describing the act that he later felt the need to retract some of his original answers as he tried to distance himself from the charge of premeditated murder.[32]

Vom Rath was brought to a hospital in Paris, where he was immediately operated on to repair damage to his spleen caused by one of the two bullets that had entered his body. Despite the attendance of Hitler's personal physician, vom Rath's condition worsened until he fell into a coma and died on the 9th of November. His body was prepared for transport back to Germany, and as Gerald Schwab notes, "The return and the funeral services which followed were conducted with all the pomp and circumstance for which the Third Reich had become famous.

---

[30] Gerald Schwab, The Day the Holocaust Began: The Odyssey of Herschel Grynszpan (New York: Praeger, 1990), 4, https://www.questia.com/read/27216298.

[31] Ibid.

[32] Ibid, 5.

The victim received honors worthy of royalty. The German people mourned the death of the young man and the well-oiled propaganda machine made the most of the opportunity."[33]

There was some speculation in Germany at the time that Grynszpan had not worked alone, or even that the Nazis had staged the killing to bring sympathy to their cause. Ironically, the death of vom Rath came on the 15th anniversary of Hitler's failed coup (the Beer Hall Putsch), which landed him in prison and compelled him to write *Mein Kampf*. The anniversary of the Putsch was the highlight of the Nazi calendar, and it ensured that all of its notable leaders would be gathered in Hitler's ideal location, the most German of all German cities: Munich. Grynszpan, however, contended that his action had been his own way of protesting the German treatment of the Jews. Under interrogation, he protested that "it's not a crime to be Jewish. I'm not a dog. I have a right to live and the Jewish people has [sic] the right to exist in this world. Everywhere I am persecuted like an animal."[34]

Not surprisingly, the Nazi leadership, in the midst of the commemoration of the Putsch, used the death of vom Rath to ratchet up their actions against the Jews and call attention to the Nazi cause. Hitler attended vom Rath's funeral, and Goebbels ordered newspapers to carry the reports of vom Rath's murder. Leading with the headline "Jewish Murder Attempt in Paris—Member of the German Embassy Critically Wounded by Shots—The Murdering Knave a 17-year-old Jew", *Volkischer Beobachter* (the party news vehicle) reported on the killing and called upon the German people to cast out the Jews: "We shall no longer tolerate a situation where hundreds of thousands of Jews within our territory control entire streets of shops, throng places of public entertainment , and pocket the wealth of German leaseholders as 'foreign' landlords while their racial brothers incite war against Germany and shoot down German officials…"[35] Goebbels himself called for "immediate action against the Jews, with the most severe consequences".[36]

Nazi control of the press meant that all German newspapers were ordered to carry the assassination story on the first page, as well as report it as a Jewish plot and call for consequences on all Jews living in Germany.[37] Though Hitler made no public speech, he attended the funeral of vom Rath and, according to Goebbels, gave orders that the police were not to attempt to rein in any actions against the Jews in retribution for the incident, allowing them instead to "for once…get the feel of popular anger".[38]

For a short time, some Jews were encouraged by the fact that Hitler's speech, given on the very anniversary of the Beer Hall Putsch in Munich, did not mention the vom Rath incident. Some hoped that this meant there would be no official call for retribution against the Jews, at least by the government. At the same time, other Jews saw the development of violence of some kind as inevitable, but even then, "no Jew could comprehend that the consequences would be so horrifyingly destructive."[39]

After vom Rath's death on the 9th, Goebbels called for the people of Germany to consider specific action against the Jewish population: "Our people must be told and their answer must be ruthless, forthright, salutary! I ask you to listen to me and together we must plan what is to be our answer to the Jewish murder and the threat of international Jewry to our glorious German Reich!"[40] Thus, while many Jews were caught entirely by surprise when Kristallnacht began,

---

[33] Ibid., 10.
[34] Bard, 5.
[35] Ibid. , 7.
[36] Ibid.
[37] Ibid.
[38] Ibid., 8.
[39] Steinweis, Alan. Kristallnacht 1938. Boston: President and Fellows of Harvard College, 2009, p. 38.

some who followed the newspaper reports saw the attacks coming. In Kehl, a group of Jews were forced to walk the streets while singing a song claiming responsibility: "We have betrayed the German Fatherland. We are responsible for the Paris Assassination."[41]

On November 8, the police commissioner of Berlin ordered all firearms in the possession of Jews in the city to be surrendered. The idea that weapon-holding Jews were some sort of threat to Berliners was 'preposterous," but it reinforced the anti-Jewish rhetoric the Germans sought to inflame and gave German mobs and officers a "valid" excuse for breaking into Jewish residences during Kristallnacht.[42]

Though there were spontaneous actions against Jews that took place even before vom Rath's death, coordinated attacks began on the night of November 9, and two incidents seem to have touched off the mass violence. First, a German newspaper in Dressau featured the names of the 204 Jewish families that still lived in the city, inciting action against synagogues and other buildings associated with the Jewish community. Second, vom Rath died at 5:30 p.m., and the news was passed on through the German press quickly and deliberately. Both of these incidents were noted in Goebbels' diary as potentially connected to "unleash[ing] the power of the people!"[43]

In the hours that followed Goebbels' declarations, Nazi leaders issued orders regarding what should occur, and some of them were conflicting. Specific directions from Goebbels included the order that German police and the SS were to stand down and allow attacks that generated spontaneously against the synagogues and Jewish businesses to take place without interruption. Historical documents and other items of value were to be seized from synagogues, and young adult Jewish males in good health were be seized for delivery to concentration camps. Some orders specifically called for wealthy Jews to be targeted for arrest, and some called for foreign Jews to be avoided because the leadership still hoped to continue their actions without condemnation from the rest of the world. The office of Rudolph Hess issued a directive that Jewish homes and shops should not be burned, while other orders gave specific addresses for the SA to attack.

In an attempt to understand the conflicting orders, Dr. Mitchell Bard, executive director of the American-Israeli Cooperative Enterprise and the director of the Jewish Virtual Library, explains that the Party often issued such "hazy directions," and as a result, party leaders became accustomed to making their own decisions. Ian Kershaw, a noted British biographer of Hitler, developed a theory of Nazi leadership style known as "working toward the Fuhrer". According to Keller, the specific design of Hitler was to gather around him men of unquestioning loyalty and ruthlessness and inspire them to lead with hate-filled rhetoric rather than direct orders. In this way, Hitler could be assured that his desires would be carried out without ever having to actually issue orders, including mass executions. While historians have searched in vain for Hitler's signature or even evidence of a verbal order for the Final Solution, for example, the "working toward the Fuhrer" thesis explains that it's not truly necessary to look for such orders. They do not exist precisely because in attempting to prove one's loyalty, impress the Fuhrer, and move up in the party ranks, many of the actual actions taken by Party leadership were designed by individuals within the party, not by Hitler himself.

At the same time, Kershaw's thesis does not mean that Hitler was unaware of the actions, or

[40] Ibid.
[41] Ibid, 108.
[42] Ibid., 39.
[43] Ibid., 41-43.

that he disapproved of them. In fact, several defendants tried at Nuremberg attempted to deny such knowledge while being confronted with documentary evidence of their own involvement in various war crimes. Instead, "working toward the Fuhrer" is an attempt to explain the inner workings of the party and to account for the apparent discrepancy between the intricate record-keeping the Germans were known for with the lack of written orders for atrocities and decisions such as the Final Solution.

Steinweiss agrees with the idea that Hitler himself had a desire to be one step removed from the ordering of violence against Jews. At the Nuremberg trials, it was decided that Goebbels' specific wording was "a transparent attempt at establishing plausible deniability for himself, Hitler, and the party." Steinweiss describes the scene of close to 36 Nazi Gauletiers streaming out of the events of the anniversary evening to locate phones, contact their home districts, and attempt to communicate the orders they had just received from Goebbels. Due to the way the information was disseminated, the lack of written orders in the initial communication, and the need for even the secondaries to communicate an unwritten order further down the line, Steinweiss says "some of the more heinous crimes committed against the Jews of Germany on November 9 and 10—specifically many of the murders—resulted, at least in part, from the orders that had been garbled or misunderstood as they were passed downward."[44]

Thus, the fact that Hitler did not directly order the attacks should not construed as a reason to excuse him or an indication that he did not know the nature of the attacks. In fact, Hitler was visited in his apartment in Munich by the city's police commissioner during the evening of the attacks and given regular updates of events as they occurred. He and Goebbels also decided on the time for the attacks to end.

Peter Longerich, in his analysis of the sometimes confusing and contradictory orders issued by the Reich, notes that additional confusion came from the fact that officers receiving orders were often left in a position of trying to discern the real desire of leadership from the stated instructions given that the Reich regularly issued instructions intended to protect the leaders from later accusation and from criticism by foreigners. In such cases, a person receiving orders might have a tendency to discount or not take seriously a condemnation of further violence or action. Even still, some of the Nazi leaders were explicit, especially Goebbels, who was directly involved in inciting actions in Munich in particular. He spent the evening observing the fallout of his "orders" and critiqued the lack of action of the Munich Gauletier, who he accused of having "cold feet and trembles for Jewish shops."[45]

Unlike an exact copy of Goebbels ' orders, the direct orders of Nazi leaders Heinrich Muller and Reinhard Heydrich regarding Kristallnacht survived intact and provide insight into the development of Nazi parameters for the coordinated attacks, as well as the minute by minute nature of policy development. As such, these documents and others are important in evaluating the historiography of Kristallnacht. One of the major issues debated by historians regarding the event is whether it should be viewed as a truly orchestrated top-down attack on Jews or whether, taking into consideration the retaliatory events that appear to have occurred spontaneously on November 7 and 8th, Kristallnacht was an organic movement of the German people that was capitalized upon by the Nazi leadership. Below are excerpts from each of the orders:

"Henrich Muller: Orders to all Gestapo Offices
11:55 PM, November 9, 1938
1) Actions against Jews, especially against their synagogues, will take place

---

[44] Ibid., p. 48.
[45] Ibid., 54.

throughout the Reich shortly. They are not to be interfered with; however, liaison is to be effected with the Ordnungspolizei to ensure that looting and other significant excesses are suppressed.

2) So far as important archive material exists in synagogues this is to be secured by immediate measures.

3) Preparations are to be made for the arrest of about 20,000 to 30,000 Jews in the Reich. Above all well-to-do Jews are to be selected. Detailed instructions will follow in the course of this night.

4) Should Jews in possession of weapons be encountered in the course of the action, the sharpest measures are to be taken...Looting, larceny etc. is to be prevented in all cases."

Muller

The prohibition against looting was emphasized not only to prevent similar incidents of the past. As the Nazi leadership knew, in order for the "anti-Semitic violence to be perceived as an expression of outrage by honorable Germans, it was important to avoid the appearance that the rioters were motivated by petty greed."[46]

Several hours after Muller's directive, Heydrich issued a second set of orders, with additional points added to the initial four. It's believed Heydrich had become concerned that the camps

---

[46] Ibid., 34.

would be flooded with more prisoners than they were prepared for, so he provided more selective criteria about who should be arrested:

"Reinhard Heydrich: To all Gestapo and SD district and subdistrict offices
1:20 a.m., November 10, 1938:
Concerning: measures against Jews in the present night.

On account of the assassination of the Leg. Sec. v. Rath in Paris, demonstrations against the Jews are to be expected throughout the Reich in the present night...the political leadership is to be informed that the German police have received the following instructions from the Reichsführer SS and Chief of Police, to which the measures of the political leadership should be adapted, appropriately:

a) Only such measures should be taken as will not endanger German life or property (i.e. synagogue burning only if there is no fire-danger to the surroundings).

b) Businesses and dwellings of Jews should only be destroyed, not plundered. The police are instructed to supervise this regulation and to arrest looters.

c) Special care is to be taken that in business streets non-Jewish businesses are absolutely secured against damage.

d) Foreign nationals - even if they are Jews - should not be molested...

5) Directly after the termination of the events of this night, the employment of the officials deployed [for the demonstrations] permitting, as many Jews - especially the well-off ones - are to be arrested as can be accommodated in the available prison space. Above all only healthy, male Jews, not too old, are to be arrested. Immediately after execution of the arrests contact is to be made with the appropriate concentration camp regarding the quickest committal of the Jews to the camp. Special care is to be taken that the Jews arrested on this order are not maltreated."

Heydrich

Geheim!

Abschrift des Blitz-Fernschreibens aus München vom 10.11.38
1 Uhr 20.

An alle

Staatspolizeileit - und Staatspolizeistellen

An alle

SD -Oberabschnitte und SD-Unterabschnitte.

Dringend: Sofort dem Leiter oder
seinem Stellvertreter vorlegen!

Betrifft:
Maßnahmen gegen Juden in der
heutigen Nacht.

Aufgrund des Attentats gegen den Leg.Sekretär vom
R a t h in Paris sind im Laufe der heutigen Nacht – 9. auf 10.
11.1938 – im ganzen Reich Demonstrationen gegen die Juden zu er-
warten.Für die Behandlung dieser Vorgänge ergehen die folgenden
Anordnungen:

1) Die Leiter der Staatspolizeistellen oder ihre Stellvertreter haben sofort nach Eingang dieses Fernschreibens mit
den für ihren Bezirk zuständigen politischen Leitungen – Gau -
leitung oder Kreisleitung - fernmündlich Verbindung aufzu -
nehmen und eine Besprechung über die Durchführung der Demon -
strationen zu vereinbaren,zu der der zuständige Inspekteur
oder Kommandeur der Ordnungspolizei zuzuziehen ist.In dieser

A telegram sent by Heydrich on the night of November 9

30,000 Jews were arrested and sent to concentration camps in the first of a massive movement of the Jewish people that would eventually see millions of Jews uprooted from their homes. By the end of the 10th, enough able-bodied men had been rounded up to supply the Dachau camp with 11,000 prisoners, Buchenwald with 9,845, and Sachsenhausen with another 9,000. Although some of these camps would become notorious during the Holocaust, this imprisonment during the November pogrom was not meant to be permanent; instead, Jews were intimidated into selling their businesses for well below their value or forced to provide evidence that they planned to emigrate from Germany in order to be released. Some left the camps in as little as six days,[47] but it is estimated that 400 Jews who were arrested during the pogrom and sent to one of the three camps died in captivity.

---

[47] Kaplan, 121-22.

A picture of 5 Jewish captives taken to Buchenwald

While there were certainly elements of the attacks that were organic, the Sturmabteilung (SA) brownshirts played the most definitive role in Kristallnacht. This was somewhat of a revival of the group's power since it had not played a central role in Hitler's Germany since 1934. When Hitler came to power, he feared the revolutionary, violent, and brawling reputation of the SA when it came to his own government's longevity, so in 1934, he ordered the major leaders of the SA arrested, had their top leader (Ernst Rohm) murdered, and essentially replaced the SA's role with Schutzstaffel (SS) soldiers who acted as his personal henchmen. Many members of the once-glorious SA were in Munich for the Nazi anniversary and certainly saw the attacks as a way to recapture their role as enforcers and holders of power.

Hitler, Goering and SA stormtroopers

In the German town of Lessum, a particularly horrible incident took place, and it was made worse by the way communications from top officials had been disseminated. The head of the local SA-Strum, Fritz K., was contacted in the middle of the night with the orders regarding Kristallnacht. Since he had somehow missed the initial orders, Lessum was starting the riots late and would need to be awakened by the SA troopers, and as the head of the SA strained to understand his orders, he asked specifically what was to be done with the Jews after their synagogues and shops were set aflame. The answer came: "Get rid of the Jews". Despite his surprise at the answer, Fritz K. interpreted the order as a directive to kill all Jews in Lessum, so he gathered the SA and gave them those instructions, over the objections of a few of the SA men. In the end, the SA approached the home of a well-known and now retired Jewish doctor of 78 years and pressured one of the objectors into shooting both the doctor and his wife. The shooter explained, "I have been instructed to carry out a difficult assignment."[48]

In the town of Aschaffenburg, the SS carried out the murders of several local Jews. A grain trader by the name of Alfons V. was captured by the SS and driven to the edge of town, where he

---

[48] Steinweis, 64-67.

was accused of general crimes such as the exploitation of German peasants, the rape of Christian women, and even the assassination of vom Rath. When Alfons V. replied that he was innocent, it is recorded that an SS man responded, "Herr vom Rath was also innocent and was a German. Now it's over for you. You have to pay for the action your people perpetrated."[49]

To avoid arrest, many Jews hid, while others decided the best plan of action was to stay mobile and out of their homes and shops. These individuals (mostly men) drove around for over 24 hours between the night of the 9th and the 10th, stopping only when necessary to refuel in hopes that the rioting would soon be over and it would be safe to return home.

There is debate concerning the actual number of people killed during the events of Kristallnacht. Some say 96, while some scholars state the number is as many as 236.[50] The official Nazi count was 91 people killed.[51] Though the majority of actions that took place were ones of vandalism and arrest, there were many who were murdered and others died of heart attacks as they were being put under arrest, having their businesses and homes destroyed, or watching loved ones being taken into custody, beaten, and/or humiliated. There were numerous suicides that took place as well.

The morning after Kristallnacht witnessed a further humiliation for the Jewish people, who were forced by the Nazis to clean up the destruction. The damage to glass alone was estimated at 24 million marks (with over 49.5 million marks in total damage), for which German insurance companies could be held liable. To ensure that the German businesses would not be liable to Jewish individuals, a quickly passed piece of legislation mandated that the money would go to the German government instead.[52] It is said that Hermann Goring was extremely angry that the glass damaged by the mobs would have to be replaced by purchasing it from Belgium, as it was an amount that represented half of the country's total output of glass for the year.[53]

[49] Ibid., 73.
[50] Brustein,. p. xii
[51] Steinweis, 61.
[52] Kaplan, 123.
[53] Bard, 196.

Picture of a destroyed synagogue in Munich

Picture of a burning synagogue in Eisenach

Picture of a burning synagogue in Siegen

Bundesarchiv, Bild 146-1970-041-46
Foto: o.Ang. | November 1938

Picture of a damaged synagogue in Berlin

Marion Kaplan, who specializes in the history of the feminist movement in Germany, offers a specific look at the impact of Kristallnacht on Jewish women. In addition to the occasional physical actions against women (including public beatings or forced marches) and the emotional and financial toll of having their husbands removed from their homes without warning, Jewish women's most common recollections involve the scattering of feathers. Kaplan explains that the memories of destroyed bedding and broken glass, involving key items from the home, represented for the women of Germany the end to any type of security and comfort for both themselves and their families.[54]

Without the protection of fathers, husbands, brothers, and sons, women were left to deal with the aftermath of Kristallnacht alone. Many gathered in public places such as factories or hospitals, and some in untouched apartments and homes, but when they finally returned to their own homes, it was mostly to dispose of what was broken because most items of value had been taken.[55] Reports by Jewish women of the large number of items of value missing from their homes certainly contradict the official orders of the Nazi party, which prohibited looting, and the reports of the Nazi's themselves in recounting the damages after the fact. Such reports always made a point to emphasize the lack of looting during the pogrom. The evidence, however, points to widespread looting by German citizens, perhaps even after the SA had done its work, and especially by German women.

The task of seeing to the release of their husbands weighed heavily on Jewish women in the weeks that followed Kristallnacht. Forced to navigate police and government channels, these women displayed remarkable courage to do so, and often without the help of friends and neighbors. One woman, struggling to save her husband, wrote, "I tried...day in and day out to find a connection that could lead to my husband's release. I ran to Christian acquaintances, friends, or colleagues, but...people shrugged their shoulders, shook their heads and said 'no'. And everyone was glad when I left. I was treated like a leper, even by people who were well-disposed toward us."[56] One survivor noted that "the highest praise goes to our wives who, without shedding one tear, inspired the hoarders, some of whom had beaten their men bloody, to respect them. Unbroken, these women did everything to have their men freed."

Children were not exempt from the horrors of persecution during the November action either. Jews living in Berlin at the time of the attacks recall memories of being sent home from school on the 10th of November because the teachers feared for their safety, even within school buildings. In order to avoid attracting the attention of angry crowds, Jewish children were sent home by alternate routes with directions not to join each other on the way, but many recall being drawn in by the scenes of destruction, including watching their synagogues burn and witnessing the leaders of their communities being humiliated and shamed.

In addition to being dismissed from their schools and camps due to fear for their safety by school and camp directors, children were directly affected by seeing the arrests of their fathers and brothers, as well as having their homes attacked. Several children had specific visual memories of their fathers speaking with Nazi soldiers while holding an iron cross or wearing decorations from their service to Germany during World War I.[57] For example, one man recalled his grandfather imploring the men arresting his father to turn back, protesting that he had given his other son, who had died in action in World War I, to the Fatherland.[58] Indeed, the humiliation of watching their father's and grandfather's vain attempts to protect them on the basis of their loyalty to Germany were some of the most poignant and devastating scenes of Kristallnacht. One

---

[54] Ibid., 125.
[55] Ibid., 127.
[56] Ibid.
[57] Bard, 43-44.
[58] Ibid., 64.

man described such a memory with difficulty: "My father went into the house and I don't even know how to tell this story. In a way, I feel very bad about it, but I can understand his pride. He went and put on his decorations from WWI on his chest, and he approached the Nazis in the street and he said 'You cannot do this to me or my family. I am a German soldier, I earned these decorations.' They certainly didn't listen. They tore off these decorations from his chest and threw them into the street. They pushed him around. I, of course, was very frightened."

Mitchell Bard supplied an account of what happened at the Dinslaken orphanage in North-Rhine Westphalia. About 50 Nazis stormed their way into the orphanage, breaking furniture and destroying books, beds, and linens. The orphanage directors, having shepherded the children outside, called for the local police to aid them but received an answer from one of the policeman: "Jews do not get protection from us! Vacate the area together with your children as quickly as possible!" This left the director with no choice but to re-enter the building where the violence continued. Though no physical harm to an orphan was recorded, Dinslaken was not the only orphanage attacked during Kristallnacht, and children who cried were told they would be burned along with the items being destroyed.[59]

Some non-Jewish German children also played a role in the events of Kristallnacht. On the morning after the attacks began, several teachers led their classes into the streets and encouraged them to participate in the action by throwing rocks, hurling insults, or just witnessing the destruction and fires. Perhaps not surprisingly, while accounts of the children's involvement were heard at post-war trials, few individual memoirs recorded the involvement of German children.[60] However, the role of German teens, whether as organized Hitler Youth members, classes of students, or simply acting spontaneously, was huge. In small towns, the youth were sometimes the sole perpetrators who carried out the burning of synagogues, and in large towns such as Berlin, boys who were emboldened by the "presence of adult authority figures who encouraged and rewarded violent behavior" as well as the "steady diet of anti-Semitic propaganda on which the boys had been nourished in the schools and in their Hitler Youth troops" contributed to burnings, lootings, and violence against Jews of all ages.

As author William Bard notes, "the destruction of synagogues, Torah scrolls, and prayer books...attacked the very soul and spirit of the Jewish people...The houses of prayer, existing for decades and in many cases, centuries, were symbols of the long-standing Jewish roots in Germany."[61] The Nazi leaders were determined to eradicate these roots, and the visual images of watching their heritage destroyed, in addition to the arrests of its male leaders, devastated the Jewish community. Though some actions against synagogues had been taken earlier in response to Hitler's whims (including one in Munich that Hitler demanded be removed by his next visit and another in Nuremberg deemed to be "spoiling the look of the city"), more historic, religious, and academic documents and religious buildings were specifically targeted during Kristallnacht. One eyewitness recalls fleeing Vienna with his mother while witnessing a crowd of people systematically burning Jewish writings: "My strongest, most physical memory of Kristallnacht was of our lorry bumping and rolling across that pile of smoldering religious books. I will never forget it."[62]

For many children preparing for their Bar Mitzvah, the intrusion of Kristallnacht meant that they would miss out on the important rite of passage, or that their studies would be disrupted.

---

[59] Ibid., 19-20.
[60] Steinweiss, p. 60.
[61] Ibid., 123.
[62] Ibid., 36.

Many young boys recalled the "smell of burning parchment" as soldiers and the Gestapo uncovered the Torah scrolls they used to prepare for the ceremony and set fire to them in the midst of households and churches. Some Jews could merely resort to smuggling some Torahs out of Germany to neighboring countries and even the United States. [63]

Not only were symbols of Jewish faith and heritage destroyed, they were also used to carry out a ritual or cultural humiliation of the Jews during the days and nights of November 7th- 10th. In addition to making well-respected Jewish men and women parade through the streets in their pajamas, Jews were forced to watch their local synagogues burn, and in some cases dance in front of them. Some Jews were forced to walk the streets in sacred objects such as prayer shawls or torn scrolls, and there were documented instances of rabbis having their beards shaved or torn out, being forced to recite Jewish prayers, or being forced to read from the Torah while being humiliated.

Even German intellectuals and artists who married Jews were subject to discrimination or persecution by the Nazis during the November pogrom. The composer Richard Strauss, once the toast of Germany, had married a Jewish woman whose family was specifically marked by Goebbels for persecution during Kristallnacht. In addition to having her family harassed and her relatives taken into custody despite Strauss' attempts to have them released, Strauss was eventually pressured to divorce his Jewish wife. He refused to do so, and though Goebbels would have liked to see his music completely eradicated from German culture, Hitler demurred. That said, Hitler and others began to ignore his work in favor of younger and more compliant artists, and Goebbels once publicly humiliated Strauss, yelling, "Tomorrow's culture is different from that of yesterday! You, Herr Strauss, are of yesterday!"[64]

Strauss in 1938

Though many Jews living in large cities could see the attacks coming, those in more rural areas and without the benefits of communication were taken aback and confused by the events of Kristallnacht. One girl described how without radio, her family and neighbors were confused by

---

[63] Ibid., 60.
[64] Evans, Richard. The Third Reich at War. P. 582-583.

the burning of the local synagogue: "It took us a while to realize that this was a coordinated effort."[65] Like many others, Jews had believed that Hitler would meet his end politically, like the Weimar leaders before him, and the sheer madness of what took place was simply unthinkable to so many who had called Germany their home for generations. In any case, the core belief that the Germans would have to recognize Jewish rights to property, privacy, dignity, and even life would soon quickly be dashed for those who stayed in the country.

A Greater Germany

Hitler's refurbishment of the German army met with widespread approval by the populace, which was understandably weary of the helpless, inferior position imposed on them by the hated treaties ending World War I. Simultaneously, however, most Germans abhorred and dreaded the notion of a second major conflict involving their nation. For several years, therefore, the Fuhrer pretended to have peaceful intent. This pretense served not only to prevent early intervention by foreign powers, who tacitly recognized Germany's right to rearm to some extent, but also reassured German citizens alarmed at the prospect of renewed war.

An expert juggler and manipulator, Hitler managed to appear "all things to all men," soothing war-weary Germans while holding out the promise of conquest and bloodshed to his aggressive Nazi followers. The conciliatory side of Hitler's act showed him as a restrained, peace-seeking statesman seeking no more than a prudent defense of Germany: "The two pledges Hitler made were, characteristically, that Germany would never yield to force on the one hand, but would strive for peace on the other. As before, he declared that Germany had no territorial demands in Europe. And he offered a series of peace pacts to reassure Germany's neighbours. All of this was merely rhetorical." (Evans, 2006, 524).

The more genuine face of Hitler, the hungry aggressor rejoicing in the strength and belligerence of Nazi society, emerged in sanguinary speeches delivered to his picked followers. During one of these menacing addresses, the American reporter William Shirer described the effect of Hitler's violent rhetoric on convinced Nazis: "Now the six hundred deputies, personal appointees all of Hitler, little men with big bodies and bulging necks and cropped hair and pouched bellies and brown uniforms and heavy boots, little men of clay in his fine hands, leap to their feet like automatons, their right arms upstretched in the Nazi salute [...] All the militarism in their German blood surges to their heads. [...] Their hands are raised in slavish salute, their faces now contorted with hysteria, their mouths wide open, shouting, shouting." (Shirer, 1942, 53).

---

[65] Ibid., 136.

Shirer

At the core of Hitler's policy lay the Four-Year Plan, overseen by Hermann Goering among others. This plan aimed to prepare Germany for war during the 1940s, clearly indicating the boundlessness of Hitler's ambitions, but intriguingly, these two leading Nazis diverged sharply regarding the Third Reich's future. Hitler wished not just to create Greater Germany but to achieve "Lebensraum," displacing, enslaving, or exterminating the Slavs to fill eastern Europe and Russia with his Teutonic "master race." This dark vision led to an endless, limitless war which Germany realistically could not win, since it would ultimately make the entire world enemies of the Reich.

Goering, on the other hand, envisioned an aggressive but far more realistic scheme. In his opinion, Hitler should build Greater Germany, then extend influence and domination into southeastern Europe via economic and diplomatic means rather than direct invasion. This would lay the groundwork for Germany as a superpower along the lines of the United States or Russia, based more on a militarily unassailable country with the overwhelming industrial and financial might to exert political influence globally.

To achieve this goal, Goering especially wanted to ensure an alliance with Britain, eschewing any steps that might prompt armed hostility from the English. Such a plan might even have succeeded, since the outside world would have perceived Germany as a grim and dictatorial but essentially rational superpower, rather than a berserk rogue state determined to conquer the world. Eventually, only Goering possessed the fortitude to tell Hitler his launch of a new world war represented a major error, and to ask him to reconsider.

That said, Goering was not the Fuhrer, and Hitler's program of building a "Greater Germany" – a territory to encompass all regions of Europe with majority German speakers, including Austria and portions of Czechoslovakia known as Sudetenland – commenced in earnest on March 7th, 1936. On this date, the Fuhrer sent 3,000 Reichswehr soldiers, supported by 30,000 more held in reserve, into the Rhineland area, a demilitarized zone created following World War I. The French remained inactive, thus permitting the Third Reich to consolidate its power over this first "recovered" territory. Given that the Rhineland formerly lay within Germany's borders, Paris likely felt unwilling to start a fresh conflagration over a region to which Germany possessed considerable claim.

In the aftermath, Hitler cheekily declared he would sign a 25 year peace treaty with the French if they agreed to create a demilitarized zone on their side of the border, but the French refused this offer, knowing it meant the destruction of the Maginot Line. Hitler, of course, managed to portray himself as a misunderstood advocate of peace, but regardless, France recoiled from any further actions following the bloodless occupation of the Rhineland. As a result, it remained an essentially passive observer during the ensuing expansion of "Greater Germany," almost up until the Third Reich's Wehrmacht rolled across its border and revealed the profound uselessness of the Maginot Line.

November 1936 also witnessed additional extension of the Third Reich's influence in Europe with the dispatch of the Condor Legion to Spain. These German soldiers assisted General Franco in his war against the Spanish Republicans and helped establish a neutral but somewhat friendly right-wing government. Moreover, the 16,000 Germans who participated gained valuable combat experience with modern warfare, while the peninsular conflict also served as a proving ground for live fire tests of new German armaments.

A picture of the Condor Legion training in Spain

Not surprisingly, the success of the Germans' operations under the noses of the western Allies encouraged Hitler to even more audacious steps. "On 18 May 1939 [...] the Legion marched proudly past in Franco's final victory parade in Madrid. Once more, international inaction had allowed Hitler free rein. The Spanish Civil War was one more example for him of the supine pusillanimity of Britain and France, and thus an encouragement to move faster in the fulfilment of his own intentions. In this sense [...] the Spanish conflict accelerated the descent into war." (Evans, 2006, 529).

Crucially for Hitler, Neville Chamberlain took the post of Prime Minister in May 1937.

Viewing the Germans as an essentially civilized people and the Slavs as a barbaric horde outside the gates of Europe, he showed an inclination to cut the Nazis considerable slack. Chamberlain placed Nevile Henderson as his ambassador to the Third Reich, and he tended thereafter to place great reliance on his recommendations. As it would turn out, Ambassador Henderson proved to be something of an asset to Hitler in maintaining uneasy but good enough relations with Britain during the early stages of Nazi adventurism. Henderson expressed his views on Third Reich aggression quite frankly: "[T]he German is certainly more civilized than the Slav, and […] also less potentially dangerous to British interests – One might even go so far as to assert that it is not even just to endeavor to prevent Germany from completing her unity or from being prepared for war against the Slav provided her preparations […] reassure the British Empire that they are not simultaneously designed against it." (Leibovitz, 1997, 103).

Chamberlain

Henderson

While Hitler likely did not see this specific memorandum, Henderson's position must have been quite clear to the Fuhrer. The signals Hitler received from the ambassador probably encouraged him to believe, not unreasonably, that Britain approved of German aggression as long as it remained focused eastward. Seen in this light, Hitler's actions seem less like those of an irresponsible rogue leader daring the British to stop him than and more like those of a man who deemed a tacit agreement existed between the European imperial powers that would allow anti-Slavic military action so long as the Germans took care not to disturb the overseas possessions of England or France.

Though it was Hitler who gave the actual orders, the British and French – and Chamberlain in particular – bear some culpability for the Wehrmacht's eastward push in the ensuing years. Chamberlain signally failed to provide any concrete aid to democracies such as Poland and Czechoslovakia, rendering them less effective as a bulwark against future Soviet aggression and making German aggression against the Soviets almost inevitable.

Simultaneously, Benito Mussolini, Italy's fascist dictator, continued his advance against the Ethiopians, but at the time, the American correspondent Shirer dismissed the Italian strongman's bombastic declarations: "Mussolini has triumphed largely with mustard gas. That's how he's beaten the Ethiopians. [...] We picked up a broadcast of him shouting from the balcony of the Palazzo Venezia in Rome. Much boloney about thirty centuries of history, Roman civilization, and triumph over barbarism. Whose barbarism?" (Shirer, 1942, 61).

Mussolini

Hitler set his sights on Austria next, but ironically, it was Mussolini who delayed the "Anschluss" (unification) of Germany and the Austrian nation. Engelbert Dollfuss, the former dictator of Austria who founded "Austrofascism" and suppressed pro-democracy demonstrators with lethal artillery fire, had been killed on July 25th, 1934 in a hail of bullets unleashed by Nazi assassins. His successor, the bespectacled Kurt Schuschnigg, continued the dictatorial Austrofascist movement, but he attempted to maintain Austrian independence and outlawed the Austrian Nazi Party.

Schuschnigg

Given this situation, Austria, too weak to defy Nazi Germany alone, relied on an alliance with Mussolini during its last few years of semi-autonomy. 1936, however, revealed the slenderness of the reed upon which Schuschnigg leaned. Mussolini required aid for his African enterprises, as the alleged "New Rome" proved too feeble to defeat hordes of ill-armed tribesmen even with the aid of bombing and poison gas, so the Italian "Duce" turned to the German Fuhrer for assistance. Hitler granted this on condition Mussolini leave Austria to fend for itself, which Mussolini accepted as the price for his dreams of winning an African empire. Austria remained independent for several years following this low-key but decisive betrayal. However, absent a collapse of the Third Reich, the outcome of the situation remained a foregone conclusion.

Hitler hesitated to pounce on vulnerable Austria, but several factors impelled him to pursue a rapid policy of Anschluss as 1937 passed. Briefly fearing he was suffering from cancer, the middle-aged Fuhrer found himself driven by the wish to achieve notable things before succumbing to his mortality. Furthermore, "[t]he heightened sense of urgency that began to grip Hitler early in 1938 had several different causes. German rearmament was progressing at a headlong pace, but other countries were beginning to rearm too, and soon the advantage that Germany had built up would be lost. At the moment, too, experience seemed to show that Britain and France were still reluctant to take firm action against German expansion. [...] But how long would the will for appeasement last?" (Evans, 2006, 534).

Thus, Hitler's actions, including the annexation of Austria, his designs on Czechoslovakia and Poland, and his launching of the Second World War (which many of his generals believed premature), emanated from the sense that he had a narrow window of opportunity. He anticipated that either his own death from natural causes or foreign opposition might thwart all his larger ambitions unless he acted on them immediately. This urgency in Nazi planning ensured that the Germans took the world by surprise with their boldness, but it also left them unprepared to exploit their early success.

Hitler called a fateful meeting in the Berlin Reich Chancellery on November 5th, 1937. Beginning at 4:15 p.m. and lasting slightly more than four hours, the meeting involved the top brass of the Nazi military machine on land, sea, and in the air. The roll call included the Luftwaffe head and number two Nazi, Hermann Goering, as well as war minister Werner von Blomberg, foreign minister Konstantin von Neurath, the Fuhrer's personal military adjutant Friedrich Hossbach, naval chief Erich Raeder, and overall army commander Werner von Fritsch. Of these men, Hitler eventually destroyed two with artificial scandals. The Fuhrer ousted Fritsch over a supposed homosexual affair, though the man involved in the homosexual relationship was in fact a completely different Fritsch. Hitler axed Blomberg over marrying a woman who formerly found employment as a sex worker.

The interior of the Reich Chancellery

Fritsch

Blomberg

On the afternoon of November 5ᵗʰ, 1937, however, these events lay in the future as Hitler concisely outlined his agenda for 1938: "'Our first objective must be to overthrow Czechoslovakia and Austria simultaneously to remove the threat to our flank in any possible operation against the West.' So the targets were to be the two states created by the Versailles peacemakers to keep Germany contained in central Europe. […] when the time came, Hitler said, 'the descent upon the Czechs would have to be carried out at lightning speed.'" (Parssinen, 2003, 13).

As the event proved, acquisition of these two nations occurred successively rather than as part of a single overall thrust. Austria's turn on the chopping block came first. Schuschnigg traveled to Hitler's lair at the famous Berghof on February 12ᵗʰ, 1938, ostensibly to smooth out the difficulties between the two countries and enable them to move forward as allies into the future. However, the reception awaiting him rapidly disabused the Austrian dictator of this rosy figment: "Hitler, tense and keyed up, received Schuschnigg on the steps of his alpine retreat with due politeness. However, as soon as they entered the great hall, with its breathtaking view over the mountains, his mood abruptly changed. When Schuschnigg remarked on the beauty of the panorama, Hitler snapped: 'Yes, here my ideas mature. But we haven't come together to talk about the beautiful view and the weather.'" (Kershaw, 2010, 355).

Hitler subsequently outlined a series of demands designed to reduce Austria to a vassal state of the Third Reich and make Schuschnigg a puppet of the Austrian Nazis. The unpleasant dish of accusations about "Austrian treason" Hitler served up to his luckless guest failed to cow the Austrian leader, as did the open threats the Fuhrer seasoned it with. However, when Schuschnigg prepared to leave after delivering a stony refusal, Hitler unexpectedly roared for Field Marshal Wilhelm Keitel. Tight-lipped, flinty-eyed, with a ramrod straight back and a small sandy mustache, Keitel bounded into the room, asking Hitler what he needed. Hitler gestured to a chair, where Keitel sat down, and responded "nothing." Schuschnigg, however, understood precisely what Hitler intended; rather than leaving, the Austrian dictator returned to his seat and, scowling in baffled rage, signed the treaty Hitler proffered.

Keitel

Key provisions of the one-sided agreement included the rehabilitation of imprisoned Austrian Nazis, the appointment of a new Minister of Security (national police commander) in the shape of a Nazi named Arthur Seyss-Inquart, and the appointment of Dr. Hans Fischbock as Austrian Minister of Finance. Seyss-Inquart would receive a death sentence at Nuremberg after the war, but with a single flourish of the pen, Schuschnigg signed control of the entire Austrian police and economy over to the Nazis. Hitler celebrated his triumph, and effectively announced his intent to pursue further annexations in the name of "Greater Germany," at a February 20th, 1938 speech at the Reichstag in Berlin: "There must be no doubt about one thing. Political separation from the Reich may not lead to deprivation of rights – that is, the general rights of self-determination. [...] To the interests of the German Reich belong the protection of those German peoples who are not in a position to secure along our frontiers their political and spiritual freedom by their own efforts." (Shirer, 1942, 93).

Seyss-Inquart, Hitler, Himmler, and Heydrich in Vienna in 1938
Hitler orchestrated the fall of Fritsch and Blomberg at this time, naming himself commander in chief of the Third Reich's armies and thus lessening the risk of internal opposition to his policies. The massive scandal surrounding Blomberg's marriage to a former sex worker also cowed the remaining Army General Staff for a time. These senior commanders appeared to feel that the marital choice of their colleague somehow besmirched their honor so deeply that they lost the

right to object to Hitler's schemes.

Meanwhile, there was a sharp divide over how to handle these developments among British officials. The majority faction, led by Chamberlain and Lord Halifax (then Lord President of the Council and soon to be Foreign Secretary) favored appeasement of Hitler and the Third Reich. The minority, spearheaded by Foreign Secretary Anthony Eden, believed in the League of Nations and called for strict opposition to German aggression, even if that led to armed conflict.

Halifax

Eden

In the end, the overt emergence of Hitler's threatening designs upon Austria strengthened the position of the appeasement faction headed by Chamberlain. Far from heeding Eden's warnings that yielding to the Third Reich's demands would make war more, not less, likely, the other British leaders came to view the Foreign Secretary as a nuisance: "At the end of 1937, there was only one question for the British Cabinet to face: how to remove Eden. Every remark he made seemed a rebuke to Chamberlain and appeasement. In February, 1938, Eden said at Birmingham that [...] 'It is not only by seeking to buy good-will that peace is made, but on a basis of frank reciprocity with mutual respect.'" (Gilbert, 1963, 76).

Eden solved the appeasers' dilemma by resigning more or less voluntarily from the post of Foreign Secretary following Schuschnigg's effective surrender to Hitler at the Berghof. This action enabled Lord Halifax to slip into the post of Foreign Secretary, putting one of Chamberlain's closest allies into a position to rubber-stamp any foreign policy decisions taken by the prime minister.

To the southeast, once Seyss-Inquart was in charge of the police, the Austrian Nazis emerged as thick as locusts and began their usual process of mass demonstrations, violence, and political bullying on a grand scale. Just three weeks after Schuschnigg's Berghof visit, the situation in Austria was so untenable that the Austrian dictator called for a plebiscite on the morning of March 9th, 1938. The proposed referendum, to be held on March 13th, would decide whether Austria chose to remain independent or opted instead for Anschluss and absorption into Hitler's Greater Germany. This bold move took Hitler and his cronies aback, particularly as they shrewdly guessed that the patriotic terms in which Schuschnigg couched his proposal made it quite likely the Austrians would choose independence. The Third Reich's leadership spent March 10th in desperate debate, infuriated but unsure how to counter Schuschnigg on such short notice. No military plans for an invasion of Austria yet existed.

By March 11th, however, the Nazis threw together a patchwork but feasible plan to defeat Schuschnigg's bold maneuver. Hitler contacted Mussolini and asked the Italian dictator to refrain from intervention on Austria's behalf. When Mussolini announced he would support Hitler's takeover and thus abandon the Austrians to their doom, the Fuhrer was ecstatic at the news: "'Please tell Mussolini I will never forget him for it, never, never, never, come what may,' a hugely relieved Hitler gushed over the telephone to Philipp of Hesse. 'If he should ever need any help or be in any danger, he can be sure that do or die I shall stick by him, come what may, even if the whole world rises against him,' he added, carried away by his elation." (Kershaw, 2010, 359).

Hitler then sent an ultimatum to Schuschnigg, asking for the plebiscite to be postponed two weeks and for the Austrian leader to hand the Chancellorship of his country over to the Nazi stooge Seyss-Inquart. Schuschnigg agreed to delay the referendum by the specified interval but initially refused to step down. However, the Austrian President convinced him to make way for Seyss-Inquart, and the same evening, Schuschnigg came onto the radio to announce his resignation in favor of Hitler's puppet. The American reporter William Shirer, then in Vienna, noted the police all sported red Nazi brassards, and shouts of "Heil Hitler! Hang Schuschnigg!" echoed frequently through the streets. The reporter then witnessed a triumphant ritual affirmation of Hitler's victory in the crucial Ballhausplatz at the Congress of Vienna building: "Twenty storm troopers are standing on one another before the building, forming a human pyramid. A little fellow scampers to the top of the heap, clutching a huge Swastika flag. He pulls himself up to the balcony, the same balcony where four years ago Major Fey, held prisoner by the Nazis after Dollfuss was shot, parleyed   with the Schuschnigg people. He unfurls the flag from the balcony and the Platz rings with cheers." (Shirer, 1942, 100-101).

Immediately prior to agreeing to resignation, Schuschnigg had cabled the English in an 11th hour bid to secure their support against Nazi aggression. With Anthony Eden gone, however, Schuschnigg's plea proved futile; Lord Halifax, the new Foreign Secretary, returned a terse, dismissive response to the Austrian: "His Majesty's Government are unable to guarantee protection." (Kershaw, 2010, 359). His last hope rebuffed, the Chancellor agreed to step down at approximately 3:30 p.m. Schuschnigg never again held political power; the Germans sent him to several concentration camps, including Sachsenhausen and Dachau, but the resourceful Austrian survived. Eventually freed by Wehrmacht soldiers who saw no point in keeping him captive as the Reich crumbled in 1945, Schuschnigg and his family fell into American hands on May 4th of that year. The former dictator moved to the United States and spent 19 years teaching political science at a prominent Missouri university. Upon his retirement, he returned to Germany, where he lived until his death in 1977 at the age of 80.

Wehrmacht soldiers entered Austria early on March 12th and Hitler himself arrived in the afternoon, greeted by throngs of exulting Austrians so dense that he found it necessary to change his itinerary due to delays navigating the ocean of cheering humanity. In the meantime, Goebbels fabricated accounts of widespread Communist looting and violence in Austria that was quelled only by the timely arrival of German saviors in uniform.

At this moment of crisis, a decisive split between Chamberlain and Winston Churchill began. Churchill wanted to issue an ultimatum to Hitler that any additional invasions on his part would lead to war with England. Churchill also wished to prepare for just such an eventuality in order to carry out the threat if Hitler refused to stop his depredations. Chamberlain, on the other hand, confined himself to almost maternal remonstrances towards the German dictator. For example, on one occasion, he "informed his sister that he would tell the Fuhrer that 'it is no use crying over spilt milk and what we have to do now is consider how we can restore the confidence you have shattered.'" (Stewart, 2001, 290).

Lord Halifax, the Foreign Secretary, naturally backed up Chamberlain's position. Both men had a vague notion that Germany needed to be stopped diplomatically, but they had no concept of how to achieve this in practice. As if to weaken their own bargaining position more, the British government sharply reduced their military spending immediately following Hitler's annexation of Austria. The Germans took note of this and went ahead with preparations to move next on Czechoslovakia.

Munich

Though most Germans tacitly or openly supported Hitler's actions and welcomed Austria's addition to the Reich, some saw the current course as leading towards probable or even inevitable disaster. Lieutenant Colonel Hans Oster of the Abwehr (Reich military intelligence) wished to topple the Nazi government, a desire which eventually matured into a plan to assassinate the Fuhrer that never came to fruition.

Immediately after the fall of Austria in the "Blumenkrieg" ("Flower War"), as the Germans dubbed the peaceful surrender to Nazi control, Oster spotted what he thought represented an opportunity when Himmler and other Nazis accused Werner von Fritsch, the army commander, of being a homosexual, a criminal and shameful lifestyle choice according to the authoritarian policies of the Third Reich. In fact, the homosexual liaison at the core of this brouhaha involved a different Fritsch entirely, a fact that emerged at the trial and resulted in Werner von Fritsch's acquittal.

Nevertheless, the trial ruined Fritsch's career despite the fact that the government openly acknowledged the accusations of homosexuality as a disproved canard. Oster attempted to use this incident as a tool to bring down the entire Nazi edifice, perhaps demonstrating why his plans tended to come to nothing: "Urged on by Oster, Fritsch challenged Himmler to a duel with pistols. According to Otto John, a legal adviser to Lufthansa with ties to the resistance, 'Oster ... thought that this would bring about the decisive confrontation between the Army and the SS and lead to the fall of the regime.' [...] In urging Fritsch to fight a duel, Oster was clearly grasping at straws." (Parssinen, 2003, 33).

Nevertheless, Oster retained his desire to bring down the Nazis, kill Hitler, and end the possibility of a Second World War through that bold action. The Lieutenant Colonel bided his time in the months of mounting crisis that followed.

Oster

Hitler's original plan to seize Austria and Czechoslovakia simultaneously and present the world with a fait accompli proved impossible. Even the mighty Fuhrer, whose boldness seemed favored by fortune in the 1930s, found his plans transformed into entirely unexpected shapes by forces outside his control.

Schuschnigg's referendum impelled Hitler to invade Austria long before he found himself in readiness to move into Czech lands, but the high population of ethnic Germans living in western Czechoslovakia provided Hitler with the pretext he needed to incorporate these areas into his growing Nazi empire. His success at taking the Rhineland and Austria without active opposition by the Western allies in general, and Britain in particular, encouraged him to indulge his ambitions with less and less restraint.

Indeed, the British attitude towards Czechoslovakia indicated that the inhabitants of the "Sceptr'd Isle" did not exactly stand ready to fight and die for that eastern European country. If anything, the British government viewed Czechoslovakia as scarcely more than a figment, and a highly annoying one at that. "Czechoslovakia, with its disgruntled minorities of Germans, Poles, Ruthenians, and Magyars, seemed to reflect in microcosm the difficulties of that earlier 'ramshackle' state. Nevile Henderson, who referred to the Czechs as 'those blasted Czechs,' had spoken to people in England, so he maintained, who regarded Czechoslovakia as a new variety of interesting flower. A colleague of his, he later recorded, had begun a dispatch to London: 'There is no such thing as Czechoslovakia.'" (Gilbert, 1963, 106).

These sentiments are made all the more ironic by the fact that in 1938, Czechoslovakia remained as a single beacon of democratic society among a miasmal bog of fascist and pseudo-fascist states. This political liberty provided one reason for Hitler's desire to seize the small but prosperous nation; its democratic success gave the lie to his propagandist declaration that the only alternative to his fascist totalitarianism was the even worse despotism of the Soviet and communist nations.

Other reasons weighed yet more heavily in the balance. Czechoslovakia's mountainous, heavily fortified western boundary presented a strategic obstacle to the Wehrmacht's freedom of maneuver in extending the Reich eastward. Furthermore, the Czechs possessed a large, modern industrial base. This juicy prize, added to Germany's already formidable manufacturing capabilities, made even more rapid armament of the Wehrmacht feasible, and it would make the destruction of the Soviet Union a realistic possibility in the absence of British and American interference.

Helping Hitler's cause, German majorities existed in many western Czech border regions, with more than 50% of the population speaking the German language and professing Teutonic rather than Czechoslovak loyalties in 1937 and 1938. The world financial crises of the 1930s hit these "Sudeten" Germans, in their "Sudetenland" regions, particularly hard, and though the Czech central government attempted to offer relief, the economic impact grew too overwhelming to counter with various policies. A secession movement arose under a former teacher named Konrad Henlein, and, though not Nazi in orientation, it adopted many tactics familiar to the brownshirts of the SA. The use of violence and intimidation at the polls became commonplace, meaning that Henlein could muster a reliable 75% majority vote in most Sudeten districts with large German populations.

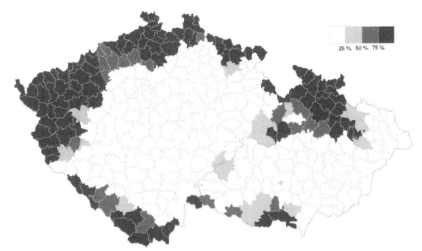

A map of parts of Czechoslovakia with heavy German ethnicity

Henlein

The Sudetenland Germans' attraction to joining the Third Reich centered on economic rather than ideological factors. Germany's economic recovery presented a tempting vision of business and employment to the reeling Sudetenland workers. Hitler's weaponry manufactures created many high-paying jobs in the Third Reich, and the Sudeten Germans longed for a slice of that newfound affluence.

Naturally, Hitler remained ready and willing to manufacture pretexts for intervention. "With Austria swallowed whole by the Third Reich, Hitler eyed Czechoslovakia the way a hungry wolf eyes a crippled rabbit. Carefully scripted riots erupted regularly throughout the Sudetenland, ostensibly in protest against Czech oppression. Hitler publicly vowed to   protect his 'defenseless' fellow Germans." (Parssinen, 2003, 36).

The May Crisis of 1938, largely a product of hysterical rumors, exercised major influence over the actions of Chamberlain and his Cabinet later in 1938. At the outset, Czechoslovak police allegedly shot and killed two German motorcyclists in the Sudetenland. More crucially, the Wehrmacht held springtime exercises near the Czechoslovakian border, generating vast alarm in both Paris and London. Though Hitler intended to seize Czechoslovakia by military force later that year, the maneuvers that catalyzed such international frenzy had nothing to do with this scheme, as the Nazis simply did not consider themselves ready to take Czech territory in late spring or early summer. The exercises represented a coincidence, a long pre-planned martial exercise with no ulterior motive which happened to coincide with the worst suspicions of those nervously watching the actions of Nazi Germany.

The British initially warned the Germans not to attack Czechoslovakia, coming very close to stating that they would intervene militarily should combat erupt. Thus, when the attack failed to materialize (due to the fact that Germans never intended their maneuvers to end with a May border crossing) the English government ascribed the absence of an attack to their own warnings. However, far from bolstering their confidence, this mistaken interpretation terrified them into future inaction. "The prime minister confided to his sister Ida that 'the more I hear about last weekend the more I feel what a damned close-run thing it was.' Chamberlain's brief flirtation with warnings to Germany was over. Even Halifax was chastened by his own boldness [...] On May 22, the day after Halifax had sent his warning to Hitler, he telegraphed the French that they could not count on British support in the event of war with Germany." (Parssinen, 2003, 37).

The English government's conception of the situation and how to deal with it remained deeply muddled and contradictory. Fear was underlying much British thinking, as well as Chamberlain's determination not to deal with the Soviets even to create a defensive pact. However, though the futile clarity of hindsight is proverbial, Britain's leaders appeared to have less of a grasp of the situation than is usually the case even in the rough and tumble of day-to-day politics. In particular, glaring contradictions in Britain's policies stand out as unworkable, and their aims stood out as contradictory and inevitably self-defeating. "Britain's strategic conception was underlined by the strength of her navy and the weakness of her army. The way to defeat Germany, it was argued, was not to pursue a head-on clash with her impressive-looking army but to use economic strangulation. This was an understandable line to take, but it logically demanded that Britain prevent Germany moving east rather than stand aside and let it happen. By going east, Germany gained the very resources that made economic strangulation a redundant policy." (Stewart, 2001, 314).

Chamberlain's fear of standing up to the Germans created a delusional state in which he thought these two incompatible aims remained simultaneously achievable. He believed he could point Germany to the east to push back the communists yet still credibly exert economic pressure on the Nazis to keep their aggression under control. For years, the Prime Minister ignored the fact that a German empire in the east rendered British attempts at economic coercion impossible.

Further exacerbating the problem, the English continued to view the Czechs with contempt bordering on hostility. In the *Daily Mail*, Lord Rothermere spoke for his fellow government officials when he declared coldly that "Czechoslovakia is not of the remotest concern to us." (Gilbert, 1963, 118). He added that if "France likes to burn her fingers there, that is a matter for France." Around the same time, the top men in Chamberlain's government expressed their hatred even more openly: "At the May 22 Cabinet meeting, reported Cadogan, the Cabinet was 'quite sensible – and anti-Czech.' In the minds of the British leaders, the attempts by this small nation to preserve their national integrity were simply irritants in the way of great-power diplomacy. Significantly, the Cabinet was, at this critical point, 'anti-Czech' rather than 'anti-Nazi'; its venom was reserved for the victim not the perpetrator of the crime." (Leibovitz, 1997, 129).

With these moves, Hitler and Chamberlain both set the stage for the Munich Agreement of 1938 and Britain's betrayal of Czechoslovakia. The Fuhrer thirsted for conquest, carried forward by faith in the Wehrmacht's fighting abilities and the Lebensraum concept that "lesser races" should be exterminated in tens or hundreds of millions to make space for a population explosion among Germans. Hitler showed himself willing to mouth platitudes to keep foreign pressure or hostility in abeyance as long as possible, even though he had no use for peace and did not intend to halt his aggression in the foreseeable future.

While aggression compelled Hitler, fear and delusion ruled Chamberlain, to the extent that the British Prime Minister convinced himself avoiding war at any price was the chief imperative of his office. Simultaneously, he betrayed his lack of faith in democracy by tacitly believing only fascist dictatorship could prevent the spread of communist violence into Europe. Though ultimately proven wrong by NATO, the most powerful military alliance in history and one created exclusively by freedom-loving democracies, Chamberlain exhibited a sort of perverse faith in Nazism as the sole viable counterweight to Soviet adventurism.

Chamberlain's position remained delicate not merely due to the intransigence of Hitler but also the fact that most Britons despised Nazi Germany and everything it stood for. Churchill and his supporters waited in the wings for the Prime Minister to slip up, enabling them to pounce, force him out of office, and institute a robust anti-Nazi policy in place of his effective collaboration. Though Churchill remained firmly anti-communist and anti-Soviet throughout his life, he refused to see the situation as a choice between supporting either one despotism or the other. He eschewed both, and history eventually proved his perspective viable.

Though the British stance against German invasion during the "May Crisis" lasted only a day, and the Cabinet backpedaled so quickly that it left no doubt of their dedication to appeasement, Hitler responded to the incident with rage. The international press reported the end of the May Crisis as a victory of Britain's firmness overawing the Fuhrer, thereby casting Hitler in the role of a weak, easily-cowed leader, and though this was obviously false, it irked Hitler. In fact, "he remained in a funk for the rest of the month, dreaming of the revenge that he would wreak on the world with his panzers and bombers." (Parssinen, 2003, 38). Incredibly, while it managed to enrage Hitler, the brief moment of British opposition to his designs for the Czechs simultaneously rendered Chamberlain's Cabinet even more pusillanimous and supine, which only goaded the Fuhrer into a more intense state of aggression. The transitory glimpse of English resolve acted on Hitler's mind like a gauntlet flung down before a duelist or the red flag waved in front of a bull. Following the momentary defiance, the Reich leader seemed determined to "prove himself."

All the while, the Sudeten German Party in Czechoslovakia received a steady stream of Nazi funding to assure that they remained a thorn in the Czech government's side. Despite his avowed intention of "wiping Czechoslovakia from the map," Hitler proceeded with some caution; the Czech army mustered 31 divisions and, though weaker than Germany's forces, possessed a moderate level of professionalism and decent equipment. Furthermore, the Sudetenland regions provided a naturally defensible frontier with their rugged landscape.

Czech soldiers in the Sudetenland in 1938

Resistance to Hitler in Britain came not from the government but from a handful of individuals. The head of the Lewis' department store chain, Lord Woolton, boycotted German goods, a move that struck a chord with the English populace. "[H]e would not trade with a Government that 'for no other reason for that of their faith persecuted one of the oldest races in the world.' The boycott was popular. 'It was what the public wanted someone to say: it gave the individual citizens something to do – a means of expressing their emotion.'" (Gilbert, 1963, 127).

Woolton

In response, Sir Horace Wilson, speaking for Chamberlain, chided Lord Woolton forcefully for interfering in foreign affairs, indicating once again how sketchy the Prime Minister's idea of democracy seemed at times. The Lord's pity for the afflicted Jews probably incensed the Cabinet further, as many British statesmen detested the luckless Jews almost as much as they did the Nazis. One anonymous but eminent individual went so far as to say, "I understand perfectly the German attitude towards these people, and I approve it fully." (Gilbert, 1963, 11). Even the brutality and sadistic oppression of Kristallnacht failed to produce any outrage or even significant discomfort among Chamberlain and his inner circle.

As the summer passed, Britain considered ways of coercing the Czechs into cooperating with Hitler's Sudetenland plans in order to preserve good relations between Germany and England. Lord Halifax, the right hand man of Chamberlain and replacement of Anthony Eden as Foreign Secretary, made a remarkable statement to the visiting German officer Wiedemann. The German recalled, "We took leave with marked cordiality, Lord Halifax asking me to tell [Hitler] that he [Halifax], before his death, would like to see, as the culmination of his work, the Fuhrer entering London, at the side of the English King, amid the acclamation of the English people." (Gilbert, 1963, 128).

The British sent Lord Runciman to Czechoslovakia in late July to attempt negotiation of a settlement between the Sudeten Germans and the Czechoslovak central government, and though Runciman did his best, with perhaps more of a bias towards the Germans than his avowed impartiality made decent, his mission proved futile. In fact, it appears to have been a sort of public relations stunt by the British government, with Runciman a luckless dupe whom the Cabinet never intended to achieve anything concrete. The Germans ignored Runciman as though he did not exist, while Chamberlain contemptuously carried out separate negotiations with the Sudeten German Party and the Third Reich without bothering to consult with Runciman.

Runciman

The Germans and Chamberlain continued to figuratively pat one another's backs throughout August. The Fuhrer stated that Germany and England represented European civilization's two pillars, while the British representatives told the German strongman that it would be a woeful situation if the world's two foremost "white races" butchered each other in a fresh war. In their private memorandums to one another, the British leaders continued to heap scorn on Czechoslovakia and dismiss the country as useless, all but talking themselves into justifying the coming betrayal of the Munich agreement.

Despite the Czechs' willingness to negotiate during August, the Sudeten Germans remained intransigent. The month also witnessed the mustering of considerable Wehrmacht forces ominously close to the Czechoslovakian border, and meanwhile, Hans Oster and his fellow conspirators, including several high ranking German officers, displayed a rather naïve faith that the British would likely come to their senses and denounce Hitler, thus giving them the opening needed to topple the whole Nazi edifice. One of the schemers, Erich Kordt, "took comfort in the expectation that the British, having been apprised of Hitler's intentions by a succession of emissaries, would soon issue such a statement. Once the British statement was broadcast in Germany (it was not yet forbidden to listen to foreign radio stations), Kordt believed that 'it would spread like wildfire. A revolutionary situation would develop as a prelude to a successful action against Hitler.'" (Parssinen, 2003, 87).

As matters developed, Oster and his fellow conspirators never received the opportunity they hoped for. Hitler launched World War II before the men could strike and prevent the eruption of another global conflict. They continued to try arranging Hitler's death throughout the war, including with explosives, but the Fuhrer proved too wily or too lucky to succumb to them. Eventually, the unfortunate officers inadvertently betrayed themselves to the Gestapo, which imprisoned them for the duration of the war, and shortly before committing suicide in 1945, Hitler spitefully ordered them hanged. Thus, they were executed without a drop, strangling slowly as the final victims of Flossenburg concentration camp. Two or three hours too late to save them, advancing American forces took the camp and found their corpses dangling from the gallows.

Chamberlain and Hitler meeting in September 1938

In September 1938 Neville Chamberlain, the Prime Minister of Britain, decided that only extraordinary measures could prevent the outbreak of another war, so he took the unprecedented step of flying repeatedly to Germany to negotiate face-to-face with Hitler, a move that perhaps inspired Rudolf Hess' later, quixotic aerial peace mission to Britain during the war. The Prime Minister summarized his decision in a report to his monarch and the symbolic head of the British government, King George VI: "The plan is that I should inform Herr Hitler that I propose at once to go over to Germany to see him ... I should hope to persuade him that he had an unequaled opportunity of raising his own prestige and fulfilling what he has so often declared to be his aim, namely the establishment of an Anglo-German understanding preceded by a settlement of the Czecho-Slovakian question." (Leibovitz, 1997, 134).

Churchill, wishing to support the British negotiating position with a show of force, suggested that the English navy should gather its forces in the North Sea, but Lord Halifax haughtily dismissed him, saying that "the British government did not intend from now onward to open personal discussions with prominent members of the House of Commons." (Gilbert, 1963, 135).

With no military forces poised to lend steel to his words, Chamberlain effectively planned to go to Germany as a suppliant, pleading for Hitler to make concessions from a more or less deliberately assumed position of weakness in order to avoid antagonizing the Fuhrer. Chamberlain dubbed his mission "Plan Z" and did not inform the rest of the government about it until he was practically ready to step onto the aircraft for Germany. He first sent a message to

Hitler stating, "I propose to come over at once to see you with a view to try to find a peaceful solution. I propose to come across by air and am ready to start tomorrow." (Stewart, 2001, 299). He told the Cabinet about the plan after Hitler agreed, on September 14th, and landed in Germany on September 15th, the following day.

This first of three visits to the Third Reich involved a long, somewhat uncomfortable and risky flight on a propeller airplane, not a 40 minute hop on a jet aircraft as would be the case in the 21st century. The trip deeply underlined Chamberlain's seriousness to both the English and the Germans, due to its difficulty and inconvenience. Even Hitler sat up and took notice.

The French, now led by Édouard Daladier, expressed some disgruntlement at the bilateral nature of Chamberlain's negotiations, as they had hoped for a trilateral council to decide the future. Nevertheless, Chamberlain went ahead and landed at Munich airport, where he was met by Nevile Henderson, the British emissary with a singular distaste for the Czechs. Chamberlain met Henderson's solicitous inquiries about his condition following the long flight with the confident assertion "I'm tough and wiry."

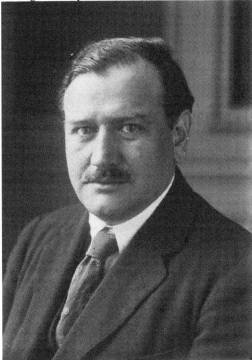

Daladier

From Munich airport, the Prime Minister traveled to Hitler's alpine manor at Berchtesgaden, where the two national leaders sat down in a well-appointed room with an interpreter and launched into a discussion of the situation after some chatter about the size of the rooms and the nature of the furnishings. A British commentator, Stang, remarked, "There was a somewhat macabre tea-party at a round table in the room with great window looking out towards Austria. The small-talk of statesmen whose only point of contact is an international emergency cynically created by the one and stoically grappled with by the other is best left in oblivion." (Gilbert, 1963, 144).

Once the initial awkward discussion about room size and windows ended, Hitler opened negotiations with a threat. The British had previously given Germany a Naval Agreement as a fairly remarkable gesture of conciliation marking their recognition of Germany's right to repudiate the arms limitations imposed by the Treaty of Versailles. The Naval Agreement permitted the Kriegsmarine to build 35 tons of naval vessels for every 100 tons possessed by the Royal Navy. When signed in 1935, the other Allies were furious with England for making such a large concession to Germany and effectively discarding the Versailles treaty, but Hitler now took the line that the Naval Agreement represented a generous concession to Britain and threatened to end it unless England agreed never to intervene in Germany's affairs under any circumstances. In the face of this aggressive opening, Chamberlain babbled, asking if the Naval Agreement would be ended before or after the Germans declared war, an absolutely meaningless procedural point.

With this initial, largely useless exchange out of the way, Hitler rapidly focused on the core of the meeting. He stated unequivocally that the Sudetenland must be removed from Czechoslovakia immediately and incorporated into Germany, leading to the disintegration of the remaining Czech territory. Chamberlain immediately stated that he conceded the point "in principle," but that the Cabinet would need to be consulted first. Of course, since the Cabinet essentially rubber-stamped the Prime Minister's decisions, this statement was tantamount to Chamberlain conceding that Hitler could take the Sudetenland, all within the first hour of negotiations. Over the course of the discussion, Chamberlain also indicated he had no objection to Germany attacking Russia.

The Prime Minister then returned temporarily to Britain. The two leaders had laid the groundwork for the Munich Agreement, but they had not yet committed anything to paper and still had details to work out. In essence, the agreement allowed Hitler to carry out any aggression he pleased east of Germany as long as he left Western Europe alone.

The following day, at 2:00 a.m., Czech President Eduard Benes made the horrifying discovery that the British had given away the Sudetenland to Germany without even bothering to consult or even notify him. Humiliated but helpless, the Czech leader protested, only to have the British respond by threatening to abandon the Czechs entirely to the nonexistent mercy of the Third Reich (something that would eventually happen). Powerless before this threat, Benes agreed to allow the Sudeten Germans to carry out a referendum regarding whether they wanted to secede from Czechoslovakia and merge with the Third Reich.

Benes

Chamberlain's second meeting with Hitler occurred on September 21st and 22nd, 1938, and this time, Hitler chose the posh Petersberg Hotel as the venue for the negotiations. The hotel, located in Godesberg (the town which gave its name to the meeting), helped to set a luxurious stage for the second conference between the two power brokers. "Magnificent rooms had been reserved overlooking the Rhine. Kirkpatrick noted that, 'Fruit, cigars and cigarettes were laid out on every table and the proprietor (the owner of the famous Eau de Cologne) had provided no fewer than fifteen samples of his products: hair lotion, shaving-cream, soap, bath salts, pomades and so on.' Kirkpatrick removed some of the latter for his wife." (Gilbert, 1963, 152).

Chamberlain expected a cordial meeting with the Fuhrer, operating under the mistaken assumption that the first meeting resolved most of the difficulties. Instead, Hitler went on the attack again, startling the Prime Minister. The Fuhrer, a practiced predator and a man skilled at dominating others, clearly sensed weakness in Chamberlain and closed in for the metaphorical kill.

This time, Hitler declared that the Sudetenland referendum was inadequate because it would require too much time, and that the Czechs must transfer control over the Sudeten regions immediately or he would repudiate the deal. Even Chamberlain balked slightly at this, since Hitler appeared to be demanding massive concessions and offering absolutely nothing in return. Chamberlain intended to sell out the Czechs, but he wanted something of value, like an agreement that the Germans would not attack France, Britain, or any of the possessions of the British Empire.

Hitler sensed he had gone too far in asking for surrender of the Czechs without offering a quid pro quo, so accordingly, he approached Chamberlain at 2:00 a.m. on September 23rd, minutes before the British leader left to catch his airplane back to Britain. Dr. Paul Schmidt, who recorded the meetings with considerable accuracy, reported, "Chamberlain and Hitler took leave from one another in a completely friendly tone after having had, with my assistance, an eye to eye conversation. [...] Hitler thanked Chamberlain for his efforts for peace. Hitler also spoke about a German-Anglo rapprochement and cooperation. [...] He went back to his old tune: 'Between us there should be no conflict,' he told Chamberlain, 'we will not stand in the way of your pursuit of your non-European interests and you may without harm let us have a free hand on the European continent in Central and South-East Europe.'" (Leibovitz, 1997, 140-141).

After that, Chamberlain left in an exuberant mood, feeling that he had gained exactly what he longed for: permanent peace between Germany and England. He had casually carved up the world between the two nations, breezily giving away Czechoslovakia and Eastern Europe to the Reich in exchange for a mere promise that Hitler would never interfere in British affairs. Upon his return to Britain, Chamberlain concealed Hitler's statements, instead providing a vague summary indicating that the Fuhrer only wished to acquire a few minor territories with ethnic German majorities. He made no mention of the German dictator's intention to expand boundlessly eastward in pursuit of Lebensraum, despite having been fully apprised of this by Hitler.

Despite his soothing and two-faced depiction of the negotiations, Chamberlain created a near-mutiny in his Cabinet. Lord Halifax, who until then supported his positions faithfully, effectively declared a position somewhat favorable to Czechoslovakia: "[I]t seems to your colleagues that you should not leave without making it plain to the Chancellor [i.e. Hitler] if possible by special interview that, after great concessions made by Czechoslovak Government, for him to reject opportunity of peaceful solution in favor of one that must involve war would be an unpardonable crime against humanity." (Leibovitz, 1997, 142).

Meanwhile, in Chamberlain's absence, Hitler returned to his usual bullying ways while negotiating with Sir Horace Wilson. At one point, Wilson noted that the Fuhrer began "shrieking" and calling Chamberlain various names "not suitable for repetition in a drawing room." The English knight remained unperturbed and even wrote off Hitler's performance as a gauche but pardonable sign of extreme strain due to the delicate negotiations; he did not realize that they represented the Fuhrer's typical method when he did not immediately get his way, or that Hitler was trying to intimidate him.

An anti-German protest in Prague on September 22

Finally, the British drew up a timetable on September 27th, 1938 that it hoped would appease both the Czechs and the Germans. This plan envisaged German occupation of two small territories outside the Czech fortification lines by October 1st, while British, Czech, and German representatives would meet in the Sudetenland on October 3rd to decide what additional Sudeten areas would be fast-tracked for handover to the Germans. On October 10th, German soldiers would enter the areas earmarked between October 3-9 by this trilateral group, and later in October, Germany, England, France, and Czechoslovakia would arrange a full-scale negotiation to finalize agreements and create a new, stable, independent Czechoslovakia without the transferred Sudetenland territories.

Though Hitler did not agree to this plan immediately, he postponed any other operations against Czech territory until he had time to speak again with Chamberlain. Thus, the British Prime Minister, the Fuhrer, the Frenchman Daladier, and Mussolini gathered in Munich on September 29th, 1938, to decide the fate of Czechoslovakia. France, Britain, Germany, and Italy did not see fit to invite the Czechs to the meeting; Chamberlain mentioned the notion obliquely at one point, but when Hitler demurred, the English Prime Minister meekly accepted his decision.

The final negotiations proved to be brief and rather perfunctory. Meeting at 12:30 p.m., Chamberlain, Hitler, Daladier, and Mussolini essentially confirmed what had already been decided. None of the exact words spoken survive due to the event's secrecy; in fact, Daladier and Mussolini found themselves excluded from the final talks between Hitler and Chamberlain. Ultimately, the Munich Agreement resembled the English plan of September 27th, but it differed in several ways. The international commission to determine which territories the Czechs would transfer to the Reich included German, English, French, Czech, and Italian representatives, and the territories would be divided into five zones, labeled from I to V with Roman numerals. Czech evacuation and German occupation of Zone I would be completed by October 2nd, Zone II by October 3rd, and so forth, with Zone IV transferred by October 8th and Zone V – potentially the broadest of all – by October 10th. Following these transfers, plebiscites would be held by the end of November to determine if the transfer would be permanent, and people living in the Sudetenland and Czechoslovakia would receive a 6 month grace period during which they could move from one territory to the other and become permanent citizens, thus allowing Czechs to leave Sudetenland and allowing Germans to concentrate there.

The four leaders appended their signatures one above another at the bottom of the document, starting with Hitler and followed by Chamberlain, Daladier, and finally Mussolini. Ostensibly, Mussolini prepared the document, but the German chancellery drew it up based on a modified form of England's September 27th plan. The agreement in its entirety read:

"Agreement concluded at Munich, September 29, 1938, between Germany, Great Britain, France and Italy

GERMANY, the United Kingdom, France and Italy, taking into consideration the agreement, which has been already reached in principle for the cession to Germany of the Sudeten German territory, have agreed on the following terms and conditions governing the said cession and the measures consequent thereon, and by this agreement they each hold themselves responsible for the steps necessary to secure its fulfillment:

(1) The evacuation will begin on 1st October.

(2) The United Kingdom, France and Italy agree that the evacuation of the territory shall be completed by the 10th October, without any existing installations having been destroyed, and that the Czechoslovak Government will be held responsible for carrying out the evacuation without damage to the said installations.

(3) The conditions governing the evacuation will be laid down in detail by an international commission composed of representatives of Germany, the United Kingdom, France, Italy and Czechoslovakia.

(4) The occupation by stages of the predominantly German territory by German troops will begin on 1st October. The four territories marked on the attached map will be occupied by German troops in the following order:

The territory marked No. I on the 1st and 2nd of October; the territory marked No. II on the 2nd and 3rd of October; the territory marked No. III on the 3rd, 4th and 5th of October; the territory marked No. IV on the 6th and 7th of October. The remaining territory of preponderantly German character will be ascertained by the aforesaid international commission forthwith and be occupied by German troops by the 10th of October.

(5) The international commission referred to in paragraph 3 will determine the territories in which a plebiscite is to be held. These territories will be occupied by international bodies until the plebiscite has been completed. The same commission will fix the conditions in which the plebiscite is to be held, taking as a basis the conditions of the Saar plebiscite. The commission will also fix a date, not later than the end of November, on which the plebiscite will be held.

(6) The final determination of the frontiers will be carried out by the international commission. The commission will also be entitled to recommend to the four Powers, Germany, the United Kingdom, France and Italy, in certain exceptional cases, minor modifications in the strictly ethnographical determination of the zones

which are to be transferred without plebiscite.

(7) There will be a right of option into and out of the transferred territories, the option to be exercised within six months from the date of this agreement. A German-Czechoslovak commission shall determine the details of the option, consider ways of facilitating the transfer of population and settle questions of principle arising out of the said transfer.

(8) The Czechoslovak Government will within a period of four weeks from the date of this agreement release from their military and police forces any Sudeten Germans who may wish to be released, and the Czechoslovak Government will within the same period release Sudeten German prisoners who are serving terms of imprisonment for political offences.

Munich, September 29, 1938.
ADOLF HITLER,
NEVILLE CHAMBERLAIN,
EDOUARD DALADIER,
BENITO MUSSOLINI."

A picture of Chamberlain, Daladier, Hitler, Mussolini, and Galeazzo Ciano taken just before the document was signed

On September 30th, Chamberlain flew back to England, where he famously waved the agreement before a crowd upon landing and told audience: "The settlement of the Czechoslovakian problem, which has now been achieved is, in my view, only the prelude to a larger settlement in which all Europe may find peace. This morning I had another talk with the German Chancellor, Herr Hitler, and here is the paper which bears his name upon it as well as mine. Some of you, perhaps, have already heard what it contains but I would just like to read it to you: 'We regard the agreement signed last night and the Anglo-German Naval Agreement as symbolic of the desire of our two peoples never to go to war with one another again.'" Later that night, from his balcony, he said one of the 20th century's most infamous lines: "My good friends, for the second time in our history, a British Prime Minister has returned from Germany bringing peace with honour. I believe it is peace for our time. We thank you from the bottom of our hearts. Go home and get a nice quiet sleep."

The British Prime Minister appeared to believe he had struck an unprecedented deal for lasting peace by crucifying Czechoslovakia and using appeasement tactics towards Hitler. However, Chamberlain could not convince some Britons of this, including Lord Halifax, who characterized Hitler as a "criminal lunatic." The Prime Minister came in for scathing contempt along with the thunderous plaudits: "[First Lord of the Admiralty] Duff Cooper thought that Chamberlain had as much chance of successfully appeasing Hitler as 'Little Lord Fauntleroy would have of concluding a satisfactory deal with Al Capone.'" (McDonough, 1998, 74).

Chamberlain's most famous critic, Winston Churchill, didn't mince words when it came to expressing his disgust with the deal: "We have suffered a total and unmitigated defeat ... you will find that in a period of time which may be measured by years, but may be measured by months, Czechoslovakia will be engulfed in the Nazi régime. We are in the presence of a disaster of the first magnitude ... we have sustained a defeat without a war, the consequences of which will travel far with us along our road ... we have passed an awful milestone in our history, when the whole equilibrium of Europe has been deranged, and that the terrible words have for the time being been pronounced against the Western democracies: 'Thou art weighed in the balance and found wanting'. And do not suppose that this is the end. This is only the beginning of the reckoning. This is only the first sip, the first foretaste of a bitter cup which will be proffered to us year by year unless by a supreme recovery of moral health and martial vigour, we arise again and take our stand for freedom as in the olden time."

For his part, in the wake of Munich, Hitler didn't even pretend to respect Chamberlain or the process that brought about the agreement. At one point, he told people around him, "Gentlemen, this has been my first international conference and I can assure you that it will be my last" On another occasion, Hitler said of Chamberlain, "If ever that silly old man comes interfering here again with his umbrella, I'll kick him downstairs and jump on his stomach in front of the photographers."

Once Munich was behind him and he had what he wanted, Hitler began a wave of anti-British propaganda, including personal insults towards Chamberlain. The Fuhrer went so far as to assert that an agreement with a democratic government must be regarded as transitory; as soon as Churchill or Eden supplanted Chamberlain, the German leader expected war, and he made his plans with that scenario in mind. In fact, he also schemed to advance west even in the absence of British provocation once he concluded his business in the east.

In the days after Munich, the Wehrmacht swarmed across the border into the Sudetenland, while the Czech army grudgingly fell back from their mountain positions and fortifications. 34 divisions of troops retreated from a formidable defensive line without firing a shot, and 175,000 ordinary people fled as well, hoping to steer clear of German control. The Czechs harbored few illusions about Hitler's character or the nature of Nazi Germany's culture and society; 50,000 more soon followed the initial panicked exodus.

A picture of Czechs leaving border lands taken by Germany

Conversely, the Sudeten Germans greeted the Wehrmacht with screaming enthusiasm, brandishing the emblems of fascism and showering the soldiers with bouquets of late-blooming flowers. The French, paradoxically, celebrated the Munich Agreement and the occupation of the Sudetenland also, to the astonishment of the American journalist William Shirer, who was in Paris on October 8th and wrote, "Paris a frightful place, completely surrendered to defeatism with no inkling of what has happened to France. At Fouquet's, at Maxim's, fat bankers and businessmen, toasting Peace with rivers of champagne. But even the waiters, taxi-drivers, who used to be sound, gushing about how wonderful it is that war has been avoided […] The guts of France – France of the Marne and Verdun – where are they?" (Shirer, 1942, 150).

A picture of Sudeten Germans welcoming the arrival of German soldiers in the Sudetenland

Germany's territorial gains in Czechoslovakia represented far more than a mere slice of real estate; the regions that contained large numbers of ethnic Germans were home to Czechoslovakia's border mountain ranges and its formidable fortifications. Thus, the Munich Agreement stripped away the country's hard outer shell and exposed its defenseless inner territories. The entire process had the effect of opening a bank vault's doors to a robber and then expecting the robber not to touch the money inside it. Not surprisingly, the Nazis went further than the Munich Agreement permitted, though they stopped short of taking over Czechoslovakia totally. The Gestapo, swarming into the country like dark locusts, arrested over 10,000 people known or suspected to have anti-Nazi opinions and moved them to the concentration camps. A decree from Hitler fired 50,000 Czechs in the Sudetenland from their jobs and gave them to Germans instead, while the Nazis simultaneously banned the Czech language in those regions they controlled.

Exceeding the terms of the Munich Agreement from the start, the Third Reich carved off two long strips of territory, giving one to Poland and another to Hungary. The Kristallnacht violence against Jews on November 9-10, 1938 also extended into the newly taken Sudeten territories, cementing Hitler's policy of hate as an official cultural characteristic of ethnic Germans both inside and outside Germany's boundaries. Through it all, Chamberlain responded to this outrage in typical fashion: "'Oh, what tedious people these Germans can be!' said Neville Chamberlain when he read the reports of the anti-Jewish riots and the measures which followed. 'Just when we were beginning to make a little progress!'" (Leibovitz, 1997, 166).

A map depicting the breakup of Czechoslovakia in the wake of the agreement
Meanwhile, the Germans continued to consolidate their position over the winter, and the Slovaks, ironically, provided the impetus for losing what little independence they themselves enjoyed. Seeing the Czechs weakened by the German seizure of the Sudetenland, they revolted against the central government and appealed to the Nazis for aid, which gave Germany the pretext to put the surviving fragments of Czechoslovakia out of their misery in early spring 1939. In yet another typical negotiation session, Hitler targeted the Czech leader Emil Hacha, an ailing man in his 60s. "Just like Schuschnigg before him, Hácha was kept waiting far into the night (while Hitler watched a popular film), then was mercilessly bullied [...] German troops were already on the move, said Hitler. When Goring added that German bombers would be dropping their payloads on Prague within a few hours, the elderly, sick Czech President fainted." (Evans, 2006, 564).

Hacha, Hitler, and Goering meeting in 1939

In response to the threats, Hacha signed over control of Czechoslovakia to Hitler on March 15th, 1939. He also called the Prague and ordered his army to refrain from firing on the Wehrmacht as they swept forward to complete their conquest. The Czechs stood down, knowing their position to be utterly hopeless. Czechoslovakia became a Reich Protectorate under the control of Reinhard Heydrich, the infamous Blonde Beast, whose assassination several years later launched a round of bloody reprisals that left the shocked, decimated Czechs unable to mount further resistance until the last few days of the war.

The Non-Aggression Pact with the Soviet Union

Another perverse byproduct of Munich is that it would set in motion the chain of events that doomed Poland.

Forged from the wreck of empires following World War I, Poland represented both a practical and a symbolic stumbling block to the ambitions of both Nazi and Soviet leaders by the late 1930s. Prussia, Austria, and Russia had extinguished Polish sovereignty on October 24th, 1795 with the "Third Partition," absorbing the Polish Commonwealth into their respective empires, and a secret treaty clause pledged all three powers to work to permanently "abolish" the existence of Poland. With that, the imperial partners drove many leading Poles into exile, but nevertheless, Polish patriotism survived, flourishing underground and emerging periodically. The Polish aided Napoleon Bonaparte with superb lancer cavalry, relishing the chance to strike back at the loathed Russians, Prussians, and Austrians, but while the Poles also hoped for restoration of their Republic, this did not occur until over 100 years after the Napoleonic Era.

The fall of the German and Russian empires in 1917 and 1918 presented Poland with its opportunity. Led by Jozef Piłsudski, the Poles founded a democratic nation in 1918 with the blessing of the Western Allies. However, the emergent, blood-soaked dictatorship of the Soviet

Union took a far different view of Poland's resurrection: "[I]n spring 1920, Lenin and Trotsky thought that they would bring their own revolution to Poland, using the bayonet to inspire workers to fulfill their historical role. After Poland's fall, German comrades, assisted by the new Red Army, would bring to bear Germany's vast resources to save the Russian revolution. But the Soviet forces on their way to Berlin were halted by the Polish Army at Warsaw in August 1920." (Snyder, 2010, 24).

Piłsudski

Already a violent, unscrupulous aggressor, the Soviet Union aimed to scoop up Poland on the way to its actual prize: Germany and the rest of Europe. Initially, the Soviets enjoyed military success, battering their way deep into Polish territory, and the Soviets' triumphalist language left scant doubt as to their intentions. Besides openly crowing that Berlin, Paris, and London headed their objective list, the communists exulted in the prostration of Poland. On July 2, 1920, General Mikhail N. Tukhachevsky told his men, "Over the corpse of White Poland lies the road to worldwide conflagration. March on Vilno, Minsk, Warsaw!"

Tukhachevsky

The tentatively pro-Soviet Prime Minister of Britain, David Lloyd George, scuppered plans to aid the Poles with arms shipments against the onrushing Bolsheviks, but Pilsudski and his colleague Wladyslaw Sikorsky refused to admit defeat. Armed with deciphered Soviet radio communications, the Polish commanders lured Tukhachevsky into an overextended position near Warsaw in August. From August 14-18, 1920, the Polish armies executed a massive encircling movement, defeating the Russians in the span of just five days. The Battle of Komarow provided the action's centerpiece; in history's last true cavalry battle, eight Soviets died for every Pole killed in action as Sikorsky's Uhlans (lancers) smashed Soviet Marshal Semyon Budyonny's dreaded 1st Cavalry Army to pieces.

Sikorsky

The war continued for some time, until finally the Russians signed a treaty in March 1921 that ended the hostilities and recognized the existence of Poland as a separate nation. That said, Poland's victory represented more of a respite than a permanent triumph; the nation, positioned between two strengthening dictatorships just a decade later in the 1930s, represented a staging area for Germany's eastward "Lebensraum" plans and the Soviets' westward "Red Europe" dreams: "Poland changed the balance of power in eastern Europe. It was not large enough to be a great power, but it was large enough to be a problem for any great power with plans of expansion. It separated Russia from Germany, for the first time in more than a century. Poland's very existence created a buffer to both Russian and German power, and was much resented in Moscow and Berlin." (Snyder, 2010, 22).

The Austrians and Czechoslovakians put up little to no resistance to Hitler's advance, but Poland offered a more serious challenge. Though in a very difficult situation, the Poles refused to yield their sovereignty without a vigorous fight. Starting in 1937, the Poles commenced a massive rearmament program, spearheaded by the construction of new factories at Starachowice, Rzeszow, and other locations. Production centered on 37mm anti-tank guns and 40mm anti-aircraft guns, but the Poles also fabricated other weapons systems in a hasty bid for deterrence and war preparation.

Money problems and a heavy reliance on imported raw materials hampered Poland's efforts at building an army. Shortages forced military contractors to produce the most urgent items first. Thus, the factories rolled out considerable numbers of 37mm anti-tank guns, but they could not spare the industrial capacity to make trucks or halftracks to tow them into action. Horses therefore towed most of Poland's anti-tank guns. Horses are slower than trucks, and they understandably tend to panic at the sound of loud explosions. The artillery required additional horses to carry ammunition and spare parts, all of which was more efficiently transported in towing trucks by the German army.

Some factors worked in Poland's favor, however. Polish experts, working from a civilian Enigma machine obtained earlier, contrived to keep abreast of German coding procedures throughout the 1930s. Despite multiple upgrades to the cryptographic technology by the Nazis, the Poles soon deciphered each fresh advance and thus obtained vast quantities of high quality intelligence on German plans and movements. "The Germans had a blind faith in their technical invincibility and consequently, at times, made careless mistakes [...] In January 1938 the Poles found that they could read 75 per cent of the Wehrmacht's cable traffic. By the summer the Poles had an impressive new code centre in the Kabackie Woods near Warsaw. A French officer, Captain Bertrand, remembered: '[...] this was the brain centre of the organization where work went on day and night in silence.'" (Williamson, 2009, 31).

The Polish military built up a stock of vehicles as well, but obviously the Poles could not match the tremendous mechanization program of the Third Reich. Aircraft, tanks, and similar hardware rolled off Polish production lines in modest numbers, and among the vehicles the Poles built were 575 TKS "tankettes." These strange little armored fighting vehicles featured a square plan, continuous caterpillar tracks, a weight of 2.6 tons, and a crew of two. Somewhat amusing in appearance, these miniature tanks mostly carried 7.62mm machine guns and served mostly as scout vehicles and mobile machine gun nests for infantry support. The Poles improved the guns on a minority of these TKS vehicles with 20mm cannons, which proved surprisingly lethal against 6-ton Panzer I and 8.8-ton Panzer II tanks. Described vividly as "cockroaches against panzers" by Polish historians, these tankettes even offered an opportunity for an "ace" to emerge in Roman Orlik, whose "cockroach" claimed a total of 13 Panzers during the 1939 invasion.

A TKS

Orlik

Poland's preparations, though energetic, failed to keep pace with the industrial might of Nazi Germany or even the backward but immense Soviet Union. Recognizing their relative weakness, the Poles sought a diplomatic solution, bolstering their strength with that of allies.

German preparations for the seizure of Polish territory or outright annexation of Poland proceeded rapidly throughout 1938 and into 1939. The Third Reich's rearmament program was underway in any case, providing cover for a military buildup near the Polish border.

Diplomatically, the German state pursued several goals simultaneously. Hitler, through intermediaries such as the slippery Joachim von Ribbentrop, sought to obfuscate his actual intent by periodically floating the idea of an anti-Soviet alliance with the Poles when talks occurred between representatives of the two nations. At the same time, von Ribbentrop regularly brought up the subject of handing over the Baltic city of Danzig and the nearby territories to Nazi control, which the alarmed Poles managed to evade while holding out hope they might comply in the near future.

Joachim von Ribbentrop

This diplomatic dance served as a mask for Hitler's purposes even as it gave the Poles a few more precious months to prepare. All the while, uncertainty about the Nazi dictator's attitude towards Poland kept the French and British from action; in fact, they sent less aid to Poland than they were inclined to for fear of disturbing a highly delicate situation. Of course, since Hitler commanded much greater industrial power than Poland, these delays ultimately aided German preparations more than those of Poland. For example, the Luftwaffe possessed 4,093 serviceable fighters, bombers, and dive-bombers on the eve of the Polish invasion, while the Poles mustered just 397. "Bomber strength was only about 20 per cent of the projected numbers and observation planes only about two-thirds of the intended figure. Although the number of fighter planes was theoretically up to strength, many were obsolescent. In general, the Polish Air Force was not capable of an offensive role." (Williamson, 2009, 25).

The Poles, understandably, remained highly suspicious of their brutal, relentless neighbors to the east, the Soviet Russians. If anything, Bolshevism represented a more alien and menacing philosophy to Polish culture than Nazism, or at least it seemed that way in 1939. The Poles maintained a non-aggression treaty with the USSR, but they were also keenly aware of its fragility.

Playing it safe, the Polish high command drew up defensive plans for an attack by either the Germans or the Soviets, but in a curious oversight, none of Poland's military planners thought to come up with a plan for a two-front war in case both of the nation's neighbors attacked simultaneously.

As it turned out, that oversight would prove disastrous. When Chamberlain visited Hitler in September 1938, Stalin became convinced that England was planning a secret pact with Germany against the Soviet Union, so he decided to try to beat them to the punch; Stalin contacted Hitler and proposed that they form an alliance, going as far as to fire his Commissar of Foreign Affairs, Maxim Litinov, a Jew who was an unacceptable ambassador to Hitler's government. Thus, throughout much of the first half of 1939, the Nazis (represented by their Moscow ambassador Friedrich Werner von der Schulenburg) and the Soviets (fronted by Stalin's diplomatic crony Vyacheslav Molotov, after whom partisans ironically named Molotov cocktails) engaged in wary, nebulous negotiations. Both powers indicated the need for political and economic cooperation, but they gave each other no concrete details; the two dictatorships clearly experienced profound distrust and were unwilling to even indicate to one another what they were willing to negotiate about.

Friedrich Werner von der Schulenburg

Molotov

With plans afoot for the invasion of Poland, Hitler pushed hard to acquire a treaty with Stalin. Molotov and Stalin initially delayed, but they finally agreed to meet Ribbentrop on August 23rd, 1939 to sign a mutual non-aggression and trade treaty which contained a secret clause regarding the annexation of Poland.

The secret clause seems, from Soviet communications, to have originated with the Soviets, and probably from a personal command of Josef Stalin delivered verbally to Molotov. It was not revealed to the world until the western Allies defeated the Nazis in 1945 and captured the treaty document, but with a flourish of their pens, Ribbentrop and Molotov abolished Poland yet again. Negotiations about earlier parts of the treaty proved lengthy and tedious, but both sides agreed to the secret clause within a few hours on the same day Ribbentrop flew into Moscow.

Though the negotiations themselves went smoothly, Stalin still put his foot down regarding some of Ribbentrop's flights of diplomatic fancy, indicating that the wounds between the two dictatorships were very far from healed under the veneer of unanimity. "[A] high-falutin preamble which Ribbentrop wanted to insert stressing the formation of friendly Soviet-German relations was thrown out at the insistence of Stalin. The Soviet dictator complained that 'the Soviet government could not suddenly present to the public assurances of friendship after they had been covered with pails of manure by the Nazi government for six years.'" (Shirer, 2011, 539).

The treaty ensuring the demise of Poland bore the name Molotov-Ribbentrop Pact, but Molotov wisely deferred to his murderous master, Stalin, on every point during the process of hammering out the exact terms by which an entire nation was doomed. The negotiations concluded with a fulsome display of false camaraderie between Ribbentrop, Stalin, and Molotov: "Stalin spontaneously proposed a toast to the Fuehrer: 'I know how much the German nation loves its Fuehrer. I should therefore like to drink to his health.' Molotov drank to the health of the Reich Foreign Minister ... Molotov and Stalin drank repeatedly to the Nonaggression Pact, the new era of German–Russian relations, and to the German nation. The Reich Foreign Minister in turn proposed a toast to Stalin." (Shirer, 2011, 532).

Molotov signing the pact

A picture of Stalin shaking hands with Ribbentrop
After a convivial evening with the man who had ordered the shooting deaths of 600,000 or
more Soviet citizens on the flimsiest pretexts and the starvation of some three million

Ukrainians, Ribbentrop flew back to Berlin in a buoyant mood. Nazi Germany found itself free to strike at Poland, though Hitler would end up delaying the attack until September 1st.

The Molotov-Ribbentrop Pact laid out the respective spheres of influence each imperial power claimed within Poland, using rivers as boundaries. The signatories attached their signatures so quickly that some of the geographic descriptions later proved erroneous. The Russians and Germans agreed on amendments to the secret protocol in order to make the division of Poland match up to actual topography. Just 18 years after pushing the Red Army out of their territory, the Poles were about to find a new horde rolling across their borders, bent on slaughter and conquest.

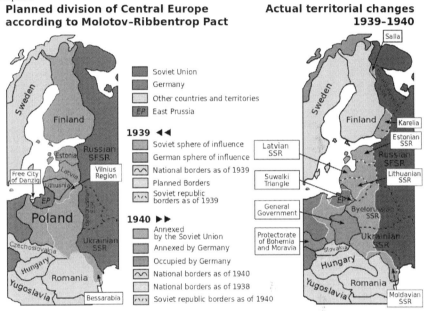

Peter Hanula's map of the plan to divide Poland

Even with the treaty signed and toasts drunk to its success, Molotov continued to play a double game. He dangled the possibility of fresh negotiations in front of the Poles even after the invasion started, decisively severing ties only when it became clear the Germans would succeed in conquering Poland. "Reluctance to give in to German pressure, to make the collaboration of the two powers official, continued after Germany attacked Poland and Britain and France declared war. As late as 5 September, Molotov offered aid to W. Grzybowski, the Polish ambassador. With the rapid collapse of Polish resistance, however, he refused to see Grzybowski for two days, then on 8 September withdrew the offer." (Watson, 2005, 171).

Meanwhile, the British and French envoys arriving in Moscow to negotiate with Stalin shortly thereafter found themselves peremptorily rebuffed with the news that the Soviet Union was no longer interested in major treaties with them. This news prompted an explosion of alarm and outrage in the government offices of London and Paris. Clearly, something insidious had taken place, and the Allies began to fear an imminent outbreak of war.

The Invasion of Poland

Huge numbers of German soldiers moved up to the Polish border as the invasion date approached. Hitler's Wehrmacht already included separate Panzer divisions whose goal was not infantry support but deep, rapid penetration of enemy territory for sweeping encircling movements. This style of warfare, known as Blitzkrieg or lightning war, was nothing new, but the Germans were the first to use it on a large scale with mechanized forces. General George S. Patton would use similar tactics to badly maul Nazi armies in western Europe just a few years later.

Heading into September 1939, the Poles had a very scant conception of the type of adversary poised to crush their nation. For all their glaring faults, the empires partitioning Poland in the 18th century had not viewed the Polish people as vermin to be massacred, but Hitler, on the other hand, made his views clear in a speech to his inner circle of generals one day prior to the signing of the Molotov-Ribbentrop Pact's in Moscow: "Our strength lies in our speed and our brutality. Genghis Khan hunted millions of women and children to their deaths, consciously and with a joyous heart. [...] I have put my Death's Head formations at the ready with the command to send man, woman and child of Polish descent and language to their deaths, pitilessly and remorselessly. Poland will be depopulated and settled with Germans." (Evans, 2009, 27).

As Hitler's words suggest, the Wehrmacht was not prepared or terribly interested in distinguishing between military and civilian targets. During the campaign, the Luftwaffe would strafe columns of civilian refugees, clearly identified as such, operating as though the civilians were advancing military formations. German tanks would fire into hospitals marked with the Red Cross emblem, and German units would round up large numbers of men, women and children and shoot them out of hand or lock them in churches or barns and set them on fire.

Joseph Goebbels' propaganda bears a considerable measure of blame for these hate-fueled actions. The Poles did indeed kill slightly more than 2,000 ethnic Germans during the first days of the invasion, a definite war crime (albeit a relatively limited one compared to the staggering atrocities of the Nazis or Soviets) but Goebbels, Hitler's propaganda minister, inflated the number killed to over 600,000, generating vast hostility towards the Poles among ordinary German soldiers.

Goebbels

Hitler originally intended his attack on Poland to occur on August 26th, 1939. The Fuhrer clearly wanted a tight timetable offering the Poles as little opportunity as possible to prepare, respond, or send out a call for help. Ribbentrop arrived in Moscow and signed the Molotov-Ribbentrop Pact on August 23rd, then flew back to Germany on August 24th. Hitler's plan to cross the border on the 26th, just two days later, would give the German forces deployed there just enough time to muster and move out.

However, British actions caused Hitler a brief hesitation and ultimately shifted the invasion back to September 1st, 1939, the date when the border crossing actually commenced. These rapid deployments were possible because the Germans began preparing as early as March 1939, when Hitler first reached the decision to invade Poland. In the meantime, forces gathered along Poland's southern border in freshly-conquered Czechoslovakia, on the west inside Germany itself, and on the north in the detached German possession of East Prussia.

The British Parliament passed the Emergency Powers Defense Bill on August 24th, 1939, which declared England's continued intention to support Poland's independent existence. Though the Third Reich and the USSR kept the clauses of the Molotov-Ribbentrop Pact related to the partition of Poland secret, the British shrewdly guessed that something of the kind might have been agreed on. The Emergency Powers Defense Bill, and the letter Neville Chamberlain sent to Hitler regarding it, referenced the Molotov-Ribbentrop Pact, stating that its existence made no difference to England's resolve to help the Poles in case of aggression.

As a result, Hitler pushed back the invasion date – "Case White" – to September 1st while he attempted to deal with the British. Simultaneously, he contacted Benito Mussolini, the fascist Italian "Duce," and hinted broadly that he hoped for Italian military support. Given the pitiful quality of Mussolini's armies, and the outstanding strength and modernity of the Wehrmacht, this appeal looks faintly absurd. He also made a strange offer to the British ambassador, Nevile Henderson: "He desired to make a move toward England which should be as decisive as the move towards Russia … The Fuehrer is ready to conclude agreements with England which would not only guarantee the existence of the British Empire in all circumstances so far as Germany is concerned, but would also if necessary assure the British Empire of German assistance regardless of where such assistance should be necessary." (Shirer, 2011, 543).

The British ignored Hitler's strange offer and signed a fresh treaty of mutual support with Poland. Around the same time, Mussolini politely rebuffed the Fuhrer's latest overtures, claiming his involvement in the Balkans and North Africa was too deep to permit aiding the Germans. Thus, Hitler, unsure of what to do, called off the attack a few hours before its scheduled beginning.

By the time Hitler decided to postpone the Polish invasion, most of his forces were already in motion. Motorized columns and tank divisions snaked through the gathering dusk towards the Polish border on the evening of August 25th, 1939. Only the use of scout aircraft, carrying officers who brought Hitler's command to halt to the advancing Wehrmacht, stopped this first advance, but in one case, this proved not to be enough. Executing his orders flawlessly, albeit orders that were rescinded shortly after he left his base, Lieutenant Albrecht Herzner led a detachment of commandos across the border into Poland, aiming for the Jablunka Pass. The Poles had set up demolition charges to close the pass and the railway tunnel it contained in the event of war, so Herzner's commandos had orders to seize the pass and disarm the charges to prepare the way for several divisions of Germans ordered to attack that way early on the morning of August 26th.

Herzner and his men had no radios, and thus it proved impossible to call them off once they left their base of operations. Indeed, the small detachment was already across the border by the time Hitler changed his mind, impossible to locate in the night-shrouded countryside. The men wore durable civilian clothing to blend in with the local population should they be spotted before reaching their objective, inadvertently illustrating the absurdity of Hitler's claims of the Poles as a separate and "inferior race" – Germans in Polish clothing were physically indistinguishable from Poles.

Herzner guided his 70 commandos unerringly to their objective 3 miles inside Polish territory, and once there, they overpowered the small unit of guards. Astonishingly, they did so without killing anyone. Even the sentries on patrol were seized, bound, and gagged without the need to cut a single throat or crush a skull. "About halfway through the tunnel, the platoon leader saw a glowing cigarette butt fall to the ground only a few feet in front of him, and then a shoe extinguished the butt. It was the sentry stationed in the middle of the tunnel who served as the contact man between the two groups at the tunnel entrances. One of the men crept forward and silently overcame the unsuspecting Pole." (Kurowski, 1997, 42-43).

The men in the guard station itself put up slightly more resistance, but after a brief exchange of gunfire and a few lobbed grenades during which two Germans were wounded, these Polish soldiers also surrendered. After clearing the barracks, the Wehrmacht commandos discovered their 70-man detachment now had over 800 prisoners, whom they locked under guard in storage sheds. Herzner's operation had gone as smooth as possible; German alpine soldiers disarmed the demolition charges, and the Nazis secured the whole Jablunka Pass area in less than half an hour.

The divisions Herzner believed to be following never appeared, but a train carrying 1,200 Polish soldiers did. However, upon learning of the situation, these 1,200 men also surrendered to Herzner's tiny band of 70 plainclothes commandos without even attempting a token resistance. The Germans placed these men under guard also.

Incredibly, Herzner's commandos remained in possession of the Jablunka Pass throughout August 26th, waiting vainly for the rumble of advancing Panzers. The German lieutenant finally managed to gain radio contact with his superiors at noon, only to discover that Hitler called off the invasion a few minutes after he left the night before. The commandos spent a tense day watching for Polish troop movements and guarding their restless horde of prisoners, but no other Polish units approached Jablunka Pass during the 26th. The approach of dusk gave the Germans the cover they needed to escape the consequences of their awkward, futile success. "That evening, the entire battle group headed back through the tunnel. It succeeded in slipping away from the Poles and headed for home. It had carried out its mission. If the war had begun at the planned hour, it would have delivered 2,000 Polish prisoners of war." (Kurowski, 1997, 44).

Naturally, the incident represented a slight but noticeable embarrassment to the Nazis. Though the Wehrmacht did not punish Herzner, the official line, issued for propaganda purposes, was that he was "insane" and inexplicably led a foray into Polish territory. In the meantime, it also alerted the Poles to one of the Nazis' objectives, and they learned the value of Jablunka Pass to the invaders through this operation. On September 1st, Col. Witold Pirszel set off the charges that choked the pass with rubble just a few minutes before the Nazis arrived on the scene at 6:00 in the morning. The damage was so extensive that the Germans did not restore full rail service through the pass for almost two years.

Immediately before the September 1st attack, the Germans carried out a "false flag" operation to provide a pretext for their Polish invasion. This grotesque plan involved bringing concentration camp prisoners to the border, dressing them in uniforms, and then murdering them at German posts near the border to represent "casualties" inflicted during fictitious Polish raids across the border into Germany. The Germans executed this plan, known as "Operation Himmler" (named after SS head Heinrich Himmler), with their usual efficiency, though nobody honestly fell for the false flag. "Heinrich Mueller, the head of the Gestapo, was put in charge of these operations. It was part of the plan that a number of prisoners from concentration camps should be dressed in Polish uniforms, given fatal injections by a doctor and at the right moment shot [...]. These victims were to be brought in under the code-words 'canned goods'. Their bodies were to be photographed for publication." (Manvell, 2007, 77).

Himmler

Mueller

These Polish "attacks" offered Hitler his excuse for a war that he had planned as far back as six months ago, and the atrocity was apparently a last minute effort to convince the British not to declare war. In this, it naturally failed, but Hitler placed no value on his prisoners' lives and seemed, at times, as though he wished to explore the furthest possible reaches of amoral disregard for human life, rights, or dignity.

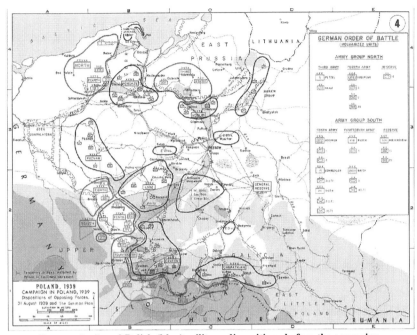

German (red) and Polish (blue) military dispositions before the campaign

German units crossing into Poland from East Prussia

With the false flags complete, thousands of Panzer I, II, and III tanks, accompanied by trucks, halftracks, and motorcycles, rolled forward towards the Polish border in the pre-dawn darkness of September 1st, 1939. Hitler launched "Case White" at last, and with it, the start of World War II, which would ultimately lead to some 60 million deaths, including his own and practically all other high Nazi officials.

Although the campaign in Poland is typically overlooked, especially in comparison to some of the incredibly large and violent campaigns in subsequent years, it was instrumental in providing the Nazi forces with experience they would use across Europe and in Russia. After all, it was in Poland that the Wehrmacht saw action for the first time, conducting what was not only an invasion but also a trial run of its new equipment and tactics. The Polish invasion proved invaluable in providing the German high command with a low-risk, high-value live fire exercise for their newly minted war machine, while the actual combat experience highlighted the remaining flaws in the system. During the campaign, the Germans honed tactics and weapon systems for the massive struggle with the Soviets, British, and United States that loomed on the horizon.

Surviving German films, taken by war photographers, show the exact moment of the border crossing. In one section, a crisply uniformed infantryman is seen raising the long, striped customs station barrier pole across a road between Germany and Poland, allowing a detachment of Nazi cavalry to trot through. Panzer tanks move forward in long lines in other segments, while halftrack prime movers tow field artillery pieces across fords and motorcycles with sidecars streak along Polish country roads.

The Wehrmacht adopted a very bold, large-scale strategy, using two huge encircling movements to chop Polish territory into thirds. Army Group North, starting from East Prussia and northern Germany, launched two main thrusts southeast, while Army Group South, based in Germany and Czechoslovakia, launched two thrusts northwest. The Germans intended these pincer movements to converge at Warsaw and Brest-Litovsk, thereby cutting off and encircling vast numbers of Polish soldiers, who would be compelled to surrender or be annihilated.

For their part, the Poles predicated their strategy on fighting a delaying action in the west, accompanied by a slow withdrawal eastward. The Poles still believed the Soviets would not attack them; in fact, a few Polish leaders, more sanguine than the rest, thought the Russians might send aid to them to help expel the Germans. They also trusted their new alliance with the British and French to provide speedy relief. Both of these Polish hopes proved hollow.

Under the overall command of Field Marshal Wilhelm Keitel, Generaloberst Fedor von Bock commanded Army Group North, while Generaloberst Gerd von Rundstedt led Army Group South. Von Rundstedt developed the Case White strategy and executed its most important maneuvers, and Bock also played his role adequately. Hermann Goering maintained close control over the Luftwaffe, viewing it as his personal domain and the key to his continued power and influence within the Nazi government. Heinrich Himmler, head of the SS and Gestapo, traveled to the front by train, hoping to realize his dream of being a powerful field commander. However, he demonstrated only tepid military skills and generally found himself ignored by the actual fighting commanders such as Bock, Rundstedt, and others. Himmler's main function proved to be overseeing some of the brutality visited upon the Polish population in the wake of the German advance.

Keitel

Von Rundstedt

One rather unexpected presence at the front was Adolf Hitler himself. Not yet weakened by illness, drugs, and his vegetarian diet, the Fuhrer watched much of the campaign's action firsthand from an aircraft window or an open automobile, including ground combat and Stuka bombardment in his itinerary. Films survive of Hitler watching from an aircraft, grim and expressionless, as explosions gut buildings in the Warsaw outskirts a few hundred feet below.

Army Group North consisted of 630,000 German soldiers in total, while Army Group South, the larger of the two (in part because of its broader and more accessible staging area in Czechoslovakia and Germany) numbered 882,000 soldiers. Against the full weight of approximately 1.5 million men, the Poles mustered somewhere between 900,000-1.2 million, though 900,000 is likely closer to the mark. 446,000 Soviet troops lurked east of the Polish border as well, awaiting the opportune moment to strike.

At the start of the war, the Luftwaffe possessed 2,315 aircraft ready to deploy and slightly more than 4,000 in total. The Polish Air Force mustered just 400 obsolete fighters and no dive-bombers whatsoever. 9,000 advanced German artillery pieces, many towed by mechanical prime movers such as halftracks, matched up against 4,300 mostly horse-drawn field artillery and anti-tank artillery pieces, which were little more than World War I surplus. These guns proved sufficient to defeat the armor of Panzer I tanks, but they had more difficulty against thicker-armored later tank models such as Panzer II, Panzer III, and Panzer IV.

A Polish bomber in 1939

A German Panzer IV

Germany enjoyed a significant edge in tanks at 2,750, while the Poles could muster only 880. While many of the tanks were light Panzer Is and Czech 38(t) models, there were also many upgunned Panzer II tanks, plus tough, hard-hitting, medium-weight Panzer III models and even a handful of Panzer IVs. In contrast, 575 of Poland's tanks were actually 2.6 ton TKS and TK-3 tankettes, of which 551 carried no weaponry heavier than a machine-gun. The 24 tankettes built with 20mm cannons proved quite dangerous to German light (and sometimes medium) tanks, but these and the 305 battle tanks (light, poorly armed, feebly armored) the Poles fielded ultimately had no chance against Nazi armor.

Technology and military doctrine both favored the Germans in the context of the era as well. The Germans considered communication key to good battlefield coordination and control, so radios were very commonplace. The Third Reich built large numbers of its tanks with individual radios, in contrast to the radio-free tanks of Poland. The Wehrmacht also made extensive use of radios in infantry units, and commanders, artillerymen, and spotters used radio communications to launch precise, timely fire missions to soften the way for their own attacks or halt those of the enemy.

Germany's army was far more mechanized than Poland's. Besides tanks and armored cars, a fleet of heavy trucks offered rapid transport of men and material. Halftracks moved artillery and ammunition to places where they were needed, and thousands of motorcycles with sidecars provided messenger service, scouting, and rapid deployment of machine gun teams. Statistics demonstrated the stark difference in mechanization between the opponents; 10% of the Polish army consisted of cavalry, while only 2% of the Wehrmacht was cavalry in 1939, a figure that was steadily shrinking too. Though a lack of fuel eventually proved the Achilles heel for German armies later in the war, this was not an issue during the Polish campaign of 1939.

In terms of doctrine, the Germans were years in advance of the Poles. Polish tanks were spread thin, assigned to supporting infantry units. The Germans clustered their armor assets into Panzer divisions which operated independently, striking rapidly and deeply into enemy territory and applying a concentration of force and firepower the Poles simply could not emulate with their diffuse armor deployments.

The Germans also utilized dive-bombers in the form of the famous Stuka. This aircraft made nearly vertical dives to deliver bombs precisely on target, enabling the rapid destruction of individual armored vehicles, squads or platoons of infantry, particular buildings (such as one housing an enemy command post or machine gun position), and so on. The Poles had no dive-bombers because they, like the other Allies, believed that the design was actually impossible, and that "anti-aircraft fire had reached such perfection that to dive below a certain level was tantamount to suicide and could not be contemplated. Again, the theory was sound, but in practice it required very steady nerves to stand at a gun while a line of dive-bombers was descending […] In practice, losses were few and the hits achieved by the dive-bomber were many." (Smith, 1998, 7).

German dive-bombers during the war

The Poles' main advantages included home ground knowledge, courage, and decent quality small arms, including rifles copied from German models and machine guns based on American designs. Led by an ossified high command that fled almost as soon as the war opened, hampered by lack of radios, equipment, vehicles, and a modern air force, the Poles' only hope was to hold out long enough for some other power to come to their aid. Despite the loud assurances of the British and French, it wouldn't happen.

On the first day of action, September 1st, 1939, the Germans' four main prongs, along with various smaller attacks, punched deep into Polish territory. The actual beginning of hostilities occurred in the north, near Danzig, which the Nazis coveted for years prior to the invasion. At 4:00 in the morning, the German vessel *Schleswig-Holstein* began shelling the Westerplatte garrison in Danzig. Soon, armored columns, coordinated by a network of radios, streamed towards the border from multiple directions and crossed it.

The Polish defenders met these initial thrusts with small arms, artillery, and cavalry attacks, occasionally supported by a few tanks. In some areas, the Germans broke through immediately, but in others, the Poles held their ground and pushed the Wehrmacht forces back. Wherever the Poles repulsed them, however, the Germans mustered again and attacked afresh until their superior mobility, firepower, and numbers broke through.

One of the toughest nuts to crack on the first day proved to be the Danzig Post Office, which was eventually isolated behind the advancing German front. The SS troops sent to seize this key point from the Polish garrison inside had great difficulty dislodging their opponents from the sturdy building. Anton Winter, a German attacker, reported, "It was simply impossible without a great number of casualties to climb over the walls and iron gate and penetrate into the building.

After the attack with the armed reconnaissance car failed, there was a short pause in the fighting. Even after a heavy army howitzer opened up fire, the defenders could still not be forced to surrender. The Poles defended the Post Office with exceptional bravery in the belief that they would be rescued by the Polish cavalry." (Williamson, 2009, 65). A flamethrower eventually drove out the 38 defenders still alive at that point, and the Germans seized ultimately executed them for "war crimes."

Meanwhile, the Luftwaffe pursued several objectives simultaneously. One of these was supporting the Wehrmacht's advance, and in this regard it was highly successful. The dive-bombers of the German air arm terrorized Polish ground troops who had otherwise faced tanks, machine guns, and artillery with composure, and the Germans designed their Stukas for maximum psychological impact: "It was known that the morale of unseasoned troops cracked when confronted by dive-bombing, which is a very personal form of aerial attack, and this was later to be played upon with the introduction of wind-siren devices on both the *Stuka* and its bombs, which added to the natural howling scream of an aircraft in a steep dive." (Smith, 1998, 7).

Unlike high-altitude bombing, which expended vast amounts of ordnance to achieve a handful of random hits, dive-bombing provided pinpoint accuracy rather similar to today's cruise missiles. An attack by a dive-bomber meant almost certain death for the target unless that target could exit the area very rapidly, and the Stukas decimated Polish soldiers who chose to stand their ground and dispersed those who did not, making them easier prey for the advancing ground portion of the Third Reich's army.

The Luftwaffe also planned on destroying the small Polish air force, but cloudy weather conditions on the morning of September 1st, along with dense fog in the north of Poland, prevented the German aircraft from effectively striking Poland's airfields. The Polish air force managed to remain operational, albeit in dwindling numbers, until September 6th, when the Luftwaffe wiped the last Polish aircraft from the sky. Similarly, the clouds also hampered Luftwaffe efforts to bomb the major and medium sized cities of Poland on the first day. By the time skies cleared and sunny weather moved in later in the afternoon of September 1st, the Luftwaffe was heavily engaged in supporting the German offensives on the ground and could spare less immediate attention to the bombing.

Though the Poles inflicted surprisingly heavy casualties on the Germans given their disadvantages, the unequal struggle tipped steadily in the Third Reich's favor as the day passed by. It was also on this day that the famous incident which fixed the idea of Polish cavalry charges against tanks occurred. Elements of the Wehrmacht's Army Group North advanced into Pomerania, including in their number the 20th Motorized Infantry Division. Moving through the Tuchola Forest, the Germans approached the town of Krojanty late in the day, meaning to seize it and obtain control of the vital railway station there.

A unit of Polish cavalry, under Kazimierz Mastalerz, a Colonel in the 4th Army of Poland, moved to intercept the 20th Motorized Infantry, and shortly before nightfall, Mastalerz's scouts reported that German infantry were present in an open field just ahead. Mastalerz, sensing an opportunity, took two squadrons of the 18th Lancer Regiment forward to the attack. The Poles rode rapidly through the forest and emerged in the infantry's rear, catching them completely by surprise. Due to his tactical advantage, Colonel Mastalerz ordered his men to charge with drawn swords rather than dismount and skirmish with their rifles. The German infantry battalion in the field quickly panicked and fled as the Poles galloped out of the woods in a line flashing with sharp-edged steel. 11 Germans died in the lightning attack, while another 9 suffered wounds from Polish sabers.

Mastalerz

Though the Poles dispersed hundreds of German infantry into the woods, their triumph proved short-lived. Six-wheeled German armored cars armed with heavy machine-guns rolled out of the forest along the road and opened a blistering fire on the cavalrymen. Unable to fight the armored vehicles of Aufklarung Abteilung 20 without their own supporting field artillery pieces, the Poles fell back immediately towards the shelter of a low hillock. On the way, a machine gun bullet struck the 1st Squadron leader, Eugeniusz Swiesciak, fatally wounding him and causing him to topple from the saddle. In a moment of ill-advised gallantry, Mastalerz turned his horse back in an effort to rescue Swiesciak. Struck by machine gun and 20mm cannon fire, the Polish colonel died on the spot, with his corpse and that of his horse falling close to where Swiesciak lay. In all, some 20-25 Poles died, and 40-50 suffered wounds.

The Poles abandoned their dead and fell back, but their attack panicked the inexperienced Germans so badly that the entire 20th Motorized Infantry halted for the day, afraid to advance further and suffer more cavalry attacks. Though this action did not save the Krojanty railway station, it did give several other Polish units in the area time to withdraw rather than being trapped and captured by the swift-moving Germans.

Later on, German tanks parked in the meadow near the bodies of dead Polish cavalrymen and their horses, and the arrival of reporters on the scene provided the finishing touch needed to transform the skirmish into the legend of brave but block-headed Polish military stupidity still current almost a century later. "The grim evidence of this encounter was discovered the following day by Italian war correspondents, who were told by German soldiers that it had resulted from the cavalry having charged tanks — and so the legend began." (Zaloga, 1982, 9).

Polish cavalry in 1939

In fact, Polish cavalry fought on horseback less than 10% of the time during the 1939 invasion. The remainder of the time, they dismounted to fight the Germany infantry rifle to rifle, while using field guns (most often old-fashioned 75mm guns) to combat advancing tanks and armored cars. Sometimes, they managed to inflict surprisingly high losses on German tanks, as when Polish cavalry used their anti-tank weapons to destroy 30 tanks and an equal number of armored cars from the 4th Panzer Army at Mokra on September 1st. Though eventually forced to retreat by concentrated German artillery fire and Stuka attacks, the Poles acquitted themselves very well considering their lack of modern equipment. They also proved the Panzer I to be a weak, practically useless tank design.

On several other occasions, German commanders misinterpreted Polish actions as charges against their tanks. When surrounded by a ring of tanks, the Polish cavalry often mounted their horses to increase speed, making a desperate rush to pass between the armored vehicles to safety. German tank crews believed these breakout attempts to be futile last-ditch lance and saber charges against their vehicles.

Over the course of the next six days, the situation worsened for the Poles and improved for the Germans. The Wehrmacht, well-equipped and highly motivated but inexperienced, continued to suffer considerable losses in both men and tanks, but the German armies remained a cohesive and effective fighting force.

On the other hand, the combat and deeply penetrating pincer movements rapidly degraded the ability of the Poles to keep resisting. The Polish air force, though gallant, died in flames where they crashed in the Polish countryside after being shot down by their German counterparts. Indeed, the Luftwaffe was the most elite arm of the Germany military at the start of the war, due in large part to the fact "they had the benefit of modern combat experience fed back from their *Legion Condor* contributions to the victory of General Franco's forces in Spain. In particular, many of the theories of army cooperation and close air support were put to the practical test and invaluable lessons absorbed." (Smith, 1998, 5). The Polish soldiers soon learned that venturing out onto roads in daylight was certain death, as any column of Polish infantry, cavalry, or vehicles was soon spotted by the Germans. Using their radios, the Wehrmacht called in the location to the Luftwaffe, whose terrible dive-bombers soon appeared to spread slaughter among the men trapped in the flat, open Polish countryside under the light of day.

A picture of a bombed Polish artillery position

Nevertheless, the need to retreat remained the driving imperative behind Polish strategy. The overall "grand strategy" of Poland was to fight a delaying action while retreating to fortified positions in the east. There, the Poles would dig in and wait for the French and British to come to their rescue by invading Germany, forcing Hitler to pull back his armies in order to protect his homeland, people, and logistical base. Moreover, the rapid encircling movements also made retreat the sole option for remaining free and alive for a few days longer. Once the double trap of the two grand Wehrmacht sweeps crashed shut, the Polish armies would be trapped in large pockets across the countryside, subject to either mass surrender or hopeless defeat in detail.

That said, actually carrying out the retreat wore down the ability of the Polish army to resist. During the daylight hours, the Poles found movement impossible under the hawk-like vigilance of the Luftwaffe. Remaining in one place, however, meant they were attacked by the Germans, forcing them to fight for much of the day. The Poles found it was possible to engage in movement free from Stuka attacks at night, but this forced the men to remain awake almost 24 hours a day. After a few days of this, the Poles were so exhausted that they began to fight more poorly, move more slowly, and suffer from lower morale and a sense of fatigue-drenched hopelessness.

With so many disadvantages weighing against them, the Poles could not maintain their defense for more than a few days, regardless of their courage and occasional local successes. Within four to five days, Polish command at all levels lost communications contact with both headquarters and with other Polish formations elsewhere in the country. Given this lack of strategic coordination, the Poles found themselves fighting blind against a highly coordinated foe whose command of the skies gave them almost total information regarding troop movements and strategic developments. "The dam burst: German mechanised columns plunged deep into Polish lines, and on 7 September the tanks of the 4th Panzer Division began appearing outside the suburbs of Warsaw. They began immediately to make attempts to break into the city itself, but showed little judgement, and on 9 September alone the Poles claimed 57 tanks from the 4th Panzer Division in intense street fighting. The second week of the war went just as badly." (Zaloga, 1982, 10).

Nazi soldiers posing with captured civilians

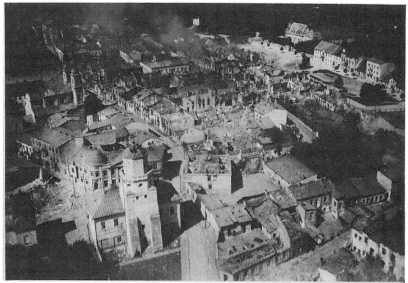
The ruins of the Polish city of Wieluń

Though the Poles were mostly thrust back and the Germans were able to keep to a rapid timetable for their blitzkrieg advance on the country's nerve centers, not everything went smoothly for the invaders. The wild card who salvaged a bit of Poland's martial reputation was General Tadeusz Kutrzeba. Finding his Army Poznan bypassed by the Germans but still fully intact, Kutrzeba launched a highly effective counterattack that took the Nazi forces almost completely by surprise. Aiming at the German 8th Army, Kutrzeba began the Battle of the Bzura, named for a river, which lasted from September 9-20 until the Poles finally succumbed to attrition and superior armaments.

Kutrzeba

The Polish high command originally assigned Kutrzeba's Army Poznan, along with Army Lodz and Army Prusy, to hold a 160 mile stretch of the Vistula against the advance of Army Group North. The line was too long for the armies to hold, however, particularly with disintegrating communications, and the Germans struck past Kutrzeba's position much deeper into Polish territory. Kutrzeba abandoned the defense of Pomerania and the Vistula River, already deep behind the advancing German front and thus no longer of strategic value, and he moved towards the capital of Warsaw from September 8-9. However, he encountered the German 8th Army and 10th Army as he did so and decided to attack, perhaps recalling the centuries-old motto of the Polish winged hussars: "First we beat the enemy, then we count them."

In the meantime, the Polish high command fled from Warsaw to Brzesc on September 7th in response to the German 4th Panzer Division attacking the capital's outskirts. This rendered the action on the Bzura less effective than it might have been by taking the high command out of the theater of operations almost entirely, but Kutrzeba's actions proved not entirely in vain, as he bought more time for additional Polish forces to escape the closing German trap.

On September 9, Kutrzeba acted on the permission he finally received from headquarters on to attack the German 8th Army. A German captain, Christian Kinder, recalling the moment when the Poles fired their first shots, said the 9th "began like every other day since the invasion of Poland. Our feet were sore as a result of the long march in the heat and dust on the uneven roads [. . .] Around eleven o'clock the columns came to a halt near the Zagaya windmill as the leading column was fired at from some farmsteads. It was clear that a major action would unfold here." (Williamson, 2009, 116).

Heavy infantry fighting throughout the 9th resulted in the Germans holding the Poles briefly, then being thrown back. The Polish lancers cut off and defeated isolated German units who thought themselves safe behind the advancing Wehrmacht front, and the Poles destroyed bridges in spots where this would hamper the Nazi's movements. The Poles relished the canned meat and good cigars they found in the staff officers' cars they seized along the roads, and morale began to rise once more. The Germans lost some 1,500 men killed and even more wounded or captured, and the Poles thrust the trailing elements of the 8th Army some 12 miles towards the main body near Warsaw.

Polish cavalry at Bzura

The 8th Army temporarily abandoned its march on Warsaw, as did other German units. Instead, on September 10th and 11th, they moved north to engage the Poles. The struggle was desperate, and the Polish soldiers inflicted heavy casualties on the Germans while sustaining many losses of their own. However, the tide slowly turned against them during days of hard fighting, in part due to lack of air support and artillery.

Pivotal action occurred at Sochaczew, a town commanding a major crossing point of the Bzura River. If the Germans took Sochaczew, they could cross the river and begin to outflank Kutrzeba's advance. Accordingly, the fighting around this objective grew fierce on September 14th and 15th. The fighting occurred over rough terrain, as one Polish participant, a commander named Klemens Rudnicki, later recalled: "The whole squadron was fighting a dismounted action with the enemy, who occupied all the surrounding dunes and sandy bush land, covering with strong machine-gun fire all the exits from the forest; bullets buzzed like wasps; the artillery began to respond; it was quite impossible to emerge from the forest [. . .] I decided to do everything possible to remain and hold out as we were for the time being, and after dark to disengage from the enemy." (Williamson, 2009, 119).

The Germans enjoyed a numerical superiority of 1.2 men to every 1 man the Poles mustered at Sochaczew, and they also outnumbered the Poles' armor by four-to-one. However, at least one incident showed that the Poles were not to be underestimated even with the tide turning against them. Though Poland's flimsy and poorly deployed tanks did not produce any "tank aces" comparable to the famous Nazi or Soviet tank aces, one man achieved remarkable results with his diminutive TKS tankette during the invasion. A 21 year old architect and officer cadet named Edmund Roman Orlik, together with his driver Bronisław Zakrzewski, made the most of the tankette's small size, maneuverability, and low profile to destroy a surprising number of Nazi tanks, including a single Panzer IV, a remarkable feat with a single 20mm cannon.

Orlik, who survived the war and received the Cross of Valor decoration, commanded one of just 24 TKS tankettes fitted with an NKM wz.38 FK 20mm gun (able to penetrate 20mm of hardened steel armor at 110 yards range and 13mm at 550 yards) rather than a machine-gun. These small armored vehicles stood 4 feet, 4 inches high, making them hard to hit and easy to conceal, as the Germans themselves acknowledged: "A Panzerwaffe officer taken prisoner in the first days of September 1939 praised the speed and maneuverability of the Polish tankette, declaring that 'such a small cockroach is very difficult to hit with a [tank] gun.'" (Magnuski, 1995, 3).

Orlik fought in support of the Wielkopolska Cavalry Brigade near Brochow during the Battle of the Bzura. On September 14th, 1939, he first made the history books when he engaged elements of the 36th Panzer Regiment, part of the 4th Panzer Division of the Wehrmacht, during the Germans' advance on Sochaczew. Moving rapidly from cover to cover, Orlik managed to destroy no less than three German Panzers, starting his career as the first armored fighting vehicle ace of World War II. He reappeared in the invasion's annals four days later on September 18th with an even more notable success.

Nonetheless, the Germans eventually defeated the Poles holding Sochaczew, thus winning the Bzura River crossing. At this point, Kutrzeba's counterattack started to collapse, but the Polish "Army Poznan" fought on doggedly for several more days even as the situation worsened. The Poles' last stand occurred near Sierakow, where the Germans brought them to bay with superior numbers and destroyed them with artillery bombardment and dive-bomber attacks. The encirclement was supported by 300 Luftwaffe aircraft, and massive howitzer batteries commanded the Polish positions from the side of the river seized by the Germans.

The Poles fought on through the 18th, however, and once again, the TKS tankettes had a role to play in the final action. Orlik, the TKS tankette ace who destroyed 3 Panzers on September 14th, repeated his feat on the 18th while supporting the Wielkopolska Cavalry Brigade. As he awaited orders near Janowka, General Abraham, the brigade's commander, arrived on the scene. The General's neck bore a bandage, covering a wound caused in the recent fighting. Abraham informed Orlik that German tanks were prowling in the vicinity and attempting to surprising the Wielkopolska horsemen. Accordingly, he ordered Orlik to take his command of three tankettes down the forest road to a nearby crossroads and hunt the Panzers before they could attack the cavalry. Orlik obeyed, leading the small squadron of TKS tankettes along the road indicated.

When the tiny force reached the crossroads, the Officer Cadet found alarming signs: "At the first intersection with the broader track, Orlik noted fresh traces of the enemy. Stopping all vehicles, he jumped out and advanced a few paces. He could clearly discern the marks of tank tracks in the sandy forest road, while the fumes of gasoline mixed with the smell of freshly disturbed earth hung in the air. […] The tank tracks were exceptionally wide. […] The Officer Cadet […] could not even guess what type of vehicles had recently passed." (Magnuski, 1995, 3).

Orlik quickly set up an ambush. He placed the two machine-gun armed tankettes in thick cover, and parked his TKS on a small hillock, concealed among young junipers. From this position, he commanded a view of the crossroads from a distance of 110-130 yards. The tankette ace and his driver barely finished setting up before Orlik spotted the outline of a smallish Panzer – likely a Czech-built 35(t) – moving along the roadway. Looking through his sight, Orlik aimed at the turret ring connecting the turret to the hull and fired. The small tankette rocked at the recoil, and a bright flash at the base of the German tank's turret indicated penetration. The tank rolled to an abrupt stop. Zakrzewski, Orlik's driver, immediately threw the diminutive armored vehicle into reverse, backing up to a new firing position to the left rear of the previous spot.

At this moment, a second tank appeared. Seeing the first German tank knocked out with smoke coming from the left side of its turret, the second vehicle swerved off the road to the right, attempting to use its stricken fellow as cover. As this tank powered across his line of sight just south of the crossroads, Orlik opened fire again, the crack of each shot deafening inside the cramped TKS. Two 20mm shells struck the second tank's armor with no success, but the third penetrated, blowing the hatches open in a rush of flame and sending a huge plume of black smoke exploding upward through the tree branches.

Zakrzewski moved the tankette again, this time forward and to the left, and at this point, a third German tank followed the first two and attempted to make a break past the crossroads and continue east. "The tank bypassed both immobilized vehicles, and then, driving at full speed and shooting indiscriminately with all its weapons (one 37mm cannon and two machine guns) fled to the east." (Magnuski, 1995, 4). Orlik originally intended to let the third tank go, but as it passed his tankette's hiding place, he found his 20mm cannon lined up for a clear shot into the Panzer's rear from a distance of 65 yards. The shell punched through the thin rear armor and destroyed the Panzer's engine, bringing it to a sudden halt.

Two of the tank crews bailed out, and Orlik managed to capture two men. He attempted to save the crew of the second tank as it was burning, but all were either dead or dying. In fact, the Polish cadet managed to drag the tank's commander clear of the conflagration, but the man died a few minutes later from his injuries. This proved to be Prince Victor IV Albrecht von Ratibor, a high-ranking German nobleman. The tank he commanded, which had survived Orlik's first two direct hits before succumbing to a third, was a Panzer IV – a powerful, well-armored medium tank, and a remarkable kill for a tiny tankette armed with a single 20mm cannon. Orlik's score of tanks was now six.

On the evening of September 18th and into the early 19th, the Poles near Sierakow were targeted by a force of Panzers, mostly 38(t) light tanks from Czechoslovakia pressed into Wehrmacht service. It was here that the tankette ace Orlik achieved his most notable success. Ordered forward to slow the Panzers' advance, Orlik maneuvered his TKS into a series of shallow sand and gravel pits just south of Sierakow itself. As the Panzers began their advance across open ground in an extended line, Orlik opened fire. The nearest German tank "brewed up," and the next three beyond it turned towards the Pole's position, firing as they came. With shells ripping the ground around his steel "cockroach" but never managing to strike it, Orlik squeezed off round after round as Zakrzewski drove desperately to and fro, trying to make the TKS tankette a difficult target. In a matter of minutes, four German tanks were burning in front of Orlik's position.

The tankette ace did not stop there, however. Driving forward past the wrecks, he engaged the 38(t)s and Panzer II's advancing on the Polish positions past their destroyed comrades. Soon the Polish architect-turned-ace had three more destroyed Panzers to his credit. At this point, however, the tank assault became so heavy that he was forced to withdraw or face certain death. Polish cavalry manning field guns managed to knock out an additional 20 Panzers, but Orlik's personal tank kill score stood at no less than 13.

When the position at Sierakow grew untenable, Orlik and Zakrzewski broke out across country along with a second 20mm-armed TKS tankette. Moving across the countryside under cover of darkness on the night of September 20, the two miniature armored vehicles got away clean and reached Warsaw. There, Orlik helped the defenders until September 28, though he did not knock out any more tanks. All his kills following that were of soft-skinned vehicles, along with a few infantry whom he picked off.

The Battle of the Bzura represented the last hurrah for the defending Polish forces. From that point on, they slid rapidly towards defeat, thanks to the combination of factors which had led to their plight during the first two weeks of the invasion. Another event sealed the doom of Poland even more assuredly; the Soviet Army, 446,000 men strong, rolled across the border into Poland on September 17 across a front 850 miles wide.

Approximately 100,000 reservists held the eastern frontier against this surprise attack, but these men were in the process of training and had only light weapons at their disposal. Polish high command sent the order to them to negotiate with the Soviets and seek safe passage to Romania. The chief generals of Poland realized that with this new force advancing from the east, their position was untenable. Ordering the reservists to fight would only result in needless butchery, with the outcome precisely the same in any case. The Soviets, however, had not come to talk. Like the Germans, they moved with a grim purpose and viewed the Poles as little more than an obstacle to their overall plans, rather than as human beings. When the reservists attempted to negotiate passage to Romania or Hungary, the Soviet soldiers simply attacked them, forcing them to fight.

The reservists, half-trained and lightly armed, suffered tremendous losses against the Soviet armies. The Russians' tactics were simple and their coordination poor, thanks to Stalin's butchery of his own officer corps during the recent "Great Purge." However, a sort of Darwinian selection occurred by which semi-capable officers came to the fore and received promotions due to the fact that they were tactically acute enough to survive combat. The famous Georgi Zhukov, who would later lead the Soviet armies against Germany, was one of these emergent leaders.

Zhukov

Some Polish reservists managed to fight their way to the borders and escape into Romania, Hungary, or Lithuania. From there, many of them eventually found their way to France and then, when the Nazis overran that, to Britain. Many others died in combat. The Soviets carried out a number of mass executions among those luckless reservists forced to surrender to them as a result of encirclement or lack of ammunition. Indeed, the fate of the Poles who fell into Soviet hands was little better than that of those who were taken by the Nazis.

By September 20, Poland's armies were effectively defeated in both the west and the east. Warsaw held out heroically for some time, but by October 6, the nation of Poland had all but ceased to exist. It now only remained for the victorious Nazis and Soviets to divide up the spoils and decide what was to be done with the unfortunate population. Poland, which had emerged from centuries of servitude in the wake of World War I, had found itself subjected to foreign conquerors again in 1939. Indeed, the men who now ruled its fate were far crueler than any who had come over its borders since the days of the Mongol hordes.

A picture of German and Soviet soldiers shaking hands in Poland

In the west, Britain and France had declared war on Germany, but they ultimately did nothing to aid their Polish allies. Their promises to hasten to the Poles' assistance in the event of foreign attack proved to be worth no more than the breath expended speaking them and the paper they were written on. The French advanced a few miles into Germany, seizing some unoccupied forest, but French soldiers refused to move outside the range of the artillery mounted in the Maginot Line, even though nearly every German soldier was redeployed hundreds of miles to the east.

The French command noted that Hitler's new method of warfare was nearly "Napoleonic" in its nature and further added, "The frontline does not exist any more and is replaced by a three-dimensional space extending on all the territory occupied by the fighting armies. Consequently the linear disposition of the troops along the frontier seems to appear totally wrong [. . .] The vital forces of the enemy have to be gradually destroyed. Their blows have to be answered by blows [. . .] The fight should be carried by independent groups of great units." (Williamson, 2009, 195).

However, despite clearly realizing (and even enunciating) this, the French acted in precisely the opposite manner by putting their full faith in a linear disposition of troops along the frontier and in fixed fortifications. A few days after venturing unwillingly over the border into Germany, the "Gallic cockerel" scuttled back ignominiously to the relative safety of the French border defenses, where the French would await their own turn on the chopping block of Hitler's insatiable aggression. With that feeble gesture, the attempts of the British and French to come to the aid of Poles abruptly ended.

In the face of defeat, the Polish government and around 150,000 of its soldiers fled abroad, ostensibly to continue the fight another day. Though many soldiers who decamped did indeed make good on this promise by fighting bravely alongside the British during the D-Day landings and the liberating drive through Europe in 1944 and 1945, the actions of the Polish government were much less defensible. The lack of modern radio communications, coupled with poor planning, had rendered the Polish command structure superfluous just a few days into the campaign. "The reality was that by the end of the first week of fighting the Polish High Command had lost control and contact with most units. Plans for counter-offensive actions tended to be overtaken by German successes. The Commander-in-Chief Marshal Rydz-Smigly was an unimaginative leader, timorous and unwilling to take risks. Several opportunities had been lost by him for counter-offensive action, most notably one for the Army Poznan to strike south in defence of Warsaw." (Prazmowska, 1995, 3).

Some of Poland's government officials fled the country as early as September 3rd, and the exodus only accelerated thereafter, with many individuals flocking to Romania in hopes of taking ship from there to France or England. However, the Romanians did everything they could to obstruct the Poles' escape without actually forbidding it, hoping to remain in Germany's good graces while also retaining diplomatic links to the Western Allies. Eventually, the Romanians allied with Nazi Germany in 1940 and were crushed by the Soviet juggernaut in 1944. After the war, the Romanians were absorbed into the Soviet empire, vanishing behind the Iron Curtain until the 1990s.

Once Hitler and Stalin conquered Poland, further negotiations took place to refine their shared boundaries. Joachim von Ribbentrop, the slippery, gloating Axis negotiator, once again flew east to meet with Molotov and Stalin. "The collapse of Poland prefaced Ribbentrop's second visit to Moscow, which marked the high point of Nazi–Soviet friendship. On 20 September, after an alarm over where the Germans would draw the demarcation line between the zones of influence of the two powers, Molotov told Schulenburg that the USSR believed that 'the time was ripe' for the two powers to establish a permanent new structure for the Polish area." (Watson, 2005. 173).

While the Nazis would never be mistaken for humane, Hitler's Wehrmacht treated the Polish people with astonishing brutality considering their close genetic and even cultural ties to German border regions. Poland's high Jewish population explains some of this mayhem, since approximately 10% of the people living in Poland at the time belonged to this religion, at least nominally. However, the Nazis viewed the blond, blue-eyed, Christian Poles as being just as subhuman as the Jews they lived alongside. 65,000 Polish civilians were shot, burned, or otherwise massacred before the end of 1939, with more to follow. The new German government lowered Polish wages to near-starvation levels, while confiscation, plundering, and rape grew endemic.

The Poles who found themselves in the areas under Soviet control fared little better. Though communism nominally preached the brotherhood of humankind and the Soviets did not embrace the concept of racial cleansing, they still viewed the Poles as little more than revolting capitalist chattel in need of brutal reeducation. The Soviets approached this matter with their typical lack of restraint: "Half a million Poles were imprisoned within Soviet-occupied Poland. Many of them were subjected to torture, beatings, killings and executions. A campaign of mass deportations began. [...] Altogether the deportees numbered an estimated 1.5 million people. In the first half of 1940, they were packed into cattle-trucks, with standing room only, and taken off in vast train convoys to collective farms in Kazakhstan and other distant locations. [...] Perhaps a third of the deportees died before the survivors were released." (Evans, 2009, 65).

The attack on Poland prompted Britain and France to enter the war, so the Nazi aggression therefore precipitated the spread of hostilities westward as well as eastward, extending the conflict around the globe as alliances triggered entry into the struggle like a series of diplomatic dominoes. Mussolini finally joined the Axis directly with the "Pact of Steel," the main effect of which was the creation of a third front in North Africa and Italy. This fatally drained manpower from Germany's eastern front, while gaining the Germans practically nothing of strategic value in return since the Italian army was close to useless.

In 1939 and 1940, however, these developments mostly lay in the future. The Germans soon invaded France, expelled the British expeditionary force from Dunkirk in short order, and began the Battle of Britain, which witnessed terror bombings of London and other British cities, as well as cities in Germany. Japan's attack on Pearl Harbor and German U-boat attacks on American shipping eventually drew the powerful United States into the war on the side of the Allies despite America's initial reluctance.

Somewhat amazingly, Chamberlain managed to survive the fall of Czechoslovakia and continued on as Prime Minister for more than a year. He had met Nazi aggression towards Poland in his accustomed style, offering to give the Germans Danzig plus a loan of 100 million pounds sterling in exchange for a promise not to enter Polish territory. Making matters worse, the Polish government looked to British and French support, and in the end, this served to undermine their efforts to protect themselves rather than providing additional military clout. Just a week or two before the German attack in September 1939, "Full-scale mobilization had been delayed in the closing days of August at the request of the British and the French." (Prazmowska, 1995, 2). In essence, neither of Western Europe's two biggest powers proved to be of any more use to Poland than they had been to Czechoslovakia in the teeth of German belligerence.

Though he continued to rule for a time, Chamberlain's days were numbered. The German invasions of Poland and the Low Countries, opposed only feebly by Chamberlain's government, finally tipped the scales against him. Soon to be replaced by the feisty and vigorous Winston Churchill, Chamberlain's last stand came on May 7th, 1940. On that day, the British government finally expressed their disgust with his failures. In a dramatic move, Leo Amery, a Conservative politician, rose during a debate over the fiasco in Norway. Directing his words towards Chamberlain, Amery quoted Oliver Cromwell as he said to the prime minister, "You have sat here too long for any good you are doing. Depart, I say, and let us have done with you. In the name of God, go!"

Chamberlain would subsequently assist Churchill during the war, showing no signs of rancor towards the man who had displaced him. However, bowel cancer soon crippled him, and he died in November 1940, his dreams of peace shattered and the survival of Britain itself hanging in the balance.

The Nazi Conquest of Western Europe

Much of World War I's most brutal action occurred in Belgium, including the region of Flanders, which also extends into northeastern France. The Allies sought to forestall the entire war by "blocking" Germany's westward advance through encouragement of Belgian neutrality, but this neutrality did nothing to stop the coming bloodbath. As fate would have it, history repeated itself a generation later when Belgium declared itself neutral, accidentally encouraging the Third Reich to invade its territories in the opening days of World War II. The moist, green Belgian countryside once again resounded to the shriek and crash of bombs, the thunder of artillery and tank guns, and the cries of wounded and dying men as the panzers and Stukas of Hitler's Third Reich plunged westward.

Stukas

Following Hitler's attack on Poland in concert with Josef Stalin's Soviet Union in 1939, France and Britain declared war on the Third Reich, starting World War II. The almost fawning appeasement offered by the ill-fated Neville Chamberlain, the helplessness of the western Allies to provide aid to Poland, and their supine acquiescence to Hitler's dismantling of Czechoslovakia, persuaded the Fuhrer he could defeat them in short order before turning against his putative eastern allies, the Soviets.

Initially, Hitler planned to begin heavy rearmament in earnest in 1943 to 1944, and he envisioned the Third Reich's confrontation with France and Britain happening somewhere from 1948-1950. However, the two nations' declaration of war following Hitler's brutal September annexation of Poland accelerated the timetable immensely. Hitler wanted to strike France in November 1939, but lack of sufficient materiel and planning difficulties delayed the invasion until May 1940.

The first decisive encounters of the German invasion of France in 1940 occurred not on French but on Belgian soil. As the strategy behind the Maginot Line made clear, French planning and strategy not only anticipated this but encouraged it in an effort to keep the Third Reich's military forces off French soil. Much of France's key industrial might operated on the northern coastal plain, so retaining this manufacturing capacity gave the French a better chance to win the conflict, remaining able to replace equipment losses rapidly. Seizure of the area would constitute a major prize for the Germans. Of course, the Belgians were far less enthusiastic about the scheme, which transformed their small country into a battlefield on which two larger nations would unleash the full fury of modern bombing, strafing, and tank warfare.

As France hoped, the Maginot Line channeled the Germans much as intended until later breakthroughs made it moot, and it actually succeeded in halting Italian dictator Benito Mussolini's massive invasion force in its tracks in southeast France. However, by that point, the French strategy suffered a crippling blow as a result of Belgian neutrality.

Two features in Belgium merited rapid seizure according to German military thinking: strongpoints and bridges. A country of many waterways, Belgium presented a notable obstacle to an invader who failed to occupy its key bridges prior to their demolition by defenders.

The Dutch had fortified the line of the Meuse River on their eastern boundary during the 1920s and 1930s, and the massive fortress of Eben-Emael formed the linchpin of these defensive positions. Eben-Emael and the other fortresses absorbed a significant portion of the Belgian military budget during the 1930s, prompting internal debate regarding the merits of various potential defense projects: "In all, the cost of construction of these forts together with Fort Eben Emael was in the region of 250 million Belgian Francs. Nevertheless, there still remained a vociferous faction within the army that believed the money would be better spent on a radical reorganization of the army and the mechanization of the cavalry with modern armoured fighting vehicles." (Dunstan, 2005, 13).

Eben-Emael, with a ground plan in the form of a diamond, defied attacks with canals, sheer concrete walls, and large anti-tank ditches, and though the Belgians officially completed the fortress in 1935, they continued to refine its defenses up until the moment the Germans seized it at the outset of their drive into France in May 1940. Eben-Emael contained a series of powerful blockhouses equipped with 60mm anti-tank guns, machine guns, flare launchers, searchlights, and casemates mounting 75mm rapid-firing artillery pieces. A single enormous, 230 ton central armored cupola mounted a pair of 120mm cannons. Armored observation domes offered 360 degree views over the surrounding landscape, barbed wire entanglements presented obstacles to enemy sappers and infantry, and sophisticated ventilation systems protected the soldiers inside from poison gas attacks. The garrison of this work consisted of 1,322 officers and men, living in underground barracks and able to hold out independently for a considerable time.

Pictures of the fort

The German plan, "*Fall Gelb,*" involved sending 28 divisions under General Fedor von Bock, grouped into "Army Group B," into Belgium, but this group could not penetrate into the Belgian interior unless several strategic bridges over the Meuse River and the Albert Canal fell rapidly into German hands. Fort Eben-Emael commanded the approach to these bridges, so the German OKW (high command) made its immediate capture the vital first objective of the entire campaign.

Von Bock

Under the German plan, Eben-Emael's capture would open the door to Army Group B's swift advance into Belgium proper. The OKW expected French and British forces to pour into Belgium from the west to counterattack Army Group B, so when this occurred, Army Group A – consisting of 7 panzer divisions and 37 other divisions – would attack through the weakly defended Ardennes Forest, break through near Sedan, and circle up towards the coast, thereby trapping the majority of the French and British armies in Belgium and cutting them off from supplies. At that point, the Germans figured their surrender would follow swiftly.

Hitler, in one of his rare moments of tactical lucidity, decided to use a revolutionary method to seize Eben-Emael quickly. A force of paratroopers and combat engineers would land on the fortress using gliders and blow its formidable defenses to pieces with the German Army's new secret siege weapon: the hollow-charge explosive. A force of hand-picked men received intensive, secretive training in this assault from late 1939 through March 1940. Dubbed "Sturmabteilung Koch" after their commander, Hauptmann Walter Koch, these men trained intensively in utter secrecy, to the extent that the Wehrmacht executed two of them by firing squad merely for revealing their presence at a nearby base to some local young women. The

Sturmabteilung consisted of four Sturmgruppe; the OKW assigned one, "Sturmgruppe Granit" ("Granite"), to take Eben-Emael, while Sturmgruppe Beton, Stahl, and Eisen (Concrete, Steel, and Iron) would simultaneously seize three key bridges.

Koch

The Germans tested and refined every detail of their brand new tactical system, until the men could land within 60 feet of a designated aiming point every time: "[T]rials of glider landings on a simulated area of Fort Eben Emael revealed that the DFS 230 required a longer stopping distance than was available, especially when landing on wet grass that was only to be expected with the dawn dew. Modifications were made by incorporating a wooden drag brake beneath the glider that dug into the ground on landing." (Dunstan, 2005, 38).

The Allies ignored several indications of a coming attack, including a French pilot reporting seeing a column of armored vehicles tens of miles long snaking ominously through the countryside towards the Ardennes Forest like a steel dragon on May 7, 1940. Warnings of an impending German attack also circulated on May 9, including a message from Pope Pius XII himself, but the alert failed to reach Eben-Emael until early on May 10, a few short hours before the attack.

Meanwhile, the fortress commander, Major Jean Jottrand, expected no aerial attack and thus made his preparations in a leisurely, confused fashion. For example, he stripped many gun positions of their crews to tear down two administrative buildings he worried might compromise his fort's fields of fire. Furthermore, some guns lacked firing pins, while another cupola set fire to its own camouflage netting with its first warning shot. Other farcical yet deadly problems plagued the Belgians; many of their guns lacked proper ammunition, and the men's grenades lacked fuses, rendering the weapons as inert as rocks.

To the east, a force of Junkers Ju-52 aircraft towing DFS-230 gliders took off from two airfields near Cologne at 3:35 a.m. The gliders, packed full of Koch's highly trained commandos, provided an icy ride, but Corporal Wilhelm Alefs reported on the aggressive mood of the men, who spontaneously began to sing "Red Shines the Sun, Make Ready:" "We didn't take off at once. There were many other planes and gliders to take off ahead of us [...] Suddenly, a jerk on the glider forced me backwards. There was a jockeying and sloshing motion as the towrope tightened and swung the glider behind the straining plane ahead. Simultaneously, we all started the chant of the paratroopers - 'Rot Scheint die Sonne, fertig gemacht.'" (Dunstan, 2005, 45).

Two of Sturmgruppe Granit's gliders separated early and landed in German territory, but the Ju-52s towed the remainder to the necessary height of 8,500 feet, drew some feeble Belgian anti-aircraft fire as they did so, and then released the gliders for their 12 minute, 16 mile glide to Eben-Emael.

Even as the men of Sturmabteilung Koch swooped toward their objectives, another group of Germans attempted to seize the nearby bridges over the Meuse. To allay Belgian suspicions, these men, called the "Brandenburgers," donned hundreds of stolen Dutch uniforms and approached under the guise of a band of soldiers from the friendly Netherlands. However, the alert Belgians figured out the ruse within moments: "The attempt on the Dutch bridges at Maastricht ended in dismal failure. There was a confused shoot-up, in which the leader of the bogus Dutchmen, Lieutenant Hocke, was killed; it was impossible to remove the explosive charges, and all three bridges blew up in the face of the waiting Panzers." (Horne, 2007, 170). This repulse caused a massive traffic jam of military vehicles on the Meuse's east bank, and later created problems for the glider-borne troops.

At around 4:30 a.m., with pale dawn light suffusing the scene, the gliders of Sturmgruppe Granit circled in at 1,000 feet of altitude through a thin morning mist. Four of Eben-Emael's machine gun turrets opened fire but the poorly maintained weapons jammed almost instantly and the defenders fired a total of 50 ineffective rounds. Once on the ground, the Germans attacked vigorously, using their 100 pound shaped charges to deadly effect. Though most failed to penetrate either the armored cupolas or the concrete emplacements making up Fort Eben-Emael, the charges killed and wounded many defenders. The powerful overpressure they created killed men underneath them outright, while the crumbling cement of the fortress fell away on the opposite side from the explosions, filling the interior with lethal concrete shrapnel. Within a quarter-hour of landing, Sturmgruppe Granit had destroyed most of the observation cupolas atop Eben-Emael and many of its most important weapons positions, and only two Germans died in this early phase of the fight.

The bell-shaped hollow-charge explosives caused enough damage, fire, and fumes to force the Belgians to retreat deep into their fortress' underground portions, and Eben-Emael's commander, Major Jottrand, squandered his final opportunity to make his fortress useful when he refused to allow the 120mm gun turret to fire on the Albert Canal bridges. The Belgians had built the turret precisely to destroy the bridges should direct demolition fail, but the major asserted he could not fire into Holland without specific high command orders. The gun crew turned their cupola back and forth in useless frustration while a drunken German, Oberjager Ernst Grechza, straddled one of the cannon barrels and gulped contraband rum from his canteen. The Germans finally put the 120mm gun turret out of action by stuffing both cannon barrels full of explosives and blowing them apart.

After that, the Germans dug in and held their position, waiting for relief. Due to the loss of the Meuse bridges, this failed to materialize until the next day, May 11, but the Belgians failed to make any effort to retake Eben-Emael. The remaining 1,000 men surrendered to the Germans and entered captivity in Germany. Granit suffered 6 dead and 18 wounded compared to the defenders' losses of 21 killed and 61 wounded.

In the meantime, Gustav Altmann's 91 men of Sturmgruppe Stahl attacked the Veldwezelt bridge despite a poor landing in heavy fog. Attacking fiercely yet efficiently, the highly trained commandos put the Belgian bunkers near the bridge out of action with their hollow-charge explosives, then took the bridge neatly at a cost of just 8 men killed in action. The Belgians counterattacked, but strikes by Stuka dive-bombers drove them back with heavy losses. That afternoon, leading elements of Army Group B crossed the Meuse on pontoon bridges and relieved Sturmgruppe Stahl, which retreated back into Germany.

Sturmgruppe Eisen under Martin Schachter, tasked with capturing the Kanne bridge, had the least success of the four Sturmgruppe. The ground fog and heavy Belgian fire disrupted the landing, and the Belgians successfully demolished the Kanne Bridge with explosive charges. Schachter's men came under heavy attack by Belgian infantry, suffering 22 dead and 26 wounded, but they took 190 prisoners and the Belgians lost 216 killed and 50 wounded. Sturmgruppe Eisen retreated under cover of darkness after failing to take their objective.

Sturmgruppe Beton, 129 men strong under commander Gerhard Schacht, attacked the Vroenhoven Bridge and took it at a loss of 7 men to the Belgians' 147 killed and 300 captured. A German soldier named Stenzel, approaching the bridge alone ahead of the main Sturmgruppe (which landed some distance to the west), singlehandedly ensured the capture by cutting the wires to the demolition charges a few seconds before the Belgian defenders triggered them.

Overall, despite the failure of the disguised "Brandenburgers" at the Meuse and the failure of Sturmgruppe Eisen, the glider operation succeeded brilliantly. The new techniques caught the Belgians utterly by surprise, while the courage, professionalism, and drive of the individual German soldiers sealed the triumph. Even absent their officers in some cases, the Wehrmacht troops showed immense personal initiative, which, as one historian points out, represented a unique advantage of the Teutonic military: "It was an outstanding example of *Auftragstaktik* - the leadership principle practised by the German armed forces for the past 200 years. This is based on trusting the skills and commitment of subordinates to perform their duties to the utmost in the execution of an agreed operational plan as defined by a commander, who also provides the necessary resources to undertake the task." (Dunstan, 2005, 59).

The entire surviving manpower of Sturmabteilung Koch received the Iron Cross 1st Class award, with the exception of the rum-guzzling Ernst Grechza, who received the Iron Cross 2nd Class due to his dangerous lack of discipline. Hitler personally awarded the officers the Knight's Cross at a special ceremony at Fuhrer Headquarters Felsennest ("Stony Aerie"), and the OKW granted all officers and men 14 days leave as further reward.

While the men of Sturmabteilung Koch enjoyed their rest and relaxation, the Allies found themselves crumpling under a series of heavy attacks made possible largely by the seizure of Eben-Emael and the nearby bridges, and despite the well-merited fame of the Panzer divisions, the Wehrmacht's blitzkrieg advance into France depended partly on air superiority as well. Controlling the skies over Poland had helped achieve Hitler's explosive victory over that nation in late 1939. Polish strategic and tactical mobility ground to a halt, since anything moving in the open suffered blistering attacks by Stuka dive-bombers. This pinned and paralyzed the whole Polish Army, winning German ground forces even greater freedom to maneuver.

Luftwaffe air support formed a key part of the *Fall Gelb* plan in all of its particulars. A fighter "umbrella" guarded the huge Panzer army moving towards the Ardennes forest and the weak point at Sedan, and air power supported the push into Belgium and broke up Belgian counterattacks against the bridgeheads across various rivers.

Another Luftwaffe mission, begun at dawn on May 10 (simultaneous with the launch of Sturmabteilung Koch), involved raiding the Allied airfields in the Netherlands, Belgium, and France. The Germans intended these sorties to knock out as many enemy aircraft on the ground as possible, and the exquisitely sunny spring weather provided perfect flying weather for airmen of both sides. In the largest series of coordinated air attacks seen in history to that point, the Luftwaffe conducted gigantic raids against dozens of airfields in the Netherlands, Luxembourg, Belgium, and France, with about 500 bombers and an equal number of fighters and dive-bombers participating in the initial May 10 assault.

The attacks in the Netherlands annihilated half of the Dutch fighter force on the ground, but some pilots managed to scramble their aircraft thanks to the Netherlands' early warning system. In the air, the Dutch found themselves facing overwhelming odds. Though their pilots fought with almost suicidal courage, the excellent aircraft and pilots of the Luftwaffe used their numerical superiority to sweep the air of opposition, leaving columns of black smoke rising into the clear blue sky as numerous wrecks dotted the landscape.

Pictures of wrecked German aircraft on May 10

Almost before the sun fully cleared the horizon, the Dutch air force effectively ceased to exist: "In the first hour the Luftwaffe's decisive tactical superiority decimated the ML's combat force; only two serviceable G.1 and ten D.21 fighters, five T.5 bombers and ten C.10 reconnaissance biplanes remained." (Dildy (2), 2015, 44). After the bombers destroyed most of the parked aircraft and fighters cleared most of the rest from the Dutch skies, German paratroopers, or Fallschirmjager, landed at the Hague and other key locations, but they encountered fierce Dutch resistance and failed to achieve many of their objectives. They did, however, gain a foothold at Waalhaven airfield, from which repeated Dutch counterattacks failed to dislodge them.

A picture of German paratroopers landing in the Netherlands

A picture of Waalhaven airfield

The German attacks in Belgium and France met with mixed success. The German bombers destroyed many aircraft on the ground, but some British fighters – chiefly Hurricanes – got into air and counterattacked the thousands of German aircraft sweeping in from the east. Many undamaged aircraft sat idle, however, and the British and French high commands vetoed a number of bold plans to launch large counterattacks.

A few Allied bombers flew against German targets, but with little success. Those in Belgium suffered 9% losses, while those flying against German airfields sustained 40% losses with practically no tactical gains. The worst showing by the Franco-British air fleet occurred when fighters attempted to support a ground attack against German-held Waalhaven airfield in the Netherlands and lost 83% casualties.

German successes on May 10th prompted the Belgians to fall back rapidly towards the Dyle River, site of the lightly fortified Dyle Line. The Belgian forces retreated so hastily, in fact, that British and French units moving to support them feared the Germans would sweep the Belgians past the Dyle before the Allies could advance that far.

As it was, the Belgians did not give permission for the British and French to come to their aid until 6:45 a.m. on May 10, nearly three hours after the initial German invasion. Thus, the British Expeditionary Force (BEF) and French 1ere Army crossed into Belgium on the morning of May 10 and moved to take up their positions on the Dyle Line. A moment of comedy occurred amid the grim preparations for war as the leading British elements attempted to "clear customs" and enter Belgian territory: "In the vanguard were the 12th Royal Lancers who were to form the forward screen alongside and to the north of the French cavalry. They were slightly delayed by a Belgian official who was unhappy with their lack of documentation for entering his country, but overcame this by driving through his barrier." (Evans, 2000, 45).

A picture of British soldiers marching to the front

The German feint by Army Group B, the so-called "Matador's Cloak," proved to be a smashing success. In response, the whole BEF, plus two French armies – the 1ere and 7ere – shifted into Belgium, putting them in a perfect position to be cut off by Army Group A's *Schwerpunkt* (main assault) through the Ardennes and the weakly held lines near Sedan.

The Allies took the Wehrmacht's bait unhesitatingly. The 1ere Army under General Jean Blanchard consisted of two Mechanized Divisions, the 2e and 3e, grouped into a Cavalry Corps commanded by General Rene Prioux, as well as 3 divisions of motorized infantry; 4 divisions of regular infantry; and a reserve infantry division. The 7ere Army consisted mostly of infantry. The BEF mustered 7 semi-motorized infantry supported by a massive but outdated artillery park of over 2,700 artillery pieces, 38 armored cars, 23 Matilda tanks armed with 40mm cannons, 77 more Matildas armed only with machine guns, and a number of machine gun armed tankettes and Universal Carriers.

Blanchard

Prioux

    The French received an enthusiastic send-off from their own people, as though victory was assured. Georges Kosak, a French lieutenant, described the festive atmosphere that accompanied the French advance to the Belgian border: "At first we pass through several small villages where the people did not seem to be informed about events; then important centres where the population mass on the sidewalks and at the windows greeting us frenziedly. French flags and garlands were hung from all windows. Women have their arms full of flowers, and their aprons full of packets of cigarettes, sweets and chocolates [...] Our hearts beat; an immense pride overcomes us." (Horne, 2007, 175).

Towns in Belgium, however, proved ominously quiet, preparing the French in some measure for their encounter with the invading Germans. The Dyle River also proved far less of a tenable defensive position than hoped; the "river" itself, a shallow stream only 20 feet wide in most places, scarcely sufficed to halt a civilian automobile, let alone armored cars and tanks with built-in fording capabilities. Making matters worse, the Dyle Line defenses consisted of small, poorly armed, widely-scattered bunkers with flimsy steel "tank fences" between them, easily knocked down in a matter of moments by the Germans.

General Blanchard of the 1ere Army sent Rene Prioux's two tank divisions forward to secure the Dyle Line, fearing his infantry would arrive too late to prevent German penetration. He did not realize the Germans wanted the Allies to advance deep into the trap of Belgium so they could be cut off and forced to surrender by Army Group A. Hitler expressed ecstatic happiness over the Allies' eagerness to take the Army Group B bait: "I could have wept for joy; they'd fallen into the trap! It had been a clever piece of work to attack Liège. How lovely Felsennest was! The birds in the morning, the view over the road up which the columns were advancing, the squadrons of planes overhead. There, I knew just what I was doing!" (Horne, 2007, 179).

By the afternoon of May 11th, the Allies occupied their positions all along the Dyle Line, but the Wehrmacht soldiers of Army Group B did not stand idle while their opponents maneuvered. Engineers threw pontoon bridges across the Meuse on May 10 and May 11 to replace those demolished near Maastricht, enabling numerous German infantry and the 3rd and 4th Panzer divisions to cross. Motorized German infantry shredded the Belgian 7eme Division when it sought to oppose the crossings, causing the Belgian 4eme Division to desert *en masse* in terror. Allied aircraft sought to bomb the Meuse bridges repeatedly, but the Motorized Flak Regiment "Goering" fought them off, along with Luftwaffe fighters from JG 27. The Allies lost 83 aircraft with most of their crews killed and only a handful surviving to be captured. In exchange, the bombers managed nothing aside from grazing one of the pontoon bridges with a 250 pound bomb.

World War II's first major tank battle developed at Hannut as the Germans and French maneuvered for tactical supremacy in the Belgian countryside. Given how the rest of the campaign turned out, it's little surprise the Battle of Hannut is largely forgotten today, but it stood out at the time as a notable French success as their tanks severely bloodied the nose of the advancing Germans and destroyed a number of Wehrmacht armored vehicles during a struggle lasting several days and involving hundreds of tanks on each side.

A picture of German soldiers inspecting disabled tanks at Hannut

As May 12 dawned, the Belgian I, II, III, and Cavalry Corps held the northern 30 miles of the line, while the BEF occupied the center and the French 1ere Army held the south between Warve and the Meuse River valley. It was here that General Rene Prioux's two armored divisions found themselves confronted by German panzers under the warm spring sunlight of a late Belgian morning. Lt. Robert Le Bel described it as "an extraordinary show which was played out about three kilometres [2 miles] away: a panzer division shaping itself for battle. The massive gathering of this armoured armada was an unforgettable sight, the more so that it appeared even more terrifying through the glasses..Some men, probably officers, walked to and fro gesticulating in front of the tanks. They were probably giving last-minute orders." (Evans, 2000, 46).

The French deployed SOMUA S-35 tanks with 47mm guns capable of piercing early-war German tank armor at most combat ranges and armor thick enough to provide cover against the main guns of 1940 variants of Panzer III and Panzer IV medium tanks. The weakness of the SOMUA lay in its one-man turret, which forced the commander to occupy multiple roles and thus reduced overall crew efficiency.

A SOMA S-35 captured by the Germans

A Panzer IV
Alongside these, the French used an equal number of Hotchkiss H-39 light tanks, armed with a

37mm gun capable of engaging German armored vehicles only at close ranges due to weak penetration against tank armor. Each division fielded 88 SOMUA S-35s and 87 Hotchkiss H-39s, the latter a stopgap due to insufficient supplies of SOMUAs.

For their part, the Germans deployed Panzer IIIs and Panzer IVs against the French, supported by the light Panzer I and Panzer II tanks with their flimsy armor and weak firepower. Supporting these, however, the Luftwaffe fielded the deadly Stuka dive-bombers, whose characteristic rising howl while diving, created by purpose-built sirens, often caused panic among those it targeted.

The "secret weapon" in the German tank arsenal, which ultimately overcame superior French guns and armor, consisted of the radio fitted into each Panzer. Only one in five – 20% – of French tanks carried a radio, so once combat began, 80% of the French tanks relied on visual signals, including merely observing the movements of other tanks and attempting to guess the intended maneuvers. The Germans' advantages in flexibility and communications ultimately permitted them to beat the French tanks in spite of their lighter armor and cannons. "Apart from a cultural obsession with radio security […] the other problem arose again directly out of the perception that tanks were only to provide support for the infantry. In such circumstances, radios were not necessary, signal flags would suffice and, once drawn up in their static lines facing the enemy, it was thought to be enough for […] a runner […] passing on orders in person by word of mouth." (Healy, 2008, 23).

The Germans moved forward with four Panzer regiments deployed abreast, with 20 Panzer IIIs leading and 12 Panzer IVs backing them up while 48 Panzer Is and IIs guarded the flanks. The French near Hannut faced 80 Panzer IIIs, 48 Panzer IVs, and 192 lighter Panzers along a 22-mile front. Each side also deployed armored cars, which chiefly served a scouting role but also skirmished viciously with one another. The Germans also held motorized infantry in reserve.

Prioux chose his ground well – the Hannut area, 18 miles east of the Dyle Line, consists of "tank country," gently rolling hills with numerous scattered groves and small clumps of forest, and hamlets to provide cover. The centerpiece of his defense consisted of a long, low ridge providing good fields of fire. Lt. Robert Le Bel's tank, from which he saw the ominous sight of the German tanks deploying, occupied a position at the heart of the French defenses, around Hannut itself. Here, sheltered by walls, hedges, and clumps of trees, the SOMUAs and Hotchkiss tanks lurked, awaiting the onslaught.

At first, the French soldiers saw nothing but an undulating cloud of dust kicked up by the treads of hundreds of tank tracks, flowing across the landscape towards them. Then the boxy shapes of tanks loomed out of the beige haze, and the French opened fire. The French tanks inflicted high casualties against the Panzer I and II tanks. At one point, a German tank commander from one of the knocked out tanks ran forward in a frenzy of frustrated rage and clambered atop a Hotchkiss tank, swinging a hammer he perhaps meant to use on its periscope. However, he missed his footing and tumbled off, crushed to death a moment later under the tank's track.

The Germans launched a strong attack on the village of Crehen and took it, driving out the French tanks and infantry. They subsequently moved on to attack Thisnes shortly after noon, and the hard-hitting Panzer IIIs and Panzer IVs destroyed 13 of the lighter Hotchkiss tanks defending Thisnes, forcing the rest to pull back.

However, at 5:30 p.m., the deep, throbbing growl of tank engines announced the approach of a French counterattack. These armored vehicles, formidable SOMUA S-35s, rolled forward, sending rounds from their 47mm guns punching through armor plates and turning panzers into shattered hulks. The battle raged fiercely until 8:30 p.m., at which point the Germans withdrew from both Crehen and Thisnes, though they destroyed four SOMUA S-35s during the fighting. The day ended with the French holding their static defense line along the Hannut ridge.

On May 13, the German commander concentrated his panzers for two narrow-front attacks designed to penetrate the French line. In the north, Horst Stumpff's 3rd Panzer Division struck at Orp-le-Grand and Orp-le-Petit, but recoiled in the face savage French counterattacks, leaving the gently rolling farmland dotted with burning wrecks. After that, Stumpff sent in his supporting infantry, and a brutal gunbattle erupted between French and German foot soldiers, neither willing to give an inch of ground to the other.

At 3:20 p.m., the 5th and 6th panzer regiments attempted another penetration, but the French, responding with commendable aggression, struck at these panzer thrusts with tank attacks of their own. The Germans called the concentrated tank melee a "Hexenkessel," or "witches' cauldron."

To the south, Johann Stever led 250 panzers of the 4th Panzer Division against the village of Merdorp, but the Germans initially enjoyed no better success than Stumpff. French armor and artillery flung his attacking forces back with heavy losses. Eventually, however, Stever's persistent attacks cut down on the numbers of surviving French tanks, and at approximately 3:00 p.m., the last two Hotchkiss tanks and 10 SOMUAs broke out westward, leaving Merdorp in Stever's hands.

May 13 witnessed additional "Hexenkessel" battles at Jandrain and Jauche. The Germans deployed their heaviest tanks, Panzer IIIs and IVs, in large numbers at these points. At Jandrain, Eberbach's panzers finally managed to destroy 8 SOMUA S-35 tanks, while the crews abandoned five more, permitting their capture. At Jauche, five remaining French tanks retreated, proving impervious to German tank gun fire. The group included Lt. Robert Le Bel: "According to the panzers' war diary, 'Fire was opened on every one of these moving tanks by PzR 6 and the PaK Kompanie, so that every tank took a large number of hits, including 7.5cm high-explosive rounds. None of the French tanks was penetrated and put out of action.' After the battle, le Bel's Hotchkiss showed impact marks from being hit by 15 A/T rounds and 42 bullets." (Dildy (2), 2015, 89).

The French armor disengaged and fell back, largely under cover of night. Prioux still had fight left in him, however. He formed a new defensive line 5.5 miles west of the Hannut line, positioning his tanks in ambush at the edge of a forest overlooking the Belgian steel "tank fences." On May 14, the Germans penetrated the fence at Perwez and fell into the French ambush. Prioux's tanks continued to crush repeated panzer attacks from 10:30 a.m. until the afternoon, when the French again withdrew.

On the following day, the Germans found themselves halted by French tanks once again near Gembloux. May 15 saw the last large-scale armored action in Belgium, however. The French high command split up Prioux's remaining tanks among the infantry, rendering them effectively useless, but at a cost of 40 SOMUAs and 94 Hotchkiss tanks, the French knocked out 222 panzers, with 48 totally destroyed and 174 crippled, thus slowing the German advance to a crawl for a remarkable span of five days.

The Battle of Hannut provided a grimly spectacular introduction to the age of tank warfare and represented perhaps the finest success of the French military during the invasion.

While Army Group B drew the Allies into Belgium and suffered a notable check at the Battle of Hannut, Army Group A hastened forward to complete the doom of the western military forces. 41,000 vehicles of all kinds, including numerous panzers, plus SdKfz armored cars, trucks, motorcycles, self-propelled guns, and other machines, moved through Luxembourg and entered the Ardennes Forest to strike at the weak point in the French line near Sedan. Sedan lay between the Allied armies in the north and the start of the Maginot Line, held only by poor quality reserve units.

Remarkably, the overall French commander, Maurice Gamelin, knew of the German movement through the Ardennes from the beginning. His reconnaissance pilots did their work well, bringing him reports of large numbers of tanks snaking along the Ardennes' winding roads. However, Gamelin dismissed these as a "rather violent feint" and continued to operate on the stubborn belief that Belgium represented the main theater of war, largely based on assumed parallels to World War I.

Many of the commanders of the German advance went on to win immortal fame during World War II, including Erwin Rommel, Heinz Guderian, and Hermann "Papa" Hoth. All drove their men hard, but the German soldiers evinced great eagerness in any case. In fact, this mood of cheerful aggression hampered the advance as units attempted to bypass each other on narrow forest roads and inadvertently created a "250-kilometer traffic jam."

Guderian

Rommel

Nevertheless, the 1,222 Panzers and supporting vehicles advanced at remarkable speed. To cut sleep to a minimum, Guderian issued pervitin amphetamines to his men, drugs given the nickname "panzer chocolate" by the men of the Heer. This early version of "crystal meth" allowed long periods of being awake and imparted a euphoric mood, but at the risk of heart attacks, suicide, psychotic violence, or a collapse into addiction.

The Wehrmacht's advance through the Ardennes only met opposition from scattered Allied forces. In the north, the Belgian Keyaerts Group, including the Chasseurs Ardennais, put up a "spirited resistance" before withdrawing to the north to rejoin the main Belgian forces on the Dyle Line, and in the south, the Germans encountered and quickly routed units of French horsed cavalry, using both armored attacks and Stuka dive-bomber strikes to disperse the lightly armed defenders. (Thomas, 2014, 31).

The Germans arrived at the Meuse on May 12 largely free from harassment by Franco-British aircraft and were confronted by relatively weak defenses. Standing on the bank of the Meuse,

Fedor von Bock confided to his diary, "Concerning Army Group A, the 4th Army has succeeded in crossing the Meuse near Yvoir and Dinant and has established bridgeheads there. The French really do seem to have taken leave of their senses." (Healy, 2008, 45). On May 13, Guderian's panzers crossed the Meuse almost unopposed, and the Germans launched a colossal Stuka dive-bomber attack of 500 sorties against the 55e Reserve Regiment, a low-quality French unit guarding the river near Sedan. General Maurice Gamelin, proving himself once again completely unfit to hold command, responded to requests for anti-aircraft guns to be sent to aid the 55e Regiment with the airy response that their squad machine guns would suffice to drive the Stukas away. These weapons, of course, lacked the range, accuracy, or striking power to even inconvenience the swiftly-descending Luftwaffe dive-bombers.

The stunned French found themselves under fire from the east bank by the deadly 88mm flak cannon, a German anti-aircraft gun which proved equally lethal against bunkers, buildings, and practically every type of armored vehicle fielded by the Allies during World War II. Guderian himself used a rubber assault boat to cross the Meuse after troops and engineers established a foothold on the west bank, and his subordinate, Lieutenant Colonel Balck, met him with a bit of jubilant, good-natured cheekiness as his boat approached shore. "He greeted me cheerfully with the cry 'Joy-riding in canoes on the Meuse is forbidden!' I had in fact used those words myself in one of the exercises that we had in preparation for this operation, since the attitude of some of younger officers had struck me as rather too light-hearted. I now realized that they had judged the situation correctly." (Evans, 2000, 52). Guderian's engineers threw three pontoon bridges across the Meuse at Wadelincourt, Glaire, and Donchery, and by midnight on the 13th, panzers poured across these temporary but expertly constructed bridges and moved on into the French countryside.

Meanwhile, Rommel's men arrived at the Meuse near Houx, a village close to Dinant, after fighting through unexpectedly stiff resistance on the eastern bank. Scouting carefully, the Germans found a long-abandoned weir connecting the two banks by way of a forested island in midstream. Waiting for complete darkness, a unit of German motorcycle troops drove their vehicles slowly across the river on the weir, establishing a bridgehead on the west bank. Though the French counterattacked strongly the next day with machine guns and mortar fire, the motorcycle soldiers maintained their foothold. Rommel's engineers rigged a cable ferry using pontoon boats intended for building a bridge, which allowed more infantry and armored vehicles to cross the Meuse, leading to expansion of the German foothold on the west bank and the eventual construction of complete pontoon bridges.

By the morning of May 14, Rommel's men moved away from the river. A handful of tanks and the 7th Rifle Regiment attacked the nearby town of Onhaye, which fell at 9:00 a.m. when 25 panzers from Panzer Regiment 25 completed the crossing at Houx and moved forward to encircle the town. The French defenders died or surrendered, giving Rommel control of a defensible position commanding the area around his crossing point. The 25th Panzer Regiment continued to spearhead the drive, reaching Morville by nightfall and extending the German position 6 miles into France.

May 14 witnessed French and British bombers and fighters attacking the pontoon bridges in the Ardennes, only to find themselves enveloped in a murderous cloud of flak. The Germans had not left their air defenses to squad machine-guns in the manner of Maurice Gamelin, instead deploying numerous flak batteries around all their river crossings. The aircraft sank two of Rommel's pontoons (though the engineers replaced them almost immediately) but inflicted no damage on Guderian's. Guderian himself reported on the futile courage of the Allied airmen:

"There was now a most violent air attack by the enemy. The extremely brave French and English pilots did not succeed in knocking out the bridges, despite the heavy casualties that they suffered. Our anti-aircraft gunners proved themselves on this day, and shot superbly." (Evans, 2000, 60).

Suffering 50% or higher losses, the remaining aircraft limped back to their airfields, with many so shredded and battered by flak bursts that they proved no longer serviceable. The Germans now held an expanding slice of French territory, well away from the main Allied forces, and nothing the local defenders attempted sufficed to halt the Wehrmacht's swift, aggressive advance.

German soldiers crossing the Meuse on May 15

The second and last major tank battle of Germany's 1940 French campaign developed at Stonne near the Sedan crossings. Here, the most deadly French tank of the time, the strangely constructed Char B1 Bis, formed the core of French resistance. Armed with a 47mm gun in its turret and a second 75mm gun bizarrely mounted in its hull, the Char B1 Bis featured 60mm armor on most surfaces, which provided protection against early German tank guns and most towed anti-tank guns also.

A disabled Char B1 Bis

One Char B1 Bis, dubbed "Joan of Arc," demonstrated this near-invulnerability when it engaged a large number of German AT guns supported by light vehicles. The tank knocked out two armored cars, but eventually lost its guns to concentrated enemy fire. Nevertheless, it survived more than 90 direct hits, many at point-blank range, while actually running over and crushing approximately 25 Wehrmacht AT guns in succession. Only a lucky shot through the side radiator port finally put a stop to Joan of Arc's rampage. On another occasion, a Char B1 Bis survived 160 direct hits.

Stonne stood on a plateau 9 miles south of Sedan, and both sides recognized it as a key point in the struggle for the Meuse bridgeheads. The French wanted to assemble a counterattack against the German crossing here, while the Wehrmacht was intent on seizing the town and plateau to forestall precisely this maneuver.

The tank expert Jean Flavigny led the French 21e Corps during the action, and the French were pitted against the 10th Panzer Division, supported by the Grossdeutschland Infantry Division. The French overall regional commander, Charles Huntziger, gave Flavigny two sets of orders, one offensive (retake Sedan) and the other defensive (hold Stonne). Flavigny had 53 Char 1B Bis at his disposal, but their supporting motorized infantry remained absent, delayed on the traffic-clogged roads. Accordingly, Flavigny opted to stay on the defensive and let the panzers come to him.

At 5:00 a.m. on May 15, shortly after a brief German artillery barrage struck Stonne, a column of 11 German tanks moved upslope towards the town and around the hairpin bend at the top. Six Panzer IV tanks led, with five lighter Panzer II tanks backing them up. As the Germans rounded the corner with the houses and church of Stonne in sight ahead, a sharp report punctured the morning air, and the lead Panzer IV slowed to a stop. A 25mm French anti-tank gun, commanded by the grizzled veteran Sergeant Durand, coolly fired several more shots into the lead tank, ensuring its disablement. The second panzer suffered a similar fate, while the third perished in more spectacular fashion by exploding violently.

The remaining panzers pushed forward nevertheless, forcing the French to pull back and form a temporary defensive line just south of Stonne. This signaled the start of a prolonged, seesaw combat in which Stonne changed hands no less than 17 times over the course of May 15-16. During the fighting, the German tanks fired so many shots at the nearly impregnable Char B1 Bis tanks that crews often abandoned their vehicles temporarily to scavenge unused shells from nearby knocked-out panzers. Feldwebel Karl Koch provided a vivid glimpse of this fighting: "After a while, a fourth tank appeared through the orchard. It was a real monster and we had no idea that France had tanks like that. We fired 20 shots at it without success. However, after a few more shots, we managed to knock off its track. [...] a fifth tank appears, another B1 firing all its weapons. [...] We fired, but could not knock it out until a ricochet hit the turret. The next shot hit it in the rear. Calm returned and we abandoned our tank again because we had exhausted the ammunition." (Zaloga, 2011, 67).

The battle turned into an infantry combat late on the 15th, but after massive French artillery strikes before dawn on May 16th, both sides committed their remaining tanks to a fresh armored encounter. Captain Pierre Billotte, France's premier Char B1 Bis tank ace – destined to survive the war, found an important labor union, and die many years later at the start of the Internet era in 1992 – now entered the fray. After knocking out one tank leading the German armor thrust, Billotte described what happened next: "The panzers following it were spaced at regular intervals on a 200-metre climb, each of them being shielded by those in front. On the other hand, I was uphill and I could fire at them from above...In ten minutes, the panzers at the head of the column were all silenced, one after the other, and I could see the ones in the rear hastily withdrawing." (Evans, 2000, 64). Billotte knocked out at least 9 and perhaps as many as 13 panzers in his attack, all without losing his own tank, "Eure."

Another French tank commander, Lieutenant Doumercq, earned a different type of fame when he cornered a German infantry platoon and crushed a number of men to death under his Char B1 Bis' tracks. Horrified by this action, both the French and Germans took to calling Doumercq "the Butcher of Stonne."

At the end of the ferocious tank fighting on May 16th, both sides withdrew their armored forces from the area around Stonne. The infantry continued to maul each other until the 23rd in a miniature reprise of World War I trench warfare, at which point the French finally withdrew and left the powdered rubble of Stonne to the Wehrmacht.

After the Germans had forced the Meuse crossings OKW, the Wehrmacht high command, ordered Guderian to halt the Germans for 24 hours to give them time to rest, regroup, and refuel. However, Guderian decided to deliberately and thoroughly flout these orders; having gained a stunning advantage over the French, he declined to sacrifice it even to give his soldiers and himself much-needed rest. Guderian rightly figured that only by keeping up the pressure could the Panzer Divisions exploit the opportunities offered by running amok in the Allied rear.

Rommel found himself in the lead on May 15th, driving in his Kubelwagen staff car alongside much better protected panzers. The Germans pushed west and took a curving path northwest as they punched deep into French territory, aiming to reach the coast of the English Channel. In this way, the Wehrmacht would encircle the BEF and much of the French Army deployed in Belgium, putting them in an untenable position and hopefully forcing their surrender.

The Germans used forests – cleared of undergrowth for firewood like most European woodland at the time and therefore offering scant obstacle to tracked vehicles – to avoid air attacks, while bypassing towns where soldiers and anti-tank guns might delay their advance. Rommel pushed out far ahead of the main force but paused on a hill crest near sunset on May 15th to survey the landscape to his rear: "Looking back east from the summit of the hill, as night fell, endless pillars of dust could be seen rising as far as the eye could reach — comforting signs that the 7th Panzer Divisions move into the conquered territory had begun." (Evans, 2000, 70).

Rommel and Guderian continued their drive on the 16th, and the French forces showed strong signs of panic as the Germans pierced ever deeper into France. Many men encountered by the Wehrmacht made no effort to attack them, instead streaming down side roads in an attempt to escape. The Germans brushed past these and moved on as the French Army assumed the role of a traffic hazard rather than an active enemy force.

At this point, the OKW nearly scuppered the successful blitzkrieg from within. Field Marshal Paul von Kleist – eventually killed by the Russians for the crime of "alienating, through friendship and generosity, the peoples of the Soviet Union" – ordered Guderian to halt, fearing the overextended German advance would suffer counterattack and annihilation. Guderian tendered his resignation, thinking this would overcome Kleist's objections, but to his astonishment, Kleist accepted it. Ultimately, Gerd von Rundstedt adroitly averted this potential crisis of command by intervening with a solution; Rundstedt's plan called for Guderian to halt but permitted him to make a "reconnaissance in force." Rundstedt left the size and nature of this "reconnaissance" totally undefined, effectively writing Guderian a blank check to do whatever he wished so long as he made the conciliatory gesture of establishing a fixed headquarters and remaining there for a while.

On May 16th, the French command sent Colonel Charles de Gaulle to make a flanking attack with a tank force on the rapidly growing German salient. This, however, was too little, too late. De Gaulle found himself commanding a pitifully small force of tanks, but he nevertheless made a brave attempt to halt the Germans near Montcornet and Serre. After an initial success against light vehicles, the French found themselves under steady attack by artillery, Stuka dive-bombers, and mechanized infantry. Towards the end of the day, de Gaulle withdrew to spare his remaining men.

De Gaulle gathered more tanks and made a new attack at Crecy on May 19th, 1940, but he again suffered a violent repulse. The 19th witnessed another disaster for the French when the highly capable General Henri Giraud fell prisoner to the Germans, prompting his 9th Army to desert en masse within hours. General Maurice Gamelin, the commander who oversaw the disastrous French defense up to that point, held a feast for his leading officers and then relinquished overall command to General Maxime Weygand.

On May 20th, just 11 days after the commencement of hostilities, leading elements of the 2nd Panzer Division under Rudolf Veiel reached the coast at the commune of Noyelles-sur-Mer, close to the mouth of the Somme River. Guderian's bold advance had cut off three French armies and the British Expeditionary Force (BEF) successfully in Belgium and the northeast corner of France.

May 21 was something of a respite for both sides, due mainly to the indecisiveness of the leaders of both the Allied and Axis forces. Guderian's and Rommel's panzer divisions held their line, reinforcing it with motorized infantry and artillery, while the OKW attempted to decide whether to strike north against the encircled French and British forces or south into France proper. Eventually, the OKW decided on a northward advance, but the order arrived in mid-afternoon and Guderian could do little more than prepare his forces for the following day's advance.

One action on May 21st resulted from personal initiative on the part of BEF commander Field Marshal John Standish Surtees Prendergast Vereker, 6th Viscount Gort. From Arras, he launched an attack southward with two understrength British infantry divisions, 16 Matilda II tanks (capable of knocking out German armor), and several dozen weakly armed Matilda I tanks. Split into two columns, his small assault unit – dubbed the "Frankforce" – attacked Rommel's men near Wailly, Agny, and Beaurains. Lord Gort's diminutive Frankforce met with initial success, destroying a number of light Panzer I and II tanks, a convoy of trucks, some light A/T guns, and taking 400 German prisoners. The Matildas' thick armor stood them in good stead, deflecting lighter German shells and persuading many Wehrmacht soldiers, including Rommel himself, that they faced a far larger battalion of Allied juggernauts. As Rommel wrote, "The anti-tank guns which we quickly deployed showed themselves to be far too light to be effective against the heavily armoured British tanks, and the majority of them were put out of action by gunfire, together with their crews, and then overrun by the enemy tanks. Many of our vehicles were burnt out." (Horne, 383). Lord Gort's 60 to 70 tanks became "hundreds" in Rommel's mind, demonstrating that even the finest commanders can succumb to irrational fear. In fact, in Rommel's memoirs, he made the mistake of claiming that five full British armored divisions attacked him from Arras.

Nevertheless, the Germans concentrated several 88mm flak gun batteries in the path of the English and soon compelled the Frankforce to retreat, leaving 9 burning hulks behind, including two highly valuable Matilda IIs. On May 22, Rommel attacked north towards Arras. A spoiling attack pinned him down for a while, but on the 23rd, he took the city and advanced past it. Guderian also sent a pair of panzer divisions north, aiming to seize Calais and Boulogne. Lord Gort and Maxime Weygand failed to meet and devise a plan, an event ascribed to the British commander's malice by the French but which actually resulted from appallingly bad communications.

Prime Minister Paul Reynaud announced the desperate situation to the French Senate in Paris that day, producing deep shock. Most government officials of France believed, up to that moment, in an imminent Allied victory. The Secretary of War, Marshal Petain – later head of the collaborationist Vichy government – argued for an armistice. Nevertheless, Weygand remained confident, albeit for reasons that might have been comical if not for the situation's deadly seriousness: "Despite his arduous experiences of the past twenty-four hours, the seventy-three-year-old Generalissimo arrived full of bounce and launched into his analysis of the situation on an evident note of optimism. 'So many mistakes have been made,' he began, 'that they give me confidence. I believe that in future we shall make less.'" (Horne, 2007, 389).

Weygand outlined a plan of bizarre optimism in which the entire trapped Allied force would turn south and "round up" the panzers in the course of one day. In the meantime, the Germans established numerous bridgeheads on the south bank of the Somme, to be used when the southward advance began. Panzers invested Boulogne on May 22nd, and on May 23rd, the British evacuated their troops at midnight. The French garrison surrendered at noon two days later on May 25th, recognizing their utterly hopeless position.

The initial investment of Calais fell to the 1st Panzer Division, but Guderian later ordered them onward to Dunkirk and replaced them with Ferdinand Schaal's 10th Panzer Division. On May 25th and 26th, the Germans attacked the city vigorously with tanks, artillery, infantry, and airstrikes by Junkers Ju 87 Stuka dive-bombers. Sir Winston Churchill and Sir Anthony Eden sent a message to the battered defenders, urging them to hold out as long as possible: "Defence of Calais to the utmost is of highest importance to our country as symbolising our continued cooperation with France. The eyes of the Empire are upon the defence of Calais, and H. M. Government are confident you and your gallant regiments will perform an exploit worthy of the British name." (Evans, 2000, 98).

Nevertheless, Schaal's fierce attacks overwhelmed the defenders. On May 27th, 47 men escaped in a yacht after hiding under a Nazi-held dock at the waterfront, but the other 3,000 British and 800 French soldiers in Calais surrendered to the Wehrmacht. With the Germans surging north all across Flanders, the British and French forces fell back towards Dunkirk, the last Channel port still in Allied possession, and the Germans closed in for the kill.

Due to their confidence in their ability to stop the Germans in Belgium and their blinkered self-assurance that no serious attack would develop elsewhere, the Allied high command had no overall plan of retreat in place when the battle for France commenced on May 10th, 1940. However, just 9 days later, with Guderian's panzers over the Meuse at Sedan in the weak point of the line and the massive forces of the Wehrmacht's Army Group A driving west along the Somme River valley towards the coast, the situation clearly called for desperate measures to salvage even part of the British Expeditionary Force.

Just eight days after the Luftwaffe bombers had streamed over the airfields of the Netherlands, Belgium, Luxembourg, and France at dawn, and glider troops seized Fort Eben-Emael on the Belgian frontier with Germany, the GHQ of the British Expeditionary Force sensed disaster clearly enough to order all non-essential personnel to be evacuated by sea from Dunkirk, Boulogne, and Calais. This May 18th mandate laid the groundwork for the next day's debates on whether to withdraw the entire BEF.

The French leader, Paul Reynaud, had recognized the hopelessness of the situation with greater speed and clarity than most. As early as May 15th, he telephoned British Prime Minister Winston Churchill with a despairing but realistic appraisal: "'We have been defeated,' Reynaud blurted in English. A nonplussed silence, as Churchill tried to collect himself. 'We are beaten'; Reynaud went on, 'we have lost the battle.' 'Surely it can't have happened so soon?' Churchill finally managed to say. [Reynaud responded:] 'The front is broken near Sedan; they are pouring through in great numbers with tanks and armored cars.'" (Lord, 2012, 2).

Reynaud

Though dwarfed by the other forces involved – the French fielded around 5 million men, of whom 2.2 million served in the northern theater, and the German invasion armies collectively numbered some 3 million – the British Expeditionary Force of some half-million soldiers possessed extraordinary significance. Almost the entire home strength of the British army, including both enlisted men and officers, resided in the BEF. If the Germans captured the BEF, England would lack any ground forces for defense. Other British soldiers existed, but deployments left them scattered around the globe.

Heated debate still raged about the advisability of retreat, with some of the British government – including, for a time, Winston Churchill – holding out hope for French commander in chief Maxime Weygand's overly optimistic plans calling for a French thrust from the south and a BEF advance from the north to defeat the gigantic German incursion along the Somme valley. Weygand, though incredibly vigorous for a mid-20th century man in his 73rd year – at one point he astounded other officers by speeding vigorously through an impromptu 100-yard sprint – emerged as something of a theatrical fantastico during France's hour of crisis. Loudly proclaiming sweeping plans capable of somehow reversing the catastrophe in utterly unrealistic periods of time – such as 24 hours – he downplayed the colossal panzer divisions as mere "penny packets" of tanks and claimed he could "mop up" the overwhelming, highly professional Wehrmacht in short order.

The British government called for the BEF to strike south in support of Weygand's alleged northward drive, and though the British ultimately carried out a remarkably successful tank raid near Arras on May 21st (until Rommel assembled a defensive line of deadly 88mm flak guns and shot the British Matilda tanks to pieces), such a move would have resulted in the BEF's swift envelopment and destruction by the hard-hitting, fast-moving Germans. Fortunately for the men of the Expeditionary Force, their commander shared none of the optimistic certainty of Weygand. Field Marshal John Standish Surtees Prendergast Vereker, 6th Viscount Gort, may have lacked imagination, but he made up for this deficiency with his clear-sighted, forthright grasp of the reality he saw in front of him.

Gort

Lord Gort took the difficult decision to withdraw the BEF rather than support Weygand's wildly impractical attack plans. The Viscount later recorded his thoughts regarding Weygand's idea of the French 9ere Army attacking northward to "close the gap" between them and the BEF, putting the Germans to rout in the process: "Reports from the liaison officers with French formations were likewise not encouraging: in particular I was unable to verify that the French had enough reserves at their disposal south of the gap to enable them to stage counter-attacks sufficiently strong to warrant the expectation that the gap would be closed." (Horne, 2007, 362).

If the two forces failed to achieve a juncture – a likely outcome, considering the battered condition of the French and the technical and numerical superiority of the Wehrmacht – the BEF would find itself trapped with no possibility of retreat. Fast-moving panzer divisions would cut it off from the coast, and the Germans could then annihilate it, and Weygand's 9ere Army, in detail.

On May 20th, just 11 days after the commencement of hostilities, leading elements of the 2nd Panzer Division under Rudolf Veiel reached the coast at the commune of Noyelles-sur-Mer, close to the mouth of the Somme River. Guderian's bold advance had cut off three French armies and the British Expeditionary Force (BEF) successfully in Belgium and the northeast corner of France.

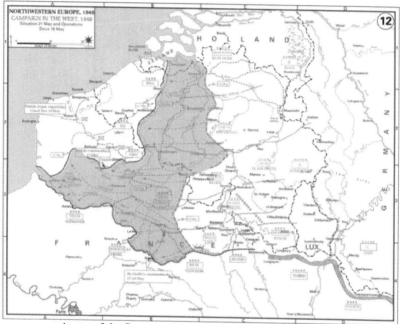

A map of the German advance (in red) by the end of May 21

The day before, on May 19th, the British Admiralty and War Office, in response to Lord Gort's firmly expressed intention to evacuate if the situation saw no radical improvement, began joint planning for the BEF's cross-Channel retreat. The planners assigned this plan the code name Operation Dynamo. Operation Dynamo called for preparing three English Channel ports – Boulogne, Calais, and Dunkirk – as potential points of embarkation. The man put in charge of this operation, Vice Admiral Bertram Ramsay, set about his task energetically, though he had little belief in its necessity or, in the event it actually became necessary, its success. Ramsay's office, among many other tasks, compiled a list of small vessels capable of evacuating men alongside large Royal Navy ships. This foresighted action helped save more than a third of the men who eventually escaped through Dunkirk.

Ramsay

Though the War Office heeded Gort enough to start planning and organizing a seaborne evacuation of the BEF, their overall belief, shared by Churchill, centered on Gort's unfitness for command. They sent Chief of the Imperial General Staff (CIGS) William Edmund Ironside, later 1st Baron Ironside, to order Lord Gort to attack southward according to the French plan. Ironside confronted Gort on May 20th, and Gort responded to Ironside's blunt commands by informing him that all but two of his divisions remained too heavily embroiled in combat to join the attack. After visiting French headquarters, Gort gloomily changed his assessment of the situation, reporting on his return to England that the French seemed unlikely to attack and that the BEF probably faced certain defeat and capture: "'I begin to despair of the French fighting at all. The great army defeated by a few tanks. [...] Personally, I think we cannot extricate the B.E.F. Only hope a march south-west. Have they the time? Have they got the food? [...] God help the B.E.F. [...] Brought to this state by the incompetence of the French Command.'" (Horne, 2007, 378).

Nevertheless, Gort went ahead and attempted the attack on Arras during May 21st using two understrength divisions, 16 Matilda II tanks (capable of knocking out German armor), and several dozen weakly armed Matilda I tanks. Split into two columns, his small assault unit – dubbed the "Frankforce" – attacked Rommel's men near Wailly, Agny, and Beaurains. Lord Gort's diminutive Frankforce met with initial success, destroying a number of light Panzer I and II tanks, a convoy of trucks, some light A/T guns, and taking 400 German prisoners. The Matildas' thick armor stood them in good stead, deflecting lighter German shells and persuading many Wehrmacht soldiers, including Rommel himself, that they faced a far larger battalion of Allied juggernauts. As Rommel wrote, "The anti-tank guns which we quickly deployed showed themselves to be far too light to be effective against the heavily armoured British tanks, and the majority of them were put out of action by gunfire, together with their crews, and then overrun by the enemy tanks. Many of our vehicles were burnt out." (Horne, 383). Lord Gort's 60 to 70 tanks became "hundreds" in Rommel's mind, demonstrating that even the finest commanders can succumb to irrational fear. In fact, in Rommel's memoirs, he made the mistake of claiming that five full British armored divisions attacked him from Arras.

Nevertheless, the Germans concentrated several 88mm flak gun batteries in the path of the English and soon compelled the Frankforce to retreat, leaving 9 burning hulks behind, including two highly valuable Matilda IIs. On May 22, Rommel attacked north towards Arras. A spoiling attack pinned him down for a while, but on the 23rd, he took the city and advanced past it. Guderian also sent a pair of panzer divisions north, aiming to seize Calais and Boulogne. Lord Gort and Maxime Weygand failed to meet and devise a plan, an event ascribed to the British commander's malice by the French but which actually resulted from appallingly bad communications.

Meanwhile, the Germans provided the final push towards evacuation. On May 22nd, after a brief delay caused by panicky misgivings on the part of the OKW HQ at the vulnerability of the highly extended Wehrmacht forces, Heinz Guderian set his panzers in motion again. Luckily for Lord Gort and the BEF, the famous panzer commander's superiors thwarted his plan of sending one Panzer Division each to Calais, Boulogne, and Dunkirk. Gort's spoiling attack at Arras caused this OKW alarm, and thus the Viscount's action unexpectedly gave him a small window of opportunity through which to escape: "I wanted the 10th Panzer Division to advance on Dunkirk by way of Hesdin and St. Omer, the 1st Panzer Division to move on Calais and the 2nd on Boulogne. But I had to abandon this plan since the 10th Panzer Division was [...] held back as Panzer Group reserve." (Guderian, 1964, 65).

By this single order, Guderian's commanders ensured that an escape route remained at Gort's disposal. They also accidentally determined that Dunkirk, and not Boulogne or Calais, became the evacuation route now known to history. Guderian understood the opportunity slipping through his fingers and vainly attempted to get his orders changed: "My request that I be allowed to continue in control of all three of my divisions in order quickly to capture the Channel ports was unfortunately refused. As a result the immediate move of the 10th Panzer Division on Dunkirk could not now he carried out. It was with a heavy heart that I changed my plan." (Guderian, 1964, 65).

The Germans accordingly attacked Boulogne and Calais first, though Guderian soon managed to "reinterpret" his orders sufficiently to bring up the 10th Panzer Division to take over the siege of Calais and detach the 1st Panzer Division to move on towards Dunkirk. Gort began his withdrawal to Dunkirk simultaneous with the northward advance of the panzers.

Boulogne fell first, while Calais' British garrison, commanded by Brigadier Claude Nicholson, received direct orders from Churchill to hold out as long as possible "for the honor of the Empire." In essence, Churchill and the War Office deliberately sacrificed Nicholson and his garrison to give Lord Gort enough time to start embarking the BEF.

Despite the magnificent late spring weather, the situation in Calais soon became ghastly, as a junior commander, Airey Neave, recounted: "It was a clear day and I could see the cliffs of Dover. The sad corpses, covered in grey blankets, had begun to stink. Shells burst among the cranes or landed in the sea. A mile out, the destroyer Wessex, struck by Luftwaffe bombs, was sinking. Black smoke from the blazing oil refinery billowed across the harbour and, to the west and south of town, there came the growing noise of rifle and anti-tank fire. The real battle was about to begin." (Evans, 2000, 98).

Events developed thick and fast for the BEF in the final week of May 1940. The Panzers reached Boulogne on May 22nd, and the last 4,368 British defenders from the 20th Guards Brigade evacuated on May 23 and 24, leaving the battered French 21e Infantry Division to surrender on May 25th after the city's Renaissance fortifications collapsed under bombardment by 88mm flak guns. Calais, invested on May 23rd, surrendered on May 26th, leaving 16,500 French and 3,500 British prisoners in German hands.

Bundesarchiv, Bild 101I-383-0337-19
Foto: Böcker | Mai 1940

The ruins of Calais after the siege

Lord Gort's decision to fully disengage the BEF and return it to England had received further impetus on May 23rd. Thanks to the Ultra code-breaking program – an invaluable intelligence tool developed partly with the aid of Alan Turing, the computing genius later tragically hounded into committing suicide by the British government for his homosexuality – the Germans, arrogantly certain their Enigma ciphers remained unbreakable, unwittingly gave the British a detailed look at their communications throughout the war. An Ultra intercept of a signal from OKW leader Walther von Brauchitsch on May 23rd commanded the two German invasion forces – Army Groups A and B – to cooperate in completing the vast encirclement of Allied armies in the north and advance rapidly to crush them. As Frederick W. Winterbotham of the Ultra program later recounted, "Lord Gort later told me it was the first of Brauchitsch's signals which influenced his decision to make for the sea as quickly as possible. He knew that if the BEF were destroyed and captured, there would be nothing to stop a Nazi occupation of Britain […] He was the complete soldier determined to save his men and possibly his country." (Winterbotham, 1974, 60-61).

Gort's choice also resulted from unfortunate experiences dealing with the French. Nominally under the command of the French general Gaston Billotte, who died in a traffic accident at one of the campaign's crucial moments – the BEF leader received almost no communication from his allies. Time and again he discovered that French units assigned to guard the BEF's flank or otherwise deployed in joint operations received new orders and moved without bothering to inform him, leaving his men perilously exposed through no fault of their own. Nonetheless, Gort remained conflicted over his decision and entertained thoughts of possibly supporting the theoretical French offensive until Billotte himself expressed scant belief in its feasibility and remarked candidly, "I am shattered with fatigue. I have nothing that can deal with the panzers." (Gelb, 1989, 84).

Prime Minister Paul Reynaud announced the desperate situation to the French Senate in Paris on the 23rd, producing deep shock. Most government officials of France believed, up to that moment, in an imminent Allied victory. The Secretary of War, Marshal Petain – later head of the collaborationist Vichy government – argued for an armistice. Nevertheless, Weygand remained confident, albeit for reasons that might have been comical if not for the situation's deadly seriousness: "Despite his arduous experiences of the past twenty-four hours, the seventy-three-year-old Generalissimo arrived full of bounce and launched into his analysis of the situation on an evident note of optimism. 'So many mistakes have been made,' he began, 'that they give me confidence. I believe that in future we shall make less.'" (Horne, 2007, 389).

On May 24th, Lord Gort and the BEF gained another precious breathing spell when the German OKW ordered all ground units halted at the Canal Line, with their advance to recommence only on the 26th. German commanders claimed, post-war, that Hitler wished to spare the British and provide them with an opportunity to escape, but other Third Reich records indicate that Hermann Goering, filled with hubris about the Luftwaffe he commanded, caused the fateful delay. The "Reich Marshal" called Hitler on the telephone on May 23rd and, full of bombast, asked him to hold back the panzers so that the British could suffer annihilation at the hands of the German air force. As Goering exulted to his second in command, Erhard Milch, after completing his conversation with Germany's dictator: "'We have done it! The Luftwaffe is to wipe out the British on the beaches. I have managed to talk the Führer round to halting the army. […] The army always wants to act the gentleman. They round up the British as prisoners with as little harm to them as possible. The Führer wants them to be taught a lesson they won't easily forget.'" (Irving, 2002, 103).

Whatever the exact cause, Hitler ordered the panzers and motorized infantry to halt and leave Dunkirk to the Luftwaffe. This left the door wide open for Gort to withdraw the BEF to Dunkirk largely unopposed and commence evacuation. Though he did so without flourish or fanfare, Gort seized his opportunity without hesitation and prepared to begin Operation Dynamo.

Late on May 25th, Lord Gort learned that the French had only a single division available for the "crushing" offensive planned against the Wehrmacht, and this hardened his resolve to march to the coast. That same day, the Luftwaffe struck Dunkirk for the first time, inflicting considerable damage, but the bombing failed to close the port on this initial day of airstrikes.

The British War Secretary, Anthony Eden, grasped the desperate situation faster than Churchill and his colleagues. Gort received a message from Eden at 4:10 a.m. on May 26th instructing him to fall back to the coast without informing the Belgians or French. Gort accordingly issued withdrawal orders to the BEF, meanwhile discussing with his French liaison, Blanchard, the establishment of a new defensive line. Obeying Eden's instructions, he tactfully refrained from mentioning this line existed solely to cover the seaborne evacuation through Dunkirk.

Eden wired a second message to Gort on the afternoon of May 26th repeating much the same message but with greater urgency. Finally, at 6:57 p.m., the Admiralty reached the same conclusion and telegraphed Admiral Ramsay at his Dover headquarters: "Operation Dynamo is to commence. It is imperative for Dynamo to be implemented with the greatest vigor."

However, some problems still remained. Very few men reached Dunkirk by the time the order finally came through due to the difficulties of extricating the BEF from Flanders. Nevertheless, Lord Gort and his commanders worked to build a well-defended line of evacuation for their units over the course of the 26th. British divisions held the western flank, while British and Belgian units held the east and the French 1ere Army held the southern approach near Lille.

Inside this protective cordon, the first 150,000 BEF soldiers and evacuating French units poured northward along every available road towards Dunkirk. Though the BEF's retreat finally started, the Stuka dive-bombers of the Luftwaffe soon detected the troop movements and circled the retreating army like vultures. Diving at high speeds, these aircraft made difficult targets for ground-based anti-aircraft forces, while their lethal effectiveness and nerve-wracking sirens frequently sent those targeted by their attacks into a panic. On at least one occasion on the 26th, however, a Stuka pilot misjudged his dive and crashed into the road surface, killing himself in a fireball while completely missing his target.

Pictures of British soldiers aiming at the Luftwaffe during an air attack

Understanding their situation in the Germans' tightening trap, many of the men falling back on the last Allied port in the north moved swiftly in spite of the Stuka attacks, mortar fire and even direct fire from Wehrmacht squads moving ahead of the main German force. Sgt. Leonard Howard of the Royal Engineers' 210th Field Company described the scene: "We arrived at the outskirts of Dunkirk at 5 o'clock in the afternoon, having walked and run 40 miles in 16 hours. Occasionally, we hadn't been able to move because we were being attacked. Survival was the main object in everyone's mind, but I remember a warrant officer walking down the road [...] Tears were streaming down his face, and he said, 'I never thought I would see the British Army like this.'" (Levine, 1988, 246).

While the men of the BEF scrambled along the roads towards Dunkirk, dodging Stuka raids or wrestling with the emotional blow of a forced retreat, Vice-Admiral Ramsay faced his own set of difficulties. The Dover organizer of Operation Dynamo had no destroyers at his disposal on May 26th for evacuation purposes; aside from a handful of supply ships, his evacuation fleet consisted of 35 ferries and other small passenger vessels and 62 flat-bottomed barges and coastal craft.

Luckily, few men waited at the seaside for rescue on the 26th; most still traversed the northward roads or held positions keeping the evacuation corridor open. Even those few proved difficult to extract, however, due to the shallowness of Dunkirk's coastal waters. Only a fraction of Ramsay's small fleet proved capable of moving in close to the beaches.

At the same time, the Luftwaffe noted the boats despite their small numbers and attacked them with strafing and dive-bombing runs. The ferry "Maid of Orleans" turned back at one point due to heavy air attack, though it returned later. The Germans also established some artillery batteries close enough to threaten the harbor, and shells plowed into the water to send white geysers of foam skyward alongside the Stuka bombs.

A picture of Stuka attacks on Dunkirk during the operation

Equipped with relatively few ships and suffering under constant German harassment, the British evacuated just 646 wounded and 3,748 unwounded men to England on May 26th. The *Rouen*, a French steamship, rescued 420 French wounded late in the day. The ships managed to deliver 12,000 gallons of fresh water for the beleaguered BEF. Still, while all of that may have perhaps been impressive from a civilian standpoint, these numbers represented a pitiful fraction of the more than 300,000 men falling back on Dunkirk in hope of escape. With that, hope waned among the British high command that even their low estimate of 45,000 soldiers rescued would prove feasible.

Ramsay, working hard to make Operation Dynamo a successful reality, appealed for more ships on the evening of the 26th. Fortunately for the Allies, a disconnect existed between middle ranking German officers who wished to prevent the British embarkation entirely and the high command (including Hitler), which seemed determined to hesitate and delay. Heinz Guderian, champing at the bit to reach Dunkirk and cut off any hope of the BEF's retreat, found himself once again thwarted by orders originating with Hitler himself: "On this day [May 26th] we attempted once again to attack towards Dunkirk and to close the ring about that sea fortress. But renewed orders to halt arrived. We were stopped within sight of Dunkirk! We watched the Luftwaffe attack. We also saw the armada of great and little ships by means of which the British were evacuating their forces." (Guderian, 1964, 67-68).

Permission to attack in the direction of Dunkirk arrived later that afternoon, and the panzers moved out in the early hours of May 27th, but the Germans found the going slow both due to the difficult terrain and continued enemy resistance by disorganized but determined French and British soldiers.

Picture of a British trawler helping the evacuation

May 27th proved an important day for Operation Dynamo in several ways. Guderian's panzers began pressing forward again in the predawn darkness, but held up by valiant, largely unsung defenses along minor canals and hedgerows by small French and British units. This day also marked the first full day of official evacuation, the order coming through at 6:57 p.m. the previous evening leaving little time for naval operations. Goering's Luftwaffe would make the most dramatic contribution to the day's events.

The HMS *Mona's Isle,* an armed boarding ship, arrived off Dunkirk harbor at first light, having run a gauntlet of shells from German batteries around Calais. However, 5 sister ships, having rescued most of the men evacuated on the 26th, found the Wehrmacht fusillade too intense and turned back to Dover rather than risk sinking.

Picture of a British gunship at Dunkirk during the evacuation

With the Germans pressing in, Lord Gort recognized the need to establish a strong defensive perimeter to keep the harbor town open. The British and French each chose a commander to hold half of the perimeter, with Lt. General Sir Ronald Adam leading the BEF III Corps and Lt. General Marie Fagalde commanding the French. The two men met in Cassel at the Hotel Sauvage at 7:00 a.m. sharp to finalize their joint defensive plan, and they chose a line of canals to serve as improvised defensive positions, the British holding the perimeter's eastern half (from Nieuport to Berques) and the French the western half (from Berques to Gravelines). The French, uninformed about the evacuation, believed this perimeter served as the base for an eventual counteroffensive.

Meanwhile, Ramsay found himself obliged to find longer routes for the evacuation ships. This proved necessary because "of the sandbars and shallows that made the waters off Dunkirk a graveyard for ships, the shortest run from Dover, covering a distance of thirty-nine miles, skirted part of the French coast and brought vessels within range of German shore batteries on the coast above Calais." (Gelb, 1989, 127).

This primary (but essentially impracticable) route bore the designation Route Z. The secondary routes included a 55-mile variant – Route X – running through partially cleared German minefields sown with 5,000 mines in 33 fields. A time-consuming 87-mile traverse, dubbed Route Y, avoided both batteries and sea mines but exposed ships for a long time to attacks by the Luftwaffe or U-boats. Ramsay sent a Royal Navy Liaison, Captain William Tennant, to coordinate the evacuation from the Dunkirk end.

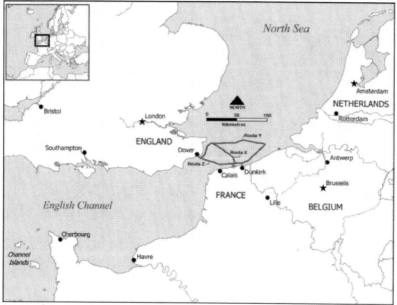

A map of the potential evacuation options

Tennant

As the sun climbed during the middle of the morning on Monday, May 27th, the air over Dunkirk filled with the roar of aircraft engines. Goering unleashed the Luftwaffe on the hated British "Island Apes," while the Royal Air Force (RAF) launched its Hurricane and Spitfire fighters from airbases in southern England in an effort to protect Dunkirk and the ships carrying out Operation Dynamo. In all, the RAF flew 257 sorties on May 27th.

While vicious dogfights erupted over the beaches and further inland, large bomber formations successfully penetrated as far as the port city and unleashed a torrent of ordnance. The German attacks came in three waves, each with a different set of objectives. The first, made up of Heinkel He 111 bombers, struck the docks and harbor facilities themselves, utterly destroying them. 5 miles of quays, 115 acres of docks, and 7 docking basins suffered annihilation during this assault (Dildy, 2010, 36). The second wave, mostly composed of Stukas, attacked the ships near

Dunkirk, sinking several. The French ships *Cote d'Azur* and *Aden*, along with a minesweeper and the British vessel *Worthtown*, suffered fatal bomb damage and sank to the bottom with considerable loss of life. The third wave, composed of nearly outdated Dornier 17Z bombers, destroyed Dunkirk's railyard and set fire to the city's oil refinery. Together, the three raids put Dunkirk's harbor facilities fully out of action before noon.

Back in England, Vice-Admiral Ramsay and his Dover staff spent a hectic day planning and organizing. Ramsay recalled 5 destroyers from Channel patrol duty to participate in the evacuation, a prudent step in the right direction. He continued to add more small ships to his fleet, while Royal Navy personnel scoured the beaches and estuaries along the Channel coast, commandeering any small seaworthy vessels they could find. In some cases, owners volunteered to crew their boats for the evacuation.

Picture of a British fisherman's boat picking up evacuated soldiers

Ramsay abandoned the shortest sea route, Route Z, as too dangerous to be practical. He despatched two minesweepers and a destroyer equipped with minesweeping equipment along the mined Route X, along with a lighthouse tender that placed buoys to mark the hopefully cleared path. A second Route X task force again included a pair of minesweepers, plus the HMS *Calcutta* – an anti-aircraft vessel – and two personnel ships and three destroyers. All of these ships traversed Route X safely, while another flotilla including six ships moved out along Route Y at 11 AM.

Throughout the day, Guderian's and Rommel's panzers continued to press forward on land, and in many areas, they broke through the ill-armed defenders, only to be pushed back by desperate counterattacks. The fighting broke up into hundreds of small actions, consisting mostly of skirmishing on a grand scale between the aggressive German advance and isolated units of British and French soldiers rallied at hundreds of locally defensible points and supported, in many cases, by only a single anti-tank gun or machine gun.

One such skirmish, at Epinette, witnessed a bizarre throwback to previous eras. There, Captain Jack Churchill carried an English yew longbow and a quiver of arrows he privately purchased before leaving England. He commanded a small section of riflemen holding a granary as a defensive position, and when Churchill spotted German infantry edging forward just a hundred feet distant, he "lifted his bow, took aim, and let fly. Hearing the twang, the riflemen blasted away. Churchill had a brief, satisfying glimpse of his arrow hitting home – right in the left side of the center man's chest. The rifles brought down three of the other Germans [...] For perhaps the last time in history, the English bow [...] had again been used in battle." (Lord, 2012, 72).

Though unable to see the overall picture, these men and countless others like them made a tremendous difference in Operation Dynamo's success. The panzer offensive, and its supporting infantry, bogged down in the face of these small but constant actions, and the evacuation corridor remained open. According to a German report from the 27th, "At every position, heavy fighting has developed – especially at every village and indeed in every house... Casualties in personnel and equipment are grievous. The enemy are fighting tenaciously and, to the last man, remain at their posts: if they are shelled out of one position, they shortly reappear in another to continue the fight." (Gelb, 1989, 136).

The Germans, unable to close their trap, dropped thousands of leaflets printed in English and French, urging the Allied troops to surrender and save themselves. The leaflets featured small but fairly accurate maps showing the Dunkirk evacuation point and warned the soldiers that they had little chance of being successfully rescued. Many Allied soldiers defiantly used the leaflets as toilet paper, but more importantly, while the Germans intended this to show the British the hopelessness of their position, the leaflets dropped on May 27th backfired. Many English soldiers, unaware of the evacuation, took new hope and began moving towards Dunkirk, and those holding defensive positions viewed the leaflets as a sign of German desperation, gaining new resolve to continue the battle in order to keep the evacuation corridor open. The Luftwaffe's propaganda effort had only stiffened the ordinary British soldier's morale and told the English where to go in order to escape.

Admittedly, the men needed all the resolve they could find, as the Luftwaffe's raid had destroyed the port's quays and docks entirely. For the moment, Tennant organized evacuations directly from the beaches, using small craft to ferry men out to the waiting personnel ships, hospital ships, and destroyers. 900 men went aboard the *Royal Daffodil*, and another 457 boarded the HMS *Canterbury*, but in all, only a disappointing 7,669 evacuees embarked.

Clouds gathered over Dunkirk on the morning of May 28th, promising a possible respite from Luftwaffe harassment. A single major raid arrived at 10:00 a.m., with semi-obsolete Dornier 17Z bombers supported by the highly effective Me 109E fighters. The German fighters shot down 8 Hurricane, 3 Defiant, and 3 Spitfire fighters at a cost of just two of their own number, but the bombing raid accomplished little. Shortly thereafter, the clouds grew even denser and torrents of rain commenced. This all but prevented effective Luftwaffe incursions over Dunkirk for the whole day, though small groups of Stukas periodically continued efforts to bomb and strafe the beaches.

Making use of this respite, the British worked feverishly at their evacuation, but trouble continued to brew elsewhere for the embattled BEF. Late in the afternoon on May 27th, King Leopold III of Belgium had opened negotiations with Hitler for the surrender of the Belgian Army. These negotiations required considerable time, but they concluded around midnight. In the early morning hours of May 28th, the Belgians – holding back considerable numbers of

German Army Group B in the east – began to surrender en masse in obedience to their King's command.

Leopold III

When the Belgians surrendered to Germany on May 28, it opened a colossal gap in the Allied lines. King Leopold III, showing consistency of character at least if not moral courage, informed the British and French of his planned capitulation only hours prior to the actual surrender, leaving them with practically no time to prepare for its disastrous military consequences. The action earned Leopold III such sobriquets as "King Rat" and "the Traitor King," nicknames he did little to disprove when he evinced more willingness to negotiate with Hitler for restoration of Belgian independence than he had shown in dealing with France and Britain, which sought to defend Belgium's freedom in the first place.

This capitulation, though perhaps unavoidable, made the danger of Operation Dynamo's failure even more drastic. Army Group B now had the potential to close in on the perimeter and add its weight to the advance of Guderian's and Rommel's Army Group A from the south and west. Luckily for the British, the Belgians presented a logistical nightmare for the Wehrmacht even in surrender. Though their defensive line cease to exist, hundreds of thousands of surrendering men now clogged the roads on the Belgian flank, temporarily blocking Army Group B's advance until they could be processed and sent to the rear. For the moment, no additional pressure fell on the evacuation from this quarter, but the whole British command structure gained fresh urgency from the disaster.

King Leopold III actually held out much longer than might be expected from a monarch trying to salvage some remnant of his army from an inevitable defeat, but this did not prevent Lloyd George from excoriating the Belgian leader in terms so hyperbolic that today, many decades distant, they seem almost like dark comedy: "'You can', he wrote in a British Sunday, 'rummage in vain through the black annals of the most reprobate Kings of the earth to find a blacker and more squalid sample of perfidy and poltroonery than that perpetuated by the King of the Belgians.'" (Horne, 2007, 524). Winston Churchill blasted the Belgian monarch's abrupt surrender in a detailed speech summarizing the repercussions: "The surrender of the Belgian Army compelled the British at the shortest notice to cover a flank to the sea more than 30 miles in length. Otherwise all would have been cut off, and all would have shared the fate to which King Leopold had condemned the finest army his country had ever formed. So in doing this and in exposing this flank, as anyone who followed the operations on the map will see, contact was lost between the British and two out of the three corps forming the First French Army." (Churchill, 2013, 174).

The Dunkirk evacuation witnessed an act of singular incompetence on this day as well. Due to his incapacity to understand an order to evacuate his wounded, Major General Henry Martin of the 2nd Anti-Aircraft Brigade instead destroyed some 100 3.7-inch anti-aircraft guns and moved all of his men, both wounded and sound, to the docks for evacuation. Though the thick clouds delayed the consequences of this ill-considered deed, it now meant that only a few batteries of 40mm Bofors guns remained to defy further Luftwaffe attacks.

May 28th also marked the start of a crucial new development whose success turned the tide and ensured the BEF's evacuation. Tennant, faced with dock facilities destroyed by Luftwaffe attacks and beaches from which small vessels extracted only a handful of men at a time, reviewed the physical embarkation points available to him and noticed the two huge breakwaters, frequently termed "moles," guarding Dunkirk's harbor entrance from massive oceanic waves. The breakwaters formed a cordon at the harbor mouth with a gap between them allowing the passage of ships. A wooden walkway 10 feet wide traversed the eastern breakwater's summit, and the concrete breakwater itself protruded 4,200 feet – some four-fifths of a mile – into the ocean. The water alongside it proved deep enough to allow a destroyer to "dock" at the mole in order to take on troops.

Tennant experienced numerous doubts about the breakwater's utility for embarking troops. He feared that the men might panic on narrow wooden walkway, lacking rails and surrounded by heaving expanses of ocean water. He also fretted that the ships might sustain damage or damage the walkway coming alongside, or that that 15 foot height difference between high and low tide would prevent successful embarkations. Nevertheless, Tennant realized this represented his sole remaining opportunity to evacuate the whole BEF in a few days rather than in a period of months he obviously did not possess.

Accordingly, he decided to experiment; using the HMS *Wolfhound* as a floating radio coordinator, he brought the steamer *Queen of the Channel* alongside the east breakwater. The boat rapidly took on 950 soldiers, proving the efficacy of the new embarkation point. The *Queen of the Channel* provided conclusive evidence that Tennant's mole rescue plan worked, but unfortunately, the test proved the gallant vessel's last voyage. "Less than halfway across the Channel a single German plane dropped a stick of bombs just astern of the *Queen*, breaking her back. [...] Seaman George Bartlett even considered briefly whether he should go below for a new pair of shoes he had left in his locker. He wisely thought better of it [...] He and the rest stood quietly on the sloping decks until a rescue ship, the *Dorrien Rose* [...] transferred them all." (Lord, 2012, 98).

Nevertheless, Tennant correctly judged the vessel's sinking moot and the mole's viability confirmed. He signaled Ramsay in Dover to redirect ships from the beaches to the eastern breakwater. Ramsay wisely trusted his subordinate and, without demur, began the complex process of signaling the numerous rescue vessels to switch over to the breakwater. He also added more small ships and further destroyers to the Operation Dynamo fleet.

A picture of soldiers on the mole awaiting rescue

The Allies experienced a busy day inland also. Though storm and rain cloaked the shore and protected Dunkirk from the worst of the Luftwaffe's abilities, this merely diverted the Me 109 fighters, Stuka dive-bombers, and Dornier and Heinkel bombers towards easier targets. Just a few miles to the south, bright sunlight bathed the landscape, revealing ground troops and vehicles clearly to the German pilots. The French soldiers protecting the beachhead took a particularly vicious drubbing yet bravely held their positions while other units continued converging on Dunkirk behind their screen.

Lieutenant General Bernard Montgomery, later famous as the rival of hard-charging American general George S. Patton, found himself in his element. During the early morning hours of May 28th, to plug the gap left by the Belgians, British high command ordered him to shift the 13,000 men of his 3rd Division northward 25 miles. Montgomery accomplished the task with zeal, using 2,000 vehicles to move his soldiers rapidly north to take up their new positions before daybreak on the 28th. Due to the necessary blackout, the drivers followed the white-painted, dimly-illuminated rear axle of the vehicle ahead of them in lieu of utilizing headlights.

Montgomery

The Germans attempted to break through across the Yser River bridge at Nieuport, but Montgomery's men – including many second-line supply personnel who armed themselves with weapons discarded by surrendering Belgians – blocked them in a desperate battle that continued throughout May 28th and most of May 29th.

While these delaying actions held the Wehrmacht at arm's length, the trickle of evacuees grew to a flood. Some 50,000 men, including Lord Gort himself, reached the environs of Dunkirk on the 28th, and Ramsay's Dover operations showed great vigor; 18 destroyers, 12 minesweepers, 18 barges, 7 personnel ships, and 3 hospital carriers worked in rotation to ferry men off the east mole, while beach evacuations continued with a force of 2 tugboats, 26 lifeboats, 18 motor launches, 17 drifters, 5 coasters, 20 other civilian vessels, 19 minesweepers, and 20 destroyers. Many men boarding the destroyers found corned beef sandwiches, cocoa, and fresh water waiting.

A picture of British destroyers dropping evacuated soldiers off at Dover

A picture of evacuated British soldiers

A picture of British soldiers boarding lifeboats

Late in the afternoon, Tennant learned of 25,000 men awaiting rescue on the beach at Bray-Dunes, 7 miles distant. Cutting cards with his subordinates to decide who should go, Tennant dispatched commanders Tom Kerr and Hector Richardson to Bray-Dunes while he and the energetic Canadian officer Campbell Clouston remained to oversee the local evacuation. When they arrived, Richardson and Kerr found the men already standing chest-deep in the sea in dense columns, awaiting rescue. A few hundred men embarked on shallow-draft vessels with great difficulty, but a few hours later, the wind kicked up a heavy surf and made even this slow progress impossible. With that, Richardson decided to send the 25,000 marching to Dunkirk.

Clouston

A picture of men awaiting rescue at Bray-Dunes

Tennant's inspired use of the eastern breakwater for embarkation and the heroic efforts of Ramsay and his staff to gather and coordinate a large flotilla made May 28th a turning point in the evacuation of the BEF. The British, and a handful of French vessels, rescued 17,804 men from Dunkirk on this day.

The next day, however, would show that the Germans still retained the ability to interdict the ships of Operation Dynamo.

A picture of the British vessel *Mona's Queen* after hitting a German mine

Under squally sunset skies on May 28th, three German S-boats left the harbor at Flushing to attack British shipping using the extended Route Y to avoid shore batteries and sea mines. Meaning "Schnellboot" or "fast boat," an S-boat was a 114 foot fast attack craft capable of speeds up 50 miles per hour. Armament of these surprisingly modern-looking advanced attack craft included two torpedo tubes, three 20mm cannons, and one 37mm Flak (anti-aircraft) cannon. The three craft bore the designations S.25, S.30, and S.34.

Their quarry, two British vessels, left Bray-Dunes at 11:00 p.m. on May 28th. Shortly after midnight, the German vessels, accompanied by a U-boat, U.62, intercepted the two ships and two others near Kwinte Buoy at one of the most vulnerable points in Route Y. S.25 and S.34 moved on in search of other prey, at which they fired their torpedoes with no effect. However, S.30, skulking near the buoy under the command of Oberleutnant Zimmerman, launched two of its four torpedoes at the HMS *Wakeful* under Commander Fisher. With the exclamation of "Good God!", Fisher spotted the pale wakes of two torpedoes spearing across the black nighttime waves towards his ship at 12:36 a.m.. The Commander ordered evasive maneuvers, causing one torpedo to miss, but the second blasted into *Wakeful*'s boiler room, detonating the boilers in a massive explosion that tore the destroyer's steel hull into two pieces. 639 of the 640 soldiers aboard died in the explosion or by drowning as the sinking ship sucked them down into the black Channel waters. Most of the officers and crew also died. 56 men, including Commander Fisher, were rescued by other British vessels combing the water for survivors.

The HMS *Grafton*, another destroyer, stayed too long in the area, circling, using searchlights, and launching flares in the vain hope of finding more men alive in the sea. The U-boat U.62 closed in and, at 2:50 a.m., fired torpedoes into the ship's stern, killing 51 men, including Commander Robinson. *Grafton's* ordeal continued as the crew of the HMS *Lydd* fired wildly in the darkness with its machine guns and 4 inch cannon, aiming at any dark shape visible against the waves. A shell struck *Grafton's* bridge and may have been the cause of Commander Robinson's death. The *Lydd* then accidentally rammed a drifter, the *Comfort,* amidships, smashing the small ship in half and sinking it, resulting in four crew deaths and killing 13 survivors from the HMS *Wakeful* aboard the *Comfort.*

In addition to this catastrophe, the British suffered the sinking of two smaller vessels by mines with all hands lost. However, in other respects, the evacuation found its rhythm. Destroyers and countless other ships queued efficiently at the eastern breakwater, while others continued to take men off the beaches with small launches. The mole was proving itself 10 times more efficient than the beach, with a destroyer loading 540 men per hour average at the mole compared to 50 per hour at the beach.

Ramsay's Operation Dynamo worked with surprising efficiency despite the chaos, panic, and occasional indiscipline in Dunkirk. The destroyer HMS *Sabre* under Commander Brian Dean made three round trips between Dover and Dunkirk on May 29th, rescuing 100, 800, and 500 men successively. The convoys achieved greater speed and increased safety when the minesweepers finally declared Route X cleared of mines and Ramsay authorized its use after a safe transit by a trio of destroyers.

Occasional moments lightened the atmosphere of panic and grim determination. One such incident occurred due to personal initiative by three enterprising continental soldiers determined to reach England on their own: "The minesweeper *Killarney* rescued three other adventurers about this time. Heading across the Channel, she encountered a raft made of a door and several wooden planks. Aboard were a French officer, two Belgian soldiers, and six demijohns of wine. All were safely transferred." (Lord, 2012, 129).

While tens of thousands of men waited, panicked, drank themselves into a stupor, or watched the southern horizon anxiously, discarded material piled up steadily around the ruins of Dunkirk. Photographs show huge numbers of round, wide-brimmed British helmets discarded in ditches like the carapaces of oversized, dead beetles. Over 100 prematurely destroyed anti-aircraft guns also dotted the streets and fields surrounding the town, and even greater destruction occurred as the British ruined their vehicles to deny their use to the Germans following the evacuation.

As a result, Dunkirk's environs transformed rapidly into a scrapyard on a scale seldom seen in the early 1940s. One survivor recalled, "New wireless sets … were placed in rows in the fields, twenty in a row, sometimes, while a soldier with a pick-axe proceeded up and down knocking them to pieces. Trucks were dealt with just as drastically. Radiators and engines were smashed with sledgehammers; tyres smashed and sawn after they had been deflated. Vehicles that were near canals were finally pushed in […] all piled on top of each other." (Gelb, 1989, 153).

Bundesarchiv, Bild 146-1973-050-67
Foto: o.Ang. | 1. Juni 1940

Pictures of abandoned material

Cloud cover persisted during the morning hours, mixing with thick black smoke from the continuing oil fires to deter Luftwaffe activity. However, in the early afternoon, the clouds rolled away and the sun blazed out. The British rightly dreaded the return of clear weather, and the Germans soon arrived in force in skies over the crater-pocked harbor. British Spitfires and Hurricanes attempted to fend them off, and shot down a few bombers and escorting fighters, but the experienced Luftwaffe pilots devastated their English counterparts.

Then, at 3:00 p.m., the much-feared Junkers Ju 87 and Ju 88 Stuka dive-bombers arrived. An initial wave of 180 Stukas began the pattern that continued through two more attacks, the third containing 55 aircraft. British anti-aircraft, crippled by loss of their 3.7 inch guns due to their erroneous destruction, only managed to down three of the attacking airplanes. The Germans, by contrast, sank a British destroyer, crippled five more, crippled the French destroyer *Mistral*, and sank 2 minesweepers, 3 trawlers, and 5 personnel ships (Dildy, 2010, 52). Several of these vessels took hundreds of crew and evacuees to the bottom with them.

An anti-aircraft gunner named Leslie Shorrock later provided an account of his turn in the long lines of men crowding down to the beaches in hopes of reaching a boat, and he witnessed the sinking of one of the destroyers: "A vast queue of men, three or four abreast, stretched from the top of the beach down to the sea, a distance of hundreds of yards. It was a very warm sunny day, with a clear blue sky, the sea appeared very calm and immediately in front of me, approximately one quarter of a mile from the beach, a large ship was slowly sinking bow first." (Longden, 2009, 44-45). German bombs also struck the mole, shredding British soldiers moving forward to embark, but they did little damage to the sturdy breakwater itself.

The assault continued until almost 7:00 p.m., when the last Stukas departed. The Luftwaffe had more available, but they chose to use them against British and French soldiers defending against the Wehrmacht's advance on the beleaguered port instead. Around the same time, Ramsay's communications with Tennant failed. Acting on a rumor that the harbor no longer supported ships, Ramsay order the evacuation suspended until he heard from Tennant or received news from his scouts. Evacuations stalled until 5:51 a.m. on May 30th, when HMS *Vanquisher*, a destroyer, moved inshore and discovered the harbor still open, the mole intact, and Tennant waiting impatiently for ships. Ramsay also lost his 8 most modern destroyers to Admiralty orders.

A picture of *Vanquisher* during the operation
Despite the issues, Operation Dynamo successfully rescued 47,310 men on May 29th, and the British and French together continued to hold a semicircular perimeter some 30 miles long. When Montgomery and his men finally received their orders to withdraw and embark at Dunkirk late in the afternoon, the French 256e Infantry Division took over holding Nieuport in place of "Monty's" Englishmen, though Montgomery's men fought near Furnes the following day.

Pictures of evacuated British soldiers at Dover

"Brauchitsch is angry ... The pocket would have been closed at the coast if only our armour had not been held back. The bad weather has grounded the Luftwaffe and we must now stand and watch countless thousands of the enemy get away to England right under our noses." – Franz Halder, May 30

The British received a welcome reprieve on May 30th when the Germans withdrew Guderian's panzer divisions and many other units to the south. Even the fiery Guderian doubted his tanks' ability to operate in the marshes and amid the web of small canals on the approach to Dunkirk. He also wanted time to carry out repairs and resupply as his vehicles prepared to enter their fourth week of action.

More crucially, the Wehrmacht began "Fall Rot" on May 30th, 1940. The initial attack into Belgium and the encircling movement through the Ardennes to the coast, Fall Gelb, had reached its end, and Hitler and the OKW now wished to drive south, conquering France before Mussolini's brave but ill-prepared army pierced the Maginot Line's alpine section.

The British also enjoyed complete immunity from the Luftwaffe on May 30th. A thick cloud deck flowed over Dunkirk at just 3,000 feet, making bombing impossible, and under this layer, dense fog reached from the clouds to the ground. Pierced by sporadic drizzle, the murk cut visibility to 300 feet. Flying in such weather with 1940 aircraft was both futile and suicidal, so the Germans kept the Luftwaffe grounded, refueling, repairing, and rearming while waiting for improved weather.

Despite the easing of enemy pressure, the British still experienced almost unbearable stress.

Huge crowds of men remained on the beaches and breakwater, some of them there for days. After baking in the sun, freezing in the rain or night, bombing, strafing, shelling, hunger, thirst, and unremitting fear, many of the men reached their limit. Sergeant Leonard Howard of the 210th Field Company of the Royal Engineers noted, "I saw British troops shoot other British troops. On one occasion a small boat came in and they piled aboard it to such a degree that it was in danger of capsizing. The chap in charge of this boat decided that unless he took some action it would, so he shot a hanger-on at the back of the boat through the head. [...] During the two days we were on the beach at least a couple of dozen men committed suicide by running into the sea." (Levine, 1988, 301).

The Admiralty returned 5 modern destroyers to Ramsay's control on May 30th, reviving the evacuation effort. Throughout the day, 53,823 soldiers, including 8,616 French *poilus*, successfully made the transit from Dunkirk to Dover aboard Operation Dynamo's ships.

On May 31st, the French confronted their British allies directly about the small numbers of French soldiers being rescued by Operation Dynamo. At a dramatic meeting, Churchill stated that the remaining soldiers would leave Dunkirk "arm in arm" on an "equal basis." Growing emotional, with tears visibly in his eyes, the British Prime Minister stated, 'We are companions in misfortune; there is nothing to be gained from recrimination over our common miseries' (Horne, 2007, 416).

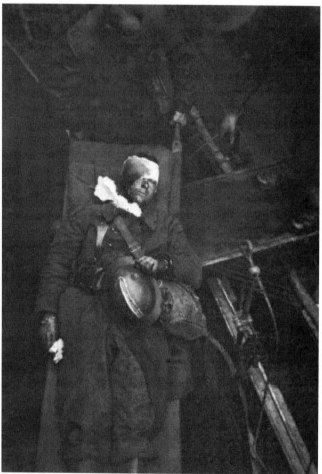

Picture of a wounded French soldier evacuated from Dunkirk

The Germans continued to press the Allied perimeter on May 31st, while the Luftwaffe launched bombing raids against Dunkirk due to good weather. These raids caused less damage than earlier attacks, however. The highly effective Stukas operated elsewhere, supporting the southward sweep of the Wehrmacht at the launch of Fall Rot, and British fighters attempted to stave off these attacks.

The German ground forces, reorganized under Kleist on May 30th following Guderian's and Rommel's departure for the new offensive, attempted to break through the shrinking Allied perimeter. For the first and last time during Operation Dynamo, British bombers attacked German troop columns; dropping 250 pound bombs on the soldiers, vehicles, and pontoon bridges of the Wehrmacht, these sorties broke up the German advance and prevented the major attack Kleist planned that day. However, German artillery general Georg von Kuchler moved his artillery up to the Yser River and opened a deadly bombardment on Dunkirk. The Wehrmacht general also made use of a pair of spotter balloons of World War I vintage; floating at the end of their tethers and guarded by Me 109E fighters, these antiquated airships proved their worth one final time. The men aboard them successfully directed Kuchler's fire with great accuracy, even landing hits on one of the destroyers as it sailed up to the breakwater.

Meanwhile, S-boats harried the escaping ships, on one occasion sinking a transport and drowning 600 of the sailors on board just a few hours from English soil. Moreover, a wind of force 3 on the Beaufort Scale raised sufficient chop in the harbor to capsize some of the small boats bringing men off the beaches, though it could not affect the east breakwater operations.

At this point, the hour for Operation Dynamo to use its "Little Ships" arrived. Celebrated in legend and even children's books, these small vessels operated with their civilian crews still in place. The calming of the sea in the early afternoon heralded the launch of this slightly surreal last-ditch effort to evacuate as many men as possible before the jaws of the German trap fully closed: "[A]t 1300hrs Ramsay ordered his recently organized armada of 'little ships' gathered at Ramsgate to sail across to Dunkirk. This ragtag regatta sailed via Route X at a stately 6 knots, over 100 boats and barges being towed by a miscellany of tugs, yachts, drifters and *schyuts*, some of them in chains up to 12 boats long. Six Tilbury tugs towed 46 lifeboats taken from ocean liners docked in London." (Dildy, 2010, 71).

Pictures of some of the "Little Ships"

Kuchler's balloon-directed artillery met these small craft with a stinging barrage, and a moderate number of civilian captains and crews, terrified by the thunderous fountains of spray kicked up by exploding shells, turned back and fled for the English coast. However, others bravely pushed forward to the beach, some of them suffering injury or death as the shells struck down. The "little ships" helped with the evacuation, though the destroyers and other ships still rescued nearly twice as many men.

Lord Gort, the BEF commander, finally left Dunkirk on May 31st. At 6:00 p.m., he boarded a minesweeper and watched the evacuation from the deck until midnight. He then transferred to a fast anti-submarine boat and left along Route X, leaving Dunkirk burning behind him. The BEF leader reached Dover at 5:47 a.m. sharp on June 1st.

May 31st witnessed the escape of no less than 68,014 men from the BEF and the French Army from Dunkirk to England aboard the wildly assorted vessels of Ramsay's fleet. This achievement made it the single most successful day of Operation Dynamo, but more than 60,000 men still remained behind.

Even before Lord Gort set foot on English soil, the sky over Dunkirk filled with the ominous drone of hundreds of aircraft engines. At 4:15 a.m. on June 1st, the ferocious scream of diving Stukas and the thunder of exploding bombs deafened the British soldiers crowding the mole and the beaches. Goring finally realized, almost too late, that the British were on the verge of escaping his Luftwaffe. Accordingly, the leader of the Third Reich's air forces recalled his Stukas from their Fall Rot support mission and hurled them at Dunkirk again.

The Germans launched five successive raids, totaling 325 Stuka sorties and 160 bomber sorties. A swarming, lethal cloud of 110 Messerschmitt Me 110s and 420 Me 109Es guarded the bombers and dive-bombers, repelling the 267 fighter sorties with Hurricanes and Spitfires the British launched against the raiders. The Germans shot down a number of English fighters while sustaining only very light losses.

Ceaselessly bombed by Stukas, pounded by Kuchler's massive guns with their balloon spotters still in place, the British fleet suffered 17 sinkings, including two destroyers. Some ships detonated or sank at once, killing many hundreds of luckless evacuees on board, but others managed to stay afloat long enough for other vessels to evacuate their passengers and crews. Gerald Ashcroft, a civilian aboard the *Sundowner*, testified to the horrors endured by the BEF and French soldiers as they attempted to escape: "The harbour mole down to the destroyer was jam-packed with soldiers so tightly they couldn't move. There were no British aircraft at all [...] The German air force was having a field day – and the fighters were coming straight along the mole, machine-gunning all the way. The troops just had to stand there. I felt very sorry indeed for them." (Levine, 1988, 312).

Relief from the strafing and bombing came only at 4:00 p.m. when thick clouds mercifully moved in again. The artillery fire continued until dark, however, as German attacks struck the perimeter, crushing it inward towards Dunkirk until the decimated British and French rallied to hold a fresh line of small canals against the determined Wehrmacht. Their doomed courage bought time for a surprising number of evacuations in light of the Luftwaffe attacks and artillery. In all, nearly 65,000 troops were evacuated, including 35,013 Frenchmen.

From this point forward, the British determined all further evacuations must occur only under cover of darkness, ceasing at first light around 3:00 a.m.. Only a few thousand British troops now remained, but tens of thousands of Frenchmen moved towards Dunkirk in hopes of rescue. Despite the increasing odds against success, the British actually managed to rescue a large number of these desperate rearguard soldiers.

Evacuations continued in the early hours of June 2nd, but as light grew, the rescue vessels retired out to sea, leaving just three ships, including the anti-aircraft vessel HMS *Calcutta*, near Dunkirk. The coast presented a hideous sight in the growing light, covered with a vast chaos of wrecked vehicles and shattered boats and ships. Corpses lay everywhere, filling the air with a penetrating, nauseating stench.

True to form, the Luftwaffe returned to bomb and strafe the ruins, attack the clumps of men scattered on the beach, and harass the three ships still in sight. The brave, energetic Canadian leader of the embarkation, Clouston, left by speedboat to Dover, where he ate and took a hot bath and slept for several hours. Then, boarding another motorboat, he left for Dunkirk once again. Tragically for the man who had selflessly risked his life for nearly a week to ensure the escape of hundreds of thousands of other men, a prowling Luftwaffe pilot spotted his motorboat and sank it. Clouston waved away another motorboat coming to his rescue, fearing it would suffer the same fate. He and his boat crew attempted to swim to some floating wreckage, but the German pilot circled back, coming in low over the waves, and machine-gunned the helpless men in the water to death.

The limits of human endurance as much as any other factor determined the winding-down of Operation Dynamo. Utter exhaustion enervated both the ship crews and the French soldiers still holding the battered, diminished defensive perimeter. Nevertheless, Ramsay's fleet made one final effort on the night of June 2-3, seeking the rescue of the remaining French soldiers. So many ships arrived, in fact, that collisions sank three in the harbor. Churchill had done his best to live up to his promise to the French.

The last ships left close to dawn on June 3rd. By then, the last, desperate effort to save French soldiers extracted an additional 46,792 men from the ruins of Dunkirk. This Herculean final night disproves later French claims of abandonment since only 6 BEF soldiers remained to be embarked alongside tens of thousands of their Gallic comrades in arms.

Finally, with the sea mostly empty of ships, General Harold Alexander sailed along the beaches, the mole, and the wrecked quays, calling out for stragglers through a megaphone. With daylight approaching and only silence answering him from the shore, Alexander finally gave the order to his crew to return to England along Route X, the final retiring ship of Operation Dynamo.

Just a few hours later, a group of several thousand French stragglers arrived on the now-abandoned eastern breakwater, too late to reach England. These men, and the other soldiers of the hard-fighting French rearguard – some 40,000 troops in all – surrendered to the Germans by 9:15 a.m. In the BEF's absence, no reason existed to die at their posts.

The British and French soldiers expected to be met with disdain in England, but for the most part they received a hero's welcome. As Captain Humphrey Bredin of the Royal Ulster Rifles recalled, "We arrived at Dover, and the only thing I remember after that was waking up in a train at a place called Headcorn in Kent where the women almost gave us a party. They invaded the train with tea, coffee and buns. It was as if we were a victorious army, and it rather embarrassed us. We felt, damn it, we'd run away." (Levine, 1988, 421).

Across the Channel, Goering continued to believe his own propaganda and ascribed a great victory to the Luftwaffe. His far more competent, realistic second in command, Erhard Milch, flew to Dunkirk for a personal inspection on June 5th. When he returned to Luftwaffe headquarters the same day, he deflated Goering's grandiose self-congratulation with an incisively accurate report: "The British army? I saw perhaps twenty or thirty corpses. The rest of the British army has got clean away to the other side. They have left their equipment and escaped [...] The fact remains that they have succeeded in bringing out practically the whole of their army, and that is an achievement which it would be hard to beat." (Irving, 2002, 105).

Milch urged an immediate invasion of southern England using Fallschirmjager paratroopers. These men, he argued, could seize airfields from which the Luftwaffe could operate against the rest of England while airlifting in additional soldiers. Goering, humbled for once by his subordinate's clear-sighted rationality, agreed, but he sheepishly admitted he had only a single paratroop division at his disposal thanks to insufficient resources. Milch seethed and predicted disaster, but he could do nothing. Another opportunity for the Germans had fallen victim to the startlingly haphazard, poorly-planned resource allocation lurking behind the superbly dangerous facade of the Third Reich military machine.

One enduring mystery of Operation Dynamo is whether Adolf Hitler forestalled the panzers from closing in and finishing off the trapped British as a deliberately conciliatory gesture towards England. Without his order to halt the panzers, leaving interdiction of the rescue chiefly in the hands of the Luftwaffe – which experienced huge difficulties with the Royal Air Force – the BEF's evacuation would have proven objectively impossible. Some German commanders claimed after the war that Hitler did indeed permit the British to escape, and the Ultra code-breaker Frederick Winterbotham believed this to be the case, an assertion buttressed by his own pre-war encounter with Hitler: "We now know that soon after Hitler ordered his tanks to stop closing in, he addressed his military staffs in France. According to one German general who was present, Hitler told them exactly what he had told me in 1934: it was necessary that the great civilization Britain had brought to the world should continue to exist [...] He went on to say that his aim was to make peace with Britain." (Winterbotham, 1974, 62).

Contrary evidence also exists, indicating that Hermann Goering's pride drove him to ask Hitler to hold back the panzers so that the Luftwaffe could win the glory. Goering exerted strong influence over Hitler, even managing to singlehandedly dissuade the Fuhrer from invading Sweden due to Goering's sentimental attachment to the nation on behalf of his Swedish wife.

Writing decades later, General Franz Halder, a staff officer for the OKW, noted, "During the following days... it became known that Hitler's decision was mainly influenced by Goering. To the dictator the rapid movement of the Army, whose risks and prospects of success he did not understand because of his lack of military schooling, became almost sinister. He was constantly oppressed by a feeling of anxiety that a reversal loomed..."

Halder

Historian Brian Bond also refuted any suggestion Hitler was feeling merciful: "Few historians now accept the view that Hitler's behaviour was influenced by the desire to let the British off lightly in hope that they would then accept a compromise peace. True, in his political testament dated 26 February 1945 Hitler lamented that Churchill was "quite unable to appreciate the sporting spirit" in which he had refrained from annihilating [the British Expeditionary Force, or BEF] at Dunkirk, but this hardly squares with the contemporary record. Directive No. 13, issued by the Supreme Headquarters on 24 May called specifically for the annihilation of the French, English and Belgian forces in the pocket, while the Luftwaffe was ordered to prevent the escape of the English forces across the channel."

Neither story is inherently implausible, and each has sufficient documentary support to make it possible yet not enough to offer a conclusive answer. In the actual rough-and-tumble of history, however, Hitler's precise motive for taking actions that led deliberately or accidentally to the escape of the BEF remain immaterial; either way, the Fuhrer made his first grave mistake of the war, though it proved by no means his last. The BEF's evacuation bolstered the British sufficiently for them to remain in the war, to the Third Reich's bitter cost.

While the Operation Dynamo evacuation through Dunkirk stands as an undisputed miracle and success in the annals of warfare, it represented salvation for a large yet limited number of the defeated Allied soldiers in France. Millions of French soldiers surrendered in the days prior to the armistice signed on June 17th, 1940. Additionally, tens of thousands of British servicemen and women remained in France, cut off, wounded or sick in a hospital, or otherwise unable to make the rendezvous at Dunkirk in time. The Germans captured approximately 40,000 British soldiers following the Dunkirk evacuation, while an additional 160,000 Allied troops contrived to escape from other ports.

A picture of British prisoners at Dunkirk

Many units simply found themselves in a position where retreat took them away from Dunkirk, such as the entire 51st Highland Regiment. The 51st Highlanders fought their way to the coastal town of St. Valery, where cliffs surrounded much of the harbor. The Royal Navy attempted to send ships to their rescue on the night of June 10th, but heavy sea fog prevented the operation. One trawler reached the port but was hit by German artillery after loading a large number of

Highlanders. The survivors found themselves forced to swim back to shore and surrender to the Germans.

The French soldiers fighting alongside the Highlanders surrendered on June 11th, 1940, and the British knew they could not fight on without their allies. Many officers put on their dress uniforms to show their British pride, while the ordinary soldiers destroyed equipment to prevent it from falling into German hands, similar to what happened at Dunkirk. The troops pushed numbers of trucks over St. Valery's cliffs to smash on the rocks below, broke many of their rifles and machine-guns, and then surrendered on June 12th.

The Germans treated many of the British with surprising harshness, while extending gentlemanly consideration to their French prisoners. Though the English captives had no way to know why the Germans manhandled them, beat them, or gave them small rations of barely-edible gruel while feeding their French captives meat and potato stew and fresh vegetables from the markets, this paradoxical behavior stemmed from a lethal ideological hatred poisoning the minds of the Wehrmacht's soldiery. According to Hitler's propaganda, Britain and the United States – each extending full rights to Jews as to other citizens – represented pawns of a worldwide Jewish conspiracy of nearly godlike power and Mephistophelian malevolence. Accordingly, the German soldiers "punished" the recently mobilized British farmhands and unwitting English officers who fell into their hands for the crime of supporting "international Jewry." All the while, the British knew nothing of the bizarre reason for the abuse and humiliation they suffered.

In fact, two small massacres even took place at the hands of certain elements of the SS Totenkopf Division. At the Le Paradis massacre, Hauptsturmfuhrer Fritz Knoechlein executed 99 soldiers of the 2nd Royal Norfolk Regiment who surrendered after a brisk firefight. Two of his victims lived to testify later: "Slowly the cries of the wounded and the noise of gunfire died down as the SS finished their deadly labours. When the attack was finally over just two men were alive. Privates Bert Pooley and Bill O'Callaghan had somehow survived, despite both being shot and having been checked over by the SS men. When night fell the two men were finally able to escape the scene." (Longden, 2009, 65).

While the other Germans occasionally proved willing to "rough up" their prisoners or deny them proper food at times, Knoechlein's actions caused outrage among those Wehrmacht commanders who learned of it, and even among some other SS officers in the Totenkopf division. Knoechlein's actions, however, met with tacit approval from SS Gruppenfuhrer Wolff, one of Himmler's right-hand men, who examined the massacre site but made no mention of the dead British soldiers. "Knoechlein was not liked by his fellow officers, who wanted to challenge him to a duel after this exhibition, which caused a considerable stir. From Hoeppner's [XVI Corps commander] staff office came demands for an inquiry. […] Eicke delayed the investigation. […] There was no court-martial for Fritz Knoechlein." (Stein, 1966, 77).

Another massacre at Wormhoudt, carried out by SS Leibstandarte "Adolf Hitler" Division soldiers, possibly under Wilhelm Mohnke, claimed 80 lives and left 15 survivors later receiving medical treatment from regular Wehrmacht medics. However, the vast majority of British soldiers taken prisoner found themselves marched to prisoner of war camps and used as laborers on farms, in factories, or in mines until their liberation.

While most of the 51st Highlanders and some 40,000 of their compatriots fell into German hands, four times as many British soldiers from other units – over 160,000 – evacuated through ports other than Dunkirk. A few thousand even contrived to escape on their own, with a few stealing small boats or receiving a "ride" from friendly French fishermen, or, in many more cases, completing the perilous crossing of the Pyrenees, traversing semi-hostile Spain, and reaching the British base at Gibraltar. From Gibraltar, most took ship to England to resume their military service, while the British military sent others directly to the new North African theater.

In the weeks following Dunkirk, small British detachments moved south and west across the French countryside, attempting to avoid detection and capture as they sought the safety of other ports. Some units managed to board trains and move across the nation towards rescue with considerable speed, though the Luftwaffe naturally targeted any rail assets it believed to be transporting soldiers.

St. Nazaire, a Breton port at the Loire River estuary, provided an exit point for many British and some French escapees from the military disaster. Other major "ports of escape" included Cherbourg, La Havre, Brest, and La Pallice. Even some smaller towns witnessed successful evacuations; just a few days after St. Valery fell, 3,000 men – 1,000 French and 2,000 English – managed to embark on a single ship at the nearby town of Veules-les-Roses, which the Germans neglected to secure until after their withdrawal. Luftwaffe air attacks failed to hit the ship, which reached Britain safely.

On June 15-16, some 30,000 men escaped from Cherbourg, the last of them withdrawing just ahead of the triumphant Germans in a miniature repetition of the Dunkirk evacuation. The French government under Marshal Petain – soon to prove himself an authoritarian after the Nazis' own hearts – surrendered on June 17th, but many French soldiers bravely continued to help the British escape, and some also fled to England to continue the struggle in the future. At Brest, 28,000 men escaped by June 19th, assisted notably by the French. Disobeying the orders of their own government and high command, the French troops formed two defensive lines and held off the Germans until the British and other Allied escapees embarked. When the Luftwaffe mined the harbor ahead of the ships, French minesweeper crews risked their lives to clear the passages rapidly. 57,000 other men, including British, French, Belgian, Dutch, Polish, and Czechoslovakian soldiers, evacuated through St. Nazaire.

Thousands of men remained in France, neither rescued by the ships nor taken captive by the Germans. These British soldiers, known as "evaders," blended in with the French, often disguising themselves as itinerant farm laborers. Frequently aided by ordinary French citizens, these men spent weeks and sometimes months moving through the countryside, looking for a way to effect an escape from France's shores alone or in tiny groups. A surprising number succeeded, reaching Gibraltar, sailing directly to North Africa and joining the British forces there, or, in a few cases, effecting escapes from the western or even northern ports. Guy Lowden, a British army captain, showed a measure of humor in a letter he wrote to his wife about the evaders' adventures in occupied France: "I think we've done all the traditional things – hidden in barns (all escapers do this, right through history); lain and trembled while the enemy rummaged about the sheds where we lay, miraculously missing the one place where we were [...] At one place there was even a pretty girl who brought us food [...] with great hunks of fresh white bread in a basket. Yes, I think all conventions have been honoured." (Longden, 2009, 157).

These escapees remain nearly forgotten by history in the aftermath of the rightly celebrated Dunkirk success, but they also form an important chapter in the evacuation. Some of the men, paradoxically, soon found themselves in France again, and then evacuated afresh, due to a doomed, quixotic gesture by the British Prime Minister hoping to shore up the disintegrating fighting spirit of the French Army and government: "Churchill made the fine moral but reckless military decision to send more troops to France [...] In June, two ill-equipped divisions were shipped to join the residual British forces on the Continent. After the armistice [...] it proved possible to evacuate almost 200,000 men from the north-western French ports to England [...] Churchill was fortunate thus to be spared the consequences of a folly." (Hastings, 2011, 76).

The British dubbed their collective evacuation efforts after Dunkirk's Operation Dynamo "Operation Ariel." Initially hampered by thick fog, the evacuation later proved feasible and, though not on as grand a scale as Dynamo, must be counted as another major success given that it rescued far more men than it left behind.

Nevertheless, despite the outcome at Dunkirk, Hitler and his generals still had reason to be pleased. The Germans now held 1,200,000 prisoners, large areas of northern France, all of Belgium and Low Countries, and could view the southern two-thirds of France as a juicy fruit ripe and ready to fall into their hands. With that, the OKW issued the order to move south from the Somme and complete the conquest of France on May 31st, 1940. The Germans mustered 143 divisions against the 60 divisions remaining to the French following the northern military catastrophe. The Germans gave this portion of their invasion the name "Fall Rot," or "Case Red" – the follow up to Fall Gelb, or "Case Yellow," the bold plan to take the north by encirclement.

Rommel led the drive south on June 5th. Other than a determined resistance from a small group of Colonial infantry holding Hengest, the Germans initially encountered only weak Allied resistance and pushed forward strongly, striking at any resistance with artillery or direct fire from the deadly Sturmgeschutz (StuG) III self-propelled guns, which proved excellent tank hunters later in the war.

On June 7th, Maxime Weygand prepared the French 10ere Army for combat against the advancing German forces. General Evans, a British commander under Weygand's command, still mustered 78 tanks and planned to use these in a concentrated flank attack on the Wehrmacht panzers when they attempted encirclement of the 10ere Army. Weygand, having learned nothing from Hannut and Stonne, ordered the furious Evans to spread his tanks out to provide static support for the infantry. He thus squandered one of the Allies' last chances to exact a high price from the Wehrmacht for their victory and sentenced the British tank crews to isolated, pointless death or capture.

Over the course of the next few days, the Germans continued to drive south across the open country between the Somme and the Seine. Isolated pockets of resistance, such as one at the small harbor of St. Valery en Caux, slowed their attack somewhat. For the most part, however, the Wehrmacht swept up the scattered French and British units they encountered as prisoners, sometimes immediately, at other times after a brief firefight, depending on the individual level of defiance found among the men of a particular unit.

On June 14, 1940, the Germans entered Paris without a fight. In fact, they arrived in the manner of a swarm of heavily-armed tourists, carrying cameras and taking each others' photographs while standing in front of various famous landmarks. The French government, of course, had declared loudly it would lead a memorable defense of the capital, only to flee four days before the first panzer-dust appeared on the northern horizon. The Germans, following them south, found enormous depots of unused weapons and ammunition, whole warehouses filled with tanks that never saw combat, and other mountains of supplies, many of which they appropriated for their own use.

A picture of German soldiers at the Arc de Triomphe

The capture failed to slow the advance. On June 15th, Guderian's troops took Langres 50 miles to the south, scooping up 3,000 prisoners as they did so. Ironically, the last acts of French defiance came from men holding the Maginot Line who refused to surrender until several days after the rest of the nation, as well as cadets at the Saumur cavalry school. 560 cadets under Colonel Daniel Michon met 10,000 advancing German troops on the Loire bridges, using their training weapons – including 10 25mm A/T guns, several machine-guns, and a handful of mortars – to defy Hitler's troops for a remarkable two-day period.

Shortly before the combat began, Colonel Michon gathered his unlikely band of young cadets and trainers in the school auditorium for a speech: "'Gentlemen, for the school it is a mission of sacrifice. France is depending on you.' One pupil, Jean-Louis Dunand, who had abandoned architectural studies in Paris to become a cadet, wrote exultantly to his parents: 'I am so impatient to be in the fight, as are all my comrades here. Times a hundred times more painful await me, but I am prepared to meet them with a smile.'" (Hastings, 2011, 75).

The brave cadets continued to fight for nearly 48 hours, until the Germans – after repeated calls for them to surrender and spare themselves – encircled the school and subjected it to withering fire from all directions. 79 cadets died and 48 suffered wounds, but they killed or wounded some 200-300 Germans. Michon led part of the student body out at night, hoping to join up with other French units to continue the struggle, while 218 cadets surrendered. In a chivalric gesture, General Kurt Feldt released all his prisoners, permitting them to return to their homes rather than interning them in POW camps.

Paul Reynaud resigned as Prime Minister of France on June 15th, appointing the "Lion of Verdun," the distinguished-looking, white-mustached Marshal Philippe Petain in his stead. Petain, 84 years old and later head of the Vichy government, appeared at this time to show frailty and only a dim grasp of his surroundings most of the time, though he was to live to 95 despite being described as "a skeleton with a chill." His main concern, he said, centered on ending the suffering of the French soldier by any means possible.

Petain signed an armistice with Hitler on June 22nd, 1940. This armistice gave the Germans northern France but left approximately 40% of French territory unoccupied and subsequently held by a fascist collaborationist government based (from July 1st onward) at Vichy. Benito Mussolini, whose Italian invasion forces were shot to ribbons by the men of the Alpine Maginot Line despite being outnumbered 10 to 1, grudgingly signed a separate peace on June 24th under massive pressure from a contemptuous Hitler. This treaty gave Mussolini a few small French towns rather than his fantasy of an Italian empire encompassing southern France.

The German Fuhrer savored his triumph with an impromptu but dramatic moment that would not be out of place in a Richard Wagner opera: "Hitler proclaimed the end of the war in the west and the 'most glorious victory of all time'. He ordered bells to be rung in the Reich for a week [...] As the moment for the official conclusion of hostilities drew near, Hitler, sitting at the wooden table in his field headquarters, ordered the lights put out and the windows opened in order to hear, in the darkness, the trumpeter outside mark the historic moment." (Kershaw, 2008, 480).

The French right wing greeted their conquest by the Germans with undisguised jubilation, as though the mauling of the French army and dissection of the country represented a mighty victory rather than a stunning defeat. The mask of doddering harmlessness soon fell from Petain; though he doubtlessly suffered from the mental effects of old age, he evinced an authoritarian, reactionary streak highly attuned to many of the Nazis' own beliefs. Openly casting contempt on the ideas of equality and freedom, Petain used his power to make himself an effective dictator. His political foes found themselves imprisoned, as did those who spoke too freely and thus committed the "felony of opinion." Though later used as the scapegoat for a wide group of right wing Frenchmen, Petain appears on the historical stage as a willing ally of Hitler and convinced, ruthless enemy of democracy following the conquest of France.

Some recent historians question whether the Third Reich intended to use Blitzkrieg tactics against France. According to the revisionist theories of these historians, the Wehrmacht anticipated a long, drawn-out war of attrition and the lightning-fast victory over the French resulted from serendipitous good fortune and French military weakness rather than deliberate German planning.

Though such questions cannot find a wholly conclusive answer now that all of the officers involved in the decision-making process are long dead, the course of the operations themselves offer significant clues to the actual German strategic intent. Taken with a final bit of objective evidence offered by Third Reich armament industry production figures, a fairly firm verdict becomes possible in this matter.

German production of weapons systems and supply of ammunition and fuel sufficed for a short war, not for a prolonged war of attrition. Hitler's delay in moving against the Soviet Union until well into 1941 highlights this fact; even the lightning campaign in France used enough resources to prompt a period of retrenchment and resupply before the next military adventure commenced. The Germans also used the same tactics and strategy as in Poland, a clear and well-documented instance of Blitzkrieg. Large-scale movements rather than slow, methodical advances provided the rule, while the Luftwaffe's Stuka dive-bombers furnished a lethal sledgehammer to break most local resistance and plunge onward deeper into enemy territory.

If anything, the OKW became frightened of their own success at one point and nearly aborted the Blitzkrieg at the time of Heinz Guderian's brief resignation. The fact that they nearly abandoned Blitzkrieg does not mean their original intention did not involve such a strategy, however. Gerd von Rundstedt's diplomatic solution and Guderian's creative use of insubordination restarted the juggernaut of Blitzkrieg and won an incredible victory for the Third Reich in just slightly more than a month.

Two other factors probably underlay the success of the Wehrmacht's "Lightning War" during the 1940 invasion of France. One involved the considerable incompetence of the French high command, especially their refusal to use their superior tanks in large, concentrated, active formations. This failed mentality was the product of ossified military thought coming from an older generation still fighting World War I in their own minds.

The other issue, the French's unwillingness to engage in another bloodbath even if it offered a chance of victory, sprang from a sort of national shock and mourning still remaining after World War I. The previous war decimated an entire generation of young Frenchmen, killing up to 38% of certain age groups. Though France's soldiers often fought with outstanding valor in 1940, the French remained collectively war-weary from the horrors of World War I. Soldiers, generals, politicians, and ordinary people vividly recalled those lying in their hundreds of thousands in the graveyards of northern France and Belgium, and preferred a relatively mild defeat to burying another generation of young men.

The Battle of Britain

As France formally surrendered, Goering's Luftwaffe moved west, deploying to newly acquired bases on the French, Belgian and Dutch coasts. To the north, they also had planes available in German occupied Norway. Hitler now trained his sights on Britain, turning his attention to destroying the RAF as a pre-requisite for the invasion of Britain. Given how quickly the Nazis had experienced success during the war thus far, perhaps the Luftwaffe's notorious leader, Hermann Goering, was not being entirely unrealistic in 1940 when he boasted, "My Luftwaffe is invincible...And so now we turn to England. How long will this one last - two, three weeks?"

Most of the British Army had been pulled off the beaches of Dunkirk by the Royal Navy at the end of May, but they left nearly all of their tanks and artillery behind. The Navy had also lost six destroyers in the process. Churchill, who had been Prime Minister only since May 10th, had insisted on a heavy RAF commitment to the French campaign, during which at least 900 planes had been lost, along with many pilots.

For Hitler, the strategic situation seemed rosy. In a series of invasions and blitzkrieg campaigns, he had effectively conquered a huge swath of European real estate, including Austria, Czechoslovakia, Poland, Norway, Denmark, Belgium, Holland and Luxembourg. His Italian allies had holdings in North and East Africa, as well as Albania. Russia had - for now - been neutralized by means of the Ribbentrop Pact. Moreover, Stalin had believed he had several years to build up his army before Germany would invade, figuring it would at least take the Germans that long to conquer France and Britain, so when France fell quickly in 1940, he worried he had miscalculated and sent his ambassador to Berlin to stall for time. Thus, in the summer of 1940, only Britain seemed to stand in defiance of Hitler. Logic suggested that she should be dealt with before Germany turned east.

From the beginning, Britain refused to play along with Hitler's script. He had expected a peace treaty with the British once France had been defeated, and but for Churchill he might have got it. Now that the stubborn bulldog was ensconced in Downing Street though, it was clear that however "generous" Hitler's peace terms might be, the British Government was having none of it. As Churchill would most famously put it after Hitler's invasion of the Soviet Union in 1941, "If Hitler invaded Hell, I would at least make a favourable reference to the Devil in the House of Commons."

If Britain were to be taken out of the strategic picture, it had to be by military means. Historically, that had always proven easier said than done. The island nation had never been an easy nut to crack: Caesar had been turned back once, as was the Spanish Armada and Napoleon. The advantages of the English Channel were obvious, but that's not to say it was impossible. The Romans had ruled Britain for 400 years, and William the Conqueror had invaded in 1066. The French intervened in the Baron's War in 1216, slipping an army ashore unopposed; and in 1688 William of Orange invaded and successfully marched on London. Surely Hitler would have felt it was a proposition well within the capabilities of the Third Reich, which was already master of most of Europe.

There's no doubt that the Wehrmacht, if safely deposited and supplied on British shores, could have done the job. Not only was the British army battered and bruised, but it lacked the tactical competence to beat the German army at this stage in the war. In the summer of 1940, however, there was no way that the Kriegsmarine could secure even temporary control of the English Channel from the Royal Navy, then the largest and most proficient in the world. Airborne troops offered no solution - they were available only in small numbers and lacked heavy equipment. They could support an invasion by grabbing key sites and holding them long enough for the tanks to arrive, but that was all. It had to be a sea-borne invasion.

Naturally, the German war leaders believed the solution to the problem of the Royal Navy would lie in the Luftwaffe. Experience during the Norwegian campaign and the Dunkirk evacuation had shown that surface ships were extremely vulnerable to pinpoint tactical bombing, something the Luftwaffe excelled at. If Germany could secure air supremacy over the Channel and southern England, then its aircraft might be able to protect German troop and supply convoys from the ravages of the Royal Navy. To do that though, they would have to first deal with the RAF.

By 1940, Britain's integrated air defense system was the most sophisticated in the world. At its sharp end were the squadrons of Fighter Command, most equipped with modern aircraft that were technically on par with anything the Luftwaffe could field. Just as importantly, the RAF was supported by a radar network and an ingenious command system designed to provide flexible and rapid response. Barrage balloons and numerous anti-aircraft batteries completed the picture.

Against this array, the Germans had a large and highly experienced air-force with state of the art equipment. In the blitzkrieg campaigns across Europe, it had given a decisive edge to her ground forces, providing tactical firepower and - importantly - shock. It had seemed as though the Luftwaffe was everywhere, likely to pounce from the skies at any moment, accompanied by the eery siren shriek of the Stuka dive-bombers. In doing so, it had swept a succession of well-equipped and well-trained air forces before it, including the RAF. Led by the supremely confident Goering, it seemed entirely plausible that the Luftwaffe would have little difficulty in clearing the skies to facilitate an invasion of Britain. On both sides of the Channel, many had a foreboding sense of awful inevitability about a German strategic advance. Newsreels of Heinkels over Rotterdam or Stukas over northern France had been stamped on the minds of millions of people across the globe. The Luftwaffe had become a latter-day bogeyman, the essential manifestation of the blitzkrieg.

For these reasons - and nobody was more prone to swallowing this kind of mythology than Hitler - Goering had convinced his Fuhrer that the Luftwaffe was up to the task[66]. There was certainly plenty of trepidation within the British high command about the prospect of a struggle with the Luftwaffe. Experience to date had not been positive. However, for a host of reasons, this campaign would be different. To begin with, Hitler was about to employ an essentially tactical air force in a strategic role.

For both sides, the air campaign which was about to open would represent a new aspect of modern warfare. The British had planned carefully for such an assault, but their resources were stretched and their morale subdued. The Germans began the campaign with a successful track record and an abundance of confidence but a less well developed understanding of strategic aerial warfare. The stakes were desperately high: for Britain, this seemed to be about nothing less than survival. For Germany, the failure to defeat Britain would leave a huge imperial power gathering strength behind its back as it inevitably turned east toward Russia. The stage was set for a unique and decisive struggle in the air.

Both the RAF and Luftwaffe had front line fighters which represented the cutting edge of aviation design for this era. Although much has been written on the competing merits of the three main types involved, technically there really was not that much to distinguish between them.

---

[66] It would not be the last time that Goering over-estimated the Luftwaffe capabilities: Stalingrad is another case in point.

The Supermarine Spitfire

The beautiful British Spitfire, with its characteristic elliptical wings, became a legendary fighter and would see active service throughout the war. It was a fast aircraft, developed directly from the Schneider Cup winning Supermarine racing planes of the 1930's. By all accounts it was a joy to fly. In most circumstances it was a good match for the German Messerschmidt 109 (Me 109), although in its battery of eight machine guns it lacked the punch of the 109's mixed battery, which included 20mm cannon. The British considered the Spitfire to be their best fighter. If this was true at all it was a very close judgement, but it was the basis for the ambition to use Spitfires mostly against German fighters, leaving the bombers to the slower Hurricanes. Lack of numbers and the desperate nature of the fighting were to make this distinction almost irrelevant, as both types were thrown into the battle wherever they were needed. The more numerous Hurricanes were slightly slower but had a better turning radius at most altitudes. They too carried eight machine guns and unlike the stressed metal Spitfires, were built with the older wood and canvas technology. This was surprisingly rugged and more easily repaired. The Me 109 sat somewhere between the two in terms of speed and turn radii. The truth was that these single seat superiority fighters were very closely matched. Other factors, such as numbers, tactical situation and pilot skill would prove much more important in the battle.

Members of the Luftwaffe sitting in front of a Messerschmidt Bf 109

The Luftwaffe also employed Messerschmidt 110's (Me 110) as heavy fighters for some of the campaign. This twin-seater had a lot more range but was totally outclassed by the Spitfires and Hurricanes, prompting a switch in tactics as the battle unfolded. Also fielded during the battle were Italian CR42 biplanes (which were also outclassed), and the oddly conceived British Defiant, a two seater fighter design with its main armament in a dorsal turret. The Defiants were quickly relegated to a night fighter role, and the Italian fighters were badly roughed up on the few occasions in which they tangled with the RAF.

In terms of bombers, the Luftwaffe employed three twin-engined medium types, as well as the famous Junkers 87 "Stuka" dive bomber. The medium bombers (by later war standards these would be termed light bombers) were the numerous Heinkel III, the Dornier 17 and the Junkers 88. All three were relatively lightly armed, with three or four defensive machine guns. All featured a glazed nose, which gave excellent visibility and placed most of the crew in the same cockpit but also created a sense of vulnerability, particularly to head-on attack. In tight formations they could provide a modicum of collective protection against fighters, but an escort was required for effective defense against significant numbers of Spitfires or Hurricanes. Although payloads were not high by late war standards[67], these aircraft were deployed in large numbers and virtually any city in England or Scotland was within their range. Unfortunately for their crews, this was not the case for the Me 109 escorts so important for their survival. The limited number of Italian bombers used during the campaign (Fiat BR 20's) were of similar characteristics - and much closer to German specification than the outdated Italian fighters.

---

[67] A Heinkel III could carry about 5,000lb of bombs; an RAF Lancaster, 14,000lb.

The Stukas, slower machines with hardly any defensive firepower, were even more vulnerable, but if they could be protected they were a highly accurate tactical weapon system capable of hitting high value individual targets like radar sites. Me 110's could also be used in this role.

Tactically, when the battle opened the Luftwaffe was much more experienced and more sophisticated than the RAF. Their fighters operated on the basis of pairs, as opposed to the RAF "finger three" formation, which was less flexible but easier to manage for rookie pilots. The Luftwaffe "fighting turn" was superior to its RAF equivalent, again relying on higher pilot competence. These systems would evolve as the campaign unfurled, with (for example) Luftwaffe fighters hampered by orders to stick closely to the bombers and the RAF experimenting with terrifying head on attacks to break up enemy formations.

In terms of raw numbers, Germany clearly had the edge as the campaign opened. In total, she had some 1000 serviceable medium bombers, 300 dive bombers, 250 heavy fighters and 850 of the vital single seater fighters available for operations on July 10. By contrast, Britain had roughly 600 operational Spitfires and Hurricanes, plus 20 of the near-useless Defiants. Italy would join the fray in September, with approximately 20 bombers and 50 obsolete fighters. Britain also had her allies, with hundreds of volunteer pilots serving in the RAF from the Commonwealth, the United States, and Hitler's conquered territories in eastern Europe. Indeed, it would be a Polish squadron which would clock up the most RAF kills during the Battle of Britain[68]. These figures are important, because at its inception the Battle of Britain was attritional. The Luftwaffe's initial goal was to incapacitate the RAF, both in numbers of aircraft destroyed and pilots killed. This ambition became blurred during the conflict, but it was the objective at the outset. And behind the numbers of aircraft, the industrial ability to replace and repair those machines, plus the number of trained pilots available, were equally important.

In addition to the men and the machines, there were other factors that played a vital role in the campaign that was about to begin. Range was the key limitation for the Luftwaffe fighter pilots. A typical sortie from northern France over south east England would allow the pilot of a Mes 109 only ten minutes over enemy territory. Oftentimes, this would be enough to make a meaningful intervention against defending RAF fighters, especially if the bombers' target was south of London. But it gave the British a real advantage, both in terms of opportunities to attack unescorted bombers and simply to dogfight for longer. The British radar system capitalized on this by allowing the British to husband their forces on the ground and scramble to intercept rather than patrolling in anticipation of a dogfight against incoming German planes. That alone was a huge force multiplier, as was the fact that the British were on the defensive. If their aircraft were shot down, a British pilot would have a reasonable chance of bailing out, parachuting to safety and rejoining the battle, sometimes on the same day. Their German counterparts faced captivity or a highly dangerous rescue in the chilly English Channel.

Finally, mention must be made of that unquantifiable but fundamental variable in all warfare: morale. German aviators had the experience and undoubtedly the confidence on entering the campaign, but as losses mounted this began to erode. The reverse was true amongst RAF aircrew, with the added component of defending the homeland. As discussed already, this battle was seen as an existential one by the British, and tenacious defense against the odds had been a hallmark of British martial culture for centuries. RAF fighter pilots saw themselves as fighting for the very survival of Britain, and in the summer of 1940 they would recall the spirit of Nelson and Drake as they cut the invader to pieces.

---

[68] 303 Squadron, flying Hurricanes.

Even before the Battle of Britain, the British had been planning to counter an aerial assault against their homeland for some years. The development of Fighter Command, particularly under Sir Hugh Dowding, had resulted in a fully integrated defensive system. This employed the latest technologies alongside thoroughly pragmatic systems of command control. Although Douhet's[69] theories on aerial warfare had been widely studied in Britain, leading to an emphasis on bomber design and production during most of the years between the two World Wars, Dowding had rejected this school. Fortunately his views had prevailed, with consequent investment from the government - just in time.

Dowding

British strategy relied upon the early detection of intruding aircraft by radar and human observers, as well as a control system which would enable such intelligence to be swiftly analyzed and acted upon. The underground telephone wires that connected command centers were therefore just as important as the high tech radar. So were the situation rooms where the battle was plotted and fighter resources allocated. Simple yet effective displays showed commanders the status of each RAF unit as the attacking enemy formations were moved across large maps. Anti-aircraft batteries were under the same command umbrella, so that they received the same warnings as the fighter squadrons and would know when to pause their barrages in order to let the fighters engage. The squadrons themselves, each of about twelve aircraft, were drilled to take off in as little as two minutes if required. Their airfields were mostly grassy strips, but a series of reserve "satellite" fields gave the whole system increased resilience.

This multi-faceted defense was organized into four Group Sectors. Number 10 Group covered Cornwall and the south west, 11 Group covered south east England, 12 Group north east

---

[69] Giulio Douhet (1869-1930), an early air war theorist who had argued that bombers would always "get through".

England, and 13 Group Scotland and the north. Inevitably, the brunt of the fighting would be borne by 11 and 12 Groups, especially the former. Ironically, the interplay of these two commands and their controversial leaders was to represent one of the gravest threats to Britain's successful defense.

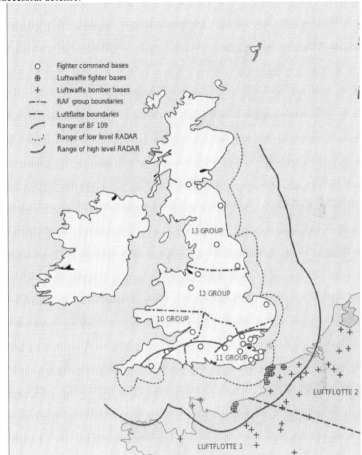

Setting aside this rivalry, Dowding's system gave him the ability to reinforce 11 and 12 Groups from elsewhere in the country. That advantage, as well as the inherent range limitations of the Luftwaffe, meant that as a last resort Fighter Command could pull back to the north of England and prepare for another round of fighting.

At the most strategic level, the British plan was a straightforward one: after all, theirs was the defensive posture. It was hoped that Dowding's sophisticated system would knock down sufficient German intruders as to make the whole enterprise impractical for the Luftwaffe. At its simplest, this is what would happen. Behind this numbers game, Churchill's Government had already moved to maximize the odds in their favor. Aircraft and component production had been dispersed, and large numbers of women were drafted in to boost production. A Civilian Repair Organization was organized to restore badly damaged aircraft. There was even a Ministry of Aircraft Production, under the energetic leadership of Lord Beaverbrook. Pilot training was accelerated and volunteers were called in from other services, such as Bomber and Coastal Commands. At the pinnacle of this effort was Churchill himself, providing superb political leadership when the country needed it most.

In contrast, Germany's planning efforts for the Battle of Britain can be summarized as complacent and unfocused. In a sense, the Luftwaffe would become a victim of its own success. Over-confidence had set in, exacerbated by Goering's arrogance. Certainly the Luftwaffe of June 1940 had a lot to be confident about, having proven the value of tactical air support in a fast moving ground campaign and, with its skilled pilots and modern aircraft, having had the better of the RAF and French Air Force. But this was to be a different campaign. The objective was strategic rather than supportive - on its own, the Luftwaffe was tasked with neutralizing the RAF. At least that much was clear, but not a great deal of thought or planning had gone in to how this was to be achieved. The Luftwaffe was simply propelled into the campaign on the back of the assumption that it must be possible given its demonstrable competence. Time was not on their side either - Hitler had stipulated that the ground invasion would take place in mid-September. Thus, brimming with self confidence, the Luftwaffe effectively chose to get on with it and let the planning take care of itself. This would become a decided disadvantage as the campaign evolved and tactics had to be changed, and it was not helped by amateurish interventions from Hitler and Goering.

All of that said, Germany deployed a powerful array of offensive airpower in a ring around the British Isles. Luftflottes 2 and 3 were based in north east and north west France respectively, with some additional Luftflotte 2 units in Belgium and Holland. Between them they were capable of attacking all of southern England, the Midlands and Wales. Luftflotte 5 in Norway was positioned to attack northern England and Scotland.

Behind the scenes, Germany was again in a weaker position than Great Britain. Albert Speer had yet to grip the problem of aircraft production in the manner that Beaverbrook had achieved - although he was to work wonders later in the war. The result was that Germany's fighter production during this crucial period fell below that of Britain's. Her intelligence assets were also problematic - an absence of reliable agents, photo reconnaissance and signals intelligence meant that the High Command had a poor understanding of what they were up against. Overarching all of this of course, was a political leadership which was arrogant, interventionist and irrational.

Speer

In planning terms therefore, despite the bluster and the German successes of the first 8 months of the war, the odds were not as stacked against the British as many at the time supposed. A highly capable and thus far unbeaten tactical air force was about to collide with a sophisticated but untested defensive system. For the young aircrew on both sides, it would be a terrifying struggle for survival, thousands of feet up in the sky.

There is still some debate as to the real beginning of the Battle of Britain, but most British historians regard it as July 10, when the Luftwaffe began to probe defenses by means of a series of sweeps and raids on Channel shipping. Of course, from the German perspective, this did not represent a serious attempt to destroy the RAF. Rather, it was a learning process, designed to establish RAF strengths and weaknesses, and even to buy some time for the preparation of a more coherent plan for the campaign.

In fact, it was a clever move, because it set up a series of small scale engagements in which the RAF tended to be at a disadvantage. Britain had always relied heavily on its coastal trade, moving bulk goods through the Channel as an alternative to more costly land transport. Coal, still the fuel that drove the economy, was one of the more important shipments. A convoy system had been employed from the outset of the war and groups of merchantmen were usually escorted by Royal Navy destroyers. This was certainly ample protection against the weak Kriegsmarine, since the Channel, shallow and heavily patrolled, was far too dangerous for sustained U-Boat operations.

The Luftwaffe, however, was another matter. Small scale raids, involving Stukas or Dornier 17's, would prey on the shipping, with squadrons of Me 109's serving as top cover. The Stukas in particular were highly effective against both the merchantmen and destroyers, as they had been at Dunkirk. For Dowding and Park (commander of 11 Group), the problem was how to respond. These raids could be viewed as diversions, and they were ever aware that Fighter Command's strength needed to be husbanded against the constant possibility of a large scale incursion by the Luftwaffe over Britain itself. Moreover, fighting over the Channel meant RAF casualties had to ditch in the sea and that the fighters were operating further from their bases. Park tended to respond with a single squadron or less, resulting in dogfights in which the inexperienced RAF pilots were badly outnumbered. The Me 109's remained high, rather than going down with the bombers, conveying another tactical advantage. The result was a steady flow of RAF casualties, and on some days quite high losses. On July 19, for example, a squadron of Defiants was shot to pieces by the far superior Me 109's.

British Defiants

Proceeding at this sedate pace, the Luftwaffe was gradually chipping away at the RAF, but it was sustaining heavy casualties too. In July, the Luftwaffe lost 123 bombers and 66 fighters to the RAF's 77 fighters. Meanwhile, the Royal and Merchant navies were suffering such steady losses that within a month the Navy had abandoned Channel convoys altogether. Round one therefore probably represented a marginal win for the Luftwaffe. But with Hitler's directive concerning a September invasion released on 16th July, it was clear that they would have to pick up the tempo.

Full scale German attacks on the British mainland began on August 12, 1940, when radar sites were hit in an effort to disrupt Dowding's early warning system. Unfortunately for the Germans, the radar system was back up and running within 6 hours, helped by the failure of the Luftwaffe to try to knock out the telephone lines and power stations that kept the system connected. This marked the beginning of operation Adlerangriff ("Eagle Attack"), the main thrust of the Luftwaffe's effort to annihilate the RAF.

Intensive air battles continued all week, and though they continued trying to target the radar systems, the Luftwaffe quickly switched their main focus to the RAF's fighter bases themselves, with places such as Manston and Biggin Hill attacked repeatedly. Throughout the week, Park's

11 Group was desperately hard pressed, and 12 Group under Leigh-Mallory was supposed to protect the bases to free up Park's fighters to tackle the incoming bombers as soon as they crossed the coast. In practice, however, Leigh-Mallory's fighters often failed to materialize at all or were too late to intervene.

Part of the problem lay in rivalry, and part in Leigh-Mallory's need to hold forces back to defend his own sector north of London, but the nub of the disagreement between the two commanders was tactical. Park believed in the effectiveness of rapid response, sacrificing numbers for tactical advantage, particularly altitude. His fighters were scrambled as soon as a threat was positively identified, usually in squadron strength. Leigh-Mallory's 12 Group, and in particular Douglas Bader, one of its most successful leaders, had developed an alternative approach: the Big Wing. Their view was that it was more useful to assemble a multi-squadron wing, involving as many as 50 fighters, before engaging the intruders. Using this strategy, however, required a long time for the squadrons to take off, climb and rendezvous before being vectored into their target. Sometimes the Luftwaffe had hit Park's bases and were heading back out over the English Channel before planes from 12 Group even had a chance to engage.

The squabbling between 11 and 12 groups meant little to the hard pressed aircrews of Goering's Luftwaffe. Flying across in broad daylight, the bombers soon learnt to fear the arrival of the RAF fighters, charging in at their formations head on[70]. Often ignoring the fighter escorts, the Spitfires and Hurricanes tore into the ponderous bombers, raking them with massed machine gun fire and sending dozens plunging to the ground in flames. Recounting what it was like, Hauptmann Rolf Schroeder 8th Staffel KG76, Luftwaffe explained, "Suddenly, the fighters split up, then attack from ahead and from the side. Look out! The fighters come in so close that one could speak to them. Pull up! Good - he misses us."[71]

To the bomber crews, it seemed that the Me 109's were never there when needed, and when they were there they were not close enough. But this was a misplaced attitude. During those early days, Luftwaffe practice was to send fighter squadrons ahead of the main bomber formations in an attempt to engage the RAF fighters before they could reach the bombers. These were sound tactics. The RAF would allot (preferably Spitfire) squadrons to deal with the Me 109's but these fighter versus fighter encounters were much more evenly matched than is often assumed. Luckily for Britain, her radar network gave her sufficient intelligence about the German build-up to allow for other fighters to be held back, fully fueled and ready to take on the bombers.

The 15th saw the most extensive fighting of the campaign, with Luftflotte V making a major effort against northern England as well as the more familiar raids in the south. Luftwaffe intelligence analysts had made a big mistake in assessing that Dowding had drawn all of his fighters south. Range constraints meant that the only escorts available to the northern raiders were the clumsy Me 110's - easy prey for a Spitfire or Hurricane. A large formation of about 50 Junkers 88 Stukas attacked without any escort at all. As a result, 13 Group had its day, scything into the enemy formations and accounting for 23 aircraft destroyed.

In the south the radar controllers couldn't believe what they were seeing on their screens. By mid-morning huge formations of bombers and fighters were assembling over the Channel. Squadron after squadron was scrambled until every single available British fighter was in the air by mid-afternoon, with literally zero reserves. Pilots were making multiple sorties too, often flying four or five missions over the course of the day.

---

[70] A tactic endorsed by Park but frowned upon by Dowding, who thought it too dangerous.
[71] Price, p77.

Fate would have it that this would be the time chosen by the Prime Minister to visit Fighter Command headquarters at Bentley Priory. Churchill sat pensively as Park and Dowding committed the last of their young men to the desperate defense of the southern airfields. Driving back to his country home during the early evening, Churchill was overcome with emotion. "Don't talk to me!" he snapped at Lord Ismay, his military advisor.

It had, indeed, been a terrible day, but Fighter Command had survived it. Goering would not have appreciated the irony represented by his latest orders, issued following a conference that took place while his aircraft were still in the air. In his directive he had instructed the Luftwaffe to desist from attacking the British radar sites, which he believed to be a waste of time. But for some three hours on the 15th, Fighter Command had been effectively blinded by damage to those same radar sites, greatly impeding its ability to react to the subsequent mass raids against the airbases.

The 15th August was also notable for the the the beginning of the chain of events which was to result in Hitler's famous decision to target British civilians, particularly in London. A small force of Me 110's had attacked Croydon airport in the London suburbs. Used as a fighter base by the RAF, Croydon was a legitimate military target, but it lay within Greater London and Hitler had specifically forbidden any attacks on the metropolis. The bombs were felt in Westminster itself. This and a later episode (possibly accidental) prompted the RAF to attack Berlin later in retaliation. The feedback from this particular mission would later have major repercussions on the unfolding Battle of Britain.

The fighting became more subdued for a few days before another massed assault on "The Hardest Day", August 18, during which both sides would suffer their highest casualties. Again the airfields were the main target and again 11 Group was hard pressed. Mistakenly believing that the RAF was down to less than 500 serviceable fighters, the Luftwaffe thought it could break their backs and launched a massive onslaught on the 18th. In actuality, the RAF was still twice as strong as German estimates, and they damaged or destroyed over 100 planes in the fighting on the 18th, while suffering over 70 damaged or destroyed planes of their own.

A German Stuka about to crash on the 18th

After a brief lull in which both sides caught their breath and the Luftwaffe assessed the damage they had wrought so far, the pattern continued for the rest of the month. In the battle of attrition, the Germans continued concentrating most of their efforts against the airfields. The key determinant for the intensity of the daily encounter was the weather. The variable summer weather meant that on inclement days, fewer raids were sent across as one base or another was blanketed in fog, or more typically, it became difficult to assemble large formations. By now the aircrews on both sides were thoroughly exhausted, welcoming these brief respites.

For the British, they also provided an opportunity to repair damaged facilities. Bases such as Biggin Hill had been hit time after time, but luckily Dowding's system had plenty of flexibility built in. Fighters could quickly change bases and there were many spare airfields. It was the support infrastructure, particularly radar and communications, that was more vulnerable. As Sgt. Gunner Ben Elswood AA Gun Battery at Biggin Hill put it, "As soon as the bombers come over and make bloody holes in the ground, we go out and fill 'em up again. Everything is in poor shape, but Jerry hadn't broken our spirit."[72]

Still, the airbases were not the only targets. Small scale raids, often at night, had begun against manufacturing centers, such as Merseyside, and as the month progressed, the Germans stepped up the scale of these raids. On the night of the 23rd, they hit a tyre factory in Birmingham with 200 bombers.

After the 18th, Goering issued a series of revisions to standing orders concerning air tactics. The dangerous Me 109's were concentrated in the Pas de Calais, under the command of Luftflotte 2. This would give them marginally more loiter time over southern England. Importantly, they were instructed to stick close to the bombers, flying at the same speed and altitude. Now deprived of most of its single seat fighters, Luftflotte 3 switched to mainly night operations. Along with that, the vulnerable Stukas were now used much more sparingly, and always with heavy fighter escorts. Similarly, the Me 110's, theoretically fighters themselves, were often escorted by Me 109's and restricted to ground attack. Luftflotte 5 in Scandinavia, which had suffered serious damage on the 15th, confined itself to small scale night raids.

Meanwhile, within Dowding's command the tensions between 11 and 12 groups had actually managed to get worse. Leigh-Mallory had not been authorized to use his Big Wing tactics, but Park continued to complain about a lack of support. Of course, 12 Group aircraft had further to fly; but Leigh-Mallory insisted that his units were not summoned in time to make a difference. The tension ran down the ranks as well, with Air Vice Marshal Keith Park complaining to 12 group on August 30, "Where in the hell were your fighters that were supposed to have protected my airfields?!"[73]

Leigh-Mallory

[72]<http://www.battleofbritain1940.net/0035.html> accessed 9.6.12.
[73] <http://www.battleofbritain1940.net/0031.html> accessed 9.6.12.

Dowding was growing tired of the tickering, and he was also growing tired of the number of his fighters that were being drawn into combat with the enemy Me 109's. He wanted to focus on the bombers, so clear instructions were given that unless the Me 109's were in company with German bombers, the RAF would not scramble to intercept them. Of course, this approach was made much more difficult by Goering's insistence on close escort. Inevitably, when the RAF attacked large mixed formations, a lot of their fighters would tangle with the escorts.

August 20 also happened to be the day Churchill gave one of the most iconic speeches of the 20th century:

"The great air battle which has been in progress over this Island for the last few weeks has recently attained a high intensity. It is too soon to attempt to assign limits either to its scale or to its duration. We must certainly expect that greater efforts will be made by the enemy than any he has so far put forth. Hostile air fields are still being developed in France and the Low Countries, and the movement of squadrons and material for attacking us is still proceeding.

It is quite plain that Herr Hitler could not admit defeat in his air attack on Great Britain without sustaining most serious injury. If, after all his boastings and blood-curdling threats and lurid accounts trumpeted round the world of the damage he has inflicted, of the vast numbers of our Air Force he has shot down, so he says, with so little loss to himself; if after tales of the panic-stricken British crushed in their holes cursing the plutocratic Parliament which has led them to such a plight; if after all this his whole air onslaught were forced after a while tamely to peter out, the Fuehrer's reputation for veracity of statement might be seriously impugned. We may be sure, therefore, that he will continue as long as he has the strength to do so, and as long as any preoccupations he may have in respect of the Russian Air Force allow him to do so.

On the other hand, the conditions and course of the fighting have so far been favourable to us. I told the House two months ago that whereas in France our fighter aircraft were wont to inflict a loss of two or three to one upon the Germans, and in the fighting at Dunkirk, which was a kind of no-man's-land, a loss of about three or four to one, we expected that in an attack on this Island we should achieve a larger ratio. This has certainly come true. It must also be remembered that all the enemy machines and pilots which are shot down over our Island, or over the seas which surround it, are either destroyed or captured; whereas a considerable proportion of our machines, and also of our pilots, are saved, and soon again in many cases come into action.

A vast and admirable system of salvage, directed by the Ministry of Aircraft Production, ensures the speediest return to the fighting line of damaged machines, and the most provident and speedy use of all the spare parts and material. At the same time the splendid, nay, astounding increase in the output and repair of British aircraft and engines which Lord Beaverbrook has achieved by a genius of organisation and drive, which looks like magic, has given us overflowing reserves of every type of aircraft, and an ever-mounting stream of production both in quantity and quality.

The enemy is, of course, far more numerous than we are. But our new production already, as I am advised, largely exceeds his, and the American production is only just beginning to flow in. It is a fact, as I see from my daily returns, that our bomber and fighter strength now, after all this fighting, are larger than they have ever been. We believe that we shall be able to continue the air struggle indefinitely and as long as the enemy pleases, and the longer it continues the more rapid will be our approach, first towards that parity, and then into that superiority in the air, upon which in a large measure the decision of the war depends.

The gratitude of every home in our Island, in our Empire, and indeed throughout the world, except in the abodes of the guilty, goes out to the British airmen who, undaunted by odds, unwearied in their constant challenge and mortal danger, are turning the tide of the world war by their prowess and by their devotion. Never in the field of human conflict was so much owed by so many to so few.

All hearts go out to the fighter pilots, whose brilliant actions we see with our own eyes day after day; but we must never forget that all the time, night after night, month after month, our bomber squadrons travel far into Germany, find their targets in the darkness by the highest navigational skill, aim their attacks, often under the heaviest fire, often with serious loss, with deliberate careful discrimination, and inflict shattering blows upon the whole of the technical and war-making structure of the Nazi power. On no part of the Royal Air Force does the weight of the war fall more heavily than on the daylight bombers who will play an invaluable part in the case of invasion and whose unflinching zeal it has been necessary in the meanwhile on numerous occasions to restrain.

We are able to verify the results of bombing military targets in Germany, not only by reports which reach us through many sources, but also, of course, by photography. I have no hesitation in saying that this process of bombing the military industries and communications of Germany and the air bases and storage depots from which we are attacked, which process will continue upon an ever-increasing scale until the end of the war, and may in another year attain dimensions hitherto undreamed of, affords one at least of the most certain, if not the shortest of all the roads to victory. Even if the Nazi legions stood triumphant on the Black Sea, or indeed upon the Caspian, even if Hitler was at the gates of India, it would profit him nothing if at the same time the entire economic and scientific apparatus of German war power lay shattered and pulverised at home.

The fact that the invasion of this Island upon a large scale has become a far more difficult operation with every week that has passed since we saved our Army at Dunkirk, and our very great preponderance of sea-power enable us to turn our eyes and to turn our strength increasingly towards the Mediterranean and against that other enemy who, without the slightest provocation, coldly and deliberately, for greed and gain, stabbed France in the back in the moment of her agony, and is now marching against us in Africa…

A good many people have written to me to ask me to make on this occasion a fuller statement of our war aims, and of the kind of peace we wish to make after the war, than is contained in the very considerable declaration which was made early in the Autumn. Since then we have made common cause with Norway, Holland, and Belgium. We have recognised the Czech Government of Dr. Benes, and we have told General de Gaulle that our success will carry with it the restoration of France.

I do not think it would be wise at this moment, while the battle rages and the war is still perhaps only in its earlier stage, to embark upon elaborate speculations about the future shape which should be given to Europe or the new securities which must be arranged to spare mankind the miseries of a third World War. The ground is not new, it has been frequently traversed and explored, and many ideas are held about it in common by all good men, and all free men. But before we can undertake the task of rebuilding we have not only to be convinced ourselves, but we have to convince all other countries that the Nazi tyranny is going to be finally broken.

The right to guide the course of world history is the noblest prize of victory. We are still toiling up the hill; we have not yet reached the crest-line of it; we cannot survey the landscape or even imagine what its condition will be when that longed-for morning comes. The task which lies before us immediately is at once more practical, more simple and more stern. I hope - indeed I pray - that we shall not be found unworthy of our victory if after toil and tribulation it is granted to us. For the rest, we have to gain the victory. That is our task."

As September began, the Germans were beginning to look for another strategy. The aerial campaign that they had anticipated lasting for three weeks at most had now been underway for eight. They were losing more aircraft and pilots than the British, but they had also inflicted considerable damage, particularly to Fighter Command's infrastructure. Near the end of August, Goering had been ramping up his attacks on air-related manufacturing, usually at night and usually in large urban areas. Other military targets had been attacked, including the major naval base at Portsmouth by 70 bombers on the 23rd. All the while, the daily assault on the airfields had continued. Where was the focus? What type of targeting was going to be decisive? Senior staff meetings wrestled with these issues on an almost daily basis. But ultimately it would be politics more than military strategy that would determine the Luftwaffe's next move.

Meanwhile, who was winning? Neither Dowding nor Goering felt that events were going entirely their way, but rhe headline figures for aircraft and crew losses strongly suggested that the RAF was having the better of it. In August, the RAF lost 426 aircraft and the Luftwaffe 774, but these are modern assessments that were unavailable to the participants at the time. Most importantly, both sides felt that they were seriously degrading the opposition, and the Luftwaffe thought that Fighter Command might be close to collapse. This was to become a factor in their new tactics.

Numbers of aircraft shot down was not the whole story either. Dowding was not receiving sufficient replacement pilots, even though aircraft production was just about keeping pace. Those that did make it to the front-line squadrons were inexperienced, many with less than ten hours solo flying time to their credit. His bases had been hard hit, some of them put out of action for hours at a time. Fighter Command was battered and reeling, but not yet down.

For Goering, things were probably worse. His crews had also taken terrible losses, and the Luftwaffe's replacement situation was worse than for the British. German aircraft production was not keeping pace with losses either. He had more aircraft than the RAF, but the gap was closing. In Goering's case however, the arrogance of the Nazi culture, the esprit de corps associated with the Luftwaffe's earlier successes, and a genuine intelligence shortfall all served to mask the degree to which it was struggling now. Essentially, the German mindset was pre-disposed to believe things were much better than they truly were.

Calculations aside, things still hung in the balance at the beginning of September. Modern historians would probably concur that even though they may not have known it, the RAF could have continued at the attritional rate they were then suffering. All other things being equal, it was a stalemate.

On August 25, the RAF had bombed Berlin. Although nowhere near on the scale of the raids that would follow in 1943, or even those the Luftwaffe had unleashed on places like Portsmouth during the Battle of Britain, it was a political embarrassment for the Nazis. Goering had assured

Hitler that no RAF plane would come anywhere near Berlin, and Hitler was furious when that was proven wrong.

The result was the speech to a largely female audience at the Sportsplast and a new Directive on September 5 ordering the Luftwaffe to focus its efforts on London. Now the strategy had changed again; Germany would attempt to terrify the British civilian population into surrender or compromise.

Two days later, on September 7, the Luftwaffe threw everything it had at southern England. 300 medium bombers, 200 Me 110's and 600 Me 109's surged across the Channel, headed for London and the surrounding area. The raids started during the middle of the morning and continued on well into the night. Squadron Leader A.V.R (Sandy) Johnstone, of the 602 Squadron RAF, recounted the Luftwaffe's raids that day. "All we could see was row upon row of German raiders, all heading for London. I have never seen so many aircraft in the air all at the same time."[74]

The British riposte fell mostly to 11 Group, with 12 Group once again experimenting with the Big Wing concept and consequently absent from its allotted task - that of protecting the airfields. Airfield defense however, was now less critical. Not only had the Germans neglected to attack the radar system, but they now chose to ignore the RAF bases as well. While the fighting swirled across the skies all day, involving nearly 1500 aircraft, at least the British fighters had the option of landing safely to refuel and re-arm.

For Park, this was fundamental. He later claimed that on September 7 the Luftwaffe had "thrown it all away." For him, this was the turning point in the Battle of Britain.[75] But it certainly didn't feel that way to the average Londoner. Huge fires raged across London's East End, which was the docklands area but also the home of London's poorest people, where thousands of tiny terraced homes were jammed in closely together. Civilian casualties were high, but as a patriotic news documentary of the period claimed, "London Can Take It". As families crammed into primitive bomb shelters in their gardens, or camped on the platforms of the claustrophobic tube stations, the last thing they thought of was capitulating to a Nazi dictatorship. London could indeed "take it", but the price was high. They called it "the Blitz", and London would be bombed every night for nearly two months.

The 7th had been a difficult day, but for Dowding's pilots at least there now followed a period of relative tranquility. The weather had deteriorated again, and it was in any case impossible for the Luftwaffe to maintain the kind of tempo it had delivered over that fateful 15 hours. For the next week there were intrusions and dogfights, as well as raids on other cities such as Liverpool, but nothing on the scale of that first assault.

At night though, it was a different matter. At this stage in the war the RAF did not have an effective night fighter force, aside from a few of the hapless Defiant aircraft that had been converted to this role, as had some Blenheim heavy fighters. There was even an experimental Beaufighter equipped with an early airborne radar set. But this was a whole new field for the British. For the most part, any German bombers operating over Britain at night had no need to worry about Dowding's fighters because the deadly Spitfires and Hurricanes were simply not capable of operations at night. Thus, the bombing against London and other cities continued almost unmolested, save for a few lucky hits from anti-aircraft batteries. It may have been quiet for the fighter boys at Biggin Hill and Duxford, but they knew that their capital city was being bombarded every night and there was very little they could do about it.

[74] <http://www.battleofbritain1940.net/0037.html> accessed 9.6.12.
[75] Orange, pp 107-8.

Fortunately for the RAF, Luftwaffe tactics were about to play into their hands once again. Goering was now being placed under growing pressure to win the campaign; the German High Command had not yet accepted that an invasion of Great Britain was unfeasible, even though Hitler himself was beginning to express some serious doubts. But if they were going to do it, they needed to do it quickly. Winter storms would soon threaten the ability to supply an army across the Channel and also seriously impede aerial operations. Goering's Luftwaffe would make one final push.

September 15th dawned rainy, but with sunshine breaking out across the south by the mid-morning there was ideal weather for daytime operations. In northern France and Belgium, hundreds of German aircraft began to assemble, the squadrons coalescing at medium altitude before heading off in a single black stream across the narrow seas. At Bentley Priory, they were ready, even more so than they had been a week earlier. The Blitz had only inflicted serious damage on 2 airbases, and even those were back up and running within hours. Thus, the RAF squadrons were replenished, reinforced and operating from fully functioning airbases.

Churchill and Dowding almost certainly had forewarning of the big push, either by Ultra decrypts from Bletchley Park or through the many British German-speaking radio operators who monitored all open transmissions. Then, of course there was radar, a fully functioning network that had been untouched by the Luftwaffe for weeks. As Wood and Dempster put it in their groundbreaking study of the campaign, "The stupidity of large formations sorting themselves out in full view of British radar was not yet realized by the Luftwaffe." [76]

The result was the most catastrophic day for the Luftwaffe of the entire campaign. British tactics were now well rehearsed, and they had the numbers to make them work. Spitfire squadrons took on the Me 109's, leaving the Hurricanes to deal with the bombers. Park was pairing his squadrons in a way that was not so dissimilar to Leigh-Mallory's proposal after all. Indeed, Bader's Big Wing made an effective appearance from its base at Duxford, throwing 50 fighters into the fray at one blow. The dogfighting lasted all day and into the evening, but the Germans had simply tried to use too many aircraft. For the British, it became a target rich environment, to coin a modern term. "157 enemy aircraft shot down!" screamed the newspaper headlines. It was probably closer to 60, but it's easy to forgive the British for exaggerating, as had both sides throughout the summer. The RAF lost 27 fighters. The Luftwaffe could not sustain such casualties - each bomber had a crew of three or four, and these aircrew were not bailing out over friendly territory.

After the debacle on September 15, German tactics changed again. It was to be the last of the massed daylight attacks, but the assault on London would continue at night. This was stressful for Londoners, but naturally night bombing was far less accurate, and with each passing day the infrastructure - firefighting and rescue services in particular - were beginning to adapt. Again, daylight Luftwaffe activity tailed off. There were a few massed fighter sweeps, on the 23rd for example, but the RAF had the confidence and capacity to scramble squadrons to take these on. The Luftwaffe's strategic impetus was permanently gone. September 15 was indeed the turning point, and it is rightly celebrated in Britain as "Battle of Britain Day".

Goering had almost run out of ideas, and Hitler was out of patience. Just like it is hard to gauge the start of the Battle of Britain, trying to determine the end of it is another area of contention. For the British, the slightly arbitrary date of October 31 has become the consensus. This is certainly arbitrary because Luftwaffe attacks on British cities - London in particular - continued for months afterwards, and it would not be for another three years before Britain could genuinely

---

[76] Wood & Dempster p231

claim to have full control of her airspace. However, the alternate argument that the battle petered out in 1941 is perhaps less plausible when it is recalled that Hitler cancelled Operation Seelowe (the proposed invasion) on December 18th. Indeed, by October 13 it had been postponed at least until 1941, making the British chronology seems the more sensible.

For those last few weeks, air battles over England would continue, but their shape and extent bore little resemblance to the huge assaults of August and September, even as Italy had joined the war against Britain and Mussolini belatedly sent a small mixed force to operate from Belgium. Italian bombers tried to raid Harwich by night on the 26th but failed to find their target. The Luftwaffe deployed the new Me109E7 Fighter-Bomber for the first time (an Me109 with a bomb-rack) and briefly, this technology discomforted the British. These planes would zoom across at high speed and high altitude, and they were just about able to hit London, still the primary target, but their payload was puny, and the RAF learned to counter them with high flying Spitfires.

The night raids continued as before, but it was clear that this was not going to neutralize the RAF, let alone knock Britain out of the war. Douhet's theory about destroying civilian morale was not going to work. During the day, small-scale Luftwaffe raids occurred regularly, usually against built up areas, but the RAF was now well versed in counter measures. Strategically, they were little more than a nuisance.

The fact was that Germany had run down the Luftwaffe, in terms of aircrew and planes. Hitler had become unconvinced and disinterested. Fatefully, his mind was now turning to Russia, and he had convinced himself that he could leave a scarred but still standing Britain behind his back. In a long battle of attrition, the RAF had come out on top, and Fighter Command was now stronger than it had been in June. Goering and his commanders had also run out of ideas. He no longer had any plan for destroying the RAF; ergo, an invasion became impossible. The advent of winter in the Channel merely confirmed that, drawing a convenient veil over Germany's folly.

On December 30, 1941, Churchill delivered an address in Ottawa to members of the Canadian government, during which he referred to the previous year's Battle of Britain and French Marshal Philippe Pétain's warning to Churchill after the fall of France that Britain would fall next. As only Churchill could put it, "When I warned them that Britain would fight on alone whatever they did, their generals told their Prime Minister and his divided Cabinet, 'In three weeks England will have her neck wrung like a chicken.' Some chicken! Some neck!"

The most obvious outcome of the Battle of Britain was that it precluded a German invasion of Britain. This had been the purpose of the German campaign, and it had been clearly frustrated. But in the decades after the decisive British victory, many historians have since argued that even had the Luftwaffe secured air supremacy over Britain, an invasion would have been a very tall order.

That is certainly true. Doubtless the Royal Navy would have suffered heavy losses in attempting to interdict an invasion fleet, but it is hard to believe that the troop barges themselves would not have been sunk in large numbers. Similarly, it should be recalled that the Wehrmacht was not well prepared for amphibious warfare. Even had they managed to cross the Channel, it would have been touch and go on the beaches.

To an extent, much of that speculation is beside the point. However risky an invasion might have been for Germany, Hitler intended to try it if he could defeat the RAF. He had therefore been defeated on his own terms, and the defeat had been made very clear to the entire world, which was arguably the most important result of the campaign. After all, it was a first, and it had demonstrated for all the world to see that Nazi Germany was not invincible. As a turning point, the Battle of Britain was particularly important across the Atlantic, where public and political opinion started to shift away from isolationism. As a result, Roosevelt and Churchill felt able to hammer out the Lend-Lease deal in December 1940, trading destroyers for bases.

Britain herself was also able to breathe a collective sigh of relief once the immediate crisis was over. Her brave young pilots had bought the country precious time to rebuild the army, and to devise strategies to strike back at Germany. Ironically, the only effective means of doing so would be a strategic bombing campaign of her own, which would dwarf Germany's blitz on British cities during the last few years of the war.

The Battle of Britain was a campaign of attrition, and in the end it was the numbers that counted. At the time, both sides had wildly over-reported losses inflicted on the enemy for propaganda purposes and through faulty intelligence. Since then, the statistical analysis of the battle has almost become a science in itself, with triumphalist early British accounts gradually giving way to more reasoned assessments. It now seems clear that the RAF outfought the Luftwaffe by shooting down many more aircraft than it lost. In crude terms, the RAF lost just over 1000 fighters, nearly all of them single seaters, while Germany lost 1600 aircraft, about 1000 of which were multi-crew medium bombers, making for much higher crew losses. British aircraft and pilot production mostly kept pace with the battle, while Germany did not. The Luftwaffe had lost nearly a third of its strength in the Battle of France, meaning that it was not at full strength for the Battle of Britain either. At its simplest, the Battle of Britain was won on the numbers, with Luftwaffe efforts finally tailing off as a consequence.

Some have argued that Germany never had the means to win in the first place. Her superior fighters lacked the range to properly protect the bombers, those bombers carried insufficient payload for strategic bombing, and Germany failed to keep pace with aircraft and crew losses. Part of this was due to hubris. Britain had a much larger and more capable fighter force than Germany had reckoned. Dowding's sophisticated defense system, largely ignored by the Luftwaffe, enabled the effective deployment of those fighters. And while the Germans thought the RAF was on the verge of collapse, Britain proved able to replace both men and machines at the required rate.

Above and beyond the resources lies the question of leadership. There never really was a plausible plan for knocking out the RAF, and much of the German effort was dissipated on fruitless attacks on civilians. Even with hindsight, it is hard to discern exactly what Hitler and Goering thought they were doing in September 1940. It hardly merited the term strategy. All this of course, was exacerbated by a poor intelligence picture and the inherent irrationality of the Nazi leadership.

As is so often the case with history, it is easy to make these points from the comfort of a 21st century armchair. In so doing one, it's easy to forget what these events meant for the participants. Thousands of brave German airmen thought they were doing the right thing for their country, and many of them died in the most horrifying of circumstances. The subtleties of grand strategy - whether or not the Royal Navy could have protected Britain without the RAF - were mostly (and naturally) lost on the pilots of Fighter Command. These young men flew up into the blue to defend their country against the odds, against a so far undefeated enemy who had swept across Europe. They were indeed "The Few", and it is unlikely that they will ever be forgotten.

The German Invasion of the Soviet Union

Hitler likely intended to attack the Soviet Union since the beginning of his expansionism in the late 1930s. However, actual planning for Operation Barbarossa, the invasion of the USSR, began only in the summer of 1940. After splitting Poland with the eastern dictatorship in 1939, Hitler's

Third Reich conquered France and the Low Countries in 1940, and it was not yet known how the Battle of Britain would play out. Nonetheless, Hitler was already thinking about the conquest of the Soviet Union.

The important artillery general Erich Marcks, later killed by an Allied fighter-bomber attack in Normandy, drew up the initial plan in August 1940. This plan envisioned two army groups, Army Groups North and South, advancing into the USSR on either side of the immense Pripet Marshes, the largest obstacle in western Russia. Soon, however, the Germans scrapped this plan in favor of a more flexible arrangement with three army groups. Army Group North, under Field Marshal Ritter von Leeb, would push for Leningrad, while Army Group Center would drive for Moscow under the leadership of Field Marshal Fedor von Bock. This formation represented the largest and best-supplied portion of the Barbarossa invasion, given its centrally important task, and while both of these army groups operated north of the Pripet Marshes, to the south of the Pripet morass, the prickly Field Marshal Gerd von Rundstedt headed Army Group South, charged with advancing through the Ukraine, taking Kiev and the Dnieper River, and preventing Soviet counterattacks from reaching the indispensable Romanian oil fields.

Marcks

Leeb

Bock

   The main thrust would lie along the axis to Moscow, according to original plans. While often compared to Napoleon Bonaparte's doomed incursion into Russia in 1812, the comparison is facile and fails to correspond to historical reality. Moscow in 1812 represented a large tract of buildings with symbolic and shelter value, but nothing more, whereas in the technological world of 1941, the Russian capital stood as the pulsing nerve center of the Soviet Union's European region – a region containing most of the USSR's population, factories, and armies. Wehrmacht panzer general Heinz Guderian spoke accurately of "the geographical significance of Moscow, which was quite different from that of, say, Paris. Moscow was the great Russian road, rail, and communications centre: it was the political solar plexus: it was an important industrial area: and its capture would not only have an enormous psychological effect on the Russian people but on the whole rest of the world as well." (Guderian, 1996, 199).

   Stalin's Red Army, for all its deficiencies, represented a modern fighting force for its day, infinitely different from the Czar's armies in 1812. The Soviet armies required massive logistical support along railways in the same manner as the Germans – which is a major reason why the Wehrmacht's encircling tactics had such a devastating effect on the Red Army in 1941. Cut off from steady supply of gasoline, diesel, ammunition, reinforcements, and food in vast quantities, the Red Army units quickly became a starving rabble on foot, with their trucks, aircraft, and tanks immobilized by lack of fuel. In fact, once they drove the Germans back west late in the war, the Soviets laid Russian-gauge railways into eastern and central Europe. Without the arteries of the railways infusing them with the varied lifeblood of war materiel, the Red Army divisions in 1944 and 1945 would have quickly halted, perhaps permanently.

Organized by a centralized totalitarian state, the Soviet rail network in the west used Moscow as the hub for practically every major rail line. The capital's colossal mustering yards maintained the rolling stock that moved all supplies to the front. Thus, had the Germans seized Moscow, this one act would cut off the northern and southern Red Army units from all ammunition, fuel, food, and reinforcements. In a matter of days, most tanks and other vehicles would cease to work, eliminating Soviet mobility on even the tactical scale. No reinforcements could reach any point beyond Moscow, and building new rail lines would take months if it proved possible at all.

As a result, control of Moscow would defeat all Soviet forces in European Russia rapidly and totally, while placing strategic and operational initiative in the Germans' hands. Moscow would provide a superb base for the winter, and the Soviet state – already loathed by most of its subjects, who understandably resented its murderous character, seizure of their property, and aggressive atheism – might well collapse. Moscow, then, represented a viable target, probably offering the key to defeating the Soviet Union in the first summer's campaign, or at least reducing it to an impotent rump state in Siberia that would likely be forced to sue for peace.

Still, the sheer size and difficult terrain of Russia presented the Wehrmacht with a vast logistical challenge, which even the Fuhrer understood. According to the war journal of Generaloberst Franz Halder of the general staff, Hitler decided to send all available anti-aircraft artillery (AAA) to support Barbarossa rather than protecting Germany proper (which would be guarded by fighter planes), indicating the Fuhrer's intention to fully commit necessary resources to the plan: "AA defense will be slightly weakened (30%) in favor of Barbarossa. [...] AAA: Fuehrer wants no serviceable piece to remain inactive. Personnel for 30 Batteries. AA Corps, of 6 [Battalions], for 6th Army ([Armored] Group 1) and [Armored] Group 2." (Halder, , 9).

This decision had a notably positive effect on operations both by providing extra flak cover for the panzer spearheads of Army Groups Center and South, and by ensuring a large number of 8.8 FlaK 36 or 37 anti-aircraft cannons on the ground in Russia. The 88mm flak gun, or "Eighty-Eight," represented the only German gun deployed in 1941 which reliably penetrated the armor of KV-1 and KV-2 tanks.

Halder further notes that the Ostheer (Eastern Army) ensured "15,000 Polish peasant carts with drivers will be made ready for Barbarossa by beginning of May," (Halder, , 34) thus ensuring that slow but effective transport, adapted to low quality Eastern European roads, would be available to the invasion force.

The Wehrmacht actually anticipated the logistical challenges of the USSR's large spaces with considerable clarity, including the lack of European-gauge railroads in the east. Though the army planned for an operation ending with the capture of Moscow in late summer or early autumn – thus neglecting winter gear – the quartermaster corps stockpiled large amounts of supplies for the summer campaign, assembled materials and pioneers to drive railroads rapidly into Soviet territory, and built up a pool of tens of thousands of tons (in cargo capacity) of trucks in 60-ton convoys.

The Germans moved men to the front from the start of 1941 on, though only a trickle of divisions arrived in the winter. The pace of deployment accelerated in March and exploded in

April. Originally, Hitler planned to launch Operation Barbarossa in mid-May 1941. However, due to an extremely wet spring which softened vast areas of terrain and swelled several rivers in the direct path of Army Group Center's and South's advance, the Fuhrer postponed the invasion until June 22nd. The last deployment started on May 23rd, one month before the launch of the attack.

Though the Germans did their best to conceal the preparations for Barbarossa through a variety of methods, mustering a heavily (though not fully) mechanized army of 3 million men could not be concealed. News arrived at the Soviet headquarters in Moscow from a wide range of sources, yet Stalin authorized no additional preparations for a potential Third Reich attack on the Soviet Union.

The murderous, primitive paranoia of the Soviet leader goes a long way in explaining this situation. Starting in 1939 and continuing into 1940, the Soviet dictator began systematically destroying his own foreign intelligence apparatus. Suspecting treachery from men who actually put their entire effort into helping Russia with intelligence gathering, Stalin repeatedly changed the intelligence chiefs at home, each previous occupant of the office dying in NKVD torture chambers or cells. Worse, Stalin had numerous agents in Europe and elsewhere in the world recalled to the USSR. When they arrived, the NKVD arrested them, tortured bizarre confessions out of them, and shot them in their underground cells, often after circus-like, sadistic show trials. The NKVD infiltrated death squads into Western Europe to assassinate those spies who defected rather than return to certain torture and execution.

The reason for this strange procedure lay in Stalin's conviction that anyone who visited the West would be suborned by capitalism and must therefore be a traitor and double agent. This had the effect of collapsing the Soviets' spy networks and casting their reports (actually, in most cases, highly accurate) into doubt in Stalin's mind.

Despite the purges, Soviet intelligence officers still reported the coming invasion weeks ahead of time. The leading Soviet agent in Japan, Richard Sorge, posed as an undercover German journalist and received brief but useful advance warning of Barbarossa. A newly arrived German officer, Lieutenant Colonel Erwin Scholl, confided a highly specific outline of the plan to Sorge over an elegant dinner at the Imperial Hotel, talking under cover of orchestral music played for the guests' entertainment. Sorge sent off a radio message to Moscow on June 1st: "Expected start of German-Soviet war on June 15th is based exclusively on information which Lieutenant-Colonel Scholl brought with him from Berlin, which he left on May 6 heading for Bangkok. He is taking up post of attache in Bangkok. Ott stated he could not receive information on this subject directly from Berlin, and only has Scholl's information." (Whymant, 1996, 167).

Sorge

The Soviet government had ordered Sorge to return to the USSR, but by guessing correctly that he would be arrested, tortured for a few days, and then killed, the agent offered a variety of excuses to postpone his return, and he still remained deeply loyal to Russia, if not the Soviet regime, thus supplying all the high quality information he could gather. Stalin, however, dismissed the warning. Having described Sorge as "a shit who has set himself up with some small factories and brothels in Japan" (Whymant, 1996, 184), the dictator and his henchmen sent back a terse reply accusing Sorge of lying.

In addition to Soviet agents, Red Army commanders near the border repeatedly sounded the alarm to Stalin, attempting to prompt the Soviet leader to authorize the movement of reinforcements up to the border. Lieutenant Fyodor Arkhipenko described the Stavka (Soviet GHQ) response to signs of German war preparations: "In the spring of 1941, German reconnaissance planes constantly violated our border and conducted [...] flights over the Soviet territory and our airfield, but there were instructions not to shoot them down and not even to scare them, but only escort them to the border. Everything was done as to postpone the war, prevent the development of attempted German provocation." (Kamenir, 2008, 69).

Additionally, since at least April 1941, the British also provided the Soviets with detailed information from their own excellent intelligent network about the impending Operation Barbarossa. The British officers providing this data to Soviets in England found themselves met with suspicious, hostile, and contemptuous questioning. Due to the earlier threat of the British to send troops to aid the Finns against the Soviet invasion of 1939-1940, and the fact that the English represented two-dimensional capitalists and thus foes in Stalin's eyes, the Soviets assumed the British and Germans worked in cahoots, actually labeling the invaluable data offered "provocation."

The use of the word "provocation" perhaps grants insight about Stalin's reasons for stubbornly refusing to believe the burgeoning flood of intelligence pointing to an imminent massive German invasion of the USSR – a mix of paranoia, arrogance, and self-delusion. Marshal Georgi Zhukov noted that Stalin's mass liquidation of the Soviet officer corps had gutted the Red Army's fighting prowess, and that "J.V. Stalin clearly knew as well that after 1939, military units were led by commanders far from being well-versed in operational-tactical and strategic education. […] It was also impossible to discount the moral traumas which were inflicted upon the Red Army and Navy by the massive purges." (Kamenir, 2008, 58).

Zhukov

Leading commissar Nikita Khrushchev, the man who eventually replaced Stalin as Soviet premier, provided a final piece of the puzzle of Stalin's actions by recording in the first volume of his memoirs the abject, helpless terror that the actual invasion plunged Stalin into. His extraordinary description is either full-blown calumny, or the portrait of a man driven into paralytic terror and despair by the arrival of an event he had dreaded but managed to delude himself would never happen: "Stalin was completely crushed. His morale was shattered, and he made the following declaration: 'The war has begun. It will develop catastrophically. Lenin left us the proletarian Soviet state, but we have sh— all over it' […] He walked out […] and went to his dacha nearest the city. […] When we came to his dacha [...] I could see from his face that Stalin was very frightened. I suppose that Stalin was thinking we had come there to arrest him." (Khrushchev, 2005, 304).

While knowing precisely what Stalin thought is impossible, these varied facts may reveal the dictator's motivation. Stalin knew that he had destroyed his own army's fighting power and felt profound fear that a war would start, he would be blamed for the subsequent disaster, and this would cause his downfall and execution. Accordingly, he adopted a pose of doing absolutely nothing that might trigger the Germans to attack, hoping to gain time to build more tanks and train new officers. In addition, he went about killing his own agents who warned of Barbarossa, and dismissing the British intelligence as "provocation," in a panicky effort to deny the possibility of his worst fears being realized even to himself.

Regardless of the exact reasons – either terrified delusion, arrogant overestimation of the Red Army's fighting capabilities, or some other cause – Stalin refused to allow the units at the border to prepare for attack. He also disallowed reinforcements even on a local level. Some commanders secretly moved a few of their rear echelon units up to the border in an effort to strengthen its defenses. They did so in secret, however, because their actions could be labeled "panic-mongering" – a type of sabotage – which could lead to anything from a simple Stavka countermanding of the order, to dismissal from their command, to outright execution.

Of course, these small preparations were far too little to counteract the steel avalanche of the Wehrmacht, which was poised to burst over the border regardless of Stalin's fears or illusions.

The borders of Europe ahead of the operation

   The Soviet Union's northern flank, guarded by the Northern Front and the Northwest Front, faced off against both Hitler's Army Group North and Finland at the start of the operation. That said, the Finns stood as limited allies of the Germans, refusing to participate in Hitler's more extreme policies but also opposed to the Soviet Union. This opposition resulted from brutal Soviet imperialism directed toward the small northern country in 1939-1940, when Stalin seized Finland's border territories and forced the Finns to accept the result. Nevertheless, the extraordinary courage, determination, and skill of the Finns in defending their nation against the Red Army led to immense Russian losses despite the USSR's overwhelming numerical superiority. Finland's fighting spirit and the possible intervention of the British ultimately prevented the nation's complete conquest.

   An interesting item of aid provided to the Germans by the Finns consisted of a stock of Red Army uniforms, weapons, trucks, and other equipment. This enabled the Germans to equip the leading units of commandos for Barbarossa with Soviet uniforms and armament, enabling successful infiltration or surprise attacks in many areas. But for the most part, the Finns actually only acted sufficiently to recover the territory ripped away from their country by the Soviets the year before, though they expected the USSR to attack them if they did not attack first in any case.

Army Group North's task consisted not only of guarding Army Group Center's left flank during its advance, but also to penetrate the marshy, forested landscape of the Baltic states, defeat the Soviet units deployed there, and seize the city of Leningrad.

The spearhead of Army Group North naturally consisted of armored units, notably Panzer Group IV under the command of Generaloberst Erich Hoepner. Hoepner would eventually be executed in Plotzensee Prison for his part in the July 20th 1944 plot against Adolf Hitler, but at the start of Barbarossa, Panzer Group IV fielded 631 tanks as part of its three panzer and two infantry divisions. Field Marshal Wilhelm von Leeb commanded Army Group North overall.

Hoepner

Fog lay thickly over eastern Poland and the Baltic region in the early morning of June 22nd, 1941, when the customary Wehrmacht artillery preparation began at 3:45 a.m. Lasting at least an hour and in some areas as much as three hours, the barrages targeted surprised Red Army units, which responded with chaotic, relatively ineffective return fire. However, the Germans used these attacks in only a few sectors; for the most part, they relied on stealth during the initial attack.

Following the initial artillery preparation, the Luftwaffe launched its attacks eastward. Messerschmitt Me-109s, Junkers Ju-87 Stuka dive-bombers, and Heinkel and Junkers bombers passed over the army formations moving forward through the first light of the new morning to pound Soviet positions. The Luftwaffe men thoroughly devastated the Soviet air force units in the region, to the extent that almost all aircraft soon redirected their efforts towards tank hunting or convoy destruction roles. By June 25th, the *I Fliegerkorps* had wiped out 1,500 Soviet aircraft, 1,100 of them on the ground.

The following infantry often saw only the carnage left by the motorized divisions in the lead and the Luftwaffe in particular. The German troops marched through summer heat, blazing sun, and dense clouds of dust, though a few paved roads existed in Lithuania. The infantry observed large numbers of Soviet corpses strewn along the way, along with the blackened hulks of burned out tanks and trucks.

At the border, the infantry broke through understrength Soviet divisions and armed work units still busily attempting to prepare a defense of the border. StuG III Sturmgeschutz assault guns moved in the fore, followed closely by*Landser* infantry in their field gray uniforms. The Germans quickly smashed the Soviet formations, but to their surprise, they discovered that the Soviets in this sector showed special zeal and determination. Many Soviet riflemen hid as the German lines surged past, then emerged behind them to open fire on their rear or ambush following units who expected no hostiles behind their own forward lines.

The 1st Panzer Division under Friedrich Kirchner and the 6th Panzer Division under Erhard Raus led the attack of Panzer Group IV in the center. Infantry armies moved on the flanks, the German 18th Army advancing on the left (north) through the coastal regions and the German 16th Army on the right (south) flank, attempting to maintain contact with the northernmost units of Army Group Center.

The 1st Panzer Division almost immediately ran into difficulties as it assaulted the town of Taurage on the Jura River. The Soviets had fortified many of the houses and fought fiercely to retain them, forcing the Germans to flush them out in detail, a task requiring most of June 22nd.

Raus' 6th Panzer Division, however, punched through to the south of Taurage and drove forward deeply against weak resistance, reaching and capturing the bridge at Kangailai, spanning the Sesuvis River, intact. The 6th Panzer Division reached Erzvilkas by nightfall on June 22nd. On the 23rd, the unit raced east toward Raseiniai, its next objective, and a pair of key bridges beyond. Rolling forward through a beautiful green landscape illuminated by summer sunlight, the Germans encountered Soviet forces dug in on the first ridges of the Samogitian highland just south of Raseiniai.

Colonel Erich von Seckendorff led his *kampfgruppe* in an attack against the ridges. The Germans worked their way forward with difficulty under heavy Soviet fire, only dislodging the Red Army soldiers two hours later when their tanks finally forced their way through a tangle of swamps and woodland to threaten the Russians' rear.

In the meantime, Erhard Raus attempted to push past this battle, along the main road, in order to seize his objective of Raseiniai. However, a single shot rang out, instantly killing the commander of the lead company as it punched through his forehead. This sniper shot, taken at extreme range, also suggested the presence of Soviet machine gunners hidden in light woodland near the road to open fire on the Germans at close range. A concealed Soviet antitank gun hit and knocked out the leading tank in the German column, but for the most part, the machine gunners fired high, as is often the case with green troops, and they soon retreated, though the Germans inflicted very few casualties on them.

Raus

Even as machine gunners retreated en masse, a group of snipers positioned in isolated fruit trees between the road and the woodland inflicted a number of casualties on the 6th Panzer Division men. As Raus himself later noted, "Snipers in the trees of a forest were no novelty to our troops, but here, for the first time, they had been found in fruit trees in the open, where no one expected them. Though doomed, they had executed their mission. They had carried it out regardless of the fact that their lives were being forfeited. That willingness to die was one of the new experiences in the ambush at Paislinis." (Raus, 2003, 18). The last few Soviet snipers scrambled out of their trees and made for the protection of the forest, but none survived the dash, cut down by accurate fire from the coaxial machine guns of the panzers.

The clever ambush delayed Raus' arrival Raseiniai, but since his *kampfgruppe* ran ahead of schedule, he arrived almost precisely on time regardless. The 6th Panzer Division men launched concentric attacks against the Soviet defenders, the tanks shattering the battalions holding the town and the supporting infantry destroying the clusters of resistance that formed. Raus' men took the two bridges over the Dubyssa River intact, and Seckendorff deployed Motorcycle Battalion 6 and other 8th Panzer Division elements on the river's east bank to establish a bridgehead.

On the evening of the 23rd, the Germans of the 6th and 8th Panzer Divisions set up their field kitchens, enjoying a hot meal along with their triumphant seizure of the Dubyssa bridges. Raus records the men watching a rose-colored sunset while savoring a quiet moment amid their rapid advance. However, their leaders felt unease, as Luftwaffe reconnaissance revealed at least 200 Soviet tanks converging on the Raseiniai area from Jonava and Kadainiai.

By the following morning, the 24th, the Luftwaffe observed the Soviet tanks in Kroki, splitting into two columns, one driving for the 6th and the other for the 8th Panzer Division. The Soviet armor struck the 8th Panzer's forward elements at Betygala, on the eastern bank of the Dubyssa River. Major General Egor Solyankin led his 2nd Tank Division units forward aggressively against the Wehrmacht.

The Germans expected the lighter BT and T-26 tanks, but the heavier tanks, including the KV-1, KV-2, and early variant T-34 armored fighting vehicles, came as a shock. An anonymous German regimental combat record from one of the units engaged described the situation: "The KV-1 and -2, which we first met here, were really something! Our companies opened fire at about 800 yards, but it remained ineffective. We moved closer and closer to the enemy, who for his part continued to approach us unconcerned. Very soon we were facing each other at 50 to 100 yards. A fantastic exchange of fire took place without any visible German success. The Russian tanks continued to advance, and all armor piercing shells simply bounced off them." (Carrell, 21).

A KV-2 tank

The gigantic KV-1 and KV-2 tanks, with their distinctive looming, boxy turrets vaguely resembling a medieval knight's helmet, crashed headlong into the Motorcycle Battalion 6 troops holding ground near Betygala. Actually running over the motorcycles and men crewing them, crushing scores of machines and soldiers, the giant tanks killed the battalion's CO, one Major Schlieckmann, in the process. The motorcycle troops fell back desperately to the west bank. The Soviet troops took the opportunity to further mutilate any wounded Germans they found, then kill them. Germans who surrendered met the same fate.

German antitank gun crews deployed and opened fire, but again, the rounds simply ricocheted off the super-heavy tank armor. The KV-1s and 2s also overran the PaK antitank guns, crushing them and their crews under their wide treads. Erhard Raus recorded the failure of even a 150mm howitzer to stop a KV at point blank range, though in this case the agile gun crew escaped unscathed to tell their tale: "One of the tanks drove straight for the howitzer, which now delivered a direct hit to its frontal armor. A glare of fire and simultaneously a thunderclap of the bursting shell followed, and the tank stopped as if hit by lightning. 'That's the end of that,' the gunners thought [...] 'Yes, that fellow's had enough,' observed the section chief. [...] someone exclaimed, 'It's moving again!' Indeed, the tank advanced again, chains rattling loudly, and crashed into the heavy gun (Raus, 2003, 23).

Solyankin launched six separate attacks during the day, but the fury of the Soviet assault gradually tapered off as the tank units exhausted their extremely limited fuel and ammunition supplies. In the meantime, while Oberst Richard Koll kept the Russians busy by counterattacking with his small, light Pz35(t) tanks (a Czech design) and a handful of Panzer IVs, the 1st Panzer Division enveloped the Soviets on their left flank and elements of the 8th Panzer Division on the right, taking Solyankin's base at Kadainiai.

Though now surrounded, the Soviets continued fighting with grim determination for two more days, attempting to break out of the encirclement. The Russians committed many more tanks to the battle, but these fell prey to the 88mm Flak guns fired horizontally as antitank weapons and 10 cm howitzers used in the same fashion. Many of the vehicles also ran out of fuel, their crews fighting on in scores of individual last stands as German infantry worked their way forward to demolish them with explosive charges. The battle ended on June 26th.

Of the 690 Soviet tanks involved in this series of running battles, known overall as the Battle of Raseiniai, approximately 50 survived. Stuka dive-bombers alone accounted for roughly 200 of the lost tanks. The Soviet infantry, utterly fatigued by days of combat with almost no rest, could not muster the energy to break out effectively either.

Despite the delay caused by the strong Soviet armor attack at Raseiniai, Army Group North continued a vigorous advance through the Baltic countries, but the Germans managed to take relatively few prisoners. In most cases, the defeated Soviets, or at least the bulk of them, managed to retreat after losing a fight rather than finding themselves encircled in huge "cauldrons" as happened on other fronts. Historians ascribe the lack of envelopments in the north to either the incompetence of Hoepner and Leeb, or to terrain conditions. The Baltic terrain indeed favored evasion and escape, with numerous forests and fields of ripe grain providing cover, swamps and sandy heaths complicating efforts by Panzer Divisions at large-scale encirclements, and overall a very different, less favorable terrain type than on the other fronts.

The infantry armies continued their advance on foot, covering an average of 15 miles per day – a considerable distance through the Baltic nations' difficult terrain, and in the teeth of summer heat and stifling dust alternating sporadically with violent thunderstorm downpours. General Georg von Küchler, commanding elements of the left flank infantry pushing along the coast, ordered his men to march from 3:00-8:00 a.m. and again from 6:00-10:00 p.m., enabling them to rest during the most intense heat.

Küchler's plan paid off, for the infantry made remarkable advances and quickly captured one city after another. The German 60th Infantry Division took Ventspils and then crossed the Dvina on June 30th. The Latvian capital, Riga, fell to this formation almost bloodlessly on the following day, July 1st.

William Lubbeck, a soldier in the Infantry Division, described the reception of the Germans in the Baltic countries. Subjected to Soviet repression, NKVD arrests and death squads, and communist collectivization efforts, the locals viewed the Wehrmacht – at least initially – as welcome liberators from their brutal Stalinist masters, as Lubbeck witnessed on his entry into Riga: "Upon entering the city on July 5, small crowds along the streets greeted us with shouts of "Befreier!" (Liberator!) and presented us with flowers or chocolate in gratitude for their rescue from the Russian occupation. While some of the population remained fearful and hid in their basements, the generally positive reception we received here and throughout the Baltic states of Latvia, Lithuania, and Estonia reinforced our conviction that our cause was just." (Lubbeck, 2010, 77).

A picture of "liberating" German soldiers

On the southern (then eastern) flank of the advance, the 16th Army also pushed forward vigorously. Using the tough, effective, ubiquitous StuG III self-propelled assault guns to good effect in support of their infantry, the German 121st Infantry Division took Kaunas on June 24th, then held it for two days against Soviet counterattacks ordered by the Front commander, Fyodor Kuznetsov.

Despite being forced to use aerial resupply and captured Red Army depots due to hostile units active in their rear, the 16th Army pushed onward, taking Dvina crossings on July 6th. The army captured no less than 24 bridges intact, greatly increasing the ability of the following units to move forward and for resupply to eventually occur.

The central motorized unit threw out a flying column, including Brandenburg regiments in Soviet trucks (many of them American Ford vehicles bought by the Soviet government even prior to Lend-Lease) and the 29th Panzergrenadier Regiment, which charged forward to seize Daugavpils in southern Latvia and take its crucial river crossings, including a railroad bridge and a major road bridge, intact on the morning of June 26th. In just 4 days, the Germans had penetrated 200 miles into Soviet territory.

At Kuznetsov's order, Major General Dmitri Lelyushenko led the 12th Mechanized Corps against Daugavpils on June 28th. Instead of one heavy armored thrust, however, he expended his units' strength in many small, piecemeal attacks during the day. Erich von Manstein's men beat off the attackers with heavy losses, ably assisted by Luftwaffe Stuka attacks that left some 200 Soviet tanks burning on the city's outskirts or in the countryside to the east. The supporting Red Air Force units lost 74 aircraft in one day.

Not for the last time, Hitler and his generals worked at cross purposes with their objectives almost within reach. While Hitler badly botched Army Group Center's potentially war-winning summer drive on Moscow, in the Army Group North area the Fuhrer perceived the correct strategy and his generals lost a golden opportunity through dithering. Franz Halder accurately described the situation in the Baltics on June 29th: "Army Group North by now should be strong enough at Dvinsk [i.e. Daugavpils] to push ahead on Ostrov, perhaps also facilitate construction of a bridge at Jakobstadt by a raid in that direction. The withdrawal movements by rail and road, which are reported to be rolling day and night from Riga toward Leningrad, are probably for the most part evacuations. It seems the Russian High Command is abandoning Lithuania." (Halder, 182).

Hitler wanted to strike hard after the retreating Soviets with Army Group North's panzers, but Leeb and Walther von Brauchitsch delayed the pursuit, leaving the panzers idle near the river crossings for six entire days. Hitler fell ill simultaneously, rendering him incapable of handling his dilatory subordinates. The pause enabled the Soviets to heavily reinforce and fortify Leningrad, which likely would have fallen readily to an immediate advance after the Germans had repelled and decimated Dmitri Lelyushenko's June 28th counterattack.

By late July, the Germans in this sector had advanced 650 miles from their starting positions but still lay 100 miles short of Leningrad. They took Tallinn in Estonia in late August, while a simultaneous attack by Finnish soldiers and German Gebirgsjager (mountain troops) in the far north took Karelia but failed to advance much farther due to the unwillingness of the Finns to do anything beyond wresting their conquered territory back from the USSR.

Both Leeb and Hitler played a role in the final act of Army Group North's failure. Leeb moved slowly, sent poorly coordinated attacks, and generally failed to exploit the many opportunities offered by the initiative of his subordinate commanders. Hitler, on the other hand, ordered Leningrad taken, obsessed with the objective and failing to see the Germans could simply bypass the city and run amok in the economically important areas beyond.

Initially led by Georgi Zhukov, Leningrad held out against the Germans' attempts to take it in late August and throughout September of 1941. After that, the Wehrmacht settled down to a siege, which inflicted immense suffering on Leningrad (and the Ostheer men thrown against it) but which permanently deprived Army Group North of its initiative and mobility.

Army Group Center provided the *Schwerpunkt,* or focal point, of the Barbarossa operation. Though the other two army groups each aimed for important objectives, Army Group Center aimed for the biggest prize of 1941: Moscow itself, via Minsk and Smolensk. This could bring about possible victory for the Germans that very summer.

For this reason, Army Group Center received the most men, the strongest logistical support, and two panzer groups, Panzer Groups II and III. Heinz Guderian, a thorny and annoying man but one of the Wehrmacht's finest armor generals, led Panzer Group II. Colonel-General Hermann "Papa" Hoth, commanding Panzer Group III, represented another highly competent commander, though one less historically famous. Field Marshal Fedor von Bock commanded Army Group Center overall.

Guderian

The Army Group launched its attack at the same time as Army Groups North and South. Guderian's and Hoth's Panzer Groups spearheaded the main advance. However, German commandos in Soviet uniforms supplied by the Finns moved forward first to secure many of the border bridges ahead of the armored formations.

Guderian's panzers, on the southern flank of the advance, crossed the Bug on these bridges, storming some and in some places using assault boats. In these attacks, the low-profile, tough, and reliable StuG III Sturmgeschutz assault guns once again proved their immense utility. The 18th Panzer Division unusually deployed 80 Tauchpanzer IIIs – Panzer IIIs modified for submersibility, using a hose to supply the engine with air and a one-way valve to expel exhaust – to crawl across the riverbed of the Bug River, generating large trails of bubbles and rolling out of the water on the far side ready to fight.

A StuG III

On the map, the route of Hoth's Panzer Group III looked easier. However, after plunging deep into Soviet territory on June 22nd and capturing three Neman River bridges, Hoth's troops encountered a "dry" obstacle nearly as troublesome as a river, on June 23rd. This consisted of "the [Rudnicki] Forest, a hilly, sandy region covered with untouched natural woods that had probably never seen a motor vehicle. All the east-west routes marked on maps as roads turned out to be unmaintained dirt roads which placed almost unbearable demands on our equipment, especially the wheeled vehicles of French manufacture. Vehicles repeatedly became stuck in deep sand." (Hoth, 2015, 71),

The retreated Soviets also set forest fires here and there, further impeding the Germans. Nevertheless, Hoth's men pushed forward with great elan, energy, and professionalism, overcoming the obstacles as they occurred. By evening, the crack 7th Panzer Division, under the dynamic leadership of Major General Hans von Funck, broke free of the Rudnicki Forest. Funck thought about trying to seize Vilnius on his own, but Hoth limited him to a reconnaissance in force beyond the city.

The Germans, to their surprise, captured many bridges intact, despite the presence of massive explosive charges on their piers or other critical structural features. Captured Soviet soldiers revealed that they often feared to detonate the bridge without specific orders to do so in an army where any action not officially sanctioned easily led to a drum-head court martial and execution. Others had received orders to blow up the bridge in their care at a specific time and feared to set off the charges early, even if they saw German armored vehicles or infantry pouring across the span – again motivated by the ubiquitous presence of murderous and power-drunk commissars throughout the Red Army.

The Wehrmacht continued driving forward with great speed despite the forested terrain and other obstacles. The Soviets mounted numerous armored counterattacks following their initial shock, yet most of these simply disintegrated under the attacks of the maneuverable, skillful Germans.

Furthermore, on the first day of operations, the Luftwaffe destroyed 768 Soviet aircraft on the ground in the Army Group Center sector. The Soviet commander of the Red Air Force in the region, Colonel I.I. Kopets – who earlier boasted of how his men would devastate the Luftwaffe fliers if battle erupted – shot himself fatally with his service pistol rather than face the wrath of Stalin. Many of his pilots died making futile lone attacks on the well-coordinated German formations.

Within three days of beginning the offensive, Army Group Center launched Hoth's Panzer Group III on the north and Guderian's Panzer Group II in the south in a gigantic double envelopment into Belarus. The pincers would close on the west side of the capital, Minsk, hopefully trapping hundreds of thousands of Red Army soldiers and capturing them in a gigantic "cauldron." Superbly planned and brilliantly executed, the encirclement of the Bialystok Salient represented one of the first large-scale "pocket battles" of Barbarossa – with many more to follow.

With deficient reconnaissance data available to him due to the speed of German advance, Luftwaffe dominance in the air, and the Red Army's crippling lack of radios below the brigade level, the commander of the West Front – Dmitri Pavlov – believed that the Germans attacked toward Grodno. As a result, sent a powerful force of tanks, including 100 massive KV-1 and KV-2 tanks and 200 T-34s, plus hundreds more T-26 and BT tanks, straight towards Grodno – and thus in between the jaws of Hoth's and Guderian's advance, deploying his heaviest armor forces into the depths of the developing pocket.

Pavlov

Battered by the Luftwaffe on their way to Grodno, the Soviet "shock group's" leading elements, the 6th Armored Corps under Major General Mikhail Khatskilevich, attacked the German 256th Infantry Division on June 25th. Initially, the Germans' antitank guns failed to harm the gigantic Soviet heavy tanks, and the StuG III assault guns of Sturmgeschütz Abteilung 210 fared little better, as Horst Slesina recorded: "Then more gun barrels grew along the horizon. A tall tank turret becomes visible followed by a gigantic tank chassis. Tanks! Giant tanks like we have never seen before! […] The shots bounce off the mighty steel walls like rubber balls […] Shrill shouts beckon the assault guns […] They rush straight at the Russians […] There is a hellish crash next to me – a direct hit on one of the assault guns!" (Forczyk, 2013, 51).

Some of the KV-2 tanks, their immense boxy turrets looming over the battlefield like towers, thundered through the German lines. Rather than turning to attack the 256th Infantry Division's rear, however, these vehicles charged onward in a move inspired more by Soviet propaganda films than tactical good sense. All eventually ran into bogs, forcing their crews to abandon them.

Next, the main force of approximately 200 tanks soon came under spirited German counterattack. Crews deployed their 88mm flak guns and succeeded in knocking out more than 10 KV and T-34 tanks. With no infantry, artillery, or air support, the Soviet tanks came under combined arms attack by the Germans, who aimed at the huge vehicles' tracks. Soon, the Germans hit and knocked out Khatskilevich's T34, killing him and demoralizing his force, which pulled back.

Pavlov, receiving new intelligence, realized the perilous situation of Boldin's shock group and ordered them to pull back to the Minsk-Warsaw road to keep the encirclement from closing. However, the men learned they operated in a trap and, already driving eastward, soon began to flee. Most of the tanks broke down or stopped for lack of fuel, while Pavlov, on the following day, abandoned his HQ and headed east.

Despite Pavlov's efforts to shift units to block the pincer movement, Guderian's and Hoth's panzers defeated these units and closed the Bialystok pocket on June 27th. The pocket remained somewhat porous, enabling some individual tanks to escape, along with Boldin himself and several other high-ranking officers.

With huge numbers of Soviets already trapped, Hoth directed his panzers to attack Minsk. While Luftwaffe raids devastated the city, the 12th and 20th Panzer Divisions pushed into the suburbs, though heavy rain on the 27th slowed them. The Soviet 13th Army, a depleted formation attempting to hold Minsk's defensive belt of 560 bunkers, retreated from the city overnight, enabling its capture by noon on June 28th.

While the two Panzer Groups continued their eastward drive, expanding the pocket by linking up again east of Minsk on July 5th, followup units began the process of defeating the surrounded Russians, now deprived of fuel for their vehicles, ammunition for their weapons, and to some degree even lacking food. In accordance with standard operating procedure, the Germans divided the Bialystok-Minsk pocket into a number of smaller pockets, then rapidly compressed these to force the surrender of the Red Army units trapped within.

In all, the Germans took 341,000 prisoners, destroying or capturing 4,799 tanks and 1,777 airplanes in the process. This cost the two Panzer Groups approximately 6% of their soldiers in killed and wounded, plus 7% to 12% of their tanks as total losses, leaving them effectively intact for further operations. The Germans destroyed Soviet tanks at a 16:1 ratio (Forczyk, 2013, 54), while infantry loss ratios sometimes reached 30:1.

Picture of a destroyed Soviet plane

German pioneers and Eisenbahntruppen (literally "Iron Road Soldiers") drove rail lines forward along multiple routes for supply, frequently exceeding a rate of 15 miles per day. 19 days into Barbarossa, they had reached a point 300 miles from the starting position. Large convoys of trucks operated from the advancing rail heads. While the Germans never managed to move as many trains as they wished or planned for, the very fact that the forward elements continued to drive forward vigorously indicates that in some fashion the mix of trains, trucks, and supply airlifts sufficed to support Operation Barbarossa through the summer of 1941.

One logistical advantage enjoyed by the Germans consisted of the extremely poor logistics of the Soviet Union. The Soviets only barely supplied their units at the best of times by creating gigantic fuel depots close behind the front lines. Moving rapidly, the Wehrmacht frequently captured their fuel depots intact, periodically winning huge quantities of gasoline and diesel, the latter useful for running captured Soviet vehicles.

As Guderian and Hoth moved forward toward Smolensk in early July, the Soviet 5th and 7th Mechanized Corps launched a counterattack against Hoth with 2,000 tanks, most of them pre-war light tanks. Battle erupted when this Soviet armor met Funck's 7th Panzer Division at Senno, approximately 80 miles west of Smolensk. In the meantime, Stalin had ordered the luckless Pavlov shot for failing to halt the Germans.

The fighting near Senno began on July 7th as multiple Soviet armor columns attacked Hoth's advance troops in pleasantly warm, sunny weather. This attack, led by Major General Vasily Vinogradov, met determined resistance by the 7th Panzer Division. Roughly handled by the tough, experienced Panzer Division, Vinogradov's tankers soon found themselves confronted by tank destroyers also. The repeated Soviet attacks managed to destroy only 8 German tanks, while leaving behind 103 burning hulks when the Russians finally withdrew.

The second Soviet commander in the debacle, Major General Ilya Alekseyenko, ignored the sounds of combat on July 7th and did not move forward to launch his own attack until July 8th.

By this time, Hoth had moved up several more panzer divisions to assist Funck's 7th in flinging back the Soviets. While the German tankers expertly maneuvered, drawing Alekseyenko's clumsily commanded armor into the fields of fire of their antitank artillery, the 20th Panzer Division under Lieutenant General Horst Stumpff adroitly smashed through the Soviet 62nd Rifle Corps, guarding the rear of the Soviet armor offensive.

Advancing 36 miles on July 9th, demolishing every Soviet unit which dared to stand in the way, Stumpff's panzers took Vitebsk and threatened to cut off the two Soviet armored corps. The Soviets fled, leaving behind a startling total of 832 tanks destroyed or abandoned, their attempted counterattack at Senno transformed into a catastrophic loss by German military skill, and accomplishing nothing except their own destruction.

Thanks to the tireless efforts of the Eisenbahntruppe, the Germans soon extended their rail lines to Minsk, where they stockpiled vast quantities of fuel for the drive on Smolensk. The offensive proceeded in leapfrog fashion, with the panzers taking a city, then advancing towards the next while the following units made the city just taken into a logistical base to support the succeeding attack.

The Germans had 687,000 gallons of fuel and 2,600 tons of ammunition in Minsk by July 12th, which they immediately funneled to the advance on Smolensk. On July 10th and 11th, Guderian and Hoth took their Panzer Groups forward across the upper Dnieper River, deliberately using poor crossing points which the Soviets neglected to guard except for trivial detachments, easily brushed aside or annihilated. Funck's 7th Panzer Division, filled with its customary elan, dashed forward 60 miles to Denisov by July 13th, chopping rapidly through the already demoralized Soviet infantry divisions in its path. Once more, Hoth in the north and Guderian in the south extended their swiftly-moving panzer divisions across the landscape like horns to encircle Smolensk, while motorized infantry rolled straight towards the city to seal the trap.

Lieutenant General Pavel Kurochkin's Soviet 20th Army held Smolensk. Marshal Semyon Timoshenko attempted to help by throwing multiple infantry units into the path of Panzer Groups II and III, but the Germans dispersed these without significantly slowing.

The jaws of the trap crashed shut around the Smolensk pocket on July 15th. General Ivan Yeremenko recorded how the infantry deployed to stop the panzer thrusts reacted when Wehrmacht armor actually appeared: "The Germans attacked with large armoured formations, often with infantrymen riding on the tanks. Our infantry were not prepared for that. At the shout 'Enemy tanks!' our companies, battalions, and even entire regiments scuttled to and fro, seeking cover behind anti-tank-gun or artillery positions [...] all operational control, contact, and co-operation were rendered impossible." (Carell, , 52).

On the same day, Lieutenant General Walter von Boltenstern led the 29th Motorized Infantry Division into the streets of Smolensk from the southwest. Swarms of StuG III Sturmgeschutz assault guns crawled forward, blowing apart the concrete pillboxes and street barricades of the Soviets. Flammpanzer flamethrower tanks followed, literally burning out the defenders of strongpoints. Large batteries of Nebelwerfer rocket launchers sent their shrieking missiles towards the defenders, and 88mm flak guns engaged and destroyed any Soviet armor that tried to stop the street-by-street advance.

Boltenstern's men took the southern half of Smolensk on the 15th. At 4 a.m. on the 16th, they forced the Dnieper crossing and began smashing every iota of Soviet resistance in the northern half of the city as well. By 11 p.m., the defenders had been captured or wiped out and the important forward base of Smolensk – intended as the jumping-off point for the attack on Moscow – lay in German hands.

Eastern Front

22 June 1941 – 1 September 1941

☐ to 9 July 1941
☐ to 1 September 1941
☐ to 9 September 1941

The extent of the German advance from June-September

With the fall of Smolensk on July 16th, Army Group Center had advanced 440 miles from its starting position in a period of just 25 days. This represented 66% of the way to Moscow; only 220 miles still separated the Germans from their objective. Additionally, the Army Group mustered some 50 mostly intact divisions, while the Soviets only had 26 divisions still available for the defense of Moscow.

During the following days, up to August 5th, the Germans battled hard to eliminate the Red Army forces caught in the Smolensk pocket. By the end of the fight, the Soviets had lost another 3,200 tanks, 3,000 artillery pieces, 1,000 aircraft, and 302,000 prisoners to the Germans.

The Soviet defenders of Mogilev still held out at this point, representing the only significant Red Army force still active west of Smolensk. Lieutenant General Vasily Gerasimenko commanded three divisions of the Soviet 13th Army holding the city, and the men under his leadership defended the metropolis with suicidal courage. Major General Heinz Hellmich, later killed at Cherbourg by 20mm cannon rounds fired from a US Air Force P-38 Lightning, led the German 23rd Infantry Division of VII Corps in an assault on Mogilev, beginning on July 20th.

Stubborn Soviet resistance continued through July 26th, when the Red Army soldiers, sensing their imminent defeat, blew up the Dnieper bridges, denying them to the Germans but cutting themselves off in the process.

The Germans fought their way into the city as the Soviets made a last desperate effort to break out westward in a truck convoy. The Germans riddled this with heavy fire, wiping out much of the force and taking 12,000 men prisoner overall. Nevertheless, Gerasimenko himself and a number of his officers managed to fight their way clear of the doomed city. When the Germans entered the streets, they found them running with brown rivulets of beer, as the Soviets had destroyed the huge Mogilev brewery's storage tanks and vats to deny the beverage to the Wehrmacht.

German soldiers at Mogilev

With Smolensk taken, the Germans drove rapidly forward and took Yelnia, creating a salient into Soviet lines. It was at this moment that Hitler's strange tendency to shy away from the culminating stroke of a military victory emerged. In France in 1940, Hitler twice halted decisive offensives and diverted the troops to secondary objectives, as if fearful of the risk of a climactic battle – or perhaps fearing success itself. He halted Guderian's drive to the coast in France, and then stopped the attack on Dunkirk until too late, missing the opportunity to deal the English a crippling blow both in human losses and morale.

With practically all of his men and officers straining forward, eager to be unleashed against Moscow, the Fuhrer suddenly decided to send Guderian south to help take Kiev and Hoth north to seize Leningrad, thus utterly dissipating the juggernaut-like onrush of Army Group Center. Hitler's generals protested strenuously, but the Fuhrer merely replied contemptuously that his commanders did not understand economics or politics. Of course, Hitler himself completely overlooked the economic and political consequences of *losing*, as the Germans might well do if they failed to capture the nerve center of Moscow and deal a fatal blow to the Soviet Union west of the Caucasus.

After much protest, Hitler allowed Hoth's men to remain with Army Group Center. Guderian's Panzer Group II, however, found itself sent south to waste precious weeks helping Army Group South capture the definitely peripheral objective of Kiev. The Soviets lacked any significant tank strength between Smolensk and Moscow during the rest of 1941 – and in fact, the German vehicles now outnumbered the utterly decimated Soviet machines by a factor of 2:1 in this region.

Marshal Georgi Zhukov launched the Yelnia Counteroffensive in early August, and fighting continued all month, with the Soviets finally breaking through and retaking Yelnia on September 6th. However, this victory failed to damage the German panzer corps, which Fedor von Bock did not commit, or the motorized infantry divisions used to support panzer breakthroughs. All of the losses inflicted by the counteroffensive fell upon the German 4th Army's infantry, and therefore failed to cripple or even lessen Army Group Center's potential for Blitzkrieg operations.

In fact, Zhukov lost an additional 75,000 casualties while inflicting approximately 10,000 casualties on the Germans. He also managed to lose most of the 300 tanks with which he began the offensive, attenuating Moscow's armor defenses even further. The Marshal, furious at the failure to achieve more, lashed out at the depleted tank divisions under his command: "105th Tank Division, despite my categorical warning about moving forward, has marked time in place for 10 days and, without achieving any kind of result, has suffered losses. In light of its inability to resolve independent combat missions, 105th Tank Division is disbanded and will turn its personnel and equipment over to 102nd Tank Division." (Forczyk, 2013, 98).

After greatly delaying the launch of the Wehrmacht attack on Moscow, Hitler ordered it to begin in late September. At this point, Guderian's Panzer Group II had to turn back northeast and fight its way back up to the Moscow area, while the rest of Army Group Center pushed forward towards the city directly.

In the ensuing campaign, the Germans inflicted defeat after defeat on the Soviets, but they suffered immense equipment losses due to the almost bottomless mud of the autumn *Rasputitsa*, or muddy season. The Germans fought into the city's suburbs, with some men claiming to see the spires of St. Basil's in the distance with their field glasses, but could go no further in the face of winter, exhaustion, and rapidly growing Soviet resistance.

The Fuhrer, of course, did not blame himself for this development. Instead, he sidelined one of his best panzer leaders, Heinz Guderian, for the remainder of the war, blaming him for the failure of Operation Typhoon. This, of course, overlooked the fact that Guderian argued strongly and repeatedly in favor of a summer drive on Moscow.

While the question of whether the Germans could have captured Moscow in the summer necessarily remains unanswerable with full certainty, it remains very likely they could have. The Wehrmacht nearly managed to take Moscow even in the teeth of the yards-deep mud of the autumn *Rasputitsa,* the onset of an extraordinarily bitter winter, and fresh Soviet reinforcements brought in from Siberia. Remarkably, they reached the suburbs of Moscow even with their vehicles and men depleted by a massive diversion of Panzer Group II to Kiev, a deteriorating logistical situation, and resurgent Soviet morale.

An offensive in August and early September might very well have driven forward through demoralized, decimated Soviet divisions with only half the strength of the Germans facing them. The Germans would have faced none of the reinforcements present later, since Stalin could not shift his Siberian divisions so quickly, and they would have been advancing over dry, firm roads in hot and dusty but operationally superior summer weather, supported by direct rail lines and a truck fleet not bogged down in the mud.

While nothing is certain in war, had Hitler permitted a summer Blitzkrieg attack straight through to Moscow, a very high probability exists that panzergrenadiers would have raised the Kriegsflagge of the Third Reich over the Kremlin – seizing the Soviet Union's crucial railway, logistical, and communications nerve center and quite possibly ending Operation Barbarossa with another Wehrmacht victory.

Picture of a German soldier passing a destroyed tank and a dead crew member in Ukraine

As with the other sectors, Russian-speaking Germans outfitted in Soviet uniforms, driving Soviet vehicles and wielding Soviet small arms – all supplied by the Finns – led the way for Army Group South. This deception enabled the Germans to quickly slaughter a number of border posts, seizing some bridges near the border with almost no resistance or chance of demolition.

At 3:15 a.m. on June 22nd, a gigantic artillery preparation swept over known Soviet positions south of the Pripet marshes. The German gunners targeted fortified strongpoints and communication centers in particular, softening up the tougher defensive works and helping to further short-circuit the already inadequate Red Army radio net. Meanwhile, assault boats packed with German soldiers rowed quickly across the rivers at the Soviet/Nazi boundary in this region. Some of the Wehrmacht units attacked so vigorously that they punched through the Soviet front lines entirely, which then flowed shut behind them, encircling these regiments or divisions in small, temporary "pockets."

The Western Bug River formed much of Army Group South's initial border with the Soviets, blocking Panzer Group I under Ewald von Kleist until the combat engineers constructed two large pontoon bridges across the flow. On the other side, Lieutenant General Mikhail Kirponos, commanding the Southwestern Front – one of the two Red Army fronts in the Ukraine – found himself defending with a sizable portion of the USSR's 1941 tank force, due to Stalin's conviction the *Schwerpunkt* would occur in the south, but such an abysmally poor communications network that he could not establish even a modicum of control until June 24th, two days after Barbarossa started.

Though the Soviets launched armored counterattacks against Army Group South as early as June 23rd, these often developed in an extremely amateurish fashion, squandering the potential of the heavily-armored and well-armed T-34, KV-1, and KV-2 tanks. In one instance, Oberleutnant

Edel Zachariae-Lingenthal with five Panzer III tanks managed to drive off a column of T-34s with ineffective, non-penetrating hits which nevertheless seemingly unnerved the inexperienced crews: "Even though at this short distance every shot was a hit, the Russians drove on without much visible effect... Despite repeated hits, our fire had no effect. It appears as if shells are simply bouncing off. The enemy tanks disengaged without fighting and retreated." (Forczyk, 2013, 57).

Major General Sergei Ogurtsov followed up this abortive push with the first major Soviet tank attack in the Ukraine, throwing 100 tanks and two battalions of motorized infantry against Gustav-Adolf Riebel's Panzer Regiment 15 near Radekhov. The German panzers, supported by field artillery and antitank guns, pulverized Ogurtsov's initial wave of light T-26 tanks and armored cars.

When the second wave, consisting of early-model T-34 tanks, moved in, the Germans found themselves in a sticky situation. The Panzer III and IV tanks – the latter still lacking the 7.5cm KwK 40 L/43 gun capable of knocking out T-34s, which only appeared in the field in the Ausf. F version of 1942 – could not damage these Soviet armored fighting vehicles. While the artillery disabled some by hitting their tracks – an unsatisfactory solution – the Germans only routed Ogurtsov's attack when the Panzer IV crews fired their grenade launchers at close range, setting the fuel drums carried on the T-34s' rear decks ablaze.

The Soviets continued to launch small, piecemeal armor attacks throughout late June and into early July, depleting their tank reserves without seriously hampering the Germans. Wehrmacht units cast out numerous motorized recon detachments, found the weak points between Soviet divisions, then penetrated these to envelop the luckless Red Army soldiers. Within a few days, Army Group South crushed Stalin's border defenses.

The Germans worked hard to break through and achieve operational freedom of movement, essential to the successful application of mobile warfare or "Blitzkrieg." On top of that, a particular bugbear of the Southwest Front existed in the person of Corps Commissar N.N. Vashugin. This power-drunk zealot, with a military tribunal and a platoon of NKVD killers in tow, haunted the headquarters of various units, beginning with Kirponos' own and extending down to local commanders attempting to stop the Germans. Vashugin proved an able, if unwitting, helper to the Wehrmacht, terrorizing and dominating the leaders facing Army Group South, demoralizing them with constant accusations and threats of execution, and ordering suicidally incompetent attacks over the objections of more knowledgeable men.

On June 27th, the advancing Germans of Ewald von Kleist's Panzer Group I, along with infantry of Hyazinth von Strachwitz, became embroiled in heavy fighting near Dubno and Brody, in a battle variously known as the Battle of Dubno, the Battle of Brody, or the Battle of Rovno. The Soviets deployed some 3,500 tanks of the 10th Tank Division and the 4th, 8th, 15th, 19th, and 22nd Mechanized Corps in an attempted encircling attack. The battle continued through June 30th, with 750 German panzers matched against 3,500 Soviet tanks, including a total of 717 T-34 and KV tanks, nearly half of the existing stock of these heavier tanks in the Red Army arsenal of mid-1941. Franz Halder's war journal notes, "Army Group South reports still heavy fighting. On the right shoulder of Armored Group 1, behind the sector of Eleventh Armored Div., a deep penetration by Russian Eighth Armored Corps in our lines, apparently has caused a lot of confusion in the area between Brody and Dubno and temporarily threatens Dubno from the southwest. This would have been very undesirable in view of the large dumps at Dubno." (Halder, 181).

A panzer division

After initial success, the Soviet attacks bogged down thanks to utter confusion among the commanders. Various parties issued orders and others countermanded them. The Germans recovered from their initially heavy losses and set about smashing their floundering opponents in detail. Luftwaffe Stuka dive-bombers devastated the Soviet armor in open country, destroying 201 tanks in one day alone. The Germans, their lighter tanks unable to easily destroy the heavy Soviet vehicles, used combined arms with antitank guns, artillery, and endless airstrikes to blow the Soviets to pieces.

As the Battle of Dubno reached its climax, the psychopathic Commissar Vashugin once more took a hand. Lieutenant General Dmitri Ryabyshev mustered the 8th Armored Corps on June 28th. He planned to attack on the 29th directly into Dubno, as soon as supporting units moved up. However, Commissar Vashugin arrived at Ryabyshev's field HQ on the road south of Dubno, already in a rage because the 8th was not advancing – despite this being the tactically sound choice.

Ryabyshev attempted to explain that he awaited more units to make a larger attack with flank support, rather than suicidally feeding his tanks in piecemeal. Another Commissar, Nikolai Popel, recorded the incredible scene which followed, though like many other men, he refused to name Vashugin in his memoirs, perhaps due to one of the many superstitions evinced by Russians: "[Vashugin] walked directly at Ryabyshev, trampling bushes with his highly polished boots. […] in a voice tense with fury, he asked, 'How much did you sell yourself for, Judas?' Ryabyshev was standing at […] attention in front of [Vashugin], confused, not knowing what to say […] Ryabyshev spoke up first: 'Comrade Corps Commissar, if you would hear me out...' 'You will be heard by military tribunal, traitor. Right here, under this fir, we'll hear you out, and right here we'll shoot you.'" (Kamenir, 2008, 205-206).

With his choices limited to a useless immediate assault or death by firing squad, Ryabyshev sent the 8th Motorized Corps into action without the supporting units that might have made the attack successful. He led his 303 tanks, including almost 100 T-34 and KV tanks, into the Battle of Dubno once again. Encountering the 16th Panzer Division, along with the German 57th and 75th Infantry Divisions, the 8th Motorized Corps recoiled after losing nearly 100 tanks, including over a dozen T-34s and 3 KV-1s.

At this point, Vashugin intervened, personally taking command and leading forward the 207 surviving tanks of the 8th Motorized Corps. The commissar, full of hubris but knowing nothing of actual combat, steered the tanks directly into a swamp. Vehicle after vehicle sank into the soft, muddy ground, brown water gurgling up to short out its engine and force its crew to abandon it. Only 43 tanks managed to pull back, leaving more than 150 destroyed by Vashugin's incompetence without a single German shot fired.

After this final disaster, Commissar Vashugin, suddenly overwhelmed with despair and probable guilt, shot himself. Khrushchev actually witnessed Vashugin's suicide, an action which undoubtedly brought great relief to all Soviet commanders in the Ukraine and might explain their somewhat improved performance thereafter. Khrushchev recalled, "[H]e said to me that he had decided to shoot himself. I said: 'What are you talking about? [...]' He answered: 'I am guilty of giving incorrect orders to the commanders of the mechanized corps. I don't want to live any longer.' [...] So I said: 'Why are you talking foolishness? If you've decided to shoot yourself, what are you waiting for?' I wanted to jolt him with some sharp words [...] But he suddenly pulled out his pistol [...], put it to his temple, fired, and fell." (Khrushchev, 2005, 310).

With the Soviet armor utterly smashed at the Battle of Dubno, the Germans secured the large, welcome fuel depots in the town, then moved on towards the Dniester. The Soviets knocked out some 200 German tanks in the battle, but of these, the Germans wrote off only 25, the remainder repaired and soon put back into service. The Soviets, by contrast, lost a minimum of 800 tanks, the vast majority lost behind German lines and therefore irretrievable.

Army Group South had won free operational space and could continue the offensive rapidly on its own terms. Ahead lay the Stalin Line, a defensive line anchored on the Pripet Marshes in the north, and beyond that, the city of Kiev, the Dnieper River, and the industrial Donbas region, all, as it seemed, ripe for the plucking.

Following the Battle of Dubno, the forces of Army Group South won operational space, giving them room to maneuver. Rundstedt kept up the pressure, moving on against the Stalin Line. This did not represent a solid fortified line but instead a series of defended strongpoints along key roads and at river crossings, stretching south from the Pripet Marshes.

Army Group South fought its way through the Stalin Line during the first week in July, facing stubborn Soviet resistance: "Three company commanders of the 108th Rifle Regiment and three officers of the 4th Armored Artillery Regiment fell on 7 July during the planned attack on Zviagel. Since 0430 hours, the battle had been raging around the Zviagel bunker line [...] At 1530 hours, after a stuka attack, our shock troops, suffering heavy losses, worked their way to the bunkers and had to engage each one of them in hand-to-hand combat." (Haupt, 1998, 24).

The German infantry crossed the immense spaces of the Ukraine, most often on their own feet. Accustomed to the confined regions of western Europe, the men of the Ostheer found themselves confronted by endless vistas familiar and even comfortable to Russians and Americans, but somewhat eerie to men of the Reich, as Gottlob Bidermann recorded eloquently: "The Ukraine steamed in the summer heat. Over wide, sandy roads and on pavement of rough stones we came into a land of unending horizons. Endless wide steppes and grain and sunflower fields bordered our way towards the east. Primitive wooden windmills dotted the horizon, and we used them as our drink and rest stations during the lonely march through a land that left us with unforgettable impressions of freedom contrasting with an overwhelming sense of emptiness." (Bidermann,

2000, 16-17).

Initial probing attacks against Kiev having failed, Kleist left an infantry army to besiege the heavily fortified metropolis while his panzers drove forward to the south of Kiev into the great eastward bend of the Dnieper River. The Soviets tried to take Kleist's rapid advance in flank in the third week of July, but ended up being encircled instead. In the huge "cauldron" at Uman, south of Kiev, Kleist's panzers encircled the Soviet 6th and 12th armies, along with part of the 18th, on the east, while the infantry advanced implacably from the west. The Soviets kept up a desperate fight well into August, but the Germans compressed and eliminated the pocket, taking 103,000 prisoners and seizing or destroying thousands of vehicles.

Kleist forced the Dnieper crossings at multiple points, no mean feat considering the river's width varied from one-half mile to a full mile south of Kiev. With his troops on the eastern bank, he prepared to strike north to cut off the huge Soviet salient with Kiev at its tip.

In the meantime, Heinz Guderian, detached from Army Group Center, attacked south across the Desna with Panzer Group II. The two panzer groups completed a classic double envelopment of the Kiev pocket on September 14th, trapping hundreds of thousands of Red Army soldiers held in place by Stalin's suicidally poor orders. Kirponos himself died trying to escape the encirclement, killed by the fragments of a mortar shell, and Kiev fell on September 18th. The Germans took over 600,000 prisoners

While Guderian turned away to the ultimately abortive late-autumn drive on Moscow, Army Group South began its push toward the Donbas industrial area, Kharkov, the Sea of Azov, and the Crimea. With the Panzer Groups newly renamed Panzer Armies, Army Group South directed its spearheads towards the Sea of Azov even before fully crushing the Kiev pocket.

Gustav Anton von Wietersheim started the action with the XIV Panzer Corps from the Dnepropetrovsk bridgehead against the Dnieper, attacking Ryabyshev's Southern Front. The panzers pulverized the Soviet rifle divisions facing them. Wietersheim led the XIV Panzer Corps southeast, then turned south, encircling and destroying the five divisions of Soviet infantry guarding the Dnieper between Dnepropetrovsk and Zaporozhe, the famous former stronghold of the Zaporozhian Cossacks. Eberhard von Mackensen assisted with the III Panzer Corps, while units of motorized infantry provided followup and mopping up.

Incredibly, Ryabyshev ignored the threat to his rear presented by Kleist's rapidly advancing Panzer Divisions. Sensing the opportunity for a fresh encirclement, the highly skilled Hans-Valentin Hube led his 16th Panzer Division in a rapid drive to Orikhiv, a place where the Red Army crushed German Mennonite militias during the Russian Civil War. Simultaneously, the German 11th Army attacked Ryabyshev's forces in front, effectively pinning them in place.

Ryabyshev managed to send the Soviet 130th Tank Brigade in a counterattack against Orikhiv, hoping to force open an escape route. However, the 13th and 14th Panzer Divisions joined Hube's 16th, forming an impenetrable blockade.

The SS Division Liebstandarte Adolf Hitler and the XIV Panzer Corps under Wietersheim – who would survive the war to die at age 90 in 1974 – smashed through fleeing Red Army units to take Berdiansk, a Ukrainian port city on the Sea of Azov, on October 6th.

Though Ryabyshev escaped, the Germans had created another massive pocket centered on Melitopol. Army Group South compressed the Melitopol pocket rapidly, annihilating the Soviet 9th and 12th Armies. 106,000 Red Army soldiers surrendered, while the Germans also captured or destroyed 210 more tanks, weakening Red Army tank stocks further. Wietersheim's drive represented another operational triumph, carrying the Wehrmacht deep into Ukrainian territory.

In the meantime, the German 6th Army pushed for Kharkov. Rain slowed their advance at first, but several gloriously sunny autumn days in mid-September provided firm roads and a boost to morale. The Soviets made occasional armor attacks and laid down harassing fire from their artillery, but their retreat resembled a rout in many instances. An officer in the 1./Sturmgeschutz-Abteilung 197, Heinrich Skodell, recorded one of many such incidents as his StuG III assault gun accompanied the 6th Army towards Kharkov: "We reached the main road to Poltava. Panic had broken out their among the retreating Russians. Pedestrians, horses, vehicles, and tanks swarmed together. We fired into their midst with two assault guns. We dispatched 10 tanks and captured 1,000 prisoners. Towards the evening, we surprised the enemy in his flank and caused unholy confusion. The Russians left an unbelievable amount of materiel and dead men behind." (Munch, 2005, 10).

The 6th Army pushed on, reaching Poltava by September 23rd. The StuG IIIs formed the advance guard, taking on tanks with AP shells and infantry with HE and machine guns. Most of the Red Army soldiers encountered seemed aged 40-50 years, some with as little as 8 days military training, and with no commissars to attempt to prevent their surrender.

Considerable pleasant weather continued until mid-October, when alternating frosts, snow, pouring rain, and sunny days slowed but did not halt the advance on Kharkov. The StuG IIIs proved extremely resilient, far surpassing the other German vehicles' ability to withstand the worsening conditions. Most remained operational despite mud, rain, bitter cold, and other adverse conditions. They spearheaded the attack into Kharkov on October 23rd, and helped seize the city completely on October 24th.

Other German forces stormed the four mile wide Isthmus of Perekop into the Crimea, taking the "Tartar Ditch" defensive works during a difficult four-day battle. Erich von Manstein's forces, along with Romanian and Italian forces, quickly subdued most of the Crimea but could not take the fortress of Sevastopol. Instead, they laid siege to it, eventually taking it on July 4th, 1942.

On November 20th, Sepp Dietrich's Leibstandarte SS Division achieved Army Group South's furthest eastward advance with their seizure of Rostov-on-Don. The Germans took the Don River bridge with a surprise attack: "The men of the 3rd Company and the efficient men of the Fellhauer Engineer Group attacked across the 500 meter steel girder bridge. A thick bundle of fuse at the bridge's foundation led to explosives, and it was skillfully cut by the engineers. [...] we surprisingly crossed to the southern bank intact and were able to surprise and disarm the bridge watch (about 30 men) by the evening meal." (Haupt, 1998, 103).

The Germans held Rostov-on-Don for only about a week. Timoshenko mounted an early winter offensive that lost many men but pushed Army Group South out of the city. Timoshenko's men pushed the Wehrmacht back to the Mius River, where Kleist established a line the Soviets could not break.

Hitler, furious at the retreat to the Mius, sacked Gerd von Rundstedt and flew to Poltava. However, after consulting with Ewald von Kleist and Sepp Dietrich, among others, the Fuhrer relented and came as close as he ever did to apologizing to one of his generals and admitting himself wrong. General Georg von Sodenstern of the infantry recorded the result: "Hitler rejoined: "Where is Field-Marshal von Rundstedt?" The latter was waiting, in accordance with instructions, in another room. There [...] a scene of reconciliation took place, in which Hitler excused himself on the grounds of a "misunderstanding," begged the Field Marshal to see that his health was restored by a period of sick leave and then once more place his incomparable services at his [Hitler's] disposal." (Messenger, 2012, 156).

Rundstedt served next in the west and never returned to Russia. In the meantime, Army Group

South dug in to repel Soviet counterattacks and wait for spring, when the assault towards the Caucasus oil fields could perhaps be resumed.

Even as the Germans were hurtling units east at the start of the invasion, commissar Nikita Khrushchev assisted in directing the effort to build up defensive works around Kiev. The task proved particularly challenging. The Irpin River, meandering just to the west of Kiev, resembles a mere brook compared to the mighty Dnieper, but presented a formidable obstacle to mechanized forces in 1941 due to the swamps and marshes of its floodplain.

The Soviets built a Kiev defensive belt along the Irpin in the late 1920s, completing it in 1930. However, Khrushchev found this in complete disrepair thanks to an order from Stalin: "There were reinforced concrete pillboxes with artillery there, but I have already mentioned how they were destroyed [...] Stalin ordered them destroyed. His intention [...] was that our command staff would not look back, but would keep its eyes fixed on the fortifications along our new border [...] Some reinforced concrete structures still existed, but there were no weapons in them [...] [We] began gathering together anything we could: rifles, cannon, and so on, with the aim of building up a defensive line somehow (Khrushchev, 2005, 315).

The Soviet 26th Army under Lieutenant General Fyodor Yakovlevich Kostenko worked on the new defensive works, while Khrushchev mobilized and organized 160,000 civilians from Kiev to assist. Working feverishly, the Ukrainians completed an impressive defensive zone in a surprisingly brief time. By the time the Germans arrived, 18 miles of antitank trenches defended the approaches to Kiev, along with 750 new concrete or log bunkers and vast swathes of barbed wire entanglements.

This impressive effort, restoring and even augmenting the original defenses, soon bore fruit. The first direct move against Kiev occurred on July 10th, when III Panzer Corps under Friedrich von Mackensen made a rapid drive directly towards the city. However, when Mackensen arrived at the Irpin, he declined to attack without infantry support (100 miles to the rear), not wishing to risk his valuable panzers in a frontal assault on a fortified, well-defended metropolis. Though the Irpin itself represented a trivial obstacle, the soft ground and swamps flanking it represented a fatally dangerous zone for armor to attempt traversing while under fire from a dense concentration of bunkers.

Khrushchev's efforts had already bought time for the defenders and citizens of Kiev. Nevertheless, the 13th and 14th Panzer Divisions and the 25th Motorized Infantry Division loomed threateningly on the Irpin's west bank for days, foreshadowing the Germans' determination to take Kiev.

On July 10th, despite the appearance of Mackensen near Kiev, Kirponos launched an attack southeast against Panzer Group I's flank near Berdychev. German Panzerjäger I tank destroyers – gimmicky modifications of the Panzer I tank with an open fighting compartment housing a 4.7 cm PaK(t) antitank gun – of Abteilung 670 had already mauled the 5th Army's tank assets near Zhitomir two days previously.

The Soviets attacked with desperate courage, committing the 9th, 19th, and 22nd Mechanized Corps against Kleist's divisions, supported by three rifle corps and all the aircraft the Soviets could still muster. Under the blazing Ukrainian summer sun, the Germans and Soviets maneuvered, fought, and died on the flat landscape, cut by riverbeds and dotted with villages, in a ferocious combat lasting nearly four days. When the three Mechanized Corps withdrew late on July 13th, only 95 tanks remained between them. III Panzer Corps shifted away from Kiev as the German 6th Aarmy's infantry finally caught up with their armor's dashing advance, and Kleist, with Panzer Group I now reassembled and the Soviet 5th Army on the retreat, decided to strike rapidly between the 5th Army and the Soviet 6th and 12th Armies to the south of Kiev.

Hitler, watching the unfolding situation of all three Army Groups in detail, issued Fuhrer Directive No. 33 on July 19th, 1941. This directive fell in perfectly with Kleist's inclinations, reading in part that "the most important object is, by concentric attacks, to destroy the enemy 12th and 6th Armies while they are still west of the Dnieper." (Forczyk, 2013, 93-94).

The situation near Kiev now took an even more disastrous turn, if possible, for the Soviets. The Stavka (Soviet supreme command) formed the 5th Cavalry Corps and 4th Rifle Corps, located east of the Dnieper, into the Soviet 26th Army, then threw this across to the river's west bank, south of Kiev, in an effort to help the 6th and 12th Armies.

Kleist devised a bold operational plan to effect the destruction of the targeted Soviet armies. He sent Mackensen's III Panzer Corps east to halt the Soviet 26th Army at the Dnieper, while the infantry of the German 6th Army continued to invest Kiev despite heavy artillery fire from the defenders. The XIV and XLVIII Panzer Corps made a swift encircling movement around the Soviet 6th and 12th Armies on the eastern side, while infantry divisions of the German 17th Army advanced from the west, acting as the hammer crushing the Soviets against the anvil of the XIV and XLVIII Panzer Corps.

As frequently happens in war, Kleist's plan did not survive contact with the enemy, but the Battle of Uman, or the Uman Encirclement, nevertheless developed into a catastrophic loss for the Soviets. Mackensen's III Panzer Corps, including the SS Wiking Division, surged eastward against the Soviet 26th Army's 10 divisions on July 15th. Simultaneously, Werner Kempf's XLVIII Panzer Corps pushed south and west, driving the Soviet 6th Army westwards toward the relentlessly advancing German 17th Army. The XIV Panzer Corps drove into the gap between the 6th and 26th Armies, increasing the isolation of the two Soviet armies in the Uman pocket. On July 18th, the XIV Panzer Corps swung east to help Mackensen's III Panzer Corps against the 26th Army.

The battle raged on throughout late July. Kempf's panzers in the east and the 17th Army infantry in the west, led by Karl-Heinrich von Stulpnagel, slowly tightened their encirclement. This gradually closed the remaining gap in the southeast through which the Soviets might have escaped, but Stalin's order to retreat only straight eastward was an impossible maneuver thanks to the dense masses of aggressive German panzer divisions in the way.

The Soviets nevertheless fought hard, surprising the Germans with the savagery of their resistance. General-Major Yuri Novoselsky led the Soviet 2nd and 24th Motorized Corps, the former mustering one KV-1 and 18 T-34 tanks alongside the T-26 light tanks still comprising the bulk of the Red Army's armor, to block the 11th and 16th Panzer Divisions.

Meeting at Monastryshchye on July 21st, the Soviet and German forces struggled in a desperate week-long battle which kept the pocket from closing immediately. This fight continued until July 27th, when loss of tanks and lack of fuel to run the remaining armored vehicles obliged Novoselsky to abandon the attack. The Soviet 18th Army attempted to intervene, but only succeeded in allowing the Germans to trap part of its manpower in the Uman Pocket also.

The German 17th Army continued its relentless advance, using the Hungarian troops of Major General Bela Miklos to conduct local mobile operations as needed. Though the 17th technically represented an infantry army, the Hungarian Rapid Corps, with slightly more than divisional strength, fielded three battalions of 38M Toldi light tanks, four motorized infantry battalions, and twice as many bicycle battalions! Despite the eccentric forces under his command, Miklos proved an able, aggressive, decisive leader.

Miklos

The leading elements of the 17th Army and the SS Leibstandarte linked up at Pervomaysk's bridge across the Bug River on August 2nd, completing the encirclement of the Soviet 6th, 12th, and part of the 18th Armies at Uman, south of Kiev. Miklos' Rapid Corps and the 9th Panzer Division met on August 3rd, strengthening the girdle of men and machines now hemming in 20 divisions of Red Army soldiers. The Germans now set about squeezing the pocket, compressing it from all sides and pounding it with artillery. The thundering barrages, creeping forward ahead of the advancing Wehrmacht and directed at concentrations of Soviet troops gathering for a breakout attempt, smashed tanks, trucks, and men with lethal impartiality.

By August 5th, the remaining Soviets found themselves packed into an area consisting of only 14 square miles. In the process, the Germans hammered the Uman Pocket with more artillery shells than they had used during the entire invasion of France, Scandinavia, and the Low Countries combined.

Finally, on August 8th, the despairing Soviets stopped fighting, permitting the Germans to round them up in vast numbers. The generals of the 6th and 12th Armies, Ivan Muzychenko and Pavel Ponyedelin, surrendered to the Germans and spent the rest of the war at the Bavarian POW camp Stalag VII-A. Liberated by the US 14th Armored Division on April 29th, 1945, the two men returned to the USSR. While Muzychenko lived out the rest of his life, Stalin ordered Ponvedelin shot in 1950.

The German OKW's final report on the Uman Encirclement described the outcome: "German troops, in cooperation with Hungarian formations, have enjoyed great success in the Ukraine […] Over 103,000 prisoners […] have fallen into our hands. 317 tanks, 858 guns, 242 anti-tank cannons and air defense guns, 5,250 trucks, twelve railroad trains, and additional war materials have been captured. Enemy losses total more than 200,000 men." (Haupt, 1998, 39).

Those men who escaped the trap almost all fled to the port city of Odessa, where they soon found themselves encircled anew, either to be taken prisoner or be evacuated by sea. The Germans paid for their victory with 4,610 killed and 15,458 wounded, a casualty ratio of 10:1 in their favor. This indicated the difficulty of the fighting, since elsewhere during Barbarossa the Germans inflicted losses at a rate of 20:1 or even 30:1.

In the wake of that fighting, the German 17th Army next advanced toward the Dnieper, pushing the Soviet units on the western bank back to the river. The 11th Army joined them, while Kleist sent Panzer Group I south to occupy the remaining territory between Kiev, the Dnieper, and the sea. The Soviets, hard-pressed by the relentless panzer divisions, used large numbers of antitank mines for the first time, inflicting some damage on their pursuers and slowing the pursuit, even as the eventual result remained a foregone conclusion.

While the Germans mopped up the western bank of the Dnieper, Kirponos, defending Kiev with Vlasov's 37th Army and the Soviet 5th Army under another skilled soldier, Lieutenant General Mikhail Potapov, did not remain wholly idle. Though lacking armor, with only around three dozen tanks still operational, Kirponos flung these against Malyn, just northwest of Kiev, on July 24th, supported by one division of cavalry and two rifle (infantry) divisions.

The Wehrmacht LI Army Corps held Malyn, anchoring the left (northern) flank of the German 6th Army, investing Kiev from the west and facing Khrushchev's bunkers and defensive works across the swampy Irpin River. The LI Army Corps flung the Russians back, but Kirponos fed more reinforcements in, with attacks continuing against the 6th Army flank for 12 days, with the last occurring on August 4th.

Once Kirponos' 5th Army recoiled, leaving the landscape around Malyn strewn with burned out Russian vehicles and windrows of Soviet corpses, the German 6th Army attempted the first serious assault against Kiev. Their commanders hoped that the Russians had depleted their forces sufficiently during the nearly two-week Malyn battle to crumple under the assault of a single German army.

General Hans von Obstfelder, then 55 years of age but destined to live to 90 and be decorated with the Knight's Cross of the Iron Cross with Oak Leaves and Swords for bravery, led his XXIX Army Corps forward across the Irpin River against Khrushchev's defensive works on August 8th. Six infantry divisions – the 44th, 71st, 75th, 95th, 99th, and 299th – rolled against the Soviet defensive belt, but found it manned and powerful: "The regiments were literally 'devoured' by forests, fire, and fanatic Russian soldiers. After four days of bloody combat, they could not force a breakthrough in the fortified positions. The commander of the 6th Army suspended the battle. The 6th Army now stood at order arms." (Haupt, 1998, 57-58).

Obstfelder

While Kirponos and the German 5th Army exchanged ineffective but costly blows, the Germans continued pushing south and east, conquering the Ukraine west of the Dnieper. The crucial turning point arrived when Stalin authorized the Soviet 5th Army elements seeking to impede this advance to fall back behind the wide river on August 16th.

By August 19th, the Germans controlled all the territory up to the Dnieper. Since the river turns southeast at Kiev and flows in that direction all the way to Dnepropetrovsk, where it turns south again, this actually enabled German forces to occupy territory far east of Kiev. Even before the Wehrmacht forced the crossings that remained intact, this placed Kiev at the point of a large, triangular salient projecting out into German-held areas. Army Group Center outflanked this salient to some degree to the north, and Gerd von Rundstedt's Army Group South lay along its southern flank. This naturally suggested pinching off the salient, and the vast numbers of men it contained, via a double envelopment far east of Kiev, with one force driving from the north and the other from the south to pinch off the salient as a huge pocket. This would necessarily force the surrender or annihilation of the men trapped within.

The plan now adopted by Hitler in fact followed exactly this pattern. The Soviet commanders on the ground were keenly aware of the possibility, but they did not dare to retreat without express orders from Stalin. The records of Soviet military action are peppered with the summary executions of Red Army generals who "retreated," even if only for the sake of prudent tactic maneuver, so the fears of Kirponos and the other men leading the Kiev defensive forces represented realism instead of paranoid overcautiousness.

Even Khrushchev, who in his memoirs frankly admitted to ordering the execution of soldiers who fell back in the face of overwhelming German attacks and prompting a junior officer's suicide, realized the perilous situation. He and Budyonny conferred about how to deal with a German encircling movement from the south, possibly hindering it long enough for the hundreds of thousands of men in the salient to escape: "After considerable thought we arrived at the following decision: to take a certain number of troops and artillery and cover our flank in the direction from Kiev toward Kremenchug, so that there, in the Ukrainian steppe, there would be something with which to block the enemy's path northward and not allow him to close the ring of encirclement. What could we take? It was obvious that the troops we had in Kiev were so far not being used. The situation there was quiet, and the enemy was making no moves against Kiev." (Khrushchev, 2005, 341).

Budyonny

The Marshal and the commissar prepared the orders and sent them to Moscow for approval. However, even withdrawing troops from Kiev to guard the salient's flank resembled a retreat too much for the Soviet Union's dictator to countenance it. Neither Stalin nor the Stavka issued any direct reply to the requested orders; instead, an aircraft arrived carrying Marshal Semyon Timoshenko, and orders for Budyonny to hand over command to the newcomer immediately.

Timoshenko

Timoshenko toured the salient and Kiev with Khrushchev. Possessing enough military acumen to correctly assess the situation, he agreed with Khrushchev that disaster loomed. However, nothing could be done, since Stalin would not hesitate to shoot any officer, even a Marshal of the Soviet Union, who ordered a retreat without his authorization – an authorization neither Timoshenko nor Khrushchev could secure.

Thus, vast hordes of Red Army soldiers awaited their doom inside the Kiev salient or the city itself, and the Germans busied themselves preparing to take this effectively sacrificial force in the iron jaws of yet another vast pocket. On September 15th, General Gotthard Heinrici wrote to his family, marveling over the Soviet failure to retreat from the trap. Of course, at that time he knew nothing of Stalin's orders: "We are just about to encircle the Russian. All troops west of Kiev will bite the dust. For some reason I cannot comprehend, the Russian has assigned his troops in the Ukraine in a way that invites us to take them all prisoners. The encirclement is getting tighter. [...] We already fight for the roads that will be essential for the enemy's retreats. While I am writing this I can hear artillery fire rolling continuously." (Hurter, 2014, 83). The incomprehensible reason, of course, resided in the deeply unmilitary but extremely meddlesome mind of Stalin. Both he and Hitler fancied themselves great generals of the caliber of Alexander the Great, Napoleon, and Gustavus Adolphus, even as they were bringing millions of their own soldiers to grief through incompetent intervention.

The wide flow of the Dnieper, approximately half a mile wide below Kiev and averaging 25 feet deep, represented a formidable obstacle that both men and vehicles required bridges to cross. The Soviets, once forced back to the eastern bank, demolished many of the existing bridges. Nevertheless, some fell into German hands, including those overlooked, those taken by daring attacks before demolition occurred, or those damaged but not destroyed and therefore fairly easy to repair.

A picture of German engineers constructing a pontoon bridge across the Dnieper

At Dnepropetrovsk, the Soviets destroyed the bridges but built a pontoon bridge to allow their own retreat once ousted from the city. However, when the Red Army engineers set off the charges on the pontoon bridge, they managed to damage it but did not break it up. The unsteady span remaining offered enough continuous surface for infantry to cross, but not vehicles. Thus, the 13th Panzer Division sent dismounted panzergrenadiers across on August 25th to establish a beachhead on the far bank, then moved engineers onto the pontoon bridge to repair it. Within a few days, the Germans restored the Soviet structure to full strength, enabling panzers, halftracks, and trucks with towed artillery to cross. The Wiking SS Panzer Division under SS-Brigadefuhrer Felix Steiner crossed on September 2nd,, indicating the engineers rendered the bridge suitable for heavy armor by that date.

Other bridges fell into German hands in a more dramatic fashion. When Stalin allowed the Soviet 5th Army to fall back to the Dnieper's east bank, those units which earlier attacked Malyn retreated through Gornostaipel to 1.8 mile long wooden bridge north of Kiev at a particularly wide part of the river. Today, the site is flooded by a large reservoir. At the time, this bridge spanned the river, connecting the banks with a large inhabited island in the middle.

The retreating 5th Army troops failed to blow up this bridge. On August 23rd at 7 PM, infantry from the German 111th Infantry Division and StuG III Sturmgeschutz self-propelled assault guns of Sturmartillerie-Abteilung 191 attacked the still-intact span. First, two StuG IIIs drove at speed onto the bridge, hoping to take it swiftly. However, one of the SPGs rolled off the edge of the bridge and plunged into the river below as it tried to maneuver around an abandoned Soviet truck, and the second StuG III retreated.

Undeterred, the Germans launched a fresh attack, led by Leutnant Kurt-Heinz Bingler in a StuG III. Infantry, some of them manhandling wheeled antitank guns forward at speed, and engineers followed. The engineers successfully cut the ignition cables to the Soviet explosives in place on the bridge before the defenders on the far bank could set off the demolition charges. Major Friedrich Musculus described the action: "The enemy dominated the bridge with anti-tank guns and machine-guns from 12 bunkers on the opposite eastern bank. […] The enemy bunkers […] were engaged with high explosives and machine-guns from all sides, and this blocked the view from their portholes. […] Once again, Lieutenant Bingler took up the lead with an assault gun. […] The assault troops reached the eastern bank with modest losses, enemy fire was erratic, and the Russian bunkers were captured in hand-to-hand combat." (Haupt, 1998, 61-62),

The drama of the Gornostaipel bridge had not yet reached its conclusion, however. Kirponos, receiving reports that the Germans captured the bridge intact, sent the bombers still available to him to attack it. These aircraft succeeded in partially collapsing areas of the wooden span, temporarily isolating 25th Motorized Infantry Division infantry on the midstream island. Nonetheless, these men found their temporary island prison something of a paradise. The bombs killed a number of fish, which the Germans retrieved, cooked, and ate, When these ran out, they went fishing successfully with hand grenades. The inhabitants had also planted numerous crops, now ripe and ready to eat, including yellow melons, grapes, tomatoes, and apricots. The men also frequently went swimming in the river.

While the Germans were enjoying this seemingly idyllic reprieve, Khrushchev had arranged for a number of gunboats to patrol the river as monitors. These Soviet river monitors interrupted the 25th Division soldiers' leisurely activities, putting troops ashore in an effort to take the island and, presumably, complete the destruction of the bridge, as Erwin Boehm later recalled: "During the morning, the Russians suddenly attacked the island. They approached the southern end in large [monitors]. We laid down heavy fire and sank two […] In spite of this, the Russians were able to get a foothold. […] a great number of them […] were now attempting to overrun our beautiful island from the south. We had to abandon our defensive positions and establish new ones further to the rear." (Haupt, 1998, 58).

The Germans landed reinforcements on the island with their own assault boats and managed to oust the Soviets from it. In the following days, the Wehrmacht's engineers busily repaired the Gornostaipel span, making it ready to play its part in the coming envelopment battle and destruction of the Soviet 5th Army.

In other areas, the Germans used boats to cross the river, establishing beachheads on the eastern shore. Gottlob Bidermann of the 132nd Infantry Division described one such crossing just north of Kanev, a city fiercely held by the Soviets for some time before they withdrew to the eastern bank or surrendered. The 132nd put soldiers across the river at Kodoriv, supporting them by artillery fire from the town of Kodoriv itself.

The Soviets counterattacked the 132nd's beachhead repeatedly, but the Germans beat them off, pushing more and more units across the river and driving inland as their strength permitted. Bidermann recounted a series of counterattacks defeated one night after dark: "The night suddenly exploded with impacting artillery rounds – and along the […] road in the northwest area […] eleven enemy attacks were repulsed between the hours of 2210 and 0250. The sunrise bore witness to the effectiveness of our defense, as countless bodies clad in khaki-brown could be seen lying in heaps before our positions. Burning vehicles littered the landscape, sending plumes of oily black smoke skyward (Bidermann, 2000, 44-45).

Army Group South's Gerd von Rundstedt continued pushing men and machines across the Dnieper at multiple points, building up a formidable array of units on the eastern shore. For the moment, these units mostly built up, only attacking to expand and improve their positions. The plan now involved waiting for the arrival of Heinz Guderian's Panzer Group II from the north, dispatched by Hitler from Army Group Center to complete the Kiev encirclement.

The Soviets continued large numbers of attacks on the Germans during this period, trying to push them back and possibly regain a foothold on the Dnieper's western bank. However, the tough Wehrmacht and SS professionals shredded these assaults, made by courageous but poorly trained, equipped, and led Red Army soldiers who often lacked sufficient rifles to fully outfit their units.

With Smolensk taken and the rail lines laid to logistically support a forward leap to Moscow, Hitler changed his plans abruptly in August, stopping the drive on the Russian capital and instead turning Guderian's panzers toward Kiev. The panzer general met with Hitler in person at the Wolfsschanze ("Wolf's Lair") in Rastenburg, Prussia, arguing in detail for a continued Moscow advance while good weather lasted, but the Fuhrer would have none of it, even as he allowed Guderian to fully express his views. Hitler then detailed his reasoning and stated his generals did not know how to run a war, a theme he would return to repeatedly, and often wildly inaccurately.

Hitler and Goering at the Wolf's Lair

Guderian did, however, secure one minor victory. Hitler's original plan called for leaving part of Panzer Group II with Army Group Center, and using another portion to attack towards Kiev. The panzer general managed to persuade the Fuhrer to let him keep his unit intact and use its entire force for the Kiev expedition. Guderian hoped this would shorten the operation, perhaps leaving enough time to strike at Moscow prior to winter.

"Hammering Heinz" flew back from Fuhrer headquarters to Panzer Group II on August 22nd, reaching his lodgings early the following morning. After snatching a few hours' sleep, the general received OKH orders: "The object is to destroy as much of the strength of the Russian Fifth Army as possible, and to open the Dneiper crossings for Army Group South with maximum speed. For this purpose a strong force, preferably commanded by Colonel-General Guderian, is to move forward, with its right wing directed on Chernigov." (Guderian, 1996, 202).

Guderian's Panzer Group II moved south from Gomel, their maneuver hindered by water obstacles and other rough terrain. In doing so, Guderian found himself with Soviet forces on both sides of his advance. Defeated but still cohesive Soviet units to the west attempted to push east, escaping from the Gomel area back to Red Army lines.

The XXIV Panzer Corps, under a general with the resounding name of Leo Dietrich Franz Geyr von Schweppenburg, received the difficult task of simultaneously attacking south and guarding Panzer Group II's right (western) flank. On the left flank, Soviet forces massed beyond the Sudost River, a tributary of the Desna. With the Sudost very low due to summer drought, Guderian recognized it as a trivial obstacle to the Red Army, assigning XLVII Panzer Corps under Joachim Lemelsen to guard this flank.

In response, Kirponos, clearly aware of Guderian's advance within hours of its commencement, found himself obliged to disperse his forces even more, facing some south and southwest in anticipation of Army Group South's northward pincer and aligning others along the Desna River to form the northern flank of the salient against Guderian's advance.

Considerable fighting took place on the southward drive, but the Soviet units proved disorganized, confused, and lacking in mobility thanks to the logistical stranglehold of German railway seizures cutting off their gasoline supply. Stavka formed two new armies, the 37th Army and the 40th Army under Kuzma Podlas, later killed near Kharkov. With supporting units falling back or fleeing and low quality recruits making up much of their force, these armies failed to do more than provide a temporary obstacle that Guderian brushed aside with ease.

Leading units of Guderian's hard-hitting Panzer Group I reached the Desna River within two days, seizing a number of bridges intact, possibly due to Soviet expectations of a slower advance. In other places, Wehrmacht engineers threw pontoon bridges across the winding Ukrainian river to allow units to pass over to the south bank.

Audacious, abrasive, and willing to stand up even to Hitler on military matters, Walter Model drove his 3rd Panzer Division south to Novgorod-Severskyi, where a major wooden road bridge crosses the Desna. At this point, the confluence of the Desna and Vit Rivers forms a "braided" flow, with an entangled profusion of channels forming scores of low-lying-marshy islands. The road bridge crosses both rivers and one of the largest of the islands at the eastern extremity of Novgorod-Severskyi, stretching no less than 2,400 feet. The Soviets had prepared the bridge for demolition, wiring a 500 pound bomb at its center (Kirchubel, 2003, 56), hanging explosives from its sides in green rubber bags, and suspending drums of gasoline from the upper wooden superstructure to complete the conflagration. Model, however, surprised the Soviets; the leading elements consisted of motorcycle troops in the extremely rugged Zundapp KS750, a motorcycle whose features included a locking differential for equally effective on-road and off-road use,

751cc motor, hydraulic brakes, a 10-gear transmission system, a high-mounted carburetor intake providing operability in deep mud or during fording, and a sidecar with a powered wheel and pintle-mounted MG34 machine gun. Immediately behind them came armored SdKfz 251 halftracks packed full of panzergrenadiers, plus engineers to disable the demolitions on the bridge. Ernst-Georg Buchterkirch, who had led the successful capture of several bridges across the Seine during the Invasion of France and personally knocked out six French tanks as commander of a Panzer, now led this attack also.

Model

Guderian summarized the results briefly but enthusiastically in his memoirs: "On my way there I received a surprising and most gratifying signal: by brilliant employment of his tanks Lieutenant Buchterkirch (of the 6th Panzer Regiment of the 3rd Panzer Division) had managed to capture the 750-yard bridge over the Desna to the east of Novgorod-Severskie intact. This stroke of good fortune should make our future operations considerably less difficult." (Guderian, 1996, 206).

Though the lack of demolition represented sheer "good fortune," as Guderian stated, the rest of the operation hinged on military skill. Artillery preparation began at 6:00 a.m. and continued for two hours, after which the motorcycle troops on their Zundapp KS750s roared forward at speed onto the bridge, engaging the Soviets in a frantic firefight with their MG34 machine guns. The Soviets returned a heavy fire, wrecking motorcycles and killing and wounding men as they raced along the span.

The German artillery dropped smoke shells on the bridge. With a sharp clattering of treads, SdKfz 251 halftracks loomed suddenly out of the gray pall, their sleek, faceted hulls suddenly disgorging squads of panzergrenadiers. Pioneers moved just behind the halftracks, snipping detonation wires on the Soviet explosives. These men cut the ropes suspending the fuel drums from the wooden superstructure, then rolled the incendiary barrels over the bridge's side into the

Desna.

Determined Soviet sappers clambered along the underside of the bridge, hanging on to wooden beams and joists. However, Panzer III tanks lined up along the German shore spotted them, directing a hail of machine gun fire at the human figures scrambling underneath the span. Dead and dying men dropped from the structure to send up fountains of spray from the Desna or Vit surface. The sappers nevertheless started several fires, which the Wehrmacht pioneers promptly extinguished.

After a desperate fight, the Soivets fell back from the bridge, leaving it in German hands. Nearby Soviet batteries opened fire with high explosive rounds, hoping to blow the bridge to matchwood, but their aim proved poor, and though the area rocked under the impact of shells, not one struck the bridge itself. The assault began at 8:00 and had succeeded by 8:30. By 9:00 a.m., the Germans cleared the bridge of wrecks, bodies, and debris, and the full stream of the 3rd Panzer Division's armor began flowing across.

On September 6th, elements of the SS Division "Das Reich" seized another Desna bridge in spectacular fashion. A battalion-strength unit of motorcycle troops, equipped with tough BMW and Zundapp motorcycles fitted with sidecars armed with pintle-mounted MG34 machine guns, the regiment "Der Fuhrer," plus engineers, raced ahead of the main division to cut off retreating Soviet troops.

As this ad hoc raiding party reached Sosnitsa, fresh orders arrived. Scouts had located an undamaged railway bridge at Makoshyno on the Desna River and the men received the command to seize this valuable asset. Arriving at the riverbank just west of a bend in the river, where the iron trestle bridge still stands in the early 21st century, the Germans awaited promised Stuka bomber support at 1:30 PM.

When 2:30 p.m. arrived with no sign of the Stukas, Guderian, who arrived in person on the scene, ordered the attack anyway. "The motor-cycle assault opened. At full speed the machines were raced over the sleepers and before the Russians could react […] the leading SS groups, whose machine-gunners in the side-cars sprayed the area with bursts of fire, had smashed through the enemy barricades. Behind the SS battalion Army engineers moved slowly cutting detonation wires […] and taking away the high explosive charges." (Lucas, 1991, 66).

SS-Sturmbannfuhrer Fritz Rentrop received the Knight's Cross of the Iron Cross for leading this attack. The bridge fell intact into German hands, providing yet another important crossing of the Desna, which was 400 feet wide at this point. Ironically, the Stukas arrived late, 27-strong, and dive-bombed the victorious SS motorcycle troops, killing 10 and wounding almost 30, thereby inflicting far more casualties with friendly fire than had the hostile fire of the surprised Soviet defenders.

In this and a number of similar actions, Panzer Group II secured a number of crossings along the length of the Desna. This galvanized the Soviet armies, nearly prostrate in recent days, to a fresh burst of activity in an effort to drive the Germans back. In some cases, they actually succeeded temporarily, though the arrival of new units eventually crushed their efforts: "By August 31st, […] The 10th (Motorized) Infantry Division succeeded in crossing the Desna, to the north of Korop, but was thrown back again to the west bank by heavy Russian counterattacks, besides being attacked on its right flank by strong enemy forces. By sending in the very last man of the division, in this case the Field Bakery Company, a catastrophe to the right flank was only just avoided." (Guderian, 1996, 208).

Though the Red Army put up a desperate final defense of the river line, knowing clearly that the movement of significant German forces to their bank spelled the end of the Kiev salient, the

Germans could not be stopped. Guderian requested and received another panzer corps, the XLVI Panzer Corps, giving him an even more potent striking force to execute his mission.

Panzer and infantry divisions poured across the Desna from the north in early September, massing like a gathering avalanche on the northern flank of the Kiev salient. With Panzer Group I and other Army Group South elements present in powerful bridgeheads on the east bank of the Dnieper, the Germans found themselves poised to deliver the coup de grace to their enemies, trapped in place by Stalin's orders.

Guderian at a command post near Kiev during the battle

The start of September brought heavy periodic rains to the Ukrainian grasslands. This signaled the start of the autumn rasputitsa, the wet season that turns Russian roads into nearly bottomless quagmires of sucking mud. A second rasputitsa occurred with the spring rains and snow melt, but the autumn version of this phenomenon proved especially grim.

Nevertheless, the Wehrmacht prepared to carry out their attack with full vigor and planning, particularly on the days without rain, when hot, sunny weather still managed to rapidly dry the roads again. On September 2nd, Field Marshal Albert Kesselring, commander of the regional air operations, flew from Army Group South's headquarters to Guderian's field HQ to confirm that German forces occupied the east bank of the Dnieper and that they stood ready for cooperative operations.

The Soviets, finding their ground forces baffled for lack of armor support, turned to raids by Ilyushin DB-3 twin-engined tactical bombers, first manufactured in 1935. Though the crews showed considerable courage in braving the whirlwind of German flak, the rather obsolete bombers inflicted only very light damage, failing to hamper the Wehrmacht buildup on either flank of the salient.

Panzer Group II continued probing for a weak point throughout the first week of September. The Russians, though unable to maneuver enough for notable counterattacks, resisted stubbornly wherever possible, clearly aware of the stakes involved. Finally, on September 9th, Walter

Model's 3rd Panzer Division found a weak link in the Soviet lines. Attacking with great élan despite the wretched weather conditions and a moderately alarming fuel situation, Model's men punched easily through the detected gap and sped south towards the next objective of Romny.

The plan now called for Guderian to break through to Romny, while Kleist would strike north towards Lubny, directly south of Romny. The forces would then link up somewhere near Lochvitsa, midway between Romny and Lubny, sealing the pocket and the doom of the men inside it.

This, of course, only represented the easternmost limit of the double envelopment. West of this point, units would drive north and south into the trapped Russians, chopping the pocket into smaller pockets that could subsequently be isolated, compressed, and eventually eliminated. Turning the larger pocket into a honeycomb of smaller pockets prevented the Soviets from mustering a force anywhere that would be large enough to break the envelopment itself.

On the 10th of September, Guderian attempted to accompany Model's drive to Romny, but he arrived only hours after the town fell due to the appallingly muddy roads. Model's men took Romny by surprise, overwhelming the Russians before they could man its strong defensive belts. However, snipers remained at large in the town, hiding in the walled gardens, so the Germans moved about in halftracks or not at all.

At 5 p.m., with the XLVI Panzer Corps arriving – including the SS Panzer Division "Das Reich" – Model conducted a detailed sweep of the town, which killed or captured all the remaining snipers or drove them out into the rain-lashed countryside. One of the Das Reich soldiers noted both the unexpected advantages and expected downsides of the rain: "At 02:00 hours rations came up. At last something hot to eat and enough bread. We advance along the side of the railway line and the Russian shells sink into the swamp which we are crossing and do not usually explode. [...] It is very tiring walking on the sleepers. [...] Our feet are suffering from being continually wet from the rain and the swamp." (Lucas, 1991, 67).

On September 9th, Kleist established another crucial bridgehead over the Dneiper. Near Kremenchug, the 257th Infantry Division under Lieutenant General Sachs conducted a "wild assault" using 150 rafts and 68 assault boats. Once they forced the river, the engineers quickly built a 650 foot long combat bridge capable of supporting heavy armor.

The 9th, 13th, and 16th Panzer Divisions crossed this pontoon bridge on the night of 11th to 12th September during an intense rainstorm that rendered the blackness over the wide river complete. Two motorized infantry divisions followed, enabling a huge force of 5 divisions to mass on the bank in preparation for attack.

Under an overcast sky at the first light of dawn, these five divisions punched north behind a rolling artillery barrage, crashing headlong into the Soviet 38th Army under Major General Nikolai Feklenko. The unexpected attack shattered the Soviet formation, leading to a rout that had the Soviets fleeing their field fortifications. Feklenko himself only escaped his farmhouse headquarters by leaping out a window at the back as Panzergrenadiers burst in the front door and killed or captured many members of his staff.

The onrush of the three leading panzer divisions pierced 40 miles forward towards Lubny in the first day alone, capturing 13,000 Russians in the process, besides destroying 75 tanks. The infantry divisions only advanced 12 miles, but nevertheless continued their dogged march in the wake of the panzers.

The 16th Panzer Division rolled onward through the night, reaching the Sula River early on September 13th, some 72 miles from the unit's starting position at daybreak the day before. Under the dashing leadership of the superbly skilled Hans-Valentin Hube, known as "Der

Mensch" and sporting a metal hand in place of the one shot away in combat at Aisne in 1914, the 16th Panzer Division hurled itself at Lubny but recoiled in the face of defenses manned by fanatical NKVD troops.

Kirponos, faced by the lethal advance of Panzer Group I from the south, ordered the Soviet 5th and 37th Armies to retreat north towards the Desna, where the German advance seemed slower. He flew out of the incipient pocket to Moscow in order to personally implore Stalin to permit him to withdraw as many men as possible from the trap, but the Soviet dictator refused. Knowing he would be executed if he disobeyed, Kirponos flew back to Kiev and resumed his command of the now hopeless defense.

Separately, Marshal Boris Shaposhnikov, the Deputy People's Commissar for Defense, and his protege Aleksandr Vasilevsky, made a last ditch effort to persuade Stalin of the necessity to save his soldiers from the grip of the Germans. Stalin authorized limited maneuvering by the 5th and 37th Armies: "In other words, this was a half-way measure. The mere mention of the urgent need to abandon Kiev threw Stalin into a rage and he momentarily lost his self-control. We evidently did not have sufficient will power to withstand these outbursts of uncontrollable rage or a proper appreciation of our responsibility for the impending catastrophe in the South-Western Direction." (Stahel, 2012, 173).

Shaposhnikov

Vasilevsky

After days of rain, the final push to close the pocket on September 14th occurred during superb, dry, sunny weather. Savoring this "panzer weather," Walter Model and his 3rd Panzer Division plunged south towards Lochvitsa. On the way, they encountered an enormous convoy of Soviet supply wagons and horse-drawn antitank artillery, guarded by a detachment of Cossack cavalry and two T-26 light tanks. The Germans immediately attacked, the panzers charging forward to strew destruction in the convoy with their machine guns and HE shells. The Russian drovers abandoned their draft animals and fled on foot, while the Cossacks kept up a brief firefight until the two light tanks "brewed up."

Having mopped up this group, the 3rd Panzer Division continued southward. Finally, they arrived at Lochvitsa, under attack by Hube "Der Mensch" and the 16th Panzer Division, who had arrived from the south: "It had been a while since the red-golden sun set. Finally, the combat group stopped on high ground and hid the vehicles behind scarecrows. The men looked over the silhouettes of the city through binoculars [...] Clouds of smoke hung over the houses, and in between the crackle of machine guns the artillery hits thudded. There was no doubt [...] a few kilometers further on were the lead elements of Army Group South." (Haupt, 1998, 75).

The leading panzer company rolled down the slope, scattering a group of Soviets who emerged from a ravine to fire briefly on the armored vehicles. Fording a brook, the leading elements of the 3rd Panzer Division rolled into Lochvitsa at approximately the same time as the leading tanks of the 16th Panzer Division. Guderian and Kleist had achieved the encirclement, penning hundreds of thousands of Red Army soldiers inside Kiev and a wedge of territory just east of it.

With the Soviets trapped, the Germans now needed to make good on their victory by capturing or killing the soldiers inside the Kiev pocket. The biggest danger lay in other Soviet forces from the east attacking the outer lines of encirclement to free their comrades. As it turned out, however, no such forces existed; the Red Army units nearby were weak and exhausted after having participated in the struggle to prevent the crossing of the Dnieper. Moreover, in anticipation of the threat against Moscow, the Soviet Stavka could not send any divisions south to aid Kirponos, let alone armies. In truth, the Soviet Union had – temporarily – run out of men. Those facing Army Group Center could not be moved for fear of exposing Moscow, while the Siberian divisions, though intact, lay at the far end of the country, much too far to be shifted in time to have the slightest effect on the outcome. With millions of men already dead, prisoners, or trapped in pockets, the USSR needed time to recruit and arm more before they could present any kind of threat to the Wehrmacht.

Throughout these dark days, Stalin continued to show a bold front, refusing to acknowledge the situation's hopelessness and describing fatalistic telegrams from the encircled commanders as "panicky." That said, it is likely he was afraid to admit his mistake and thus possibly invite his own toppling and execution, the fate that often befell a discredited dictator, and one remarkable action reveals that he in fact understood the magnitude of the disaster he engineered at Kiev. Despite his aversion to bringing any foreigners onto Russian soil, and his pathological paranoia about the hated West, the Soviet strongman sent a secret letter to British Prime Minister Winston Churchill. This letter read, in part, "If [...] a second front in the west seems unfeasible to the British government, then perhaps some other means could be found of rendering the Soviet Union active military aid against the common enemy. [...] Britain could safely land 25–30 divisions at Archangel or ship them to the southern areas of the USSR via Iran for military cooperation with the Soviet troops on Soviet soil." (Stahel, 2012, 225).

Sent on September 13th, this letter revealed the panic, possibly even terror, under Stalin's blustering surface. His suggestion that the British land in the south indicates a desperate fantasy of saving Kiev, an impossibility even had Churchill agreed right away, and it was indicative of a man feeling so trapped as to give way to self-delusion and wishful thinking.

Meanwhile, most of the Soviets streaming east from the disintegrating formations had only light weapons or none at all, and thus could not break out through the German cordon. In a few places, the dreadful KV-1 tanks appeared, leading groups of men trying to escape. In some cases, these vehicles actually managed to push through and escape eastward, while in others, the Germans used Stuka dive-bombers and 88mm flak guns used as direct fire antitank weapons to destroy them.

The Soviet 5th, 21st, 26th, and 37th Armies lay inside the Kiev pocket. As the operations to annihilate them began, the Luftwaffe flew over the "cauldron" with near impunity thanks to the destruction of all Soviet airfields inside the area. Cleverly, the German Stuka pilots looked for clumps of forest alongside major roads running through the pocket, dropping bombs among the tress. Though they usually could see nothing except treetops, the Luftwaffe men assumed that densely-packed groups of Russian men and vehicles likely sheltered there during the day, trying to hide from air attacks before continuing nighttime attempts at escape. Soviet eyewitness accounts indicate the efficacy of this tactic. While some bombs fell into unoccupied groves, many plunged directly into thickly concentrated Soviet units, blasting apart dozens of men and vehicles with every hit. In some cases, the use of incendiary bombs flushed Soviet units into the open, where the Germans strafed them relentlessly.

Staring defeat in the face, some of the Soviets turned to gruesome torture in revenge for their impending destruction. Eric Kemmeyer, an SS man, described one such scene, which was so ghastly the local German commander shot a large group of Soviet prisoners in response: "[I]n a small depression covered with apricot trees, was a small group of men whispering together. I pushed my way through them and shrank in horror [...] The small trees were bearing fruit, very strange fruit – German soldiers. They were not a pretty sight, with their arms tied high behind them to the weak branches, their jackboots off and their legs burnt and carbonized up to their knees. So distorted were their faces that even seasoned soldiers had to look away." (Stahl, 2010, 53-54). According to Kemmeyer, the Soviets had soaked the 102 prisoners' feet in gasoline, without getting the accelerant elsewhere on the men's bodies, and then set them afire. By burning the lower extremities, the men would eventually die from shock and generalized bleeding, but only after hours of excruciating agony – a method of execution dubbed "Stalin's socks."

More men preferred to surrender than to take such revenge, however, which only served to further inflame their already ruthless enemy. Nor could the Wehrmacht make their encirclement airtight, given the huge spaces involved and the unfamiliar terrain. Forests, river and stream beds, and darkness all gave cover for groups of Soviet soldiers or even individual men attempting to escape eastward.

The Germans caught many of these escapees nevertheless. The Wehrmacht troops took men in uniform prisoner, while those Red Army soldiers who discarded their telltale uniforms in favor of civilian clothes risked being hanged or shot as partisans if captured. In the end, approximately 15,000 soldiers eluded the Germans, rejoining their comrades in the east, while some 50 tanks broke out.

Some of the Soviets, unaware of the Germans' plans and deeply loathing the Soviet Union (with its own vast catalog of massacre, torture, engineered famine, and brutal political repression) actually sought to defect to the Germans rather than to escape the trap. One group of 200 men fought their way back to the Dnieper with submachine guns and grenades, killing the commissars who tried to stop them. Once they arrived at the Dnieper, they surrendered to the Germans. A Soviet soldier described the scene: "In our regiment, the division commissar gathered the privates and commanders and started to incite the people to get going, in order to force our way east. […] The Red Army soldiers became agitated. Our regimental commander called out to the privates: 'Who do you obey? Away with the damned Chekist!' The commissar instantly drew his revolver and shot. The commander fell down. Our second lieutenant and a group of Red Army soldiers jumped on the commissar – in less than a minute he was torn to pieces." (Berkhoff, 2004, 13).

Those who remained true to the Soviet Union's colors often found themselves under low-level but persistent sniper fire from the local inhabitants, who hoped to regain their national independence from the Soviet empire. Others, by contrast, received shelter, food, and other help from the local people, who attempted to help the escape the encirclement.

At army headquarters, General Franz Halder observed in rather colorful fashion that "enemy formations are bounding off the encirclement ring like billiard balls" (Stahel, 2012, 245). Soon enough, however, the Germans acted to stop even this futile activity. The LI Army Corps under Walter von Seydlitz-Kurzbach plunged south, cleaving the pocket in two and linking up with XXXIV Army Corps under General Alfred Wager, advancing north from the Dnieper. This junction occurred on September 18th.

On September 16, 1941, the German 71st and 296th Infantry Divisions spearheaded the attack by the XXIX Corps into Kiev proper (Kirchubel, 2003,66). The Germans fought their way forward through dense defensive works over the next three days, while the Soviet commissars attempted to bolster the defenders' morale by playing Stalin's speeches over numerous loudspeakers mounted throughout the defensive zone. A Wehrmacht eyewitness recorded the excitement the Germans felt at the sight of the city finally visible in the distance ahead of them: "Then a new tree-covered ridge rose, and beyond that, we could see what made our hearts beat faster: Kiev's characteristic towers rising clearly in the morning haze! […] To the right, we could make out the large iron bridge over the Dnepr, and behind it two additional bridges leading out of the center of the city." (Haupt, 1998, 80).

Encountering bunkers and dug-in Soviet tanks turned into quasi-pillboxes, the 95th Infantry Division worked to clear these obstacles. The 77th StuG III Battalion, made up of 21 Sturmgeschutz III assault guns, worked their way forward alongside the 95th, fulfilling their original role as anti-bunker weapons (later almost totally eclipsed by infantry support and tank hunting). These StuG IIIs still featured the short-barreled 7.5 cm KwK 37 L/24, useful in the cramped spaces of fortified sectors and urban areas, but later underwent upgrade to the 7.5 cm KwK 40 L/43 and soon the L/48, whose increased barrel length suited it better to anti-tank action.

The low, tough-looking StuG IIIs crawled forward through the maze of Soviet bunkers, the deep purring rumble of their engines punctuated by the crash of firing as they sent their shells punching through the concrete of enemy strongpoints. German infantry with demolition charges and flamethrowers also worked their way forward.

The assault guns likewise played an important role once the Germans penetrated into the streets of Kiev itself. The armored vehicles moved up to fire high explosive (HE) shells into any buildings held tenaciously by the Soviets. Sd.Kfz 250 halftracks with pintle-mounted MG34 machine guns worked in cooperation with the StuG IIIs, laying down suppressing fire to keep antitank infantry at bay.

The Germans also utilized heavy artillery concentrations, with rolling barrages moving just ahead of their troops and smoke screens deployed to block Soviet lines of sight. A Wehrmacht participant later recalled the action: "[N]ow we looked calmly at the towers on the horizon and knew for sure that it would not be long before we would climb those towers of Kiev. […] Friendly shells of all calibers were roaring over us. […] Then our smoke shells were fired. In front of the Bolshevik positions an enormous smoke screen expanded, as if suddenly a large theater curtain was dropped in front of the enemy. This was the signal for the […] infantrymen to attack." (Haupt, 1998, 80-81).

The Soviet artillery answered, sometimes hitting the Germans, but often suffering from lack of well-trained forward observers and simply pounding areas of terrain that the Germans avoided. The Wehrmacht's gunners provided counter-battery fire also, gradually silencing the fire of the Soviet guns. All the while, commissars and other political officers roamed through the Soviet lines, shooting men who tried to fall back from their positions. As the situation deteriorated, the Soviets retreated anyway, or surrendered, sometimes killing their unit's commissar as a prelude in order to prevent being gunned down by him.

Several days of heavy fighting carried the Germans forward through the deep defensive lines encircling Kiev. On September 19, with multiple divisions piercing the city's defenses, Soviet resistance finally began to suffer irreversible collapse. Major General Wilhelm Stemmermann's 296th Infantry Division burst through the northern defenses close to the Dnieper's banks, penetrating almost 16 miles during the morning of the 19th. At the same time, the 95th Infantry Division and 99th Rifle Division pushed into the southern suburbs of Kiev, then fought their way into the streets. Elements of these two divisions reached the city center at around 11:00 a.m. There, they triumphantly raised the Kriegsflagge of the Third Reich – a variant on the standard Swastika flag with four black and white arms forming a crucifix-like quartering of the field behind the main emblem, and the Iron Cross of the German military in the canton. The Germans officially took Kiev on the 19th of September, though patchy combat continued for days as Soviet units made last stands here and there in the streets.

The German commanders and men felt the elation natural to soldiers overcoming a difficult obstacle, but Kiev had one more surprise in store for them. The Soviets left a number of large explosive devices hidden in the metropolis, which they detonated remotely following their departure. The Soviet engineers placed this ordnance in the buildings they deemed most likely to be occupied by the Germans, including an arsenal building near the famous Monastery of the Caves. The Soviets also booby trapped the Grand Hotel and other locations likely to house German officers.

The Germans, delighted at finding the buildings intact, moved into precisely those structures the Soviets had prepared with lethal masses of explosives. Soon the explosions began, taking a heavy toll on the unprepared invaders. A huge cache of explosives demolished the Grand Hotel, blowing dozens of German officers, including Colonel Hans Heinrich Ferdinand Freiherr von Seydlitz und Gohlau of the Wehrmacht General Staff, to fragments.

These "parting gifts," according to some historians, helped trigger the Einsatzgruppen massacre at Babi Yar. General Gotthard Heinrici briefly noted the booby traps in a letter written to his wife on September 29th, with a pertinent afterthought: "The situation in Kiev is […] quite unpleasant, because the Russians have hidden a great amount of mines and incendiary devices which cause lots of detonations. The kind of warfare we witness here has nothing to do with a decent battle." (Hurter, 2014, 89).

The remote control detonations took place on September 24th, setting fire to large tracts of the city. All told, the Soviet demolition experts and saboteurs did their work well; walls of flame roared through conquered Kiev so rapidly that they trapped and killed as many as 200 German soldiers, burning them to death alongside the luckless inhabitants. Only after five days did the conflagrations burn out or succumb to fire extinguishing efforts.

In addition to the explosives which actually detonated, the Germans and Ukrainians assisting them located 670 more incendiary charges, many equipped with timers. Red Army saboteurs also remained in the city, carrying out arson attacks with Molotov cocktails. Other charges which the Germans failed to locate continued exploding sporadically through the middle of October, leveling more housing and leaving at least 15,000 Ukrainians without shelter at the onset of winter.

The destruction of much of their city, and the Soviets' attempt to firebomb their much-prized opera house, rekindled the rage of the Ukrainians, smoldering in any case after the 3.9 million deaths of the communists' genocidal Holomodor in the early 1930s and the political repression and death squads following it. General Heinrici noted the effects of Soviet rule on the Ukrainians: "[T]he first thing the village folk ask is: When do we get our land back that has been taken away from us? […] Everybody tries to display a poor lifestyle in order not to be persecuted or shot as a property owner. […] Even worse, however, is the people's fear of the party and its representatives. No one dares to do anything on their own responsibility, but waits for an order so as not to be punished." (Hurter, 2014, 81).

The Germans arrogantly failed to notice or exploit this anti-Soviet feeling, which could have netted them tens of thousands of recruits, or, at minimum, the willing assistance of an anti-communist population. Instead, the Germans swept the city for hunting rifles and other civilian arms which might be used to resist them, and instituted a savage martial rule. Ultimately, many of the Ukrainians managed to conceal their civilian rifles, supplemented by weapons scavenged secretly from the battlefield, to begin a fierce partisan movement. The vigorous partisan warfare generated by the Germans' harrowing treatment of the local inhabitants would prove a thorn in the Wehrmacht's side and greatly increase the difficulties of resupply.

After accelerating the process of destroying the Southwest Front, expending precious months in the process, Guderian turned his Panzer Group II northeast for Hitler's belated drive on Moscow. In the meantime, Army Group South pushed onward to the limits of its endurance, taking the industrial region between Kiev and Kharkov and seizing the Crimea, but failing to take Kharkov itself or the Donbas industrial region in 1941.

A picture of some of Kiev's ruins

While the final drama was playing out in Kiev, the Germans continued their relentless compression of the encirclement along the perimeter. The two large pockets soon became three smaller ones, along with a handful of fragmentary holdouts, all firmly gripped in the claws of

Panzer Groups I and II and their supporting infantry armies.

Timoshenko had authorized a full withdrawal to Psel on September 16th, but the maneuver was no longer feasible at that point for most of the men inside the pocket. Kirponos refused to believe the authorization carried any weight. Still anticipating a firing squad if he withdrew, he asked for explicit permission from Moscow for the retreat. Late on September 17th, Stalin transmitted grudging approval for the abandonment of Kiev, but specified no other acceptable retreat, leaving Kirponos once again in an impossible bind.

The Germans now began crushing the remaining pockets, where the Soviets, densely packed into dwindling islands of terrain, made ideal targets for Stuka formations and panzer attacks. A 3rd Panzer Division medic described the shambles in one such pocket near Kiev on September 19th: "Chaos reigns. Hundreds of trucks and cars, interspersed with tanks, are scattered over the land. Often the occupants were overcome by fire when they tried to get out and they hang from the doors, burned into black mummies. Thousands of corpses lay around the vehicles (Haupt, 1998, 82).

With no hope left, Mikhail Kirponos attempted to escape the trap on September 20th, 1941. Accompanied by 2,000 men from the Soviet 5th Army and the Southwestern Front headquarters unit, Kirponos reached Drukovshina, 9 miles south of Lochvitsa, before Wehrmacht units caught him, tantalizingly close to safety. Elements of the German 3rd Panzer Division spotted the Soviet convoy and rolled forward to the attack. The deafening crack of tank guns and the thunder of exploding shells rang out as the panzers went into action. Moments later, the vicious clatter of machine guns and the snap of rifles joined the din. The heavy, skillfully directed German fire quickly began to break up the Soviet column.

Soviet anti-tank gunners set up their weapons to fire on the advancing panzers, but high explosive shells smashed the guns and tore the crews to bloody ribbons. The Germans also quickly knocked out the thin-skinned BA-10 and BA-20 armored cars accompanying the convoy. Seeking a defensible position, the Soviets retreated into Shumeikovo Woods, a clump of forest near a collective farm.

The Russians fought desperately for their lives, using the trees and a ravine as cover. The equally determined Wehrmacht soldiers closed in, and a furious gun-battle lasting five hours followed. The Soviet officers fought alongside their troops, and the Germans killed Kirponos in action when they opened fire with mortars: "German mortar shells exploded all around, and, although Kirponos was soon wounded, he continued to direct his forces [...] the Soviet troops not only repelled the enemy attacks but also launched occasional counterattacks of their own. Suddenly General Kirponos [...] quietly groaned and slumped over on his side, as yet another shell fragment struck the commander's body. Kirponos died within two minutes." (Maslov, 1998, 27).

The Soviet soldiers, still desperately holding off the Germans, buried the Colonel-General in a hastily excavated grave near a stream. As the Germans finally broke through the defending lines on the eastern side of the woodland, most of the surviving Soviets shot themselves rather than be captured. Nevertheless, the Wehrmacht took several hundred prisoners, including the Soviet 5th Army commander, Lieutenant General M.I. Potapov, who had been knocked unconscious by the shock of a mortar shell exploding nearby.

In a strange footnote to Kirponos' death, a commissar escaped from the encirclement carrying the commander's comb and pocket mirror. He brought these objects to Khrushchev, then at Poltava, east of the encirclement. After receiving these personal effects of the dead general, Khrushchev talked with the commissar further: "He said there was still a chance to penetrate to those areas. I asked him, since there was such a possibility, to go back and remove from Kirponos's service jacket his Gold Star signifying Hero of the Soviet Union. He had always worn it. And the man did go! There were marshes in the area that were hard to cross with mechanized equipment, but this man overcame those obstacles and returned, bringing the Gold Star with him." (Khrushchev, 2005, 344).

One of the last high-ranking officers to escape the encirclement alive, Lieutenant General Fyodor Kostenko, reported that the people along the way fed and sheltered him and the small band of men accompanying him. Kirill Moskalenko, by contrast, who escaped a few days earlier, attempted to hide in a cowshed, from which a peasant woman wielding a pitchfork had evicted him. Those who eluded the trap barely succeeded in doing so, whether they were common soldiers or generals; many others found themselves forced to surrender, or died either deep within the crushed salient or close to escape in the manner of Kirponos.

In the short term, the Battle of Kiev reaped spectacular results for the Germans, destroying a large portion of the remaining Red Army that had existed at the start of Operation Barbarossa. While deaths are unknown – but assuredly a vast total – the Red Army suffered 85,000 wounded, and the Germans claimed no less than 665,000 Soviet soldiers captured. In response to the colossal numbers of prisoners taken during the operation, Hitler engaged in bombastic flights of fancy: "I declare today – and I declare it without reservation – the enemy in the East has been struck down and will never rise again." (Axell, 1997, 182).

A map of Germany's push deep into Russia during the operation

Anyone who knows a trivial amount about World War II knows how Germany's invasion of the Soviet Union ends, but as just about every history written about Operation Barbarossa readily indicates, far from representing an inevitable loss, Operation Barbarossa bears many of the hallmarks of a highly successful campaign carried out with forethought, a superb degree of professionalism, and the conception and execution of a logistically supported *Schwerpunkt* on a titanic scale. The comparison between Napoleon's and Hitler's campaigns too often obscures the profound differences between the two invasions of Russia, especially when German planners carefully researched Napoleon's campaign in order to avoid its mistakes well before the operation was underway.

The main advance of the Germans, centered on driving towards Moscow, did not suffer defeat due to either the size of Russia or the Soviet opposition. The Wehrmacht smashed the Soviets in nearly every encounter during Barbarossa, while their few setbacks had essentially no strategic importance. The German work battalions performed magnificently, driving railways forward quickly enough to keep Army Group Center fully supplied even as it moved rapidly from the Third Reich's previous border. Using the railways and the immense, well-organized masses of trucks extending their logistic reach, the Wehrmacht pushed railways as far as Smolensk, establishing a massive railhead there. The Germans' method of defeating the spaces of the Soviet Union consisted of extremely rapid railroad construction. This technique represented a viable way to overcome the challenges that defeated the earlier invader, Napoleon, who lacked such technology.

The use of strategic military railway-building brought the Germans within striking distance of Moscow by early August, after shattering most of the Red Army. And unlike Napoleon's campaign, which seized the city to virtually no effect in 1812, the Nazi capture of Moscow would have had a profound impact on the course of the Eastern Front. In the early 19th century, a capital city merely represented a large concentration of people. In the 20th century, however, Moscow held a considerable portion of the Soviet Union's manufacturing capability – as much as 25% – and represented a key rail hub for the entirety of European Russia. Had the Germans seized it, they would have attained a stranglehold on the supply lines for Leningrad and other peripheral areas and forces, compelling their surrender or weakening them enough for rapid destruction.

Adolf Hitler himself represented the single factor preventing a crushing victory of the Wehrmacht over the Soviet Union in summer 1941. The Germans had devised methods of overcoming the huge expanses of Russia and the Soviets' scorched earth policy at the same time. Their forces, though equipped with a large number of arguably obsolete Panzer I, II, and III tanks, possessed the professionalism, skill, and fighting spirit that the Red Army lacked utterly. They could not, however, overcome their own dictator's mental limitations. Hitler created strategic plans of sweeping boldness, then, once in motion, flinched away from the decisive encounter, halting or diverting his forces. The Fuhrer did the same twice in France alone, halting the panzer drive to the coast, and then, more disastrously, stopping his men short of crushing the British Expeditionary Force at Dunkirk.

In France, the Germans remained overwhelming enough that the mistakes did not punish Hitler's glaring errors. France fell nevertheless and the Fuhrer learned nothing. In Operation Barbarossa, Hitler launched his mechanized divisions at Moscow, then, against the advice of most of his generals, shrank away from the crucial battle which would almost certainly have given him victory in the east. Instead, he diffused the steely tidal bore of the Wehrmacht advance into many feeble eddies, spending its force on secondary objectives and waiting until the autumn mud and the onset of winter before resuming the drive on Moscow, which ultimately led to a narrow defeat around the Russian capital.

As the historian R.H.S. Stolfi, an eloquent advocate of Hitler's scuppering of an almost certain seizure of Moscow and Wehrmacht victory in August to early September 1941, put it, the Fuhrer expressed a strangely defensive attitude while in possession of the most mobile, flexible offensive force the world saw prior to America's combined arms military of 1945: "The age of tanks may soon be over. [...] If we accomplish our European missions our historical evolution can be successful. Then in the defense of our heritage, we will be able to take advantage of the triumph of defense over the tank to defend ourselves against all attackers." (Stolfi, 1992, 222).

Hitler's fatal flaw as a wartime leader lay in his refusal to seize the fruits of Blitzkrieg because of his fear of the climactic battle. He won in France despite this deep flaw because the French and British collapsed even without the delivery of a knockout blow, but when the Fuhrer shrank from dealing a potential deathblow to the USSR by taking Moscow in summer rather than dispersing the Ostheer's energy in attacks on Leningrad and Kiev, he cast away the war-winning opportunity Operation Barbarossa delivered to him within two months of crossing the Soviet Union's border. Simultaneously, he ensured the eventual defeat of the Third Reich in a war of attrition that hampered its unique military strengths while exploiting its material weaknesses.

Operation Barbarossa was designed to be conducted with a high level of brutality. According to one German officer, "this war, will be very different from the war in the west...Commanders must make the sacrifice of overcoming their personal scruples." (Reid, p.22) In June 1941, the German High Command announced the "Commisar Order," in which captured political officers were to be immediately shot, while civilians were to be subjected to "collective measures" and German soldiers were absolved from potential prosecution for crimes like rape and murder against the Soviet population.

The German offensive consisted of three army groups: one moving north toward Leningrad, a second moving due east toward Moscow, and a third heading south toward Kiev. By September 1941, Germany's high command estimated that their forces had captured 2.5 million prisoners, killed nearly 5 million Russians, taken 18,000 tanks, 22,000 field guns, and destroyed 14,000 aircraft. The first major Russian city in their path was Minsk, which fell in only six days, and in order to make clear his determination to win at all costs, Stalin had the three men in charge of the troops defending Minsk executed for their failure to hold their position. In the future, Russian soldiers would fight to the death rather than surrender, and that July, Stalin exhorted the nation, "It is time to finish retreating. Not one step back! Such should now be our main slogan. ... Henceforth the solid law of discipline for each commander, Red Army soldier, and commissar should be the requirement — not a single step back without order from higher command."

Captured Soviet equipment in 1941 near the beginning of Operation Barbarossa.

Although the Germans were making incredibly quick progress on the Eastern Front, Edwin Erich Dwinger marveled at the strength and determination of the Russian soldiers even as they were being overrun by German troops, writing:

"Several of them, burnt by flamethrowers, had no longer the semblance of human faces. They were blistered, shapeless bundles of human flesh. A bullet had taken the lower jaw of one man. The scrap of flesh which sealed the wound did not hide his trachea, through which breath escaped in bubbles.

Five machine-gun bullets had shredded into pulp the shoulder and arm of another man, who was without any bandages. The Germans offered no medical help to their prisoners.

Not a cry or a moan escaped the lips of these wounded, who were seated on the grass. Hardly had the distribution of food begun than the Russians, even the dying, rose and moved forward. The man without a jaw could hardly stand. The man with one arm clung with his arm to a tree trunk. Half a dozen of them rose, holding their entrails in with one hand.

They do not cry. They do not groan. They do not curse. There is something mysterious, inscrutable, about their stern stubborn silence." (Hoyt, p. 41)

While the German invasion progressed quickly during the early stages, German atrocities committed against conquered Russian populations helped unify Russian resistance against the German advance and also convinced the Russians that the only possible outcomes of the war were victory or annihilation. Even though the Russians were losing the war, their will to fight strengthened around a growing hatred for the Germans and their tactics.

Certainly their resolve was tried during the first terrible months of fighting, as Germany surrounded Leningrad and then headed toward Moscow. The worst fighting, however, was in the Ukraine. Though badly outnumbered and destined for defeat, the Soviet soldiers held off the Germans around Kiev and thus spared Moscow while it was reinforced. They suffered the worst defeat in Red Army history, but were praised as heroes by their countrymen.

Picture of a German soldier walking past a dead Soviet and a burning tank in Ukraine.

In September, as winter months approached, Germany continued to advance across the countryside. This led Stalin to implement his famous "scorched earth" policy, ordering the retreating soldiers to leave nothing behind that the advancing Germans might be able to use. He also approved the formation of small bands of guerilla fighters who would remain behind the retreating army and harass the advancing German forces. These two strategies, along with Germany's ever thinning supply line, created quite a handicap for Hitler's army.

To his credit, Stalin took a page out the Royal Family of England's book and remained in Moscow even when the city was evacuated and the Germans were only fifteen miles away. He lived and worked in a bomb shelter just under the Kremlin, acting as self-appointed Supreme Commander-in-Chief and overseeing every move made by the army. He bided his time and waited until November, when the German army was forced by bad weather to end their forward movements. The Germans had reached the vital resource centers in Russia that they were aiming for, but the sheer size of Russia had enabled the Soviet Union to mobilize millions more to fight, requiring the Germans to dig in and prepare for long term sieges, even while the notoriously harsh Russian winter was setting in.

The German attack lost momentum due to a number of reasons, most importantly because of their overextension in the drive toward Moscow, the coming winter (and their lack of preparation for it), and the Russian reserve units that entered the war from the Siberian front. By December 1941, the German high command made the decision to pull back from their relentless drive toward Moscow, but when the 1st Panzer Division was engaged by Soviet troops, the Germans were caught by complete surprise because they believed there were no reserve Russian troops. Instead, seven Soviet armies pushed west against the center of the German forces. As German general Franz Halder put it in his diary in 1941, "The whole situation makes it increasingly plain that we have underestimated the Russian colossus...divisions are not armed and equipped according to our standards, and their tactical leadership is often poor. But there they are, and as we smash a dozen of them the Russians simply put up another dozen. The time factor favours them, as they are near their own resources, while we are moving farther and farther away from ours. And so our troops, sprawled over the immense front line, without depth, are subject to the incessant attacks of the enemy."

Not only were German forces stretched thin, but the cold and snow were causing their tanks to malfunction. At the same time, German troops, who were not outfitted for the cold, were suffering from severe frostbite and other problems related to the winter weather. The Russian attack created a bulge in the German Army Group Center, and as German leaders were unable to reinforce those positions, the Russians proceeded to force a 50 mile deep gap in the German line. While some German officers at the front advocated a full retreat, Hitler refused, and this caused many to question whether the leaders back in Germany understood the gravity of the situation on the Eastern Front.

The German push into Russia during 1941

For the people of Leningrad, information about the German advance was difficult to come by, especially because most reports from the Soviet Union were shrouded in propaganda that ordinary citizens had to decipher in order to understand the true situation. As the Germans made their way to within 30 miles of the city, rumors spread that Leningrad had not yet been bombed because Hitler was saving it for his (nonexistent) daughters to take control of. The authorities tried to stop the rumors by creating laws against spreading "false rumours provoking unrest amongst the population," "disclosing military secrets," as well as arresting "defeatists" who were not patriotic enough for Soviet leaders.

At the same time, Leningrad's city leaders tried to deflect attention away from the war by indulging in some rumor-mongering of their own, mostly through stoking fears of spies who were helping to signal German Luftwaffe pilots. As Yelena Kochina wrote in her diary, fear of spies spread like "an infectious disease,"

> "Yesterday near the market a little old woman who looked like a flounder dressed in a mackintosh grabbed me:
>
> 'Did you see? A spy for sure! she shouted, waving her short little arm after some man.
> 'What?'
> "His trousers and jacket were different colours.'
> I couldn't help but laugh.
> 'And his moustache looked as though it was stuck on.' Her close-set angry eyes bored into me.
> 'Excuse me...' I tore myself away. Before pushing off, she trailed me for several steps along the pavement.
> But...even to me many people seem suspicious, types it would be worth keeping an eye on." (Reid, p. 53)

During the first four weeks of the German invasion, the citizens of Leningrad engaged in preparedness drills, even though it seemed to them as though the war remained a distant event. Roughly 50,000 residents, mainly women and children, had also been sent 60 miles to the southwest to build new defenses along the Luga River. As one woman recalled of her experiences building defenses, their orders were to "dig anti-tank ditches (1.2m deep) and breastworks (supposedly 1m high). Though our only tools were shovels, axes and stretchers [to carry soil], we set to work enthusiastically. The days were sunny and hot. We worked from 5 a.m. to 8 or 9 p.m., with a two or three hour rest after lunch. We were well fed but there was no tea, except for what our landlady made us from lime flowers. Physically it was very tough, and after two weeks, trying to lift a stretcher, I suddenly found I couldn't straighten up again."

While some workers were injured on the job, others were fired upon by the German Luftwaffe. One recalled:

> "Our whole laboratory dug anti-tank trenches around Leningrad today. I dug the earth with pleasure (at least this was something practical!)....Almost all the people working in the trenches were women. Their coloured headscarves flashed brightly in the sun. It was as if a giant flowerbed girdled the city.
> Suddenly the gleaming wings of an aeroplane blotted out the sky. A machine gun started firing and bullets plunged into the grass not far from me, rustling like small metallic lizards. I stood transfixed, forgetting completely the air-raid drill that I had learned not long before." (Reid, p. 57)

By July 4, the Germans had made their way near the Luga Line, where Soviet General Georgy Zhukov ordered his Northwestern Army Group to hold the defensive positions there against German attacks. By this time, the German attack was beginning to lose steam because of the terrain, climate, and the Germans' lack of reliable maps. The summer dust was an especially serious problem, as it made it difficult for German resupply transports to run efficiently.

Zhukov

On July 13, the Soviets launched a counterattack against the 8th German Panzer Division, driving it back away from the Luga, and for the city of Leningrad, the counterattack meant a reprieve from the anxiety gripping the city over a potential German attack. Many citizens wondered whether a German attack or siege on the city would lead to a famine, as had occurred during the Russian Civil War of 1921-22, and others wondered whether or not they should evacuate the city. For Leningrad's city officials, evacuation of valuables had already started once the German offensive was confirmed by Russia's leaders. For example, the Hermitage, a Leningrad museum, packed up over 1,000 crates on July 1 and shipped them to a secret location away from the city. A second train left Leningrad on July 20 with over 700,000 items from the Hermitage's collections.

Leningrad's leaders also instituted a policy of rationing on July 18, which meant manual workers received 800 grams of bread a day, white collar workers received 600 grams, and "dependents" were given 400 grams. Other food items which were rationed included meat, cereals, butter, and sugar. At the beginning, these ration levels were considered "generous" and in some cases represented an improvement in diet for some poor residents.

On August 8, the Germans began to concentrate their efforts at the Luga Line, the major defense position protecting Leningrad. The German advance came in three parts, with General Georg-Hans Reinhardt's panzer division attacking the northern sector of the Luga Line, General Erich von Manstein's 8th Panzer Division cutting the Soviet defense in two at the Kingisepp-Gatchina railway line, and Georg von Kuchler's Eighteenth Army advancing on the city of Novgorod to the southwest. Stalin became extremely agitated upon learning of the German advance, fearing that the German armies were moving into position to outflank Leningrad and cut off communications with Moscow, and he sent a terse message to the commanders of the Soviet forces in the north that were failing to hold off the German advance: "It appears to us that the High Command of the Northwestern Army Group fails to see this mortal danger and therefore takes no special measures to liquidate it. German strength in the area is not great, so all we need to do is throw in three fresh divisions under skilful leadership. Stavka cannot be reconciled to this mood of fatalism, of the impossibility of taking decisive steps, and with arguments that everything's being done that can be done." (Reid, p. 66)

Georg-Hans Reinhardt

Erich von Manstein

Georg von Kuchler

The Northwestern Army Group was in tatters, with its 22 rifle divisions fighting along a 250 miles front. Not only were Soviet troops stretched thin, they also lacked vital equipment such as heavy weapons and radios. When a Soviet general near Lyuban responded to Stalin's message, he requested not only more troops but also semi-automatic weapons to replace the antiquated rifles that the infantry had been using. In his response, Stalin begrudgingly agreed: "We've already let you have three days' worth of production, you can have another three or four days...We'll send you more infantry battalions, but I can't say how many...In a couple of weeks, perhaps, we'll be able to scrape together two divisions for you. If your people knew how to work to a plan, and had asked us for two or three divisions a fortnight ago, they would be ready for you now. The whole trouble is that your people prefer to live and work like gypsies, from one day to the next, not looking ahead. I demand that you bring some order back to the 48th Army, especially to those divisions whose cowardly officers disappeared the devil knows where from Lyuban yesterday...I demand that you clear the Lyuban and Chudovo regions of the enemy at any price and by any means. I entrust you with this personally..." (Reid, p. 67)

As the Germans closed in on the city, the citizens of Leningrad formed volunteer units as a wave of patriotism swept the population, but Soviet documents admitted that this Leningrad army, called the *narodnoye opolcheniye* ("People's Levy"), was made up of "professors, judges, directors, and some plain invalids." While the People's Levy began as a volunteer movement, it quickly became near-compulsory, and seven volunteer divisions, totaling 31,000 people, were sent to the front between July 4 and July 18. Each division was made up of people from the same district, so men from the same workplaces and families were able to remain together. Among factory workers who volunteered, many of them were skilled workers who had been exempted from the draft and were the best of Leningrad's industrial workers. Among non-factory workers, volunteers were engineers, scientists, artists and students who represented some of the most talented men in the city.

As volunteering for the People's Levy became all but compulsory, recruitment targets were divided by district and by the number of eligible residents in those districts. For city leaders trying to organize evacuation efforts, as well as for factory managers who were trying to transform their workplaces for defense production, it was a struggle to retain the manpower to keep their efforts going. Not surprisingly, many of the people who were registered for the volunteer regiments did not realize what they were being asked to do; they assumed that they would be used as civil defense forces, or as a home guard in case the Germans entered Leningrad. Instead, they quickly learned that they would be sent to the front. In July and August of 1941, 70,000 of these volunteers died, many of them due to lack of training and equipment.

It was not until August 24 that the Soviet leadership finally acknowledged that the Germans had advanced close to Leningrad and were on the city's doorstep:

"Comrades! Leningraders! Dear friends! Over our beloved native city hangs the immediate threat of attack by German-Fascist troops. The enemy is trying to break through to Leningrad. He wants to destroy our homes, to seize our factories and plants, to drench our streets and squares with the blood of the innocent, to outrage our peaceful people, to enslave the free sons of our Motherland. But this shall not be. Leningrad - cradle of the proletarian Revolution - never has fallen and never shall fall into enemy hands...

Let us rise as one man in defence of our city, our homes, our families, our honour and freedom. Let us perform our sacred duty as Soviet patriots and be indomitable in the struggle with the fierce and hateful enemy, vigilant and merciless in the struggle against cowards, alarmists and deserters; let us establish the strictest revolutionary order in our city. Armed with iron discipline and Bolshevik resolve we shall meet the enemy bravely and deal him a crushing blow!" (Reid, p. 93)

As Leningrad prepared for the coming German attack, city leaders made a major mistake by failing to evacuate the surplus population before the siege began. According to Soviet sources, on August 29, 636,283 people had been evacuated out of the city. This meant that roughly 2.5 million civilians remained in Leningrad, as well as another 343,000 from surrounding towns caught in the German siege ring. 400,000 of these civilians were children, and over 700,000 were other non-working dependents. The failure of city officials to properly evacuate Leningrad inevitably added to the large death toll and increased the tragedy of the situation.

The reason for the failure to properly evacuate the city is because Soviet leaders prioritized industrial and institutional evacuation over the non-working population. Therefore, the preparations that did take place privileged moving 92 Leningrad defense plants to the east, along with 164,320 workers at those plants. Additionally, problems with the railway lines increased the chaos surrounding Leningrad's preparations; many trains were overloaded, and when the Germans cut the railway link to Leningrad, over 2,000 carloads of machinery were still awaiting removal and remained in the freight yards.

By August 25, Leningrad was nearly surrounded, with only a tenuous path leading to the east, so Stalin sent a five-man special commission to the city to help plan its defense. Stalin's commands were fanciful and impossible to put in place, but the commission, fearful of disappointing him, responded affirmatively to them. Stalin ordered the commission to place tanks "on average every two kilometers, in places every 500 meters, depending on the ground" along a 120 kilometer defense line where "the infantry divisions will stand directly behind the tanks, using them not only as a striking force, but as armored defense. For this you need 100-200 KVs [a Soviet armored tank]. I think you could produce this quantity of KVs in ten days...I await your swift reply." (Reid, p.105) The commission remained in Leningrad for about a week, where they attempted to implement Stalin's orders.

On August 29, the Germans seized control of the town of Tosno, roughly 25 miles from Leningrad. Furious at the Red Army's failure to defend Tosno, Stalin telephoned two members of the social commission, Vyacheslav Molotov and Georgy Malenkov, and said, "I have only just been informed that Tosno has been taken by the enemy. If things go on like this I am afraid that Leningrad will be surrendered out of idiot stupidity, and all the Leningrad divisions fall into captivity. What are Popov and Voroshilov doing? They don't even tell me how they plan to avert the danger. They're busy looking for new lines of retreat; that's how they see their duty. Where does this abyss of passivity of theirs come from, this peasant-like submission to fate? I just don't understand them. There are lots of KV tanks in Leningrad now, lots of planes...Why isn't all this equipment being used in the Lyuban-Tosno sector? What can some infantry regiment do against German tanks, without any equipment?...Doesn't it seem to you that someone is deliberately opening the road to the Germans? What kind of man is Popov? How's Voroshilov spending his time, what's he doing to help Leningrad? I write this because the uselessness of the Leningrad command is so absolutely incomprehensible. I think you should leave for Moscow. Please don't delay." (Reid, p. 106)

As the Germans proceeded closer and closer to Leningrad, Molotov and Malenkov increased the pace of arrests and deportations of Leningraders suspected of being Trotskyites, Zinovievites, Mensheviks, and anarchists, as well as priests, Catholics, former officers in the tsarist army, "former wealthy merchants," "white bandits," "kulaks,." and people "with connections abroad", which included "diversionists," "saboteurs," and "antisocial elements." One witness of a mass arrest noted "about a hundred people waited to be exiled. They were mostly old women; old women in old-fashioned capes and worn-out velvet coats. These are the enemies our government is capable of fighting - and, it turns out, the only ones. The Germans are at the gates, the Germans are about to enter the city, and we are busy arresting and deporting old women - lonely, defenseless, harmless old people." (Reid, p. 107)

The German encirclement of Leningrad

Russians in Leningrad marching to the front.

Soviet tanks advancing to the front.

As a result of the surprise attack and the pace of the German advance, the siege of Leningrad began in earnest by September 1941. For most Germans and Soviets, the fight over Leningrad seemed like one that would quickly be decided. At the time, the entire German offensive seemed unstoppable, as Army Group North had surrounded Leningrad while Army Group Center had captured Smolensk eight weeks earlier and was now making its way toward Moscow. In the south, Army Group South was close to encircling four Soviet armies and was in the process of taking Kiev. It seemed like the Soviet Union was on the brink of collapse, and in fact, Stalin sent a desperate message to Churchill on September 4 imploring him to open a second front in France or the Balkans by the end of the year to divert 30-40 German divisions away from the Eastern Front.

As the German forces pushed forward, rumors spread that they had begun sending Russian citizens from occupied regions to ask Soviet army commanders to surrender. Stalin wrote to his commanders overseeing the defense of Leningrad (Zhukov, Zhdanov, Kuznetsov, and Merkulov):

"It is rumored that the German scoundrels advancing on Leningrad have sent forward individuals - old men and women, mothers and children - from the occupied regions, with requests to our Bolshevik forces that they surrender Leningrad and restore peace.

It is also said that amongst Leningrad's Bolsheviks people can be found who do not consider it possible to use force against such individuals...

My answer is - No sentimentality. Instead smash the enemy and his accomplices, sick or healthy, in the teeth. War is inexorable, and those who show weakness and allow wavering are the first to suffer defeat. Whoever in our ranks permits wavering, will be responsible for the fall of Leningrad.

Beat the Germans and their creatures, whoever they are...It makes no difference whether they are willing or unwilling enemies. No mercy to the German scoundrels or their accomplices...

Request you inform commanders and division and regimental commissars, also the military council of the Baltic Fleet and the commanders and commissars of ships." (Reid, p.126)

The Germans advanced up to about 10 miles away from the city center of Leningrad by September 24, but at that point, the German commanders realized their overextended armies could not continue to push eastward. Instead, they requested permission from Hitler to dig in and move to the defensive. In the fighting up to late September, the German Army Group North had suffered 190,000 casualties, while the Soviets lost even more men. It is estimated that the combined number of men killed, missing or taken prisoner for the Soviet Baltic Fleet and Northwestern Army Group was 214,078, and an additional 130,848 were wounded. This amounted to two-thirds of their original troop strength.

Soviet soldiers in a trench along the front in September 1941

Soviet soldiers carry a wounded soldier.

The prolonged siege and lack of movement in the northern front of Operation Barbarossa was due to a compromise by the German High Command in which Hitler and his generals disagreed on whether Leningrad or Moscow should be the focal point of the German advance. Hitler believed that Leningrad needed to be captured first, and after the destruction of the Baltic Fleet and capture of the city's manufacturing capabilities, the Germans could then begin their final push to Moscow. However, his top generals, Halder and Brauchitsch, did not want to spend the equipment and manpower that it would take to capture Leningrad and instead wanted to drive on toward the Soviet capital. In the end, the German High Command reached a compromise in early September that if Leningrad was not taken by the middle of the month, panzer units would be diverted from the north to the south in the push toward Moscow. Although this seemed like a relatively small matter, the consequences would be far-reaching, because Army Group North would be able to tighten the siege ring around Leningrad but never amassed enough manpower to overwhelm the city. Thus, the Germans missed their best opportunity to capture Leningrad in the fall of 1941, and from that time on, their advance in the northern sector ground to a halt.

Part of the reasoning behind the siege was that the Germans did not really know how to proceed if they captured both Leningrad and Moscow. Hitler wanted to destroy both cities and "make them uninhabitable", and in a planning session on September 21st, German leaders outlined the options available to them:

"1. Occupy the city; in other words proceed as we have done in regards to other large Russian cities. Rejected, because it would make us responsible for food supply.

2. Seal off city tightly, if possible with an electrified fence guarded by machine guns. Disadvantages: the weak will starve within a foreseeable time; the strong will secure all food supplies and survive. Danger of epidemics spreading to our

front. It's also questionable whether our soldiers can be asked to fire on women and children trying to break out.

3. Women, children and old people to be taken out through gaps in the encirclement ring. The rest to be allowed to starve:

a)   Removal across the Volkhov behind the enemy front theoretically a good solution, but in practice hardly feasible. Who is to keep hundreds of thousands of people together and drive them on? Where is the Russian front?

b)   Instead of marching them to the rear of the Russian front, let them spread across the land. In either case there remains the disadvantage that the remaining starving population of Leningrad becomes a source of epidemics, and that the strongest hold out in the city for a long time.

4. After the Finnish advance and the complete sealing off of the city, we retreat behind the Neva and leave the area to the north of this sector to the Finns. The Finns have unofficially made it clear that they would like to have the Neva as their country's border, but that Leningrad has to go. Good as a political solution. The question of Leningrad's population, however, can't be solved by the Finns. We have to do it." (Reid, p. 133)

The plan for the northern sector was set in place in a memo that was sent to Army Group North on September 28, detailing the change in plan from a ground assault into a siege that would emphasize starvation and air raids:

"According to the directive of the High Command it is ordered that:

1. The City of Leningrad is to be sealed off, the ring being drawn as tightly as possible so as to spare our forces unnecessary effort. Surrender terms will not be offered.

2. So as to eliminate the city as a last center of Red resistance on the Ostsee [the Baltic] as quickly as possible, without major sacrifice of our own blood, it will not be subjected to infantry assault...Destruction of waterworks, warehouses and power stations will strip it of its vital services and defense capability. All military objects and enemy defense forces are to be destroyed by firebombing and bombardment. Civilians are to be prevented from bypassing the besieging troops, if necessary by force of arms." (Reid, p. 130)

Once the siege had started, the Luftwaffe dropped incendiaries and high-explosive bombs on Leningrad. The bombing was worst in the first weeks of the siege and then let off when the German 8th Air Corps was sent to Moscow, and again when winter set in and the freezing temperatures grounded all aircraft. In all, roughly 69,000 incendiary and 4,250 high-explosive bombs were dropped on Leningrad. While bombings occurred at night, German troops fired on the city during the day, so there was little respite for the city's residents. Historian Anna Reid explained in *Leningrad: The Epic Siege of World War II, 1941-1944*, "Shelling, many felt, was actually worse than bombing, since bombardments were not preceded by an alarm. From 4 September to the end of the year the Wehrmacht's heavy artillery pounded Leningrad 272 times, for up to eighteen hours at a stretch, with a total of over 13,000 shells...The rumour that some shells were filled only with granulated sugar, or held supportive notes from sympathetic German workers, was a soothing invention."

Damage done by German artillery in Leningrad.

Nurses help the wounded after a German barrage in the city.

"At this period, too, Leningraders resorted to their most desperate food substitutes, scraping dried glue from the underside of wallpaper and boiling up shoes and belts. (Tannery processes had changed, they discovered, since the days of Amundsen and Nansen, and the leather remained tough and inedible.)" – Anna Reid, *Leningrad: The Epic Siege of World War II, 1941-1944*

As the siege progressed during the fall and winter of 1941, Leningrad continued to produce war-making material such as guns, tanks, shells and mines, but the majority of the goods produced in Leningrad did not go to the northern sector or efforts to lift the siege. Instead, Leningrad's production went to help protect Moscow in the central sector, which meant Leningraders were left to suffer as coal that could have been used to heat homes were used for war production, and the transport capacity that could have brought food into Leningrad instead was used to send munitions to the capital. By December, Leningrad's factories had been shut down and the German siege ring had been closed so that nothing could get out of the city, so the massive production efforts of late 1941 that supplied Moscow ended up being very costly for Leningrad. While the German lines and focus across the theater had made it too difficult for them to assault Leningrad with ground forces, the Soviet Union's focus on producing for the central sector meant that the Russians were unable to muster the forces and weaponry necessary to keep a land route open. Had the Red Army been able to accomplish this, Leningrad's defense factories could have continued production, and the civilian losses would have been much less.

Another problem was that Soviet leaders went into the siege unprepared. When the last road connecting Leningrad to the rest of Russian was closed by the German advance, city leaders estimated that they only had enough food reserves for one month. Thus, if the siege was not quickly lifted, the city would have to depend only on the food it could gather from inside the siege ring. But even for the food supplies that were in the city, Soviet officials failed to spread out the supplies in order to minimize the threat of aerial bombardment. Thus, when the Badayev warehouse, which was filled with food, was bombed on September 8th, many Leningrad residents believed that nearly the entirety of the city's food supplies had been destroyed. This had an enormous effect on lowering morale, as did the smell of burning ham and sugar that filled the air as the warehouse burned.

Citizens trying to procure wood in October 1941.

After the Badayev warehouse bombing, city officials decided to gather food from outlying areas within the siege ring. While this brought the harvest in to help city residents, it also meant that farmworkers, who did not qualify for rations, were deprived of food. Farm families were allowed fifteen kilograms of potatoes per person per month, with the rest being relinquished to requisitioning parties sent out from Leningrad to the countryside. Any farmers who failed to give up their potatoes were "held responsible under wartime law" and could be punished for their actions. Taking foodstuffs from the countryside continued throughout the first winter of the siege, and it is estimated that three-fifths of the flour and grain, a quarter of the livestock, and over half of the potatoes that supplied the city came from farm families' stores.

As food supplies dwindled, alternatives were devised to feed Leningraders. For example, flax-seed cake became the grains rationed to the populace, and sheep guts and calf skins (from the city's tanneries) became meat rations. At the same time, the rationing system did not equally distribute food to all residents, because it privileged feeding industrial workers and soldiers and practically ignored office workers, the elderly, children, and the unemployed. The rations were also cut again and again as the siege wore on, and when rations fell to their lowest levels, manual workers (a little over one-third of the population) were given 350 grams of bread per day and 125 grams for everyone else. This meant that non-manual workers were given the equivalent of 460 calories per day, and while this was the amount officially cited by Soviet leaders, the fact that bread was increasingly baked with fillers to save on flour meant that most residents were not able to reach even that calorie level.

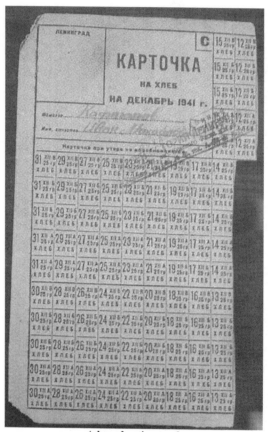

A bread ration card

As a result, the physical decline of Leningrad's residents was rapid, as they went from being relatively untouched by the war to suffering the destruction and death caused by the siege. Within 3 months, things were dire, as noted by one resident:

"People turn into animals before our eyes. Who would have thought that Irina, always such a quiet, lovely woman, would be capable of beating her husband, who she has always adored? And for what? Because he wants to eat all the time and can never get enough. He just waits for her to bring something home, and then throws himself on the food...

The most grisly sight in our apartment is the Kurakin family. He, back from exile and emaciated by years in prison, is already beginning to bloat. It's simply horrible! Of his wife's former love, there is little left. She is constantly irritated and argumentative. Their children cry and beg for food. But all they get is beatings. However, the Kurakins are no exception. Hunger has changed almost

everyone." (Reid, p. 176)

An old Russian woman pulling an emaciated man.

By the end of 1941, the German offensive on the Eastern Front was beginning to bog down, and while the Germans had encircled Leningrad, their efforts moving toward Moscow were slowing. However, despite the fact the Germans were encountering difficulties, the Soviets were not yet able to take advantage of the changing momentum. At Leningrad, Soviet troops attempted a number of breakouts on November 2, 9, 11, and 13, but they all failed, and given the Soviet army's inability to break out, the city disintegrated more and more as time wore on.

Aside from the toll that the rationing system took on individuals and families, government agencies also began to stop functioning. When the fire department ceased operations, buildings that had been hit by German bombs burned for days, and when the hospital system became overwhelmed by the sheer number of entrants into Leningrad's health care facilities, reports to city officials told of how "bedlinen has not been washed since 15 January...The wards are completely unheated, so some patients have been moved into the corridors, which have temporary stoves. Due to the very low temperatures patients cover themselves not only with hospital blankets but with dirty mattresses and their own coats...The lavatories are not working and the floors are not being washed." (Reid, p.216)

While the hospital infrastructure was creating problems, disposing of dead bodies was also a major problem. As one resident wrote about the dead at Erisman Hospital:

"Each day now eight to ten bodies are brought in on sleds. And they just lie there on the snow. Fewer and fewer coffins are available, so too the materials to make them. The bodies are wrapped in sheets, blankets, tablecloths - sometimes even in curtains. Once I saw a small bundle wrapped in paper and tied with string.

It was very small - the body of a child.

How macabre they look on the snow! Only occasionally an arm or leg protrudes from the crude wrappings...It reminds me of a battlefield and of a doss-house, both at the same time." (Reid, p. 216)

Sick and injured children in a hospital.

The Leningrad Party Committee officially closed 270 factories during the winter of 1941/1942, but the rest hardly functioned at all. Aside from the workers who had died, factory managers complained that "hundreds of people fail to appear for work, and nobody pays any attention. Every day the number absent without leave rises...After the district Party Committee told the management that their behavior sheltered truants, in the course of two days they brought proceedings against seventy-two absentees. But this was not the end of [the management's] mistakes. Of the 72 cases half had to be sent back again, for lack of evidence." (Reid, p. 220).

The Soviets also had to worry about Moscow from nearly the beginning of the invasion. The genesis of Operation Typhoon lay in Fuhrer Directive 35, which did not actually call directly for taking Moscow. This Directive, again showing more strategic sanity than generally credited to Hitler, ordered "a decisive operation against Army Group Timoshenko, which is conducting unsuccessful offensive operations on Army Group Centre's front. It must be destroyed decisively before the onset of winter. [...] after destroying the main mass of Timoshenko's group of forces [...] Army Group Centre is to begin pursuing enemy forces along the Moscow axis." (Forczyk I, 2006, 12).

The OKW, cooperating with Field Marshal Fedor von Bock, the commander of Army Group Center, interpreted this directive very generously as they prepared plans in August and early September. In keeping with their fixation on Moscow, these men made the Soviet capital their main objective, as opposed to merely pounding Russian general Semyon Timoshenko's armies into submission. They code-named the scheme "Operation Typhoon."

Bock

Timoshenko

    The German lines of supply experienced numerous problems in Russia – though the Soviet forces suffered even greater logistical headaches much of the time, in part due to the paranoid irrationality of Soviet totalitarian government – and relied heavily on truck transport. Hitler ordered no less than 3,500 new trucks sent to Army Group Center during the preparations for Operation Typhoon to carry gasoline, supplies, and ammunition. Moreover, 307 additional tanks also reached the Eastern Front for Operation Typhoon, of which 50 were Panzer IV medium tanks, 166 were Panzer III medium tanks (already undergunned for the era), and the balance Czech-based Pz-38(t) light tanks (Forczyk II, 2013, 116). In all, the Wehrmacht mustered 70 divisions for the Operation; 47 infantry divisions comprised the bulk of Army Group Center, but 15 Panzer divisions (mustering at least 1,000 tanks) and 8 motorized infantry divisions gave the expedition both mobility and teeth. The Germans organized these divisions into six armies.

    Soviet forces found themselves outnumbered by anywhere from 1.5:1 to 2:1 in personnel and various kinds of equipment, but with Moscow at their backs, the men facing the Wehrmacht killing machine exhibited fanatical courage and determination. The waning year also strictly limited the operational days before foul weather set in. Approximately 894,000 Soviet soldiers formed three fronts facing Army Group Center. These men, deployed in an amateurish manner by their inexperienced commanders, benefited from the support of 849 tanks, consisting of 47 KV-1 heavy tanks, 94 T-34 medium tanks, and hundreds of largely obsolete light tanks. These ragged, exhausted men, with little ammunition and few supplies, found themselves concentrated close to the front due to grandiose Stalinist plans for an offensive.

Soviet T-26 light tanks at the battle

A Soviet T-34 tank during the fighting

Lieutenant General Ivan Konev commanded the main portion of the front, with six armies at his disposal. Commanding the reserve force of six armies behind him, Semyon Budyonny remained convinced of the superiority of horsed cavalry to tanks – and, indeed, of lances to rifles. "Pulya dura, shtyk molodyets," his favorite aphorism derived from Suvorov, translates as "the bullet is a fool, the lance is a stout fellow," and Budyonny proved grimly faithful to it by viciously participating in the judicial murder of Mikhail Tukhachevksy, the modernizer of Soviet tank warfare. The sly survivor Andrei Yeremenko, meanwhile, commanded four armies on the Bryansk Front, guarding Moscow's southern flank.

Konev

Budyonny

Russian cavalry at Moscow

During the operations, the Panzer III and Panzer IV tanks proved inferior to the Russians' T-34 and KV-1 tanks, but German tactics more than evened the balance. Heinz Guderian noted that during the Third Reich's and Soviet Union's brief alliance, questions by visiting Soviet military men made him suspect that the Soviets might have superior tank designs: "The Russian officers in question firmly refused to believe that the Panzer IV was in fact our heaviest tank. They said repeatedly that we must be hiding our newest models from them, and complained that we were not carrying out Hitler's order to show them everything. The military commission was so insistent on this point that eventually our manufacturers and Ordnance Office officials concluded: 'It seems that the Russians must already possess better and heavier tanks than we do.'" (Guderian, 1964, 84).

The Germans' tanks did not lack its own advantages, however. Every German tank included a powerful radio, while only 1 in 10 Russian tanks possessed a radio, usually with a very short range and weak signal. The panzers operated as part of a sophisticated radio net connected to all levels of command, making precise coordination possible and providing invaluable real-time information to the panzer commanders.

The inexperienced Russian crews also fought fully "buttoned up," depriving their commander of clear vision of the situation. Worse, they often neglected to turn on the tank's ventilation system, resulting in violently sick or fully incapacitated crews from ammonia fumes. Soviet commanders also frequently committed tanks in small groups, squandering their effectiveness, though some showed tactical acumen equal to any panzer commander of the Third Reich.

The Germans originally planned to launch Operation Typhoon in mid-September, giving themselves two additional weeks prior to winter's arrival to execute their design, but delays set in, however. Army Group Center lay at the end of extremely long overland supply lines, and due to lack of rail transport in many locations, panzers had to drive up to 600 miles under their own power while mustering for the offensive. After traveling so far over Russia's appallingly bad roads, the Germans spent considerable time repairing and overhauling the battered vehicles.

A picture of a vehicle stuck in mud on a road outside Moscow

While the Germans prepared, the Soviets dug in, even though the Russians believed the Germans would mount their next offensive in the south to pierce even deeper into the Soviet Union's underbelly. Heinrich Haape reported, "East of the Mezha, the Russians prepared a strong system of trenches, bunkers, tank-traps and barbed-wire entanglements. They laid minefields, reinforced their front-line troops, brought up supplies and gathered their strength to stand against us once more. We had to sit helplessly ... and listen to stories brought back by our patrols of the rapidly developing Russian defensive system." (Stahel I, 2013, 55).

Guderian opened operations on September 30th, but the Soviets initially mistook his thrust for a feint since the majority of Army Group Center remained immobile. Thus, the Battle of Moscow began fully at dawn on October 2nd, 1941, in approved Wehrmacht style; a huge artillery bombardment swept over the Soviet positions at 5:30 a.m. sharp, pulverizing and stunning the frontline defenders. Luftwaffe bombers followed the rolling curtain of artillery fire, dropping their lethal payloads on the Russian soldiers, after which panzers rumbled forward through the gray predawn gloom, the armored spearhead followed by swarms of experienced, highly trained Wehrmacht infantry.

Guderian

The tanks achieved dramatic breakthroughs, commanded by such armored warfare luminaries as Heinz Guderian (leading Panzer Group 2), Hermann Hoth (in charge of Panzer Group 3), and Erich Hoepner (Panzer Group 4's talented leader, destined to end his life slowly strangling in a piano wire noose after the July 20th, 1944 bomb plot against Hitler). With dry conditions under a clear sky and bright sun, the panzers traversed the Russian roads up to 12 miles on the first day, and since the Soviets only had light tanks with green crews, the German armored forces scarcely believed their good fortune.

Hoepner

Hoth

A picture of German panzers at the battle

General Erhard Raus' 6th Panzer Division, forming the leading unit of Hoth's Panzer Group 3, pierced even deeper into Soviet territory. The division reached the upper Dnieper 18 miles from the starting point on the first day and, critically, took two good bridges intact. This had the effect of both securing Hoth's line of advance and denying the Russians in the sector any easy retreat past the river. Nevertheless, the Soviets attempted a withdrawal that night, as Raus reported: "That night I ordered the renewed employment, by the entire division, of the defensive hedgehog tactics that *Kampfgruppe* Raus had routinely utilized in its drive through the Baltic countries. […] Enemy troop units were moving all around the entire system of panzer hedgehogs as soon as darkness fell."

Raus

Meanwhile, the German infantry encountered stiffer resistance. Though badly mauled by artillery, bombing, and tank attacks, the Soviet infantry rallied bravely and fought hard to hold their remaining positions. Here and there the Germans suffered notable casualties, but eventually, the Soviet infantry succumbed, and the penetration broadened and strengthened. During the advance, the German infantry frequently found large piles of Soviet soldiers already killed in passing by tank machine guns. One particular item of note in the first days of the offensive consisted of wrecked American-made Jeeps, whose strange appearance drew the curiosity of the Wehrmacht soldiers (Seaton, 1993, 76-77). These vehicles marked the first trickles of Lend-Lease, destined to grow into a flood that kept the Soviet Union in the war.

October 3rd witnessed even more successes for the Germans, while the situation rapidly worsened for the Soviets. Arthur Wollschlaeger led four panzers into the city of Orel and captured it with its strategically vital bridges and railroad yards intact. As his tiny force seized the city of 140,000 inhabitants, Wollschlaeger noted, "City life was still in full swing. When the citizens of Orel saw us, they fled into the buildings and side streets, white as ghosts." Wollschlaeger's men represented the very tip of Guderian's Panzer Group 2, while Guderian's men encountered and routed a rifle battalion consisting of Russian women near Orel on the same day, another strange sight for the all-male Wehrmacht. Other units found the machinery of disassembled factories stacked in the railyards, ready for shipment eastward but now unexpectedly overtaken by the German advance (Seaton, 1993, 77).

With the skies still clear, the roads firm and dry, and the Luftwaffe providing close air support when needed, Hoth and Hoepner's Panzer Groups each pushed 30 miles past the starting point. Both Ivan Konev and Andrei Yeremenko requested Stalin's permission to fall back, fearing another vast encirclement such as those which already yielded 3 million prisoners to the Germans during the previous three months, but the Soviet dictator curtly refused. Understandably fearing summary execution or torture in NKVD cells followed by a show trial and execution, the Red Army commanders held their ground as the tide of German armor and infantry penetrated deep into their rear. A Soviet commander attempted to attack the flank of Raus' 6th Panzer Division on the 3rd near Kholm in order to stop or delay the advance of Hermann Hoth's Panzer Group 3. 100 Soviet tanks took part, but they attempted the attack through thickly wooded terrain, which dispersed them into small, uncoordinated groups. The Germans quickly deployed PaK anti-tank guns and 88mm Flak guns and shot the attack to pieces, claiming 80 kills in a matter of hours and forcing the remaining Soviet armor to retreat.

The Wehrmacht and the German population showed the same incredulous reaction to the fresh advance despite its initial successes. Nobody understood why the war continued following the massive defeats inflicted on the Soviet Union, but Stalin's ideological intransigence and the Russians' clear awareness that Hitler intended their literal extermination as subhumans obviously gave the Soviets plenty of motive to keep fighting. Of course, that determination was less clear to those who were constantly being given Goebbels' propaganda, and Hitler addressed his people in Berlin, reiterating that the fresh offensive would smash the Soviet army and end the threat of communism forever.

Though the ground attack moved forward initially with the inexorability of a juggernaut, the Luftwaffe failed to master the skies over the region near Moscow. Spread thin over a huge space, the German pilots fought with skill and professionalism but found the Soviet air forces much superior to the barely-trained draftees dying in hordes on the ground. On October 5th, Heinz Guderian himself narrowly avoided death when Soviet bombers attacked his airfield headquarters at Sevsk, destroying some German planes on the runway and shattering the windows of the room where Guderian and his staff stood conferring.

A picture of Soviet planes near Nazi positions around Moscow

Picture of a downed German plane being shown off in Moscow

During October 3rd and 4th, the Panzer Groups attacked and maneuvered to trap entire Soviet armies in "pockets" – in the vivid German terminology "Hexenkessel" or "witches' cauldrons" – where surrender would quickly follow. In the south, Guderian's panzers sought to create a pocket around Bryansk, while Vyazma formed the center of another encirclement made by the planned juncture of Hoth's and Hoepner's Panzer Groups. Luftflotte 2 of the Luftwaffe supported the panzer thrusts constantly, directing devastating Stuka dive-bomber airstrikes anywhere that Soviet infantry or armor concentrated in an effort to resist the offensive.

Konev, understanding all too well the fate awaiting his armies if the double envelopment closed its jaws around them, launched multiple counterattacks in addition to the ill-fated tank attack near Kholm on October 3rd. The fighting continued for three days, through October 5th, during which the Germans destroyed dozens of Soviet tanks but lost significant (albeit lesser) numbers of their own.

Despite the Soviet attempts, the encirclement annihilated the Soviet 43rd Army and trapped the 20th and 24th Armies within a hostile girdle of Wehrmacht men and steel. The commanders at the OKH headquarters, visited by Hitler himself on October 4th, showed great energy and verve, expecting another stunning victory, and the Fuhrer spoke airily of Guderian driving through to Tula and then Moscow. However, the inexorable specter of supply failures began to manifest itself almost simultaneously with his visit, the first sign that the Wehrmacht simply lacked the means to carry out Operation Typhoon as planned. Guderian called for 500 cubic meters of gasoline but received only 20% of that on October 6th, seriously slowing his advance, and a chorus of similar requests came in from Hoth, Hoepner, and their subordinates as their efforts to maneuver began faltering even before completing the Bryansk and Vyazma encirclements. Exacerbating the problem, the Germans' tanks all featured gasoline engines due to procrastination by Hitler's engineers, while the Soviets' diesel tank engines needed far less fuel by volume to continue operating. The Panzer I tank included a diesel engine, but its obsolescence prevented its fielding on the eastern front, at least in a mainline combat role.

As the Germans slowed, the Soviets stepped up their counterattacks. T-34 tanks delivered a startling reverse to the 4th Panzer Division, part of Heinz Guderian's Panzer Group 2, near Mtsensk on October 6th. The German defeat came despite their superior numbers, with 56 panzer III and IV tanks facing off against 45 T-34s and other Soviet tanks. The 4th Panzer Division commander, Langermann-Erlencamp, repeatedly attacked on October 7th, 8th, and 9th, but the Soviet commander, Mikhail Katukov, skillfully used flanking attacks to destroy most of the Division's panzers and held on to Mtsensk, halting a small but significant part of the Operation Typhoon advance in its tracks.

Katukov

On October 5th, at around noon, Stalin finally realized the folly of his orders for Konev and Yeremenko to hold their ground. The crucial moment arrived when scouting aircraft found an unopposed column of German armor and infantry, 12 miles in length, approaching Yukhnov with no Soviet forces between it and Moscow, 114 miles distant. The Soviet dictator ordered a new defense line called the Mozhaysk Defense Line between the column and Moscow, while giving Konev and Yeremenko full authorization to retreat.

As the Soviets finally changed plans, the Germans struggled to close the encirclement during the end of the first week in October and into the start of the second week. Fedor von Bock feuded savagely with several of his subordinates, causing further delays, but even still, nearly 79,000 prisoners fell into German hands even before the Vyazma Pocket's closure, along with hundreds of tanks, artillery pieces, soft-skinned vehicles, and aircraft, signaling yet another crushing defeat for the Red Army.

Facing disaster, Stalin recalled Marshal Georgy Zhukov from Leningrad on October 7th and sent him to review the situation. Zhukov managed to convince Stalin not to execute Konev by asking for the disgraced general to be made his second in command – Konev's predicament, after all, was completely the result of Stalin's own incompetent orders – and quickly realized that the dictator had doomed his own armies by refusing earlier permission to retreat. Zhukov even dared to praise Konev's performance: "Shooting Koniev will not improve anything or encourage anyone. It will only produce a bad impression in the army. Shooting Pavlov was no use at all. Everyone knew that Pavlov should never have been put in charge of anything larger than a division … But Koniev is not Pavlov – he is an intelligent man. He can still be serviceable."

Zhukov

Stalin inquired belligerently whether Zhukov counted Konev as a personal friend, but the Soviet commander remained adamant and Stalin eventually backed down. Some accounts suggest he threatened to kill both men if Moscow fell, but regardless of these possible threats, Zhukov focused on building the Mozhaysk Defense Line after his elevation to command in place of Konev on October 10th. He did little to relieve the men trapped in either hexenkessel, appearing to view them as a sunk cost, but he appreciated the time their sacrifice bought him. Though his staff discussed airdropping food, fuel, ammunition, and medicine, no flights ever took place for that purpose.

Despite supply difficulties and desperately brave Soviet resistance, the hard-charging Heinz Guderian completed the Bryansk encirclement by October 6th, trapping the Soviet 3rd, 14th, and 50th Armies. Yeremenko attempted to coordinate the efforts of the armies under his command, but he gradually lost radio contact with the units comprising them, and radio communications with Moscow failed also. Yeremenko, despite his deep fear of Stalin's wrath, ordered his men to break out and escape much sooner than Konev did to the north, recognizing the hopelessness of the situation and choosing to possibly incur the Soviet dictator's wrath by disobeying his foolish orders.

Picture of a Soviet radio operator during the battle

As a result, the Germans completed the two enormous encirclements successfully even while suffering fuel shortages and considerable casualties due to dogged Soviet counterattacks. The Soviets continued fighting despite their encirclement, forcing the Wehrmacht to commit 28 divisions to their destruction and greatly weakening the thrust towards Moscow. Ultimately, 514,000 Soviet prisoners fell into the Third Reich's hands, the largest single surrender of Operation Barbarossa to date.

Though Stalin had thrown away another eight armies through his strategic blundering, the weather abruptly changed and did more to impede the Germans than the Red Army. Heavy rain fell on October 6th and 7th, immediately crippling the Wehrmacht's mobility, and tanks and other vehicles used extra portions of already scarce fuel fighting their way laboriously through the muck. Fleeing Soviet journalist Vasily Grossman gloated, "There's rain, snow, hailstones, a liquid, bottomless swamp, black pastry mixed by thousands and thousands of boots, wheels, caterpillars. And everyone is happy once again. The Germans must get stuck in our hellish autumn." (Stahel I, 2013, 81).

Guderian's encirclement at Bryansk proved relatively porous due to his lack of manpower, while the Vyazma "hexenkessel" showed considerably greater security. Nevertheless, large numbers of Red Army soldiers escaped eastward, even as the majority died or surrendered in the two pockets. The Germans reduced the Vyazma pocket systematically on October 8th and 9th with merciless artillery and bombing attacks, combined with massive infantry advances. General Erhard Raus vividly described some of the action during the closing of the Vyazma pocket on

October 9th, when he said that the 6th and 7th Panzer Divisions, working together, "resembled a mighty battleship, smashing all targets within reach with the heavy caliber of its broadsides. Artillery and mortar shells from 300 throats of fire hailed down on the Soviet batteries and tanks. Soon the Russian tanks were in flames, the batteries transformed into smoking heaps of rubble, and the lines of skirmishers swept away by a swath of fire from hundreds of machine guns."

Also on October 9th, Hans von Greiffenberg, in command of the Vyazma pocket forces, ordered the encircled Soviets eliminated with extreme vigor. He gave a simple directive: "All corps have the order: 'Forwards, forwards, forwards!'" The Soviet 19th Army attempted to break out of the encirclement on October 10th, supported by other units, but Hoepner's Panzer Group 4 and the 23rd Infantry Division under Major General Heinz Hellmich fought this breakout attempt and eventually pushed it back. That said, the 19th Army's effort to extricate itself cost Hoepner's and Hellmich's men dearly thanks to the intense fighting, and the Germans noted with dismay that the Russians fought with great tenacity, with 5 men dying for every 1 who surrendered. This was the case even though appallingly bad Soviet logistics meant that at least half of the Red Army soldiers carried no weapons at all; they simply followed the armed men so that when these died, they could arm themselves with the fallen man's rifle. Not surprisingly, the Wehrmacht soldiers could hardly believe what they were seeing.

The drive on Moscow slowed and stuttered to a near halt as the weather continued worsening. Though the panzers negotiated the mud with considerable difficulty, the wheeled trucks and horse-drawn supply wagons bringing them gasoline could not maneuver at all. German engineers struggled to "corduroy" the roads with logs, but the process remained time consuming and the bumpy drive damaged the worn, overused trucks further. General Raus noted that most of the tanks had now been driven continuously for 6,000-7,000 miles, and that in the absence of spare parts, the men kept them running by cannibalizing other tanks. This, of course, reduced the number of working vehicles as effectively as combat losses, though the general noted forlornly that the hulls might be salvageable for eventual remanufacture.

As heavy snow fell on October 9th and 10th, the Germans contrived to force an advance despite the staggering obstacles. Junkers Ju-52 aircraft airlifted several hundred tons of fuel daily to the advance units, enough to permit a laborious forward movement, and some commanders pressed their SdKfz 251 Hanomag halftracks into service as improvised fuel trucks, gaining a little mobility at the cost of depriving their infantry of the protection of these early armored personnel carriers.

Meanwhile, on October 10th and 11th, the Soviets continued their frantic efforts to break out of the "pockets." Frequently, single companies of German motorized infantry blocked the path of division-sized Russian units, and in some cases, these small forces found themselves under constant attack for 24 continuous hours. Mikhail Lukin, commander of the Soviet 19th Army, did his utmost to organize the men for a successful breakout. The Red Army soldiers siphoned the gasoline out of their wheeled vehicles, such as trucks and command cars, and used it to fill the engines of tanks and artillery tractors, deemed to be the highest value assets still in the encircled forces' protection. The Soviet artillery fired off all their remaining shells at pre-designated targets such as railyards and then destroyed their guns to keep them out of German hands.

The attack aimed for the village of Bogoroditskoye, across the Bobria River and through low-lying swampy ground that the Soviet soldiers soon dubbed "the Valley of Death." At the last minute, Lukin found it necessary to deal with the anxieties of an important subordinate: "At this moment, General V.P. Vashkevich, upon whom I was placing all hopes, raised objections regarding the timing of the attack and the haste with which the divisions were being committed into battle, so again I had to try to convince him […] that if we didn't break out that night, next day the enemy would crush us […] We said our farewells, shook hands, and he left."

Vast numbers of Soviet soldiers died as they attempted to push through the German defenses over open ground. Machine guns raked the crowd, rifle fire picked off single men, and artillery, mortars, and direct fire from the deadly 88mm anti-aircraft guns shredded human flesh and vehicular steel with impartial brutality. Some men managed to break out eastward, and those who did so at night frequently escaped, but during the day, mobile panzer units relentlessly hunted and slaughtered fleeing soldiers who managed to survive the lethal cordon surrounding the pockets. Still, the sheer desperation of the Soviets to escape made a lingering impression on their tormenters. The 11th Panzer Division officer Walter Shaefer-Kehnert described the surreal vision of a Soviet breakout attempt: "I saw one of these attacks coming early in the morning. We were sitting on the top of the hills, there was fog going down to the river valley, and when the fog came up it was like a herd of vehicles and men coming up by the thousand and it made your blood freeze."

Most of the men trying to escape ended up as prisoners or as jumbled, shattered corpses freezing in the churned mud. The 111th Panzer Grenadier Regiment alone took 3,000 prisoners and killed 2,000 more men in the course of two days, sustaining considerable losses in killed and wounded in the process. In the meantime, von Greiffenberg's soldiers pressed into the Vyazma pocket from the west, squeezing the remaining Soviets into a smaller and smaller area. Vast columns of hundreds of thousands of prisoners stumbled westward through the deep, clinging mud of the roads, including Lukin himself. His staff eventually abandoned him in a peasant hut after a bad leg wound rendered him practically immobile. The Germans took him prisoner, eventually amputated his leg when they could not save it, and attempted to recruit him for the Wehrmacht, an effort which ultimately failed.

Many of the men taken prisoner died in any case, often in a far more lingering and excruciating manner than those cut down by machine gun fire and high explosive shells. Some German guards reported starving soldiers literally tearing one or two of their comrades to pieces daily and devouring them in desperation. At one location in Poland, the Germans penned 100,000 luckless Soviets in the open inside a huge barbed wire entanglement and simply guarded them until every single one starved to death, while shooting any who attempted to escape.

Though some Germans felt pity for the Russians taken prisoner and then murdered by inches in this fashion, other exhibited savage indifference or hatred, showing how completely totalitarian propaganda could transform otherwise ordinary men into hardened killers. Maximilian Siry, a German officer, felt that the Wehrmacht's defeat stemmed from their excessively lenient and gentle treatment of prisoners: "One mustn't admit it openly, but we were far too soft. All these horrors have landed us in the soup now. But if we'd carried them through to the hilt, made the people disappear completely – no one would say a thing. These half measures are always wrong. […] We've seen that we cannot conduct a war because we're not hard enough, not barbaric enough." (Stahel II, 2015, 44-45).

Vashkevich, on the other hand, was one of the few who successfully broke out that day. He gathered portions of the 1282nd and 1286th Rifle Regiments 12 miles away from the breakout point, along with some artillery units and naval infantry. The men slept while Vashkevich and his officers kept watch for other escapees throughout the day, but only a bare handful joined them. As the sound of firing died away, Vashkevich realized that the bulk of the 19th Army remained trapped or had perished, so he led his men eastward.

The 20th and 24th Soviet Armies, also penned in by the Vyazma encirclement, attempted to break out as well. Most Russian records of these two armies remain classified even as of the early 21st century, but a few radio messages reproduced in various official records indicate the same mix of desperate courage and chaos as was the case with the 19th Army. One radio operator reported no less than three generals dying while leading a single vain effort to burst through the German lines on October 13th.

By the morning of the 14th, the 20th and 24th Armies ceased to exist as fighting forces. Many men surrendered, particularly when the Germans promised them food over loudspeakers (a promise immediately broken in most cases). The luckier or more experienced hid in swamps and, if undiscovered by the Germans, survived with food supplied by the local peasants.

Conversely, the Bryansk hexenkessel proved much trickier to seal due to lack of sufficient men, so far more Soviet soldiers escaped from it to fight another day. A bold advance by Major General Wolf Trierenberg split this pocket in two, and the Germans moved to reduce the northern pocket first, using Sturmgeschutz (StuG) III self-propelled assault guns to move through the dense forests near Bryansk and slaughter the trapped Soviets. These low-profile, turretless armored vehicles packed a considerable punch with their 75mm guns, capable of firing high explosive (HE) rounds at infantry or armor-piercing (AP) rounds at tanks.

The Russians fought back with the vigor that might be expected by cornered soldiers, even as the Germans overwhelmed them with better equipment and sheer fighting skill. On October 10th, a large section of the Soviet 50th Army burst out of the northern Bryansk pocket and retreated eastward. Few others from the unit managed to escape after that date.

The southern Bryansk pocket suffered more systematic reduction. Guderian used the hammer of a number of mechanized and foot infantry divisions advancing from the west to crush the Soviets against the anvil of his Panzer corps deployed to prevent their escape in the east. Small groups of Soviets slipped through the tank cordon on October 10th as the trapped 3rd and 13th Armies battered against the Wehrmacht cage containing them, and on October 11th, a massive Soviet attack pierced the defenses at the juncture of the 25th and 29th Motorized Infantry Divisions, enabling many men to escape.

Yeremenko himself only barely eluded capture on October 13th. Though he exhibited a slippery personality capable of surviving in Stalin's psychotically paranoid high command – A.M. Vasilevsky underlined Yeremenko's "ability to weasel his way out, pull the wool over someone's eyes, and his skill at groveling"– the Colonel-General displayed almost reckless courage in combat situations. After suffering a dangerous wound from an exploding shell, he narrowly escaped aboard a Polikarpov Po-2 medical evacuation biplane with advancing panzers only 600 feet away.

October 13th also marked the final end to major operations in the Vyazma pocket as the infantry forces pushing from the west met the panzers and motorized infantry blocking the eastern retreat. Over half a million Red Army soldiers surrendered, while hundreds of thousands more lay dead. Even the Germans seemed aghast at the landscape, carpeted for many miles with shattered and dismembered human corpses, with actual mounds of dead soldiers rising at the points where breakout attempts met concentrated fire.

The battle at Vyazma had an oddly demoralizing effect on both sides. The Germans marveled at the endless hordes of Soviet soldiers, and though they had only lost 48,000 killed and wounded, morale suffered a heavy blow as the ordinary soldiers began to believe they would never return home alive. Meanwhile, the Soviet army and citizenry, aware that the hordes were not in fact endless, felt grief and fear at the colossal defeat the seemingly unstoppable Wehrmacht juggernaut inflicted on Moscow's defensive armies.

Marshal Zhukov took the initiative in stiffening resolve among his men with a widely distributed order sent out on October 13th. Besides lengthy and detailed threats of the deadly fate awaiting "traitors" who fled, retreated, or abandoned equipment, the Marshal struck a confident patriotic note: "Now, in order to offset this failure [at Leningrad], the fascists have undertaken a new adventure – an offensive on Moscow. The fascists have thrown all their reserves into this offensive, including untrained [soldiers] and every sort of random rabble, drunkards, and degenerates. [...] At this moment, everyone, from private to the highest commander, must valiantly and selflessly fight as one for their Motherland, for Moscow."

Fighting in the Bryansk pocket continued far longer than in the Vyazma pocket, but here again a German victory, albeit a costly one, slowly emerged. The combat raged on past October 13th, when the by-then nominal commander of the Soviet forces, Yeremenko, received his evacuation by air. On that same day, the Soviets used the dense forest to close into actual melee with the infantry of the Grossdeutschland Division, leading to a huge bayonet battle in the woodland. The Soviets inflicted heavy losses and killed two men who had received the extremely rare Knight's Cross decoration, and the Grossdeutschland soldiers were so infuriated by the losses that they took no prisoners that day, leaving the forest tracks heaped with mangled corpses. As fighting continued through October 18th, the Russians fought doggedly but with increasing despair, but Guderian's men finally wiped out the southern pocket on the 18th, freeing them at last for a new advance. Most trapped Soviet political officers shot themselves, knowing the hatred the Nazis held for them, and Soviet prisoners who turned over a commissar to the Einsatzgruppen could expect better treatment and more food as a reward. Many wounded Russian soldiers also committed suicide, knowing their chances of surviving captivity approached zero, or they simply asked other men to shoot them. With no medical care available, many badly wounded men gave themselves the mercy of a bullet rather than die in agony over hours or days, sometimes exhorting their comrades to avenge them before pulling the trigger. One recalled, "A lieutenant in command of one platoon, who'd been wounded in the attack, before shooting himself said, 'Tell them, brothers, how we died here, and to take revenge for us!' Private F.P. Chukharev, a radio operator who'd been wounded in the chest, wanted to shoot himself with the lieutenant's revolver. However, the medic Maletsky bandaged him and convinced him the wound wasn't fatal." (Lopukhovsky, 2013, 362).

Around 68,000 men escaped from Vyazma, while 23,000 eluded capture at Bryansk. The rest joined the endless columns totaling close to 4 million prisoners being driven westward. These men, starved, dehydrated, and constantly beaten by the German guards in an effort to make them move faster, died by the thousands on the road. The Germans shot anyone who fell behind, and German vehicles simply ran over any prisoner who collapsed from exhaustion during the march. Nearly 2 million men soon died in German captivity, mostly from starvation and the disease accompanying it.

Many of the men who escaped continued eastward in the hopes of rejoining the Red Army, others remained behind as partisans, fearing that their return in defeat would lead to their execution and the arrest of their families, as per Stalin's Order #270. Many of these newly minted partisans lived only a short time, because the Germans ruthlessly rounded up real or suspected partisans in the following months and executed tens of thousands of them, nearly destroying Soviet guerrilla forces for some time.

Meanwhile, those men who escaped the Germans and rejoined the Red Army forces to the east often experienced another sort of difficulty. Operating almost by the standards of tribal warfare, the Soviets viewed soldiers who eluded capture and fled to fight another day, even from a desperate situation, with a mix of suspicion and contempt bordering on hatred. The Soviets operated by an unspoken but clearly identifiable rule that a soldier who retreated rather than die – however uselessly – at his post, very closely resembled a traitor and counterrevolutionary. Officers who ordered their men to surrender almost always suffered summary execution when they returned home, explaining the numerous officer suicides in units too broken and defeated to continue fighting.

As a result, escapees met with interrogation by the NKVD, and while many escaped this process unscathed, others whose stories seemed thin or whom the interrogators simply disliked found themselves sent to Siberian labor camps where death from starvation, abuse, and disease frequently awaited them.

Even as the battles to reduce the Bryansk and Vyazma pockets still raged, Fedor von Bock used some of his units to push forward towards Moscow, where only ragtag units of militia and NKVD policemen guarded the approaches to the capital, perhaps numbering 90,000 in all. The German engineers, working tirelessly in conditions of bitter cold, wet, and filth, rendered some roads passable by digging drainage ditches alongside them and stabilizing them with corduroy logs, but other roads remained impassable liquid mires.

A picture of a Russian road completely swamped with mud during the operation

A picture of Russian soldiers standing guard west of Moscow
Two Panzer Corps formed the leading elements of this continuing German offensive. The jowly Adolf-Friedrich Kuntzen led the 57th Panzer Corps, while the keen-minded and extremely able Leo Geyr von Schweppenburg commanded the 26th Panzer Corps. Kuntzen's northern push moved very slowly, hampered not only by the mud but by constant Soviet roadblocks. The T-34 tanks showed themselves far more mobile over mud and wet ground thanks to their wide tracks, but while the Germans eventually upgraded their other tanks with wider tracks also, the Wehrmacht had none available in 1941. Kuntzen's column reached Medyn, 84 miles from Moscow, on October 11th, 1941, while Schweppenburg met with poorer success in the south and remaining stalled near Mtsensk thanks to Soviet resiliency. Despite Stalin's ill-advised massacres of his own tank officers, new, successful tank commanders were emerging there through a process reminiscent of natural selection.

Fedor von Bock showed a rather cavalier disregard for concentration of force by dispatching the 1st Panzer Division under Eugen Walter Kruger far to the north to seize Kalinin. Totally ignoring supply and fuel problems, von Bock further stated that Kruger would use Kalinin as the staging point for operations 30-40 miles further north, at a moment when even a few miles' advance often presented astounding difficulties. Undeterred, Kruger's men pushed north to Kalinin on October 12th and 13th, frequently mixing with swarms of Soviet soldiers fleeing along that road from the disastrous Ryazma fight. Lieutenant Colonel Walther Wenck engaged in a bit of drollery when he described the bizarre situation of German and Russian formations jostling for use of the same roadway: "Russian units, although not included in our march tables, are attempting continuously to share our road space, and thus are partly responsible for the delay of our advance on Kalinin. Please advise what to do?' The message was returned: 'As usual, 1st Panzer Division has priority along the route of advance. Reinforce traffic control!!'"

The Germans pushed into Kalinin on the 13th, finding a city utterly unprepared for their arrival, and combat soon erupted. Kruger's 1st Panzer Division experienced a hard fight to take the objective, and the Wehrmacht barely established a marginal foothold in the city the first day. The second day, October 14th, witnessed a heavy German assault from the western side of the town, and the Wehrmacht soldiers, including motorcycle troops, two panzer companies, artillery, and a battalion of flamethrower equipped tanks, pushed to the city center shortly after noon. The Flammpanzer II flamethrower tank crews enjoyed a brief moment of glory as their usually ineffective vehicles cleared building after building and accelerated the advance by panicking many defenders who wished to avoid burning to death.

At 6:00 p.m., the Germans successfully seized one of the Kalinin bridges across the Volga intact; they later found the whole structure wired with explosives which the Soviets neglected to set off. The Germans removed the explosives and set a force to guard each end of the precious bridge. Fighting for other portions of the city continued for days.

The town of Staritsa, near Kalinin, also became a focus of fighting. With its pontoon bridge across the Volga offering an alternative to the two bridges in Kalinin proper (which the Germans feared the Soviets would demolish), the town presented a tempting prize. The German 6th Infantry Division under Auleb moved against it, but they met stiff resistance from the Separate Motorized Rifle Brigade under A.N. Ryzhkov. Ryzhkov held Staritsa until October 20th, tying down an entire German infantry division for a critical week.

In an effort to help hold Kalinin, the Soviets shifted the 180th Fighter Regiment of the 46th Mixed Air Division from Rzhev to the Kalinin airfield on October 13th. The first aircraft to arrive, under the command of a Captain Timofeyev, found the airport apparently abandoned, and when the Captain touched down briefly, a German soldier appeared and fired at his I-16 airplane, prompting him to take to the air again.

Lacking radios, the men could not warn the rest of the Regiment away. Later, the Regiment's head, Captain Sergeyev, landed on the field alongside his adjutant Lt. Klusovich, both piloting MiG-3 fighters, after a skirmish with Junkers Ju-87 Stukas supporting the German advance. The Captain observed some peculiar vehicles, probably SdKfz 250 or 251 halftracks, parked alongside the airstrip. Though Klusovich opened his canopy and shouted urgent warnings to Sergeyev, the Captain walked towards the vehicles and was seized by a truckload of Germans almost immediately. One German rifleman scrambled up on Klusovich's wing, but the adjutant shot the man with his pistol and got airborne again amid a storm of bullets. The Germans savagely murdered Sergeyev, perhaps in reprisal for the shot rifleman, and dumped his body beside the airstrip, where it remained for two months. (Radey, 2012, 59).

Temperatures fell sharply and 8 inches of snow fell on October 17th, exacerbating German troubles yet further. Hitler and the OKW had actually issued large quantities of winter clothing for the soldiers in Russia, but the railways were occupied with moving fuel and replacement vehicles up to the front and shuttling cattle cars full of suffering, dying prisoners back for slave labor in Germany. As a result, most of this excellent gear remained stockpiled in Polish warehouses for months to come.

Before the cold could consume them, on the 18th and 19th, the temperatures warmed and endless sheets of rain fell, turning the mud into a watery swamp. The forces freed by the destruction of the Vyazma pocket pushed eastward again, encountering hastily built but powerful defensive positions near Mozhaisk. The Soviet defenders fought with stubborn courage, but the Wehrmacht managed to finally overrun them in days.

Hard fighting permitted the Germans to break through Zhukov's Mozhaisk Defense Line at multiple points by October 19th, but the OKH (High Command on the Eastern Front) almost immediately began squandering any chance to exploit the breakthrough. Even the overly optimistic Fedor von Bock, commander of Army Group Center, balked at the new schemes emanating from headquarters in general and Franz Halder in particular. At a moment when the hard-fighting soldiers of Army Group Center found themselves exhausted, worn out, hungry, possessing badly battered equipment, and nearly out of ammunition and fuel, Halder concocted a grandiose scheme to send part of von Bock's forces 210 miles northeast past Kalinin to Vologda, while dispatching Guderian 150 miles southeast to Voronezh – all while still planning to take Moscow.

Halder

On October 17th, Kruger's 1st Panzer Division actually attacked past Kalinin – still not pacified after four days of vicious street fighting – in the direction of Torzhok, but after pushing forward 18 miles and traveling approximately half the distance to Torzhok, the panzers encountered such heavy resistance that further advance became impossible. When the Soviets cut the road behind them, Kruger and his dashing panzer crews were forced to turn around and fought their way back to Kalinin.

All the while, both Halder and Fedor von Bock developed a fixation with keeping hold of Kalinin, now rendered utterly useless by the inability to advance against further Soviet pressure. Soldiers and tanks whom von Bock should have otherwise directed to Moscow found themselves sent to Kalinin instead, with orders to hold it in anticipation of a mighty northeastward offensive possible only in the fantasies of deluded OKH officers. Large amounts of men and material struggled through the deep mud of the Kalinin road, subject to frequent strafing by Soviet aircraft, on October 18th and 19th, draining away the strength needed if Operation Typhoon might yet succeed.

Kalinin proved a mortal wound to the drive on Moscow. The attack towards Torzhok cost 45 tanks, mostly Panzer IVs that were almost impossible to replace before spring, and the Germans counted more than 1,000 abandoned supply trucks mired on the Kalinin road, either hopelessly bogged down in thick, sucking ooze, smashed by Russian air attacks, or both. Smaller disasters also struck; an enterprising Soviet tank crew drove their KV-1 heavy tank into Kalinin proper on the evening of the 18th, and these tanks, proven able to shrug off over 75 hits from the German anti-tank guns of 1941, appeared rarely but had a devastating effect when they did arrive. In this case, all attempts to destroy the KV-1 failed as it ranged up and down the streets, running over anti-tank guns and blowing trucks and halftracks to pieces with HE shells.

Meanwhile, to the south, Leo Geyr von Schweppenburg's 26th Panzer Corps remained halted at Mtsensk by repeated Soviet armor attacks using the hard-hitting T-34 and KV-1 tanks. This remained the case on October 20th, 9 days after his initial arrival, and Hitler, the OKW, and the OKH now found themselves in a dilemma of their own making because their numerous triumphalist propaganda announcements of the imminent fall of Moscow prevented them from halting the offensive, fearing that morale in Germany itself would collapse in that event. For his part, Goebbels, the Nazi propaganda minister, evinced distress verging on a frenzy of despair. The architect of thunderous bombast about the conquest of Moscow and the surrender of the Soviets, the small, spare Goebbels now regretted his own extravagant language.

Attempts to meet the soaring claims of propaganda now directly – and fatally – dictated German military decisions during the Battle of Moscow, but on the other side, Stalin showed himself by no means certain of holding Moscow when he ordered the evacuation of certain personnel and much of the government on October 15th. This order caused rioting and looting among the people themselves on October 16th and 17th, as they were understandably infuriated by the apparent cowardice of their leaders after months of forced labor and propaganda calling for limitless sacrifice. With only a vague idea of war developments and news of the Wehrmacht just 60 miles distant, the people's mood turned ugly.

Underneath the immediate disaffection with the Moscow leadership lay a deeper current of anti-communism which the Germans, classifying the Russians as subhumans and brutalizing them accordingly, failed to exploit as they could have. Zhukov already warned Stalin that "half the peasantry" hated communism, and Alexander Osmerkin, a Moscow painter, expressed a similar loathing for Soviet totalitarianism and a tragically misplaced hope in German deliverance: "[T]here'll be no Cheka, and we will have free contact with Europe. I've burned my certificates, cleared out all compromising material from my apartment – the Marxist classics and the portraits and the rest of the filthy Bolshevik rubbish. Good Lord, I think, is it really all coming to an end?"

The Soviet dictator, declaring that he had expected larger upheavals, appeased the populace with assurances of their defense, the reopening of many places of work and business, and resumption of all salaries. The NKVD shot a few persistent looters and arrested approximately 100 citizens (plus over a thousand military deserters), but even their repression seemed low-key. Order returned, for the most part, by October 20th.

As the unrest hovered over the capital, Zhukov and other Soviet leaders worked diligently to prepare the city for defense. The Soviets drafted hundreds of thousands of women to dig 4,800 miles of anti-tank ditches and other earthworks around the city, while other construction efforts led to the building of immense stretches of barbed-wire entanglements, tank traps, and barricades. The Russians disassembled the machinery of over 500 factories and shipped the capital goods east by rail for reassembly deeper in the Russian interior. At the same time, the gulag organizer, torturer, and serial rapist Lavrenty Beria oversaw rigging a thousand major Moscow buildings with numerous explosives, often fitted with anti-magnetic housings to prevent easy detection. If the Germans took the city, these explosives would detonate, quite likely killing many men (as similar experiences at Kiev would demonstrate). Locations prepared in this manner included the NKVD offices, factories, the Bolshoi Theater, the mint, meat-processing plants, trolley and bus stations, railway stations, telegraph and telephone buildings, and even the Kremlin itself.

Pictures of Russian barricades being erected during the campaign

A picture of Moscow residents receiving military training

A picture of the Bolshoi Theater and its protective camouflage

Moscow enjoyed no immunity from German attack despite the absence of Wehrmacht ground forces. Though its airplanes suffered numerous technical failures as the weather grew colder, the Luftwaffe carried out regular night raids against the city, but with 600 large searchlights and a plethora of anti-aircraft guns, plus some early Lend-Lease fighter aircraft from the U.S. and Britain, Moscow's air defenses proved very difficult for the Germans to penetrate. A few daytime raids struck at the thousands of women laboring to build ditches and set up barbed wire entanglements on the approaches. Flying low, these scattered aircraft strafed the workers, killing a few dozen here and there but failing to slow the work due to its enormous scale.

The Germans continued attempting to press forward up to October 21st and 22nd, but the weather made the roads only slightly passable, and the Wehrmacht could not traverse the open fields at all. Zhukov threw every available man into obstructing German progress along the roads, and since they were compelled to follow these narrowly circumscribed routes, German columns met Soviet units head-on rather than bypassing or encircling them. This type of fighting nullified many German advantages, leading to slow progress and heavy losses, while the survivors suffered incredibly from cold, wet, hunger, and exhaustion.

At Maloyaroslavets, on the bank of the Luzha River, 3,500 Soviet cadets were deployed to delay the Germans with orders to hold out up to a week if possible. The determined youngsters arrived at Maloyaroslavets on October 11th and proved impossible to dislodge before the 18th, obeying their orders to the letter. Following two to three days of fighting, the Luftwaffe futilely dropped propaganda leaflets over Maloyaroslavets which read, "Valiant Red Junkers! You have fought valiantly, but now your resistance no longer makes sense. The Warsaw highway is ours almost to Moscow itself! Within another day or two we will be entering it. You are true soldiers. We respect your heroism! Come over to our side. You will receive a friendly reception, tasty food, and warm clothes from us. This leaflet will serve as your pass."

After overcoming incredible hardships and difficulties, the Germans finally reached the end of their strength at the high water mark of Kamenskoye on October 18th, 42 miles distant from

Moscow. Encapsulating both realistic situational awareness and surprising humor in a single phrase, the panzer commander Wilhelm von Thoma declared, "The spirit is willing, but the truck is weak." (Stahel I, 2013, 246). The Germans noted that the depth of mud now buried some horses up to their heads if they ventured into it, and it submerged some bogged-down trucks completely.

While the weather itself presented an almost insurmountable obstacle, the Soviets added to the Germans' problems. Incessant attacks under the overall command of Konev – spared by Zhukov's intercession but threatened again by Stalin with execution should he fail – struck Kalinin, forcing the men committed to its defense to hang on grimly to the increasingly ruined city. Other determined Soviet attacks hammered different parts of the Wehrmacht line on October 25th and 26th. These proved better led and better equipped than the luckless masses of men butchered so easily in the summer and autumn campaigns, but the Red Army still suffered from poor troop quality and the deep Stalinist disregard for attempting to preserve human life and thus build up a pool of experienced veteran soldiers.

Divisions arriving from Siberia, freed by the supine inaction of Germany's ally Japan, greatly bolstered the forces available to Zhukov in late October. As Guderian himself remarked in his later writings, "The soldiers wondered at the time why, when Hitler declared war on America, Japan did not do likewise against the Soviet Union. A direct consequence of this was that the Russian forces in the Far East remained available for use against the Germans. These forces were being moved at an unprecedented speed and in great numbers to our front. The result of this policy of Hitler's was not an alleviation of our difficulties, but an additional burden of almost incalculable weight. It was the soldiers who had to carry it." (Guderian, 1964, 138).

A picture of Russian soldiers in Moscow marching to the front

Though the Germans built a railhead as far forward as Vyazma to bring in supplies and completed it on October 23rd, this still left nearly 70 miles between the nearest railway and the fighting front. With mud anywhere from 3-6 feet deep on the roads and the open country an impassible marsh, efforts to bring fuel, food, and ammunition forward proved barely sufficient to maintain the Wehrmacht in place. In the meantime, Hitler and army headquarters both continued to plan far-flung operations to penetrate hundreds of miles beyond the current positions, with no practical hint of how to achieve such miracles.

Heinz Guderian, dauntless to the last, launched a final attack along the highway towards Tula on October 23rd. This highway, ultimately leading to Moscow, remained in better condition than most Russian roads, and it benefited from concentrated German engineering efforts with corduroy logs laid across it. Guderian used his tanks as personnel carriers, thus saving fuel otherwise utilized by SdKfz 251 halftracks for the same purpose.

The Soviets attempted to stop this drive, led by a task force under Colonel Heinrich Eberbach, a brave, snub-nosed man who would survive the war and die in 1992 at the age of 96 after assisting materially in organizing the postwar Bundeswehr. However, Guderian found a weak point, and the Germans punched readily through most of the defenses thrown up to impede them. Eberbach reached Tula, a city of 250,000 people, on October 29th, but he received a bloody nose when he attempted to seize the metropolis from elements of the Soviet 50th Army with a surprise attack.

At precisely this moment, when Guderian just might have penetrated all the way to Moscow from the south, Hitler and the OKW intervened to strip away a number of crucial units for a proposed (and utterly impractical) late-season push towards Voronezh. In fact, on October 23rd, Hitler and his cronies went so far as to order Guderian to abandon his drive on Tula and Moscow and divert his entire army to Voronezh, far away to the southeast. In response, Fedor von Bock, commander of Army Group Center, openly rebelled against Hitler's will for the first time. Appalled and shocked at the nonsensical change of plans, he refused to communicate the orders to Guderian. Making things even more complicated, the OKW reversed its orders once again on October 28th and commanded Guderian to continue to Tula. Such massive, random changes in strategic direction undermined Bock's confidence and highlighted the rapidly growing detachment from reality characterizing the Third Reich's upper echelons.

Faced with impenetrable mud, the Germans opted on October 30th to suspend further operations until cold weather hardened the ground enough to allow a fresh advance towards Moscow. This gave the Wehrmacht men some time to recuperate and resupply, but, as von Bock feared, it also gave the Russians time to bring in fresh Siberian divisions. The German halt lasted well into November, while the days shortened and fighting continued along the largely fixed fronts where the Wehrmacht and Red Army forces abutted one another. A meeting between the commanders of the OKH occurred on November 13th, 1941, at Orsha. This riverside Belarusian city of 37,000, home base of the train-bombing partisan Konstantin Zaslonov and his men, eventually became the site of several Nazi concentration camps, likely due to convenient rail access.

Pictures of Russian mortar and artillery teams preparing for battle

A picture of a Russian scouting unit near Moscow

A picture of a Russian patrol team in a Moscow suburb

With the ground hardening at last in bitter cold, the Orsha conference decided on a double envelopment of Moscow in the approved Wehrmacht fashion. Panzer Group 3 (Hoth) and 4 (Hoepner) received orders to move north of Moscow via Klin, while Guderian's Panzer Group 2 and other elements struck to the south and then east through Tula, still in Soviet hands.

As the Germans waited out the weather, Stalin had taken a calculated risk to bolster the morale and confidence of his people. He ordered two entire divisions withdrawn from the front to provide the men for a gigantic, triumphal parade in Moscow on November 7th. This weakened the front temporarily, but only during a brief window while the Germans showed no signs of moving in any case. Stalin addressed the Muscovites and his soldiers in ringing terms: "The whole world is looking at you, for it is you who can destroy the marauding armies of the German invader. The enslaved peoples of Europe look upon you as their liberators. […] Be worthy of your mission! The war that you are fighting is a war of liberation, a just war. May you be inspired in this war by the valiant image of our great ancestors – Alexander Nevsky, Dmitri Donskoi, Kuzma Minin, Dmitri Pozharski, Alexander Suvorov, Mikhail Kutuzov."

The speech and martial display restored Moscow's confidence in the Red Army and in their dictator. It also achieved great fame in the following months during screenings around the world, but ironically, the film shown did not depict the actual speech in Red Square. The film crew arrived after the parade, since Stalin ordered it shifted forward two hours from 10:00 a.m. to 8:00 a.m., and they initially reacted with visible terror when NKVD men approached them. However, the NKVD and Stalin proved exceptionally mellow and sympathized with the crew rather than ordering them sent to labor camps or killed. Stalin gave his speech a second time indoors while the relieved men filmed him, and the film of the speech was circulated to Britain, the United States, and elsewhere. Thus, ironically, the speech that attracted such vast praise actually occurred in a makeshift studio rather than amid the living throngs of Moscow.

A Soviet propaganda poster that reads "Let's make a stand for Moscow!"

Hitler also made speeches at nearly the same time, seeking to repair the damage the premature October announcements of victory had done. The bombastic lies remained in the minds of both soldiers and civilians, however, and the obvious falsity of the promises sapped the Germans' will to fight, but on November 8th, in Munich, the Fuhrer offered yet another claim of victory after a lengthy peroration in which he clearly made batteries of excuses for the failure to produce an actual victory: "Never before has a gigantic empire been shattered and defeated in a shorter time than the Soviet Union has been this time. This could occur and succeed only thanks to the unheard-of, unique bravery and willingness to sacrifice of our German Wehrmacht, which takes upon itself unimaginable strains. What all the German arms have accomplished here cannot be expressed by words. We can only bow deeply before our heroes."

No amount of backpedaling, however, concealed the fact that Goebbels' thunderous declarations of triumph had no substance whatsoever. At the same moment that Stalin mobilized the patriotism of his formerly doubtful and rebellious citizenry, Hitler's and Goebbels' lies rebounded on them to destroy the Germans' belief in the possibility of winning. Though the soldiers fought on bravely and with immense skill, the poison of doubt and disbelief filled it from the Battle of Moscow onwards.

Army Group Center rolled into motion once again on November 15th, this time over roads frozen hard and fields likewise hardened by the cold. By now, however, Zhukov commanded a much larger force of regular soldiers, numbering some 240,000 men, as opposed to the scratch force of 90,000 militia volunteers and NKVD at his disposal in October. The Soviet marshal, watching the situation closely, launched multiple spoiling attacks against both pincers of the German double envelopment. These met with mixed success, but they served at least to slow the Germans and deplete their already decimated ranks further. "One such attack, by Group Belov against Guderian's right flank, caught the German 112th Infantry Division with no antitank weapons that were effective against the attacking T-34s. The result was a panicked retreat by most of the division on 17 November, an event almost unprecedented in the German Army." (Glantz, 34).

However, the 44th Cavalry Division from Tashkent did not fare nearly so well during their spoiling attack in the north against Hermann Hoth's men near Klin. The brave but poorly led Soviets attempted a traditional cavalry charge against the modern infantry and artillery of the German 106th Infantry Division and died almost to a man amid a storm of HE shells and machine gun bullets. They literally inflicted zero casualties on the Germans, as one Panzer Grenadier described: "We could not believe that the enemy intended to attack us across this broad field, which lay open like a parade ground before us. But then three ranks of cavalry started moving towards us. Across the sunlit field the horseman rode into the attack bent over their horses' necks, their sabres shining. The first shells exploded in their midst and soon a thick black cloud hung over them. Torn scraps of men and horses flew into the air. It was difficult to distinguish one from the other."

Hoth led his Panzer Group 3 (now called the 3rd Panzer Army) against the Soviet 16th Army commanded by Konstantin Rokossovsky and the 30th Soviet Army, between Kalinin and Klin. Desperate fighting followed for days as the Germans slowly hammered the 16th and 30th Armies back and reached Klin on November 24th.

A picture of officers from the 16th Army, with Rokossovsky in the middle

Rokossovsky asked for permission to withdraw slightly to give his men room to maneuver and to counter German outflanking moves on both flanks, but Zhukov ordered him to remain in place. Predictably, this immobility led to disaster. The Germans outflanked Rokossovsky's 16th Army precisely as he expected and seized a number of bridges intact, enabling further advance. The popular, lionized General Ivan Panfilov, a luminary of the defense along the Moscow highway in October, died to a German shell, demoralizing the entire 16th Army further. When it finally retreated, the 3rd Panzer Army swept triumphantly into Klin. From there, Hoth's men took the crossings of the Volga-Moscow Canal on November 28th, securing a path across one of the few remaining major obstacles. Hoepner's 4th Panzer Army, operating in tandem with Hoth's 3rd, reached a position just 12 miles from the Soviet capital. German officers using their binoculars could now see the city's buildings in the distance.

In the south, Guderian had worse luck. The T-34 spoiling attack by P.A. Belov halted his entire advance for a day, and it only resumed on November 18th. After that, the efforts to take Tula bogged the Germans down in a desperate fight at the very end of an extremely extended supply line. On November 26th, Belov led the newly formed 1st Guards Cavalry Corps, consisting of approximately a division of tanks, an engineer unit, and a detachment of BM-13 Katyusha multiple rocket launchers, in a fierce attack against the 17th Panzer Division, routing it and preventing Guderian from taking Tula or advancing further on his leg of the encirclement.

Fedor von Bock's final effort to reach Moscow began on December 1st when he committed the German 4th Army under Kluge down the highway connecting Minsk and Moscow, but the attack came to a crashing halt at Naro-Fominsk, stopped by the 1st Guards Motorized Rifle Division and then broken on December 5th by simultaneous attacks on both flanks by the Soviet 33rd Army.

Seeing the Germans halted in all directions, the Soviets launched a series of counterattacks beginning at 3:00 a.m. on December 5th. By now, at least 3-4 feet of snow lay on the ground and the nighttime temperature hovered around 0 degrees Fahrenheit, chilling the poorly dressed Germans with bitter cold. Still, even as they were forced to retreat, the Germans maintained order for the most part and limited the gains made by the Soviets.

Pictures of German soldiers surrendering

In the north, General Erhard Raus prepared his 6th Panzer Division for the drive into Moscow when the temperature dropped sharply to -30 degrees Fahrenheit, halting his vehicles in their tracks. The Russians launched their first attack against Hoth's leading elements the same day, though without initial success. One German recalled, "At that moment a sudden drop in the temperature to -30°F, coupled with a surprise attack by Siberian troops, smashed Third Panzer Army's drive on Stalin's capital. By building 6th Panzer Division's defense around Colonel Koll's last five panzers, we held off the initial attack by the Siberians, who presented prime targets in their brown uniforms as they trudged forward through the deep snow. This local success facilitated the division's disengagement (Raus, 2003, 90).

Stalin and the Stavka botched their strategy once again, failing to encircle even one major Wehrmacht unit despite their efforts to imitate German envelopment methods. The Soviet soldiers, though brave and tough, still lacked the skill, experience, and keenly professional individual initiative characteristic of their Third Reich counterparts.

That said, the Soviet counteroffensive shoved the Germans away from Moscow and began the slow process of pushing the Germans back further, even if it did not achieve the kind of stunning victory Stalin craved. The retreating Germans destroyed the equipment they could not bring with them, packing tanks with dynamite to detonate them, setting trucks on fire, and "spiking" artillery pieces by exploding charges in the barrel.

Moreover, the weather often hindered the Soviets nearly as much as the Germans, or in some cases more, since the Wehrmacht now fell back towards its own railheads and found resupply progressively easier. Even the T-34 tanks found the deep snow hard to maneuver through, and Soviet air attacks proved largely ineffective. Though the Russians deployed ski troops and attempted the use of sleighs as personnel carriers, these men could not carry heavy weapons and routinely found themselves massively outgunned by the Germans.

The Germans remained formidable adversaries and the outcome of the war in the east remained in the balance for several more years until strategic disruption and Lend-Lease tipped the scales against the Reich. Nevertheless, as machine gun bullets hummed above the snow and the wintry trees shattered amid the thunderous orange bursts of artillery and tank gun shells, by December 11, 1941, the Battle of Moscow proper was well and truly over.

The opening phases of Operation Typhoon – up to the end of the twin pockets at Vyazma and Bryansk in mid-October – had provided the Wehrmacht with yet another stunning victory, and the Soviets lost close to a million men killed, wounded, and captured. A large number of the wounded also died as a result of being abandoned in hostile territory during cold weather. Huge amounts of materiel also fell into German hands or suffered destruction at the hands of the Wehrmacht. The Germans appropriated many Russian trucks, whose simple design and rugged characteristics matched the country's road conditions very well, and while the number of German casualties mounted steadily throughout this period, at no point did it reach crippling levels.

After the fall of the pockets, however, German mobile warfare came to an end. Channeled into mud-filled roadways by sodden pastureland, impenetrable woods, or huge Russian minefields, the Wehrmacht found themselves forced to launch frontal attacks during which the Russians either halted them or slowed them greatly while inflicting numerous losses. The Germans lost thousands of trucks and several thousand tanks, a very grievous blow which delayed the resumption of truly mobile warfare almost indefinitely. With their logistics in shambles and fuel, ammunition, food, and winter clothing lacking, the Wehrmacht were forced onto the defensive and never fully recovered the initiative.

Of course, the largest of the Third Reich's failures lay in the strategic sphere. Rather than concentrating for a massive *Schwerpunkt* to punch through to Moscow and seize it decisively, Army Group Center constantly detached units to open new fronts, take new towns, and launch offensives in fresh directions. Large numbers of men diverted to Kalinin and Voronezh, among other unimportant objectives, drained the strength of the main push and contributed even more than any other factor. Though it's often forgotten in hindsight, the Germans' defeat in the Battle of Moscow was not a foregone conclusion, and the Soviets came very close to losing their capital despite the bravery of their soldiers, the depth of the mud, and the incompetence of the OKW and OKH.

Things wouldn't get any better for Nazi Germany in the aftermath. Hitler took over direction of the war from the General Staff following the Battle of Moscow, and though the Fuhrer actually did no worse than the unrealistic, bungling, arrogant men he now overrode, he certainly didn't do any better either.

Meanwhile, the Soviets mustered new strength, armed themselves with vast quantities of weapons and vehicles sent by Britain and the United States, and gradually overwhelmed the now mostly immobile Germans in a war of attrition, the only type their strategists could win.

A Russian stamp commemorating the 60th anniversary of the Battle of Moscow

The Start of the North African Campaign

"The more I see of war, the more I realize how it all depends on administration and transportation. It takes little skill or imagination to see where you would like your army to be and when; it takes much more knowledge and hard work to know where you can place your forces and whether you can maintain them there." – General Archibald Percival Wavell

World War II in Africa is often remembered for the epic confrontation between Generals Bernard Montgomery and Erwin Rommel in the broiling wastes of the western desert. This campaign, of course, certainly did take place, but in the grand scheme of things, El Alamein and the advance on Tunisia amounted to nothing more than the concluding chapters in a much longer and more detailed operation.

Montgomery

Rommel

To understand the North Africa Campaign of World War II, it is necessary to see North Africa in a wider context than just the Maghreb and southern Mediterranean. The prize at the center of the campaign was Egypt, the Suez Canal, and the geopolitical hinterland of this region, which included not only the Mediterranean, but the Red Sea. These positions were of major strategic value for global shipping, and North Africa also held symbolic value for the Italians, who were in search of a revived Roman empire under Mussolini. For the Allies, it was the only theater of war where the fight could be taken to the enemy, making it a means to relieve pressure on Britain in the vital summer of 1940 and then on Russia when Hitler's attentions turned east in 1941.

At the outbreak of World War II in September 1939, the Axis powers, for all intents and purposes, consisted of fascist Germany and Italy under the respective leadership of Adolf Hitler and Benito Mussolini, with Hitler very much the First Among Equals. Hitler's preoccupation, however, was with Europe, in particular the conquests of Great Britain and then the Soviet Union. He had not initially factored North Africa into German strategic planning and was content to leave operations within that theater to the Italians and Il Duce, his Axis partner. The Italians certainly were present in North and North East Africa, and better armed and equipped than the British in the early phases of the war. All things being equal, they certainly should have been able to attend to that theater without an excess of German involvement.

However, Italy arrived as a latecomer to the great "scramble for Africa". The rise of fascism in Italy and across Europe during the early part of the 20th century breathed new life into the guttering flame of the Italian Empire. The late 19th and early 20th centuries marked an age of massive European expansion and the rise of competitive European imperialism worldwide. This marked the preamble to WWI, during which the great power blocs of Europe exorcised an innate belligerence in a bloody contest, settling the matter of empire between the victors and the vanquished.

The principal powers involved in this process were British, French and German, the Ottoman and Russian Empires being largely static and already in decline. The rapid partition of Africa from 1885 to WWI marked the final chapter of the great European imperial adventure, after which a steady decline set the tone for post-World War II decolonization. The Portuguese, of course, were major landholders in Africa, but they did not rank among the first tier of European powers, and neither, for that matter, did the Italians.

A map of Italian possessions in Africa in 1942

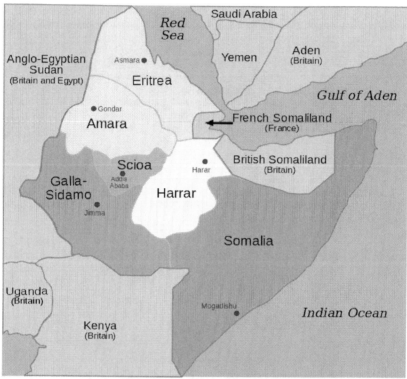

A map of North East Africa at the start of the war

Italy retained in her possession the Libyan coast and the two relatively impoverished African territories of Eritrea and Somalia. Mussolini, however, wanted more, but in the aftermath of the rapid European takeover of Africa in the closing decades of the 19th century, very little of substance remained for the Italians to claim as their own. The lone exception was the sprawling feudal kingdom of Ethiopia, which remained aloof and surprisingly resistant to European influence and occupation until as late as 1936, when the Italians finally succeeded in annexing the territory. The first Italian advance into Ethiopia from Italian Somaliland took place in 1887, but it was halted soon afterward at the Battle of Dogali, an Italian military disaster that resulted in the slaughter of some 500 Italian troops.

Opting for a political offensive as an alternative, the Italians maneuvered for territory and eventually succeeded in securing control of the important Red Sea port of Massawa through threats and aggressive posturing. This minor coup was deployed by the Italians as a political spearhead for a further claim on the colony of Eritrea, which offered a morally slim but ultimately successful basis upon which to claim that Ethiopia, as a whole, had placed itself under Italian protection.

Ethiopia was, however, still substantially ruled by its traditional monarchy, with whom the Italians enjoyed a cordial, although occasionally tenuous relationship. Matters came to a head in

1895, with the first Italio/Ethiopian War, which saw an Italian force of 17,000 men at arms advancing against an Ethiopian force of 80,000 mixed infantry and cavalry, under the command of Emperor Menelik himself. The two armies met at Adowa—or Adwa—some 200 miles from Massawa, and no more than 20 miles inside Ethiopian territory. Here, the Italians suffered yet another overwhelming and humiliating defeat and were thereafter effectively driven from the territory. They would not contemplate any further advance on the Kingdom for another 40 years.

It was the dramatic 1922 March on Rome by Benito Mussolini and the Blackshirts of his National Fascist Party that set the tone for renewed imperial impetus in Africa. The result was the Abyssinian Campaign—or the Second Italio/Abyssinian War—which was briefly fought between October 1935 and May 1936, resulting in the successful overthrow of the Ethiopian Empire and the triumphant occupation of the territory by the Kingdom of Italy. To consolidate this achievement, vast resources and energy were funnelled into this region and Libya, to fortify and protect both in preparation for even greater Italian advances.

Mussolini

On the basis of these occupations, Mussolini hoped to gain even more African territory from the British, as Italy increasingly allied itself with a belligerent and militarily dominant Germany. Bearing in mind how much African territory had fallen under British protection and how weakly defended it was relative to Italy's strength, it was not inconceivable at that particular moment that the Kingdom of Italy might rise out of the ashes to claim the lion's share of imperial Africa.

On paper, Italian military resources in the region were formidable when weighed against the handful of native regiments and eccentric colonial formations standing between it and British Africa. By June 1940, Italian forces in East Africa had comprised four command sectors, with a total of 300,000 men. Italian entrenchments concentrated around the mouth of the Red Sea presented the first major strategic challenge of the war for the Allies. Control of the Red Sea was pivotal to the survival of Egypt, which, in turn, was critical to British control of the Suez Canal and the Sudan. Although the British had retained a formidable naval presence in the Mediterranean, the Italians controlled the Tyrrhenian Sea, and Axis air and naval facilities on the islands of Sicily and Sardinia tended to neutralize Allied bases on Malta. Allied access to the Canal Zone was achieved only at the astronomical cost of some 50 percent of every naval convoy that made it through. It was, therefore, often necessary for British and Allied shipping routes to take the long but relatively safe sea voyage around the Cape of Good Hope and up the east coast of Africa in order for men, munitions, and supplies to reach East Africa, the Far East, Australia, and of course, parts of North Africa itself.

The French position in Djibouti, overlooking the Mandab Strait between British Somaliland and Aden, was initially of advantage to the Allies, but with the fall of France in June 1940 and the advent of the Vichy Government a month later, this advantage disintegrated. A nominal air supply corridor still remained in operation between the port town of Takoradi on the Gold Coast, via Nigeria, Chad, and Khartoum. This route, however, was dependent on Allied retention of Anglo/Egyptian Sudan and the safety of British interests along the west coast of Africa, and it was hardly a practical alternative for shipping convoys.

In defense of the British position in North and East Africa stood an anaemic Allied force under the command of General Archibald Wavell, commander-in-chief of the Middle East. Under Wavell's command were no more than 45,000 men unequally scattered over Egypt, Sudan, British Somaliland, and northern Kenya. Clearly, the situation for the Allies in the region was perilous.

Wavell

For the Italians, a golden opportunity existed to slip a noose around the Allies' neck in Africa, which might have altered the course of the war from the onset. Indeed, during these critical moments of the war, the Allies might have easily been crushed by the Italians between Libya and Italian East Africa, in which case Egypt and the Suez would have easily fallen into Axis hands. From as early as 1938, the British had been aware of this potential, but no one at that time could have predicted that France, with its strong presence in Algeria, Morocco, Tunisia, and Djibouti, would not stand among the Allies as a firm partner in the region. When France collapsed, however, the situation in North and East Africa radically shifted in favour of the Axis powers. The burden of defense fell, at least in the short term, on the shoulders of the colonies of British Africa. Britain, imperiled as she was on her own shores fighting the Battle of Britain, could do little to help.

On June 10, 1940, Italy declared war against France and Britain, and the game was on. The Italians opened what came to be known as the East Africa Campaign with a cautious and probing bombing operation, conducted along the length of the ill-defended border between Somalia and Kenya. Similar attacks were also launched against vulnerable Allied shipping convoys in the Red Sea. However, despite massive concentrations of Italian armor and manpower north of the Kenya-Somalia border, no meaningful land invasion followed.

The situation was similar in Sudan. The Italians held the strategic advantage, and with British defenses attenuated along a vast, desert frontier, a concerted Italian invasion during the opening months of the war could hardly have failed. The principal strategic advantage in the Italians taking control of the Sudan would have been a link-up between Italian Libya and Italian Sudan, which would, in turn, have isolated British Egypt on all sides. This would have effectively throttled Allied shipping in the Red Sea, which, in combination with Italian control of the Tyrrhenian Sea and its approaches to North Africa, would have destroyed the fighting capacity of the Allied Middle East Army. However, in July 1940, the Italians squandered this obvious opportunity, contenting themselves with a series of limited incursions into Sudan and a low-level, aerial campaign against a limited Royal Air Force presence in the skies of Sudan. The result was the withdrawal of the British garrisons of Kassala and Gallabat, which were occupied and fortified by the Italians.

In the summer of 1940, Britain was at her most vulnerable, reeling under the weight of the evacuation at Dunkirk and preparing for the Battle of Britain. Military support and supplies still made it through, and every effort was made to hold on in North Africa, but there was little hope should the Italians choose to make the best of their advantage. Ultimately, these moments of vital Allied weakness, when the British bulldog was down and inviting nothing but a good kick, were inexplicably wasted by the Italians, who preoccupied themselves with the defense of static positions until, in due course, the opportunities were lost.

Elsewhere, the Italians were somewhat more proactive. Before any dramatic invasions of British Africa east of the 25th Meridian and south of the Sahara could be contemplated, it was necessary for the Italians to neutralize Allied defense of the British Protectorate of Somaliland. British Somaliland, as distinct from Italian Somaliland, was a minor, British, overseas territory, established as a protectorate in 1888, primarily encompassing the modern region of Puntland, lying adjacent to the mouth of the Red Sea, to the more significant British naval port of Aden. It was because the territory lay at the southern entrance to the Gulf of Aden—and thus the Red Sea with its main port of Berbera just a hundred miles across the straits from Aden—that it was of such strategic value to the British. These two ports controlled Red Sea access, and the loss of the former, although not necessarily catastrophic, would certainly have inhibited the dominant Allied position.

Despite this, the British military situation in Somaliland was fundamentally untenable. Although British Prime Minister Winston Churchill, conscious of domestic morale, insisted it be defended at all costs, General Wavell realized that the price in manpower to do so would not be justified by its retention. Much to Churchill's fury, rather than reinforce the region, Wavell ordered a strategic retreat with a stiff rearguard action to make the Italians pay as heavily as possible in blood and armor for their first major acquisition of the campaign.

Churchill in 1941

This set the stage for the Battle for British Somaliland. On August 3, 1940, after a heavy initial Italian air and artillery action, a force of some 25,000 mixed Italian and native regiments crossed the frontier in two columns supported by tanks and armored cars. A relatively minute British garrison of 1,600 troops prepared to meet and interdict the approaching columns as they began an ordered retreat toward the port of Berbera, where preparations for an evacuation were already underway. The principal action of this brief campaign was the Battle of Tug Argan. The main Italian column pursued the retreating British from the city of Hargeisa towards Berbera, along the principal trunk road passing through what was known as the Tug Argan Gap. This natural bottleneck offered the British the opportunity to mount a major ambush from a series of low-lying hills. On the afternoon of August 10, the Italian column came within view of dug-in Allied defenders. The following morning, as the sun rose over the desert, a concentrated artillery bombardment preceded a series of Italian infantry assaults that steadily drove the British defenders back, although at an enormous cost in Italian and indigenous Somali lives.

This action lasted until the morning of August 16, when, just ahead of an Italian encirclement,

British defenders slipped away. While still interdicting the advancing Italian column to the outskirts of Berbera, the first British troops embarked on Royal Navy transporters for the short journey across the Gulf of Aden. Allied Somali servicemen were given the choice to either leave or stay. Most opted to stay and were allowed to retain their arms.

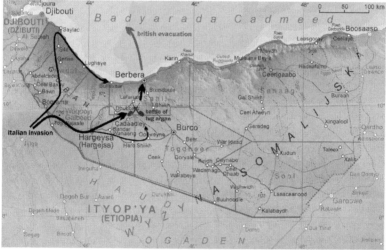

A map of the region

The Italians took control of what would briefly be Italian Somaliland, but they seemed, once again, curiously reluctant to follow up with the advantage. They dug in and waited, apparently abandoning any further interest in both the wider, strategic war in North and East Africa, and Mussolini's lavish ambition to conquer British Africa.

The British, on the other hand, now reinforced in Kenya by South African troops, were prepared to start moving to retake their own territory and liberate those claimed by the Italians. Two divisional columns were formed under the respective commands of British Generals Alan Cunningham and William Platt, and poised to penetrate Italian-held territory, the former from the Northern Territories of Kenya and the latter from Sudan/Eritrea. The main thrust of this combined operation was from the south, where a mixed British and Commonwealth force, comprised primarily of South African, Kenyan, and Rhodesian elements, including numerous native detachments from the West African Frontier Force and the Kings African Rifles, began to push the Italians back.

Interestingly, front-line combat was often fought between opposing native regiments, and as Italian native battalions began to defect to the Allies, it became clear the Italians were on the run. By the beginning of February 1941, the Allies were in control of southern Somalia. By March, they were steadily advancing along the *Strada Imperiale*, a superb blacktop military road running from Mogadishu to Harar, and headed for the ultimate objective of Addis Ababa, the Ethiopian capital.

The city of Harar fell on March 26, and Dire Dawa fell four days later. A week later, advance columns of the Allied southern offensive entered and effectively occupied Addis Ababa. There, they found order being maintained by the highly disciplined *Polizia dell'Africa Italiana*, who then formally relinquished responsibility. Soon afterward, a force was sent north under the command of South African Major General Dan Pienaar to link up with British and Commonwealth forces advancing south. The campaign officially ended with Emperor Haile Selassie's return to Addis Ababa on May 5, 1941, precisely five years after being forced to leave the capital of his kingdom upon the Italian occupation on the same date in 1936.

The other great African theater of World War II was, of course, the North African Mediterranean hinterland, and the Western Deserts of Egypt and Libya. Here, the struggle for dominance over the vital shipping lanes of the Mediterranean and Suez Canal consumed Allied and Axis powers in a nail-biting struggle for Egypt's ultimate control.

At the outbreak of war, the British were well-established in Egypt, as they had been since their victory in the 1882 Anglo/Egyptian War. The territory had proved vital to Allied interests during World War I, and it was no less vital now. The British, however, were under siege on their own islands. The risky evacuation at Dunkirk was still fresh, and Operation Sealion, the German air assault on Britain's shores and cities, was in full effect. As a result, it was only with great difficulty, and at enormous cost, that the British were able to retain control of Egyptian territory.

Across the 25th Meridian, however, just 250 miles to the west, the Italians were no less established in Libya, and they were as interested in seizing the Suez Canal as the British were in holding it. At the onset of war in September 1939, the Italians were somewhat isolated in their North African position, surrounded on every side by British (Egypt) and French (Tunisia, Algeria, Niger, Mali, and Chad) territories. The French, as an Allied power, stood firmly in the British corner, but by the summer of 1940, the French in Algeria and Tunisia had officially declared support for Vichy France, and the Free France movement had yet to fully establish itself.[77] Most senior French military and civil officials in Morocco, Algeria, and Tunisia were Vichy appointees, and although they did not, in many cases, command the loyalty of French garrison troops—and certainly not the French *Armée d'Afrique*—French forces throughout the region were nonetheless supine, and no longer available to support the Allied position.

The Italians were now in a position to contemplate an invasion of British Egypt. The Italian invasion of British Somaliland was complete, and the Italian mood was confident and aggressive. For Mussolini, this was the stuff of dreams. With the British holding on by the skin of their teeth and isolated at the mouth of the Nile, the eastern Mediterranean was *mare nostrum*, and the road to Cairo from Tripoli seemed wide open.

On the morning of September 9, 1940, a month after the fighting at Tug Argan, Marshal Rodolfo Graziani ordered the drawbridge of fortress Libya dropped, and the Italian 10th Army surged forth upon the perilously thin line of British defenses in what was codenamed *Operazione E*. The British were immediately driven back apace as Italian forces, comprising some five divisions, a tank brigade, and 300 aircraft, quickly took the defended positions of Sallum, Ḥalfāyah Pass, and Sidi Barrani. Then, the Italian columns abruptly halted and did what Italian military expeditions had so far consistently done. At Sidi Barraini, 40 miles or so into Egypt, they paused for reflection, resupply, and succor, and as they waited, they dug fortifications in the desert of the most impenetrable kind. Thereafter, despite fulminating demands from Mussolini himself, Marshal Graziani could not be induced to penetrate any deeper into Egypt.[78]

---

[77] The Free French was a French military and political organization in exile, formed in 1940 under the leadership of General de Gaulle. Based in London, the movement organized forces that opposed the Axis powers in French Equatorial Africa, Lebanon, and elsewhere, and cooperated with the French Resistance.

[78] Graziani claimed logistical and resupply issues, which, in combination with operational timidity, brought an effective halt to the Italian advance.

Graziani

This allowed the British vital time to regroup and reinforce, and in December 1940, Operation Compass was launched under the overall command of General Wavell. In a mobile campaign, the Italian 10th Army was swiftly routed and pitched into retreat. A headlong pursuit followed, spearheaded by the 7th Armoured Division, the legendary Desert Rats, and supported by a variety of British and Commonwealth troops. It was during this advance that the important port of Tobruk was taken, mainly by Australians troops, and held for 241 days, despite the ebb and flow of Allied military fortunes.

Meanwhile, the Italians surrendered an extraordinary 138,000 prisoners, hundreds of tanks, over 1,000 artillery pieces, and numerous combat aircraft. It was in every respect an utter rout, and by mid-February, the Italians had been driven back past Tobruk and Benghazi to El Agheila in the Gulf of Sirte, at which point Wavell was forced to pause to consider other regional flashpoints. By then, the British had stretched their supply lines, and with exhausted men and crumbling equipment, the advance was called off. The best equipped units were then taken out of the theater and redeployed to Greece to take part in Operation Lustre. In the aftermath of the failed Italian invasion of Greece, Allied forces were moved into the theater in anticipation of German intervention.

As these events were taking place, Hitler sensed both crisis and opportunity, and the Fuhrer responded by dispatching the newly constituted *Africa Korps* to Libya under the command of the legendary General—later, Field Marshal—Erwin Rommel. The Afrika Korps, or *Deutsches*

Afrikakorps, remains one of the most storied units of World War II. Although it existed for a little over two years, it carved an indelible mark on the fabric of military history, in part due to the way it was used as a tool in the hands of its bold, gifted, creative commander, the famed Desert Fox.

An anti-tank unit in the Afrika Korps

The Afrika Korps began as a minor expeditionary force comprising two tank divisions (the 5th Light Division—later redesignated 21st Panzer Division, and the 15th Panzer Division) operating nominally under the Italian chain of command. Advance units arrived in North Africa under the codename Operation *Sonnenblume* in February and March 1941, and Rommel was initially under orders to simply reinforce the Italian position. With a little German help, Hitler was of the opinion the Italians could hold their own in North Africa, and his offensive focus was on Russia. Rommel's orders were to work with the Italians and act purely in a defensive capacity, as Hitler did not want to divert resources to a theater he regarded as secondary.

Rommel, however, had no intention of doing this. He was not necessarily aware of the launch of Operation Barbarossa—the invasion of Russia—at that point, and he saw it as his duty to exploit what local opportunities were available. The British had, after all, positioned within artillery range of Tripoli, exhausted at the end of a 1,300 mile supply line. With bold and determined action, the conquest of Egypt and the Suez was entirely possible, and the great fatted calf that was British Africa might have also been available for the taking. What began as probing attacks against British positions accelerated quickly into a breakneck pursuit, pushing the British back 1,000 miles. With the exception of Tobruk—where the besieged garrison was holding out—the British were thrown out of Cyrenaica in less than a fortnight.

As surprised as the British were, the German High Command was perhaps more surprised still, and Rommel was again warned against any actions requiring reinforcement. Meanwhile, in June 1941, the British launched Operation Battleaxe, an ill-fated counteroffensive that quickly broke against strong German defensive positions. With both sides exhausted and ill prepared, an operational pause came into effect that lasted from the end of June to November 1941.

German tanks during Operation Battleaxe

During this period, a comprehensive reorganization was undertaken behind British lines. The local military administration was split into two commands, with one for Syria and Palestine and another for Egypt. Both of these came under new Commander-in-Chief Sir Claude J.D. Auchinleck, Wavell's successor—Wavell had moved on to the post recently vacated by Auchinleck, that of commander-in-chief of the Indian Army. In Egypt, the Army of the Nile—later to resonate through history as the Eight Army—came under the local command of General Sir Alan Cunningham, fresh from his victories in East Africa.

Auchinleck

The North Africa Campaign had developed into a contest of armor and mechanized infantry, and vital to the organization of both forces was reconnaissance. Desert warfare in World War II gave rise to a number of specialist units operating under specific conditions, some of which—like the Special Air Service or the SAS founded by Colonel David Stirling—would evolve and survive, while others—such as the Long Range Desert Group—would gradually dissolve as the focus of the war moved north to Europe. The Long Range Desert Group, or the LRDG, was the brainchild of Brigadier Ralph Bagnold, a scientific explorer who had, prior to the outbreak of war, began to utilize motorized transport for scientific work and research in Egypt. He was one of the adventurous and resourceful men—among whom might be numbered Thomas Edward Lawrence, the legendary Lawrence of Arabia—who combined the artistic and intellectual with the manly art of war. Bagnold developed an informal catalogue of desert survival techniques, breaking new ground in where and how a motor vehicle might be used, behind the wheel of a Ford Model T.

In 1940, Bagnold tested the concept of forming a unit of long-range reconnaissance experts equipped for desert travel who might range far behind enemy lines in a fleet of specially modified vehicles. He ran the idea past General Wavell, who turned out to be an eager listener. Bagnold warned of the likelihood of an Italian raid on Aswan in southern Egypt, which would link southern Libya with northern Ethiopia, effectively severing the vital British link between Egypt and Sudan. Without effective reconnaissance, he argued, the British had absolutely no idea what the Italians were up to in the deep desert. He proposed a small group of motorized light patrols be created, manned by specially trained volunteers equipped with the most desert-worthy vehicles available, capable of achieving 1,500 miles of travel, in an entirely self-contained and mutually supporting capacity.

Wavell agreed, and Bagnold was more or less given a blank check to do what needed be done to get the group off the ground. Volunteers were not difficult to find, but Bagnold made a point of recruiting colonials, particularly Kiwis and Rhodesians. Initially, the group comprised just two Kiwi patrols of 30 men each, two of which were typically officers and remainder other ranks. It is perhaps noteworthy that many of the volunteers for this unit were willing to accept a reduction in rank, so the "other ranks" in this case were quite often commissioned officers drawn from other units.

A typical patrol of the LRDG was made up of three men per vehicle: a driver, a gunner, and a third man who would be either the unit navigator, cook, fitter, signaler, medical orderly, quartermaster, sergeant, or 2IC. They were equipped with American-made, 30-cwt Chevrolet trucks, customized for desert duty. Armaments varied but usually consisted of a .303 Lewis Gun or Vickers machine gun mounted alongside the front passenger's seat or on the leading edge of the flatbed—sometimes both—and a rear-facing companion for the sake of hot extraction. Navigation and communication equipment consisted of a wireless truck, carrying a standard army issue No.11 wireless set and a Phillips radio for navigational time signals. The navigation truck itself was equipped with a theodolite, maps, air navigation tables, and other sundry equipment.

As both armies dug in and reconsolidated, the Long Range Desert Group ranged the dunes and vast gravel plains of the western desert, facilitating covert SAS and commando operations, gathering intelligence, and interdicting the enemy with hit and run actions against the long Axis supply lines.

As all of this was underway, the Short Range Desert Group—the scathing, frontline soldier's name given to the jaunty and un-bloodied staff officers stationed in Cairo, armed with their gin-slings and fly whisks—were hard at work preparing the logistics for General Claude Auchinleck's planned offensive. This massive mobilization of manpower and equipment, second perhaps only to the later buildup in preparation for the invasion of Europe, was codenamed Operation Crusader and pivoted on one very simple plan.

The main thrust of the operation was to be launched in late November. The first force—named XXXth Corps and led by the 7th Armoured Division and its support groups—was to move from Fort Maddalena, an abandoned Italian fortification lying just inside Italian territory, some 80 miles inland from the coast, heading round in a northwesterly direction toward the besieged port of Tobruk. En route, it expected to meet, engage, and destroy the bulk of Axis armor positioned on the outskirts. Parallel to this, formations of the second force—or XIIIth Corps—would move to outflank Rommel's fortified positions on the frontier, were situated on the coast at Bardia and Sollum. Upon receiving a signal, the besieged Tobruk garrison would sally forth, penetrating southeast to link up with the advancing British columns.

As military lore often dictates, few operational plans survive contact with the enemy. On a cold desert afternoon on 17 November 1941, Operation Crusader began with the sound of a mass mobilization resonating along the lonely desert frontier. German forward reconnaissance observed the commencement of a major operation, and by dusk, the first Allied armoured columns began to move forward, advancing into Libya through gaps in the wire north of Fort Maddalena. At dawn the following morning, the support group followed.

Initially, the attack proceeded well. The Germans, it appears, had been taken completely by surprise, initially presenting the spearhead of British armour with no opposition at all. On the following day, the advance continued. After a sharp engagement with enemy armour, units of the 7th Armoured Division succeeded in capturing the strategic aerodrome at Sidi Rezegh, situated just 12 miles south of the Tobruk perimeter.

The following morning, November 20, a counterattack by German tanks was repulsed. Soon afterward, the British Support Group infantry appeared on the scene. With an apparently fair wind behind them, it was decided they'd storm the escarpment to the north of the Sidi Rezegh aerodrome, and thereafter, push across the main coast road, known as Trigh Capuzzo, toward El Dedu in order to rendezvous with the Tobruk garrison.

Having anticipated this, Rommel had been busy taking the measure of the British attack overnight, and he was ready to respond by sunrise. On November 21, the 21st Panzer and Italian Ariete 132nd Armoured Divisions began moving northeast at a brisk and confident pace toward British positions. One of the longest, bloodiest, and most embittered actions of the North African Campaign, the Battle of Sidi Rezegh, was about to begin.

Before dawn on November 20, the Kings Royal Rifle Corps had taken over the Sidi Rezegh landing ground from the Armoured Brigade, digging in under the constant barrage of enemy fire, the unnerving sight of large bodies of enemy armour, and infantry massing to the west and the north. Despite this, in the early hours of the morning of the 21st, orders were issued to commence planned attacks on the steep escarpment north of the Sidi Rezegh landing ground, which would put the Allies in command of the main coast road, thus cutting off the only Axis line of communication from east to west. There was little alternative at that point, bearing in mind it was level terrain, in comparison to a simple frontal assault executed across the landing-ground itself. The plan called for the concentration of artillery fire on enemy positions, immediately followed by a carrier assault from offshore, after which the battalion would form up and cross the starting line at precisely 0800h, in what was classic British Army attack strategy.

A picture of German panzers at Sidi Rezegh

A picture of German prisoners at Sidi Rezegh

By noon all objectives had been achieved, and overall, the attack was deemed a success. In all, 700 Italian prisoners were taken, and the opening phase of Operation Crusader appeared to have passed successfully, with most objectives achieved. However, dawn the following morning revealed a somewhat different picture, however. The ocean-facing slopes of the escarpment were now covered with enemy vehicles, including tanks, and soon a steady shelling of Allied battalion positions began. At the same time, the sound of a heavy bombardment from the south grew increasingly louder as the depleted 7th Armoured Division was incrementally forced back by the superior weight of German and Italian armour. At about 1300h, German armour positioned to the north of Sidi Rezegh began to move. Supported by an intense artillery barrage, the massed formation swept past the left flank of the British armoured brigade, turning on the unprotected infantry positions from the rear.

With nothing but anti-tank rifles and a few two-pounders for the reply, the infantry was helpless. In due course, after a stiff but futile resistance, their positions were overrun. Five officers and 50 other ranks—later joined later by roughly another 100—were the only ones to escape the rout, with almost the entire personnel of three British companies being reported missing. That evening, what transport there was available was gathered, and the survivors of the battalion hurriedly organized. Then, amidst the glowing ruins of battle, a withdrawal began.

As all of this was taking place, British armoured brigades were engaged in no-less harrowing fighting in the neighbourhood of Sidi Rezegh. There, a deadly tank battle had been underway for two days between the light Allied Honey and Valentine tanks and the much heavier German Mark IIIs and Mark IVs. Axis forces, advancing in a northeasterly direction with the intention of crushing the Support Group and the 5th South African Brigade—which had, by then, advanced south of Sidi Rezegh—succeeded in overrunning South African positions and consigning the brigade to the same fate as the King's Royal Rifle Corps, effectively destroying it as a fighting formation.

In the meantime, preparations for the break-out of the garrison were complete in Tobruk, and the operation commenced three hours before dawn on 21 November with an artillery barrage from the guns of Tobruk. This action involved the Polish Brigade and the 4th Royal Tank Regiment, along with the King's Dragoon Guards and 2nd Black Watch, supported by the machineguns of the Northumberland Fusiliers. The operation ultimately failed, thanks to actions happening overnight, and the inability of the relieving force to hold its position at Sidi Rezegh.

Casualties sustained were heavy, with the Black Watch being hit particularly hard. The area around Sidi Rezegh and El Duda devolved into an extended bout of chaotic fighting that would ebb at night and flare during the day. A melancholy landscape of burned-out tanks, plumes of black smoke, and the debris of battle greeted the dawn of every day.

By November 23, however, formation reports revealed the ultimate loss of Sidi Rezegh, and a failed relief of Tobruk, at a heavy cost in casualties. As a consequence, General Allan Cunningham appeared to suffer something of a crisis of faith, concluding that the best course before him lay in withdrawal. Auchinleck, however, refused to consider this, and promptly passed command of the Eighth Army on to General Neil Ritchie, who until then had served as Deputy Chief of Staff.

Neither side emerged from the operation unscathed, but Rommel was perhaps able to recover more quickly from the brawl, thanks to the work of his disciplined and highly organized recovery sections. It was this that allowed him to retain the advantage of his overwhelming superiority in armor. Tactical failings, however, can sometimes ruin the best equipped army, as the Italians had frequently shown. Rommel inexplicably opted against striking what might have been a killing blow to the depleted British formations, plunging behind their lines in order to raid and harass their lines of supply and communication instead. As he did, Allied forces moved in to recapture Sidi Rezegh, which allowed the Tobruk Garrison to link up and thus secure an excellent tactical position across the main coast road, effectively isolating Rommel from his rear bases and supply lines.

A British Crusader tank passing an abandoned Panzer on November 24
This swung matters back in favor of the Allies. Positioned now to the east of the Tobruk/Sidi Rezegh corridor were the 21st Panzer and Ariete Divisions and to the west, the 15th Panzers and

various Italian infantry divisions. The contest in and around Sidi Rezegh resumed once again with all its former ferocity as the isolated Axis units sought to fight their way back. On December 1, 1941, the attackers succeeded in punching a hole through British lines, and an orderly and gradual German withdrawal back to their El Agheila base followed. The Germans were forced to fight a rearguard action against determined, opportunistic British pursuit on their way back, which continued to Gazala, some 40 miles along the coast road west of Tobruk.

At this point, Rommel gathered his armor and turned around to fight. The Germans were aided in no small part by inclement weather bogging down Allied transports, grounding aircraft, and starving British forces of supplies and fuel. By December 16, Rommel had succeeded in reaching Ajedabia on the western edge of Cyrenaica. Three weeks after that, he was home behind his familiar fortified line at El Agheila. The year 1941 ended with battle lines drawn essentially as they had been nine months earlier.

The Eastern Front in 1942

Operation Barbarossa was designed to be conducted with a high level of brutality. According to one German officer, "this war, will be very different from the war in the west...Commanders must make the sacrifice of overcoming their personal scruples." (Reid, p.22) In June 1941, the German High Command announced the "Commisar Order," in which captured political officers were to be immediately shot, while civilians were to be subjected to "collective measures" and German soldiers were absolved from potential prosecution for crimes like rape and murder against the Soviet population.

The German offensive consisted of three army groups: one moving north toward Leningrad, a second moving due east toward Moscow, and a third heading south toward Kiev. By September 1941, Germany's high command estimated that their forces had captured 2.5 million prisoners, killed nearly 5 million Russians, taken 18,000 tanks, 22,000 field guns, and destroyed 14,000 aircraft. The first major Russian city in their path was Minsk, which fell in only six days, and in order to make clear his determination to win at all costs, Stalin had the three men in charge of the troops defending Minsk executed for their failure to hold their position. In the future, Russian soldiers would fight to the death rather than surrender, and that July, Stalin exhorted the nation, "It is time to finish retreating. Not one step back! Such should now be our main slogan. ... Henceforth the solid law of discipline for each commander, Red Army soldier, and commissar should be the requirement — not a single step back without order from higher command."

Captured Soviet equipment in 1941 near the beginning of Operation Barbarossa.
Although the Germans were making incredibly quick progress on the Eastern Front, Edwin Erich Dwinger marveled at the strength and determination of the Russian soldiers even as they were being overrun by German troops, writing:

"Several of them, burnt by flamethrowers, had no longer the semblance of human faces. They were blistered, shapeless bundles of human flesh. A bullet had taken the lower jaw of one man. The scrap of flesh which sealed the wound did not hide his trachea, through which breath escaped in bubbles.

Five machine-gun bullets had shredded into pulp the shoulder and arm of another man, who was without any bandages. The Germans offered no medical help to their prisoners.

Not a cry or a moan escaped the lips of these wounded, who were seated on the grass. Hardly had the distribution of food begun than the Russians, even the dying, rose and moved forward. The man without a jaw could hardly stand. The man with one arm clung with his arm to a tree trunk. Half a dozen of them rose, holding their entrails in with one hand.

They do not cry. They do not groan. They do not curse. There is something mysterious, inscrutable, about their stern stubborn silence." (Hoyt, p. 41)

While the German invasion progressed quickly during the early stages, German atrocities committed against conquered Russian populations helped unify Russian resistance against the German advance and also convinced the Russians that the only possible outcomes of the war were victory or annihilation. Even though the Russians were losing the war, their will to fight strengthened around a growing hatred for the Germans and their tactics.

Certainly their resolve was tried during the first terrible months of fighting, as Germany surrounded Leningrad and then headed toward Moscow. The worst fighting, however, was in the Ukraine. Though badly outnumbered and destined for defeat, the Soviet soldiers held off the Germans around Kiev and thus spared Moscow while it was reinforced. They suffered the worst defeat in Red Army history, but were praised as heroes by their countrymen.

Picture of a German soldier walking past a dead Soviet and a burning tank in Ukraine.

In September, as winter months approached, Germany continued to advance across the countryside. This led Stalin to implement his famous "scorched earth" policy, ordering the retreating soldiers to leave nothing behind that the advancing Germans might be able to use. He also approved the formation of small bands of guerilla fighters who would remain behind the retreating army and harass the advancing German forces. These two strategies, along with Germany's ever thinning supply line, created quite a handicap for Hitler's army.

To his credit, Stalin took a page out the Royal Family of England's book and remained in Moscow even when the city was evacuated and the Germans were only fifteen miles away. He lived and worked in a bomb shelter just under the Kremlin, acting as self-appointed Supreme Commander-in-Chief and overseeing every move made by the army. He bided his time and waited until November, when the German army was forced by bad weather to end their forward movements. The Germans had reached the vital resource centers in Russia that they were aiming for, but the sheer size of Russia had enabled the Soviet Union to mobilize millions more to fight, requiring the Germans to dig in and prepare for long term sieges, even while the notoriously harsh Russian winter was setting in.

The German attack lost momentum due to a number of reasons, most importantly because of their overextension in the drive toward Moscow, the coming winter (and their lack of preparation for it), and the Russian reserve units that entered the war from the Siberian front. By December 1941, the German high command made the decision to pull back from their relentless drive toward Moscow, but when the 1st Panzer Division was engaged by Soviet troops, the Germans were caught by complete surprise because they believed there were no reserve Russian troops. Instead, seven Soviet armies pushed west against the center of the German forces. As German general Franz Halder put it in his diary in 1941, "The whole situation makes it increasingly plain that we have underestimated the Russian colossus...divisions are not armed and equipped according to our standards, and their tactical leadership is often poor. But there they are, and as we smash a dozen of them the Russians simply put up another dozen. The time factor favours them, as they are near their own resources, while we are moving farther and farther away from ours. And so our troops, sprawled over the immense front line, without depth, are subject to the incessant attacks of the enemy."

Not only were German forces stretched thin, but the cold and snow were causing their tanks to malfunction. At the same time, German troops, who were not outfitted for the cold, were suffering from severe frostbite and other problems related to the winter weather. The Russian attack created a bulge in the German Army Group Center, and as German leaders were unable to reinforce those positions, the Russians proceeded to force a 50 mile deep gap in the German line. While some German officers at the front advocated a full retreat, Hitler refused, and this caused many to question whether the leaders back in Germany understood the gravity of the situation on the Eastern Front.

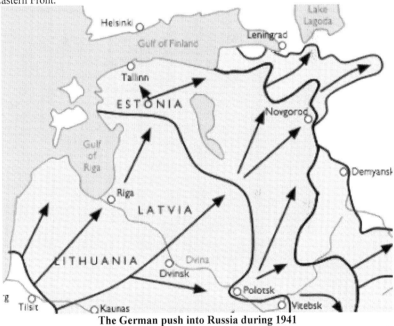

The German push into Russia during 1941

For the people of Leningrad, information about the German advance was difficult to come by, especially because most reports from the Soviet Union were shrouded in propaganda that ordinary citizens had to decipher in order to understand the true situation. As the Germans made their way to within 30 miles of the city, rumors spread that Leningrad had not yet been bombed because Hitler was saving it for his (nonexistent) daughters to take control of. The authorities tried to stop the rumors by creating laws against spreading "false rumours provoking unrest amongst the population," "disclosing military secrets," as well as arresting "defeatists" who were not patriotic enough for Soviet leaders.

At the same time, Leningrad's city leaders tried to deflect attention away from the war by indulging in some rumor-mongering of their own, mostly through stoking fears of spies who were helping to signal German Luftwaffe pilots. As Yelena Kochina wrote in her diary, fear of spies spread like "an infectious disease,"

> "Yesterday near the market a little old woman who looked like a flounder dressed in a mackintosh grabbed me:
>
> 'Did you see? A spy for sure! she shouted, waving her short little arm after some man. 'What?'
>
> "His trousers and jacket were different colours.'
>
> I couldn't help but laugh.
>
> 'And his moustache looked as though it was stuck on.' Her close-set angry eyes bored into me.
>
> 'Excuse me...' I tore myself away. Before pushing off, she trailed me for several steps along the pavement.
>
> But...even to me many people seem suspicious, types it would be worth keeping an eye on." (Reid, p. 53)

During the first four weeks of the German invasion, the citizens of Leningrad engaged in preparedness drills, even though it seemed to them as though the war remained a distant event. Roughly 50,000 residents, mainly women and children, had also been sent 60 miles to the southwest to build new defenses along the Luga River. As one woman recalled of her experiences building defenses, their orders were to "dig anti-tank ditches (1.2m deep) and breastworks (supposedly 1m high). Though our only tools were shovels, axes and stretchers [to carry soil], we set to work enthusiastically. The days were sunny and hot. We worked from 5 a.m. to 8 or 9 p.m., with a two or three hour rest after lunch. We were well fed but there was no tea, except for what our landlady made us from lime flowers. Physically it was very tough, and after two weeks, trying to lift a stretcher, I suddenly found I couldn't straighten up again."

While some workers were injured on the job, others were fired upon by the German Luftwaffe. One recalled:

> "Our whole laboratory dug anti-tank trenches around Leningrad today. I dug the earth with pleasure (at least this was something practical!)....Almost all the people working in the trenches were women. Their coloured headscarves flashed brightly in the sun. It was as if a giant flowerbed girdled the city.
>
> Suddenly the gleaming wings of an aeroplane blotted out the sky. A machine gun started firing and bullets plunged into the grass not far from me, rustling like small metallic lizards. I stood transfixed, forgetting completely the air-raid drill that I had learned not long before." (Reid, p. 57)

By July 4, the Germans had made their way near the Luga Line, where Soviet General Georgy Zhukov ordered his Northwestern Army Group to hold the defensive positions there against German attacks. By this time, the German attack was beginning to lose steam because of the terrain, climate, and the Germans' lack of reliable maps. The summer dust was an especially serious problem, as it made it difficult for German resupply transports to run efficiently.

Zhukov

On July 13, the Soviets launched a counterattack against the 8th German Panzer Division, driving it back away from the Luga, and for the city of Leningrad, the counterattack meant a reprieve from the anxiety gripping the city over a potential German attack. Many citizens wondered whether a German attack or siege on the city would lead to a famine, as had occurred during the Russian Civil War of 1921-22, and others wondered whether or not they should evacuate the city. For Leningrad's city officials, evacuation of valuables had already started once the German offensive was confirmed by Russia's leaders. For example, the Hermitage, a Leningrad museum, packed up over 1,000 crates on July 1 and shipped them to a secret location away from the city. A second train left Leningrad on July 20 with over 700,000 items from the Hermitage's collections.

Leningrad's leaders also instituted a policy of rationing on July 18, which meant manual workers received 800 grams of bread a day, white collar workers received 600 grams, and "dependents" were given 400 grams. Other food items which were rationed included meat, cereals, butter, and sugar. At the beginning, these ration levels were considered "generous" and in some cases represented an improvement in diet for some poor residents.

On August 8, the Germans began to concentrate their efforts at the Luga Line, the major defense position protecting Leningrad. The German advance came in three parts, with General Georg-Hans Reinhardt's panzer division attacking the northern sector of the Luga Line, General Erich von Manstein's 8th Panzer Division cutting the Soviet defense in two at the Kingisepp-Gatchina railway line, and Georg von Kuchler's Eighteenth Army advancing on the city of Novgorod to the southwest. Stalin became extremely agitated upon learning of the German advance, fearing that the German armies were moving into position to outflank Leningrad and cut off communications with Moscow, and he sent a terse message to the commanders of the Soviet forces in the north that were failing to hold off the German advance: "It appears to us that the High Command of the Northwestern Army Group fails to see this mortal danger and therefore takes no special measures to liquidate it. German strength in the area is not great, so all we need to do is throw in three fresh divisions under skilful leadership. Stavka cannot be reconciled to this mood of fatalism, of the impossibility of taking decisive steps, and with arguments that everything's being done that can be done." (Reid, p. 66)

Georg-Hans Reinhardt

Erich von Manstein

Georg von Kuchler

The Northwestern Army Group was in tatters, with its 22 rifle divisions fighting along a 250 miles front. Not only were Soviet troops stretched thin, they also lacked vital equipment such as heavy weapons and radios. When a Soviet general near Lyuban responded to Stalin's message, he requested not only more troops but also semi-automatic weapons to replace the antiquated rifles that the infantry had been using. In his response, Stalin begrudgingly agreed: "We've already let you have three days' worth of production, you can have another three or four days...We'll send you more infantry battalions, but I can't say how many...In a couple of weeks, perhaps, we'll be able to scrape together two divisions for you. If your people knew how to work to a plan, and had asked us for two or three divisions a fortnight ago, they would be ready for you now. The whole trouble is that your people prefer to live and work like gypsies, from one day to the next, not looking ahead. I demand that you bring some order back to the 48th Army, especially to those divisions whose cowardly officers disappeared the devil knows where from Lyuban yesterday...I demand that you clear the Lyuban and Chudovo regions of the enemy at any price and by any means. I entrust you with this personally..." (Reid, p. 67)

As the Germans closed in on the city, the citizens of Leningrad formed volunteer units as a wave of patriotism swept the population, but Soviet documents admitted that this Leningrad army, called the *narodnoye opolcheniye* ("People's Levy"), was made up of "professors, judges, directors, and some plain invalids." While the People's Levy began as a volunteer movement, it quickly became near-compulsory, and seven volunteer divisions, totaling 31,000 people, were sent to the front between July 4 and July 18. Each division was made up of people from the same district, so men from the same workplaces and families were able to remain together. Among factory workers who volunteered, many of them were skilled workers who had been exempted from the draft and were the best of Leningrad's industrial workers. Among non-factory workers, volunteers were engineers, scientists, artists and students who represented some of the most talented men in the city.

As volunteering for the People's Levy became all but compulsory, recruitment targets were divided by district and by the number of eligible residents in those districts. For city leaders trying to organize evacuation efforts, as well as for factory managers who were trying to transform their workplaces for defense production, it was a struggle to retain the manpower to keep their efforts going. Not surprisingly, many of the people who were registered for the volunteer regiments did not realize what they were being asked to do; they assumed that they would be used as civil defense forces, or as a home guard in case the Germans entered Leningrad. Instead, they quickly learned that they would be sent to the front. In July and August of 1941, 70,000 of these volunteers died, many of them due to lack of training and equipment.

It was not until August 24 that the Soviet leadership finally acknowledged that the Germans had advanced close to Leningrad and were on the city's doorstep:

> "Comrades! Leningraders! Dear friends! Over our beloved native city hangs the immediate threat of attack by German-Fascist troops. The enemy is trying to break through to Leningrad. He wants to destroy our homes, to seize our factories and plants, to drench our streets and squares with the blood of the innocent, to outrage our peaceful people, to enslave the free sons of our Motherland. But this shall not be. Leningrad - cradle of the proletarian Revolution - never has fallen and never shall fall into enemy hands...
>
> Let us rise as one man in defence of our city, our homes, our families, our honour and freedom. Let us perform our sacred duty as Soviet patriots and be indomitable in the struggle with the fierce and hateful enemy, vigilant and merciless in the struggle against cowards, alarmists and deserters; let us establish the strictest revolutionary order in our city. Armed with iron discipline and Bolshevik resolve we shall meet the enemy bravely and deal him a crushing blow!" (Reid, p. 93)

As Leningrad prepared for the coming German attack, city leaders made a major mistake by failing to evacuate the surplus population before the siege began. According to Soviet sources, on August 29, 636,283 people had been evacuated out of the city. This meant that roughly 2.5 million civilians remained in Leningrad, as well as another 343,000 from surrounding towns caught in the German siege ring. 400,000 of these civilians were children, and over 700,000 were other non-working dependents. The failure of city officials to properly evacuate Leningrad inevitably added to the large death toll and increased the tragedy of the situation.

The reason for the failure to properly evacuate the city is because Soviet leaders prioritized industrial and institutional evacuation over the non-working population. Therefore, the preparations that did take place privileged moving 92 Leningrad defense plants to the east, along with 164,320 workers at those plants. Additionally, problems with the railway lines increased the chaos surrounding Leningrad's preparations; many trains were overloaded, and when the Germans cut the railway link to Leningrad, over 2,000 carloads of machinery were still awaiting removal and remained in the freight yards.

By August 25, Leningrad was nearly surrounded, with only a tenuous path leading to the east, so Stalin sent a five-man special commission to the city to help plan its defense. Stalin's commands were fanciful and impossible to put in place, but the commission, fearful of disappointing him, responded affirmatively to them. Stalin ordered the commission to place tanks "on average every two kilometers, in places every 500 meters, depending on the ground" along a 120 kilometer defense line where "the infantry divisions will stand directly behind the tanks, using them not only as a striking force, but as armored defense. For this you need 100-200 KVs [a Soviet armored tank]. I think you could produce this quantity of KVs in ten days...I await your swift reply." (Reid, p.105) The commission remained in Leningrad for about a week, where they attempted to implement Stalin's orders.

On August 29, the Germans seized control of the town of Tosno, roughly 25 miles from Leningrad. Furious at the Red Army's failure to defend Tosno, Stalin telephoned two members of the social commission, Vyacheslav Molotov and Georgy Malenkov, and said, "I have only just been informed that Tosno has been taken by the enemy. If things go on like this I am afraid that Leningrad will be surrendered out of idiot stupidity, and all the Leningrad divisions fall into captivity. What are Popov and Voroshilov doing? They don't even tell me how they plan to avert the danger. They're busy looking for new lines of retreat; that's how they see their duty. Where does this abyss of passivity of theirs come from, this peasant-like submission to fate? I just don't understand them. There are lots of KV tanks in Leningrad now, lots of planes...Why isn't all this equipment being used in the Lyuban-Tosno sector? What can some infantry regiment do against German tanks, without any equipment?...Doesn't it seem to you that someone is deliberately opening the road to the Germans? What kind of man is Popov? How's Voroshilov spending his time, what's he doing to help Leningrad? I write this because the uselessness of the Leningrad command is so absolutely incomprehensible. I think you should leave for Moscow. Please don't delay." (Reid, p. 106)

As the Germans proceeded closer and closer to Leningrad, Molotov and Malenkov increased the pace of arrests and deportations of Leningraders suspected of being Trotskyites, Zinovievites, Mensheviks, and anarchists, as well as priests, Catholics, former officers in the tsarist army, "former wealthy merchants," "white bandits," "kulaks,." and people "with connections abroad", which included "diversionists," "saboteurs," and "antisocial elements." One witness of a mass arrest noted "about a hundred people waited to be exiled. They were mostly old women; old women in old-fashioned capes and worn-out velvet coats. These are the enemies our government is capable of fighting - and, it turns out, the only ones. The Germans are at the gates, the Germans are about to enter the city, and we are busy arresting and deporting old women - lonely, defenseless, harmless old people." (Reid, p. 107)

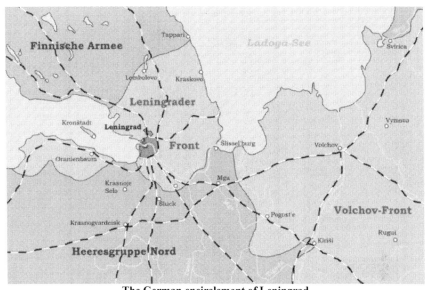

The German encirclement of Leningrad

Russians in Leningrad marching to the front.

Soviet tanks advancing to the front.

As a result of the surprise attack and the pace of the German advance, the siege of Leningrad began in earnest by September 1941. For most Germans and Soviets, the fight over Leningrad seemed like one that would quickly be decided. At the time, the entire German offensive seemed unstoppable, as Army Group North had surrounded Leningrad while Army Group Center had captured Smolensk eight weeks earlier and was now making its way toward Moscow. In the south, Army Group South was close to encircling four Soviet armies and was in the process of taking Kiev. It seemed like the Soviet Union was on the brink of collapse, and in fact, Stalin sent a desperate message to Churchill on September 4 imploring him to open a second front in France or the Balkans by the end of the year to divert 30-40 German divisions away from the Eastern Front.

As the German forces pushed forward, rumors spread that they had begun sending Russian citizens from occupied regions to ask Soviet army commanders to surrender. Stalin wrote to his commanders overseeing the defense of Leningrad (Zhukov, Zhdanov, Kuznetsov, and Merkulov):

"It is rumored that the German scoundrels advancing on Leningrad have sent forward individuals - old men and women, mothers and children - from the occupied regions, with requests to our Bolshevik forces that they surrender Leningrad and restore peace.

It is also said that amongst Leningrad's Bolsheviks people can be found who do not consider it possible to use force against such individuals...

My answer is - No sentimentality. Instead smash the enemy and his accomplices, sick or healthy, in the teeth. War is inexorable, and those who show weakness and allow wavering are the first to suffer defeat. Whoever in our ranks permits wavering, will be responsible for the fall of Leningrad.

Beat the Germans and their creatures, whoever they are...It makes no difference whether they are willing or unwilling enemies. No mercy to the German scoundrels or their accomplices...

Request you inform commanders and division and regimental commissars, also the military council of the Baltic Fleet and the commanders and commissars of ships." (Reid, p.126)

The Germans advanced up to about 10 miles away from the city center of Leningrad by September 24, but at that point, the German commanders realized their overextended armies could not continue to push eastward. Instead, they requested permission from Hitler to dig in and move to the defensive. In the fighting up to late September, the German Army Group North had suffered 190,000 casualties, while the Soviets lost even more men. It is estimated that the combined number of men killed, missing or taken prisoner for the Soviet Baltic Fleet and Northwestern Army Group was 214,078, and an additional 130,848 were wounded. This amounted to two-thirds of their original troop strength.

Soviet soldiers in a trench along the front in September 1941

Soviet soldiers carry a wounded soldier.

The prolonged siege and lack of movement in the northern front of Operation Barbarossa was due to a compromise by the German High Command in which Hitler and his generals disagreed on whether Leningrad or Moscow should be the focal point of the German advance. Hitler believed that Leningrad needed to be captured first, and after the destruction of the Baltic Fleet and capture of the city's manufacturing capabilities, the Germans could then begin their final push to Moscow. However, his top generals, Halder and Brauchitsch, did not want to spend the equipment and manpower that it would take to capture Leningrad and instead wanted to drive on toward the Soviet capital. In the end, the German High Command reached a compromise in early September that if Leningrad was not taken by the middle of the month, panzer units would be diverted from the north to the south in the push toward Moscow. Although this seemed like a relatively small matter, the consequences would be far-reaching, because Army Group North would be able to tighten the siege ring around Leningrad but never amassed enough manpower to overwhelm the city. Thus, the Germans missed their best opportunity to capture Leningrad in the fall of 1941, and from that time on, their advance in the northern sector ground to a halt.

Part of the reasoning behind the siege was that the Germans did not really know how to proceed if they captured both Leningrad and Moscow. Hitler wanted to destroy both cities and "make them uninhabitable", and in a planning session on September 21st, German leaders outlined the options available to them:

"1. Occupy the city; in other words proceed as we have done in regards to other large Russian cities. Rejected, because it would make us responsible for food supply.

5. Seal off city tightly, if possible with an electrified fence guarded by machine guns. Disadvantages: the weak will starve within a foreseeable time; the strong will secure all food supplies and survive. Danger of epidemics spreading to our

front. It's also questionable whether our soldiers can be asked to fire on women and children trying to break out.

6. Women, children and old people to be taken out through gaps in the encirclement ring. The rest to be allowed to starve:

a)   Removal across the Volkhov behind the enemy front theoretically a good solution, but in practice hardly feasible. Who is to keep hundreds of thousands of people together and drive them on? Where is the Russian front?

b)   Instead of marching them to the rear of the Russian front, let them spread across the land. In either case there remains the disadvantage that the remaining starving population of Leningrad becomes a source of epidemics, and that the strongest hold out in the city for a long time.

7. After the Finnish advance and the complete sealing off of the city, we retreat behind the Neva and leave the area to the north of this sector to the Finns. The Finns have unofficially made it clear that they would like to have the Neva as their country's border, but that Leningrad has to go. Good as a political solution. The question of Leningrad's population, however, can't be solved by the Finns. We have to do it." (Reid, p. 133)

The plan for the northern sector was set in place in a memo that was sent to Army Group North on September 28, detailing the change in plan from a ground assault into a siege that would emphasize starvation and air raids:

"According to the directive of the High Command it is ordered that:

3. The City of Leningrad is to be sealed off, the ring being drawn as tightly as possible so as to spare our forces unnecessary effort. Surrender terms will not be offered.

4. So as to eliminate the city as a last center of Red resistance on the Ostsee [the Baltic] as quickly as possible, without major sacrifice of our own blood, it will not be subjected to infantry assault...Destruction of waterworks, warehouses and power stations will strip it of its vital services and defense capability. All military objects and enemy defense forces are to be destroyed by firebombing and bombardment. Civilians are to be prevented from bypassing the besieging troops, if necessary by force of arms." (Reid, p. 130)

Once the siege had started, the Luftwaffe dropped incendiaries and high-explosive bombs on Leningrad. The bombing was worst in the first weeks of the siege and then let off when the German 8th Air Corps was sent to Moscow, and again when winter set in and the freezing temperatures grounded all aircraft. In all, roughly 69,000 incendiary and 4,250 high-explosive bombs were dropped on Leningrad. While bombings occurred at night, German troops fired on the city during the day, so there was little respite for the city's residents. Historian Anna Reid explained in *Leningrad: The Epic Siege of World War II, 1941-1944*, "Shelling, many felt, was actually worse than bombing, since bombardments were not preceded by an alarm. From 4 September to the end of the year the Wehrmacht's heavy artillery pounded Leningrad 272 times, for up to eighteen hours at a stretch, with a total of over 13,000 shells...The rumour that some shells were filled only with granulated sugar, or held supportive notes from sympathetic German workers, was a soothing invention."

Damage done by German artillery in Leningrad.

Nurses help the wounded after a German barrage in the city.

"At this period, too, Leningraders resorted to their most desperate food substitutes, scraping dried glue from the underside of wallpaper and boiling up shoes and belts. (Tannery processes had changed, they discovered, since the days of Amundsen and Nansen, and the leather remained tough and inedible.)" – Anna Reid, *Leningrad: The Epic Siege of World War II, 1941-1944*

As the siege progressed during the fall and winter of 1941, Leningrad continued to produce war-making material such as guns, tanks, shells and mines, but the majority of the goods produced in Leningrad did not go to the northern sector or efforts to lift the siege. Instead, Leningrad's production went to help protect Moscow in the central sector, which meant Leningraders were left to suffer as coal that could have been used to heat homes were used for war production, and the transport capacity that could have brought food into Leningrad instead was used to send munitions to the capital. By December, Leningrad's factories had been shut down and the German siege ring had been closed so that nothing could get out of the city, so the massive production efforts of late 1941 that supplied Moscow ended up being very costly for Leningrad. While the German lines and focus across the theater had made it too difficult for them to assault Leningrad with ground forces, the Soviet Union's focus on producing for the central sector meant that the Russians were unable to muster the forces and weaponry necessary to keep a land route open. Had the Red Army been able to accomplish this, Leningrad's defense factories could have continued production, and the civilian losses would have been much less.

Another problem was that Soviet leaders went into the siege unprepared. When the last road connecting Leningrad to the rest of Russian was closed by the German advance, city leaders estimated that they only had enough food reserves for one month. Thus, if the siege was not quickly lifted, the city would have to depend only on the food it could gather from inside the siege ring. But even for the food supplies that were in the city, Soviet officials failed to spread out the supplies in order to minimize the threat of aerial bombardment. Thus, when the Badayev warehouse, which was filled with food, was bombed on September 8th, many Leningrad residents believed that nearly the entirety of the city's food supplies had been destroyed. This had an enormous effect on lowering morale, as did the smell of burning ham and sugar that filled the air as the warehouse burned.

Citizens trying to procure wood in October 1941.

After the Badayev warehouse bombing, city officials decided to gather food from outlying areas within the siege ring. While this brought the harvest in to help city residents, it also meant that farmworkers, who did not qualify for rations, were deprived of food. Farm families were allowed fifteen kilograms of potatoes per person per month, with the rest being relinquished to requisitioning parties sent out from Leningrad to the countryside. Any farmers who failed to give up their potatoes were "held responsible under wartime law" and could be punished for their actions. Taking foodstuffs from the countryside continued throughout the first winter of the siege, and it is estimated that three-fifths of the flour and grain, a quarter of the livestock, and over half of the potatoes that supplied the city came from farm families' stores.

As food supplies dwindled, alternatives were devised to feed Leningraders. For example, flax-seed cake became the grains rationed to the populace, and sheep guts and calf skins (from the city's tanneries) became meat rations. At the same time, the rationing system did not equally distribute food to all residents, because it privileged feeding industrial workers and soldiers and practically ignored office workers, the elderly, children, and the unemployed. The rations were also cut again and again as the siege wore on, and when rations fell to their lowest levels, manual workers (a little over one-third of the population) were given 350 grams of bread per day and 125 grams for everyone else. This meant that non-manual workers were given the equivalent of 460 calories per day, and while this was the amount officially cited by Soviet leaders, the fact that bread was increasingly baked with fillers to save on flour meant that most residents were not able to reach even that calorie level.

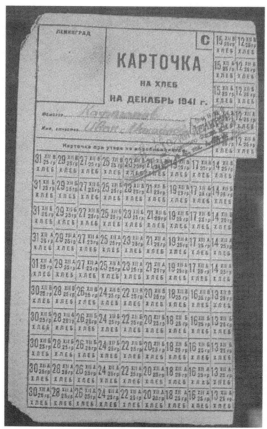

A bread ration card

As a result, the physical decline of Leningrad's residents was rapid, as they went from being relatively untouched by the war to suffering the destruction and death caused by the siege. Within 3 months, things were dire, as noted by one resident:

"People turn into animals before our eyes. Who would have thought that Irina, always such a quiet, lovely woman, would be capable of beating her husband, who she has always adored? And for what? Because he wants to eat all the time and can never get enough. He just waits for her to bring something home, and then throws himself on the food...

The most grisly sight in our apartment is the Kurakin family. He, back from exile and emaciated by years in prison, is already beginning to bloat. It's simply horrible! Of his wife's former love, there is little left. She is constantly irritated and argumentative. Their children cry and beg for food. But all they get is beatings. However, the Kurakins are no exception. Hunger has changed almost

everyone." (Reid, p. 176)

An old Russian woman pulling an emaciated man.

By the end of 1941, the German offensive on the Eastern Front was beginning to bog down, and while the Germans had encircled Leningrad, their efforts moving toward Moscow were slowing. However, despite the fact the Germans were encountering difficulties, the Soviets were not yet able to take advantage of the changing momentum. At Leningrad, Soviet troops attempted a number of breakouts on November 2, 9, 11, and 13, but they all failed, and given the Soviet army's inability to break out, the city disintegrated more and more as time wore on.

Aside from the toll that the rationing system took on individuals and families, government agencies also began to stop functioning. When the fire department ceased operations, buildings that had been hit by German bombs burned for days, and when the hospital system became overwhelmed by the sheer number of entrants into Leningrad's health care facilities, reports to city officials told of how "bedlinen has not been washed since 15 January...The wards are completely unheated, so some patients have been moved into the corridors, which have temporary stoves. Due to the very low temperatures patients cover themselves not only with hospital blankets but with dirty mattresses and their own coats...The lavatories are not working and the floors are not being washed." (Reid, p.216)

While the hospital infrastructure was creating problems, disposing of dead bodies was also a major problem. As one resident wrote about the dead at Erisman Hospital:

"Each day now eight to ten bodies are brought in on sleds. And they just lie there on the snow. Fewer and fewer coffins are available, so too the materials to make them. The bodies are wrapped in sheets, blankets, tablecloths - sometimes even in curtains. Once I saw a small bundle wrapped in paper and tied with string.

It was very small - the body of a child.
How macabre they look on the snow! Only occasionally an arm or leg protrudes from the crude wrappings...It reminds me of a battlefield and of a doss-house, both at the same time." (Reid, p. 216)

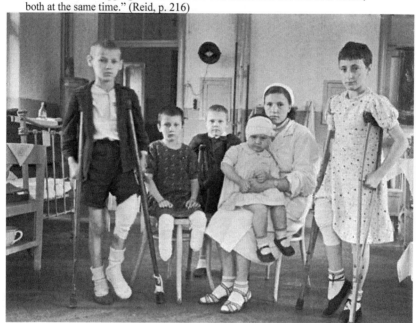

Sick and injured children in a hospital.

The Leningrad Party Committee officially closed 270 factories during the winter of 1941/1942, but the rest hardly functioned at all. Aside from the workers who had died, factory managers complained that "hundreds of people fail to appear for work, and nobody pays any attention. Every day the number absent without leave rises...After the district Party Committee told the management that their behavior sheltered truants, in the course of two days they brought proceedings against seventy-two absentees. But this was not the end of [the management's] mistakes. Of the 72 cases half had to be sent back again, for lack of evidence." (Reid, p. 220).

On January 22, 1942, Moscow's State Defense Committee finally ordered the evacuation of Leningrad. The evacuation route went across Lake Ladoga, which had frozen over and gave the Russians a way out of the siege ring. For residents of Leningrad, acceptance into the evacuation program meant having to complete paperwork and pass checks in a very short period of time and also having to wrap up personal and familial affairs before leaving the city. Each evacuee was only allowed to bring 60 pounds of luggage with them, and due to the lack of transportation in the city, they were forced to drag these personal effects with them to the departure point at Finland Station, which was an extremely difficult task considering the condition of most residents. Only those medically cleared were allowed to depart the city, which meant that many families had to make tough decisions about leaving behind loved ones who were too sick.

Supplies being unloaded from Lake Ladoga in 1942

Even those who were lucky enough to depart the city faced a harrowing journey. Although official Soviet propaganda told stories about evacuees being treated to a comfortable journey that included plenty of food, the evacuation was actually an extraordinarily difficult ordeal. Evacuees had to bribe people for food and transportation, and even with bribes, the journey remained difficult. As one evacuee wrote of the early part of his trip, "I waited, hungry and unfed like everyone else (despite the fact that in Leningrad we had been promised three meals a day and given the appropriate coupons). At about 5 p.m., I found the man in charge but he fobbed me off with some meaningless nonsense or other, and I realized I wouldn't be going anywhere soon. The lorries came and went, but the people in charge chose who to let on themselves, not following any sort of list or queue...I approached the boss once again, telling him that I was ill and that I was going to join my son, a decorated soldier." (Reid, p. 276)

Furthermore, Leningraders weren't the only ones being transported. There was also the removal of peasants and war refugees that could more appropriately be described as a forced deportation that removed ethnic Germans and Finns, as well as "criminals" and "socially alien elements." If Leningraders experienced hardships in the evacuation process, those facing forced evacuation fared even worse. Between the start of the war and October 1942, roughly 128,000 people were deported out of the siege ring. Evacuations continued throughout the winter but ended in the spring when Lake Ladoga was no longer sufficiently frozen and could not handle the passage of trucks over the melting ice.

For those who were not evacuated, residents of Leningrad encountered some incidents of crime. There were reports of trade school students stealing bread from city residents as they returned from the food lines. Theft was also an issue for the city's abandoned children, many of whom were teenagers too old to be accepted into the city's orphanages (who did not take in children over the age of 13). City authorities had to worry about the possibility of bread riots, and though no major riots actually occurred, a few near-riots unnerved officials, especially in January and February 1942. Anna Reid described one such scene: "People were being allowed into the shop ten at a time. At one point, when the next ten were being allowed in, everyone behind rushed forward and started trying to break down the doors. A pair of policemen tried to hold back the crowd. Finally they began telling lies, promising that people would be let in as soon as the crowd took a few steps back. When the crowd did so they locked the doors and announced that the shop was closed and everyone could go home. There were shouts, complaints - some had not eaten for two days, others had starving children." (Reid, p. 282)

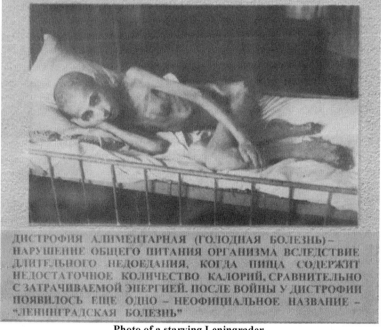

ДИСТРОФИЯ АЛИМЕНТАРНАЯ (ГОЛОДНАЯ БОЛЕЗНЬ) – НАРУШЕНИЕ ОБЩЕГО ПИТАНИЯ ОРГАНИЗМА ВСЛЕДСТВИЕ ДЛИТЕЛЬНОГО НЕДОЕДАНИЯ, КОГДА ПИЩА СОДЕРЖИТ НЕДОСТАТОЧНОЕ КОЛИЧЕСТВО КАЛОРИЙ, СРАВНИТЕЛЬНО С ЗАТРАЧИВАЕМОЙ ЭНЕРГИЕЙ. ПОСЛЕ ВОЙНЫ У ДИСТРОФИИ ПОЯВИЛОСЬ ЕЩЕ ОДНО – НЕОФИЦИАЛЬНОЕ НАЗВАНИЕ – "ЛЕНИНГРАДСКАЯ БОЛЕЗНЬ"

Photo of a starving Leningrader

An actual incident did occur at "Bread Shop no. 318" when "the crowd burst in, incited by a person unknown, and dragged away 100 kg of bread. We managed to arrest a few people. At Bread Shop no. 399 about 50 kg of bread were looted by the crowd, but not one looter was arrested. A group fell upon Bread Shop no. 318's cart, which had been bringing in the new delivery. On the night of 7 January two people were discovered hiding under the shop counter. They were found to be carrying knives. The same day Shop no. 20 on Gas Prospect was robbed. Similar incidents took place in the Smolniy and other districts." (Reid, p. 283)

Leningraders were also killing each other for food or ration cards. In the first half of 1942, there were 1,216 arrests for such murders. Many city residents were afraid of being attacked by unknown persons while walking on the streets, but police reports indicate that most incidents involved people killing family members, co-workers, and neighbors. On top of that, the most high profile crimes during the first winter of the siege involved cannibalism, the ultimate act of desperation. One resident noted, "Not long ago Prendel told us that corpse-eating is on the rise. In May [1942] his hospital dealt with fifteen cases, compared with eleven in April. He had to - and still has to - give expert advice on whether cannibals are responsible for their actions. Cannibalism - a fact. He told us about a cannibal couple who first ate the small corpse of their child, then entrapped three more children - killed them and ate them...For some reason I found what he was saying funny - genuinely funny, especially when he tried to exonerate them. I said, 'But you didn't eat your grandmother!' After that I just couldn't take his cannibal stories seriously. It's all so disgusting - cannibals, roofs with holes in them, blown-out windows, pointlessly destroyed cities. Oh yes, the heroism and romance of war!" (Reid, p. 286)

According to police records, twenty-seven people were arrested for cannibalism in December of 1941, and that number rose to 356 in January 1942, and then 612 in February. 300 were arrested in March and April, and then as summer came, arrests for cannibalism declined almost totally until winter. By December 1942, when incidents of cannibalism seemed to be finally ending, 2,015 people had been arrested for the crime. Leningrad's municipal laws did not include anything on cannibalism, so Soviet officials prosecuted suspected cannibals for "banditry." Of the 1,913 cannibal cases brought before the courts by June 1942, 586 were sentenced to death and 668 were sentenced to serve prison terms of between 5-10 years.

Other incidents of unrest occurred in the city, but it never turned into open revolt against Soviet leaders. In early 1942, after the Red Army had won a victory at Moscow and Soviet offensives began around Leningrad in an attempt to lift the siege, city residents began to gain hope, but the army failed to dislodge the Germans, and the increased rations that Soviet officials had promised Leningraders failed to materialize. Instead, rations were actually reduced even further, destroying morale in the city and increasing the strain among residents who tried to get their hands on food. As one resident wrote, "Queue numbers are written down and handed out. When people have got theirs they hurry off to warm themselves up. But others, arriving later, sometimes weasel their way in, writing out new numbers...6 a.m. arrives but still the shop is closed. It's still shut at seven, at eight. Then at nine, if she feels like it, the manager finally opens up, and everyone pushes inside, packing it full to bursting. All the glass in front of the cash desk has been smashed, the counters are pushed aside and so on." (Reid, p.297)

Grain arriving to Leningrad in 1942.

Although most Leningraders never reached the point of open confrontation with party leaders, some residents were openly critical of them. One worker at a machine-tool factory was arrested after posting a pamphlet criticizing the Soviet leadership: "Working Leningraders! Death hangs over Leningrad. Two or three thousand people died daily. Who is to blame? Soviet power and the Bolsheviks. They assure us that the blockade will be lifted and food norms raised, but it turns out to be lies, as everything Soviet power has promised proved to be lies. Seize the city leadership! Save yourselves and the Motherland, or death awaits!" (Reid, p. 301) In 1941 and 1942, Soviet leaders arrested 9,500 people for political crimes, and while one-third were members of the intelligentsia, the rest were peasants and workers. Once arrested, conviction was almost a guarantee, as only 6% of cases ended with not-guilty verdicts (Reid, p. 304), and though most of the convicted Russians were incarcerated and not executed, incarceration was not necessarily a better alternative because many prisoners died of starvation. Roughly 2,000 inmates died each month during the first winter of the siege, and prisoners were also forced to work on the Ice Road and in gulags within the siege ring, where many died from "exhaustion."

Hitler's plans for 1942 included capturing Leningrad, as well as Operation *Blau*, his plan for a southward push toward the Caucasus and Central Asia, but the Germans apparently didn't realize that they were already dangerously overstretched along the Eastern Front. Making matters worse, the Red Army was beginning to make use of its superior reserves, which began to include women. Women had originally been drafted into the army to fill support positions, but by the spring of 1942, they were being trained and sent to the front as fighter and bomber pilots, anti-aircraft gunners, observers, snipers, mine-clearers and infantrymen. By the end of the war, roughly 800,000 women had served in the Red Army.

As the German offensive along the Eastern Front ground to a halt, one of the problems that German leaders pointed to after the war ended was the effect of the winter weather on German units. The winter of 1941-1942 was especially cold, even by Russian standards, and the Germans found that the weather was an "unforeseen catastrophe, paralyzing everything. On the Leningrad front, with a temperature of 42 degrees below zero, not a rifle, not a machine-gun nor a field-gun has been working on our side." (Reid, p.314) Meanwhile, German soldiers were reduced to either stealing clothing and blankets from Russian peasants, or taking clothing and boots from Russian corpses left on the battlefield. As one German soldier wrote about their desperate situation: "Their felt boots, unfortunately, we have to cut from their feet, but they can be sewn back together again. We're not yet as bad as the 2nd Battalion, who chop the dead Russians' legs off and thaw them out on top of their stove in their bunker." (Reid, p. 316)

Like the German soldiers, the Russians also suffered from the extreme cold of the winter, and many of the Red Army soldiers stationed within the siege ring also starved to death due to disorganization, theft, and corruption. While at its lowest, Russian soldiers were supposed to receive 500 grams of bread and 125 grams of meat per day, but they often received very little food. An infantryman named Semen Putyakov described the dire conditions of soldiers at Leningrad when he wrote about his experiences. On January 8, he wrote, "Gnawed on horse-bones during wood chopping. Hunger, hunger. My swollen face isn't going down. They say there'll be ration increases, but I don't believe it." In describing the other men in his unit, he wrote about their "disgusting starvation deaths" and how "it would be better to die in battle with the fascists" than to starve to death within the siege ring (Reid, p.317).

Starvation forced Russian soldiers into extreme acts including killing food carriers who were taking food up to units on the front because they were failing to get their allotted amount of food. As one army officer recalled, "In early January 1942 the divisional commander started getting urgent calls from regimental and battalion commanders, saying that this or that group of soldiers hadn't been fed, that the carrier hadn't appeared with his canteen, having apparently been killed by German snipers. Thorough checks revealed that something unbelievable was happening: soldiers were leaving their trenches early in the morning to meet the carriers, stabbing them to death, and taking the food. They would eat as much as they could, then bury the murdered carrier in the snow and hide the canteen before returning to their trenches. The murderer would go back to the place twice a day, first finishing off the contents of the canteen and then cutting pieces of human flesh and eating those too. To give you some idea of the numbers I can tell you that in my division in the winter of 1941-2, on the front line alone – taking no account of units in the rear – there were about twenty such cases." (Reid, p. 320)

Even though the soldiers stationed at Leningrad were in poor condition, Stalin ordered them to join a winter offensive that first winter because he believed the attack would allow the Soviet Union to recapture Smolensk, parts of Ukraine, and liberate Leningrad. While 326,000 troops took part in the offensive, General Kirill Meretskov, the commanding officer in charge, pleaded for more time to plan the attack and to maneuver his units into position. Instead, Stalin refused to back down from his original timeline of an early January attack, and in the end, Meretskov likely decided to comply because of his fear of being purged, a fate that had occurred to many Red Army officers during Stalin's rule.

As Meretskov no doubt feared, the lack of coordination among Red Army units resulted in the Soviets inflicting little damage to the Germans, and they were unable to drive them back from Leningrad and the other cities. As the German General Franz Halder summed up in his diary in January, "Continued enemy attacks, but nothing on a major scale." A second attack in February did gain a measure of success when the newly created Soviet Second Shock Army managed to force a pocket in the German lines, but even as 100,000 Soviet soldiers held the pocket, their attempts to widen it were unsuccessful, and on March 2, Hitler ordered German units under the command of Georg von Küchler to cut the pocket off from the main body of the Soviet army. The Germans were successful at trapping the Second Shock Army, with only a small corridor connecting it to the main body of the Soviet forces. By mid-March, the spring thaw had made the corridor impassable, and the Second Shock Army was no longer able to receive supplies from the main body of the Red Army. As one survivor of the Second Shock Army recalled of the desperate situation the Soviet soldiers found themselves in, "We were completely helpless, since we had no ammunition, no petrol, no bread, no tobacco, not even salt. Worst of all was having no medical help. No medicine, no bandages. You want to help the wounded, but how? All our underwear has gone for bandages long ago; all we have left is moss and cotton wool. The field hospitals are overflowing, and the few medical staff in despair. Many hundreds of non-walking wounded simply lie under bushes. Around them mosquitoes and flies buzz like bees in a hive... The main problem, though, was hunger. Oppressive, never-ending hunger." (Reid, p. 325)

Eventually, the remnants of the Second Shock Army attempted a breakout, during which many soldiers were either killed or captured. In the aftermath of the war, the surviving members of the Second Shock Army became part of a Soviet narrative that claimed they had engaged in deliberate mass defection to the enemy. Some survivors were hanged for treason, and others had to treat their time in the army as a secret.

Overall, the winter offensive from January-April 1942 along the Leningrad and Volkhov Fronts saw 308,000 Soviet casualties out of 326,000 troops committed to the assault. As one Russian soldier recalled of the offensive that "you couldn't help thinking and comparing: why are the Germans so well-trained, while all we do is try to overwhelm them with numbers? Why do they use technology and brains, while all we've got is bayonets? Why is it that every time we attack, our blood flows in rivers and our dead pile up in mountains? Where are our tanks?" (Reid, p. 329-330)

In the spring and summer of 1942, continued setbacks hit the Red Army. In addition to the defeat of the Second Shock Army, a Russian army of 200,000 men was encircled and forced to surrender at Kharkov, while the Soviets also lost the strategically important port of Sevastopol, home of Russian's Black Sea Fleet, where 106,000 Soviet troops defended the city for about five months against a combined 203,000 German and Romanian soldiers until Stalin finally conceded the port city.

Meanwhile, as the spring thaw made its way to Leningrad, the city's survivors began to return to a measure of normality, even as many city residents dealt with guilt over the death of family and friends over the past winter. As Lidiya Ginzburg wrote of Leningrad's "Siege Man":

> "Siege people forgot their sensations but remembered facts. Facts crept slowly out from the dimness of memory into the light of rules of behavior which were now gravitating back to the accepted norm.
> 'She wanted a sweet so much. Why did I eat that sweet? I needn't have done. Any everything would have been that little bit better'... Thus Siege Man thinks about his wife or mother, whose death has made the eaten sweet irrevocable. He recalls the fact but cannot summon up the feeling: the feeling of that piece of bread, or sweet, which prompted him to cruel, dishonorable, humiliating acts."
> (Reid, p. 334)

For Soviet leaders in Leningrad, the most important issue as spring began was to prevent outbreaks of disease. This required mobilizing citizens to collect the thousands of corpses that had been unburied during the winter, and the cemeteries, which were already overflowing, became mass graves for the winter dead. City leaders also tried to mobilize the remaining city residents into a gardening drive so that the starvation of the previous winter would not be repeated if the siege was not lifted during the year. Leningraders created vegetable gardens in public parks and squares, while many residents also created vegetable boxes in the windows of their apartments.

Leningrad's leaders also continued to take large quantities of food from the peasants living in rural areas within the siege ring. Understandably, this left the peasants irate with the rest of Leningrad's residents, and their resentment occasionally took the form of open defiance toward the Soviet government. As one Russian peasant woman stated, "I can't wait for Soviet rule to end. It has bankrupted the peasants, left us hungry and barefoot, and now you're stripping us naked. But I'm not going to bow down before you fine gentlemen. Your reign's coming to an end. You sent all the good people out of the village, but just you wait, it'll be your turn next." (Reid, p. 347)

By the spring of 1942, Germany no longer had the strength to launch a massive offensive as they had done a year earlier, but Hitler nevertheless ordered the German armies forward in an attempt to access oil from the Caucasus and grain from Ukraine to continue their war effort. Meanwhile, Hitler targeted Stalingrad as the site of a potential German attack, since it was both an important industrial center and held symbolic importance as the namesake city of the Soviet leader.

Hitler's plan for his 1942 offensive was to target the Russian south by attacking Stalingrad, which he would use "as a fulcrum, while the main armies wheeled south to occupy the Caucasus." (Hoyt, p. 86) As Field Marshal Kleist would later recall, "The capture of Stalingrad was subsidiary to the main aim. It was only of importance as a convenient place, in the bottleneck between the Don and the Volga [rivers], where we could block an attack by Russian forces coming from the East. At the start Stalingrad was no more than a name on a map to us." (Hoyt, p. 87)

The area of operations in southern Russia during 1942.
The Soviets knew what the Germans planned to do, and Stalin decided that they would counter the German attack. Stalin ordered his units around the Crimea to attack Field Marshal Erich von Manstein's army, but because it had been reinforced by two Panzer divisions and by General Wolfram von Richthofen's 4th Air Fleet, the numerically superior German forces were able to clear the Kerch Peninsula, with Russian losses estimated at 100,000 prisoners and 200 tanks lost. A second Russian offensive was launched along the Volkhov River by General Andrei Vlasov, but again the Germans defeated the Russian forces and captured Vlasov and his staff. A third offensive was launched by Marshal Timoshenko against German positions at Kharkov, but while the Soviets were able to force the Germans back, they were not able to push them back as far as Stalin had hoped.

Field Marshal Erich von Manstein's army
As the Russian attack failed to achieve their aims, the Germans launched a summer offensive, which they called Operation Blau. The army units involved in Blau were split into two groups, and they forced their way east before coming together around Timoshenko's forces. Timoshenko had earlier asked Stalin for permission to withdraw his troops as the Germans approached, but when the request was refused by the Soviet leader, he was forced to engage, losing all of his equipment and a large number of men. Soviet estimates put his losses at 75,000 soldiers, while the Germans claimed they had taken 240,000 prisoners. Besides the loss of manpower, the Soviets lost the bulk of their tanks, which gave the Germans a roughly 10-1 advantage.

The success of Operation Blau convinced Hitler that he needed to widen the scope of his plans, and that using Stalingrad as a hinge for a German sweep to the south was not enough. Instead, he now decided that the Germans needed to capture Stalingrad in addition to taking the Caucasus. Meanwhile, the Russians believed Stalingrad was the key to their defense. The city was the center of industrial operations in the entire region, and with a population of 600,000, it was the most important port on the Volga that the Soviets still controlled. As Stalin came to realize the importance of Stalingrad to Russia's southern defenses, he had 180,000 civilians build defenses around the city. The city's Defense Committee organized eight "annihilation battalions" that were composed of 11,000 men to fight off paratroopers, and streets were blocked with barricades in case of street fighting. Finally, Stalin had industrial goods and foodstuffs moved to the eastern part of the city, and the Soviets also evacuated some of the women and children from the city.

The German push towards Stalingrad from May-July 1942.

On July 23, 1942, the German attack on Stalingrad began, and the German Army Group B, which comprised the attacking forces, was split into four subgroups. The northern group was made up of two panzer, two motorized, and four infantry divisions, and this group was supposed to commence its attack on July 23 and capture the bridge over the Don River at Kalach. The second group was made up of one panzer division and two infantry divisions, and this group was supposed to attack on July 25 and focus on the central area of Oblivskaya-Verkhne-Aksenovsky. The third group was also focused on the center and was supposed to clear Russian forces stationed on the west of the Don to open the road to the Volga River. Finally, the southern group, which was made up of one armored division, one motorized division, and four infantry divisions, was supposed to cross the Don on July 21 and move toward Stalingrad from the south.

By now, the Germans knew that fighting the Soviets here would hardly be a cakewalk, and as one soldier recalled of the fighting:

"I retain nothing from those terrible minutes except indistinct memories which flash into my mind with sudden brutality, like apparitions, among bursts and scenes and visions that are scarcely imaginable. It is difficult even to try to remember moments during which nothing is considered, foreseen, or understood, when there is nothing under a steel helmet but an astonishingly empty head and a pair of eyes which translate nothing more than would the eyes of an animal facing mortal danger. There is nothing but the rhythm of explosions, more or less distant, more or less violent, and the cries of madmen, to be classified later, according to the outcome of the battle, as the cries of heroes or of murderers. And there are the cries of the wounded, or the agonizingly dying, shrieking as they stare at a part of their body reduced to pulp, the cries of men touched by the shock of battle before everyone else, who run in any and every direction howling like banshees. There are the tragic unbelievable visions, which carry from one moment of nausea to another: guts splattered across the rubble and sprayed from one dying man onto another, tightly riveted machines ripped like the belly of a cow which has just been sliced open, flaming and groaning, trees broken into tiny fragments, gaping windows pouring out torrents of billowing dust, delivering into oblivion all that remains of a comfortable parlor. And then there are the cries of the officers and noncoms, trying to shout across the cataclysm to regroup their sections and companies. That is how we took part in the German advance, being called through the noise and dust, following clouds churned by our tanks to the northern outskirts. All resistance was overwhelmed and once again everything was either German or dead, and a sea of Russian soldiers had drawn back into the limitless confines of their country." (Hoyt, p. 110)

With the Russians seemingly on the verge of defeat, Hitler made the decision to transfer five divisions to the Leningrad Front and send two panzer divisions to France, where a rumored Allied invasion might take place. As the Germans advanced on Stalingrad, Stalin turned over command of the forces in the south to General Vasily Chuikov, who brought the 51st Army and 208th Infantry Division with him. These units had been lost in the scuffle as Soviet leaders scrambled to bring units from across the eastern portion of the country to defend the area surrounding Stalingrad. Upon arriving at the Stalingrad front, Chuikov reorganized the defenses in the area, but Stalin decided to tinker with the army leadership and appoint General Andrey Yeremenko as commander of what he called the Southeastern Front. This meant that there were two major commands, the Stalingrad Front and the Southeastern Front, and both were headquartered in Stalingrad.

Vasily Chuikov

Andrey Yeremenko
On August 6, General Chuikov's defenses held against a German attack, but to the northwest, the German 6th Army surrounded the Russian 62nd Army, and over the next four days, the Germans attacked and captured most of its soldiers. The Germans continued to move toward Stalingrad, and by mid-August the German southern subgroup had reached a point 40 miles from the city, while in the northwest, German troops were about 60 miles away. On the morning of August 21st, German forces surprised Russians defending the Don River, and after taking those positions, engineers placed 22 bridges across the river so that the V Panzer Corps could cross. It seemed to the German High Command that Stalingrad was about to fall, and they began plans to sweep toward Moscow.

Picture of Germans advancing toward Stalingrad.

On the morning of August 23, German bombers dropped a thousand tons of bombs to soften up Stalingrad's defenses as panzers continued to move toward the city. Along with the soldiers who made up the defense forces, industrial workers were mobilized to help with the defense of the city. The panzer columns made their way toward the city with little resistance, but while the Germans believed victory was imminent, the Soviets planned to defend Stalingrad. As Soviet military leaders told General Yeremenko, "You have enough strength to annihilate the enemy. Combine the aviation of both fronts and use it to smash the enemy. Set up armored trains and station them on the Stalingrad belt railroad. Use smoke to deceive the enemy. Keep the enemy not only in the daytime but also at night. Above all do not give way to panic, do not let the enemy scare you, and keep faith in your own strength." (Hoyt, p. 126)

Picture of a German divebomber over Stalingrad.

By the night of August 23, German forces had cut the front in two by breaching Soviet defenses on the left flank. German units had entered the northern suburbs of the city but were unable to make it further than that, even though the Luftwaffe had run an estimated 2,000 bomber runs on Stalingrad. Yeremenko reported to Stalin that some city officials wanted to blow up the factories of Stalingrad and move the goods within the city across the Volga River, but Stalin viewed these potential actions as a willingness to surrender and forbade anything less than the full defense of the city.

On the morning of August 24, the 16th Panzer Division's Group Drumpen attacked the north-most industrial suburb of Stalingrad, which was called Spartakovka, but the panzers of Group Drumpen had made such rapid progress to Spartakovka that they had actually outrun their infantry support in the 3rd and 30th Motorized divisions. In fact, the 3rd motorized was 12 miles behind Group Drumpen, while the 60th was over 20 miles behind. As a result, while Soviets on the path to Spartakovka were quickly overrun by Group Drumpen, the panzers were stopped by Russian defensive positions once they reached the suburb. The combination of Russian defenses, rifle battalions and worker militias were able to hold the German forces, and by noon the Russians launched a counterattack using tanks that came straight from the city's factories. By the end of the day on the 24th, Soviet forces held approaches to the city from the north, and the German advanced units had been forced backward roughly a mile. Meanwhile, the Soviet 35th Rifle Division moved south and cut the German communications, while the 16th Panzers were being attacked from all sides by Soviet units. On August 25, the Regional Communist Party Committee of Stalingrad issued a proclamation that stated, "Comrades and citizens of Stalingrad! We shall never surrender the city of our birth to the depredations of the German invader. Each single one of us must apply himself to the task of defending our beloved town, our homes, and our families. Let us barricade every street; transform every district, every block, every house, into an impregnable fortress." (Hoyt, p. 134)

While the Soviets had stopped the German advance in the north for now, the 6th German Army attempted to enter Stalingrad from the southwest. The Soviets repelled the German advance here as well and even attacked German forces, but their troop strength was not sufficient to force them back away from the city. Over the next three days, the two sides were held in a stalemate, and General Chuikov reported:

"From time to time a German shell would burst in the river, but this indiscriminate shelling was not troublesome. From a distance we could see that the pier was crowded with people. As we drew closer many wounded were being carried out of the trenches, bomb craters, and shelters. There were also many people with bundles and suitcases who had been hiding from German bombs, and shells.

When they saw the ferry arriving they rushed to the pier with the one idea of getting away to the other side of the river, away from their wrecked houses, away from the city that had become a hell. Their eyes were grim and there were trickles of tears running through the dust and soot on their grimy faces. The children, suffering from thirst and hunger, were not crying but simply whining and stretching out their little arms to the water of the Volga." (Hoyt, p. 135)

On August 29, the 4th Panzer Army attacked the Soviet defenses and penetrated both the 64th and 62nd Russian armies, and as the 4th Panzers made their way forward, thousands of troops from the Russian 126th and 208th Divisions were captured. General Hermann Hoth, who was leading the charge, asked General Friedrich Paulus to attack from the north in hopes of trapping the Russians, but Paulus was worried that his position in the north was vulnerable to a Russian attack and therefore decided not to move toward Hoth's units. When the Russian danger in the north was alleviated on September 2, Paulus finally committed his troops, but the delay had allowed the Russian forces in the area to escape the trapping maneuver.

Hermann Hoth

Friedrich Paulus

Germans advancing to Stalingrad in September 1942.

A picture of Stalingrad taken in September 1942.

As the fighting raged around Stalingrad, Stalin called General Georgy Zhukov to Moscow, where he named him the deputy commander of Soviet forces. Stalin sent Zhukov to Stalingrad with three new armies and told him, "The situation in Stalingrad is getting worse. The enemy is 3 versts [two miles] from Stalingrad. They can take Stalingrad today or tomorrow, unless the northern group of troops gives help urgently. Get the commanders of the troops of the north and northwest Stalingrad Front to attack the enemy without delay and get to the relief of Stalingraders. No delay can be tolerated. Delay at this moment is equivalent to a crime. Throw in all aircraft to help Stalingrad. In Stalingrad itself there is very little aviation left. Report at once on all measures taken." (Hoyt, p. 137)

Georgy Zhukov

On September 5, Zhukov sent the 24th Army to attack German forces, and though the attack failed, they were able to draw the Germans away from Stalingrad for a short period to relieve the pressure on the city's defense forces. Meanwhile, to the south of Stalingrad, the German 4th

Panzer Army again began to move toward Stalingrad, but when they approached the suburbs of Krasnoyarmeysk and Kupersnoye, the Russian defenses began exacting a heavy toll on German troops who were trapped in the narrow streets of the suburbs. Even the German panzers had problems here once the Russians effectively used Molotov cocktails to destroy them. The problem for the Germans was that they failed to adapt to urban warfare, instead continuing to use the tactics that had been so successful in the wide-open spaces leading up to Stalingrad.

A picture of Soviet defenders lodged in Stalingrad's suburbs.

Despite the problems the Germans were facing in street fighting, General Paulus still believed the Germans would soon take the city, and on September 12, he told Hitler that he expected to take the city within a few days. When a new German offensive began on September 13, they targeted the Mamayev Hill, the location of the command center of the 62nd Army. The German leadership hoped that they could move from there straight to the banks of the Volga River, and to soften up Russian defenses, the Luftwaffe again engaged in constant bombardments that allowed the German troops to gain ground on the Russians. The Luftwaffe bombing runs also stopped the Russians from counterattacking, and by midday, German tanks and motorized infantry had engaged in the fighting. Although the Russians inflicted heavy losses on the Germans, the attacking forces believed they had won once they reached the city center, and some German soldiers began drinking and celebrating in the streets.

However, while the Germans were massing in the city center, General Chuikov assembled a battalion with nine tanks toward the center, and Russian snipers began picking off celebrating German forces who still believed that they had captured the city. A reserve unit of tanks was deployed to keep the Germans from breaking through to the Volga, and when they held out until the next day, the Russians were reinforced by the Rodimtsev Division arriving from the east side of the Volga.

Soviet reinforcements crossing the Volga and landing on the west bank.

As the Russians tried to dislodge the Germans from the city, they engaged in tactics that were designed to keep the Luftwaffe from attacking their units. For example, they set up defensive positions at street intersections, and as German panzers were funneled tightly through the street networks toward these defensive positions, Soviet "storm troops" engaged them, taking out their infantry accompaniment. The close-quarters combat meant that the Luftwaffe was unable to bomb Russian positions without endangering their own troops. The fierce fighting took its toll on both sides, as one German soldier later described:

> "I know in my bones what our watchword 'courage' means - from days and nights of resigned desperation, and from the insurmountable fear which one continues to accept even though one's brain has ceased to function normally. I know that one can call on all the saints in heaven for help without believing in any God, and it is this that I must describe, even though it means plunging back into a nightmare for nights at a time, for that is the substance of my task to reanimate with all the intensify I can summon, those distant cries from the slaughterhouse.
>
> Too many people learn about war with no inconvenience to themselves. They are about Verdun or Stalingrad without comprehension, sitting in a comfortable armchair, their feet beside the fire, preparing to go about their business the next day, as usual. One should really read such accounts under compulsion, in discomfort, considering oneself fortunate not to be describing the events in a letter home, writing from a hole in the mud. One should read about war in the worst circumstances, when everything is going badly, remembering the torments of peace are trivial, and not worth any white hairs. Nothing is really serious in the tranquility

of peace. Only an idiot could be disturbed by a question of a salary. One should read about war standing up, late at night, when one is tired, as I am writing about it now at dawn, while my asthma attack wears off. Those who read about Verdun and Stalingrad and expound theories later to friends over a cup of coffee, haven't understood anything. Those who can read such accounts with a silent smile, smile as they walk, and feel lucky to be alive..." (Hoyt, p. 146)

Bundesarchiv, Bild 183-B22413
Foto: Pfreundtner | September 1942

German artillery advancing on Stalingrad in September.

Picture of street fighting in Stalingrad.

Fierce fighting continued within the center of the city, and the central railroad station changed hands four times as both sides sent forces back and forth against the building. General Chuikov described the situation at the railway station: "By this time we had nothing left with which to counterattack. General Rodimtsev's 13th Division had been bled white. It had entered the fray from the moment it had crossed the Volga, and had borne the brunt of the heaviest German blows. They had to abandon several blocks of houses inside central Stalingrad, but this could not be described as a withdrawal or a retreat. There was nobody left to retreat. Rodimtsev's Guardsmen stood firm to the last extremity, and only the heavily wounded crawled away. From what those wounded told us, it transpired that the Nazis, having captured the station, continued to suffer heavy losses. Our soldiers, having been cut off from the main forces of the division, had entrenched themselves in various buildings around the station, or under railway carriages - usually in groups of two or three men - and from there they continued to harass the Germans day and night." (Hoyt, p. 152)

On September 18, the Luftwaffe was sent to the northwest to engage with Russian troops who had been ordered to attack German positions in an effort to take pressure off of Stalingrad, but once the German airplanes were out of the way, the Russians commenced an attack on the northern part of the city. The attack failed to dislodge the Germans, but it demonstrated the extent to which both sides were stretching themselves in an attempt to gain an advantage.

Some of the toughest fighting took place around the grain elevator at the northern edge of Stalingrad, beginning on September 20. As one Soviet soldier recalled, "In the elevator the grain was burning. The water in the machine guns evaporated, the wounded were thirsty but there was no water near. This was how we defended ourselves twenty-four hours a day for three days. Heat, smoke, thirst, our lips were cracked. During the day many of us climbed up to the highest points in the elevator and from there fired on the Germans. At night we came down and formed a defensive ring around the building. Our radio equipment had been knocked out the first day and we had no contact with our units." (Hoyt, p. 150). German soldiers broke through Russian defenses and moved up the stairs in hand-to-hand fighting, and though the Russians initially drove them back, the Germans were able to take the grain elevator on the night of September 20.

The next day, September 21, the heavy fighting moved to the Red Square, where the main arenas of battle were a nail factory and the Univermag department store, which had been converted into the headquarters of the Guards 42nd Regiment's 1st Battalion. German artillery fired on the Univermag building, and then German infantry entered. In the fighting that ensued within the building, every officer in the battalion headquarters was killed, while retreating survivors moved slowly back all the way to the banks of the Volga River. In their last position, the survivors, about 40 men in all, held out in a three-story building for five days. One of them explained, "At a narrow window in a semi-basement we set up the heavy machine gun, with our emergency supply of ammunition - the last belt of cartridges I had decided to use at the most critical moment. Two groups, six in each, went up to the third floor and the attic. Their job was to break down walls and to prepare lumps of stone and beams to throw at the Germans. A place for the seriously wounded was set aside in the basement..." (Hoyt, p. 150)

By the last week of the month, the German leadership believed victory was imminent, to the extent that Goering sent a message to General Wolfram von Richthofen at the front asking him to inform Goering as soon as victory was achieved. Hitler was also frantically awaiting word of victory at Stalingrad, becoming gradually more upset as Stalingrad continued to hold out and thereby delay his plans for that city and the Causasus. In the meantime, fighting continued to rage around Stalingrad, and by now the German positions were close enough that they could steadily shell river traffic on the Volga. They ended up sinking two ships: the *Borodino*, which was filled with wounded soldiers; and the *Joseph Stalin*, which resulted in the drowning of 1,000 women and children.

Russian commanders tried to reinforce the center city, but they encountered difficulty in both procuring additional men and moving them to the front lines, as one Soviet remembered: "There were times when these reinforcements were really pathetic. They'd bring across the river - with great difficulty - say twenty new soldiers, either old chaps of fifty or fifty-five or youngsters of eighteen or nineteen. They would stand there on the shore, shivering with cold and fear. They'd be given warm clothing and then taken to the front line. By the time these newcomers reached this line, five or ten out of twenty had already been killed by German shells, for with those German flares over the Volga and our front lines, there was never complete darkness. But the peculiar thing about these chaps was that those among them who reached the front line very quickly became wonderfully hardened soldiers. *Real frontoviks*. (Hoyt, p. 154)

As the Germans gained more control over the city center, they were able to utilize the east-west orientation of the streets, which coincided with their direction of attack, to their advantage. German tanks were able to fire down the streets from one end to the other, and their heavy guns were used to destroy buildings as well. This forced the Russians to change tactics again for the street fighting, as General Chuikov noted: "City fighting is a special kind of fighting. The buildings in a city act like breakwaters. They broke up the advancing enemy formations and made their forces go along the streets. The troops defending the city learned to allow German tanks to come right on top of them - under the guns of the antitank artillery and antitank riflemen; in this way they invariably cut off the infantry from the tanks and destroyed the enemy's organized battle formation." (Hoyt, p. 154)

Bundesarchiv Bild 101I-817-2571-04
Foto: Ollig | 1942 Herbst

Picture of German soldiers engaged in street fighting in Stalingrad on September 23.
Even though Russian tactics disabled or destroyed a number of tanks, German forces occupied most of the center of the city by September 24. Still, the battle for Stalingrad was far from over, as Russian artillery located on the east bank of the Volga River fired continuously at German positions within the city. These artillery batteries played a crucial role in keeping the Germans from overrunning all Soviet positions, as Konstantin Simonov recalled: "We could certainly not have held Stalingrad had we not been supported by artillery and katyushas on the other bank all the time. I can hardly describe the soldiers' love for them. And as time went on, there were more and more of them, and we could feel it. It was hard to imagine at the time that there was such a concentration of guns firing shells at the Germans, morning, noon, and night, over our heads." (Hoyt, p. 155)

By now, Hitler's patience was entirely gone, and when Stalingrad still hadn't completely capitulated, he fired his army chief of staff, General Halder, and replaced him with General Paulus. Paulus had the Nazi flag raised over the Univermag building to signal their control over the center of the city, but Paulus understood that German forces did not control Stalingrad. In fact, they only had a tenuous hold on the areas that they did control.

As German forces advanced in late September, they began their assault of Stalingrad's industrial districts. By this time, the Germans controlled nearly 90% of the city, but pockets of Russian soldiers continued to hold out in buildings across Stalingrad. At the same time, the Soviets continued to send reinforcements into their positions in the city, bringing the new troops across the Volga at night even as German artillery shelled the boats.

By the end of September, the Russians and Germans were at a stalemate, but General Zhukov, commanding officer of the Stalingrad Front, knew that the Soviets would have an advantage going forward. Zhukov estimated that units from both sides had been badly damaged by the fighting: "As for the Soviet troops, they had suffered such heavy casualties in the fierce fighting on the approaches to Stalingrad, and were to suffer more within the city itself, that they were unable to defeat the enemy with existing forces." At the same time, Zhukov knew that "von Paulus's Sixth Field Army and Hoth's Fourth Tank Army, two of the Wehrmacht's most effective striking forces, had been so weakened in the grueling fighting for Stalingrad that they would be unable to complete the capture of the city." (Hoyt, p. 159)

Soviet defenders in Pavlov's House in Stalingrad withstood German attacks from September–November 1942.

A German soldier with a submachine gun in Stalingrad in October 1942.
While 100,000 new Soviet troops had been brought to Stalingrad by early October, Russian troops were being killed so quickly that Chuikov still only had 53,000 soldiers at his disposal at the beginning of the month. However, even as these reinforcements were being sent to Stalingrad and depleted in the fighting, 27 new divisions were secretly being assembled in staging areas behind the front. The Soviets had critical advantages in that they could move men and machinery toward Stalingrad more quickly than the Germans could. Zhukov also knew that he would soon have T-34 tanks at his disposal, which were the newest, most technologically advanced Soviet tanks that were coming off the assembly lines. Just as importantly, Russian officers had gained valuable experience during the German invasion and were no longer an officer corps paralyzed by the fear of Stalin's purges.

By the start of October, Zhukov and Stalin both believed that by the middle of November, the Soviets would be strong enough to launch an offensive to dislodge the Germans. At that point, they would have at their disposal 11 armies, 900 tanks, and 1,115 aircraft. Of course, the Soviets could only launch that future offensive against the Germans as long as the current forces within Stalingrad held the line and kept the Germans within the city until the new forces could be deployed.

Aiding the Soviet cause was Hitler himself, who was consumed with the idea of a German victory at Stalingrad. Some of his officers attempted to convince him that the best course of action was to withdraw for the winter, regroup, and then continue the offensive the next year, but Hitler was not interested in such a plan. In fact, Hitler spoke to the German people, emphasizing his goals: "We had three objectives: (1) To take away the last great Russian wheat territory. (2) To take away the last district of coking coal. (3) To approach the oil district, paralyze it, and at least cut it off. Our offensive then went on to the enemy's greatest transport artery, the Volga and Stalingrad. You may rest assured that once there, no one will push us out of that spot." (Hoyt, p.

160)

Hitler's insistence that German forces in Stalingrad could not retreat made them targets for all kinds of creative Soviet attacks. A major problem for German commanders was the way Soviet troops used the sewers as passageways to attack them. Russian soldiers would come out of manholes, fire at the rear of German columns marching along the streets, and then duck back into the sewers before the Germans knew what was occurring. As German General Hans Doerr put it:

"The time for conducting large-scale operations was gone forever; from the wide expanses of steppe land, the war moved to the jagged gullies of the Volga hills with their copses and ravines, into the factory area of Stalingrad, spread out over uneven, pitted, rugged country, covered with iron, concrete and stone buildings. The mile, as a measure of distance, was replaced by the yard. G.H.Q.'s map was the map of the city.

For every house, workshop, water tower, railway embankment, wall, cellar and every pile of ruins, a bitter battle was waged, without equal even in the first world war with its vast expenditure of munitions. The distance between the enemy's army and ours was as small as it could possibly be. Despite the concentrated aircraft and artillery, it was impossible to break out of the area of close fighting. The Russians surpassed the Germans in their use of the terrain and in camouflage, and were more experienced in barricade warfare for individual buildings..." (Hoyt, p.163)

On October 3, the Germans who had been pressing into the industrial districts prepared an attack against the Red October tractor factory in which three infantry divisions and two panzer divisions would participate. However, the Russians were able to ferry reinforcements to their positions from across the Volga, and because of the increased troop strength from these reserves units, the German attack was stopped. The close-quarters nature of the combat was perhaps best exemplified on October 12, when a German advance of one block in the industrial district cost them the lives of four battalions worth of soldiers. The next day, a Russian counterattack gained just 200 yards before being stopped.

Hitler, who was becoming increasingly frustrated that Soviet forces were halting the German advance, gave General Paulus an ultimatum by making October 15 the deadline for capturing Stalingrad. Thus, on October 14, General Paulus sent five divisions against the Red October factory in what was called "the final offensive." In addition to these ground forces, the Luftwaffe sent all available planes to attack Soviet defensive positions. As General Chuikov later described the scene, "They bombed and stormed our troops without a moment's respite. The German guns and mortars showered on us shells and bombs from morning until night. It was a sunny day, but owing to the smoke and soot, visibility was reduced to 100 yards. Our dugouts were shaking and crumbling like a house of cards. By 11:30 AM 180 tanks broke through to the stadium of the Tractor Plant. By 4 P.M. The troops were encircled but still fighting." (Hoyt, p. 166)

By midnight of the 14th, the Germans had encircled the tractor plant, but fighting continued between Russian and German troops within the workshops of the factory. A Soviet recalled, "We reckoned that the Germans had lost 40 tanks during the day and in the Tractor Plant there were 2,000 German dead. We also suffered very heavy losses during the day. During the night 3,500 wounded soldiers and officers were taken across the Volga; this was a record figure." (Hoyt, p. 166)

A German soldier's perspective of the fighting around and within the Red October tractor factory similarly described the carnage that soldiers experienced:

"The captain came up and told the men they had to clear the factory of the

Russians inside, probably factory militia.

Of course there was no question of argument. With dry mouths, we moved forward into the factory buildings, which were littered with hundreds of large objects - ideal for snipers and as bad as possible for us. The relatively large size of our force was in no way reassuring. Even if we overwhelmed them in the end, each bullet they fired was bound to hit someone, and if I should be the only casualty in a victorious army of a million men, the victory would be without interest to me. The percentage of corpses, in which generals sometimes take pride, doesn't alter the fate of the ones who've been killed. The only leader I know of who finally made a sensible remark on this point, Adolf Hitler, once said to his troops, 'Even a victorious army must count its victims.'

...The first two sheds were empty. Perhaps our prisoners had been telling the truth. But our orders were to check the whole place Our group surrounded the entire factory complex and then began to move toward the center. We passed through a series of enormous barnlike buildings which seemed to be on the point of collapse.

The wind was blowing hard and the buildings echoed with sinister creaking sounds. Otherwise everything was quiet except for the occasional clatter made by one of our men deliberately shoving aside some metal object or overturning a pile of crates." (Hoyt, p. 167)

Soviet soldiers fighting around the Red October factory.

A German sniper at Stalingrad.
As the Germans pressed the attack, they were met by 8,000 Russian soldiers from the Soviet 37th Guards Division and several thousand armed factory workers. The Germans managed to take the factory, but both sides suffered heavy losses, with the Russians losing roughly 75% of their troops in that area.

Even though the Germans had dislodged the Russians from that sector of the industrial district, Russian soldiers continued to hold out in areas, and across the Volga, Soviet artillery batteries inflicted damage against German units. German ground troops continued to gain ground inch by inch, but by October 19, they had lost air superiority, and Russian aircraft now replaced Luftwaffe planes over Stalingrad for basically the first time since the battle had started.

In mid-October, Hitler suspended virtually the entire German offensive on the Eastern front except at Stalingrad, revealing his strong desire to capture the city, but for General Paulus, the situation at Stalingrad was growing critical. Even though German forces were advancing through the city, their troop strength was being depleted, and the troops that remained in fighting condition were exhausted. Paulus requested additional troops, but after Hitler sent him reinforcements from the German Replacement Army, the only additional troops that Paulus could procure were those from areas of the Eastern Front that were not currently engaged against the Russians. German operations in the industrial district of Stalingrad were estimated to be depleting troop strength by one division every five days.

On October 26th, the German 100th Division attacked and was able to make its way to within 400 yards of the banks of the Volga River, near the last ferry landing the Russians held on the western bank of the river. Capturing it would stop the Soviets from being able to send reinforcements and supplies to their troops in Stalingrad, and the men of the 100th Division cheered as the Volga came into sight, firm in the belief that they were finally on the verge of victory. However, when the Germans continued the attack the next day, they discovered that the

Russians had been able to reinforce their positions with two battalions that had crossed the river that night. The Russians held out until the evening, stopping the Germans from capturing their last ferry landing, but at a cost of a battalion's worth of dead soldiers.

Meanwhile, the Russians had been sending reinforcements to the Soviet 65th Army, stationed along the Don River south of Stalingrad. German reconnaissance had discovered the massing troops, and General Paulus forwarded these reports to Army Group B, which then sent them ahead to Hitler, but Hitler chose to ignore these reports. Instead, Hitler relied on advisers who assured him that because of their high death rates, the Russians did not have any important reserves left. At the end of October, General Paulus issued a statement to his troops: "The summer and fall offensive is successfully terminated after taking Stalingrad. The 6th Army has played a significant role and held the Russians in check. The action of the leadership and the troops during the offensive will enter into history as an especially glorious page. Winter is upon us. The Russians will take advantage of it. It is unlikely that the Russians will fight with the same strength as last winter." (Hoyt, p. 178)

The Germans continued to push the attack, and on November 9th, the German battalions in the industrial district pushed forward, capturing the Commissar's House and pushing Russian troops there down to an area on the shore that was 400 yards wide and 100 yards deep. In five days of fighting, the Russian combat engineers lost a thousand men, while the 138th Division only had a few hundred men left standing. Elsewhere in the industrial district, the Soviet 62nd Army was isolated into three groups while withstanding a German attack, but they held their ground.

All the while, the goal of the Russian efforts at Stalingrad was to stall the Germans while the new army massing in the south made its way into the city. Although Russian casualties continued to be extremely high, they achieved their goal, and on November 19th, Operation Uranus commenced. With that, Russian units in the south marched toward Stalingrad to attack General Paulus' flank, but when Hitler was informed of the movement of Soviet forces to the south, he wasn't terribly concerned, in part because General Paulus, in an attempt to curry favor with Hitler, had exaggerated Soviet troop strength for the forces opposing the German 6th Army at Stalingrad. Since his reports suggested five times as many Soviet troops as actually were present on the Stalingrad Front, this most likely furthered Hitler's belief that they were grinding down Russia's troops and their war-making capabilities. This is probably also the reason why he chose to ignore reports of the Soviet buildup south of the city until they began Operation Uranus.

As a result, Hitler continued to believe that whatever suffering his German forces faced at Stalingrad, the situation among Russian troops must be worse. As he relayed to Paulus, "The difficulties of the fighting at Stalingrad are well known to me, but the difficulties on the Russian side must be even greater just now with the ice drifting down the Volga. If we make good use of this period of time we shall save a lot of blood later on. Therefore I expect that the commanders will once again fight with their usual dash in order to break through to the Volga, at least at the ordnance factory and the metallurgical works, and to take these parts of the city." (Hoyt, p. 183)

Through Hitler's urgings, Paulus called on his troops to capture every part of the city before the Russian offensive arrived, and this renewed German attack initially looked like it would push the Russians across the Volga and capture the entire city within 24 hours. The Russians held just isolated positions throughout the city, and these were all under attack from German artillery fire. As one German officer wrote of their progress:

"We have fought during fifteen days for a single house, with mortars, grenades, machine guns and bayonets. Already by the third day fifty-four German corpses were strewn in the cellars, on the landings, and the staircases. The front is a corridor between burnt out rooms; it is the thin ceiling between two floors. Help comes from neighboring houses by fire escapes and chimneys. There is a ceaseless struggle from noon to night. From story to story, faces black with sweat, we bombard each other with grenades in the middle of explosions, clouds of dust and smoke, heaps of mortar, floods of blood, fragments of furniture and human beings. Ask any soldier what half an hour of hand-to-hand struggle means in such a fight. And at Stalingrad, it has been eighty days and eighty nights of hand-to-hand struggle. The street is no longer measured by meters but by corpses.

Stalingrad is no longer a town. By day it is an enormous cloud of burning, blinding smoke; it is a vast furnace lit by the reflection of the flames. And when night arrives, one of those scorching, howling, bleeding nights, the dogs plunge into the Volga and swim desperately to gain the other bank. The nights of Stalingrad are a terror for them. Animals flee this hell; the hardest stones cannot bear it for long; only man endures..." (Hoyt, p. 184)

Even as the Germans were trying to snuff out the last pockets of resistance in Stalingrad, Operation Uranus began, and Soviet forces moved slowly until they encountered resistance from the Romanian 3rd Army, which had earlier been dispatched by Hitler to reinforce the German flank. The Romanians provided some resistance against the Soviet armies even though their equipment was outdated, and it was not until Russian commanders decided to feature their tank divisions that they overcame the Romanian forces. The Soviet forces of Operation Uranus then moved toward the rear of the German 6th Army, where they met General Ferdinand Heim's XLVIII Panzer Corps. Some confusion over the deployment of the Panzer Corps gave the Russians an opening, allowing them to penetrate 30 miles into the German lines at Blinov. The remaining Romanian units retreated from the battlefield, and General Paulus was ordered to stop all offensive operations in Stalingrad and divert three panzer divisions and an infantry division to the south to help stem the tide of the Russian attack on the flank of the 6th Army.

Romanian soldiers at the Battle of Stalingrad.

The lines around Stalingrad on November 19, 1942.

The next day, November 20, the German reinforcements from Stalingrad helped stop the Russian 21st and 65th armies from creating a pocket surrounding them, but they were unable to stop the larger envelopment of German units. By the end of November 20, the 4th Panzer Army was cut in two, and the Russians had created a pocket surrounding Stalingrad. As the Russians moved to close the pocket, Hitler emphasized that the forces engaged at Stalingrad had to remain there and not retreat away from the city. He also tried to reinforce his divisions in the area with two panzer divisions, one mountain division, and two infantry divisions, but these were all the reinforcements Hitler was able to muster on the Eastern Front.

As Operation Uranus progressed, the Russian troops from the Stalingrad Front and the Southeastern Front completed their maneuvers and joined together, enveloping the German 6th Army between the Volga and Don Rivers. On the night of November 22, General Paulus reported to the headquarters of Army Group B, "The Army is encircled. The South front is still open east of the Don. The Don is frozen over and can be crossed. There is little fuel left; once it is used up, tanks and heavy weapons will be immobile. Ammunition is short. Provisions will last for six more days. Request freedom of action. The situation might come to abandonment of Stalingrad and the northern front." (Hoyt, p.194). However, when that message was sent to Hitler, he continued to insist that his forces must not retreat from Stalingrad, and he believed the Luftwaffe could airlift supplies into the enveloped troops of the 6th Army even though his chief of staff and the head of the Luftwaffe were trying to convince him that the inclement weather would not allow for such an airlift.

On November 23rd, Paulus sent a new message to Army Group B: "Murderous attack on all fronts. Arrival of sufficient air supplies is not believed possible, even if weather should improve. The ammunition and fuel situation will render the troops defenseless in the very near future." (Hoyt, p. 194). When no reply came from Hitler to Paulus, the general sent one more message:
"Mein Fuehrer:
Ammunition and fuel are running short. A timely and adequate replenishment is

not possible.

I must forthwith withdraw all the divisions from Stalingrad itself and further considerable forces from the northern perimeter.

In view of the situation I request you to grant me complete freedom of action."

(Hoyt., p. 195)

Yet again, Hitler refused to allow a retreat and reiterated his demands to Paulus that the 6th Army hold their ground at Stalingrad. Even while Hitler refused to allow Paulus to order a retreat, General Walther Seydlitz-Kurzbach of the LI Corps ordered the 94th Infantry Division to retreat out of the northeastern sector of the pocket. Seydlitz-Kurzbach's idea was that the retreat by the 94th Infantry would force Paulus to call a general retreat. However, by retreating, the 94th Infantry was forced to move across open fields that left them vulnerable to enemy fire. While one German officer had estimated that a third of the division would be killed during the retreat, the entire division was wiped out. This convinced the remaining German units not to attempt a retreat, so they remained at their positions within the pocket.

When Hitler learned of the actions of the 94th Infantry, he was furious at Paulus, who did not actually know what had occurred when he was contacted by radio. On the morning of November 24, Hitler sent Paulus orders under the highest priority decree ordering him to defend the Volga Front and the Northern Front at all costs. Hitler then asked Goering whether the Luftwaffe could supply the 6th Army, and when Goering answered in the affirmative, the decision was made. This meant that the Luftwaffe had to land 500 tons of supplies every day, which was a virtually impossible task, but Goering stood by his belief that it could be done.

As the Germans stayed in place, Russian forces, after routing the Romanian units south of Stalingrad, moved 134 divisions toward the city. As Russian tank divisions moved westward to take a position in the German rear, infantry units moved east to create a ring around the Germans. The Russian plan to push Germany out of the Eastern Front centered on Stalingrad. General Zhukov, who oversaw Operation Uranus, had at his disposal 7 of the 9 reserve armies that had formed since Germany commenced their invasion of the country. The goal was to destroy the German 6th Army, and then push westward to make sure the Germans would not be able to invade Russia again.

On November 24, Field Marshal Erich von Manstein, who had taken command of Army Group Don, provided some hope to the beleaguered 6th Army by announcing that he wanted to help relieve their position, but that he needed them to cut a supply channel to the southwest. Manstein wanted to create a two-pronged attack: one would be a diversion to the west, and the second would move toward Stalingrad, where he hoped a simultaneous push by Paulus and the 6th Army would allow them to break out and link up with his divisions. However, even as Manstein was preparing to take action, the 6th Army remained dependent on the Luftwaffe to supply them, but they were having great difficulty getting past Russian fighter planes that targeted these German transport planes. The loss of transports as they attempted to fly supplies into the 6th Army meant that they were only able to fly in 200 tons of supplies per day rather than the 500 tons required.

By November 28, General Zhukov spoke with Stalin, and during their conversation, Zhukov devised a plan to wipe out the 6th Army. The Russians would hold two tank groups of 100 tanks each to repel any attempted relief offensive, and meanwhile, they would attack the 6th Army and split them into two groups. From there, the weaker group would be destroyed first, and then the entire Soviet army would descend on the remainder of the 6th Army at Stalingrad. Stalin approved this plan, and with that, the Soviets simultaneously began preparations to attack the German Army Group Center in order to keep those divisions from aiding the 6th Army.

As the Russians prepared for their new offensive, General von Manstein began his relief mission by sending his 23rd Panzer Division, LVII Panzer Corps, as well as the Romanian 4th Army and two Luftwaffe divisions forward toward Stalingrad. Manstein's overall plan involved three parts. First, he would attack the town of Kotelnikovo to the northeast of his position. After that, German units along the Chir River would attack out of the Chir bridgehead, and finally, the 6th Army would break out to the south. This last part of the plan was not communicated to Hitler, who still wanted it to remain in Stalingrad.

When von Manstein began his relief offensive to the north, he took Soviet forces in that area by surprise. The German forces pushed back the Soviet 51st Army and then continued on their 60 mile drive toward General Paulus and the 61st Army. In three days, von Manstein's drive had made it 25 miles and had also made it across the Aksai River, which had been fortified by the Russians with 120 tanks and two infantry divisions. But while von Manstein advanced, the Russians launched an offensive of their own aimed at forces von Manstein had gathered to the southwest. These southwestern units were made up of the Italian 8th Army, as well as one German division and two battalions of another division. Also in the area was the German 27th Panzer Division. When the Russian offensive hit the German and Italian forces, the Italians, who were not used to the fighting on the Eastern front, panicked and ended up losing half of the 250,000 soldiers that made up the 8th Army. A second German position at the town of Nizhne Chirskaya also was forced back by a Russian force of four infantry divisions, which pushed the Germans back across the Chir River.

The one area in which the Germans were having success was along the southeastern portion of the Soviet pocket surrounding Stalingrad, where a superior German force threatened to open the pocket and allow the 6th Army out. On the night of December 18, von Manstein sent Major Eismann, an intelligence officer, into the pocket to make contact with Paulus, who he was having difficulty communicating with because the Russians were jamming their radio contact. When Eismann reached Paulus and gave him Manstein's views of the breakout, Paulus became indecisive and seemed to favor remaining within the pocket, as Hitler had ordered him to do, rather than attempt the breakout to link up with Manstein's forces. Paulus finally agreed to the planned breakout, but he was convinced by General Arthur Schmidt that he should not move until Hitler had approved the plan for the breakout, which had been codenamed Operation Thunder Clap. Hitler, however, refused to allow Operation Thunder Clap to proceed and instead remained steadfast in his refusal to leave the Stalingrad region.

Thanks to Hitler's refusal and the Luftwaffe's inability to provision their forces, the situation for the soldiers of the German 6th Army was becoming critical. By December 26, they only had two days' worth of bread, and the next day, the last of the fuel was rationed out. Von Manstein tried to convince Hitler to allow the breakout, but Hitler instead diverted one of the divisions engaged in von Manstein's drive to the Chir River region to bolster forces under attack there. As Manstein stated, "This measure means dropping for an indefinite period the relief of the Sixth Army, which in turn means the Army would now have to be adequately supplied on a long term basis. In Richthofen's opinion no more than a daily average of 200 tons can be counted on. Unless adequate supplies can be assured for Sixth Army the only remaining alternative is the earliest possible breakout of the Sixth Army at the cost of a considerable risk along the left wing of Army Group. The risks involved in this operation, in view of the Army's condition, are sufficiently known." (Hoyt, p. 230)

Hitler still refused to allow the 6th Army's attempt to breakout, and in the meantime, Soviet forces to the west of Stalingrad continued to inflict damage on German units. General Nikolai

Fyodorovich Vatunin reported to Stalin that in two weeks of fighting in the west, he had destroyed 17 divisions, taken 60,000 prisoners, killed 60,000 soldiers, and had taken their supplies. As General Zhukov assessed at the end of 1942, "The successful strikes of the Southwest and Stalingrad Fronts against the enemy forces in the areas of Kotelnikovo and Morozovsk finally sealed the fate of von Paulus' forces encircled at Stalingrad. Our troops in a brilliant execution of their assignment broke up von Manstein's attempt to reach the trapped Germans." (Hoyt, p. 232)

In fact, Soviet forces had created a critical situation for German forces in the south of the Eastern Front. Not only was Stalingrad enclosed, but Russian advances in the Caucasus had put Army Group A in danger of being isolated. This meant that of the three German army groups operating in the south, the 6th Army had been enveloped, Army Group A was in danger of the same fate, and von Manstein's Army Group Don had been split into three sections and had lost half its fighting force during their drive north.

On January 8, Russian emissaries offered Paulus the opportunity to surrender, but even though the 6th Army was encircled, it would still be a difficult battle to wipe them out. Paulus refused to answer, and after waiting two days for an answer which did not arrive, the Russians began their assault of the 6th Army. By the end of the fourth day of the assault, eight German divisions on the western side of the pocket had been destroyed, and on January 14, Pitomnik airfield was captured by Russian forces, which meant that the Luftwaffe relief effort, already struggling mightily due to the number of transport planes that had been shot down, had now virtually ceased.

Bundesarchiv, Bild 183-E0408-0022-001
Foto: o.Ang. | Januar 1943

German defenders in Stalingrad in January 1943.

By this point, the only thing keeping the Russians from overrunning all German positions in the south was the 6th Army at Stalingrad. While it had been decimated and was on the verge of breaking, the 6th Army still had 200,000 soldiers, so they required a large amount of Soviet attention, but without the presence of the 6th Army, all German divisions along this portion of the

Eastern Front were in danger of being destroyed. While Hitler had continually believed the 6th Army was not in mortal danger, by January 1943, he finally understood that the 6th Army was basically lost, but he continued to believe that German forces could regroup and mount a renewed spring assault on the Russians.

The Desert Fox and the Fate of North Africa

When the Italian offensives in North Africa failed at the beginning of the war, Hitler sensed both crisis and opportunity, and the Fuhrer responded by dispatching the newly constituted *Africa Korps* to Libya under the command of the legendary General—later, Field Marshal—Erwin Rommel. The Afrika Korps, or *Deutsches Afrikakorps*, remains one of the most storied units of World War II. Although it existed for a little over two years, it carved an indelible mark on the fabric of military history, in part due to the way it was used as a tool in the hands of its bold, gifted, creative commander, the famed Desert Fox.

An anti-tank unit in the Afrika Korps

The Afrika Korps began as a minor expeditionary force comprising two tank divisions (the 5th Light Division—later redesignated 21st Panzer Division, and the 15th Panzer Division) operating nominally under the Italian chain of command. Advance units arrived in North Africa under the codename Operation *Sonnenblume* in February and March 1941, and Rommel was initially under orders to simply reinforce the Italian position. With a little German help, Hitler was of the opinion the Italians could hold their own in North Africa, and his offensive focus was on Russia. Rommel's orders were to work with the Italians and act purely in a defensive capacity, as Hitler did not want to divert resources to a theater he regarded as secondary.

Rommel, however, had no intention of doing this. He was not necessarily aware of the launch of Operation Barbarossa—the invasion of Russia—at that point, and he saw it as his duty to exploit what local opportunities were available. The British had, after all, positioned within artillery range of Tripoli, exhausted at the end of a 1,300 mile supply line. With bold and determined action, the conquest of Egypt and the Suez was entirely possible, and the great fatted calf that was British Africa might have also been available for the taking. What began as probing attacks against British positions accelerated quickly into a breakneck pursuit, pushing the British back 1,000 miles. With the exception of Tobruk—where the besieged garrison was holding out—the British were thrown out of Cyrenaica in less than a fortnight.

As surprised as the British were, the German High Command was perhaps more surprised still, and Rommel was again warned against any actions requiring reinforcement. Meanwhile, in June 1941, the British launched Operation Battleaxe, an ill-fated counteroffensive that quickly broke against strong German defensive positions. With both sides exhausted and ill prepared, an operational pause came into effect that lasted from the end of June to November 1941.

German tanks during Operation Battleaxe

During this period, a comprehensive reorganization was undertaken behind British lines. The local military administration was split into two commands, with one for Syria and Palestine and another for Egypt. Both of these came under new Commander-in-Chief Sir Claude J.D. Auchinleck, Wavell's successor—Wavell had moved on to the post recently vacated by Auchinleck, that of commander-in-chief of the Indian Army. In Egypt, the Army of the Nile— later to resonate through history as the Eight Army—came under the local command of General Sir Alan Cunningham, fresh from his victories in East Africa.

Auchinleck

The North Africa Campaign had developed into a contest of armor and mechanized infantry, and vital to the organization of both forces was reconnaissance. Desert warfare in World War II gave rise to a number of specialist units operating under specific conditions, some of which—like the Special Air Service or the SAS founded by Colonel David Stirling—would evolve and survive, while others—such as the Long Range Desert Group—would gradually dissolve as the focus of the war moved north to Europe. The Long Range Desert Group, or the LRDG, was the brainchild of Brigadier Ralph Bagnold, a scientific explorer who had, prior to the outbreak of war, began to utilize motorized transport for scientific work and research in Egypt. He was one of the adventurous and resourceful men—among whom might be numbered Thomas Edward Lawrence, the legendary Lawrence of Arabia—who combined the artistic and intellectual with the manly art of war. Bagnold developed an informal catalogue of desert survival techniques, breaking new ground in where and how a motor vehicle might be used, behind the wheel of a Ford Model T.

In 1940, Bagnold tested the concept of forming a unit of long-range reconnaissance experts equipped for desert travel who might range far behind enemy lines in a fleet of specially modified vehicles. He ran the idea past General Wavell, who turned out to be an eager listener. Bagnold warned of the likelihood of an Italian raid on Aswan in southern Egypt, which would link southern Libya with northern Ethiopia, effectively severing the vital British link between Egypt and Sudan. Without effective reconnaissance, he argued, the British had absolutely no idea what the Italians were up to in the deep desert. He proposed a small group of motorized light patrols be created, manned by specially trained volunteers equipped with the most desert-worthy vehicles available, capable of achieving 1,500 miles of travel, in an entirely self-contained and mutually supporting capacity.

Wavell agreed, and Bagnold was more or less given a blank check to do what needed be done to get the group off the ground. Volunteers were not difficult to find, but Bagnold made a point of recruiting colonials, particularly Kiwis and Rhodesians. Initially, the group comprised just two Kiwi patrols of 30 men each, two of which were typically officers and remainder other ranks. It is perhaps noteworthy that many of the volunteers for this unit were willing to accept a reduction in rank, so the "other ranks" in this case were quite often commissioned officers drawn from other units.

A typical patrol of the LRDG was made up of three men per vehicle: a driver, a gunner, and a third man who would be either the unit navigator, cook, fitter, signaler, medical orderly, quartermaster, sergeant, or 2IC. They were equipped with American-made, 30-cwt Chevrolet trucks, customized for desert duty. Armaments varied but usually consisted of a .303 Lewis Gun or Vickers machine gun mounted alongside the front passenger's seat or on the leading edge of the flatbed—sometimes both—and a rear-facing companion for the sake of hot extraction. Navigation and communication equipment consisted of a wireless truck, carrying a standard army issue No.11 wireless set and a Phillips radio for navigational time signals. The navigation truck itself was equipped with a theodolite, maps, air navigation tables, and other sundry equipment.

As both armies dug in and reconsolidated, the Long Range Desert Group ranged the dunes and vast gravel plains of the western desert, facilitating covert SAS and commando operations, gathering intelligence, and interdicting the enemy with hit and run actions against the long Axis supply lines.

As all of this was underway, the Short Range Desert Group—the scathing, frontline soldier's name given to the jaunty and un-bloodied staff officers stationed in Cairo, armed with their gin-slings and fly whisks—were hard at work preparing the logistics for General Claude Auchinleck's planned offensive. This massive mobilization of manpower and equipment, second perhaps only to the later buildup in preparation for the invasion of Europe, was codenamed Operation Crusader and pivoted on one very simple plan.

The main thrust of the operation was to be launched in late November. The first force—named XXXth Corps and led by the 7th Armoured Division and its support groups—was to move from Fort Maddalena, an abandoned Italian fortification lying just inside Italian territory, some 80 miles inland from the coast, heading round in a northwesterly direction toward the besieged port of Tobruk. En route, it expected to meet, engage, and destroy the bulk of Axis armor positioned on the outskirts. Parallel to this, formations of the second force—or XIIIth Corps—would move to outflank Rommel's fortified positions on the frontier, were situated on the coast at Bardia and Sollum. Upon receiving a signal, the besieged Tobruk garrison would sally forth, penetrating southeast to link up with the advancing British columns.

As military lore often dictates, few operational plans survive contact with the enemy. On a cold desert afternoon on 17 November 1941, Operation Crusader began with the sound of a mass mobilization resonating along the lonely desert frontier. German forward reconnaissance observed the commencement of a major operation, and by dusk, the first Allied armoured columns began to move forward, advancing into Libya through gaps in the wire north of Fort Maddalena. At dawn the following morning, the support group followed.

Initially, the attack proceeded well. The Germans, it appears, had been taken completely by surprise, initially presenting the spearhead of British armour with no opposition at all. On the following day, the advance continued. After a sharp engagement with enemy armour, units of the 7th Armoured Division succeeded in capturing the strategic aerodrome at Sidi Rezegh, situated just 12 miles south of the Tobruk perimeter.

The following morning, November 20, a counterattack by German tanks was repulsed. Soon afterward, the British Support Group infantry appeared on the scene. With an apparently fair wind behind them, it was decided they'd storm the escarpment to the north of the Sidi Rezegh aerodrome, and thereafter, push across the main coast road, known as Trigh Capuzzo, toward El Dedu in order to rendezvous with the Tobruk garrison.

Having anticipated this, Rommel had been busy taking the measure of the British attack overnight, and he was ready to respond by sunrise. On November 21, the 21st Panzer and Italian Ariete 132nd Armoured Divisions began moving northeast at a brisk and confident pace toward British positions. One of the longest, bloodiest, and most embittered actions of the North African Campaign, the Battle of Sidi Rezegh, was about to begin.

Before dawn on November 20, the Kings Royal Rifle Corps had taken over the Sidi Rezegh landing ground from the Armoured Brigade, digging in under the constant barrage of enemy fire, the unnerving sight of large bodies of enemy armour, and infantry massing to the west and the north. Despite this, in the early hours of the morning of the 21st, orders were issued to commence planned attacks on the steep escarpment north of the Sidi Rezegh landing ground, which would put the Allies in command of the main coast road, thus cutting off the only Axis line of communication from east to west. There was little alternative at that point, bearing in mind it was level terrain, in comparison to a simple frontal assault executed across the landing-ground itself. The plan called for the concentration of artillery fire on enemy positions, immediately followed by a carrier assault from offshore, after which the battalion would form up and cross the starting line at precisely 0800h, in what was classic British Army attack strategy.

A picture of German panzers at Sidi Rezegh

A picture of German prisoners at Sidi Rezegh

By noon all objectives had been achieved, and overall, the attack was deemed a success. In all, 700 Italian prisoners were taken, and the opening phase of Operation Crusader appeared to have passed successfully, with most objectives achieved. However, dawn the following morning revealed a somewhat different picture, however. The ocean-facing slopes of the escarpment were now covered with enemy vehicles, including tanks, and soon a steady shelling of Allied battalion positions began. At the same time, the sound of a heavy bombardment from the south grew increasingly louder as the depleted 7th Armoured Division was incrementally forced back by the superior weight of German and Italian armour. At about 1300h, German armour positioned to the north of Sidi Rezegh began to move. Supported by an intense artillery barrage, the massed formation swept past the left flank of the British armoured brigade, turning on the unprotected infantry positions from the rear.

With nothing but anti-tank rifles and a few two-pounders for the reply, the infantry was helpless. In due course, after a stiff but futile resistance, their positions were overrun. Five officers and 50 other ranks—later joined later by roughly another 100—were the only ones to escape the rout, with almost the entire personnel of three British companies being reported missing. That evening, what transport there was available was gathered, and the survivors of the battalion hurriedly organized. Then, amidst the glowing ruins of battle, a withdrawal began.

As all of this was taking place, British armoured brigades were engaged in no-less harrowing fighting in the neighbourhood of Sidi Rezegh. There, a deadly tank battle had been underway for two days between the light Allied Honey and Valentine tanks and the much heavier German Mark IIIs and Mark IVs. Axis forces, advancing in a northeasterly direction with the intention of crushing the Support Group and the 5th South African Brigade—which had, by then, advanced south of Sidi Rezegh—succeeded in overrunning South African positions and consigning the brigade to the same fate as the King's Royal Rifle Corps, effectively destroying it as a fighting formation.

In the meantime, preparations for the break-out of the garrison were complete in Tobruk, and the operation commenced three hours before dawn on 21 November with an artillery barrage from the guns of Tobruk. This action involved the Polish Brigade and the 4th Royal Tank Regiment, along with the King's Dragoon Guards and 2nd Black Watch, supported by the machineguns of the Northumberland Fusiliers. The operation ultimately failed, thanks to actions happening overnight, and the inability of the relieving force to hold its position at Sidi Rezegh.

Casualties sustained were heavy, with the Black Watch being hit particularly hard. The area around Sidi Rezegh and El Duda devolved into an extended bout of chaotic fighting that would ebb at night and flare during the day. A melancholy landscape of burned-out tanks, plumes of black smoke, and the debris of battle greeted the dawn of every day.

By November 23, however, formation reports revealed the ultimate loss of Sidi Rezegh, and a failed relief of Tobruk, at a heavy cost in casualties. As a consequence, General Allan Cunningham appeared to suffer something of a crisis of faith, concluding that the best course before him lay in withdrawal. Auchinleck, however, refused to consider this, and promptly passed command of the Eighth Army on to General Neil Ritchie, who until then had served as Deputy Chief of Staff.

Neither side emerged from the operation unscathed, but Rommel was perhaps able to recover more quickly from the brawl, thanks to the work of his disciplined and highly organized recovery sections. It was this that allowed him to retain the advantage of his overwhelming superiority in armor. Tactical failings, however, can sometimes ruin the best equipped army, as the Italians had frequently shown. Rommel inexplicably opted against striking what might have been a killing blow to the depleted British formations, plunging behind their lines in order to raid and harass their lines of supply and communication instead. As he did, Allied forces moved in to recapture Sidi Rezegh, which allowed the Tobruk Garrison to link up and thus secure an excellent tactical position across the main coast road, effectively isolating Rommel from his rear bases and supply lines.

A British Crusader tank passing an abandoned Panzer on November 24
This swung matters back in favor of the Allies. Positioned now to the east of the Tobruk/Sidi Rezegh corridor were the 21st Panzer and Ariete Divisions and to the west, the 15th Panzers and

various Italian infantry divisions. The contest in and around Sidi Rezegh resumed once again with all its former ferocity as the isolated Axis units sought to fight their way back. On December 1, 1941, the attackers succeeded in punching a hole through British lines, and an orderly and gradual German withdrawal back to their El Agheila base followed. The Germans were forced to fight a rearguard action against determined, opportunistic British pursuit on their way back, which continued to Gazala, some 40 miles along the coast road west of Tobruk.

At this point, Rommel gathered his armor and turned around to fight. The Germans were aided in no small part by inclement weather bogging down Allied transports, grounding aircraft, and starving British forces of supplies and fuel. By December 16, Rommel had succeeded in reaching Ajedabia on the western edge of Cyrenaica. Three weeks after that, he was home behind his familiar fortified line at El Agheila. The year 1941 ended with battle lines drawn essentially as they had been nine months earlier.

Protected by the combined defenses of salt marshes and minefields, Rommel waited for resupply and reinforcement, which, with German efficacy, were not long in coming. Within three weeks, his losses in terms of manpower and equipment had been replaced, and his forces were joined by two fresh Italian Divisions, the Littorio and Sabrata. The Allied troops confronting Rommel at El Agheila had become vulnerable due to extended supply lines and exhausted troops. They were situated at the end of attenuated supply lines stretching back over 1,000 miles to Cairo, largely isolated from reinforcement, and critically short of supplies and ammunition. Axis gunners now had a commanding view of British forward positions and made good with their heavy guns, which easily outranged the Allied 25-pounders.

On January 21, 1942, these static lines finally snapped, and the game was on again. Three German columns, each strongly supported by armour, broke out of El Agheila, pressing the British back toward Ajedabia, in this, the latest yaw in an ongoing see-saw struggle. Once again, the Allies were in retreat along the coast road. By the end of the first week of February, Rommel was pressing hard against the South Africans south of Gazala, the line holding and the position briefly stabilized. It was, nonetheless, a bitter pill for the Eighth Army to swallow. All that had been won by the hard fighting and sacrifice of the weeks and months prior was quickly lost. Rommel had so grown in stature— thanks to his extraordinary daring and aggression—he was often compelled to travel to Berlin and Rome in the midst of the advance to personally receive the plaudits and congratulations of Hitler and Mussolini.

For the British, however, this was arguably the lowest point of their campaign. Churchill himself remarked, "Before Alamein, we never won a victory and after it never suffered a defeat." El Alamein had yet to be fought, and for the time being, the Mediterranean fleet was depleted by grim and costly convoy runs, while the Royal Air Force in Malta had been reduced to a remnant. Although the position was extremely tense along the Gazala line, positions remained static. The British had adopted the "box" defense system, which consisted of strongly fortified positions with 360 degree defenses and vehicles and armaments dug in below ground level. Held by determined troops, these structures represented formidable defensive positions, although static by nature.

Meanwhile, Rommel had, once again, formulated a simple plan of attack. The Italian infantry divisions were to deliver three holding attacks on the British forward positions, the first in the north near Gazala, the second where the *Trigh Capuzzo* (the desert road) cut the center of the British line, and the third in the south, near Bir Hacheim. Alongside these, the Afrika Korps and Littorio Division, with a force of 350 tanks, were to outflank British-defended positions in the south, delivering a lightning blow in the rear with the intention of capturing Tobruk and the airfields in its vicinity.

Australian forces at Tobruk

At daybreak on May 27, in the searing heat of late spring, the attack commenced. Stiff opposition was almost immediately registered from the 25-pounders and light tanks of the 1st and 7th Armoured Divisions, as well as constant harassment by the Royal Air Force. In spite of this, Axis Panzer groups succeeded in reaching El Duda and Sidi Rezegh by afternoon, where they were held and eventually obliged to fall back after a ferocious tank battle south of Tobruk.

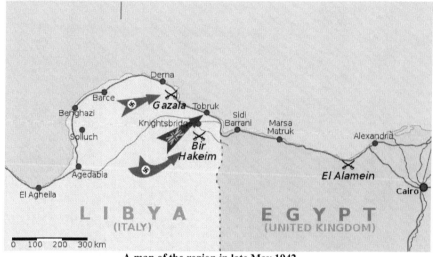

A map of the region in late May 1942.

By early June 1942, Rommel had switched his focus to Bir Hakeim, which held a strategically important position along the Gazala line. This city, which was defended by French troops, was attacked by Axis forces for 10 days, but as French troops desperately tried to hold the strategically important location, the British made the decision not to reinforce them. The French commander, Brigadier-General Pierre Koenig, asked for permission to withdraw his forces as water and ammunition ran low, and on June 10, his men left the city. A German soldier noted his surprise in an account: "During the first ten days of our attack against the French the British had remained amazingly calm. The 'Ariete' Division alone was attacked by them on 2 June, but it defended itself stubbornly. After a counterattack by the 21st Panzer Division the situation again there became quiet."

The British had given up the initiative, and it was Rommel and the Germans who pressed forward. Axis forces attacked at Knightsbridge and El Adem on June 12, and in the combined battles, the British lost roughly 120 tanks. After this point, the situation continued to worsen for the British, and one of the biggest issues was that Auchinleck, as the newly appointed Commander-in-Chief of British North African forces, had overlapping responsibilities that did not allow him to focus his energy on Rommel's threat. At the same time, mistakes by Auchinleck's subordinates allowed Rommel continued opportunities to attack British forces, like the British inability to hold Tobruk. Although Auchinleck ordered his men to reinforce the garrison there, his subordinates, Generals Ritchie and Gott, decided that the garrison could hold out on its own even though the defenses around the city were weakened from previous fighting.

After his victories at Knightsbridge and El Adem, Rommel decided to concentrate a large percentage of his forces on attacking Tobruk. The British 4th Armoured Brigade attempted to stall the German advance on Tobruk, but in the ensuing battle on June 17 against German panzers stationed between Belhamed and El Adem, the British lost another 30 tanks, crippling Britain's tank capabilities in the area. When the Germans attacked Tobruk on June 20, the city's defenders had little chance of holding out against superior German firepower, and by the end of the first day, the battle was basically over. Once their mopping up operations had been completed, the Germans had captured the city and 33,000 prisoners.

Axis forces inspect an abandoned British tank.

The defenders at Tobruk were ill-equipped and had inadequate defenses for such a large-scale German attack, yet British leaders had believed that Tobruk was "impregnable," as Captain B.L. Bernstein wrote. His disbelief at the loss of Tobruk was confirmed when he wrote that "the whole thing was a ghastly mistake!" Likewise, Churchill was taken completely by surprise at the loss of Tobruk, as he had also misunderstood the strength of forces stationed there. Churchill was in Washington, D.C. meeting with Roosevelt when he was notified of Tobruk's defeat, and as he said to Roosevelt, "Defeat is one thing, but disgrace is another." (Latimer, p. 51)

Emboldened by the victory at Tobruk, Rommel next decided to launch simultaneous efforts against Egypt and the island of Malta, believing that he could take both locations before the British were able to regroup and mount a serious defense. While his logistics support was continually being stretched to the breaking point, Rommel believed that they could keep up, and he argued with other German military officers who thought he was being too reckless. Although Hitler backed Rommel's plan, it was eventually curtailed so that the attack on Malta was suspended while the Germans concentrated on an advance against Egypt.

As the Axis forces moved toward Egypt in late June, the British brought together scattered groups of forces to create a defense that included 159 tanks and infantry units that were combined from a number of divisions. As the Germans began their attack, the British Desert Air Force played an important role by neutralizing the Luftwaffe and thereby preventing Rommel from enjoying air support. Meanwhile, the ground battle was a confused jumble, with both sides making mistakes in the fighting; Rommel could have been surrounded early on, but instead his 21st Panzer Division was able to scatter the New Zealand Division that was opposing them. The British, believing the New Zealanders had been wiped out, ordered a withdrawal that left their X

Corps isolated at Matruh. The X Corps was forced to remain in their position for a day and then attempt a breakout during the night, leaving 6,000 prisoners and 40 tanks behind. On the morning of June 29, the forward elements of the 21st Panzer Division surprised a British column near Fuka and took another 1,600 prisoners. At this point, Rommel believed victory was imminent and told his subordinate, Hauptman George Briel, "Well Briel, you will advance with your men to Alexandria and stop when you come to the suburbs. The Tommies have gone. When I arrive tomorrow we'll drive into Cairo together for a coffee." (Latimer, p. 54)

Rommel in June 1942.

With the battle turning against the British, Auchinleck ordered a withdrawal to the Alamein line, 60 miles from Alexandria, on June 26, where the British defensive line included a massive artillery defense. The British strategy also included remaining as mobile as possible, "unimpaired by the necessity for defending fortified positions." By July 1, as Axis forces moved toward the Alamein line, it seemed as though the British had been defeated, and German propaganda called for the women of Alexandria to "[g]et out your party frocks, we're on our way!" The Royal Navy evacuated Alexandria, and British officers in both Alexandria and Cairo tried to burn secret documents in preparation for the cities being taken.

British infantry in defensive positions at El Alamein in July 1942.

An advancing German panzer ahead of the First Battle of El Alamein
The Alamein line had geographic features that would be crucial for the British defensive line.
At Alamein, a natural barrier to the south meant that in order to outflank the defensive forces, as
Rommel had done time and again in his drive toward Egypt, the Germans would have to go far
to the south and cross a portion of the Sahara. Meanwhile, in order for an attacking force to
engage the Alamein line, they would be funneled into three areas due to the layout of hills and
rivers in the area. Therefore, the British could concentrate their forces in these areas, but their
preparations at the Alamein line were hastily constructed, and they only had one full-strength
infantry division ready by July 1. Fortunately, the Germans were also encountering some
problems, as they experienced "the diminishing power of the offensive" that had left their troops
"exhausted by victory."

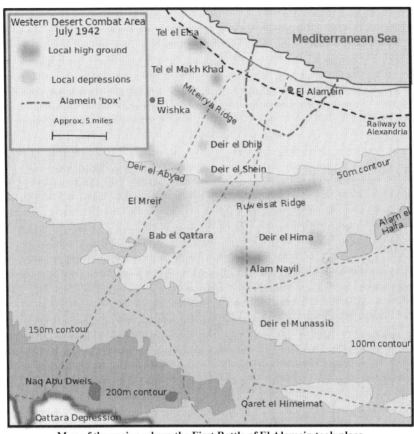

Western Desert Combat Area
July 1942

Local high ground

Local depressions

━ ━ ━ ━ Alamein 'box'

Approx. 5 miles

Tel el Eisa

Tel el Makh Khad

El Wishka

Miteirya Ridge

Mediterranean Sea

El Alamein

Railway to Alexandria

Deir el Dhib

Deir el Abyad

Deir el Shein

50m contour

El Mreir

Ruweisat Ridge

Alam el Halfa

Bab el Qattara

Deir el Hima

Alam Nayil

150m contour

Deir el Munassib

100m contour

Naq Abu Dweis

200m contour

Qaret el Himeimat

Qattara Depression

Map of the region where the First Battle of El Alamein took place.

Over the next four weeks, the confused jumble of operations and disconnected actions that made up the First Battle of El Alamein would stop Rommel and save Egypt from the Axis onslaught. As the German attack at Alamein began in early July, the 3rd South African Brigade fought off a German attack in the center, while the 18th Indian Brigade also faced a German attack at Deir el Shein. After eight hours of fighting, the Germans were able to destroy the Indian Brigade, forcing the British to withdraw. At this point Auchinleck believed his lines were overextended and he abandoned positions at Bab el Qattara and Naqb Abu Dweis and instead created mobile units with the New Zealand Division and the 5th Indian Division, which would respond to German attacks and back up other defensive positions.

Further to the south, the Germans and British tried to outflank each other with little success, but on July 2, Auchinleck believed the Germans were stretched to their limit: "Auchinleck explained that Rommel was now fully extended and that his advanced troops were now dangerously exposed. So it was essential that the Eighth Army, seriously disorganized, was given a few days to reorganize and establish defense positions at Alamein. The answer – all the fighting troops which could be rallied would be formed into a striking force to bloody the enemy's nose within the next twenty-four hours…So the CinC assumed the duties of the corps, division, brigade and even battalion commander, collected together a miscellaneous force from the remnants of Eight Army, and gave orders direct to those involved." (Latimer, p. 61)

Shortly after this British attack was launched, they stopped Rommel's advanced troops and had taken 3,000 prisoners, thanks in part to assistance by the Royal Air Force and Royal Navy. The Royal Air Force provided cover for ground troops and also continued to neutralize the effectiveness of the Luftwaffe, while the Royal Navy's dominance of the Mediterranean made it extremely difficult for Axis forces to receive both supplies and reinforcements from Europe. When Rommel ordered another attack to stem the tide at the Alamein line on July 3, he found that his troop strength was down to around a tenth of its strength and he only had 26 tanks, which were opposed by over 100 in the British 1st Armoured Division. Rommel halted the attack on account of the exhaustion of his troops and his low troop levels.

The British now outnumbered the Germans and were being reinforced more quickly. While the British were gaining the advantage, they were still plagued by mistakes, as "there followed a week of missed opportunities for the British and thereafter, more weeks of costly and mismanaged operations." (Latimer, p. 63) Furthermore, the British were still fighting in improvised divisions that jumbled the chain of command. By July 7, Auchinleck had decided on a plan of attack in which British forces would take the ridge of Tel el Eisa, his Australian division would take Tel el Makh Khad, and his South Africans would move along the coast road. Once these objectives had been accomplished, his forces would move forward to Deir el Shein.

On July 10, two companies attacked Tel el Makh Khad and then withdrew in what was described as an engagement that "appears to have achieved little but the bewilderment of the participants." The attack at Tel el Eisa was more successful, with British forces there being supported by heavy artillery, air support, and tanks from the 44th Royal Tank Regiment. At Tel el Eisa, they were able to capture 106 prisoners and four guns before overrunning an Italian position and capturing a further 800 prisoners. The most significant action at Tel el Eisa, however, was the capture of the German 621st Radio Company, which severely hampered their efforts at communication and provided the British with intelligence on the combat readiness of German forces and the plan of battle for the Axis army.

Destroyed panzers at Tel Al Eisa

Two days after the Germans lost these positions, they launched a new attack against the Alamein line using the 21st Panzer Division, supported by all the infantry and air support they could bring to bear, but this attack was stifled by British artillery fire. At this point, it seemed like neither side had the overwhelming force necessary to overrun the other side, leaving one of Auchinleck's subordinates to write a letter complaining that the army needed "a commander who will make a firm plan and leave his staff to implement it, crash through with it; and once the conception is under way, move about the battlefield himself and galvanize the troops who are looking over their shoulder." (Latimer, p. 66)

After a period of no major offensive movements, Auchinleck pushed forward once more, ordering an attack for July 21 that would engage both the German main positions and their southern flank. However, the attack began poorly when a division of New Zealand infantrymen were counterattacked by German panzers without any tank support, causing the deaths of 700 soldiers. At the same time, the Fifth Indian Brigade attacked to the west, with the 23rd Armoured Brigade making a parallel attack. The 23rd Armoured faced some difficulties as they lost tanks to mines, as well as anti-tank and tank guns, but by the end of the day they had reached their objective 3.5 miles to the west of where the Indian infantry stopped. As one British soldier recalled of the fighting in this sector, "I saw great clouds of black smoke. Then the wreckage of the attack coming back. The tank wounded, half-naked. Mortar bombs falling… there must have been a kind of madness at the Army Command, a feeling that there was a once and for all chance to drive the enemy back and that all risks must be taken in the hope of success. The kindest thing that can be said is that tired men do make mistakes." (Latimer, p. 70)

By the end of the day, the British had made some headway, but their losses had been heavy. The 23rd Armoured Brigade lost half of their 87 tanks, and the 2nd New Zealand Division had suffered 904 casualties, including 69 officers. Even with these losses, the British command decided to continue pushing forward; on July 22, after preliminary operations by the South Africans, they ordered the 9th Australian Division to push 6,500 yards west and then 4,500 yards to the south. The 9th Australian Division, which had already undergone two weeks of almost continuous fighting, faced heavy artillery and machine-gun fire as they attempted to advance to their objective. They gained ground but failed to reach their goal, and in the process, they suffered 270 casualties along with 50 missing. Included in these figures were all company commanders (who had been killed), and their replacements became casualties as well.

Australian guns at the First Battle of El Alamein

Auchinleck next ordered a major offensive, codenamed Manhood, on July 24 and 25 that involved a converging attack on German positions by the XXX Corps, 1st Armoured Division, and 69th Brigade from the 50th Northumbrian Division. An enemy counterattack overran the 6th Durham Light Infantry and the 5th East Yorkshire Regiment of the 69th Brigade, and with the failure of the southern portion of the attack, the 2nd Regiment, 28th Battalion became isolated and was forced to surrender as panzers coming from three directions began to surround them. The failure of operation Manhood cost the British a further 65 casualties and 489 missing from the 28th Battalion, 600 casualties from the 69th Brigade, and 32 tanks from the 6th and 50th Royal Tank Brigades. As Percy Lewis, a soldier whose first action was during operation Manhood, stated, "It was a frightening experience, we were green-horns and officers tried to comply with the training book as taught but it didn't work out." (Latimer, p. 71)

Although the British had incurred heavy losses from their attacks at the Alamein line, they were nearly able to break through the German defenses. As Oberst Fritz Bayerlein, Panzerarmee Chief of Staff wrote, the British forces "very nearly succeeded in breaking through our positions several times between the 10th and 26th. If you could have continued to attack for only a couple more days more you would have done so. We then had no more ammunition at all for our heavy artillery and Rommel had determined to withdraw to the Frontier if the attack was resumed." (Latimer, p. 72)

Casualties had been high for both sides. The Axis lost 2,300 Germans and 1,000 Italians killed, 7,500 Germans and more than 10,000 Italians wounded, and 2,700 Germans and 5,000 Italians taken prisoner. Meanwhile, the British and Commonwealth forces lost over 13,000 men. In the end, the First Battle of El Alamein was a tactical stalemate, but that represented a strategic Allied victory because the Germans had not been able to overrun them in Egypt. Rommel subsequently (and conveniently) blamed issues with the supply lines and the inferior abilities of the Italians, reporting, "then the power of resistance of many Italian formations collapsed. The duties of comradeship, for me particularly as their Commander-in-Chief, compel me to state unequivocally that the defeats which the Italian formations suffered at Alamein in early July were not the fault of the Italian soldier. The Italian was willing, unselfish and a good, and, considering the conditions under which he served, had always given better than average. There is no doubt that the achievement of every Italian unit, especially of the motorised forces, far surpassed anything that the Italian Army had done for a hundred years. Many Italian generals and officers won our admiration both as men and as soldiers. The cause of the Italian defeat had its roots in the whole Italian military state and system, in their poor armament and in the general lack of interest in the war by many Italians, both officers and statesmen. This Italian failure frequently prevented the realisation of my plans."

With the Americans entering the North African theater, the presence of a new Anglo-American command structure gave Churchill the opportunity to reorganize the British high command. Auchinleck, who had up to this point held both Commander-in-Chief and operational command duties for the Eight Army, was fired and replaced with Harold Alexander as Commander-in-Chief and Bernard Montgomery as operational commander, both of whom Churchill believed would be more successful against the Germans. As one British officer recalled of Churchill's last meeting with Auchinleck prior to his firing: "Here, he said, or here…We were along with him [Churchill], as Brooke had gone up the line. It was a bit like being caged with a gorilla. Eventually the Auk [Auchinleck] said, 'No sir, we cannot attack again yet.' Churchill swung around to me. 'Do you say that too? Why don't you use the 44th Division?' 'Because, sir, that division isn't ready and anyhow, a one division attack would not get us anywhere.' Churchill rose, grunted, stumped down from the caravan and stood alone in the sand, back turned to us. I wondered if he was thinking himself in Lincoln's shoes, when Lincoln dismissed McClellan at Harrison's Landing." (Latimer, p. 90)

Ironically, Montgomery wasn't the first choice for command of the Eighth Army, but the original replacement, General William "Strafer" Gott, was killed when his plane was shot down shortly after taking command. In describing Auchinleck's replacements, Alexander and Montgomery, Harold Rupert Leofric George Alexander, third son of the Earl of Caledon, wrote, "Both of them completely imperturbable and efficiency itself, and yet two totally different characters. Monty with his quick brain for appreciating military situations was well aware of the very critical situation that he was in, and the very dangers and difficulties … acted as a stimulus … they thrilled him and put the sharpest of edges on his military ability. Alex, on the other hand, gave me the impression of never fully realizing all the very unpleasant potentialities of our predicament. He remained entirely unaffected by it, completely composed and never to have the slightest doubt that all would come right in the end." (Latimer, p.92) Alexander and Montgomery ended up working well together. Alexander took on the high-level leadership of British forces, dealing with politicians (and especially with Churchill) to make sure his troops were well-supplied and reinforced, while he let Montgomery have full control over day-to-day operations in North Africa.

Montgomery

Alexander

As the British reinforced their North African positions and awaited the arrival of American units, German intelligence informed Rommel of the increasing amount of American-made supplies making their way to the British, and he assumed that American entry into North Africa was imminent. With American entry forthcoming, Rommel figured he had only a small window to execute an attack before his forces were so outnumbered by the Anglo-American forces that victory would be impossible. In April, May, and June of 1942, Axis forces were reinforced by 22,900 men, and in July and August, 36,200 more men arrived. In terms of German plans, Friedrich von Mellenthin, a German staff officer, summarized them when he wrote, "The British excelled at static warfare, while in mobile operations Rommel had proved himself master in the field ... But Hitler would never have accepted a solution that involved giving up ground, and so the only alternative was to try and go forward to the Nile, while we still had the strength to make the attempt." (Latimer, p. 106)

Furthermore, Rommel lacked respect for the British, who he believed were amateurish in their military planning, so he planned an attack with little reconnaissance and intended to fight a decisive battle behind the British front, as he had done at Gazala, "in a form in which the great aptitude of our troops for mobile warfare and the high tactical skill of our commanders could compensate for our lack of material strength." But Rommel was also in a critical situation, because his already low-level of supplies were lessened further due to Hitler's emphasis on the Eastern Front, as well as the Royal Navy's increased attacks on German and Italian shipping in the Mediterranean. Another major blow, which Rommel would not know about until much later, was that British intelligence had intercepted and decrypted his transmissions laying out his attack plans.

By knowing the German plans ahead of time, Montgomery was able to plan a diversionary raid on the German supply lines as the German attack was supposed to commence. The Germans were ultimately delayed in their attack, which gave the British more time to fortify their positions, and when the Germans finally began their attack in early September, Rommel's main goal of Alam Halfa, which he believed was the key to defeating the British defensive positions, was heavily reinforced and backed up with Royal Air Force planes. Their bombing runs on the advancing German troops "absolutely pinned my troops to the ground and made impossible any safe deployment or any advance according to schedule." (Latimer, p. 111) Montgomery later wrote about the effect of Allied airpower during the battle, "The moral effect of air action is very great and out of all proportion to the material damage inflicted. In the reverse direction, the sight and sound of our own air forces operating against the enemy have an equally satisfactory effect on our own troops. A combination of the two has a profound influence on the most important single factor in war—morale."

Rommel's plan called for a rapid penetration of minefields around Himeimat and Munassib during the night of August 30 and 31 so that by 0330 hours his armored formations would be facing north and ready to move forward at first light. Instead, German armor came upon minefields that were much heavier than the Germans expected, and they also came under attack from Royal Air Force fighters. Rommel, understanding that the element of surprise was now gone, decided that his armored divisions needed to force the British armored units into a decisive battle.

At 1330 hours, after a refueling stop, the German panzers engaged the 22nd Armoured Brigade near Alam Halfa Ridge. The British had three regiments deployed there, along with anti-tank guns and a reserve regiment that was stationed two miles away. When the German panzers drove into the center of their formation, the attack began. As Major A.A. Cameron recalled of the tank engagement: "I saw tank after tank going up in flames or being put out of action, and this included my own when the big gun became unserviceable. However, the German advance had been momentarily checked and, although in the fog of battle it was difficult to know which of their tanks had been knocked out (German tanks seldom went on fire,) the great thing was that they were not coming on in front." (Latimer, p. 112)

The technologically superior Panzers seemed to be winning the battle, but as they moved forward toward the anti-tank guns of the 1st Rifle Brigade, the reserve Royal Scots Greys engaged the panzers, and the combined tanks of the Scots Greys and the anti-tank fire of the 1st Rifle Brigade forced the panzers to withdraw. This tank battle represented Rommel's best attempt to reach the Nile River Delta. Although he attacked again the following day with the 15th Panzer Division, fuel shortages did not allow him to bring as many panzers to bear as he had the previous day. Montgomery did not realize that these two battles represented the end of the German offensive, so he continued to scramble to reinforce the units that had been engaged by the panzers.

Rommel withdrew his forces back to their August 30th position, all the while taking fire from Royal Air Force fighters. Rommel himself came under fire from six air attacks, and his interpreter, Wilfried Armbruster wrote that they had "never experienced bombing that was anything like last night. Although we were well dispersed on Hill 92, the bombs came very close … Our combat echelon has had many men killed, three Flak 88s were hit and several ammunition trucks." (Latimer, p. 113) Meanwhile, the British raid on the German supply lines commenced on the morning of September 1, with members of the 15th Battalion paving the way for the 40th Royal Tank Regiment to raid the German positions. As the infantry of the 15th Battalion began making their way toward the Germans, they were met by heavy fire and eventually were forced to withdraw. Although the raid was aborted, the British learned that the Germans were defending with mines and barbed wire, which could be overcome with cooperation between infantry, artillery and tanks.

On September 3, the British launched Operation Beresford, a major attack of their own in the southern sector, but it again failed to create a decisive outcome. Beresford was costly for both sides, with 1,859 German casualties and 113 lost panzers, 1,051 Italian casualties and 11 lost tanks, and 1,750 British casualties and 67 lost tanks. Although the British did not gain ground during Beresford, it was considered to be a defeat for the German and Italian forces, and von Mellenthin later called it "the turning point of the desert war." For the Axis armies, the Allied naval and air forces were able to constrict Rommel's supply line, and the Royal Air Force in particular established what Rommel called a "paralyzing effect" on his armored vehicles. Finally, Montgomery had the British fight a "static battle from prepared positions," which negated the Germans' mobility advantage. After this battle in the south, Montgomery decided to hold his position there and refocus his efforts to the north while also buying time for reinforcements and training.

Montgomery believed that while his troops had been engaged in fighting with the Germans for a lengthy period of time, they lacked proper training and a proper understanding of military maneuvers, so in the fall of 1942, units which were recalled from the front lines for "rest" were subjected to training regimens that were supposed to prepare them for the large-scale engagements that he had planned for the future. As one soldier noted when he was recalled from the front lines to a rest area, "In a rest area you either dug holes all day and guarded dumps all night or you trained all day and guarded dumps all night. This rest area was different. You trained all day and then you trained all night. Not every day and every night – but almost." (Latimer, p. 120) However, when Churchill learned that Montgomery was delaying offensive operations to train his troops, he became furious. Churchill believed the British needed to press the Germans, in part because he wanted the British to beat the Germans before relying on American assistance, and he had fired Auchinleck in part because he often needed to be goaded into attacking.

As it turned out, Montgomery's delays were fortuitous, because the Germans suffered a huge blow in late September 1942 when Rommel was forced to return to Germany after suffering from various ailments that finally caught up to him. Although Rommel had been dealing with circulation and blood-pressure problems, chronic stomach and intestinal catarrh, and nasal diphtheria, he most likely would not have left his command but for the fact he was convinced a British attack would not occur for 6-8 weeks, which would give him a window to return to Germany, recover, and then return to North Africa. When he reached Berlin to begin his recuperation, Rommel found that his reputation and previous victories actually hurt him, because his requests for more supplies and manpower in North Africa were rejected by military officials who pointed to his ability to do more with less.

Georg Stumme replaced Rommel in the interim, but before he left, Rommel created a defensive plan for his forces that abandoned the mobile tactics they had been so successful with in previous engagements. With the Royal Air Force dominating the skies and the extremely low supplies of fuel that the Germans had on hand, Rommel instead decided to create a web of static defensive positions encircled by minefields that would allow the Germans to withstand Anglo-American attacks and then quickly launch counterattacks. The outer edges of the German defense were wired and mined to a depth of between 500 and 1,000 yards. After that, the Germans positioned weapon pits for machine-gun and light mortars, then a second minefield, and finally, the main German defensive positions. The Germans laid a total of 249,849 anti-tank mines and 14,509 anti-personnel mines.

Stumme

In terms of total troop strength, the Axis army in North Africa now consisted of four German divisions and eight Italian divisions, along with the German-Italian Panzer Army that consisted of the 15th and 21st Panzer Divisions, the 90th Light Division, the 164th Division, the Ramcke Parachute Brigade, and three Italian corps (the X, XX, and XXI. Rommel had serious doubts about the effectiveness of his Italian forces, so whenever he was given the opportunity, he sandwiched Italian units between German units in order to "stiffen the Italians' resolve."

As the Germans prepared their defenses, the British were busy scouting these positions, either through captured intelligence reports or from Royal Air Force sorties flown over the Axis forces. The Germans were able to reinforce their troop strength to the 75% level, as opposed to the 30% that they were at in mid-summer, but they were still unable to get an adequate amount of supplies to their North African troops. In August 1942, the British sunk 25% of the general cargo and 41% of the fuel that the Axis powers were sending across the Mediterranean, while in September the British became even more systematic in their targeting of Axis shipping, with the Royal Navy and Royal Air Force pairing with intelligence services to target tanker ships. Royal Navy vessels destroyed two Axis convoys departing Greece on September 6, and a few days later, they spotted and tracked a major fuel convoy and sunk one of the main fuel-carrying ships. A few days later, a Royal Navy taskforce, supported with RAF fighters, came upon the remaining ships in the convoy, and one British pilot wrote about the ensuing attack: "two bright orange flashes on the vessel, stern and amidships. I swung the aircraft round and we could all see two great columns of water going above her masts. It was clear that both torpedoes had hit … Very quickly thick grey smoke began to come out of the ship. The destroyers closed in and within five minutes a heavy smoke pall lay all over the ships. We could plainly smell the smoke in the aircraft; it smelt oily and acrid." (Latimer, p. 140)

Even when supplies did reach North Africa, the Axis forces had trouble moving them overland to the front. The Italians had no fighter cover for their transports, and the Germans refused to provide Luftwaffe planes to do the job, so the Italians avoided using ports within range of British airfields. This meant they had to land supplies at Tripoli and Benghazi and then had to make the long haul to the front. An example of the problems of supplying troops came in terms of feeding German soldiers; with problems getting their usual fare of bread and potatoes to the front, German soldiers had to make due with biscuits that one soldier called "cement plates." He ruefully added, "I felt sorry for the fellows who did not have good teeth because you had to grind it." (Latimer, p. 142)

Another major problem for troops at the front was the lack of quality water. While British troops had a pipeline that ran from Alexandria, Axis troops had to obtain water from old wells that were of poor quality. The water was often brackish, and the chemical treatment that had to be applied to make it drinkable also made it further unpalatable. As Lieutenant Joachim Schorm recorded in his diary, "Where would you find anybody in Germany who would drink water of this color and taste? It looks like coffee and tastes horribly of sulphur." (Latimer, p. 143) Soldiers of both sides faced also had to deal with flies that swarmed seemingly everywhere. One point of contention between German and Italian units was the German belief that the poor hygiene that Italian troops practiced made their areas breeding grounds for flies, but British soldiers also had to deal with flies, and each soldier was ordered to kill fifty flies per day. As H. Metcalfe recalled, "eating and drinking became a work of art, one hand waving back and forth over the food, the other hand waiting, then a quick rush to the mouth before they pounced again. They were around mouth, eyes, face, anywhere there was moisture. They settled on the rim of hot cups of tea in dozens." (Latimer, p. 143).

While the Germans dug in on defense, the British also prepared for a major engagement by secretly moving men and weaponry forward from the rear. From September 6 - October 22, flights of 20-30 bombers flew missions over German and Italian cities like Tobruk, Matruh, Sollum, Bardia, Benghazi, and even as far away as Suda Bay (Crete) and Navarino (southwest Greece). On October 9, a heavy raid on Luftwaffe airfields all but ended their effectiveness in North Africa, and heavy bombing by Royal Air Force planes signaled the beginning of Britain's offensive. Planes spent the next five days continuously bombing German and Italian positions, while on the ground, British, New Zealand, and Australian units moved into position. On the morning of October 23rd, the 21st Squadron Royal Engineers were briefed as to their role: "I know I'm speaking to young men only 20 or 21 years old, but I have to give it to you straight: right behind you is a whole division relying on you sappers to open the lanes for the tanks and infantry to pass through. Also behind you are a thousand guns. They will put up a terrific barrage as you sappers go in. Some of you will be killed, or lose an arm or leg, because Jerry will be trying to stop you. There will be mortaring, Stuka dive bombing and the rest." (Latimer, p. 174)

As they began heavy artillery fire and aerial bombardment to soften the Axis defenses, British troops made final preparations for the battle ahead, but as one soldier noted, the "prelude to the battle was a nightmare…we worked from dusk to dawn each night, and as the flies and heat made it virtually impossible to sleep during the day, we entered the battle in a fair state of exhaustion. Working conditions were appalling: the Alamein position had been fought over several times and the whole area was littered with decomposing corpses, some unburied and others whose graves had been uncovered by the wind. The stench of putrefaction was all-pervading and the air thick with dust and horrible desert flies." (Latimer, p. 171)

On the eve of battle, British forces enjoyed overwhelming tank superiority over the Germans and Italians. The British had 1,029 tanks at the front (267 of which were Shermans, advanced enough to be able to stand their ground against the German Panzer Mark IV "Specials"), as well as another 200 tanks in reserve. The Germans only had 218 operational tanks, while the Italians had 278. The British superiority was therefore more than 2:1, which was an important advantage but still less than the 3:1 ratio that was generally believed necessary to attack prepared positions. Naturally, British troops were on edge all day on October 23, and as one soldier recalled: "Perhaps the worst of the suspense was over…"

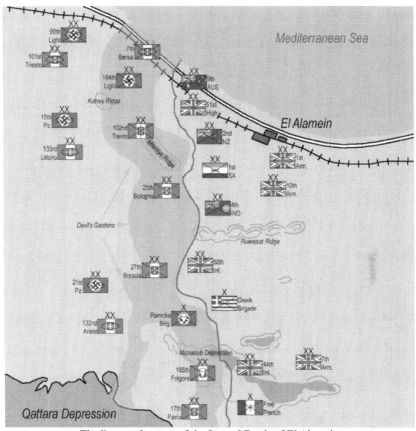

The lines at the start of the Second Battle of El Alamein

The next morning, when the pre-attack artillery barrage began, 882 field and medium guns participated in softening up the Axis' forward positions. An Allied soldier recalled, "No fury of sound had ever assailed our ears like that before, it cuffed, shattered and distorted the senses, and loosened the bowels alarmingly. I was more than startled, I was shocked, and needed to know that everyone else was there. When I could focus, the faces I saw first looked blanched and then flushed brightly in a kaleidoscope of passionately flickering hues as every line and every detail was etched into relief by the flashes from muzzles of the guns...hundreds of guns almost hub to hub, all bucking, recoiling, spitting fire and snapping like a pack of vicious terriers, all at once, it was sheer horror...The constant drill by which our army life had been ruled was now our saving grace, and even before the initial shock had been fully absorbed we fell into the routine of performing all our tasks automatically." (Latimer, p. 177)

A picture of the Allied artillery barrage to start the battle

While the Germans suffered few casualties during the British artillery barrages, their communications suffered heavily, and this disruption would be critically important as German commanders were unable to gain information on where and to what depth their positions were being attacked and penetrated. At German headquarters, there was mass confusion when the British advance began: "The great weight of shell fire made it seem possible that the enemy was beginning an offensive. At midnight it seemed that the enemy had penetrated the outpost line in a few places and was advancing towards the main defense line." (Latimer, p. 179)

After the Allies fired over half a million shells, the attack, dubbed Operation Lightfoot, began with infantry advancing and engineers clearing the mines for the tanks. By 0200 on the 24th, 500 tanks began advancing forward, but across various parts of the line, the Allies were surprised by the depth of the German minefields, which slowed the attack. Nonetheless, Montgomery still hoped to break through in the north and begin a rout.

A German mine explodes as Allied tanks cross a minefield.

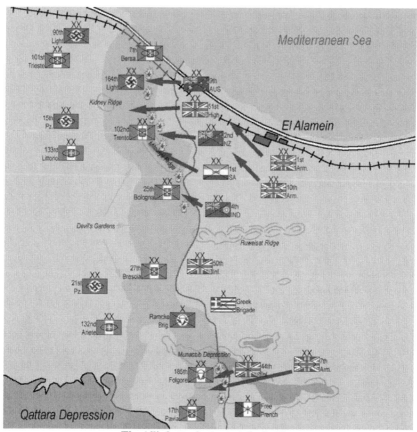

The Allied attacks to start the battle.

On the far north, the 24th Australian Brigade commenced by beginning a dummy attack to draw the Germans' attention, while south of them, the 9th Australian Brigade, 20th Australian Brigade, and 26th Australian Brigade all breached the outer rim of German and Italian defenses and began to cross the minefield leading to the main defensive positions. To the left of the Australians, the 51st Highland Division, consisting of seven battalions, swept forward through an "expanding funnel" to a final objective located three miles away, and the 5th Black Watch cut barbed wire and paved the way for units behind them to move forward as well.

The fighting in the forward positions was fierce and bloody. Once the German and Italian soldiers overcame their initial surprise over the attack, they defended as best they could in their forward trenches. Some units suffered heavy casualties during the fighting, and as E.M. Scott recalled, "The Masterton boys [where 22nd Battalion recruited] came through fairly well. Went in that night with twenty-five in that platoon and reached the objective with twelve. It is remarkable the stuff we went through that night without sustaining a great number of casualties.

Some of course were unlucky and some grand soldiers and great mates are no more…the rotten part about an attack is that it must go on, and if your best mate goes down beside you, you can't stop. It seems hard and callous, but it's unavoidable. The stretcher bearers and the lightly wounded following up attend to them." (Latimer, p. 189)

Behind the initial infantry push came the British tanks, which began navigating the minefields a few hours after the infantry battalions had made their way forward. The tanks had problems navigating the minefields, and as one tank driver recalled, his tank was making its way forward when he spotted a New Zealander waving his hat: "I swerved to miss him, there was a bloody great flash and the New Zealander floated through the air over the gun. The tank seemed to lift off the ground about six feet and clouds of dust filled the inside. The offside track had been blown off by a mine. I got out with the tank Commander to see what we could do for the New Zealander – the rubber of the tank track had pitted his face like shrapnel." (Latimer, p. 204) Tanks that were immobilized by mines were immediately vulnerable to enemy fire, and even though sappers worked feverishly to clear paths through the minefield, a number of tanks were hit by mines.

Although the British units were making their way forward, it was in a confused and chaotic manner. As a liaison officer from the 4th Indian Division reported from the front, "Progress not as quick as expected. Lanes through minefields nowhere nearly through. Appalling congestion in lanes. Armour head to tail in single file in both lanes, treading on heels of infantry (and suffering from considerable shelling)…Not much fun for leading tanks as they got to end of cleared lane…At once came up against anti-tank screen. Even Italian anti-tank guns made good shooting. Artillery busy being organized to help infantry forward. New units untrained to do own fire and movement…All kept engines running whole time even when not in action and soon ran dry. Troubles of getting petrol convoy up to them through congested lanes. A petrol convoy did arrive eventually behind Miteiriya, did not disperse and got bombed. One of best Hun air actions of the battle." (Latimer, p. 212)

Although Rommel was rushing back to the front from Germany almost as soon as the battle started, the Germans suffered a disaster when Stumme apparently suffered a heart attack after coming under enemy fire during the 24th. With Stumme dead and Rommel at least a few days away from arriving, the Germans were deprived of their two most important commanders as the Allies cleared mines and gradually pushed forward throughout the 24th. All the while, the Royal Air Force ran sorties that softened up Axis positions.

Allied bombing at El Alamein.
That night, Montgomery traveled to the 2nd New Zealand Division Headquarters to assess the situation at this critical position at the front. After being briefed by the 2nd Division's officers, Montgomery realized that further losses in this sector could mean losing the battle because of the location's strategic importance. He therefore made the decision to withdraw the 10th Armoured Division and rest the New Zealanders. He also changed the direction of operations, ordering the main thrust to now move through the northwest, through the 9th Australian Division's area.

On October 25th, as the British were shifting operations to the northwest, an Axis counterattack against the London Rifle Brigade created a short but crucial engagement in which Axis tanks, including Italian M13s and German Mark IIIs, engaged the Rifle Brigade's infantry units' dug-in positions that were supported by anti-tank guns. The Axis tanks were trying to utilize their superior firepower against what they believed was a weak spot in the British line manned only by infantry, but anti-tank fire halted their forward momentum, and as their tanks were hit, the crews tried to escape: "One Italian officer was hoisting himself out when a 6-pounder shot hit him in the chest and he literally disintegrated." In their withdrawal from the engagement, Axis units were forced to leave 14 tanks behind. This counterattack revealed the

Axis strategy of trying to engage infantry units with tanks, but it also showed the problems tank attacks had when fighting dug-in infantry positions effectively supported by anti-tank guns. Even if successful, their tank strength would be depleted, and with an already unfavorable tank ratio against the British, this strategy might gain the Germans and Italians some territory, but they would still lose in terms of material strength.

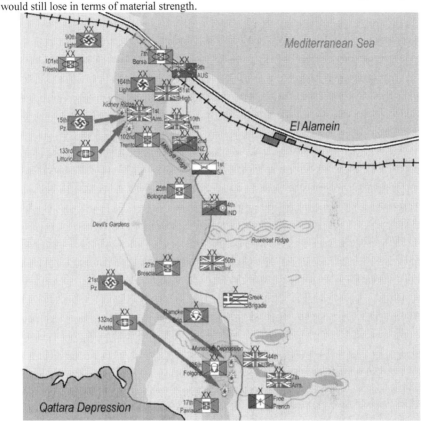

The Axis counterattack

Late on the 25th, Rommel returned to take command of the Axis forces, but he found the situation to be critical. British artillery had done heavy damage to the German and Italian defensive lines, and while they had prevented a breakthrough, they were unable to dislodge the enemy from their positions. Additionally, Axis forces were suffering from fuel shortages that were limiting what they were able to accomplish. As one officer told Rommel, "The fuel situation permitted only local counter-attacks by our panzer units which were standing ready immediately behind the threatened sectors of the front." He also explained, "Only small supplies of fuel remain close to the front." (Latimer, p. 230)

As the British began their attack in the northwest, their plans revolved around a hill that they called Trig 29. This was a hill that rose only 20 feet, but it was the highest area in the sector and overlooked the entire area surrounding it. If the British were able to take the hill, they would have a nearly unobstructed artillery position from which to decimate the Axis defenses. To take Trig 29, the 9th Australian Division was ordered to attack north toward the sea, and with support from the 1st South African Division and the 26th Australian Brigade, they were then ordered to take the hill.

The Allied push in the early morning hours of October 26.
When the attack commenced at midnight on October 26th, the lead companies of infantry moved forward through heavy defensive fire to a position 200 yards short of Trig 29. After securing this location, armored carriers moving in rows of four pushed forward, and as infantrymen leaped out and charged, they overwhelmed the German and Italian defenders. For the rest of the 26th and 27th, the Australian and South African soldiers holding Trig 29 were subjected to heavy Axis artillery fire and counterattacks, but they were able to hold on.

On October 27th, Montgomery ordered another push forward that involved taking two positions called Trig 33 and Kidney Ridge. This led to a major tank battle in which the British assaulted Axis defensive positions only to be pushed back by a counterattack made by Italian M14 tanks. In the initial part of this battle, British forces were hit heavily, with the 47th Royal Tank Regiment and the 24th Armoured Brigade having to withdraw because of the heavy losses they suffered. Because of the importance of this area to Axis defenses, the Germans poured reinforcements into the area, and as Major-General Raymond Briggs recalled, "News had just reached me that the 21st Panzer Division was on the move from the south to join the 15th Panzer Division opposing us. I knew that every tank would be needed at short notice, as indeed they were a few hours later, to take on the two divisions. I had to balance the possible destruction of the Rifle Brigade against the necessity to conserve my tank state. My reluctant decision was that I must leave the infantrymen to fight it out themselves." (Latimer, p. 249)

As the battle raged on, infantrymen and anti-tank crews attempted to stem the Axis counterattack and hold their position. One Allied soldier described the scene: "[O]ne of our [anti-tank] chaps crawls from his trench and with bullets ripping into the sand around him, runs stooping over to a 6-pounder fronting north, extracts a shell already in the breech and creeps back with it to his own gun which faces the panzer. It's amazing how the [machine-gun] stream misses him, but he calmly puts the shell in, takes steady aim, and fires. Immediately there's an explosion from the panzer." (Latimer, p. 252) As the engagement ended, Axis forces had lost 70 tanks, while the British forces lost 16 carriers and 10 guns, along with a large number of infantry deaths.

Bundesarchiv, Bild 101I-783-0107-14A
Foto: Dörsen | 1941 April - Mai

A disabled British Sherman tank at the battle.

The Axis command, realizing the dire situation they were in, ordered a number of counterattacks that were halted by British artillery fire, but both Montgomery and Churchill were frustrated by the inability to push forward faster, and at one point Churchill complained, "Is it really impossible to find a general who can win a battle?" After a few days of action that did not provide a decisive breakthrough, Montgomery ordered a new attack, codenamed Supercharge, that would take place on November 1. Meanwhile, Montgomery sought to consolidate the gains that his troops had made in the north by resuming operations in the south. To do this, he brought his New Zealand divisions back into action, where they would be supported by the 2nd Armoured Brigade, the 7th Motor Brigade, and the 8th Armoured Brigade. As they moved out, one soldier recalled, "As far as could be seen, to both left and right of us, men were advancing with their rifles in the porte position, their bayonets glinting in the pale moonlight. Full moon had been days ago so it was quite dark...As we advanced, the feeling of pride and exhilaration was unmistakable. We didn't realize or think of the danger we were in; we were doing a job and the thought of being killed or wounded was far from our minds...I remember seeing forms sink to the ground but our orders were to keep going and not to stop for wounded or dying. Later we passed slit trenches with forms slouched over them facing in our direction ... " (Latimer, p. 284)

In moving through the minefields to their starting positions, the British encountered some problems as enemy artillery and mortar fire not only hit transports and carriers but also knocked out mine markers so that 29 tanks failed to reach their starting point on time. At 0520 hours, the commanders at the front decided to delay for half an hour, and then a further delay meant that units did not begin moving forward until 0615. The forward tanks, the Warwickshire Yeomanry and the Royal Wiltshire Yeomanry, were quickly pinned down by enemy fire, and the Third Hussars moved into an anti-tank gun line that knocked out A Squadron almost immediately, while C Squadron's leader and second in command were immobilized, causing that squadron's tanks to lose cohesiveness.

The Warwickshire Yeomanry managed to move forward and take out an Italian anti-tank gun position, but they were suffering heavy losses, as Lieutenant H.S. Robertson reported, "At dawn our tanks came up and began fighting their battle right in amongst us, manoeuvring for position and firing while what seemed like every tank and anti-tank gun in the Afrika Korps fired back. Solid shot was ricocheting all over the place and there was H[igh] E[xplosive] too. The whole show was fantastic. Some of our lads had to skin out of their trenches several times to avoid being run over. One Sherman backed towards me. The Tankie saw me, worked round my trench, and stopped a yard or so away. I looked up, and there was a ruddy great gun-barrel hanging over my head. There was one hell of a bang, and showers of sand came down on top of us. The Boche fired back, but missed: we heard the shell go by a few feet away." (Latimer, p. 288)

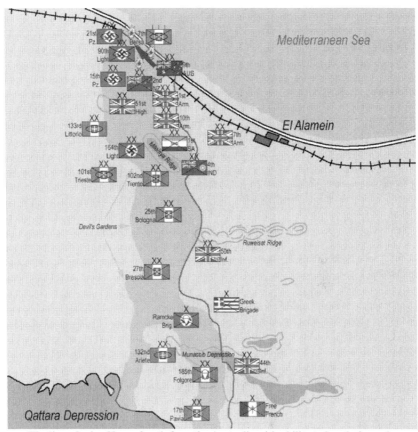

Mediterranean Sea

El Alamein

Devil's Gardens

Ruweisat Ridge

Qattara Depression

Munassib Depression

The lines during November 1 show the Australians' inability to break through.
Although the Australians were unable to break through at the beginning of the operation, over the next few days, the Allies managed to drive a wedge into the Axis positions, and with Rommel's panzer strength dwindling, there were basically no reinforcements at his disposal to plug the hole in his lines. Montgomery later reported, "If the British armour owed any debt to the infantry of the Eighth Army, the debt was paid on November 2 by 9th Armoured in heroism and blood." In the drive forward, the 9th Armoured lost 70 vehicles and more than half of their tank crew of 400 men. When one Allied general asked the 9th Armoured's leader, John Cecil Currie, where his tanks were, Currie pointed to a small group of tanks. When the general responded, "I don't mean your headquarters tanks, I mean your armoured regiments. Where are they?" Currie explained, "There are my armoured regiments…"

By the evening of November 2, Rommel began ordering a withdrawal of his forces, and he sent an aide to deliver a message to Hitler that read, "The army's strength was so exhausted after its ten days of battle that it was not now capable of offering any effective opposition to the enemy's next break-through attempt...With our great shortage of vehicles an orderly withdrawal of the non-motorised forces appeared impossible...In these circumstances we had to reckon, at the least, with the gradual destruction of the army." Despite telling Hitler that the battle was inevitably lost, Rommel received a directive on the afternoon of November 3: "To Field Marshal Rommel. It is with trusting confidence in your leadership and the courage of the German-Italian troops under your command that the German people and I are following the heroic struggle in Egypt. In the situation which you find yourself there can be no other thought but to stand fast, yield not a yard of ground and throw every gun and every man into the battle. Considerable air force reinforcements are being sent to C.-in-C South. The Duce and the Comando Supremo are also making the utmost efforts to send you the means to continue the fight. Your enemy, despite his superiority, must also be at the end of his strength. It would not be the first time in history that a strong will has triumphed over the bigger battalions. As to your troops, you can show them no other road than that to victory or death. Adolf Hitler"

This forced Rommel to stop his order to withdraw and uphold Hitler's order that "you can show no other road than that of victory or death." Late that night, as Rommel grappled with Hitler's orders, he discussed the situation with Major Elmar Warning and reached the conclusion that following Hitler would be suicidal: "If I do obey the Führer's order then there's the danger that my troops won't obey me...The Führrer is crazy." (Latimer, p. 296)

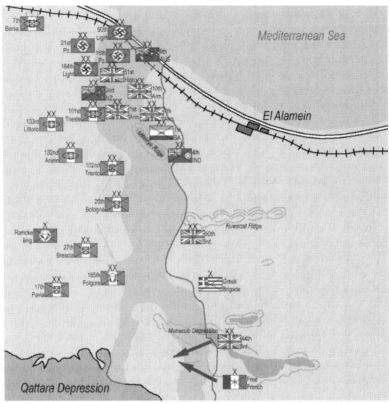

The lines on November 3

Due to Rommel's initial orders and Hitler's response urging the Desert Fox to remand them, Axis forces along the front were in a state of flux. Rommel initially attempted to halt the order to withdraw after it had been in effect for 15 hours and ordered his troops to stand firm, but then he began to waffle over whether to disobey Hitler's directive. Ultimately, he ordered a partial withdrawal to a prepared position behind their lines. Naturally, this left Rommel's troops in a state of confusion and chaos; some troops had already been withdrawn, and then the back and forth movement of transports and carriers that his orders had caused created congestion that made it impossible for effective troop movement. As this was going on, the thin line of German and Italian troops on the front line continued trying to hold off the British advance.

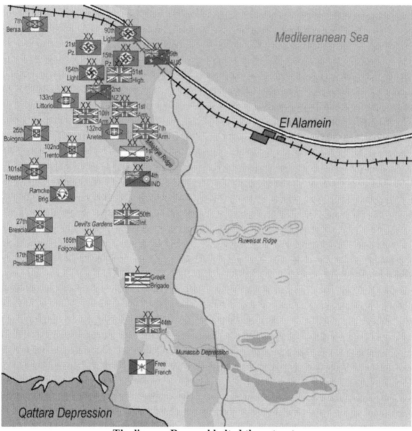

The lines as Rommel halted the retreat.

Meanwhile, the British were preparing for H-Hour, which was set for 1800 hours. As the attack commenced on the night of November 3, British officers in the 152nd Brigade received reports that the Axis forces were retreating. They decided to quickly move forward, where they were repelled by artillery and anti-tank fire, but elsewhere along the line, British forces encountered little resistance as they moved on. One Allied soldier noted, "The more we advanced the more we realized that the Italians did not have much fight on them after putting up a strong resistance to our overwhelming advance and they started surrendering to our lead troops in droves. There was not much action to see but we came across lots of burnt out Italian tanks that had been destroyed by our tanks. I had never seen a battlefield before and the site [sic] of so many dead was sickening."

By the early hours of November 4th, a number of British regiments had made decisive breakthroughs against the Italian divisions in the north, and by daybreak on the 4th, British commanders received news of victory. Rommel reported, "The picture in the early afternoon of the 4th was as follows: powerful enemy armoured forces...had burst a 19-kilometre hole in our front, through which strong bodies of tanks were moving to the west. As a result of this, our forces in the north were threatened with encirclement by enemy formations 20 times their number in tanks ... There were no reserves, as every available man and gun had been put into the line. So now it had come, the thing we had done everything in our power to avoid – our front broken and the fully motorised enemy streaming into our rear. Superior orders could no longer count. We had to save what there was to be saved."

As Allied units chased the Italians across the desert, they had to surrender en masse due to their lack of ammunition and other resources like food and water. A writer for *Time* magazine wrote that for the Italians, It was a terrific letdown by their German allies. They had fought a good fight. In the south, the famed Folgore parachute division fought to the last round of ammunition. Two armoured divisions and a motorised division, which had been interspersed among the German formations, thought they would be allowed to retire gracefully with Rommel's 21st, 15th and 19th light. But even that was denied them. When it became obvious to Rommel that there would be little chance to hold anything between El Daba and the frontier, his Panzers dissolved, disintegrated and turned tail, leaving the Italians to fight a rear-guard action."

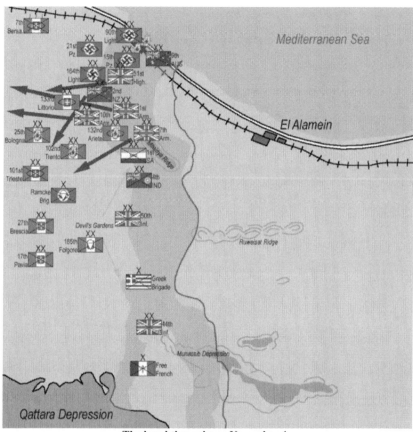

The breakthroughs on November 4.

Mountains of historical analysis and endless reevaluations of strategy and tactics have pointed to Rommel's disregard for the real issues of logistics and supply, and his tendency to thrust forward when the right tactical opportunity presented itself, regardless of how his rear echelon staff and supply chain would keep up. The see-saw nature of the campaign is an indication of how both sides tended to rush to the offensive and then fall back on the defensive as distances outstripped supply and forces became depleted. Montgomery, with a more considered approach, broke this cycle, and with the Germans on the run and the Americans preparing to land on the French North African coast, Montgomery had all of the tools in his hand to mount the spectacular advance that would forge his reputation into the future.

The victory at El Alamein was incredibly decisive for a number of reasons. First, it showed the Allies the importance of a strategy that involved artillery and air-support, and that the Allies were superior to the Axis forces in this regard. Later in the war, as they fought in the European theater, German prisoners of war asked to see the "artillery machine gun" that the Allies had in their arsenal and were shocked to find that the rapid firing artillery that they so feared was not due to new technology but simply the skill of Allied artillery units. Moreover, while Rommel revealed himself to be a master tactician, Alamein, like Stalingrad and the Marne, showed the importance of staying within the army's supply lines and not overextending.

The objective of Operation Torch was to neutralize the Vichy French presence in North Africa, regarded, at that point, as an extension of Axis power, and to encircle German and Italian forces in Tunisia in preparation for an invasion of southern Europe. Under Allied pressure in the east, surviving German and Italian forces were falling back on Tunisia, the point closest to Axis naval and air bases in Sicily and Sardinia.

In the wake of the attack on Pearl Harbor, President Franklin D. Roosevelt had favored an early Allied landing in Europe, but Churchill and other Allied commanders felt the logistical demands of the tactic would simply be too great at that point in the war. An Allied advance into "the soft underbelly" of Europe would have a better chance of succeeding if it were mounted from North Africa under conditions of victory in that theater. Bearing in mind the reversal of Axis fortunes in the preceding weeks, the time was certainly ripe.

At the onset of the war, Hitler had not applied much importance to North Africa as a theater, and he was, therefore, reluctant to commit resources to it. He regarded the southern Mediterranean as an Italian responsibility, preferring to commit German resources to Europe, and Russia in particular. Upon the German occupation of France early in the war and the establishment of the collaborationist Vichy government, the Germans agreed not to occupy Vichy France directly, having cautiously assumed French forces and colonial administrations loyal to Vichy would offer an effective buffer. With North Africa and southern France in compliant hands and with Spanish neutrality, there seemed no immediate cause to engage German forces in North Africa. The Italian defeat forced the German High Command to revise this policy somewhat, but even then, Hitler did not appear to recognize the strategic importance of North Africa, nor did he acknowledge the obvious potential of the boot of Italy as an avenue of Allied re-entry into Europe.

The question of where, precisely, the Vichy French in North Africa stood was central to Allied planning. General Dwight D. Eisenhower was appointed the overall commander of Allied ground, naval, and air forces (Commanding General, European Theatre of Operations), and it was he who was charged with devising the practical logistics of mounting an amphibious American operation directly from the United States.[79] It could not be determined how the Vichy French authorities—or French forces in the region—would respond to an Allied invasion, and this lay at the heart of Allied concerns. There was also some uncertainty at precisely how the Spanish fascist dictator General Francisco Franco would react. He might, on the one hand, sense the general flow of events and retain Spanish neutrality, but should he counter by bringing Spain into the war on the German side, he would be in a strong position to thwart, or at least complicate, Allied plans. Spain controlled a portion of Morocco (Ceuta) and was certainly positioned to compromise British Gibraltar, which was, of course, the key to Allied naval control of the western Mediterranean.

---

[79] The Allied Naval Commander of the Expeditionary Force would be Admiral Sir Andrew Cunningham, and his deputy was Vice-Admiral Sir Bertram Ramsay, who would plan the amphibious landings.

American troops on a landing craft in late 1942

Eisenhower

At Roosevelt's request, the U.S. *chargé d'affaires* to the Vichy government, Robert D. Murphy, was dispatched to Algeria to sound out the local French. The French commander, Admiral Jean François Darlan, was a Vichy appointee and known to be pro-Nazi, so he would no doubt oppose Allied forces, despite a junior command that was anti-German in general. The question was how Vichy French forces on the ground would respond to a command to resist an Allied landing. Although it was generally acknowledged that they would resist, it was hoped this would not be with any particular determination or commitment. What had been indicated was that French naval deployments were likely to pose a greater risk than land forces, which, in the end, proved to be the case. Allied commanders concluded French Vichy forces were unlikely to fight, and as a consequence, U.S. troops were instructed not to engage the French unless they themselves came under attack.

Murphy

Darlan

Over the question of precisely where and when to stage the amphibious landings, Eisenhower grappled with his own planning committees and Allied command in London, eventually agreeing to three landings in Algeria and Morocco, the furthest east being Algiers. His own preference was for a landing—or a series of landings—much closer to the frontier between Algeria and Tunisia, shortening the distance for an expeditionary force to travel in order to achieve the objective of closing in on Axis forces besieged in the territory. The argument against this was that the reduced but still powerful Axis forces in Tunisia would oppose the landings, while inexperienced American troops would be forced to fight to gain a bridgehead.

In the end, Eisenhower accepted an Allied plan that envisaged three amphibious task forces simultaneously seizing key ports and airports in Morocco and Algeria, primarily targeting the cities of Casablanca on the Atlantic coast of Morocco, Oran in western Algeria, and the capital city of Algiers itself. The Western Task Force, earmarked for the Moroccan landings, comprised American units under the command of Major General George S. Patton, with Rear-Admiral Henry Kent Hewitt commanding naval operations. The units engaged in this branch of the operation comprised the U.S. 2nd Armored Division and the U.S. 3rd and 9th Infantry Divisions, some 35,000 troops in total, transported across the Atlantic from the United States in a convoy of over 100 ships.

The Central Task Force, directed at Oran, comprised some 18,500 troops of the U.S. 1st Infantry Division and the U.S. 1st Armored Division. This convoy sailed from Britain under the command of American Major General Lloyd Fredendall, with naval forces commanded by British Commodore Thomas Troubridge. The Eastern Task Force, intended for Algiers, was commanded by British Lieutenant-General Kenneth Anderson, and it consisted of a brigade of the British 78th and the U.S. 34th Infantry Divisions, along with two British commando units (No. 1 and No. 6 Commandos), totalling 20,000 troops. Ground forces during the landing phase were to be commanded by U.S. Major General Charles W. Ryder, commanding general of the 34th Division, while naval forces were commanded by British Vice-Admiral Sir Harold Burrough. American supporting air operations were under the command of Major General James Doolittle, under the overall command of General Patton. British air operations fell under the command of Air Marshal Sir William Welsh.

The campaign commenced at dawn with the landing of the Western Task Force on November 8, 1942, at three points on the Moroccan coast: Safi to the south of Casablanca, the coastal settlement of Fedala to the north, with the largest landing, comprised of some 19,000 men, at the main port of Casablanca, Mehdiya/Quneitra. In the hope that French forces occupying the latter would comply, no preliminary bombardment was ordered, although French troops did indeed respond with artillery, and U.S. casualties were taken. Nonetheless, the landing was nonetheless executed successfully.

At Safi, chosen to land the Western Task Force's medium tanks, some minimal French sniper activity was noted, but the landing went ahead largely unopposed. By November 10, the western operation was complete, and U.S. armor and infantry began to move up the coast to join the action in Casablanca, where the landing was somewhat delayed due to navigational difficulties. The first wave was met by French artillery before a bombardment by Allied carriers offshore, and Allied air interdiction cleared the way. A sprawling and indecisive naval battle, the Battle of Casablanca, was fought between French and U.S. ships during November 8-16, resulting in the destruction of a French cruiser, six destroyers, and six submarines. Two U.S. destroyers were also damaged.

The Central Task Force fared better. The arrival of a French naval convoy on the scene as Allied minesweepers were clearing a route in caused a brief hiatus, and landing craft were damaged thanks to the unexpected shallowness of the water, but on the whole, three successful landings were executed. A detachment of the U.S. 1st Ranger Battalion neutralized French artillery positions, the only significant action being a French naval interdiction halting an effort to land U.S. infantry directly to the quayside in order to forestall any possible effort by the French to destroy the harbour facilities. Two Allied ships were damaged by French warships in harbour, most of which were destroyed in a later attempt to break out.

A U.S. Air Force airborne operation was mounted parallel to the landing of the Central Task Force, aimed at the capture of local airports, the first ever major airborne operation mounted by the United States.

In the meantime, the Eastern Task Force, directed toward Algiers, was preceded by an orchestrated French Resistance coup within the city, the capital of Vichy French North Africa, where key targets were seized including the telephone exchange, radio station, and governor's house. At the same time, Murphy attempted to negotiate official French cooperation but failed, and the landings went ahead against very light French resistance.

The Algiers Operation was split across three beaches, two to the west of the city and one to the east. To the west, elements of the U.S. 34th Infantry Division and the British 11th Brigade Group, drawn from the 78th Infantry Division, made landfall under the command of U.S. Major General Charles W. Ryder. The middle landing was comprised of a U.S. 168th Regimental Combat Team, taken from the 34th Infantry Division and supported by the British 6th Commando and most of the 1st Commando. To the east of Algiers, elements of the U.S. 39th Regimental Combat Team landed alongside the U.S. 34th Division, supported by the five remaining troops from the British 1st Commando. A floating reserve was provided by the British 36th Brigade Group, taken from the British 78th Division. All French coastal batteries had been put out of action by the French Resistance. In one instance, the landings were warmly welcomed by French troops.

The only notable action in this sector took place in the port of Algiers itself, where, in Operation Terminal, two British destroyers made the attempt to land a party of U.S. Army Rangers directly onto the quayside in order to prevent the French from destroying port facilities and scuttling their ships. The landed troops, however, pushed quickly inland, and the city was surrendered to the Allies at 1800h.

On November 10, two days after the combined operation, General Darlan, the commander of the Vichy forces, made a deal with the Allies and Eisenhower in particular, offering him recognition as French "High Commissioner" of North Africa in exchange for ordering a formal halt to all French resistance. French troops still at large immediately quit the fight, linking up with the Allies for the most part.

When news of this reached Hitler, he ordered an immediate German occupation of Vichy and sought to reinforce Axis positions in Tunisia, while in Toulon, where the French Fleet had been headquartered, every important ship was scuttled. The French *Armée d'Afrique*, the North African arm of the French Armed Forces, immediately sided with the Allies, providing a significant addition to available Allied forces.

The writing was on the wall. The Eighth Army, under the command of General Montgomery, was closing in on Tunisia from the east, and General Patton, having consolidated and organized the combined Allied Expeditionary Force, began to move in from the east as well.

Patton

The Eastern Front in 1943

On January 21st, the Russians finally broke through the German lines when the Russian 57th Army forced open a three-mile gap in the German defense. The German soldiers there had run out of ammunition, and the lack of fuel meant there was no way to transport more to them from another sector. On January 22, General Paulus sent a message to Hitler asking for permission to surrender. Hitler refused, and when Paulus argued that his men were nearly out of ammunition, Hitler again told him that he needed to continue fighting.

On January 24, the chief of operations from the 6th Army contacted von General Manstein to update him on their situation: "Attacks in undiminished violence are being made against the entire western front which has been fighting its way back eastward to the Gorodische area since the morning of the 24th in order to form a hedgehog in the tractor works. In the southern part of Stalingrad the western front along the city outskirts held on to the western and southern edges of Minima until 4 P.M. Local penetrations were made in that sector. The Volga and the northeastern fronts are unchanged. The conditions in the city are frightful, where twenty thousand unattended wounded are seeking shelter among the ruins. With them are about the same number of starved and frostbitten men and stragglers, most of them without weapons, which they lost in the fighting. Heavy artillery is pounding the whole city area. Last resistance along the city outskirts in the southern part of Stalingrad will be offered on January 25 under the leadership of energetic generals fighting in the line and gallant officers around whom a few men still capable of fighting have rallied. The tractor works may possibly hold out a little longer." (Hoyt, p.264)

As Russian forces moved into the city, they went from house to house, where many German soldiers simply surrendered. On January 31, Paulus surrendered as Russian forces neared the 6th Army headquarters. Not surprisingly, the Russians treated German prisoners as poorly as the Germans had treated theirs. When the Battle of Stalingrad ended in February 1943, 91,000 soldiers were captured by Russian forces, and of these, tens of thousands died of hunger and typhus. When these prisoners were later moved to prison camps, thousands more died. In all, when the last of the German survivors were allowed to return home in 1955, only 5,000 survivors remained.

German prisoners in Stalingrad.

A Soviet soldier follows a German prisoner.

Paulus and his chief of staff taken prisoner.

In addition to the destruction of the German 6th Army, the Hungarian, Romanian and Italian armies that had been sent to the Eastern Front to fight under Hitler were also destroyed in the fighting. It was at Stalingrad that the German alliance was undone, and after losing there, German forces were never able to match the Soviet Red Army, which continued to grow in manpower and machinery. The total costs of the engagement at Stalingrad are staggering; there were between 500,000 and 800,000 German casualties, while the Soviets suffered an estimated

1,129,619 casualties.

The center of the city of Stalingrad after the battle.

Wreckage in Stalingrad after the battle.

Soviets disposing of German dead after the battle.
Stalingrad proved to be Germany's high water-mark against the Soviet Union, and for the rest of the war, they were in a constant state of retreat. As the Red Army chased them out and retook more and more of the countryside, they were appalled by the treatment both soldiers and civilians had received at the German's hands. Over 4 million Soviet prisoners of war had died of starvation, sickness and other forms of mistreatment, and as part of the "Final Solution," the Germans had also killed all the Jews they captured, as well as civilians of any other ethnic group Hitler didn't care for. It seems that their thought process was that the more Soviet people they killed, the fewer they'd have to deal with later. It has been estimated that the invading Nazis completely razed over 10,000 Russian villages to the ground, slaughtering all the inhabitants they could get their hands on.

As word of the German genocide spread throughout the Soviet Union, it had a galvanizing rather than weakening effect. Instead of surrendering to the invading forces in hopes of receiving fair treatment, the Soviet peasants would hide in the woods when they heard of an approaching German army. From there, they would organize guerrilla groups that would strike at the Germans from all angles, picking off sentries, disrupting supply lines and spreading chaos. Likewise, the Russian soldier knew that he had a better chance of survival in the field of battle than if they were taken prisoner, so they were more than willing to fight to the death.

A Soviet propaganda poster depicting Hitler, Mussolini, Goering and Goebbels retreating. The poster's caption reads, "Death to the German Occupiers!" The words on the tank's red flag say, "Forward to the west!"

Ultimately, Leningrad's delivery would come in the aftermath of the Battle of Stalingrad. As the fighting at Stalingrad reached its climax, Stalin ordered another attempt to liberate Leningrad, which by this time was down to one-fifth of its pre-war population. This new offensive was codenamed Operation *Iskra*, and it began with a two-hour barrage that included 4,500 guns, which paved the way for the Soviets to push their tanks forward across the Neva

River on pontoons. By January 12, 1943, Soviet troops had liberated the town of Shlisselburg, and residents of Leningrad became excited by the possibility of lifting the siege. One civilian noted:

> "The entire city is waiting... Any moment now! People are saying that our fronts – the Leningrad and Volkhov – have joined up. Officially nothing is known...
>
> Somewhere guns are booming. The all-clear has just sounded. Ordinary siege life goes on, but everyone is waiting. Nobody says anything – nobody dares to, in case a wrong word gets to wherever our fate is being decided, and changes it all. I'm perplexed and bewildered. I can't find a place for myself. I try to write and can't." (Reid, p. 374)

However, after the initial breakthrough of January 1943, little progress was made around Leningrad. Instead, in the early part of 1943, the focus of Soviet efforts centered on the center and southern portions of the Eastern Front, where Stalin hoped to build on his victory at Stalingrad. Rostov-on-Don was liberated in February, Kharkov was liberated in July, and after a great tank battle, Kursk was safe by the end of August.

The Soviet victory at Stalingrad came after the Allies' victory in North Africa in late 1942, and by the early months of 1943, the Allies looked to press their advantage in the Pacific and Western Europe. The United States was firmly pushing the Japanese back across the Pacific, while the Americans and British plotted a major invasion somewhere in Western Europe to relieve the pressure on the Soviets. On September 3, 1943, the Russians gained more relief along the Eastern Front when the Allies opened a second front and drew German attention with an amphibious invasion of Sicily, marking the beginning of operations in Italy.

In late September 1943, German troops all along the Eastern Front were in a general retreat, and German commanders tried to convince Hitler to withdraw from Leningrad. They argued that the retreat among forces in the south and center were leaving German troops in the north dangerously exposed to a renewed attack by the Soviets. Hitler ended up partially agreeing to a retreat by allowing his northern troops to withdraw to the "Panther Line," a defensive works built behind the Narva River. This shortened the northern front, but the ring around Leningrad remained in place.

In the fall of 1943, the Red Army liberated Smolensk and then moved on to Kiev, and meanwhile, Soviet General Leonid Govorov began plans for a final liberation of Leningrad: three Russian armies, whose combined size was three times larger than the German Army Group North, would converge on Leningrad. The attack began on January 14, 1944 with a heavy bombardment of German positions, and the Germans were quickly overwhelmed, finally completing the liberation of Leningrad after nearly 900 days.

The liberation of the city brought a mix of joy and sadness for the city's residents. As 12 year old Irina Bogdanova recalled after the announcement of liberation, "Then after a few minutes, in a corner of the dormitory, someone started crying. Then in another corner, another child, until we were all crying. And none of us wanted any breakfast or lunch. Not until suppertime were the teachers able to coax us into the dining room. It was because we suddenly realized that nobody was waiting for us. Living in the children's home we hadn't thought about this, we'd just been waiting for the war to be over. Only with victory did we have to come to terms with life again, with all that we had lost." (Reid, p. 391)

Olga Fridenberg mourned her mother following the city's liberation: "Now I have so much time, I feel cast away in it. All around me it stretches away into infinity. I want to fill it by doing things, by moving about in space, but nothing helps…Only late in the evening do my spirits revive somewhat – another day is over. Relieved, I lie down and for seven hours am blissfully unaware of time…waking up in the morning is frightful – that first moment of consciousness after the night. I am here. I am in time again." (Reid, p. 391).

When the war finally ended, the city's residents yearned for a return to normal life, but Stalin's rebuilding efforts showed that there would be a new normal, especially the fact that Communism, which some had regarded as a temporary thing, was now acknowledged to be here to stay. Living standards did slowly improve in the late 1940s and early 1950s, but this period also saw renewed repression by the Soviet government, especially in targeting Leningrad's intelligentsia. Even some of the city's Communist party leaders were caught up in purges, and a number being executed in the "Leningrad Affair" between 1949-1951, during which 69 Party officials were executed or exiled and 145 of their relatives faced the same fate. As Dmitri Likhachev wrote, Leningrad would face a "siege within" lasted nearly 40 more years of Soviet rule.

The military actions of previous years set up the conditions resulting in the Battle of Kursk in July 1943. Following the utter devastation wreaked on the unprepared Red Army in 1941 during Operation Barbarossa, the Germans encountered steadily increasing Soviet pressure. A sort of seesaw alternation of offensives ensued, in which the Germans went on the attack during the summer months and the Soviets counterattacked in winter.

Hitler's "Fall Blau" offensive in 1942 aimed to seize the Caucasus oil fields, but failed to do so. Instead, stripping the rest of the Wehrmacht lines of units led to the encirclement and destruction of the 6th Army at Stalingrad. The Soviets carried out a strong counteroffensive in southern Russia and the Ukraine during the winter of 1942-1943. The Red Army seized the city of Kharkov, then lost it again on March 14th, 1943.

Though the Wehrmacht eventually contained the Soviets, the attack created a massive salient centered on Kursk. A pause followed as the spring "Rasputitsa" – the Russian thaw, which turns dirt roads and fields alike into seas of sticky mud a yard deep or more – brought both armies to an effective halt.

The Kursk salient, jutting from Soviet into German territory, measured 74.5 by 118 miles, or around 8,700 square miles, approximately the same size as the entire U.S. state of New Jersey. Containing huge numbers of Soviet soldiers and tanks, it made an extremely tantalizing target for a battle of encirclement, such as those that devastated the Red Army in 1941 and to a lesser degree in 1942. If the Germans could "pinch off" the salient at the base, the Soviet war effort might suffer a sufficient blow for Stalin to seek peace.

The attack on the Kursk Salient – codenamed Operation "Zitadelle" or Citadel – also represented a slave raid on a giant scale. With serious manpower issues, the Germans needed slaves to increase factory production and make large numbers of the new, advanced tanks and aircraft their scientists developed. Hitler hoped Citadel would yield hordes of prisoners to man the Third Reich's factories.

The coming offensive provoked a surprising amount of argument in the high commands of both the Wehrmacht (OKW) and the Red Army (STAVKA). Stalin wanted another bold offensive, and Deputy Commander-in-Chief Marshal Georgi Zhukov and Chief of General Staff Marshal Aleksandr Vasilevsky found themselves called upon to muster all their courage and oppose their dictator's wishes. Zhukov declared:

it will be better if we wear the enemy out in defensive action, destroy his tanks, and then, taking in fresh reserves, by going to an all-out offensive, we will finish off the enemy's main grouping (Healy, 1992, 10).

At the STAVKA meeting on April 12th, 1943, the two Marshals held their ground against Stalin – an act of considerable valor in itself. Where Hitler might demote a recalcitrant general in a fit of pique, Stalin ordered men shot or sent to labor camps for similar daring. However, the Soviet dictator listened, perhaps impressed by the two men's boldness. Zhukov also carefully wove promises of offensives into the chiefly defensive plan, and his own reputation for extreme aggression doubtless gave weight to his words.

Georgi Zhukov in 1941

Stalin also possessed intelligence from several foreign sources indicating German interest in attacking at Kursk. The German communist Rudolf Roessler, remaining out of Hitler's reach in Switzerland, obtained swift, accurate information on Wehrmacht decisions through his still-unknown OKW contacts, the "Lucy Ring," and passed them on to Stalin. The "Cambridge Five," including the infamous Kim Philby and the "Fifth Man" John Cairncross, confirmed this data with intelligence stolen from the British ULTRA program. Stalin disregarded this information until Zhukov confirmed it, however.

Stalin agreed to let the Soviet generals meet the Germans on the defensive, turning the Kursk salient into a gigantic fortress on which the Wehrmacht would hopefully dash itself to pieces. With their supreme leader's approval finally secured, the Soviet commanders set about their task with thoroughness and gusto.

The Soviets eventually committed ten armies to the Kursk region, though they did not deploy all of them immediately. The north flank of the salient, designated the Central Front, faced the German staging area and rail-head at Orel, and fell under the command of the tall, powerfully-built Marshal Konstantin Rokossovsky. The southern half of the salient, commanded by Marshal Nikolai Vatutin, bore the name of the Voronezh Front. The Soviets anchored the Voronezh Front on Oboyan and Prokhorovka – small points on the map soon to become immortally famous in history.

Nikolai Vatunin

Behind the two main fronts, to the east, lay the Steppe Front with reserve and counterattacking forces under the former lumberjack Ivan Konev, who established a formidable reputation for skilled military deception and who proved himself the equal in brutality of any Einsatzgruppen commander with his evident relish in massacring thousands of German POWs.

The Soviets set about building a triple layer of echeloned defenses around much of the Kursk salient's perimeter, featuring every kind of defensive work that time and resources permitted them to use. Anti-tank ditches, "Pakfronts" of dug-in anti-tank guns, barbed wire entanglements, bunkers, firing pits, and every other kind of prepared position soon formed a belt 30 miles deep around the salient's rim. The Red Army used not only its soldiers but approximately 300,000 drafted civilians and tens of thousands of POWs to build the defenses. Most of the civilian work crews consisted of women.

Guessing the heaviest Wehrmacht attacks would fall at the base of the salient in an effort to cut it off with a pincer movement, Vatutin and Rokossovsky built their strongest defenses there. Huge minefields covered much of the landscape, along with obstacles intended to channel the Germans into prepared kill zones. The Russians set up and preemptively sighted in vast concentrations of artillery on the most likely assault routes. The Red Army offered cash premiums of 200 to 1,500 rubles to men who actually knocked out Wehrmacht tanks, with the amount varying by method.

Since the Soviets planned immediate counterattacks once the Wehrmacht attack subsided, they also created a whole-new formation. This formation, the tank army, originated with General Pavel Rotmistrov, who presented the idea first to Lieutenant General Nikita Khrushchev, then to Stalin himself:

I gave the tankers' opinion that it was necessary to organize and improve the mass employment of tanks, for which it was necessary to create tank armies of   homogenous composition, and to reexamine their use on the battlefield. […] Stalin   received   me   and listened to me attentively. He then approved all my proposals.   Several   days   later,   the decision to create the 5th Guards Tank Army took place   (Zamulin, 2010, 47).

Of course, formation of the tank armies on short notice proved difficult and some were filled out with obsolete early war Soviet tanks or with flimsy M3 Lee light tanks from America, known by the grim but clever nickname of "the Coffin for Seven Brothers." Each tank army needed approximately 5,000 trucks to support its mobility, including bringing up supplies of 600 tons of fuel daily. Without the tens of thousands of U.S. Lend-Lease trucks available to the USSR in 1943, Rotmistrov's tank armies would have proved impossible. Even with this aid, a severe shortage of trucks existed.

The M3 Lee

The tank armies took part in Kursk, particularly in the famous Battle of Prokhorovka. They also led the counter-punch once Operation Citadel foundered. The Germans also possessed formidable fortifications, including barbed wire, minefields, and improvised bunkers, designed to soak up the initial push of any Red Army attack and leave it prey to the mobile German divisions.

Hitler's anticipation of another offensive victory did not represent as far-fetched an expectation as it might appear. Though the Red Army's fighting and leadership qualities improved rapidly in late 1942 and into 1943, the Wehrmacht still repeatedly demonstrated its superiority and capacity to smash even extremely powerful Russian formations through use of maneuver and flexible, aggressive tactics.

Exactly one year prior, on July 5th, 1942, Zhukov launched an attack by 700 tanks near Orel, only to see his assault obliterated by the Germans in a huge tank battle that cost his forces 500 armored fighting vehicles. The indomitable Walther Model – who once made even Hitler quail with a frosty glare – crushed Operation Mars, a Soviet attack against the Rzhev Salient, in November 1942, encircling the Russian offensive forces and reducing no less than 1,800 of their 2,300 tanks to burning hulks.

Walter Model

In light of such triumphs, victory over an opponent who outnumbered the Germans just 1.3:1 in some areas and a maximum of 2:1 (in certain types of aircraft) in the Kursk Salient appeared plausible to the Fuhrer and some of his generals.

A number of experienced Wehrmacht commanders demurred, however. A see-saw debate continued through the first half of 1943 between Hitler and the generals who favored an offensive on one side, and those who opposed an attack on the other. Hitler's will obviously would prevail, but such excellent commanders as Heinz Guderian, Erich von Manstein, and Hans von Kluge continued to argue against the attack.

Heinz Guderian

Guderian, a famous panzer leader, suggested concentrating all available units into a single force and attacking just one side of the salient with maximum concentration of force. The northern side, supported by the rail-head at Orel, provided an obvious choice for this move. Erich von Manstein, an extremely capable general with a string of victories to his credit, preferred luring the Soviets out of their prepared positions in the Kursk Salient, and, once their offensive drove deep into German lines and overextended itself, pinching it off and wiping it out in detail.

Erich von Manstein

On April 15th, the Fuhrer proclaimed:

This attack is of decisive importance. It must be a quick and conclusive success. It must give us the initiative for this spring and summer … Every officer, every soldier must be convinced of the decisive importance of this attack. The victory of Kursk must shine like a beacon to the world (Kershaw, 2009, 636).

Nevertheless, to the rising distress of even those generals in favor of it, the offensive suffered multiple postponements. Hitler moved the date from May to June and finally to an unspecified moment in July. The German defeat in North Africa made rapidity essential before American and British troops reached Europe. However, the Fuhrer wanted to wait until his engineers and factories finished a number of new fighting vehicles.

Hitler relied on the deployment of a several new and "secret" weapons systems to tip the scales in favor of the Wehrmacht. These included the formidable Panzer V Panther heavy tank, the Panzer VI Tiger, and the enormous Sd. Kfz. 184 Ferdinand, also dubbed the Elefant. The Brummbär infantry support gun, a massive self-propelled gun with a short-barreled 15cm howitzer for armament, also debuted during Citadel.

The performance of the Tigers in their first-ever action against Soviet T-34 tanks at Tomarovka on March 13th boosted German hopes for the new weapons system still higher, as Erhard Raus later recounted:

our Tigers took up well-camouflaged positions and made full use of the longer range of their 88mm main guns. Within a short time they knocked out sixteen T-34s [...] and when the others turned about, the Tigers pursued the fleeing Russians and destroyed eighteen more tanks. Our 88mm armor-piercing shells had such a terrific impact that they ripped off the turrets of many T-34s and hurled them several yards. The German soldiers [...] immediately coined the phrase: "The T-34 tips its hat whenever it meets a Tiger" (Raus, 2005, 191).

Hitler dithered and delayed, which enabled a massive Soviet buildup in the Kursk Salient. Offsetting this advantage, the Wehrmacht also gained additional time to move men, materiel, and supplies into Operation Citadel's staging areas. Each unit shifted the region committed the Wehrmacht more irrevocably to a "showdown" near Kursk.

The Third Reich's supreme leader only decided on the exact date for Citadel's launch – July 5th, 1943 – on July 1st. Nevertheless, the excellence of Soviet spying ensured that Stalin, the STAVKA, and the field commanders knew this date within 24 hours of Hitler issuing his top-secret command, totally denying the Wehrmacht either strategic or tactical surprise. Though the Germans attempted to conceal the date – for example, by having Erich von Manstein participate in an award ceremony with the Romanian leader Ion Antonescu on July 3rd in Bucharest, then board his headquarters train surreptitiously and immediately journey towards the front – their deceptions failed completely.

The Germans and Soviets mustered the maximum number of men, tanks, other vehicles, and aircraft available for the battle of Kursk. Both the OKW and the STAVKA knew the encounter constituted the main and decisive action of summer 1943. Its outcome would determine the shape of the "Ostfront" conflict in 1944 also. Therefore, neither side held anything back when mustering their armies for the crisis.

Walther Model led the northern force, directed against Rokossovsky's Central Front. Model's force, the 9th Army, included 800 tanks, with only 45 Tigers. The Germans deployed the 83 available Elefant (Ferdinand) tank destroyers in this sector, supported by Brummbär self-propelled howitzers and Borgward IV radio-controlled demolition tanks.

A Group of German Soldiers at Kursk
Model received no Panzer V Panthers and his best tanks consisted of Panzer IV Ausf. H

vehicles, outgunning the T-34s but slower due to their gasoline engines (as opposed to the vigorous diesel engine of the T-34). The 9th Army also included 196 Sturmgeschutz StuG Ausf. G self-propelled guns (SPGs) and 31 Sturmhaubitze StuH 42 self-propelled howitzers.

Air support for the 9th Army came from 686 combat aircraft of Luftflotte 6, including many excellent Focke Wulf Fw-190A fighters, commanded by Robert von Greim. Artillery support consisted of 3,630 tubes plus 165 of the infamous Nebelwerfer rocket launchers, variously dubbed the "Screaming Mimi," the "Howling Heinie," and the "Moaning Minnie." Though Model commanded 15 infantry divisions as part of the 9th Army, only eight of these saw action during Citadel. Total manpower in all branches stood at approximately 335,000 (Frankson, 2004, 18).

Rokossovsky, by contrast, deployed 711,575 men (both combat troops and non-combat support personnel) on the Central Front. His armored forces consisted of 1,785 tanks and self-propelled guns (SPGs). Of these, 456 comprised the 2nd Tank Army, led by Lieutenant General Aleksei Rodin. T-34/76s made up approximately 7 out of 10 of Rokossovsky's tanks, with the remainder T-70 light tanks, the latter practically useless against Panzer IIIs and IVs. Rokossovsky also had around 40 KV-1 heavy tanks.

Panzer III and Panzer IVs

The Soviets fielded a few SU-152 tank destroyers – the famous "Zveroboi" or "Beast Fighter," so called because it combated "Panthers" and "Tigers" – at Kursk. The most common SPG, however, consisted of the SU-76, a lightly-armored, open-topped tank destroyer known by a number of unflattering nicknames due to its vulnerability and the high lethality of serving in these machines. The Soviet soldiers called the SU-76 the "Suka," or "Bitch," as well as the "Golozhopy Ferdinand," or "Bare-Ass Ferdinand."

12,453 artillery tubes, anti-tank guns, and mortars supported the Central Front, together with 1,050 aircraft. Rokossovsky's force also mustered 41 rifle divisions, many of them close to their notional strength of 9,600 men apiece. These soldiers showed far higher morale and possessed much better equipment and training than the untrained and often unarmed unfortunates sent to their doom by Stalin in 1941 and early 1942.

In the south, Vatutin and his Voronezh Front found themselves pitted against Erich von

Manstein and a stronger Wehrmacht force. Manstein's Army Group South

Luftflotte 4 supported Army Group South

The first moves near Orel occurred after night fell on July 4th when thousands of German sappers crawled forward into the gigantic minefields guarding the approaches to the Central Front. Probing carefully at the ground and lifting out the mines they located to clear lanes through the extensive minefields, these men proved their outstanding professionalism by clearing one mine per minute per man for hours. By early morning on July 5th, they had prepared routes through the minefields for the attacking vehicles and infantry, marking these with short stakes and tape.

Zhukov, knowing the exact hour of the German deployment, ordered a preemptive artillery barrage on the suspected Wehrmacht mustering positions at 2:20 AM on the 5th. Thousands of guns opened fire, lighting up the sky with their muzzle flashes and shaking the earth with a furious, staccato barrage of explosions. The Soviet gunners hit almost no Germans, but managed to destroy almost all the stakes and route tape laid by the Wehrmacht sappers, erasing nearly every sign of the lanes through the minefields.

The intensity of Russian artillery fire, despite its poor aim, prompted Model to order a 2.5-hour delay in the attack while German artillery engaged in counterbattery fire. The Soviets' excellent artillery outranged that of the Wehrmacht, however, and only the frontline artillery batteries lay within reach of the Germans' lighter guns.

Accordingly, Luftflotte 6 sent forward their massed formations of medium bombers and Stuka dive-bombers to pound Russian defensive positions and batteries. Focke Wulf FW-190A fighters screened these vulnerable aircraft, and soon engaged an aggressive counterattack by the Soviet 16th Air Army.

Rather than enjoying full air superiority, the Germans found themselves plunged into an aerial struggle as ferocious and uncertain as the battle unfolding on the ground. Lieutenant General Sergei Rudenko botched the deployment of his brave pilots and their improved-quality aircraft by sending them in "penny packets" rather than immense formations, however. During 2,088 sorties, Luftflotte 6 shot down 100 Soviet aircraft (83 of them fighters) at a cost of 25 of their own aircraft (Forczyk, 2014, 49).

Sergei Rudenko

Model, a brilliant defensive general, proved himself somewhat less acute while on the offensive. Instead of a rapid *Schwerpunkt* with his panzers, followed up by mechanized infantry, the Third Reich general opened his attack with infantry on foot, deployed in sequential fashion that reduced their impact even further. The Soviet 13th Army fought back fiercely, while the Germans negotiated a landscape rendered deadly by the 503,000 anti-tank and anti-personnel mines the Soviets laid along the salient's northern face.

The 78th Assault Division led the attack, a unit at full strength and including many experienced veterans. The first 45 Elefant (Ferdinand) tank destroyers crawled forward in support, "brewing up" Soviet tanks with lethally accurate rounds from their long-barreled 88mm guns. The 78th Assault Division took heavy losses, however, and nearly found itself brought to a complete halt at Hill 257.7:

> Studded with bunkers supported by dug-in tanks, the Russian position was a nightmare version of the kinds of defenses Americans would encounter two years later on Okinawa. It quickly won the nickname "Panzer Hill" […] The Ferdinands went forward anyway. Enough of them reached the defenses, and enough infantry managed to follow, that the hill fell to close assault—a polite euphemism for a series of vicious fights in which bayonets were civilized weapons (Showalter, 2013, 63).

The desperate struggle of the 78th Assault Division carried it forward only 3 miles by nightfall, a trivial distance compared to the number of miles to Kursk itself, the target of the drive. However, greater success attended the trio of panzer divisions and four infantry divisions Model sent towards the strongpoint of Ponyri. Led by Major General Mortimer von Kessel, the 20th Panzer Division blasted their way forward in the van, moving behind a rolling barrage of artillery fire. They took the town of Bobrik and extended the 9th Army's advance to five miles on the first day.

Nearby, the 45 Tiger tanks provided to 9th Army wreaked havoc out of proportion to their numbers, nearly succeeding in reaching the rear of the Soviet 81st Rifle Division and running amok there. The massive, boxy tanks engaged infantry, bunkers, and AT guns just as often as enemy tanks, using high explosive (HE) shells to deal with these threats.

In the case of towed anti-tank guns, the Tigers often conserved ammunition by simply running them over and crushing them under their treads. In some instances, Soviet infantry with no anti-tank weapons stood their ground against the steel giants with suicidal courage, achieving nothing except raising the levels of carnage higher, as a Tiger commander described:

> Red soldiers appeared in front of the tank. We drove directly into a defensive position. "Coax [i.e. 'coaxial machine-gun']!" The brown-clad figures rose in masses, kneeling and standing, firing with their machine-pistols and rifles against our steel armor. A few pulled back. […] They could not stop us. Those who were not cut down by the bursts of our machine gun fire were run over (Lochmann, 2008, 144).

The Germans forced their way approximately five miles deep into Rokossovsky's Central Front on the first day of Operation Citadel, creating a salient 9 miles wide in the base of the Kursk Salient. This effort came at high cost, however, particularly to Model's already scarce infantry. As firefights and artillery bombardment continued throughout the night, the Germans retrieved and repaired as many damaged tanks and tank destroyers as possible, preparing for the renewed struggle on the next day.

During the night, Rokossovsky decided to commit much of Rodin's 2nd Tank Army and the independent 19th Tank Corps to a counterattack early on July 6th. Motivated mainly by fear of his dictator – Rokossovsky "still remembered having his teeth smashed out by the NKVD while in prison and had no intention of giving Stalin a chance to condemn him for inactivity" (Forczyk,

2014, 51) – hectored Rodin into an ill-advised piecemeal attack against German panzers standing on the defensive.

Konstantin Rokossovsky

Hampered by their own infantry and defensive positions, the first elements of the 2nd Tank Army finally approached Bobrik at 10:40 AM. The T-34s rolled forward across over a mile of open ground towards a village where dozens of Panzer VI Tiger tanks lurked. Under a light overcast with rain showers falling, the 107th Tank Brigade under Polkovnik Nikolai Teliakov advanced bravely towards the silent village.

Suddenly, the thunderous whipcrack sound of long-barreled 88mm tank guns ripped through the air. Tank after tank slewed to a halt, punctured by massive shells, torn apart from within by the orange blast of explosions, shedding tracks and turrets as the detonations tore them apart. In just three minutes, the Tiger gunners destroyed 45 of Teliakov's tanks at no loss on their side.

The 164th Tank Brigade, seeing Teliakov and his men slaughtered in a furious storm of shells, swung wide in an effort to avoid Bobrik and ran headlong into the 2nd Panzer Division. In the vicious fight that followed, the 164th lost 23 of its 50 tanks, but managed to destroy 10 Panzer IVs and tank destroyers before retreating.

Once the Luftwaffe once again drove Rudenko's luckless airmen from the immediate vicinity – destroying 91 Soviet fighters at a cost of 11 of their own – Model ordered the advance resumed on a six-mile front, advancing towards Ponyri. The day cleared around noon and the temperature soared into the upper 80s under a brilliant, baking sun. The tank crews drove with their hatches open for fresh air as the 2nd Panzer Division, the 20th Panzer Division, the 505th Tiger Battalion, and a number of infantry divisions pushed forward against the 2nd Tank Army and the defending Soviet infantry.

Ponyri, the goal of this push, remained out of reach on July 6th. Instead, a brutal struggle involving tens of thousands of men on each side developed as the Germans pushed relentlessly but gradually forward. Soviet and Wehrmacht tanks clashed, leading to rapidly mounting armor losses on both sides.

Curtains of artillery fell, and fighter-bombers and ground-attack aircraft, including the famous Shturmovik, hunted tanks and infantry concentrations amid the rolling folds of the plains, the burning villages, clumps of trees, and tall fields of rye. The two sides tore at each other with every weapons system available, from rifles and machine guns to Nebelwerfer and Katyushka rocket launchers to the heaviest artillery and bombs.

Over the next five days, the Germans pushed their way forward in brutal fighting until they finally reached Ponyri on the 10th and into the 11th. This "Stalingrad of the Steppes," as the combatants dubbed it, became the focus for extremely intense fighting for days. The Soviets distributed a pamphlet describing the life and heroic death of Konstantin Blinov, Hero of the Soviet Union, in bombastic terms to rouse their tank soldiers to fighting fury:

At Ponyri, Blinov did not leave the battlefield for three days. An expert soldier, he was sent to the most crucial points in our defenses. Wherever Blinov came with his tank, the enemy was sure to sustain a defeat. [...] Blinov destroyed six enemy tanks, eight antitank guns and nine weapon emplacements; with machine gun fire and the treads of his tank, he killed 350 Germans (Fowler, 2005, 55).

The men of both sides exhibited heroic courage and endurance in what became a pounding, relentless battle of attrition. Thousands died and thousands more sustained wounds, necessitating their difficult evacuation from the battlefield when their comrades could rescue them. Though Model reached Ponyri, he could not push beyond it in the teeth of Soviet grit, determination, numbers, and lethal concentrations of artillery.

Reaching the town hollowed out 9th Army, inflicting 50,000 casualties on the Germans, the loss of 400 tanks, and the destruction of 500 aircraft. Though Soviet losses ranged higher, and Germans eventually retrieved and repaired many of their knocked out tanks to fight again, Model's 9th Army could do no more. The full extent of its achievement during Operation Citadel consisted of penetrating 10 miles into Soviet lines before further advance grew impossible.

A frequently underrated contribution to the attack of the 9th Army in the north came from the 83 "Ferdinand" Sd. Kfz. 184 heavy tank-destroyers of schwere Panzerjager-Abteilung 653 and schwere Panzerjager-Abteilung 654, better known to history by the name of "Elefant." These massive vehicles weighed in at 70 tons combat weight and consisted of a Tiger tank hull with a massive, boxy superstructure mounted at the rear.

A Disabled Elefant

With armor up to 7.87 inches thick (200mm), the Elefant provided a sort of moving fortress on the battlefield, capable of sustaining numerous hits from Russian tank guns from the frontal angle without being knocked out. Armament consisted of the long-barreled 8.8cm Pak 43/2 L/71, which combined the devastating hitting power of the 88mm German anti-tank gun with the long-range accuracy of a barrel 71 calibers long (hence the designation L/71). Elefant crews noted successful hits on some Russian tanks at ranges of 1.8 miles (3,000 meters) during the Kursk engagement.

Historians note the Elefant's slow speed (19 miles per hour at maximum in optimal conditions), tendency to mechanical problems, and relative vulnerability to Soviet anti-tank teams when unsupported by their own infantry due to the lack of an external machine gun. While correct, these criticisms ignore the immense combat power the Elefant demonstrated during the battle at Kursk.

When deployed during the battle, Borgward IV Schwerer Ladungstrager radio controlled demolition vehicles moved ahead of the Elefants to clear mines. These 3.5 ton remote-controlled vehicles cleared lanes through the thick Soviet minefields, and also knocked out some anti-tank gun positions. Unlike smaller radio controlled vehicles used by the Wehrmacht such as the Goliath "beetle tank" tracked mine, the Borgward IV dropped its explosive charge and then moved away before detonation, enabling reuse.

42 Sturmpanzer Brummbär infantry support guns armed with short-barreled Skoda 15cm (6 inch) howitzers, organized into three squadrons of 14 Brummbär vehicles apiece, followed the advancing Elefant units. These massive, lumbering mobile artillery turrets fired indirectly over the Elefants to give them close-range heavy artillery support.

Unteroffizer J. Bohm expressed the qualified but widespread appreciation of Elefant crews for their massive, lumbering tank destroyers in a July 19th after-action report:

The main gun is very good. It destroys every tank with one or two rounds, even the KV II and the sloped American ones. [...] The Ferdinand has proved itself. They were decisive here, and we cannot go against the mass of enemy tanks today   without a weapon of its type. [...] The engine is recognized as weak for the tonnage   and the track is a bit narrow. If the vehicle is modified according to combat   experiences, it will be fantastic! (Munch, 2005, 53).

Bohm recommended manufacturing 10 Elefants for every one then in service.

Out of the 83 Elefants engaged in combat at Kursk, the Russians destroyed only 13 (some demolished by their own crews when retrieval proved impossible). The Soviets knocked others out, and mines or engine fires disabled some, but the Germans retrieved all of these and put them rapidly back into service, in part thanks to their extremely rugged design. Due to their weight each Elefant required towing by 5 prime mover halftracks.

In exchange, the Elefants achieved 502 confirmed tank kills and destroyed approximately 200 anti-tank guns and 100 pieces of field artillery. The leading Elefants, directly engaged in combat, killed an average of 15 Soviet tanks apiece during Kursk, and one, under Lieutenant Heinrich Teriete, destroyed 22 tanks in just one day of combat, July 14th, 1943, winning the Lieutenant the prestigious Knight's Cross of the Iron Cross award.

Heinz Groschl, a Porsche engineer accompanying the units, reported on the Elefant's juggernaut indestructibility:

Hull – Has proved itself impervious to rounds. Except for one penetrating hit to the side near the rear ventilation motor housing (76 mm) and besides many scars, everything has remained intact. [...] Practical experience has shown however, that the engine gratings are a weak area. Apart from Molotov cocktails, a direct hit from artillery [...] on or near the gratings can set the vehicle ablaze (Munch, 2005, 55).

Far from being the "white elephant" portrayed by many historians, the Elefant proved utterly devastating in action against Soviet armor. Only its sluggish speed and limited numbers prevented it from exercising a more decisive role in Operation Citadel.

Vatutin and Manstein squared off against each other along the Voronezh Front, where the Wehrmacht's Army Group South – including a number of elite SS armored divisions – prepared to land an even heavier blow against the Kursk Salient than Model launched in the north. A belt of approximately 440,000 mines, both anti-personnel and anti-tank, defended this face of the salient, behind which the Soviets manned their formidable triple defensive line.

One of the key anchors of the third, innermost line of defense lay at Prokhorovka Station, a railway stop near Skorovka. An insignificant stop on the rail line prior to 1943, military preparations transformed it into a linchpin of the defensive line. The Soviets placed a large supply depot and equally massive ammunition dump at Prokhorovka, supplying the 6th Guards Army. The railway made replenishment of these materiel stockpiles swift and efficient. The 2nd Air Army built a major airfield at Prokhorovka, while the 5th Guards Tank Army located its headquarters at Skorovka.

A formidable task confronted Manstein. Unlike the open "tank country" in the northern Kursk Salient, here natural defenses augmented the incredible maze of earthworks, tank traps, and dugouts created by the Soviets. Relatively common terrain features included woodland, tracts of ravines and broken ground, small rivers, swamps, marshes, many villages, and a number of farms.

Nevertheless, Vatutin's headquarters identified 13 viable attack routes for Manstein's heavy armor. Knowing of the SS units massed opposite them, Lieutenant General Mikhail Chistyakov, commander of the 6th Guards Army, exhorted his men immediately before the forces clashed, referring to them by the Soviet appellation of "Guards" units:

> In front of you stand Hitler's Guards formations. We must expect the main effort of the German offensive on this sector (Fowler, 2005, 59).

On July 4th, 1943, elements of the Fourth Panzer Army advanced at 3 PM and took several hilltops that provided essential artillery observation posts. The main attack came some 12 hours later, beginning at 3 AM on July 5th and involving the advance of Army Group South's large force of panzers. The army deployed over 100 Tigers and 200 Panzer V Panthers, along with hundreds of Panzer IVs, most upgunned and fitted with armored skirts to provide extra protection to their vulnerable tracks.

The day came clear and with the promise of intense heat, though violent thunderstorms overnight generated more of the omnipresent mud that bedeviled both armies on the Eastern Front. The first move came in the air and developed thanks to an effort by the 2nd and 17th Soviet Air Armies to seize the initiative.

Large squadrons of Soviet Yak-3 an Ilyushin Il-2 fighters arrived at 4:20 AM, escorting 150 Shturmovik ground attack aircraft and several detachments of bombers. The Soviets hoped to catch the Luftwaffe still on their airfields, where the Shturmoviks could strafe them with their automatic cannons and the bombers destroy the Stukas and other aircraft, besides pitting the airstrips with craters.

The Germans, however, showed themselves alert and extremely active. The signals intelligence crews picked up a sudden spike in radio transmissions from the identified Soviet Air Army communications centers, and immediately telephoned the airfields. Even before long-range German radar detected the signatures of the incoming aircraft, ground crews pushed Stukas and bombers hastily off the sides of the rough airstrips and rolled out Messerschmitt Bf-109 and Focke-Wulf Fw-110A fighters to counter the challenge.

So swiftly did the highly professional crews and pilots work that by the time the incoming Soviet formations arrived, the German fighters already circled high in the sky, waiting for their prey. The Russians flew in low, expecting to strafe and bomb the airfields from a low altitude for maximum effect. The experienced Luftwaffe pilots dove against them like stooping hawks, taking the surprise attack by surprise. Soon, Soviet wrecks littered the landscape, and the rest fell back in the face of stinging German assaults.

No sooner had the Luftwaffe fighters chased off the Soviet incursion than 400 Stuka dive-bombers and medium tactical bombers swept forward to hammer the Soviets' prepared positions ahead of the panzer assault. The men of the 6th Guards Army held their ground with grim doughtiness as German bombs rained down and the Stukas descended again and again, their wing sirens shrieking as they plunged to deliver their lethal payloads on Russian artillery and antitank positions.

Behind the front lines, General Mikhail Chistyakov ensconced himself in the small apple orchard of a farm, expecting the German attack to shatter on the first line of defenses. General Mikhail Katukov, twice named Hero of the Soviet Union, and his aide Lieutenant General Nikolai Kirillovich Popel, arrived to inform him that, instead, Army Group South's elite SS armored units were breaking through the first line of entrenchments and that Chistyakov's al fresco headquarters lay in their path. As Popel later wrote:

> On the table were cold mutton, scrambled eggs, a carafe with chilled vodka to judge by the condensation on the glass, and finely sliced white bread – Chistyakov was doing

himself well (Fowler, 2005, 77).

In this manner, Chistyakov first learned from his less complacent subordinates that the heavy panzer attacks succeeded in punching through the Voronezh Front's outer boundary despite the frenzied efforts of the Russian soldiery to repel them.

Even the mighty panzer formations might have failed against the intricately interlocking trenches, bunkers, obstacles, tank traps, and antitank gun positions if not for the steady, accurate airstrikes provided by hundreds of Stukas. Junkers Ju 87G-1 and Henschel Hs 108B ground attack aircraft, armed with paired 37mm cannons, stalked the field, attacking Soviet armored units moving up to support the infantry lines.

Manstein tasked Army Group Kempf with driving through the Soviet lines on the right of the attack, guarding the eastern flank of the advance from counterattack. General Hermann Breith commanded this large detachment, which consisted of the 6th, 7th, and 19th Panzer Divisions, plus Heavy Panzer Battalion 503 containing Tigers and three battalions StuG III Sturmgeschutz self-propelled assault guns. Altogether, this force consisted of 300 Panzer VI, III, and a handful of Panzer II tanks and "Flammpanzer" flamethrower tanks, augmented by 45 Tigers and 75 StuG IIIs.

Delivery of the main *Schwerpunkt* fell to the responsibility of the 4th Panzer Army, commanded by Generaloberst Hermann Hoth. The 4th Panzer Army consisted of two Panzer Corps. The II SS Panzer Corps, led by the highly professional SS-Obergruppenfuhrer Paul Hausser, contained three elite SS-Panzergrenadier Divisions, *Leibstandarte Adolf Hitler*, *Das Reich*, and *Totenkopf*. These amounted to 327 tanks and 95 assault guns, including StuG IIIs and Hummels.

Paul Hausser

The other half of 4th Panzer Army, deployed on the left, comprised the XLVIII Panzer Corps, led by General Otto von Knobelsdorff. One of the regular Wehrmacht's finest divisions, the *Grossdeutschland* Panzergrenadier Division, formed the core of this formidable unit, and included 45 Tigers, 200 Panthers, and 120 Panzer IVs and Panzer IIIs in its roster, while commanded by a man with the resounding name of Hyazinth Graf Strachwitz von Gross-Zauche und Camminetz. The 3rd and 11th Panzer Divisions and the 167th Infantry Division rounded out the XLVIII Panzer Corps, which mustered 450 tanks and 45 assault guns overall (Nipe, 2012, 47-49).

Army Group South's strategic reserve consisted of three seasoned divisions, the SS-Panzergrenadier *Wiking* Division together with the 17th and 23rd Panzer Divisions.

The advancing German forces met ferocious, almost fanatical, resistance from the Soviets, a far cry from the panicked levies of the first years. The XLVIII Panzer Corps slogged forward in an endless series of hard-fought battles for the next section of trenches and bunkers, pushing 3 miles into Soviet lines on the first day.

The 3rd Panzer Division seized the fortified town of Korovino on the extreme left. Meanwhile, *Grossdeutschland* and the 11th Panzer Division cooperated to attack Cherkassoye. Brave anti-tank squads of Soviets attempted to scramble up on the panzers and destroy them by attacking antitank mines to their turrets; some succeeded. The Wehrmacht finally dislodged Cherkassoye's valiant defenders through use of flamethrower tanks, whose ghastly effectiveness seared itself into the minds of the Germans also:

A flamethrower crewman from Das Reich wrote of the "strange feeling to serve this destructive weapon and it was terrifying to see the flames eat their way forward and envelop the Russian defenders." A more matter-of-fact veteran of the day mentioned [...] in passing that ever since then he had been unable to tolerate the smell of roast pork (Showalter, 2013, 80).

The Soviets managed only localized counterattacks on July 5th, which the Wehrmacht also rolled up as they continued to press slowly forward. However, on July 6th, the Soviets moved up additional rifle battalions and tank brigades in larger counterstrikes against the still-advancing Wehrmacht. The Panzers continued to roll forward towards their next objective of Oboyan, fighting against the usual complex of defenses.

The Germans encountered General Mikhail Katukov's 1st Tank Army, having pushed clean through the 6th Guards Army. Many of Katukov's tanks occupied dug-in positions, despite the protests of his political officer, Nikita Khrushchev. However, a number of Katukov's vehicles also remained mobile, and at around noon, he threw these forward in a spoiling attack against the *Leibstandarte Adolf Hitler* Division.

Mikhail Katukov

The *Leibstandarte*'s Tiger detachment met the Soviet vehicles in a head-on encounter near Yakovlevo, where the II SS Panzer Corps had now pierced no less than 20 miles into the salient, a menacing development the Soviets could not ignore. One of the *Leibstandarte* tank commanders later described the action:

On separate slopes, some 1,000 meters apart, the forces faced one another like   figures on a chess board […] They rolled ahead a few meters, pulled left, pulled   right, maneuvered to escape the enemy crosshairs and bring the enemy into their own fire. […] After one hour, 12 T-34s were in flames. The other 30 curved wildly   back and forth, firing as rapidly as their barrels would deliver. They aimed well but   our armor was very strong. We no longer twitched when a steely finger knocked on   our walls (Fowler, 2005, 83-85).

The armored spearheads of Manstein's advance pushed forward with the Tigers in the fore, Panthers and upgunned Panzer IVs guarding the flanks, and less well armored tanks following in support. Nikolai Popel expressed astonishment at the sheer numbers of German vehicles. Though the Russians fought desperately, the Tigers and other Wehrmacht tanks caved in the 1st Tank Army and continued their advance.

Behind the lines, repair crews worked ceaselessly to retrieve knocked out or broken down panzers, repair them, and send them back into action. Most hits temporarily disabled a vehicle rather than annihilating it; even after the Kursk action concluded, permanent losses and write-offs remained a surprisingly small item.

Katukov himself remained unconvinced of the value of armored counterattack, though the remote but hovering presence of Stalin, always questioning why his commanders did not immediately go on the offensive, encouraged these reckless actions anyway. Katukov later wrote:

Let the fascists come crawling forward in the hope that at any moment, they'll   succeed in breaking out into operational space. Let the Hitlerites get enmeshed in our defenses and die. We, in the meantime, will be grinding down the enemy's   materiel and manpower. Once we bleed their units white and smash the fascists' armored fist, then the suitable moment will ripen for launching a mighty counterattack (Zamulin, 2010, 114).

The Germans fully broke through the first of the three Soviet lines of defense and pierced the second at one location by the end of July 6th. The Wehrmacht forces continued to push forward steadily on July 7th, 8th, and 9th, despite increasingly large and desperate counterattacks by the Soviets. Progress naturally slowed considerably for the Germans, and some of the commanders began to wonder if withdrawal represented the best option.

For his part, Vatutin committed every unit available to prevent a breakthrough into the "operational space" behind his three lines of defense. He knew clearly that once the Germans reached this relatively undefended ground, they could cut off hundreds of thousands of Soviet soldiers from their lines of supply and force their surrender. The Wehrmacht had already taken copious amounts of prisoners, but if the whole Kursk Salient fell, the Red Army's capacity to undertake offense action would likely vanish for the rest of the year, quite possibly forcing Stalin to sue for peace.

Army Group Kempf, meanwhile, had established a defensive line along the east of the German advance. There, as Theodor Busse, a German infantry general on Manstein's staff, remarked, they "stood like a rock wall" (Newton, 2002, 20), defending the tree belt along Koren Creek against Soviet counterattacks. In addition to using this natural strongpoint for defense, the Kempf group also managed to throw several bridgeheads across the Donets river, which might prove useful for later advances.

Though the Wehrmacht continued to advance and push against the second defensive line, their fighting strength slowly frayed. Damage to tanks and the loss of men took their toll on the army's ability to maintain operations over the longer term. Nevertheless, the Germans continued their efforts with consummate professionalism and steely determination – a resolve matched fully by their Soviet opponents.

The German offensive stalled on July 9th, leading to a conference among the leading German commanders. Hermann Hoth recommended a fresh assault, and Manstein supported him provisionally. Once he visited the frontline units personally and observed conditions for himself, Manstein gave Hoth approval for his renewed offensive.

Hermann Hoth

The 4th Panzer Army resumed its attack on July 11th and finally punched through the stubborn defenses that halted it two days before. The *Totenkopf* Division successfully crossed the

Psel River on pontoon bridges, penetrating this stubbornly held line of defense. Other breakthroughs occurred, and this laid the groundwork for the most famous moment of the entire Battle of the Kursk Salient.

Late on July 11th, the II SS Panzer Corps under SS Obergruppenfuhrer Paul Hausser – a long-faced Prussian officer and SS fanatic who survived the war and lived until 1972 – moved forward to take up positions to attack Prokhorovka Station. Hausser deployed *Das Reich* on the right of his formation, *Liebstandarte* in the center, and *Totenkopf* on the left. At this moment, Vatutin decided to commit the entire 5th Guards Tank Army in an effort to halt the relentless German advance, now poised for a fatal breakthrough.

The Battle of Prokhorovka on July 12th, 1943, taking place near Prokhorovka Station, developed naturally out of the sequence of events leading up to it. Several frequent historical assertions about this battle constitute little more than mythology, though many historians continue to quote them. The research of post-Soviet Russian historians and the rediscovery of accounts by German generals and SS panzer leaders, however, paint a very different picture from the accepted view.

One myth states the Battle of Prokhorovka represented the biggest tank battle in history in terms of the number of vehicles engaged. While massive, several other battles actually involved more tanks, including the abortive Operation Mars in 1942 against the Rzhev Salient. Prokhorovka certainly stands among the top five largest tank encounters of world history, but is at best the second largest and perhaps the third or fourth.

The other myth is that the Soviets won an overwhelming victory and wiped out the German panzers at Prokhorovka. In fact, this springs from a false picture presented to Stalin by Red Army commanders seeking to prevent their own execution. In reality, though damaged by the massive, courageous Soviet attacks, Manstein's panzer formations decimated the 5th Guards Tank Army and its supporting units, then continued advancing through July 17th, pushing forward and achieving the position necessary for a decisive breakthrough, prevented only by Hitler's decisions.

The Soviet commander Vatutin viewed the situation with understandable alarm on July 11th, 1943. On July 9th, it appeared the Wehrmacht thrust finally exhausted its momentum in the second defensive line. But on July 10th, and even more strongly on July 11th, the Third Reich juggernaut rolled forward again, breaking through defensive lines and crushing the local counterattacks sent against it.

German Advancement towards Prokhorovka on July 11th.

Nikolai Vatutin – a capable man of high professionalism who inspired loyalty in his subordinates through his thoughtfulness and high regard for them, but who earlier suffered arrest, persecution, and extraction of several teeth in a Soviet dungeon – listened to a report from Pavel Alekseyevich regarding the fighting power of German armor and suggested tactics to counter it:

'The fact is that the Tigers and Ferdinands not only have strong frontal armor, but also a powerful, long-range direct fire 88mm gun. In that regard they are superior to our tanks, which are armed with 76mm guns. Successful struggle with them is only possible in circumstances of close-in combat, with exploitation of the T-34's greater maneuverability and by flanking fire against the side armor of the heavy German machines.' 'In other words, engage in hand-to-hand fighting and take them by boarding,' the *front* commander said (Zamulin, 2010, 268).

These tactics formed the basis for much of the later myth about Prokhorovka, but it remains one thing to propose tactics and another to successfully execute them. Nevertheless, Vatutin had little choice. The rail-head at Prokhorovka supplied many of his forces with ammunition, fuel, and food, making it a choice target for the Germans in any case. He also wanted to save the Soviet 48th Rifle Corps, in imminent danger of finding itself encircled and destroyed by the II SS Panzer Corps.

Above all, perhaps, he received dark hints by telephone from Stalin about retribution visited on parties unknown if the Germans reached the rear in the Prokhorovka area. Vatutin and his fellow commanders might experience a "nine-gram pension" – that is, be shot in the base of the skull – if the Wehrmacht broke through.

The 5th Guards Tank Army, and several other tank battalions Vatutin and Lieutenant General Rotmistrov managed to collect, moved forward and prepared for action to the north of Prokhorovka on July 11th. Part of the myth about the battle states that the Soviets managed complete surprise against the II SS Panzer Corps on July 12th. However, documentary evidence demolishes this view. The Germans did not stumble suddenly on the Soviet force; rather, they rapidly gained clear awareness of the Soviet preparations and stood on the defensive to receive the counterattack, a completely correct tactical response playing to the strengths of the Tigers and Panzer IVs against the T-34/76s.

An impossible task in an era of reconnaissance aircraft, assembling nearly 900 tanks and assault guns took many hours and could not be hidden in the rolling farmland near Prokhorovka. Besides aerial scouting, the men of *Leibstandarte* heard the roar of numerous tank engines in the early morning and carried out a brief but useful probing attack in the direction of the Soviet lines, which confirmed the buildup of heavy armor concentrations.

The Soviets attempted artillery support for their attack, which provided additional warning to the Germans but, for once, proved too haphazard to inflict much damage. The attached artillery of *Leibstandarte,* by contrast, inflicted considerable harm on the Russians. Worse, the Ju-87 Stukas, upgraded with a pair of 37mm cannons for tank busting, soon crisscrossed the skies, accompanied by bombers. Hans Rudel, the famous Stuka ace, tore into the advancing Soviet armor columns with gusto:

"The first flight flies behind me in the only cannon-carrying airplane.... In the first attack four tanks exploded under the hammer of my cannons; by the evening the total rises to twelve. We are all seized with a kind of passion for the chase...." (Showalter,   2013, 151).

Unleashed by the radio code phrase "Steel! Steel! Steel!," the entire 5th Guards Tank Army rolled forward at full speed towards and past Prokhorovka. Violet smoke erupted all along the line as the Germans fired their purple smoke shells, a color-coded signal indicating a tank attack. The crews ran to their vehicles and took up final fighting positions, choosing the military crest of long slopes where possible to give them a clear field of fire and good lines of sight. The Tiger crews, experienced men almost to a man, parked their Tigers at a slant so that the angled front armor presented an even greater thickness to the T-34 shells and caused most to harmlessly carome off even at point-blank range.

As the Soviets charged full-throttle across several miles of open ground, the Tigers and Panzer IVs began a terrible, methodical harvest of machines and men. Shell after shell screamed through the air to rupture hulls, set engines on fire, blow turrets off, and reduce human flesh to charred paste. Despite this lethal storm, the T-34s came on, followed by T-60 light tanks and SU-76 "Golozhopiy Ferdinand" assault guns.

SS-Obersturmfuhrer Rudolf von Ribbentrop (still alive as of New Year's 2016) led a section of 7 Panzer IVs in defense of a shallow valley. Positioning his tanks just below the top of a long slope overlooking a Soviet anti-tank ditch with a single bridge across it, Ribbentrop hammered the swarms of Soviet tanks with his vehicle's 75mm high velocity gun, while the other vehicles did the same. The densely packed T-34s crashed into the ditch in their effort to advance, and even after crossing the bridge, fared little better:

Burning T-34s drove into and over one another. It was a total inferno of fire and   smoke, and impacting shells and explosions. T-34s blazed, while the wounded tried   to crawl away to the sides. The entire slope was soon littered with burning enemy   tanks. We remained behind the smoldering wreck. Just then I heard my loader   report: "No   more   armor-piercing available!" (Kurowski, 2002, 197).

All along the line, the merciless scene repeated itself. Under an overcast sky (giving place later to thunderstorms) the Germans pounded Vatutin's tank force and its reserves to pieces. At one place, the Germans surrounded 93 T-34s and destroyed them all. After the battle, Hausser attempted to count them, lost track, and finally achieved a total by scrambling amid the giant steel carcasses with chalk, writing large numerals on each tank to reach a total.

Many of the T-34 tanks carried spare, unarmored fuel containers on their exterior. While this helped them achieve greater range, it also made them a species of rolling incendiary bomb, dangerous to neighboring vehicles and extremely fatal to their crews. Usually, tank crews needed to use an armor piercing (AP) round against an enemy tank to destroy it. However, the Germans soon discovered they could use high explosive (HE) rounds against the T-34s successfully, thus effectively increasing their onboard supply of anti-tank rounds. An HE hit on the fuel set it afire and destroyed the tank as surely as though it fell victim to a huge Molotov cocktail. In at least one case, this flammability led to a spectacular event commemorated by both sides.

A trio of Tigers, including those of Tiger ace Michael Wittman and that of Georg Lotzsch, engaged and destroyed 18 T-34s on one flank of *Leibstandarte*. After knocking out most of the tanks, Wittmann and Lotzsch witnessed three Russians emerge from a burning T-34 tank, two of them carrying a badly wounded friend. The two men hurried to a shell crater and placed the injured man in it for protection, while the Germans held their fire. Then, to the astonishment of the SS tank crews, the two Soviet tank crewmen climbed back into their holed and burning T-34/76. A moment later, it lurched forward directly towards Lotzsch's Tiger. Lotzsch

ordered an advance, to get clear of the smoke. The gunner fired—and the shell bounced off. The Russian kept coming and rammed the Tiger. As flames covered both tanks, the German suddenly backed up. At five yards' distance, the T-34 exploded (Showalter, 2013, 154).

Lotzsch's tank suffered only cosmetic damage from the explosion and immediately rejoined the fight, but the unknown, heroic Soviet crewmen entered legend. In an embellishment on the sober if surprisingly sympathetic German account, the Soviets claimed both tanks detonated in a rather cinematic fireball when the T-34 rammed the massive 45-ton Tiger.

Later Soviet accounts of the battle portray the T-34s boldly dashing into close contact with the surprised German tanks and destroying them en masse, though at considerable cost to themselves. The historicity of the Soviet triumphalist propaganda is clearly disproved by a few facts. The Soviets claimed they destroyed 400 German tanks – but the actual total tank strength of the II SS Panzer Corps on the day of battle numbered 211, with around 100 more undergoing repair far behind the front lines. They also claimed the destruction of 70-100 Tiger tanks, yet in fact the German force had only 15 Tigers on the day of Prokhorovka, none of which suffered destruction.

The muster reports of the two sides' tank units, paradoxically only studied by historians some 60 to 70 years after the battle, provide a much better picture of the outcome. These indicate German losses of approximately 70 tanks, most of which proved capable of repair. This still represents around a third of the Wehrmacht vehicles involved, and shows the desperation of the fighting and the determination of the outmatched Russians to come to grips and defeat their enemies.

On the Soviet side, Red Army documents show a stunning drop of 650 tanks in the 5th Guards Tank Army by July 13th. Of these, the Soviets eventually retrieved and repaired approximately 400. However, with the Germans left in possession of the battlefield, repair only occurred after the Germans later retreated for other reasons. For all practical purposes, the 5th Guards Tank Army's roster fell from 800 to 150 tanks during the Prokhorovka fight.

The German General Theodor Busse provided a succinct summary of the situation in describing the battle, and also noted the continued advance, which only ended after July 17th when Hitler called off the offensive:

Fourth Panzer Army repulsed all attacks on 12-13 July without losing a foot of ground. For Army Group South, 14 July brought complete success along the entire front, and the enemy's offensive power appeared to have been broken. The requirements for cleaning out the southern bank of the Psel from Prokhorovka to a point north of Peny had been established. Pertinent orders for this operation had been issued (Newton, 2002, 24).

The Battle of Prokhorovka, in fact, represented a rather costly German victory. The courage, grit, and determination of the Red Army tankers remains undeniable. They gave their utmost and succeeded in inflicting relatively heavy losses on the elite SS tank units despite the enormous disadvantages they fought under. The Germans, of course, showed equal courage, great skill, and enjoyed the use of notably superior fighting machines.

In the end, the famous Battle of Prokhorovka differed only somewhat from the fight at Bobrik. The T-34/76 crews found themselves forced to attack over open country against adversaries whose tank guns could easily knock them out over a mile away, while their own guns only proved effective at ranges of 80 yards or less. Their only option involved racing forward as quickly as possible, trying desperately to close the distance, while continuing to fire in the hope of an extremely lucky shot.

The Germans, in a highly professional manner, stood on the defensive once they realized the Soviets targeted them with a major tank attack. Their seasoned SS gunners picked their targets and fired accurately, destroying tank after tank. The upgunned Panzer IVs proved deadly also, though more vulnerable to Soviet 76mm guns. Their long-barreled high-velocity 75mm cannons threw their shells with much greater velocity and accuracy than the short-barreled 76mm guns on the Soviet tanks.

Prokhorovka, in fact, generated enough accurate reports despite the myths forged for public consumption that the Soviets immediately began an improvement program to redesign the T-34. The resulting T-34/85, armed with an 85mm gun, outmatched Panzer IVs and could destroy Panthers and Tigers, though the two heaviest German tanks remained notably superior to all T-34 models in both firepower and protection.

At the same time that Army Group South's elite Panzergrenadier units fought the Battle of Prokhorovka, events unfolded elsewhere rendering their hard-won victory moot. With the 9th Army brought to a halt against the Central Front due to lack of sufficient panzers, the Soviets loosed a counterattack towards Orel on July 12th under the operational name Operation Kutusov.

The offensive involved three Soviet armies – the 3rd and 63rd Armies under Colonel-General Markian Popov, detached from the Briansk Front, and the 11th Guards Army from the Western Front under General Vasily Sokolovsky.

Popov's offensive proved amateurish and blundering in the extreme. Directed at German defensive belts held by the 56th and 262nd Infantry Divisions, the luckless Soviet soldiers found themselves sent directly ahead into minefields, barbed wire entanglements, and defensive positions with interlocking fields of fire. Receiving almost no tactical direction whatever from their commander, the Russians suffered heavy losses and pushed forward only three miles before being brought to a halt.

Sokolovsky's 11th Guards Army attack represented a very different matter. This aggressively led force struck a sector commanded by the incompetent Generaloberst Ernst Fackenstedt, whose 5th Panzer Division lost 55 of its 100 Panzers permanently (as against *Leibstandarte's* permanent loss of just 7 tanks at Prokhorovka).

On July 13th, Walther Model in the north began withdrawing all units of the 9th Army from the modest 10-mile incursion they drove into Soviet lines. With Soviet counterattacks threatening Orel and the lifeline of its railway, Model needed all his troops to fend off the risk of encirclement. He reported:

"Already today it can be concluded from the scale of the offensive against 2. Panzerarmee that the enemy has set as his aim the complete conquest of the Orel Salient... radical changes have taken place during the last forty-eight hours. [...] The center of gravity of all operations has shifted to the panzer army. Here the crisis has continued to develop at unprecedented speed" (Nipe, 2012, 51).

Model managed to extricate most of his men from the potential trap, and joined his forces with those already in place opposing the Soviet advance. During the next two weeks, the Soviets slowly forced the Germans back, taking considerable losses in the process. The Elefant or Ferdinand tank destroyers proved even more lethal on the defense than on the attack in the open country where the combat occurred. Eventually, however, the Germans packed them on to trains and sent them elsewhere for refitting, before deploying some to other areas of Russia and some to Italy to fight the newly landed American and British allies.

Despite this northern counterattack, Manstein believed his Army Group South remained poised for a decisive breakthrough. While *Leibstandarte* withdrew somewhat to be refitted, repaired, and rearmed, and the men received a much needed rest period after the immense stress of a week of lethal combat, *Das Reich* and *Totenkopf* continued to press forward, taking river crossings and tactically valuable hills in preparation for an expanded offensive into the soft interior of the Kursk Salient.

Manstein asked Hitler to release the three Panzer Divisions held in reserve for Army Group South, intending to use them to break through and attain yet another stunning victory over the Red Army. His men already held 24,000 prisoners, the largest number taken for over a year in a single action. During the first week of the offensive, the Soviets lost tanks at a rate of approximately 10 vehicles destroyed for every 1 lost by the Germans. Manstein's notion of a larger strategic victory may not have been a mere pipe dream.

Nevertheless, Hitler refused to release the Panzer Divisions, squandering all the effort and sacrifice put into carrying out his Kursk attack by his hard-fighting German soldiery. Allied landings in Sicily on the night of July 9th to 10th opened Operation Husky, threatening the Italian mainland and opening a second front on the Eurasian continent. British deceptions cleverly misled Hitler into suspected an imminent Balkans landing also.

Faced by this situation, Hitler ordered the Kursk offensive halted and some of the divisions transferred west for refitting and redeployment against the Americans and British. The crucial meeting occurred on July 13th, when Hitler convened several of his commanders, including Manstein, at his "Wolf's Lair" or Wolfsschanze in the Masurian Forest of East Prussia (Poland).

Hitler employed his usual technique of letting his generals argue to an impasse and then stepped in to resolve the situation. The attack would be called off, though he allowed Manstein to pursue a few local objectives first, and several of the best divisions would be transferred to the Balkans – where the Fuhrer expected an attack that nevertheless never materialized – and the rest would go to Italy. The final German offensive on the Eastern Front reached its end with a few words from the Third Reich's supreme leader.

Though the Battle of Kursk represented the first major Soviet victory on the Eastern Front for some time, it left the German army largely intact as a fighting force. The Wehrmacht retained its cohesion despite its personnel losses. The Germans retrieved most tanks damaged or knocked out in Kursk, repaired them, and returned them to action. Only the most shattered found no further use – the mechanics cannibalized the worse cases for parts to repair other tanks of similar make.

However, Kursk proved a highly important watershed. The battle presented the last strategic offensive by the Wehrmacht during the war, and stood as the turning point at which initiative changed irrevocably to the Soviets. The Red Army remained on the offensive for the rest of the war. Though Model, "the Fuhrer's Fireman," defeated individual offensives time and again, the Wehrmacht lost ground rapidly and steadily as the Soviet titan ground forward.

Soviet soldiers continued to show great bravery and developed moderate fighting skills as the war continued. Their officer corps grew more professional, operating as much as possible in a professional manner. However, Stalin remained something of a burden on his subordinates. He eschewed encirclements, as the first of these failed to achieve what he hoped for.

Rather than realizing the Red Army would improve with practice, he insisted on frontal assaults in all circumstances and at all times, preferring a febrile "patriotic" zeal to maneuver and scientific warfare. This, of course, cost the Soviets millions of additional dead, as the Germans tore at the Soviet "human waves" with the ferocity of a wounded predator. Nevertheless, the Soviets used tactics at a local level whenever possible, as their junior officers learned by experience.

Much of the explanation for the German failure at Kursk lies with the sheer numbers of Soviet soldiers, tanks, aircraft, and artillery involved. The Soviets prepared the Salient as a trap for the Germans with a colossal amount of human ingenuity and effort. The thirty mile deep defensive lines around the salient's boundaries proved sufficient to soak up the Wehrmacht's efforts.

A German Soldier's Grave at Kursk

In the north, where Kluge and Model lacked enough tanks, the Citadel attack failed to penetrate very far into the prickly, lethal thickets of the salient's defenses. The massed panzers in the south punched much deeper into the defensive belts and nearly broke through, though still at heavy cost. Infantry support also proved lacking. With not enough infantry, the Wehrmacht found themselves forced to use tanks to hold positions and guard flanks, eroding the Schwerpunkt's offensive drive even exclusive of casualties.

One possibly critical factor seldom explored in histories of Kursk involved the respective engine designs of Wehrmacht and Red Army tanks. Stalin, in a rare flash of insight, ordered his designers to produce only tanks with diesel engines. While Hitler manifested a brief flirtation with diesel during the early war years, he allowed the factory engineers to talk him out of its implementation:

> Hitler expressed interest in developing a diesel tank engine – which he recognized offered savings in fuel and improved range – but German engineers fobbed off such ideas as 'too difficult and too time consuming,' so it was allowed to slide. If any word

describes the state of German tank design at the start of Barbarossa, it is mediocrity (Forczyk, 2013, 21).

However, diesel engines in tanks provided superior power, speed, and mobility to the vehicle. The T-34 of the Soviets used a diesel engine and showed great strategic and tactical mobility. While the Tigers, Panthers, and Elefants (Ferdinands) of Hitler's Citadel offensive proved devastating in combat with T-34s, KV-Is, KV-IIs, and various Lend-Lease tanks, they simply lumbered along too slowly to close the "pincers" of Citadel's encircling movement in the time allotted.

A Disabled T-34

Their slow strategic speed also enabled the Soviets to move numerous reinforcements into place to impede or block each arm of the offensive. Faster tanks might well have moved rapidly enough to thrust deeper into the salient's base before all of the Stavka's reserve armies could deploy to halt them. At the very least, diesel Panthers, Tigers, and Elefants would have permitted a more extensive pincer movement, increasing the chance of Hitler green-lighting further offensive operations.

While the Germans opened World War II – and, indeed, their actions in Russia during Operation Barbarossa – with "Blitzkrieg" tactics, these worked chiefly due to the nearly static tactics and strategy of their opponents. Though the Panzers represented formidable fighting machines, their mobility began and ended at a very low level. Their successful maneuvering in the early phases of the struggle only happened because the mobility of their adversaries proved even poorer. In effect, the Germans enjoyed initial luck in their enemies compensating for glaring flaws in their weapon systems.

The French in 1940 had tanks as lethal to the German tanks of their era as the Wehrmacht's own Tigers and Panthers later proved to T-35s and M4 Shermans. However, they remained hamstrung at the operational level due to the rarity of radios, leading to each tank fighting in isolation and thus succumbing to coordinated "packs" of weaker but better coordinated German armor. In other cases, the panzers simply bypassed the French tanks and allowed Luftwaffe air strikes to deal with them.

In the Soviet Union of 1941, Stalin ordered his men to hold position regardless of circumstances, making them easy prey for German encirclement and capture. These successes, in fact, probably tricked the Germans into believing their mobility surpassed that of all possible opponents. Kursk amply proved this view incorrect.

However, instead of focusing on improving their current tank models and then building them in large numbers, the Third Reich dissipated its remaining productive energy on bizarre experiments with a series of super-heavy tanks, such as the Panzer VIII Maus. This 287-ton monstrosity had a maximum speed of 12 mph and an off-road range of just 39 miles. The Germans built only two, neither of which saw action.

The Battle of Kursk, in effect, prompted the Germans to embrace the mobility problems of their armor design and exaggerate them to the point of caricature, while the Soviets created the upgraded T-34/85 on the same basic chassis and then built tens of thousands of these highly mobile tanks. Kursk's aftermath made the Wehrmacht cling to its weaknesses and the Red Army cleave to its strengths. Unsurprisingly, the Red Army won. This outcome can be said to be the main consequence of Operation Citadel.

Operations in Italy

The Anglo-American strategic conference held at Casablanca between January 14th and 24th, 1943, decided the course of the war during that year. The American negotiators at the Anfa Hotel proposed a modest landing in France to establish a beachhead for later operations. The British, by contrast, preferred Sicily, and rapidly prevailed in the debate: "'If I had written down before I came what I hoped the conclusions would be,' one British planner noted, 'I could never have written anything so sweeping, so comprehensive, and so favourable to our ideas.' Wedemeyer, the chief [American] army planner at Casablanca, bluntly concluded 'that we lost our shirts... One might say that we came, we listened, and we were conquered.'" (Stoler, 2000, 103).

The Americans' plan, developed by Dwight D. Eisenhower with notable skill and speed, bore the codename Operation Roundup. This scheme, eventually used as the basis for developing Operation Overlord (the D-Day landings), envisioned setting 48 divisions ashore in France during spring of 1943, supported by over 5,000 aircraft.

A picture of General Eisenhower in North Africa with (foreground, left to right): Air Chief Marshal Sir Arthur Tedder, General Sir Harold R. L. G. Alexander, Admiral Sir Andrew B. Cunningham, and (top row): Mr. Harold Macmillan, Major General W. Bedell Smith, and unidentified British officers.

However, the material strength needed to carry out a plan of this scale did not exist at that stage of the war. The Anglo-Americans lacked sufficient ships in early 1943 to transport a force so large despite the United States' remarkable industrial output, while aircraft production also lagged behind the necessary totals. Supplying the force after landing would likely have proven a logistical impossibility. Furthermore, the Luftwaffe still controlled European skies, not yet decimated by America's lethal P-51 Mustangs and other high quality, well piloted, and numerous aircraft of the late war period.

The British, in exchange for an American agreement to land in Sicily rather than their preferred target of France, offered the concession of strengthening their military presence in Burma, leading to the eventual deployment of over a million soldiers against the southwestern frontier of the Empire of Japan. The English also noted the strategic advantages gained by opening the Mediterranean route to Lend-Lease shipments to the Soviet Union, a forecast revealed as accurate by the result.

While even greater strategic gains would likely have accrued from seizure of Sardinia, placed opposite the central Italian coast and permitting an immediate strike at Rome, one major factor militated against this choice. Sardinia lay outside the range of Allied air bases on Malta. Anglo-American commanders and planners feared devastating Luftwaffe attacks against the transport ships with no air cover. Sicily, on the other hand, lay within range of the Maltese airfields – the decisive factor in choosing it as the target.

Meanwhile, the Third Reich's commander of the Mediterranean theater, Field Marshal Albert Kesselring – dubbed "Smiling Albert" by the Allies due to his frequent, toothy, self-confident smiles in many surviving photographs – deemed it probable the Anglo-American forces would attack Sicily. He based this belief on the fact that it represented the easiest "stepping stone" into southern Europe, that the Allies possessed the means to attempt such a landing, and that they would do so as quickly as possible in order not to lose the momentum gained by their victory in Tunisia.

Accordingly, Kesselring – a superb tactician – strengthened Axis forces on Sicily considerably, gave orders to improve its defensive works, and dispatched paratroop General Paul Conrath of the Hermann Goering Division to command German forces on the island. Kesselring recorded the conference leading up to the defense in his memoirs: "'It makes no difference,' I told them, 'whether or not you get orders from the Italian army at Enna. You must go into immediate action against the enemy the moment you ascertain the objective of the invasion fleet. I can still hear General Conrath of the 'Hermann Goering' Panzer Division growl in reply: 'If you mean to go for them, Field-Marshal, then I'm your man.' I returned home feeling pretty confident (Kesselring, 1954, 194).

Kesselring and Rommel

Conrath (left) and Goering
Tardiness in preparation cost the Allies an easy seizure of Sicily. Thanks to Hitler's stubborn, irrational insistence on holding the last scrap of African territory still in German hands – in Tunisia – to the last, and losing over 100,000 men in the process, Wehrmacht efforts remained

focused in Africa for several months in the spring of 1943. 9 of the 10 divisions earmarked to spearhead the Operation Husky invasion stood idle during this period, while only a skeleton garrison held the island.

The German forces assembled to hold Sicily, or at least to delay the Allied advance there, consisted of various units sent by Hitler and the OKW to reinforce the doomed Afrika Korps remnant in Tunisia. Kesselring, clear-sighted enough to see deployment to North Africa, and who sentenced these forces to almost immediate surrender as the Allies crushed the remaining German foothold there in an iron grip, diverted them to Sicily instead.

Though neither man commanded large portions of the Sicilian defense force, Kesselring tasked two officers, Colonels Ernst-Gunther Baade and Bogislaw von Bonin (who worked as a journalist after the war), with organizing the disparate elements into working military units. Assisted by a small but able staff of experienced veteran officers, Baade and Bonin worked hard and rapidly, setting up chains of command and arranging for efficient delivery of supplies. Baade's abilities prompted his superiors to overlook his eccentricities: "In the field, he wore a black beret with a tartan plaid ribbon, with a huge claymore (a double-edged broadsword formerly used by Scottish Highlanders) at his side instead of the traditional Luger. [...] Baade was a gentleman who believed in chivalry. He was also personally brave and professionally competent; hence, he had no problems in the Afrika Korps, despite his peculiarities. [...] he led patrols wearing a kilt." (Mitcham, 2007, 32).

While the Germans sent men and materiel to aid in holding the island, the Allies, though allowing the invasion force to stand idle, undertook massive preparations of their own. The logistical corps of both the American and British armies worked around the clock, stockpiling huge amounts of food, medical supplies, ammunition, spare parts, and gasoline for their invading soldiers. Seeing to every detail, the assiduous quartermasters even accumulated a store of 144,000 condoms, a large stock of chewing gum, and a supply of rat traps to deal with vermin.

The supply corps earmarked another vast collection of supplies to assist the Sicilian population, while scrambling to arrange for the shipment of no less than 38,000 tons of food and 160,000 tons of coal to supply the 19 million people in Italy's south each month (Atkinson, 2007, 57). The Anglo-Americans also worked to obtain donkeys for transporting supplies through Sicily's hot, harsh, rugged landscape.

In the days leading up to Operation Husky, both Axis and Allies bombarded the Sicilian population with propaganda. The Germans persuaded the Sicilians that the American soldiers were rapists almost to a man, causing the local men to expend vast efforts hiding their female relatives. For their part, the Allies air-dropped millions of leaflets, some quite pithy: "One message warned, 'Germany will fight to the last Italian'" (Atkinson, 2007, 56).

The Americans and British each offered a unique contribution to the preparations for Operation Husky, the hugest seaborne landing then attempted in the history of warfare. Superior quality landing craft and pontoons proved the indispensable element provided by the United States. The backbone of the landings, without which moving nearly 200,000 men ashore rapidly would have proven impossible, consisted of the DUKW.

Predictably but aptly dubbed the "Duck," the DUKW amphibious transport rolled off General Motors Corporation (GMC) assembly lines in thousands between 1942 and 1945, eventually totaling over 21,000 vehicles. DUKWs, based on a heavily modified 2.5-ton truck chassis, showed extraordinary seaworthiness, surviving 20-foot waves kicked up by 70 mph winds to deliver troops safely to the beach in some instances. Successful deployment of Allied forces through the violent surf present during the initial Husky landings would have been impracticable without the superb American landing craft.

The Duck

The other vital American contribution came from the Navy's Construction Battalions, or Seabees: "Navy engineers [...] countered with Project GOLDRUSH: a floating pontoon that could be towed or carried in sections on the LSTs, then bolted together to form an articulated bridge across the water gap from sandbar to beach. Tests in Narragansett Bay had proved the bridge could bear a Sherman tank." (Atkinson, 2007, 60).

While the Americans' vehicular "know-how" readied imperative landing equipment, British intelligence went into overdrive with extraordinary and remarkably successful deception measures. Bombing missions struck Axis targets from Romania to Sicily, softening up the Luftwaffe's airfields without betraying the final destination of the coming attack. Large Royal Navy convoys carried out repeated feints towards Greece, Sardinia, Sicily, and the north coast of France to confuse the German high command regarding the place the inevitable blow would fall.

MI5 and other British intelligence forces achieved their masterstroke with Operation Mincemeat, however. This elaborate deception centered on a corpse and a briefcase full of falsified military papers. Lieutenant-Commander Ewen Montagu and Flight-Lieutenant Charles Cholmondeley devised Operation Mincemeat, which MI5 and other committees then adopted. Montagu summarized key points of the scheme in a memo: "A body is obtained from one of the London hospitals [...] it is then dressed in army, naval, or air force uniform of suitable rank. The lungs are filled with water and the documents are disposed in an inside pocket. The body is then dropped [...] at a suitable position where the set of the currents will probably carry the body ashore in enemy territory." (Macintyre, 2010, 17).

Montagu

Cholmondeley
Vice Chief of the Imperial General Staff Lieutenant General Sir Archibald Nye wrote an actual letter to General Sir Harold Alexander, discussing many military matters, most of them extremely accurate and verifiable. In the letter, however, he also described a planned attack on Greece by British divisions launched from Egypt and another attack on Sardinia, with a third attack on Sicily as a purely diversionary measure. Nye wrote the letter with verve and skill, apparently immensely enjoying his part in the deception.

Nye

Alexander

Montagu's plan next called for obtaining a corpse to serve as the "carrier" of the letter. A Welsh homeless man named Glyndwr Michael died at St. Pancras hospital at age 34 after desperately eating bread crusts smeared with rat poison, which fatally damaged his liver. MI5 operatives skillfully transformed the starving Glyndwr into Major William Martin of the Royal Marines. Known for decades only as "The Man Who Never Was," Glyndwr received a Royal Marines officer's uniform, plus other details such as a false photo of his nonexistent fiancée "Pam" and other personal items stuffed into the pockets.

The picture of "Pam"

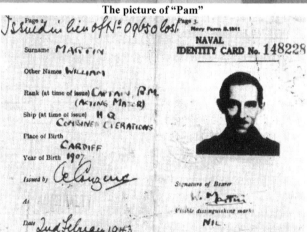

Issued in lieu of Nº 09650 lost

Surname MARTIN

Other Names WILLIAM

Rank (at time of issue) CAPTAIN, R.M.
(ACTING MAJOR)

Ship (at time of issue) H Q
COMBINED OPERATIONS

Place of Birth CARDIFF

Year of Birth 1907

Issued by

At

Date 2nd February 1943.

NAVAL
IDENTITY CARD No. 148228

Signature of Bearer
W. Martin

Visible distinguishing marks
NIL.

Major Martin's ID card

Montagu and his agents fitted the corpse with a life vest and a briefcase, handcuffed to the wrist, in which they placed Sir Archibald Nye's letter along with other, genuine military documents. They then packed "Major William Martin's" body into a vacuum sealed metal cylinder full of dry ice and placed it aboard the submarine HMS *Seraph*, commanded by Lieutenant Norman Jewell.

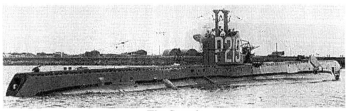

The *Seraph*

The Seraph sailed from Greenock, Scotland on April 18th, 1943, and arrived off Huelva, Spain on April 30th. The British chose Huelva due to an onshore current and their knowledge that a German Abwehr (military intelligence) officer operated in the port at that time. "Major William Martin" would appear as the victim of a military airplane crash, drowning at sea and drifting ashore due to tides and currents.

As the sailors eased Glyndwr Michael's corpse, disguised as Major William Martin, into the sea, Jewell, contrary to his orders, read the 39th Psalm aloud: "Lord, make me to know mine end, and the measure of my days, what it is: that I may know how frail I am. Behold, thou hast made my days as an handbreadth; and mine age is as nothing before thee: verily every man at his best state is altogether vanity..."

A Spanish fisherman soon found the corpse and brought it to the attention of the authorities. Just a few hours later, the Spanish brought the body to the British vice-consul, minus the briefcase and its documents. The British government arranged for Glyndwr Michael's body to receive a burial with full military honors. His tombstone, in Huelva, identifies him as William Martin, though a 1998 addition states, "Glyndwr Michael, Served as Major William Martin, RM." The stone also declares, "Dulce et Decorum est pro Patria Mori" ("It is sweet and seemly to die for one's country").

The Spanish eventually returned the briefcase also, with the documents showing clear signs of opening and resealing. This news caused immense rejoicing in British intelligence circles. Copies of the documents reached Hitler in late May, and the Fuhrer initially expressed skepticism as to their reality. However, his leading intelligence analyst, Baron Alexis von Roenne, who secretly loathed Hitler and the Nazis and made sure to support every piece of Allied disinformation he obtained, endorsed the document's authenticity, which immediately convinced the Third Reich's dictator. Hitler accordingly issued an order: "It is to be expected that the Anglo-Americans will try to continue the operations in the Mediterranean in quick succession. The following are most endangered: in the Western Med, Sardinia, Corsica and Sicily; in the Eastern Med, the Peloponnese and the Dodecanese. ... Measures regarding Sardinia and the Peloponnese take precedence over everything else." (Macintyre, 2010, 195-196).

Ironically, the Italians and Mussolini, normally incompetent and situationally unaware, saw keenly through the ruse accepted by their Teutonic allies. Italian intelligence indicated again and again that the whole weight of the gathering Allied invasion forces would fall upon Sicily alone. Time and again, the Duce forwarded accurate reports on Anglo-American intentions to the Fuhrer, only to be ignored contemptuously by both the German leader and the intelligence officers of the Abwehr.

Mussolini

As a result, Hitler diverted vast numbers of men slated to defend Sicily to other theaters instead. He sent 10,000 soldiers to Sardinia, 10 divisions to the Balkans, and seven divisions to Greece. The Fuhrer's orders also sent large torpedo boat detachments from Sicily to the Aegean Sea, stripping forces that might have sunk many landing craft. In the event, Sicily only received around 20,000 reinforcements rather than the 200,000 or so at Hitler's disposal in early June 1943. The dead Glyndwr Michael served his country well indeed.

Overall command of the Allied land forces in Sicily lay with General Sir Harold Alexander, a Briton of immense ego and dubious military capacity. Though Dwight D. Eisenhower commanded the Anglo-American effort overall, Alexander exercised direct control over the invasion's actual planning and execution, and the general remained in command of the Italian theater for much of the war's remainder, winning eventual promotion to the rank of Field Marshal.

Under Alexander, Lieutenant General George S. Patton commanded the American contingent, while General Sir Bernard Montgomery – familiarly dubbed "Monty" – led the British forces. Patton, a brash, headstrong eccentric, would develop into one of the most successful American commanders of the war, and he already showed a "maverick" streak and tendency to act on his own initiative regardless of orders. Meanwhile, Montgomery, another aggressive commander, held his American allies in immense scorn, a fact clearly emergent on the battlefields of Sicily.

Patton in Sicily

Monty

Major General Guy G. Simonds led the 1st Canadian Infantry Division, a significant unit in the Sicilian campaign. An enthusiast for all things Montgomery, Simonds added a disconcerting, frosty aloofness to "Monty's" characteristics, making him less than popular with the men under his command, in contrast to his role model: "Tall, lean, and bronzed by the North African sun […] Simonds had grey-blue eyes that were as steady and unnerving as Montgomery's. His jet-black hair was set off by a little wave at the temples, his moustache thin and turned up at the ends. [...] A Winnipeg Free Press reporter commented: 'He's a marvelously keen observer who can put the picture into words without any need to write a long report about it. That's the Montgomery style.'" (Zuehlke, 2008, 42).

Simonds

Patton's American force operated under the name of the U.S. 7ᵗʰ Army, consisting of the 2ⁿᵈ Armored Division, the 3ʳᵈ and 9ᵗʰ Infantry Divisions, and the 82ⁿᵈ Airborne Division. Lieutenant General Omar Bradley's II Corps added two more divisions to this roster, the 1ˢᵗ Infantry (the "Big Red One") and the 45ᵗʰ Infantry. In all, the United States contributed 66,000 men to the initial invasion force.

Montgomery's British 8ᵗʰ Army comprised the 1ˢᵗ Airborne Division, the 13ᵗʰ Corps under Lieutenant General Miles Dempsey, made up of the 5ᵗʰ Division and the 50ᵗʰ Northumbrian Division, and the 30ᵗʰ Corps, led by Oliver Leese and including the 51ˢᵗ Highland Division and the 1ˢᵗ Canadian Division. 115,000 men from all corners of the British Empire mustered for the first landings.

Allied vehicle and artillery strength also reached impressive totals. One thousand eight hundred pieces of field artillery, 600 tanks, and 14,000 other vehicles – ranging from armored cars to trucks, Jeeps, and halftracks – came ashore with the landing force. The Americans fielded most of these vehicles; the British complained of their own mobility-limiting lack of vehicular support and relatively weak tank forces, while the Canadians made use of American-built M1 tanks alongside British and Canadian vehicles.

This gigantic force would move ashore carried or supported by 2,590 ships. 1,839 of these consisted of shipborne landing craft providing transport from the troopships to the beach; of these, the American DUKW (an amphibious troop transport) and LST (Landing Ship Tank, for tanks and other vehicles) proved instrumental in the landing's success. 1,670 combat aircraft and 835 transport and support aircraft offered air support and delivered paratroopers to the Sicilian operation. As more reinforcements arrived, Allied troop numbers eventually swelled to 467,000 men.

Notable British aircraft included the hard-hitting Supermarine Spitfire, scourge of the Luftwaffe during the Battle of Britain, and the Hawker Hurricane, an aging but still useful design. The Americans contributed B-17 and B-24 bombers, C-47 transport aircraft, and P-38 Lightnings, the last of which soon established a formidable reputation among German soldiers subjected to their relentless strafing.

At the moment that the first British and American boots thudded into the sand of Sicily's southern beaches, around 230,000 Italians and 40,000 Germans garrisoned the island. Axis troop totals remained vague and uncertain throughout the struggle, as some units arrived as reinforcements at the same time as others withdrew to the Italian mainland. The highest Wehrmacht troop total reached an estimated 65,000, while the Italians never numbered more than a quarter million men.

Albert Kesselring held overall theater command, in the same manner as Dwight D. Eisenhower on the Allied side, but the supreme commander of Axis forces on Sicily nominally remained Italian General Alfredo Guzzoni. Guzzoni led the Italian 6th Army, consisting of 44 divisions in all. Italian armored strength consisted of just 148 tanks, the majority Renault R35s from France, and the rest either L3 tankettes or Fiat 3000 tanks, essentially useless for 1943's armored warfare. 68 Semovente assault guns supplemented this force, of which 24 Semovente da 90/53s represented the only Italian vehicles capable of knocking out an Allied medium tank, despite their own trivial armor protection.

Guzzoni

Though Guzzoni commanded the German forces on paper, in reality the Wehrmacht soldiers viewed him and all other Italian military men with scorn. Lieutenant General Frido von Senger und Etterlin occupied the role of de facto commander of all German units in Sicily, though he technically remained a liaison officer on Guzzoni's staff. A tough, skilled soldier, Etterlin showed little love for Nazism and once point-blank refused an order from Hitler to massacre 200 prisoners.

Etterlin

The German forces in Sicily consisted of two main units, supplemented by a large number of Luftwaffe ground personnel. The 15th Panzergrenadier Division under Lieutenant General Eberhard Rodt mustered three regiments of Panzergrenadiers, equipped with SdKfz 250 and 251 halftracks (the armored personnel carriers and infantry fighting vehicles of World War II), plus a tank battalion numbering approximately 60 tanks, mostly outdated Panzer IIIs and more modern Panzer IVs, the latter approximately equal in firepower and armor to an American M1 tank. Rodt proved a skilful defensive commander despite a lackluster record during the war up to that time.

The Hermann Goering Panzer Division, led by Lieutenant General Paul Conrath, fielded a mixed bag of paratroopers, three understrength Panzergrenadier battalions, and tank units, the latter including 53 Panzer IIIs, 32 Panzer IVs, 20 Sturmgeschutz StuG III self-propelled assault guns (used in both infantry support and tank hunter roles), and 17 of the new Panzer VI Tiger tanks. The Tiger, a tremendously powerful tank with nearly impervious armor for its era, remained plagued with appalling mechanical problems in Sicily, only later resolved by further engineering efforts. Despite his macho boasting to Kesselring, Conrath proved notably inferior to Rodt in the role of battlefield commander.

Shortly after Operation Husky commenced, tough and experienced general Hans-Valentin Hube – called "der Mensch" after his performance in Stalingrad – arrived to take over command of the defense. Portions of the 14th Panzer Corps, the 29th Panzergrenadier Division, and the 1st Fallschirmjager Division also provided reinforcements.

Hube

While the Germans and Italians worked busily to fortify Sicily's northern coast during May and June, Allied reconnaissance aircraft thoroughly scouted the island's shores. Kesselring dismissed the existing defensive works as so much "gingerbread" and set about creating formidable defenses in the north, particularly near some of the major cities. Anglo-American pilots snapped numerous photos showing the Italians and Germans frenziedly completing these fresh defenses, but other photographs revealed only weak, strung-out defenses along the southern coast of Sicily. The Axis commanders remained smugly convinced the nearly continuous sandbars in this region would deter any attacker, unaware of the capabilities of American DUKWs or Project Goldrush's pontoons.

The Allied commanders, originally planning landings on the northern coast, switched the focus to a southern beachhead, supplemented by airborne assaults at key inland positions. Eisenhower and the other generals reaffirmed their choice of a southern approach after receiving photos revealing Sicilian women from nearby villages bathing in the sea at the selected attack points, accidentally confirming that the Axis had mined neither the beaches nor the adjacent waters.

The island of Pantelleria lay in the path of the invasion fleet, along with several other islands making up the Pelagian archipelago. A small, rocky island with many cliffs, Pantelleria boasted a large airstrip from which Italian and German aircraft might strafe and bomb the armada. Despite a formidable number of batteries, the 10,000 draftees garrisoning the island possessed little experience and even less fighting spirit. Vice Admiral Gino Pavasi understood the position's weakness, but Mussolini deemed it impregnable.

The Allies set about proving the Duce wrong on May 18th, 1943, when the Royal Navy threw a blockade around the island and relentless bombing attacks began. The Anglo-Americans expected a fairly rapid capitulation. As Eisenhower remarked, "Admiral Cunningham, in particular, agreed with me that the place could be taken with slight cost. We based our conviction upon the assumption that most Italians had had a stomachful of fighting and were looking for any good excuse to quit." (Mitcham, 2007, 40).

By June 6th, the Allies dropped 900 tons of bombs on the harbor and Italian defenses. From June 6th to June 11th – the date chosen for actual landings – the Allied bombing efforts increased dramatically and continued 24 hours a day, with 4,000 tons of bombs dropped in just four days. Aerial photographs show the harbor and island invisible under a vast, windswept pall of smoke from structures and vehicles set alight by the munitions, and perhaps not surprisingly, many of Pavasi's unwilling soldiers deserted.

On the morning of June 11th, Pavasi attempted to surrender, but the Allies failed to receive his message. Accordingly, the British 1st Infantry Division under Major General Walter E. Clutterbuck conducted landings with rubber assault boats. In just a few hours, the sturdy British infantry collected 11,000 Italian prisoners, while Pavasi surrendered for a second time – successfully this time – in an underground hangar built by the Duce's engineers. British casualties consisted of one man wounded by several ferocious bites from a local donkey, while the entire bombardment and assault cost no more than 200 Italian lives. The Allies captured the island's brand new airstrip intact.

Pictures of Italian prisoners on Sicily

The nearby island of Lampedusa fell on the following day, providing the Allies with another good airfield within striking distance of Sicily, while Linosa and Lampione – the latter totally undefended – passed into British hands on June 13th. The systematic seizure of the Pelagian archipelago shook Hitler's confidence in the information provided by Operation Mincemeat, but not enough for him to shift the 17 spare divisions at his disposal out of Greece and the Balkans to defend Sicily.

The time between the fall of Pantelleria on June 11th and the invasion of Sicily on July 10th, 1943 witnessed systematic Allied air attacks on German airfields and other important assets in Sicily and southern Italy. Keeping up the pretense of an eastern Mediterranean operation, numerous sorties flew against targets in Greece and even the Balkans during the same period. The Luftwaffe fought back but generally had the worst of most encounters. Hermann Goering, seeing Kesselring as a possible replacement, gutted the core of experienced Luftwaffe commanders in the Mediterranean by ousting them in favor of men of his choosing. Inexperienced crews and aircraft rapidly falling into obsolescence likewise crippled Luftwaffe efforts against the Allies. Kesselring's numerous attempts to bomb the gathering invasion fleet succeeded in sinking only nine ships between April and July.

Intense strain showed in the relations between the German and Italian governments, as each suspected the other of harboring the intentions that they did in fact possess. Mussolini and his government maneuvered for a way to extricate themselves from the war, while asking the Third Reich for vast stocks of modern weaponry and vehicles, while Hitler plotted a German seizure of the Italian peninsula. Kesselring, caught in the middle, attempted to set up a defense of Sicily that respected the Italian Army's right to manage the defense of its nation's territory while preserving independence of action for the Wehrmacht units that would likely provide the greater part of the defensive effort.

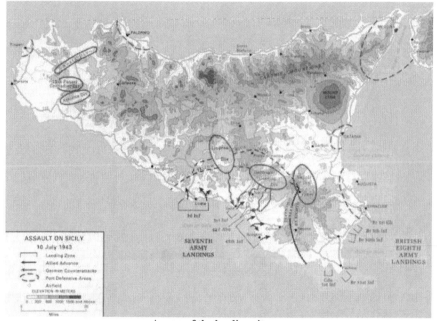

A map of the landing sites

The day before the invasion fleet launched, July 8ᵗʰ, 1943, most of the men already waited aboard the ships. Ominously – though most of the men lacked the meteorological knowledge to spot the coming trouble – the sea lay smooth and motionless as a mirror under a blast furnace sun. Confined below decks in case Axis reconnaissance aircraft passed over, the men sweltered in stifling conditions, checking their gear or writing letters.

Lieutenant Commander Richard C. Steere, an MIT meteorologist known for such uncannily accurate forecasts that Patton called him "Commander Houdini," reported that a polar front would produce a windstorm on the following day, July 9ᵗʰ, while the fleet sailed for Sicily. In response to Patton's queries, Steere also confidently predicted the windstorm's cessation by "D-Day," July 10ᵗʰ. He also suggested that Sicily itself, blocking the northern gale, would reduce wave heights in its lee.

Early on the morning of the 9ᵗʰ, the huge armada set sail across the Mediterranean towards Sicily. Nearly 3,000 vessels, including flat-bottomed LSIs (Landing Ship Infantry) and LSTs (Landing Ship Tank) alongside escorting destroyers and numerous other craft, left their North African berths and set out across the darkened Mediterranean. Calm prevailed for a few hours, but then the windstorm Steere predicted swept in from the northwest. The sea turned an ominous green color and gathered itself into hurrying mountains of sliding, battering water topped with wild crests of foam. At around noon, when the armada drew parallel with Malta, the gale achieved extraordinary violence, with winds of 35 miles per hour (Beaufort scale 7) and 16 foot wave heights reported.

As the ships pitched and tossed alarmingly on the tumultuous sea, filled with frightened, vomiting soldiers, Patton called for Steere and asked him whether the invasion could go ahead. Steere boldly stuck to his prediction that the winds would cease before the next day. The only members of the expedition seemingly unperturbed by the "Mussolini wind," as the soldiers colorfully dubbed their airy tormenter, were the pack donkeys: "'Ship rolled thirty degrees and pitched fifteen,' a naval officer recorded. 'Donkeys were unconcerned, and seemed to enjoy their hay splashed with salt water.'" (Atkinson, 2007, 65).

At around the time Patton queried Steere about the weather forecast, the commander of the Canadian contingent received information that a highly placed spy in Mussolini's government claimed a remote-detonated minefield lay exactly in his assigned path. Unwilling to turn back but nervous, the commander asked Simonds his opinion of the matter. The cold, aloof Canadian officer considered it briefly before dismissing the report as false, as indeed it was. Even Simonds, however, appeared nervous in the face of the worsening gale, warily watching the huge waves crash against the ship.

The ships drew close to Sicily after nightfall on the 9th, with an early morning landing scheduled for Saturday, July 10th, 1943. At 9:00 p.m. that night, the winds dropped sharply, seemingly vindicating Steere's predictions, and the men prepared to go ashore in an almost cheerful mood. However, when the invasion armada approached within eight miles of the Sicilian coast, the "Mussolini wind" increased again suddenly, growing even more violent than during the day.

"Commander Houdini's" prediction had been incorrect this time, but the attack went ahead anyway. Bombers struck the shore defenses shortly before the ships came into range, lighting up the northern horizon with brilliant flashes of light, followed by a wavering glow from incinerated crop fields. Soon the defenders on the shore at the chosen points of attack heard, above the sound of the wind and ocean, a deep rolling, throbbing sound from thousands of ship engines straining against the gale-driven waters.

A visually spectacular, lethally violent pageant began at 2:45 a.m. on July 10th. Moving ahead of the troop ships, Royal Navy destroyers moved inshore, using gigantic spotlights to sweep the Sicilian coastline and pick out targets for their powerful guns. The Luftwaffe and Italian air forces sprang into action, dropping searingly bright magnesium flares on parachutes to illuminate the ocean for miles and braving a storm of flak to strafe, bomb, and dive-bomb the approaching vessels. An eccentric British anti-aircraft officer, Derrick Leverton, who also worked as an undertaker and commanded his battery wearing a helmet, blue swimming trunks, and sandals due to the heat, described the approach to Sicily's shore at H-Hour: "With flares, searchlights and blazing fires, plus the vivid chromatic effects of bomb bursts and shell explosions, all of Sicily so far as the eye could reach was like nothing in the world so much as a huge pyrotechnical show." (Macintyre, 2010, 241). Leverton, an incorrigible optimist despite his profession and his disconcerting habit of referring to trenches and foxholes as "graves," continued to enjoy the scenes immensely, even expressing gratitude for a splash of cool seawater thrown up refreshingly by a near miss from a Stuka dive-bomber.

Even as the Allied landing craft undertook the final push towards the Sicilian coast, other Anglo-American soldiers already occupied a few scraps of Sicily's territory. The participants in two airborne insertions named "Husky 1" and "Ladbroke" suffered disastrously from poor planning and execution of the plan, but nevertheless, they caused disproportionate confusion and demoralization in the Italian and even some of the German troops, who believed them far more numerous than they were.

3,405 paratroopers from the 505th Parachute Infantry Regiment, supplemented by the 3/504th, set out under the command of Colonel James Gavin in 226 C-47 transports. Separated and confused by the darkness and the high winds, the aircraft dropped the paratroopers in a haphazard manner, some landing in the British sector and the rest scattered in small groups across the countryside. A few units managed to take their objectives, mostly minor bridges and road junctions, but most ended up lost. These men attacked Italian targets of opportunity, and, ironically, these widely-scattered assaults on Italian patrols, ambushes of small units, and destruction of bunkers or flak emplacements convinced even the Germans that as many as 40,000 American paratroopers were running amok in Sicily's interior. In his book about the invasion, Samuel Mitcham explained, "Spontaneously, small raiding parties led by junior officers […] stalked through the dark countryside, creating fear and confusion among German and Italian soldiers […] In a manner reminiscent of Indian warfare tactics of America's Old West, these stealthy raiders, many wearing war paint and with their heads shaved, lay in wait in the darkness along roads." (Mitcham, 2007, 73).

Gavin

An even greater fiasco developed with the British "Ladbroke" glider landing. An assemblage of British-made Airspeed AS.51 Horsa wooden gliders, plus a handful of American-made metal framed Waco CG-4A gliders, numbering 144 in all, left Tunisia late on July 9th, towed by 109

American C-47 Skytrain transports and 35 British A.W.41 Albemarle glider tugs. The Anglo-American leadership ordered these 1,700 men to take the Ponte Grande Bridge across the Anapo River. The commanders hoped to duplicate the crisp and well-oiled use of gliders by the Germans during the seizure of Fort Eben-Emael at the start of hostilities. Instead, they sacrificed many men for negligible gain.

Almost totally inexperienced at towing gliders, battered by gale-force winds, confused by the darkness, and alarmed by numerous bursts of flak that seemed closer in the night, the pilots released the Horsa and Waco craft too soon and too low. The airmen released most of the gliders at heights of 2,000 to 4,000 feet, often too low to gain needed lift and maneuvering room, and frequently did so before actually reaching the Sicilian coast. Approximately half of the gliders crashed into the ocean, some plunging totally beneath the waves and carrying hundreds of men to their doom. Others shattered on the surface, or managed a belly landing and floated for some time, permitting the men inside to hack their way free and find suitable wreckage to cling to. One lucky crew landed safely – though accidentally – in Malta, and another in the south Tunisian desert.

While many men drowned and Italian machine gunners on the shore killed others mercilessly as they floated helpless in the water, some managed to hold out until rescued when daylight came, showing perhaps a touch of British understatement as they did so: "'We went under almost instantly,' Flight Officer Ruby H. Dees recalled. 'When I reached the surface, the rest of the fellows were hanging on the wreckage.' An officer clinging to another fractured wing murmured to a British major, 'All is not well, Bill.'" (Atkinson, 2007, 90).

Meanwhile, the Italians shot down many of the gliders that actually reached land, scattered over a 30 mile front rather than concentrated in one place. Explosives and grenades aboard the gliders cooked off as they crashed, shattering the craft and the men inside them. Around 12 landed near the Ponte Grande, with one crashing so spectacularly that only a single man out of 30 emerged alive.

Out of 2,057 glider troops launched at the beginning of the attack, 87 men actually reached the bridge. This small force gallantly took and held the Ponte Grande for several hours, but by 4:00 p.m., the Italians wounded or killed all but 15 of the British. The British soldiers finally surrendered, and they found themselves marched off by a diminutive, swaggering Italian officer. Just a few minutes later, however, a patrol of soldiers from a Northamptonshire unit rescued them and took the Italian officer prisoner, and a band of Royal Scots Fusiliers arrived at the bridge via an overland march and took it intact, proving "Ladbroke" an utterly futile waste of human lives.

The British 8th Army under Montgomery landed on Sicily's southeast coast. In most sectors, the few coastal batteries present succumbed quickly to bombardment by destroyers and other supporting ships offshore. Elements of at least two Italian Coastal Divisions occupied the areas attacked, but did little other than skirmish lightly with the British before retreating, though they did capture some 174 British Ladbroke glider troops, along with a handful of stray American paratroopers.

A picture of Allied forces off shore

In conjunction with that, Miles Dempsey's 13th Corps landed further north on Sicily's east coast, with the 5th Division landing along the beaches designated "Acid North" just south of the city of Syracuse. Dempsey tasked them with seizing the important objective of the Syracuse-Augusta naval base, a major Italian facility and fortress in eastern Sicily. The 50th Northumbrian Division came ashore to the south at "Acid South," landing points near the city of Noto.

The rest of the British 8th Army, Oliver Leese's 30th Corps, landed along a 25 mile stretch of Sicilian coast divided into three zones, Bark East, Bark South, and Bark West, including the Pachino Peninsula at the island's southeast corner and some of the shore west of it. The 1st and 2nd Canadian Infantry Divisions landed in the Bark West sector and moved to secure Pachino Airfield. The English and Canadians faced heavy surf and difficult landing conditions in the darkness, but almost no hostile fire. By 6:45 a.m., the 8th Army found itself well-established on shore at the start of a clear, hot, sunny day.

A picture of British soldiers coming ashore

Further to the west, the U.S. 7th Army came ashore at their own designated landings, Cent – near Scoglitti, about 15 miles west of the Canadian disembarkation points – Dime – near Geta – and Joss – on a 10 mile stretch of coast flanking the town of Licata, a picturesque bluffside town. American objectives included several small airstrips within a short distance of the coast.

The U.S. 45th Infantry Division landed along the coast in the "Cent" sector, around Scoglitti. The "Thunderbirds" met little resistance from human adversaries, but suffered considerable losses during their landing from natural forces. Coming ashore through a violent, chaotic nine-foot surf, landing craft collided or smashed to pieces on jagged, half-submerged rocks, drowning scores of men. The Americans pushed inland, taking ground rapidly as the Italians fled in wild disorder or surrendered, as at San Croce Camerina: "When [Lieutenant Colonel Felix L.] Sparks arrived in the village, he was greeted by dozens of white flags fluttering from windows. Five hundred Italian soldiers had given up without the loss of a single American life. 'Those goddamn Italians came right out with their hands up,' Sparks recalled, 'with their bags packed, ready to go to the States.'" (Kershaw, 2012, 36).

The 3rd Infantry Division landed in the Joss sector, seizing Licata and pushing inland. The U.S. 1st Infantry Division – the famous and relatively experienced "Big Red One," named for its unit insignia of a crimson number one on an olive green shield, came ashore in the center of the American landings near Gela. The battle of Gela on July 10th, continuing into the 11th as the Germans launched a counterattack against the beachhead, represented the only serious fighting during the initial invasion.

The 1st and 4th Ranger Battalions, among the first American soldiers ashore, encountered minefields in addition to machine gun fire from the Italian defenders and artillery fire from heights commanding the beach and town from a distance of several miles. One luckless Ranger officer, in the lead, stepped on a mine which blew his torso open. He turned to the men behind him, his beating heart exposed, and exclaimed, "I've had it." Other Rangers suffered wounds from exploding mines, and the Italians successfully set off demolition charges that destroyed the Gela pier. After a surprisingly vigorous firefight, the Rangers ejected the Italians – men of the 18th Coastal Brigade under Major Rubellino – from Gela, taking 200 prisoners in the process. The 26th Infantry Regiment leapfrogged inland to take the tactically useful high ground near Ponte Olivo, while the 16th Infantry Regiment took another commanding position at Piano Lupo, though only after a fierce struggle against determined Italian soldiers in a string of machine-gun nests.

In the meantime, the Italian artillery swept the beach with shells so persistently that the "Big Red One" abandoned the idea of offloading their artillery there. Instead, the landing craft carrying the vital guns shifted to the Joss landing zone to the west, greatly delaying their deployment.

By mid-morning, the Italians launched a major three-pronged counterattack, including troops from the Livorno Division. Dozens of Renault R-35 and Fiat 3000 light tanks supported each of the infantry columns as they advanced courageously against the dug-in Americans. No U.S. tanks yet supported the infantry due to difficulties in clearing the minefields while under Italian artillery fire. Light scouting aircraft deployed from the ships offshore served as spotters, despite being hunted ruthlessly by prowling Messerschmitt Bf-109D fighters. With their aid, the USS *Shubrick*, USS *Savannah*, USS *Boise*, and HMS *Abercrombie* fired their guns at a range of ten miles and successfully destroyed a number of Italian tanks. The Rangers then worked their way forward aggressively with bazookas, using the broken ground to get close to the Italian tanks and destroy more of them. With their routes of advance clogged by shattered, burning hulks, and with fierce fire directed at them by the Americans, the Italian soldiers finally withdrew, though not before taking a handful of prisoners from the 26th Infantry Regiment.

Scarcely had the Italians retreated when the ominous, faceted shapes of Panzer IV tanks appeared amid clouds of dust, advancing from the north at about 1 PM. The Hermann Goering Division's panzers attacked the 16th Infantry Division at Piano Lupo and overran their positions, then continued down towards the beachhead itself. At this point, heavy fire from the warships offshore brought the German tanks to a temporary halt.

Truck-mounted infantry of the 15th Panzergrenadier Division, supported by the full force of 17 Panzer VI Tiger tanks, also launched an attack, capturing the entire 1st Battalion of the U.S. 180th Infantry Regiment. They were finally halted when the Tigers entangled themselves in an olive grove. The day ended indecisively as the Germans pulled back slightly to regroup and Patton's 2nd Armored Division put their first M4 Shermans ashore despite moderately effective bombing attacks by the Luftwaffe.

A Sherman tank on Sicily after the landing

A picture of materials being towed ashore

The Battle of Gela continued on the next day, July 11th, 1943. A pleasantly mild morning soon turned into a scene of chaos and mayhem as over 30 Panzer IVs and 30 Panzer IIIs rolled forward against the 26th Infantry Regiment, smashing through it amid a storm of bullets and shells and rolling down towards the beach. Out of 60 M4 Shermans then ashore, only four remained serviceable, the remainder having thrown their tracks. Patton himself landed as the German tanks advanced closer and closer to Gela and the beachhead, swaggering about fearlessly and barking orders.

The tide turned gradually as Patton called for the ships offshore to shell the German tanks. Directed with deadly accuracy by spotters on the ground and in the air, the naval gunners destroyed tank after tank. Daring American soldiers, many of them Rangers, worked close to the steel giants to fire bazooka rounds into their underside or engine compartments. When the Germans finally began to withdraw at 2:00 p.m., they left 43 tanks behind, a figure that both U.S. Army and Wehrmacht records independently corroborate. Among these, 10 of the mighty Tigers had suffered destruction from naval shells. Bazooka teams accounted for six Panzer III and IV tanks out of the total. Patton described the failed attack as "the shortest Blitzkrieg in history" (Macintyre, 2010, 245), and German losses numbered 630 men killed or wounded while the Americans sustained 175 killed and 665 wounded.

As the Americans worked to consolidate their positions following the German counterattacks, July 11th witnessed another airborne disaster in the form of Husky 2, a parachute drop intended to provide inland support to the Gela landings. As the C-47 aircraft passed over American positions carrying the 82nd Airborne, the U.S. troops on the ground opened fire on their own aircraft to deadly effect. Omar Bradley watched the results with horror: "Like a covey of quail the formations split as pilots twisted their ships to escape [...] Ready lights flashed in the darkened cabins and parachutists tumbled out of the twisting aircraft. Some landed on the division fronts where they were mistaken for German raiders and shot while hanging in harness." (Porch, 2004, 426).

Bradley

    Another stain on the American front occurred on the 11th as well. After a hard fight to take the miniscule Biscari airfield, during which both Italians and Panzergrenadiers with armored halftracks inflicted heavy losses on the attacking American soldiers, and snipers nestled among the wrecked aircraft exerted a heavy toll, two Americans decided to take vengeance into their own hands. One, Sergeant Horace T. West, gunned down 37 prisoners in front of several other stunned soldiers, keeping nine for interrogation while two managed to escape. In the same sector, Captain John Compton assembled a firing squad and massacred another 36 helpless captives. West and Compton, when brought to book for these open atrocities, claimed they thought Patton's bloodthirsty speeches constituted an order to kill all prisoners. Compton escaped punishment, though he died a year later in combat in Italy, unmourned by his contemptuous fellow officers. West, though sentenced to life imprisonment, escaped with a year's confinement due to Bradley's fear that news of the massacre would induce the Germans to kill all Americans who fell into their hands – and that the American press might censure him.

To the east on July 11th and 12th, the British 8th Army advanced vigorously inland, encountering little resistance for the moment. The Syracuse-Augusta naval base fell almost without a shot being fired, and the Italian commander in Augusta itself surrendered before the first British soldier reached the town. The nominal commander of the Syracuse-Augusta base, an admiral, remained ignorant of his charge's fall until told of the event the following day at his posh headquarters in Catania. Wehrmacht Colonel Wilhelm Schmalz fought a series of delaying actions against the British with the small German forces immediately available to him near Syracuse and Augusta. With the powerful 8th Army moving rapidly northward, supplied and reinforced via Syracusan airfields and harbor facilities captured undamaged, Schmalz found himself obliged to give up Augusta on July 11th.

Though the Allies possessed enough air superiority to theoretically dominate the skies over Sicily, the Axis' aircraft continued to bomb the beaches heavily through the 11th and 12th. In fact, the Americans at Gela saw very little of their allegedly impervious fighter support. The SS *Richard Rowan*, a Liberty Ship carrying huge stores of gasoline and ammunition, took a direct hit from two bombs dropped by an Italian-piloted Stuka dive-bomber, and the ship detonated spectacularly.

A picture of the Liberty ship *Robert Rowan* exploding after being bombed by a German plane

The Luftwaffe and a handful of Italian pilots carried on a valiant effort against the invasion force despite being vastly outnumbered, forced to use bomb-pitted runways, and starved for fuel, ammunition, and ground support. Their efforts, though necessarily strictly limited, likely represented the most competent and organized Axis response to Operation Husky during the initial 48 hours.

On July 12th and 13th, and into the following days, the British 8th Army pushed north despite Schmalz's efforts to slow it, penetrating to the Plain of Catania south of Mount Etna. Catania itself, in the foothills, and the Gerbini Airfield, represented the new prize following the fall of Syracuse and Augusta. With Catania in their hands, the British might threaten Messina itself in the extreme northeast of Sicily. The seizure of Messina would cut the Germans off from retreat and likely force the surrender of the entire Axis garrison.

As the British crested the high ground above the Catanian plain and moved down towards the Simeto River, a line defended by tough, determined Wehrmacht soldiers, a spectacular panorama opened before them under the blazing, searing Sicilian sun. The English officer David Cole described the scene: "The panorama before us was magnificent. Thirty miles to the north, dominating the horizon was the huge, misty, snow-capped conical mass, 10,000 feet high, of Mount Etna [...] Along the coast, the city of Catania was dimly visibly, shimmering in the heat. All this would have constituted a picture of great beauty and tranquility, had it not been for the thud of shells, with their tell-tale puffs of black smoke, exploding near the river." (Hastings, 2011, 401).

Ben Aveling's picture of Mount Etna

The Americans also pushed forward vigorously in the face of collapsing Italian units. The 3rd Division proved exceptionally mobile due to special training insisted upon by its commander, Major General Lucian Truscott. While most units favored a standard marching pace of 2.5 miles per hour, Truscott preferred a minimum of 4 mph, and records show an average speed of 5 mph for the 3rd Division's infantry even on the steep, sunbaked Sicilian roads. Moving at this rapid pace, the men of the 3rd covered 15 miles inland by the time Eisenhower arrived to receive Patton's report in person on July 12th.

The Thunderbirds of the U.S. 45th Infantry Division continued inland and, on July 15th, debouched onto Highway 124 between Vizzini and Caltagarone. Highway 124 led to the northeast, in the direction of Mount Etna and the central portion of the German defenses. No sooner had the men begun their march up the highway, however, when they encountered elements of the 51st Highlanders, also using the roadway to advance.

Montgomery, learning of the situation, openly showed his total contempt for his American allies by ordering them to vacate Highway 124 forthwith and leave it entirely for the 8th Army's use. Patton, wishing to avoid a diplomatic incident, ordered his men to obey. With nowhere else in the rugged countryside to go, the U.S. 45th Infantry turned around and marched directly south towards the landing beaches. Both Bradley and Patton expressed outrage most of their soldiers also shared: "'My God,' US II Corps commander Omar Bradley exclaimed to Patton, 'you can't allow him to do that.' As far as Bradley was concerned, Montgomery's theft of the road was 'the most arrogant, egotistical, selfish and dangerous move in the whole of combined operations in

World War II.' […] in private [Patton] exploded. 'Tell Montgomery to stay out of my way or I'll drive those Krauts right up his ass,' he raged." (Kershaw, 2012, 39).

A relatively quiet but very bitter rift between the allies resulted from this obvious, and quite deliberate, snub. The Americans' green soldiers fled at Kasserine Pass half a year previously, so Montgomery – and to a large extent, Alexander as well – dismissed them haughtily as a nation of cowards. The fighting prowess of the Americans at Gela, now experienced and toughened by combat in Tunisia, escaped the British commanders totally.

Patton, seething with rage and viewing Eisenhower as little more than a British apologist and stooge, was determined to seek his own objectives. He planned to take the U.S. 7th Army north to capture Palermo, a port on the northern Sicilian coast. From there, his forces could strike east along coastal Highway 113, bypassing Etna and its German defenders to the north and, with luck, seizing Messina before the British.

Meanwhile, as the British moved down into the Catanian plain, they discovered that it provided poor country for tanks, contrary to their hopes. The dense network of stone walls dividing the arable land and the hardy stone cottages of the farmers made an ideal setting for smaller German forces to ambush and set up 88mm flak guns in anti-tank positions, delaying the advance and steadily inflicting casualties.

Operation Fustian followed – a British airborne landing to take the Primosole Bridge across the defended Simeto River. Around midnight on July 13th to 14th, another force of gliders and paratroopers flew in to take the bridge. The British now took their turn with a hideously costly friendly fire incident, wildly riddling their own aircraft with machine gun fire and flak, while German flak batteries also savaged the luckless, aerial troops. Forty aircraft, seeing the suicidal nature of the mission, turned around and flew back to Tunisia, their pilots refusing to die in a hail of their own army's fire.

To make matters worse, the Wehrmacht's 1st Fallschirmjager Division chose that night to land and reinforce Schmalz's defenders, as ordered by Adolf Hitler personally. The British and German paratroopers landed very close to one another and confused firefights erupted across the darkened landscape. One hundred and thirteen British paratroopers reached the Primosole Bridge and took it, but only held it for part of the 14th before German counterattacks forced them to retreat or suffer annihilation. One of the remaining Tiger tanks parked at a position commanding the bridge methodically sent shell after shell into the defenders, its thick armor immune to any weapons the British carried.

The British finally battled their way forward and took the bridge on July 16th, but by this time, the Germans had formed a thoroughly prepared defensive line just beyond the river, one that the British would not break until the start of August.

On July 17th, Patton, who had been brooding at his coastal headquarters, abruptly ordered an aircraft prepared and flew across the Mediterranean to Alexander's headquarters in the bayside town of La Marsa, Tunisia. Alexander, whom one Briton described as "bone from the neck up" (Atkinson, 2007, 130), listened to Patton's plan to drive on Palermo and studied the maps as the American general excitedly pointed to key highways, positions, and routes.

Alexander, guessing despite his lack of intelligence that Patton would act with or without approval, assented in order to maintain the appearance of authority. In fact, Patton had already ordered a "reconnaissance in force" to the port city of Agrigento, and Darby's 1st and 4th Rangers, together with three battalions of the fast-marching 3rd Infantry Division, approached the city through an almond orchard and stormed it even as Patton and Alexander talked far to the south, taking 6,000 Italian prisoners in the process.

The Americans met little resistance as they marched steadily north, though fleeing or surrendering Italians sometimes clogged the roads and slowed the pace. The leading elements of the U.S. 3rd Infantry Division, including Truscott himself, reached Palermo on July 22nd, to be greeted by a series of mass surrenders among the Italians garrison. The cheering inhabitants showered the American troops with flowers and lemons as they moved along the streets to survey the harbor, choked with the wrecks of 44 large ships and hundreds of smaller craft.

Patton himself arrived on July 23rd and took up residence in the ancient but still usable palace. At a cost of 300 men, the Americans had captured some 53,000 Italians and a handful of Germans, in addition to killing or wounding 2,300. The U.S. 7th Army now effectively held western Sicily and, more importantly from Patton's viewpoint, enjoyed full access to Highway 113 along the coast. By July 28th, American engineers rendered Palermo's harbor 30% functional again.

The Americans struck east along Coastal Highway 113 and the interior Highway 120 on July 23rd. The Germans, of course, fought for every valley, chokepoint, and pass along the way in an effort to delay them. The 45th Infantry began the advance but the 3rd Infantry gradually supplanted them as the 45th grew more exhausted and depleted.

During the advance, Patton's nerves wore to a frazzle, and it remains conceivable that he suffered a partial nervous breakdown. Alternating between screaming, wild rages and equally uncontrollable fits of sobbing at the admittedly appalling sight of mangled casualties, the general put a permanent stain on his reputation with several incidents that have since passed into legend. He shot a Sicilian civilian's mule and had it and the man's cart hurled off the side of a bridge the animal obstructed.

Even more damaging, he slapped and punched several soldiers for "cowardice," though one proved to be in a dazed state from severe malaria, fever, diarrhea, and dehydration, and another suffered from a combination of dehydration and actual shell-shock. On August 20, Patton received a letter from Eisenhower informing him that his conduct with respect to two of his soldiers was unacceptable and that he must apologize. It was a humiliating blow, but it could have been much worse, since Eisenhower had been under pressure to level formal charges and prosecute Patton, which would have ended his career. Patton had slapped Charles Kuhl after Kuhl explained that he was in the hospital for combat fatigue because he was more nervous than wounded, to which Patton responded, "You hear me, you gutless bastard? You're going back to the front." Kuhl described the second incident in a letter to his father: "General Patton slapped my face yesterday and kicked me in the pants and cussed me." Kuhl would later explain, "I was suffering from battle fatigue and just didn't know what to do."

The famous slapping incidents almost finished Patton, but it was Eisenhower's belief in his indispensability as an aggressive combat general, rather than any sense of friendship, that kept him in his post. Historians vary as to why Patton behaved this way. He had an old-fashioned view of combat fatigue, believing that it was merely cowardice, and he was dealing with the issue of thinning ranks and "malingering" of men who wanted to leave the front. He might also have been unable to control his mood swings, or perhaps he was simply exhausted. All of these factors may have played a role. In May 1943, Patton noted, "The publicity I have been getting, a good deal of which is untrue, and the rest of it ill considered, has done me more harm than good. The only way you get on in this profession is to have the reputation of doing what you are told as thoroughly as possible. So far I have been able to accomplish that, and I believe I have gotten quite a reputation from not kicking at peculiar assignments."

Initially the press was persuaded not to run the story but it inevitably leaked during a

November radio broadcast back in the U.S. Eisenhower rode out the storm, and Patton received support from Roosevelt while he was passing through Sicily on his way back from the Tehran Conference. Patton repeatedly apologized, believing that he would pay for the mistakes with his career, and when Clark's army - including most of Patton's troops - attacked the Italian mainland, he would be left with staffing duties. He traveled around the Mediterranean, not quite believing Eisenhower's assurances about his future, but this was part of an Allied ploy. The Allies knew that the Germans rated Patton highly, and thus his appearance in a series of locations would cause intelligence confusion as they theorized about the next Allied invasion. Thus, Patton visited Cairo, Malta and Algeria to sow seeds of doubt, even if he was not happy to play decoy

However, that was all in the future, and in the meantime, to the east, Montgomery's decision to block the U.S. 45th Infantry Division now had seriously negative consequences for the men under his command. The Hermann Goering Division, noting the retreat of the Americans, turned their entire strength against the British 8th Army. Making matters worse, Montgomery now needed to take two objectives rather than focusing on just one – Vizzini and Catania, the latter now reinforced by German paratroopers (Fallschirmjager) of the 1st Parachute Division – thus dividing and weakening his forces.

The British holding the Primosole Bridge on July 14th fought off numerous German counterattacks, but eventually used up their ammunition and retreated to avoid capture. The 50th Division struck at the Primosole Bridge on July 15th, but the Germans resisted fiercely, delaying the British recapture of the structure until late on the 16th. Montgomery, rather than concentrating his forces after gaining this key crossing, split them further, sending the 51st Canadian Division to take Paterno, between the 13th Corps (attacking towards Catania) and the 30th Corps (advancing through Vizzini).

By July 19th, Montgomery realized his error and asked for American assistance. At that point, however, the U.S. 7th Army, fully occupied in its northward offensive, ignored his request entirely. Alexander declined to order the Americans to rejoin the 8th Army's push, though he sent the 78th Division from Tunisia to reinforce Montgomery.

Hube took over from Guzzoni in directing the defense on July 22nd, 1943. The next day, July 23rd, the Americans began a grueling assault on Nicosia, destined to last until July 27th, when the Germans retreated towards Etna in good order. During the same period, and onward through the 29th, the exhausted British regrouped, while continuing to press against the Etna defense line at multiple points.

The British launched many attacks towards Catania, but the 1st Fallschirmjager and Hermann Goering troops repulsed each bloodily from their well-prepared positions. Dozens of these attacks occurred, with the aftermath of one sufficing for a description of the bleak results of each of the others: "Heavy machine-gun and small-arms fire greeted the brave attackers who again suffered high losses. The dead and wounded lay in rows before the German position and the cries of the wounded were heard for the rest of the night. The next morning some of the wounded British troops were rescued by the Germans." (D'Este, 2010, 295).

During these exchanges, the 1st Fallschirmjager Division established a rather schizophrenic reputation for itself among its enemies. On the one hand, its men's frequent use of the exclamation "Heil Hitler," especially when captured, convinced the British of the paratroopers' fanatical Nazism. On the other hand, the German airborne soldiers went to considerable lengths to retrieve wounded Britons and provide them with the same medical care as their own troops, a chivalric gesture amid the brutal fight of attrition south of Etna's looming volcanic cone.

On July 29th, the British resumed their offensive – "Operation Hardgate" – and managed to take Centuripe and Regalbuto by August 3rd. This attack used the 78th Division – newly arrived from North Africa – and the 1st Canadian Division, aiming for Adrano. The 13th Corps facing Catania now largely held its positions, tying down the Hermann Goering division but playing little aggressive role beyond that.

Schmalz, still conducting a brilliant defense, used tactics described by the British Major Hugh Pond: "All 8th Army's assaults started in the same way […] the Germans were by now used to it and their reaction was to get as many men as possible under cover, leaving just a few sentries […] As the shelling ended, or went over, they reoccupied their defensive positions and came up fighting." Colonel Schmalz estimated that the enemy fired […] thirty thousand shells on one kilometer of front in a one-and-a-half hour period. He lost two men killed and eight wounded." (Mitcham, 2007, 189).

At Regalbuto, the Engineers of the Hermann Goering Division fought furiously, supported by the infantry and a few tanks. They deployed the Wehrmacht's multiple rocket launchers, officially named Nebelwerfers but nicknamed "Moaning Minnie" or "Screaming Mimi" by the Allies, to deadly effect. Only after days of hard fighting in sheer ravines and along knife-sharp ridges did the British and Canadians finally dislodge their tenacious Teutonic opponents. "'B' Company reached the base of Tower Hill first and quickly drove off the few Germans who had hung around to meet the Canadians. Leapfrogging past, 'C' Company pushed to the summit in time to see the last of the two estimated companies of paratroops that had fought to stem their assault legging it down the other side. The outflanking movement, by the battalion, succeeded in smashing this strongpoint and opening the way for the advance on Adrano." (Zuehlke, 2008, 287).

As the Americans continued their advance on July 29th, they ran up against the 15th Panzergrenadier Division at the mountaintop town of Troina. A strongpoint of the German defenses around Mount Etna, Troina represented an important objective because Highway 120, a key route of advance through the jagged Sicilian countryside, ran through it. The U.S. 1st Infantry Division, the "Big Red One," supplied many of the soldiers, though the 39th Infantry Regiment of the 9th Infantry Division also participated.

Under the overall command of Omar Bradley, the immensely popular Terry Allen led the effort, along with Theodore Roosevelt III, the immensely good-natured and equally courageous grandson of the famous president. Bradley secretly harbored a venomous hatred for both men, but he concealed it while he used them to take Troina.

Allen

The Germans held Troina in force, with a tactically advantageous position commanding the only practicable route of approach from the west, a bare valley five miles long. The double-spire Norman church furnished an excellent observation post for German spotters and officers. The Americans began the battle in possession of Cerami, an oleander-shaded hilltop town facing Troina from the west.

The Americans initially believed Troina weakly defended, but the Germans swiftly disabused them of that mistaken notion. On July 31st, the 3,000 men comprising the 39th Infantry Regiment, under Lieutenant Colonel Jack Toffey, moved forward under cover of night late in the evening, flanking Highway 120. However, the German defenders – under the personal command of Eberhard Rodt – and four battalions of Italian soldiers led by Giacomo Romano – awaited them in trenches and camouflaged firing positions. Met by a furious hail of machine gun and mortar fire, and the concentrated bombardment of 88mm flak guns and other Wehrmacht field artillery whose smokeless powder made them difficult for the Americans' supporting gun crews to pick out for counterfire, the 39th Infantry retreated after a sharp firefight.

Rodt

Realizing the strength of Troina's defenses, the Americans attempted to outflank the town. The 26th Infantry Regiment circled to the north of Troina, taking Monte Basilio after two days of hard fighting, heavy artillery fire, and counterattacks by the Panzergrenadiers. The 18th Infantry Regiment attempted to encircle the position from the south, taking Monte Salici and facing equally strong German and Italian resistance. The 39th and 16th Infantry advanced directly up the valley on either side of Highway 120.

The fight for Troina lasted from August 1-5, with the Americans slowly pushing forward from cover to cover, while machine guns, mortars, and artillery fired back and forth, sending metallic death and equally lethal stone fragments showering through the harsh ridges and valleys of the Sicilian countryside. The end of the fight came on August 6th. Hube, now commanding the defense of Sicily, judged the Etna Line untenable in the first week of August, so he ordered the Hermann Goering Division to pull back from Catania on August 4th, abandoning the town to the British 8th Army, and he gave similar orders to abandon Troina to the U.S. 7th Army on August 5th.

On August 6th, Americans advancing to the edge of town found it abandoned by the Wehrmacht, leaving behind maggot-filled corpses, ruinous desolation, and a highly distressed population who nevertheless welcomed the coming of the Americans. Bradley, a coldly vindictive man despite his undoubted military skills, "celebrated" the victory by immediately relieving his personal enemies, Terry Allen and Theodore Roosevelt III, from command, to their despair and to the lasting outrage of their men, among whom both commanding officers enjoyed great popularity.

Hube had, in fact received authorization from Kesselring on August 2nd to abandon Sicily entirely. Knowing that Hube had his finger on the pulse of combat more accurately than he did from afar, Kesselring left the timetable of withdrawal to Hube's initiative. Though the Allies now pushed the Germans back almost to the Messina peninsula in the island's extreme northeast, with the British advancing from the south and the Americans from the west, some fight still remained in Hube and his sturdy, veteran Wehrmacht soldiers.

The Germans dug in afresh along the San Fratello Line, though Hube also began orderly, large-scale withdrawals by ferry across the Straits of Messina to the Italian mainland at the same time, drawing down the remaining Axis presence on the island. The 29th Panzergrenadier Division, a new unit of reinforcements led by General Walter Fries, held the San Fratello Line against the Americans, making use of the steep, avalanche-prone Nebrodi Mountains with their dense cork, oak, and beech forests as natural defensive positions.

The 3rd Infantry Division, still moving at "Truscott's Trot," advanced along Coastal Highway 113 and engaged the 29th Panzergrenadier Division (nicknamed the "Falcons") near San Fratello itself in early August. The hard-fighting Panzergrenadiers brought the U.S. soldiers to a standstill, though the Americans also proved unwilling to give ground, leading to vicious stalemate fighting along the rugged Sicilian coast.

August 8th proved a pivotal day in the German defense. The British captured Bronte, an important defensive position in the new defensive line, and the Americans succeeded in seizing Cesaro. Hube, already withdrawing the 29th Panzergrenadiers from San Fratello east along Highway 113, found himself astonished by American audacity when the 3rd Infantry Division used landing craft to conduct a surprise landing in the rear of the San Fratello positions.

Hube, now seriously alarmed that the British, Americans, or both might break through his defenses and seize Messina, greatly accelerated the withdrawal process. On August 9th to 10th, Wehrmacht soldiers occupied the Tortorici Line, designed to protect the crucial road junction at Randazzo, now the key to escape for many German units still at risk of being cut off and captured by the aggressively advancing allies. Axis presence in Sicily shrank to one corner of the island, exclusive of huge numbers of Italian prisoners. The invasion of Sicily was nearly complete.

As the clock ran out on the Axis occupation of Sicily, Patton grew desperate to accelerate his own advance, hoping to reach Messina prior to the deeply hated "Monty." Recycling the same maneuver used at San Fratello, Patton order Lieutenant Colonel Lyle Bernard to outflank the Tortorici Line along Highway 113 by sea, using an amphibious attack at Brolo on August 11th. Truscott objected, judging the maneuver a suicide mission for his men, but Patton, his eye on Messina, bullied him into compliance.

The 2nd Battalion landing at Brolo in the rear of the Germans, supported by the cruiser USS *Philadelphia* and six destroyers, soon found they had indeed bitten off more than they could chew. Counterattacked powerfully by the desperate Wehrmacht, Bernard withdrew his command to Mount Cipolla, where he hoped to make a last stand. Throughout the 11th, the Americans desperately held off the Panzergrenadiers and their supporting Panzers, occasionally helped by naval gun fire from the skittish USS *Philadelphia*.

The U.S. soldiers sustained 177 wounded and killed, but the Germans proved more interested in escaping than in destroying his force. Once they drove him and his men to Mount Cipolla, the Wehrmacht troops lost interest in them, attached their guns to prime movers, and drove off rapidly along Coastal Highway 113, abandoning the Tortorici Line. On that same day, August 11th, the 15th Panzergrenadiers began their evacuation across the Strait of Messina to Italy, leaving the Hermann Goering division to handle much of the remaining defense.

The key road junction at Randazzo fell to a collaborative Anglo-American attack on August 13th. Participants included the British 78th Division and the U.S. 9th Division, and the loss of this position prompted the Hermann Goering Division to abandon Taormina and move north on

Highway 114, leaving the roadway behind them defended by huge quantities of land mines and booby traps. These lethal devices slowed the British pursuit sufficiently to allow the Hermann Goering's soldiers to reach Messina largely unmolested and begin their own evacuation.

Hube, comparing the adroit German escape to the British evacuation at Dunkirk earlier in the war, correctly predicted that its success would greatly bolster German morale: "The end of the Sicilian campaign is actually a full success. After the initial fiasco, the fighting as well as the preparation and execution of the evacuation, with all serviceable material and men (including the wounded) went according to plan." (Mitcham, 2007, 222).

The final race into Messina took place during August 15th to 17th, and the Americans "won" the race by a few hours, with several platoons from the 45th Infantry Division – the Thunderbirds – entering the city outskirts late on the 16th and moving deeper into the city on August 17th. Darby's Rangers and more Thunderbirds entered the city shortly after dawn, followed by British armor in the mid-morning. Patton arrived at 10:00 a.m. to receive the formal surrender of the city officials, shortly before a British officer arrived in an armored car to do the same, just slightly too late.

The meeting naturally provoked banter on both sides: "'Where you tourists been?' asked GIs when the British arrived just two hours later. 'Hello, you bloody bastards!' replied British tankers. [...] Patton entered the shattered city later that day, a phalanx of press and photographers in his wake. A senior British officer greeted him with a snappy salute. 'It was a jolly good race,' said the gracious limey. 'I congratulate you.'" (Kershaw, 2012, 42).

A bombed-out wreck, Messina offered little to the conquerors, though the populace who had not fled showered them with flowers and grapes as they marched through the streets. Patton, however, appeared radiant, his place on newspaper front pages across the globe momentarily assured.

The Anglo-American air forces and naval groups, each under their own independent command and seeing little need to confer with Eisenhower, Alexander, Montgomery, or Patton, made almost no effort to stop the German evacuations from Sicily. The Germans themselves expressed astonishment that no major attacks came, and they even began evacuating by day as well as night.

The German units emerged battered but fairly intact, while the Italians suffered devastating casualties: "Total Italian losses were about 4,680 killed, 5,000 wounded, and about 152,000 missing or captured [...] German losses were 4,561 killed, 4,583 missing, and 5,523 captured for a total of 14,667; a further 13,532 were wounded and evacuated [...] Allied losses were 2,237 killed and 5,946 wounded in the Seventh US Army, and 2,062 killed and 7,137 wounded in the British/Canadian 8th Army." (Zaloga, 2013, 89).

Despite his brief brush with personal triumph, Patton found himself in the crosshairs of scandal and hatred following the seizure of Messina. Almost immediately, news of the slapping incidents broke, enraging almost the entire U.S. 7th Army against its commander. Patton apologized to both men involved publicly, but the damage was done. While some troops cheered him, the 1st Infantry Division – the "Big Red One" – gathered its entire 15,000 men to hear a victory speech from Patton. When the general finished, the men, still furious enough to "shoot" Patton due to the slapping incident and because they knew he had permitted Bradley to replace their heroes Roosevelt and Allen, sat in deep silence with expressionless faces rather than cheering. One man, with a nearly sublime sense of irony, remarked loudly, "That f****ing f***er of a general f***ing swears too much." (Atkinson, 2007, 172).

Meanwhile, in the Allied high command, the matter of where to land in Italy became a matter of pressing importance. Churchill favored a northerly landing, memorably and colorfully remarking, "Why should we crawl up the leg like a harvest-bug from the ankle upwards? Let us rather strike at the knee … Tell the planners to throw their hat over the fence." (Atkinson, 2007, 136).

Ultimately, many far-reaching consequences followed from Operation Husky. The Italians ousted Mussolini, leading to his imprisonment, rescue by the Nazis, and reestablishment of a rump Fascist state in northern Italy. For their part, the Germans used the time taken by the Allies in expelling them from Sicily to occupy much of Italy in detail, creating a new front.

Of course, the Allies also gained some advantages. They carried out the amphibious assault with superb professionalism, even if the accompanying airborne drops proved catastrophically bungled. Perhaps most importantly, the Allied forces gained invaluable experience in amphibious operations that would later be put to good use during the D-Day landings in Normandy a year later. The U.S. Army also gained the battle experience needed to quickly become one of the most formidable Allied armies during the war.

The Mediterranean route also opened for Lend-Lease shipments to the Soviet Union, increasing the flood of materiel by 27% annually. On top of that, the USSR also benefited immensely by the removal of many German divisions earmarked for a fresh 1943 offensive – 17 redeployed to the Balkans and Greece alone – which also gutted Hitler's Kursk offensive. With so many men and vehicles stripped from the Eastern Front, the balance tipped from deep uncertainty to a steady (though brutally costly) Soviet advance.

In fact, Operation Husky interrupted Operation Citadel in southern Russia at its most crucial moment. The Germans had penetrated two of three Soviet defensive lines and were poised to encircle and capture another vast horde of Russians. Had Citadel carried forward, the Wehrmacht stood a good chance of regaining the initiative in the east, pushing the Soviets back in a series of fresh defeats. Instead, Hitler decided to defend Italy, allowing the Soviets to counterattack and gain the initiative for themselves, grabbing momentum that they never relinquished. Operation Husky decisively switched the Third Reich to a losing, defensive strategy, and it had succeeded largely due to the Nazi failure to reinforce Sicily, which in turn resulted from the deception of Operation Mincemeat.

In that sense, from a certain viewpoint, the fate of Sicily, Operation Citadel, and Hitler's "Thousand-Year Reich" all hinged on a Welsh pauper named Michael Glyndwr and the clever scheme of Ewen Montagu and Charles Cholmondeley, two junior British officers with an idea straight from the pages of a pulp adventure novel.

The immense difficulties Sicily's rugged terrain caused to the Allied forces, and the successful delaying actions fought by small numbers of well-led German soldiers, inspired Hitler and his generals to garrison Italy as an obstacle to British and American advance. A relatively limited number of Wehrmacht troops used the endless series of mountain ridges and defensible hilltop towns to slow the offensive to a crawl, tying down large numbers of Western troops and frequently inflicting heavy casualties.

The situation cut both ways, of course. With Mussolini deposed and the defense of Italy falling exclusively to German soldiers, divisions crucially needed elsewhere remained tied down opposing the Allied advance. With a seaborne invasion of France already planned for the spring or summer of 1944, American general Dwight D. Eisenhower deemed the Italian theater strategically crucial in lessening the Atlantic Wall's defenses: "It is essential for us to retain the initiative […] If we can keep him [i.e. the German enemy] on his heels until early spring, then the more divisions he uses in a counteroffensive against us, the better it will be for

OVERLORD." (Atkinson, 2007, 255).

Following the initial fall of Mussolini from power in Sicily's wake, the new Italian government signed a treaty with the Allies. Though ostensibly secret, the treaty soon leaked out, partly thanks to incautious announcements by the BBC. In response, the Germans occupied much of Italy, deploying 16 divisions, including crack Waffen-SS units seasoned on the Eastern Front. 720,000 Italian soldiers fell into German hands, much of the peninsula suffered Third Reich occupation by mid-September 1943, and Hitler installed Mussolini as the figurehead satrap of a northern Italian dictatorship.

Albert Kesselring, known as "Smiling Al" due to his nearly inevitable cheerful, confident, toothy grin, commanded the theater overall on the Wehrmacht side. He managed to wrest considerable independence of action from Hitler at a 1943 conference, freeing himself from the Fuhrer's nervous micromanagement.

Kesselring and Rommel
Under Kesselring's expert leadership, the Germans fell back northward methodically, fighting a

major delaying action at Volturno in mid-October. The Wehrmacht then established themselves on the Reinhard Line, a temporary defensive front meant to delay the Allies until the Germans finished preparing the stronger Gustav Line, stretching from Gaeta to Ortona and anchored on the formidable strongpoint near the early medieval monastery of Monte Cassino, as Kesselring described in his memoirs: "On 4 November advanced Allied patrols were observed there. I had full confidence in this naturally very strong position and hoped by holding it for some length of time, perhaps till the New Year, to be able to make the rear Gustav Line so strong that the British and Americans would break their teeth on it." (Kesselring, 1954, 226).

In broad outlines, the Allied strategy witnessed the British Eighth Army under the tenacious but extremely undiplomatic Bernard Montgomery advancing up the eastern, or Adriatic, side of the Italian peninsula. The United States Fifth Army, meanwhile, pushed up the western side of Italy flanked by the Tyrrhenian Sea, directly towards the key town of Cassino. General Mark Clark led the Americans; the general showed many traits of an ambitious, smooth, conceited publicity-seeker and drew censure both at the time and later. Nevertheless, he also displayed determination, grit, and hard-driving aggression.

Montgomery

Clark

Cassino dominated Route 6, also known as the Via Casilina, a main highway artery and the only western Italian road at the time capable of supporting an aggressive advance by a large, motorized army. The ancient Appian Way or Route 7, closer to the coast, ran through numerous marshes and crossed many canals, and therefore seemed much less attractive to the Americans with their large numbers of trucks, tanks, and other vehicles.

These maneuvers and positions set the stage for the one of the largest land battles in World War II. The battle would consist of four main encounters, beginning in the bitter, rainy, mud-drenched weather of January 1944 and continuing through sunny, warm days of May 1944. The final shots of the Battle of Monte Cassino rang out just a few days before the Allies surged ashore in the decisive D-Day landings in Normandy on June 4th, 1944.

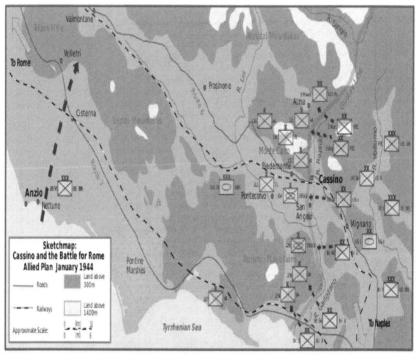

A map of the plan of attack for the First Battle

The Italian terrain and weather greatly increased the hardship of the Allied soldiers attempting to break the Gustav Line in early 1943. The bare, stony valleys of the Italian mountains provided little shelter from either meteorological conditions or hostile people. Sheer slopes made maneuvering difficult and often trapped men in natural killing grounds overlooked by mountains and hills occupied by the enemy.

With little soil in many locations, digging foxholes or trenches frequently proved impossible, leaving soldiers exposed to enemy fire. Additionally, practically all ordnance and even small arms fire kicked up showers of lethal stone shrapnel from the loose scree present everywhere, with razor-sharp shards of rock tearing into unprotected bodies and faces. The Germans, standing on the defensive, usually had positional advantage.

In the winter, when the first battle of Monte Cassino commenced, constant rains soaked the harsh landscape. This produced clinging, sucking mud which bedeviled both sides. Additionally, fog frequently blanketed the landscape in winter, further depressing men already disheartened by high casualties, physical misery, and the fact that many had fought for years in North Africa before being sent to a fresh, extremely lethal encounter with no intervening period of recuperation. As one description put it, "Fog in front of the outposts, fog in front of the enemy, fog in front of the hotels, fog for taking away the wounded, fog for bringing up ammunition, fog, fog, fog [...] There was no longer any day; there were only two species of night, one yellowish and full of clouds, that did not allow you to see and took you by the throat, the other full of flashes, of glimmers of light, of bursts of machine-gun fire, of fearful noises." (Caddick-Adams, 2013, 6).

The Cassino area, thickly fortified with pillboxes, mines, and other emplacements, fell under the immediate command of the superbly skilled Wehrmacht leader Generaloberst Heinrich von Vietinghoff. The XIV Panzer Corps, a key unit in the defense, served under the leadership of another extremely capable officer, Lieutenant General Friedrich von Senger und Etterlin.

Vietinghoff

Senger

Vietinghoff knew that the Allies, against whom he fought the relatively successful Volturno delaying action, must come up Route 6, which ran directly through Cassino, if they wished to penetrate into the Liri Valley and advance beyond to Rome. The impregnable mountain barriers of the Apennines blocked any armored advance on the "Eternal City" save along this single axis. Accordingly, German artillery and spotters occupied the mountain ridges around Cassino, commanding every inch of the approaches.

The Americans, newly-minted but extremely courageous Allied Italian units, and many others fought their way slowly north towards Cassino during late December and early January. The Germans made good use of the terrain, reducing the Allied advance to a grinding pace and inflicting numerous casualties.

The soldiers of both sides performed prodigies of valor, interspersed with moments of panicked flight, during the brutal attritional struggle. The Allies successfully forced the Wehrmacht soldiers out of one position after another, but generally at a high cost in killed and wounded. Moreover, their formidable air power proved relatively ineffective amid the violent winds and rainstorms of the Italian mountain winter.

Picture of a B-17 flying over Monte Cassino and its famous abbey

The Allies arrived near Cassino on January 10th and launched their first attacks almost immediately. The French Expeditionary Force (FEC) delivered the first blow on the night of January 11th to 12th, 1944, under the leadership of the brilliantly intelligent, extremely cordial and well-liked French General Alphonse Juin. A superb commander, Juin found himself well-served by his colonial troops, the 2nd Moroccan Division and the 3rd Algerian Division.

Juin

The Moroccans proved extremely capable in alpine warfare, originating as they did from the Atlas Mountains. Known as Goumiers, these men wore British helmets, long vertically striped tunics, American boots, and carried as many guns, machine-guns, knives, and daggers as they could lay their hands on. Formidably brave, they also acquired an unfortunate reputation for rape and atrocity – partly based on the facts of a number of appalling incidents, and partly founded on hysterical exaggeration among the panicked and demoralized civilian population.

Juin's FEC soldiers moved forward through heavy rain and snow, achieving complete surprise as they attacked on the far right flank of the Allied position. Mark Clark envisioned flanking maneuvers by one corps on each flank to encircle Cassino and a direct attack by two additional corps (the British 10th Corps and the U.S. 2nd Corps) across the Garigliano, Rapido, and Gari Rivers. The bold plan, making use of strong encircling movements in the best tradition already demonstrated time and time again by the Wehrmacht, deserved more success than it actually achieved.

The Moroccan division attacked the 5th Gebirgsjager Division north of Cassino in the darkness, first slaughtering the outposts with their curved daggers, then attacking larger defensive positions with grenades and mortars. The Gebirgsjagers – elite German mountain troops with considerable fighting experience – nevertheless found themselves caught completely by surprise and pushed back with heavy losses.

The Algerian division, to the Moroccans' left, attacked the eminence of Monna Casale, also held by elements of the 5th Gebirgsjagers. Here, the Germans managed to put up stiffer resistance, and daylight found the Algerians still battling up the slopes. Nevertheless, they secured the peak by noon. A seesaw battle for the Monna Casale occupied the whole afternoon, with the Gebirgsjager troops finally breaking off late in the day after suffering startling decimation.

The FEC continued their forward drive throughout the following six days, with bitterly-fought small actions between the skilled Gebirgsjagers and equally effective Goumiers as the two sides contested each gully, crag, and slope. The colonial troops finally reached the end of their tether on January 17th. Alphonse Juin asked Mark Clark for just one more division as reinforcements to punch through to the Liri Valley, thus totally outflanking Cassino and forcing the garrison's retreat or surrender.

Senger, the German commander in the sector, recognized the peril but had no reinforcements to back the final lines of defense. Juin's correct assessment, however, ran headlong into Mark Clark's skepticism. By January 17th, he prepared to unleash British and American troops directly towards the Cassino position. Neglecting to visit Juin's position personally, he dismissed the French general's call for an additional division – and thus threw away an excellent chance to destroy the Gustav Line just six days into the fighting. His decision resulted in a bloodbath lasting for 123 more days.

On January 17th, the British 10th Corps attacked across the Garigliano River near the coast. The Wehrmacht defenders, men of the 94th Infantry Division supported by several tanks on loan from the Hermann Goering Panzer Division, met the British with ferocious counterattacks and determined resistance as soon as their assault boats crossed the Garigliano. Part of the 2nd Royal Scots Division came ashore from landing craft but found themselves bogged down under fire in the midst of huge German minefields.

A German panzer at the battle

American soldiers and tank at the battle
Despite the courage and skill of the German 94th Infantry, the British 56th Division and others fought with equal valor and tactical acumen, gradually pushing their Wehrmacht opponents back. This enabled more English troops to cross the Garigliano, creating a major bridgehead by nightfall on January 19th.

With the French halted on their extreme left flank, Vietinghoff and Senger realized that the British were now poised to outflank Cassino, crossing the Aurunci Mountains to surge into the undefended Liri Valley. Kesselring, told of the situation, immediately sent two Panzergrenadier Divisions, the 29th and 90th, to block the British advance. While waiting for the reinforcements to arrive, the 15th Panzergrenadier Division detached a single regiment to stiffen the 94th Infantry.

On the 19th, the British 46th Division tried to cross the Garigliano upstream to prepare the ground for a major U.S. Army crossing. However, only a tiny number of men managed to cross. The river, swollen to a muddy, roaring torrent by days of heavy rain, swept boats and pontoon bridges away with equal force. The British made over a dozen attempts to cross, none of which succeeded.

The U.S. 2nd Corps' attack in the center proved an unmitigated disaster. The 36th National Guard Division, "Texas," advanced late on January 20th, across marshy ground thick with deep mud and encumbered by barbed wire entanglements and minefields. The men attempted to cross the swollen Rapido River in the darkness, but the 15th Panzergrenadier Division, an extremely experienced elite unit, shredded them with a blistering fusillade of mortar, rifle, and machine gun fire.

With most rubber assault boats punctured almost instantly by German fire, only a few men crossed successfully, where they either died or surrendered when they discovered their hopeless situation. The Americans tried again on the night of January 21st, attempting to build a bridge under cover of night to send Sherman tanks across the Rapido. The Panzergrenadiers prevented this also, forcing the U.S. soldiers and engineers to retreat with a lethal, sustained hail of fire.

The engineers also provided relatively poor guidance to the soldiers on their way down to the riverbank. For their part, the troops proved less than enthusiastic about the crossing in the teeth of what they deemed a superior force, as one engineer recounted, "The infantrymen I talked with didn't like night fighting and lacked confidence in their ability to knock out the enemy in a night engagement." (Blumenson, 1993, 338).

The centerpiece of Mark Clark's attack failed so badly that Senger believed it to be a minor diversionary attack, when in fact the American general meant it to be a stunning body blow to the German resistance.

The Allies did not intend the attack on Cassino as a simple slogging match, understanding quite clearly the cost of such an operation. Instead, they planned a landing at Anzio by an entire army corps, the U.S. 6th Corps, to outflank the Gustav Line and force the Germans' withdrawal to avoid encirclement. The Allied command, though in possession of a sound plan, put it in the hands of a poorly chosen leader, Major General John P. Lucas. The Anzio landing occurred on schedule on January 22nd, 1944.

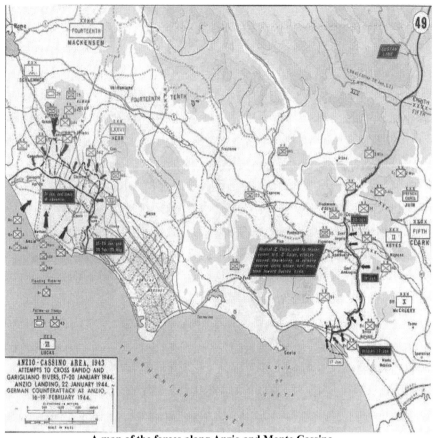

A map of the forces along Anzio and Monte Cassino

American soldiers at Anzio

Lucas

Despite achieving total tactical surprise, Lucas squandered the opportunity to run amok in the Gustav Line's rear by remaining supinely in Anzio. Winston Churchill, with his typical verve, excoriated Lucas' failure with a colorful description: "Instead of hurling a wildcat onto the shore all we got was a stranded whale." (Caddick-Adams, 2013, 53). Lucas permitted the Germans to bottle his force up uselessly in Anzio, while Churchill continued to hurl accurate but futile verbal barbs at the incompetent American general.

A later German report also expressed surprise at Lucas' inaction: "The Allies on the beachhead on the first day of the landing did not conform to the German High Command's expectations. Instead of moving northward with the first wave to seize the Alban Mountains... the landing forces limited their objective. Their initial action was to occupy a small beachhead." (Blumenson, 1993, 362).

Regrouping and consolidating their positions after these successes and failures, the Allied forces renewed their attack in earnest on January 24th. On the right flank, history repeated itself, with Alphonse Juin and his tough Goumiers winning tactical successes they could not exploit due to Mark Clark's stubborn refusal to believe Juin's reports or send him the reinforcements he wanted.

The Moroccan Goumiers performed astonishingly, seizing Monte Santa Croce, 3,700 feet tall, while buffeted by frigid gale-force winds and raked incessantly by German machine gun, mortar, and artillery fire. The Moroccans hauled themselves up ice-coated cliffs using pitons and ropes alone while subjected to the rage of man and nature, and succeeded in ousting the tough Gebirgsjager from the soaring height.

The main thrust of the French pushed for Monte Cifalco, however, where batteries of German 75mm mountain guns kept up a murderous fire on Allied positions. The German unit, under the command of Captain Anton Auggenthaler, fought back fiercely, slowing the advance of the FEC men to a crawl despite their nearly suicidal courage.

However, Clark's headquarters sent fresh orders diverting the French towards another objective, a ridge called the Colle Belvedere, five miles due north of Monte Cassino. The new goal, besides having considerably less immediate tactical value than Monte Cifalco, appeared impracticable to the men actually on the ground. The commander charged with leading the first advance, General Joseph de Monsabert, responded angrily when he received the order, "Storm Belvedere? Who's dreamed up that one? Have they looked at it? You'd have to first cross two rivers [...] then smash through the Gustav Line in the valley, and finally, all the time attacking the Boche, climb more than 2,000 feet over a bare rock pile, itself heavily fortified, that can be fired on from Cifalco and the rest of the summits round that. It's pure wishful thinking! It's a crazy gamble!" (Caddick-Adams, 2013, 62).

Monsabert

Almost miraculously, the Moroccans, led by French and Moroccan officers, managed to seize the Colle Belvedere on January 25th by ascending a vertical fissure in the rock under cover of mist. The German artillery and infantry still exacted a heavy toll, but the FEC soldiers pushed on to take the additional objective of Monte Abate in the morning of January 27th, though the Germans bloodily evicted them again before noon.

Another seesaw battle erupted for the Colle Belvedere on the 28th and 29th, with first one side and then the other seizing control of the ridge after brutal combat. At one point, a train of 80 resupply mules started for the French lines, but German shells aimed from Auggenthaler's battery killed 78 of them, scattering ammunition and food over the mountainside. The FEC soldiers held the Colle Belvedere at sundown on the 29th.

Auggenthaler himself died to counterbattery fire during the fighting, which claimed 1,481 Allied soldiers killed and wounded against approximately 1,200 Germans. Preventing a full French breakthrough required Senger to commit 17 of the 44 Wehrmacht and SS battalions available to him for the Cassino defense.

The Americans, in the meantime, launched their own offensive across the Rapido River towards the German-held village of Cairo and several nearby hills. Preceded by a half-hour barrage, the U.S. 34ʰ Division, nicknamed the "Red Bull," advanced through the thick mud to the river, which, though icy, they successfully waded in the darkness, taking some ground beyond it.

Morning light on the 25th revealed the Red Bull Division's positions to every German battery on the nearby hills and mountains, however. A storm of shells began falling amid the luckless GIs, raising fountains of mud and earth while shattering human bodies as well. The fire grew so intense that the division pulled back hastily to the Allied side of the Rapido to avoid pointless decimation.

Showing great determination, the American soldiers continued their attempts to push across the Rapido, attacking until ferocious artillery fire compelled them to retreat and regroup. However, by the 27th, the men, under Charles W. Ryder, established a tenable position on the north bank of the Rapido. From there, they took two key hills Point 213 and Point 56, in addition to the village of Cairo on the 29th.

The 148th Regiment of the 36th Division "Texas" joined in also, taking Monte Manna on the 34th Division's right and linking up with the left flank of Juin's FEC units. With a solid Allied front now established on the north side of the Rapido, elements of the 34th Division, assisted by American tanks, actually fought their way into the outskirts of Cassino itself. The Americans fought with desperate courage but could not penetrate deeply into the town.

Senger, noting the lack of activity in the British 10th Corps on the left of the Allied line, took a huge gamble and stripped his defenses there, moving the 90th Panzergrenadier Division and its seasoned, eccentric commander Ernst Baade – who often wore a Scottish kilt and broadsword as part of his battlefield regalia – to block the Americans.

Pushing towards the Monte Cassino peak, crowned dramatically by the ancient, richly decorated monastery, the Americans pushed onto ridges they named "Snakeshead" and "Phantom." The brutal fighting continued in searingly cold, windswept conditions until February 4th, by which time pure exhaustion and cold forced a pause on the men of both sides. The lull lasted for three days.

The final assault of the First Battle of Cassino began on February 7th, involving nearly all of the 34th Division and supporting regiments from several other divisions. M4A3 Sherman tanks from the U.S. 756th Tank Battalion supported their advance as best as they could in the mountainous terrain. The American soldiers pushed forward amid bursting shells, regardless of the long stone splinters that tore through their comrade's faces and bodies. Over the succeeding few days the 168th Regiment, in the advance, reached the high water mark of the First Battle's main offensive on February 12th.

They pushed the Germans back and came within a few yards of the monastery walls atop the looming "Monastery Hill." Frustratingly, the American soldiers came within one mile of a breakthrough into the Liri Valley before the Germans finally halted them. At one point, according to an eyewitness: "On February 5 an Allied patrol, during an artillery barrage, ventured within thirty meters of the perimeter of the monastery and easily succeeded in ejecting from a cavern about twenty German soldiers, who were made prisoners. The abbot and the monks, knowing full well that the number of Germans in the neighborhood of the monastery was very small, then regarded as imminent the occupation of the abbey by the Allies." (Bloch, 15).

Though the advance represented a remarkable achievement of American arms, demonstrating the maturation of the U.S. Army towards a more professional organization, human flesh and blood could achieve no more. The attack came to a halt under intense German fire, then slowly drew back. The exhausted men could push themselves no further, and fell back to defensive positions lower on the slopes. The First Battle of Cassino ended with the Germans still in possession of the town, castle, and Monastery Hill. The Gustav Line remained intact despite the immense strain placed upon it.

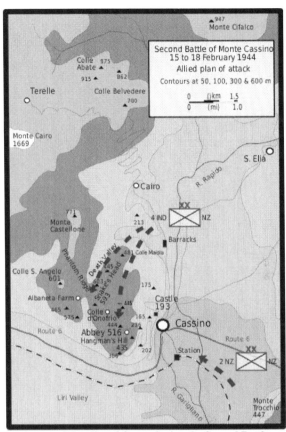

A map of the aligned forces during the Second Battle

General Mark Clark launched the Second Battle of Cassino a few days later in response to the arrival of reinforcements detached from the British Eighth Army on the Adriatic front. The British found the Gustav Line as impenetrable on the peninsula's Adriatic flank but, averse to losses after their World War I losses, proceeded with much greater caution and therefore halted to await more favorable weather.

The overall commander, General Sir Harold Alexander, therefore decided to shift three divisions from the temporarily halted British Eighth Army to the U.S. Fifth Army, still on the offensive. These included the 2nd New Zealand Division, the British 78th Division, and the 4th Indian Division. The last of these, the British 78th Division, reached the Cassino battlefield on February 17th, whereupon Clark formed the three units into the II New Zealand Corps. This fresh force provided the soldiers for the Second Battle of Cassino. Sir Bernard Freyberg, a skilled and experienced commander, led the Corps overall.

Alexander

Freyberg

All the Fifth Army commanders knew the reinforcements would be quickly committed to a new assault, but the precise location involved some debate. Clark, in fact, felt intimidated by Freyberg's formidable reputation and long, successful command history, and wanted no Eighth Army troops added to his force, though he possessed sufficient diplomacy to welcome the newcomers warmly. "Tiny" Freyberg, standing more than six feet tall, apparently even made the shorter Clark feel physically inadequate.

Freyberg possessed a military record studded with hard-fought actions. He commanded the garrison of Crete during the German airborne invasion, inflicting high losses on the Fallschirmjager paratroopers through skillful use of his men. Though forced to abandon the island, he successfully evacuated more than half of his command. He also played a crucial role in the pivotal North African battle of El Alamein, greatly assisting Montgomery in securing his famous victory.

A picture of German paratroopers at the battle

The New Zealanders initially believed their removal from the Eighth Army line heralded a spell of rest and recuperation in a more favorable clime. The sullen glow of Mount Vesuvius ahead, however, soon disabused them of this pleasant daydream. The men traversed the final miles up Route 6, the Via Casilina, through a landscape dotted with water-filled shell craters, their transport vehicles negotiating a "busy highway running through a rain-sodden and dejected landscape, past the litter of battle and grey stone buildings wasted by war and splashed with mud. It was under the tight control of American military police, models of brisk, or even brusque, efficiency, and the strange driver felt at first like a bucolic drayman plunged into the traffic stream of a metropolis." (Caddick-Adams, 2013, 173-174).

Before these men experienced their turn in the deadly struggle at Monte Cassino, however, a tragic and notorious event unfolded. Their arrival, in fact, precipitated the bombing of the Monte Cassino Monastery itself. To his credit, General Mark Clark believed an attack on the monastery itself unnecessary, and even detrimental to the Allied cause in several ways. He believed the repeated German assertions, backed up by statements by the Holy See and the monks of the Abbey themselves, that the formidable structure remained unoccupied by the Wehrmacht. Though the Germans prepared positions close under the monastery's cliff-like 150-foot walls, they scrupulously avoided occupying it due to its high historic value.

Clark thought Senger's assurances of non-occupation could be taken at face value, which indeed they could. He also accurately predicted that bombing the location would only inflict pointless civilian casualties. Furthermore, he judged the Germans would use such an action for highly effective propaganda against the Allies.

Moreover, the American commander of the U.S. II Corps, Geoffrey Keyes, offered his own opinion of the situation. Keyes possessed considerable martial ability, and even drew a compliment from George S. Patton himself, who remarked that Keyes had "the best tactical mind of any officer I know." (Atkinson, 2007, 334). Keyes thought that bombing the monastery would reduce it to ruins that would provide the Germans with excellent cover for snipers and artillery observers, precisely foreseeing what, in fact, happened.

Keyes

Sir Bernard Freyberg originated the idea of destroying the Abbey and drove it home forcefully. He indicated the need for it to be "blown down" as soon as he arrived on the scene in early February, and he lodged a formal request to that effect on February 12th, the same day the Americans retreated from their "high tide mark" 100 feet from the monastery walls. He gave the request to General Alfred M. Gruenther, Clark's Chief of Staff, who passed it on to Clark, then visiting the encircled troops at Anzio.

At this critical moment, Clark permitted his feelings of inferiority towards the decorated, lionized Freyberg to influence his choice. He stated that if Freyberg were an American commander, he would turn him down flat. After arguing with Freyberg, however, he felt sufficiently intimidated to attempt to pass responsibility on to Sir Harold Alexander, overall commander of the two Allied armies. Alexander adroitly "passed the buck" back to Clark, stating that he supported Freyberg's request to bomb the Abbey but that the final decision lay with Clark.

Amid all these efforts to shunt the decision to other people and thereby avoid responsibility, Freyberg held to his hard line. His persistence ultimately won the day. Clark argued with the New Zealander again following Alexander's slippery response, but acquiesced after Freyberg truculently declared Clark would bear the blame if the assault failed due to German snipers and spotters in the monastery. Clark later stated, "I said then that there was no evidence the Germans were using the Abbey for military purposes. I say now that there is irrefutable evidence that no German soldier, except emissaries, was ever inside the Monastery [...] the bombing of the Abbey [...] was a tactical military mistake of the first magnitude. It only made our job more difficult, more costly in terms of men, machines and time." (Bloch, 1976, 48).

Still, blame for the operation must rest squarely on General Clark's shoulders. Though General Tuker of the 2nd New Zealand Division and Lieutenant General Sir Bernard Freyberg initiated the action with their arrogant insistence that the Monastery "must be" occupied by the Germans or that it "certainly would be," Clark exhibited a clear lack of moral fiber in surrendering to their demands for what he clearly knew represented a disaster for the men under his command.

He characterized the bombing as a "tactical military mistake of the first magnitude" – an assessment proven amply correct by the sequel – and knew this at the time he issued the order for the attack. No personal coercion, such as that suffered by Stalin's luckless generals (who frequently found themselves obliged to follow an incorrect course of action or die in front of a firing squad), applied to Clark in the armies of the western democracies. Unable to stand up to the badgering of a pair of foreign officers, Clark decided to carry out an action he knew would achieve nothing valuable, would likely kill hundreds of civilians, and could endanger the lives of tens of thousands of men under his command if the bombing actually strengthened the Wehrmacht Cassino position, which it did. Clark's surrender decisively proved him unfit for command.

The day before the bombardment, February 14th, the Americans made an effort to clear Italian civilians from the Monastery by dropping hundreds of leaflets in Italian, declaring their intention to bomb it and urging everyone to leave the compound. The inhabitants retrieved some of the leaflets and brought the matter to the abbot's attention. Unfortunately, the Americans neglected to mention the date of the bombing, and the abbot, Gregorio Diamare, arranged an evacuation with the Germans, to take place at dawn on February 16th. This, as it happened, represented a timetable exactly 20 hours too late to save the 800 refugees and assorted monks inside the Abbey from the bombing, though neither the Italians nor the Germans knew this.

On the morning of February 15th, Clark withdrew to his headquarters at Presenzano, 15 miles from Cassino, apparently motivated by a desire to avoid witnessing or hearing the devastation unleashed by his orders. Ironically, the crew of one of the first bombers mistook Presenzano for Cassino and dropped its bombs, aiming for Clark's headquarters building. Sixteen bombs fell, narrowly missing Clark's location.

Ultimately, the bombing killed 100 of the 800 civilians sheltering in the monastery, wounded 150 to 250 more, and reduced the magnificent, ancient structure to a ghastly ruined shell. The 13th Strategic Air Force dispatched its bomber into an unusually bright, sunny sky to destroy the Abbey. The first wave included 142 B-17 Flying Fortresses and dropped 253 tons of bombs, mostly "blockbusters" designed to rupture reinforced masonry and destroy buildings. The ordnance lived up amply to its name, bursting the massive walls like papier mache and reducing the monastery to a gigantic rubble-choked crater.

The war correspondent Christopher Buckley described the monastery under attack: "A moment later a bright flame such as a giant might have produced by striking titanic matches on the mountainside, spurted upwards at half a dozen points. Then a pillar of smoke five hundred feet high broke upwards into the blue. For nearly five minutes it hung around the building, thinning gradually upwards into strange, evil-looking arabesques such as Aubrey Beardsley at his most decadent might have designed." (Whiting, 1974, 117).

A second wave arrived at 1:00 PM, including 47 B-25 Mitchell bombers and 40 Martin B-26 Marauder bombers. These aircraft pummeled the Abbey's smoking wreck with 100 additional tons of bombs, followed by a furious artillery bombardment from the batteries in the Rapido River valley and the surrounding heights in Allied hands. The soldiers expected to attack as soon as the artillery bombardment ended, but, to their rage and bafflement, no attack order came. The assault actually occurred days later, giving the Wehrmacht considerable time to occupy the ruins and set them in order for defense.

Aerial photos showing the damage

A picture of the ruined monastery from the ground

Militarily, Clark's action provided the Germans with a key strongpoint that greatly prolonged the struggle and ultimately led directly to tens of thousands of Allied deaths. Senger himself commented succinctly, "The bombing had the opposite effect to what was intended. Now we would occupy the abbey without scruple, especially as ruins are better for defense than intact buildings. In time of war one must be prepared to demolish buildings which are required for defense. Now the Germans had a mighty, commanding strongpoint, which paid for itself in all the subsequent fighting." (Bloch, 1976, 35). Thus, Tuker and Freyberg's cocksure badgering of the easily intimidated Clark, far from guaranteeing the safety of their New Zealand troops, in fact ensured their slaughter during the Second Battle of Cassino.

As the campaign continued on, Alphonse Juin requested that the new II New Zealand Corps join his Moroccans and Algerians to break through the last defenders between them and the Liri Valley. The French general still wished to complete the encirclement begun a month before and halted only due to lack of reinforcements. However, General Clark disallowed this, instead choosing to deploy the New Zealanders against Cassino and Monte Cassino in place of the exhausted, depleted 34th Infantry Division. As a reason, he cited the difficulty of supplying such a large number of troops by mule train, an objection with some merit but perhaps not enough to counterbalance the immense gains possible if Juin broke through into the Germans' rear.

When the Second Battle began in earnest, Cassino, the monastery, Castle Hill, and Hangman's

Hill (so named due to a half-wrecked electric pylon on its summit that resembled a gallows) stood at an angle of the Gustav Line with Allied positions to the immediate north and east. To the north, the 4th Indian Division occupied the lower sections of Snakeshead Ridge, which slopes up southward to the main east-west ridgeline atop which the monastery stands. To the east, the 2nd New Zealand Division occupied low ground on the far side of the Rapido River, flowing close along the eastern side of Cassino itself.

The battle plan called for the 4th Indian Division to attack south up Snakehead Ridge, taking the main ridgeline and the monastery at its eastern end. At the same time, the 2nd New Zealand Division's orders called for an attack westward along the railroad passing over the Rapido River, taking the station just south of Cassino and from there take the southern fringes of Cassino. This would permit tanks to push along Route 6, which curves around the base of the Monte Cassino height on the south and then enters the Liri Valley.

Brigadier Lovett of the 7th Indian Brigade led five battalions of soldiers from the British Empire south up the bare, rocky slopes on February 17th, 1944, starting the Second Battle of Cassino. The Rajputana Rifles sought to recapture several high points lost when the Americans fell back to make place for the 4th Indian Division, while several battalions of Gurkhas attacked towards the monastery. The attack met with devastating fire from the German defenders. Thanks to their relative positions, the Germans enfiladed the slope, firing at the attacking men from the side as well as from directly ahead. Exposed on bare, stony ground, the Rajputs and Gurkhas suffered heavy casualties. The determined Gurkhas pushed nearly to the Abbey walls, like the Americans before them, but finally retreated, leaving the mountainous slopes strewn with dead and dying men. The German Fallschirmjagers – the elite "Green Devils" holding the main ridge – counted a minimum of 400 corpses left behind.

At 9:30 PM on the same day, the 28th Maori Battalion spearheaded the 2nd New Zealand Division's attack westward across the Rapido River. Moving forward determinedly, the Maoris engaged in fierce gun battle with the German defenders, forcing them back along the line of Route 6 and the railroad tracks. Cutting their way through barbed wire entanglements, negotiating minefields where lurking subterranean ordnance exploded suddenly to leave men screaming with their feet blown off and legs shredded by mine fragments and stone splinters, the Maoris drove the Wehrmacht troops out of the train station and off a tactically advantageous rise nearby known as the "Hummocks."

Combat engineers in bulldozers followed the 28th Maori Battalion, filling shell craters and ditches to create a practicable route for the tanks intended to support the infantry. However, one of the obstacles proved too large to quickly fill. The first gray of dawn found the bulldozers still frantically backing and advancing, trying to fill the gap. Spotted almost immediately by Germans on the heights, the exposed engineers came under a blistering artillery barrage that soon halted their work.

The 28th Maori Battalion found itself clinging forlornly to the railroad station and the Hummocks, shelled by German mountain batteries and unsupported by tanks or other infantry. In an effort to assist, II New Zealand Corps headquarters ordered their own artillery to fire numerous smoke rounds around and above the Maori positions, preventing accurate aim by the German artillerymen.

This move gave the men of the 28th Battalion some respite, and the Allied artillery continued to blanket their positions in smoke. The wily Senger soon devised a method of turning this to his advantage, however. Later in the afternoon, German forces advanced stealthily through the smoke and launched a sudden counterattack against the Maoris, turning their own smokescreen against them. Outnumbered and nearly cut off, the battalion retreated swiftly back across the Rapido River to their starting positions. The Second Battle of Cassino ended quickly in Allied failure.

At the same time that the Second Battle developed, the Wehrmacht launched a concentrated counterattack against the American "beached whale" at Anzio. Though the Americans defeated this effort to push them back into the sea, it hardened the resolve of General Clark and the other Allied commanders to keep up the pressure on the Gustav Line with as little interruption as possible. The Allied high command in Italy decided that breaking through the Gustav Line required a massive attack in the Cassino vicinity by both the U.S. Fifth Army and the British Eighth Army. Codenamed Operation Diadem, this plan eventually saw the light of day as the fourth and final Battle of Cassino. However, shifting numerous elements of the British Eighth Army through the Apennines to their starting positions, and preparing the Fifth Army for action, required both considerable time and better weather. The commanders decided on May 1944 as the best time for the operation.

In the meantime, Freyberg's II New Zealand Corps found themselves slated for fresh action. Keeping the Germans off balance, and perhaps achieving a lucky breakthrough that would obviate Operation Diadem, lay at the core of the Third Battle of Cassino. This action received the codename Operation Dickens, after Charles Dickens, who visited the Monte Cassino monastery in 1859 and marveled both at its historic treasures and at its opulent richness compared to the squalid poverty of the nearby towns and villages.

Clark granted Freyberg extensive authority and autonomy in working out the details of Operation Dickens. The New Zealand leader once again demonstrated his fascination with colossal bombing raids as a preparation for his attack. The head of American air forces in Italy, General Arnold, concurred with Freyberg, though some of his colleagues strongly demurred: "Break up every stone in the town behind which a German soldier might be hiding. When the smoke of the last bombers and fighters begins to die down, have the ground troops rapidly take the entire town of Cassino." (Blumenson, 1993, 436).

The 6th New Zealand Brigade, a force of three battalions holding the northern edges of Cassino, would fall back from the town, after which a gigantic carpet bombing attack would level Cassino and, hopefully, kill most of the Germans holding it as a strongpoint. Freyberg's opponents, the 1st Fallschirmjager Division under the Knight's Cross holder General Richard Heidrich, fought him on Crete earlier in the war. This fact likely influenced Freyberg's tactical decisions also.

The attacks following would occur at multiple points along the line. The 4th Indian Division would shift their route of attack, eschewing the bare slopes around Snakeshead Ridge in favor of an assault on Castle Hill and up a defile leading to the monastery. This might offer slightly more shelter from enfilading fire than the open slopes just to the west. American and New Zealand tanks would support this attack along a special road built from the village of Cairo by combat engineers. The road theoretically enabled armor to climb as far as Point 593 and from there close in on the ruined monastery.

Simultaneously, the 6th New Zealand Brigade would advance into Cassino following the cessation of bombing. Tanks of the 19th Armored Regiment would attack in support, adding extra punch to the infantry assault. Freyberg insisted Operation Dickens wait until three successive days of dry, sunny weather hardened the ground enough for armor to use it without bogging down.

As the heavy rains continued day after day, however, the start of Third Cassino remained elusive following its February 20th planning. The Allied air forces also needed better weather to carry out Freyberg's carpet bombing of Cassino. In the meantime, approximately 500 men in total from the 4th Indian Division and the 2nd New Zealand Division suffered injury or death from skirmishing and shelling.

The skies finally cleared, and stayed clear, on March 12th, 1944. The Third Battle of Cassino accordingly began on March 15th – a possibly ominous date for those who recalled William Shakespeare's famous line "beware the Ides of March." In response to the warm, sunny weather, flowers bloomed everywhere. The soldiers' letters and diaries took note of violets, anemones, and other blossoms contrasting with the grim, shell-scarred battlefield. Spring also brought the return of less welcome organisms, however, such as clouds of mosquitoes in the swampy ground near the dammed Rapido River. Allied light bombers sprayed insecticide over the low ground to reduce the risk of malaria among the tens of thousands of men packed into the valley.

Vast waves of Allied aircraft, totaling 600 in all, struck Cassino at 8:30 AM on March 15th, carpet-bombing the hapless town into a hill of nearly undifferentiated rubble. As a follow up, 750 artillery tubes launched a three-hour bombardment of the wreck once the last bombers circled away to the southeast. The German Fallschirmjager Major Rudolf Böhmler later attempted to describe the result of the attack: "The very first wave enveloped Cassino in a pall of dark grey dust, hiding from view the horror below, where men, houses and machines were being blown to pieces. In this hell, it seemed as though all will to resist must be quenched... and all life be brought to an end. As wave succeeded deadly wave, the inferno seemed endless." (Caddick-Adams, 2013, 182).

Ian Eaker, a U.S. Air Force general watching the attack from several miles away alongside Freyberg and a half-dozen other generals, remained highly skeptical of the effectiveness of the bombing. Despite the colossal physical forces unleashed, causing violent shocks to run through the stone under the men's feet even at three miles' distance, Eaker guessed the Germans would simply use the ruins as defensive positions and the destruction represented a futile gesture.

The Fallschirmjagers holding Cassino took heavy casualties from the bombardment, with somewhere between 220 and 230 killed. Nevertheless, they represented some of the finest German infantry, elite soldiers with intensive training and the professional calm and toughness born out of years of experience. They waited out the attack in whatever shelter they could find – cellars, culverts, and prepared positions, or even caves at the base of the looming hill behind the town. Then, once the bombers circled away and the artillery fire ceased, they emerged briskly to set up countless defensive positions in the rubble, awaiting the expected Allied attack.

The war correspondent Sergeant Len Smith later expressed the admiration many friends and foes alike felt for the fierce, determined Green Devils: "They survived the terrific air and artillery bombardments that leveled all of Cassino except the schoolhouse, the jail and the Continental Hotel and came back to fight like demons. They turned every inch of Allied destruction into a strongpoint for themselves: they fought off the best the Allies had to offer, yielding only to death. To them must be accredited a great defensive victory, for, at least, they delayed by many months the liberation of Rome." (Whiting, 1974, 127).

Their general, Heidrich, and the overall commander of the Cassino defense, Senger, both remained close to Cassino in keeping with the standard Wehrmacht procedure. Senger, in fact, walked alone to Heidrich's headquarters through Allied shellfire, noting the smells of fresh earth and scorched iron characteristic of an artillery bombardment.

Late in the afternoon, as the mountain winds pushed away the pall of dust and smoke hanging over Cassino, the New Zealand troops moved south from Cairo. The 25th Battalion advanced cautiously in the lead, backed up by the 26th Battalion. The men ejected the Germans from Cassino's medieval castle on Castle Hill at 4:45 PM, and handed it over to soldiers of the 5th Indian Battalion moving up to cover their flank.

As the New Zealanders moved into the rubble-choked outskirts of Cassino, moving towards the Continental Hotel (actually the "Excelsior Hotel"), a stone jail, and a nunnery which appeared as the key points on Cassino's northern fringe, the lethal buzzsaw sound of German MG-34 and MG-42 machine guns sliced the air, soon joined by the vicious thud of exploding grenades. The Fallschirmjagers, already in position, greeted the New Zealand troops with intense fire from their numerous automatic weapons.

The imprudence of the bombing rapidly grew apparent as the tanks rolled up to the edge of Cassino. The chaotic hills of stone rubble and broken timbers completely blocked the armored vehicles. The crews clambered out and desperately attempted to open a way through the wreckage with shovels and picks, while subjected to deadly fire from the Germans.

Worse followed when a few Shermans actually managed to enter the town along Route 6. A Panzer IV tank, lurking inside the ruined lobby of the Continental Hotel, fired lethally accurate shots into each Sherman that managed to penetrate the outer cordon of rubble. Soon burning Sherman M4A3 tanks dotted Route 6, adding their bulk to the other obstacles encumbering the Allied advance. Senger credited the solitary Panzer IV tank with a key role in defeating the entire attack on Cassino.

Risking their lives in a courageous effort to open other avenues of advance for the tanks, combat engineers drove their bulldozers forward, only to come under sniper fire. Some cellars still held trapped Germans, and the British troops, moved to pity by their despairing screams, attempted to dig them out with their bare hands. Most such attempts failed and the Germans drowned as heavy rain began again overnight. Other Germans surrendered as the New Zealanders overran their positions, and proved to be surprisingly composed despite the ferocious shelling. Only 1 of 300 prisoners taken, in fact, showed any symptoms of shell-shock, despite immediate examination by trained psychiatrists.

Above the town, the Rajputana Rifles and the Gurkhas fought their way up the zigzagging road towards Hangman's Hill, about 300 yards short of the monastery itself. The fight to reach Hangman's Hill occupied many hours, as the men encountered ambush after ambush and negotiated hairpin turns in the face of relentless German fire. A steady stream of wounded poured back down the mountain, often carried in slings attached to mules, while corpses piled up wherever a firefight occurred.

Tremendous rains continued to fall as the New Zealanders gradually took the eastern two thirds of Cassino during the following two days. Some tanks forced their way into town and fired high explosive rounds into any suspected Fallschirmjager position. Wallowing through flooded craters and slithering through deep, sucking mud, the miserable, drenched men slowly wrested control of the town from the Germans. The convent fell on March 16th, and the botanical gardens on March 17th.

On the 18th, most German resistance centered around the Continental Hotel and the Hotel des Roses in the western section of the town. The Allies controlled approximately two thirds of Cassino, though "control" remained relative. In some buildings, New Zealand or a few American soldiers occupied the interior while Germans lurked on the roof, shooting anyone who attempted to bring them under fire and periodically dropping grenades into the lower floors. Attacks on the two hotels met with bloody repulses.

Each side had a vicious surprise prepared for the other on March 19th. The Germans struck first, counterattacking the castle and Castle Hill in an effort to retake the medieval structure and thus isolate the Rajputs, Gurkhas, and Essex soldiers on Hangman's Hill. The 4th Fallschirmjager Regiment's 1st Battalion gathered in the predawn darkness on Point 236, then rushed the castle, wiping out an advance post on Point 165 on their way. By now, several companies of British soldiers from the Essex Battalion held the ancient fortress.

Unable to determine the relative positions of the Germans and the Rajputs, the British defenders of the castle relied on small arms rather than artillery and mortars in the desperate fight. The first wave almost broke into the castle interior but the British troops smashed the assault with Bren gun fire and grenades. The Germans fled, but only briefly.

At 7:00 AM, German artillery laid down a dense smokescreen on the approaches to the castle. The Fallschirmjagers attacked again, hurling scores of grenades as they attempted to scale the walls. Enfilading fire from several machine guns and rounds from 3-inch mortars eventually drove them back, but the number of men fit for combat inside the castle fell from 150 to 60, and several machine-guns malfunctioned due to overheating. Much of the fighting occurred at very close range, as the youthful Major Denis Beckett, one of the garrison's commanders, recounted: "Eventually I climbed on top of a wall, exposing head and shoulders. I was a complete bloody fool to do this, but I could see no alternative. Anyway, a little runt of a Boche [i.e. German] chucked a grenade at me and I was lucky not to get it on the head." (Parker, 2004, 230-231).

A third attack at 8:00 AM also failed, after which the two sides agreed to a brief truce during which the hostile soldiers intermingled, cooperating in removing their wounded for treatment. The Fallschirmjagers refused to admit defeat, however. A tiny group of Green Devils wormed their way forward unobserved and planted an explosive charge under the castle's north wall. A sudden thunderous blast ripped the medieval stonework asunder, bringing a large section of the castle down in an avalanche of masonry that killed 20 more of the few men still holding the fortress. Fallschirmjagers dashed through the smoke and dust, spraying fire ahead of them from their submachine guns. The Essex soldiers met them with a lethal fusillade of machine gun fire that cut most of the men down and forced the remnants to retreat. The Fallschirmjager battalion now had only 40 men still mobile out of an original force of 200.

Though this represented the Fallschirmjagers' last effort, they delayed an attack to be launched from Hangman's Hill towards the monastery as the Allies attempted to reinforce the castle. Freyberg and his subordinate commanders, however, failed to change a crucial part of their plan. The day before, 37 tanks and tank destroyers, mostly American but a few crewed by New Zealanders, successfully climbed the road prepared by the engineers to a hidden hollow just below Snakeshead Ridge, known as the Madras Circus. This powerful force of tanks, totally concealed from the Germans, lurked only a short distance from the monastery itself. Already on high ground, they had a clear run to the Abbey along the saddle of the ridge. Unfortunately, Freyberg and his officers completely forgot to radio the tanks and tell them that the infantry advance from Hangman's Hill would arrive much later than planned.

As a result, the tanks and tank destroyers rolled out at the appointed time, but found no infantry to support them. Instead, they approached the monastery unsupported, met by swarms of Fallschirmjagers with Panzerfausts (rocket-propelled grenades) and Panzerschrecks (German bazookas). The tanks' promising attack, almost certain to succeed if properly coordinated with infantry, instead resulted in a massacre. The Germans knocked out almost a third of the force – 12 tanks – in short order, taking the surviving crews prisoner, while the rest of the vehicles retreated hastily to Madras Circus.

Down in the town on the 19th, history repeated itself grimly. The Maoris and New Zealanders advanced bravely on the Continental Hotel, but the solitary Panzer IV in the lobby continued to devastate the attackers with accurate fire. The Fallschirmjagers showed considerable initiative, infiltrating past the attackers and then counterattacking them from the rear with grenades and machine guns, filling the rubble-choked streets with dead and wounded men.

The men on Hangman's Hill found themselves cut off, unable to advance or, for some time, retreat. Late on the 19th, elements of the British 78th Infantry Division took over defense of the half-ruined castle, allowing the remaining 34 Essex soldiers to retreat down the slippery mountainside in the gathering darkness.

During the next few days, the assault petered out. By March 23rd, the Third Battle of Cassino ended, though continuous bombardment and sniping by both sides continued. The New Zealand troops now held Castle Hill, the castle itself, and part of Cassino. Many units, including much of the 4th Indian Division, suffered casualties of 70% to 80%, losing most of their best men and finding their fighting spirit broken by the nearly futile slaughter.

Freyberg's reputation suffered greatly, while the German "Green Devil" Fallschirmjagers won global renown for their skill, courage, and relentless aggression. The Battle of Monte Cassino developed steadily into a material setback for the Allies and a propaganda coup for the embattled Third Reich. However, according to Albert Kesselring, it also prompted a decisive shift in Allied strategy and tactics away from a methodical, formal method towards a swifter, dynamic way of making war closer to the German approach.

Arrangements for the Fourth Battle of Cassino, or Operation Diadem, began at the same time Freyberg was making his plans for the Third Battle. Grander in scale and more complex, Operation Diadem took much longer to prepare. While the bombers flattened Cassino and the New Zealanders, Maoris, Gurkhas, Rajputs, and Essex men fought on the harsh slopes or amid the sodden rubble of the town, their leaders continued working on the preparations for the largest assault on the Gustav Line.

After the third battle, the Allies withdrew the decimated units and moved fresh ones into their positions. These men found a bizarre, hideous landscape full of craters and wreckage, strewn thickly with abandoned equipment, corpses, dismembered human limbs, and helmets, some of them still with heads in them.

The grotesque litter dispirited the men even before combat began. Both sides continued shelling each other, while the Allies also launched repeated bombing raids on the German positions, albeit on a smaller scale than the colossal bombardment of "Operation Dickens."

While the armies prepared for the climactic encounter and the weather slowly warmed, the Allies and Germans both kept up a brisk "leaflet war." Vast numbers of expertly produced propaganda leaflets passed back and forth between the sides, delivered via empty artillery shells stuffed full of documents and fitted with a small ejection charge. The soldiers of both sides read these leaflets with interest, since they provided one of the only reliefs from the tension-filled boredom of their existence.

The leaflet writers attempted to make their creations not only effective as propaganda, but also intriguing in some fashion so that soldiers would keep them longer and read them repeatedly. Many took the form of cartoons, with amusing characters taking the place of notable leaders. Others included objectively useful information in addition to their propaganda content, such as advice on how to avoid malaria or other ailments, how to improve hygiene, and the like. Some contained material verging on "pin-up" art, such as a leaflet aimed at the British showing a grinning American pulling up the skirt of a slim Italian woman to expose one of her buttocks. Yet others provided advice on malingering successfully by simulating illness. In one highly successful case, "The Allies produced a special weekly newspaper for the German frontline troops called *Frontpost*, which was fired into German lines. An interrogator of prisoners of war was amazed when one of his charges requested a copy 'as if this was a regular service to which he had subscribed.'" (Parker, 2004, 263).

While the men clung to their positions in ruined buildings, craters, or small rock shelters known as sangars that took the place of foxholes, amid the stench and horror of thousands of unburied corpses, the Allied armies shifted steadily into position for a sledgehammer blow designed to crack the Gustav Line's Tyrrhenian Sea end wide open.

If the Allies' tactical performance during the earlier stages of Cassino left much to be desired, their strategic acumen proved a brilliant counterbalance. The Allied generals managed to hoodwink even the extremely intelligent and militarily knowledgeable Albert Kesselring regarding their true intentions. While moving seven fresh divisions to the Monte Cassino area, they successfully made it appear as though only a holding force remained in front of the monastery. Kesselring believed Sir Harold Alexander no longer wished to attack at Cassino and that no action would be forthcoming there.

Simultaneously, large scale deception operations, including huge practiced seaborne landings and permitting the Germans to intercept falsified orders, conveyed the idea the Allies planned a huge amphibious assault at Civitavecchia. This port city, far up the coast of the Tyrrhenian Sea and well north of Rome, made a logical choice for such an operation. Kesselring swallowed the bait, sending two powerful divisions to Civitavecchia and allowing Senger, the skilled commandant of Cassino's defense, to go to Germany on leave in early May, just in time for the unexpected attack at Cassino.

It is axiomatic in war that a successful attack against defended positions requires at least three to one odds, and the Allies enjoyed such odds at Cassino by May. The Allies mustered 108 battalions, 2,000 tanks, 1,600 artillery tubes, and 3,000 supporting aircraft – including reconnaissance planes, transports, bombers, fighters, and fighter-bombers.

Though the Germans remained almost totally unaware, this huge force stood poised to attack on May 11th, 1944, the same day that Vietinghoff, commanding alone in Senger's absence, sent a morning report to Kesselring's headquarters that stated, "There is nothing special happening."

From left to right, a formidable multinational array waited for the advance order on May 11th. The U.S. 85th and 88th Infantry Divisions now held the ground closest to the coast on the extreme lift. Just to their right, securing the Garigliano bridgehead, Alphonse Juin's FEC corps waited, now bolstered by additional Goumiers and two fresh divisions. The British XIII Corps – consisting of two Canadian divisions (infantry and armored), 8th Indian Division, the British 4th Division, the British 78th "Battleaxe" Division, and the British 6th Armored Division – confronted Cassino itself.

Occupying the salient on their right stood the Polish II Corps, comprising the Polish 2nd Armored Brigade and two infantry divisions, the 3rd Carpathian Division and the 5th Kresowa Division. Lieutenant General Wladyslaw Anders commanded the corps. Taken prisoner by the Soviets during the joint Third Reich-USSR invasion of Poland, he spent time imprisoned by the communists, at one point undergoing torture in the cellars of the infamous Lubyanka. Freed when Hitler attacked Russia, Anders commanded Polish forces in exile and lived in England after the war until his death in 1970. Clark tasked the Poles with taking the key position of Monte Cassino itself.

The Germans suspected nothing as dusk fell on May 11th. The regular artillery exchange between the sides stopped at 10 PM as the German gun crews' shift came to an end and fresh men took their place. Deep silence hung over the battered valley and the shell-pocked mountains surrounding it under the Italian night sky.

At precisely the moment of 11 PM as indicated on radios tuned to the BBC channel, a giant fusillade erupted from all 1,600 artillery pieces along a front of 20 miles. The flashes of gun muzzles, streaks of fire in the sky, bursting flares, and exploding shells turned the night into a sudden kaleidoscope of violent flashes. The sound of the guns firing and the explosions blended into a continuous roll of deafening thunder so loud that men could barely hear one another when shouting at a range of a few feet.

The Allied soldiers watching recorded feelings of awe and exhilaration at the almost elemental outpouring of firepower unfolding before them. The Germans felt very different emotions, but returned fire as best they could with their outnumbered artillery. The initial bombardment lasted continuously for 40 minutes.

Shortly after midnight in the early morning of May 12th, the Americans of the 85th and 88th Divisions – mostly inexperienced draftees fresh from the United States – started off the advance, but soon found themselves pinned down by the German 94th Division opposing them. By contrast, Alphonse Juin's FEC tore into the German defenders near Monte Maio vigorously, pressing the German 71st Division back fiercely and once again proving the Moroccans' and Algerians' alpine combat skills: "After the French had captured the Monte Maio, the German 71st Infantry Division began to disintegrate. A number of gaps began opening in its line and the Algerians and Moroccans moved at ease over the slopes of the mountains. Units of Goumiers in their drab-striped gowns traversed impossible ground, outflanking and outmaneuvering enemy positions." (Ford, 2004, 81).

Over the following few days, the Americans pushed forward gradually, until the German 94th Division retreated as part of the general Wehrmacht pullback from the Gustav Line. At that point, the Americans advanced swiftly along Route 7, linking up with men breaking out from the Anzio beachhead on May 23rd and establishing a continuous American line along the coast.

Juin's FEC soon took Monte Maio and pushed swiftly through the Aurunci Mountains, soon moving along the heights overlooking the Liri Valley and laying the groundwork for the Allied drive along Route 6 to Rome.

The main encounter of the battle, however, occurred at the line's center, where the British XIII Corps fought their way through to the Liri Valley and Route 6 beyond Cassino, and the right, where Anders' Poles battled for the ridgeline and ultimately took the ruined monastery itself, signaling the end of the German defense.

One strange and somewhat amusing contribution to the Allied effort at Monte Cassino originated with a bear named Wojtek. Polish soldiers serving in Iran in 1942 as part of the "Anders' Army" (made up of Polish POWs released from Soviet gulags following Hitler's invasion of the Soviet Union) adopted the bear as a cub. Proving intelligent and trainable, Wojtek became a unit mascot, noted for his love of beer and honey and his ability to smoke cigarettes provided a friendly human lit them for him. In the absence of such a person, Wojtek simply ate the cigarettes. Numerous photographs survive showing the bear riding in the cab of Bedford MWD 15cwt trucks, on transport ships, or relaxing with soldiers of his unit.

Pictures of Wojtek

In order to bring their pet with them when shifted from Iran to Europe, the Poles of the 22nd Artillery Supply Company enlisted Wojtek in their unit as a private, later promoted to corporal. Wojtek worked as an ammunition carrier at Monte Cassino. Independent confirmation of the bear's capabilities came from the letters and accounts of Allied soldiers ignorant of Wojtek's history, such as the Scottish Black Watch soldier John Clarke, who recounted, "We went to look and found a battery of Polish gunners setting up for a barrage. The gun site was hidden in a clearing within a large wood. As we watched, suddenly out of the wood came a large bear, walking on its hind legs. It seemed to be carrying something. […] The bear went up to the trail legs of the artillery gun and placed a shell on the ground. The bear then went back into the wood and returned with another shell. By this time, we had realised the bear was tame and most likely a circus bear. We just went on our way." (Orr, 2010, 155-156).

Wojtek essentially worked as a volunteer. A highly imitative creature, he watched the men carrying ammunition boxes and shells, then simply did the same. However, he did not do so on command, and stopped whenever he felt the need for a nap or a meal. The Polish soldiers, delighted by his presence, adopted a unit badge showing Wojtek on his hind legs carrying a shell, which soon became official.

Wojtek the bear survived the Monte Cassino battle and the war as a whole, traveling to Scotland with the Polish men who fought in the desperate encounter. Initially stationed at a farm where he carried large fence posts in the same manner he had carried artillery shells, the bear was eventually sent to the Edinburgh Zoo, where he ate vast quantities of apples as well as snacking on cigarettes thrown to him by Polish veterans, and lived until 1963. Some former soldiers, when visiting, leaped into his enclosure to roughhouse with the bear, whose demeanor grew animated when he heard people speaking Polish. Bronze statues of Wojtek stand in Edinburgh and Krakow, the latter unveiled on the 70th anniversary of Monte Cassino in 2014. Others stand in London and Canada, commemorating the most famous non-human soldier at Monte Cassino.

As for actual human soldiers, the British XIII Corps crossed the Rapido River as part of the assault, with the British 4th Division crossing near Cassino itself along the much-traveled railroad line, and the 8th Indian Division near San Angelo. One of the British soldiers, John Clarke, reported the lethal problems encountered by the 4th Division during their crossing: "'To cross the river, folding canvas boats had been sent from Burma. They had only arrived a few hours before zero hour. Attacking infantrymen assembled the boats and set off across the swift-flowing river.

Many were simply swept away to their deaths.'" Other men drowned within yards of setting out. Their boats sank almost instantly because the canvas sides were riddled with holes caused by insects which had infested them during their storage in the Far East." (Orr, 2010, 161).

On the far side, dense minefields awaited the British and Indian troops, blowing off feet and mangling legs and genitals. German counterattacks struck the weak bridgeheads repeatedly early on May 12th, and Fallschirmjager machine gunners slipped forward to spray men crossing the river or gathering on the far bank at point-blank range.

British combat engineers attempted to throw pontoon bridges over the river to bring up tanks, but the Germans soon made the area untenable. Canisters of black smoke attached to tripwires provided dark spots in the white morning fog that picked out exactly where the British engineers labored for the still-undaunted German mountain batteries. Furious, accurate artillery fire destroyed trucks and bulldozers and reduced scores of men to shredded, burned piles of flesh and bone. When the Germans opened fire with Nebelwerfer rocket launchers – the infamous "Screaming Mimis" or "Moaning Minnies" in Allied parlance – the engineers retreated.

With a bridge indispensable, the engineers returned that afternoon and began building one on their shore of the Rapido. Once it was completed, they planned to use a bulldozer to push it along log rollers down to the river. The Germans greeted this project with furious barrages of fire, killing and wounding some of the volunteers working on the bridge and greatly slowing its construction. Nevertheless, it slowly took shape, and by 4 AM, appeared ready for use.

The bulldozer pushed the bridge forward, but as it approached the bank under heavy fire, the machine suddenly came to a halt. Bullet holes in its radiator caused its engine to overheat and seize up. The nearby armored unit brought up a Sherman tank, and, despite heavy mortar fire that killed some of the engineers nearby, managed to shove the bridge into the Rapido at 4:45 AM on May 13th. A unit of Sherman tanks crossed almost immediately, simultaneously proving it sturdy enough for use and securing the far end.

The first infantry unit across the bridge, from the 4th Division, was the 6th Black Watch, a famous Highlander unit from Scotland. The men advanced with bagpipes skirling amid the fog, smoke, and darkness, which raised the spirits of the other soldiers waiting to cross. Though met by intense small arms fire, the British soldiers flooded across the bridge, establishing a decisive bridgehead on the German side of the Rapido.

Meanwhile, the 4th Indian Division took San Angelo and pushed its own way inland against heavy resistance. Soon, the Indian and British soldiers linked up to form a continuous front and moved forward slowly and inexorably. The Allied advance lacked tactical finesse – in fact, it represented a sort of slow-motion human wave tactic little different from the appallingly costly charges of the Red Army.

The Germans fought with superb skill and élan, inflicting numerous casualties on the lumbering formations of their opponents. But in the attritional battle Sir Harold Alexander forced, the Allied troops pushed them back and wore them down with sheer weight of numbers. No matter how many fell wounded or dead, the British could send in more men to fill the gaps. The Germans had no reinforcements, so their defending force shrank gradually but inevitably.

Up on the heights, the Poles attempted an attack designed to pass by Snakehead Ridge, cut through a ravine, and emerge behind the main ridge line – Phantom Ridge. There, Anders hoped, they could attack the German positions from the south and overwhelm them. Despite heroic courage, however, the Poles could not break through and fell back with heavy losses, leaving Phantom Ridge in German hands.

Only on May 16th did the Poles finally fight their way onto Phantom Ridge. On that day,

British tanks reached Route 6 beyond Cassino, almost completing the isolation of the town. Kesselring ordered Vietinghoff to withdraw to save his remaining men. Reluctantly, the Fallschirmjager and Gebirgsjager troops abandoned their positions on the ridge, in the monastery, and in Cassino during the nights of May 16/17 and May 17/18.

A British officer, not realizing the Germans eluded encirclement with the same consummate adroitness they showed in a tactical defense, declared bombastically and extremely inaccurately: "We were going in for the kill. The Poles were sweeping round from the right; we, two and a half miles away in the valley, were on our way to seal it off from the left. It shouldn't be long now. And once we had cut the Highway the very qualities that had made the Monastery an impregnable bastion for so long would turn it into an equally formidable death-trap. For so long the guardian and protector of its garrison, it would round on them in its death-throes and destroy them." (Whiting, 1974, 176).

The Battle of Monte Cassino itself ended on the morning of May 18th. Polish troops of the 3rd Carpathian Division climbed into the monastery, accepting the surrender of 17 Fallschirmjager troops still inside, and capturing three wounded paratroopers they found in a makeshift hospital in one of the monastery's crypts. A makeshift Polish flag soon waved over the ruins, while the tough, experienced Polish soldiers wept as they listened to the *Krakow Hejnal,* the medieval bugle signal of their conquered homeland.

A picture of German prisoners following the battle

Following the German retreat from Monte Cassino, the Wehrmacht formed a fresh defensive line at the Hitler Line, a few miles beyond the now broken Gustav Line. However, this improvised defense lacked the prepared strength of the Gustav Line. Most of Vietinghoff's and Senger's artillery pieces lay abandoned around Monte Cassino, either spiked by having explosive charges put in their barrels or captured by the Allies.

The Hitler line crumbled after just two days' fighting, leaving the road to Rome open. Sparking yet more controversy, General Mark Clark opted for the "photo op" operation of seizing Rome rather than attempting the encirclement of the retreating German forces. This gave the Allies some interesting souvenir photographs and a minor propaganda boost, but it enabled most of the Wehrmacht soldiers to escape and fight again another day, which they did with their usual determination and skill despite their seemingly inevitable defeat.

For his part, Kesselring believed the Allied commanders changed their strategy and tactics in response to German propaganda: "I believe this development was due to a cardinal error of our German propaganda, which could not do enough to taunt the enemy for their lack of initiative, thereby goading them into a gradual change of operational principles. The method of cautious and calculated advance according to plan with limited objectives gave place to an inspirational strategy which was perfected through the months remaining till the end of the war." (Kesselring, 1954, 264).

While ill-advised taunts about the Allies' slow, lumbering command and maneuver style undoubtedly helped the transition he noted, the incredible bloodbath at Cassino likely contributed even more. Fighting in a slow, methodical fashion clearly did not save lives – over 60,000 men lay dead around Cassino following the 129 day brawl. Speed, daring, flexibility, and the capacity to quickly seize opportunities even if the methods or routes taken proved "unorthodox" clearly not only produced victories more quickly and surely, but also conserved the lives of Allied soldiers.

Monte Cassino showed the worthlessness of the "tried and true" military techniques on the modern battlefield. Eisenhower and the Allied high command in France may well have given Patton more leeway for his aggression and initiative with the grim lessons of the Battle of Monte Cassino in mind, leading to the rapid collapse of Wehrmacht defenses across France once the Allies achieved a breakout from Normandy after D-Day.

D-Day

Over the last 68 years, the story of D-Day has been taught across the West, and people from Russia to the United States are familiar with some of the operation's unprecedented, history-making facts. The Normandy landings, codenamed *Operation Neptune,* were the amphibious landings of *Operation Overlord,* the Allied invasion of France. The landings, consisting of an initial airborne landing followed by a subsequent amphibious attack began at midnight on June 5-6 1944. United States' General Dwight D. Eisenhower was Supreme Commander of the Allied Expeditionary Force, while British General Bernard Montgomery was given overall command of ground forces. The massive armada of *Overlord* was to be the largest invasion force and amphibious operation in history, and on June 6 alone, 170,000 troops were landed across five sectors of beaches spread over a 50 mile area on the Normandy coast.

The United States' landing beaches were codenamed Utah & Omaha, Juno was the Canadian target, while Sword and Gold Beaches were to be attacked by the British forces. As everyone knows, after a day of endless and bloody battles, the Allies were able to breach the German defenses and establish a beachhead in Normandy. While the Allied forces were fighting for a single objective, the experiences in each sector were far different for the men who fought there.

All nations have their recollections of World War II entrenched in their collective memories. Britain will never forget the debacle of Dunkirk and the existential threat which it faced in 1940, standing alone against the unstoppable Nazi war machine following the defeat of France. For France, its rapid defeat and occupation will forever be etched in its collective memory. And no American could forget Japan's devastating, surprise attack on Pearl Harbor on December 7, 1941. However, D-Day is the one event of World War II that all nations attach utmost significance to. Today it is remembered for spelling the beginning of the end for Nazi Germany, but it was the most complex war-time operation ever executed, and Eisenhower himself was aware there was a high probability that the invasion would be defeated, which would set the Allies back at least a year in Western Europe if not longer.

To put the difficulties the Allies faced into context, the Normandy invasion was the first successful opposed landings across the English Channel in over eight centuries. Strategically, the campaign led to the loss of the German position in most of France and the secure establishment of a new major front. In a wider context, the Normandy landings helped the Soviets on the Eastern front, who were facing the bulk of the German forces and, to a certain extent, contributed to the shortening of the conflict there.

The origins of Operation Overlord and the attacks on D-Day had their origins years before June 6, 1944. As far back as early 1942, when President Roosevelt was debating where to put American forces, the Allies, which now included the Soviet Union by necessity, did not agree on the war strategy. The Germans and British were fighting in North Africa, and the British lobbied for American help in North Africa, where British General Montgomery was fighting the legendary "Desert Fox," General Erwin Rommel. At the same time, Soviet premier Josef Stalin vehemently argued for the Allies to open up another front in Europe that would help the Soviets, who were facing the brunt of the Nazi war machine in Russia.

General Montgomery

President Roosevelt ultimately sided with the British and sent American troops to North Africa, so they could help the British oppose Rommel. While this left Russia to handle the Nazis on the European continent singlehandedly, it left Rommel facing armies in his front and rear. The Allies eventually gained the upper hand over Rommel after the Second Battle at El Alamein near the end of 1942, which induced the Germans to leave the theater.

With Italy and Germany both having been defeated in North Africa, the Allied troops there were now free to be used in an invasion of Europe. In addition, North Africa provided the Allies a potential staging ground for an invasion of the southern part of the continent, while an invasion force from Britain could threaten from the west. Hitler now had to worry about the Allies invading not only from Britain but also from North Africa.

Before Churchill and Roosevelt made their strategic decisions for 1943, the German army suffered a massive blow in February 1943 at Stalingrad, where a major surrender of troops marked the beginning of the end for Hitler's armies in Russia. Still, it would take another two years for the Red Army to gradually push the Nazis west out of Russia and back toward Berlin. Stalin still desperately needed Allied action on another front.

In July 1943, less than half a year after the surrender at Stalingrad, the Allies conducted what at the time was the largest amphibious invasion in history, coordinating the landing of two whole armies on Sicily over a front more than 100 miles long. Within weeks of the beginning of the Allied campaign in Italy, Italy's government wasted no time negotiating peace with the Allies and quickly quit the war, hanging Mussolini in the process.

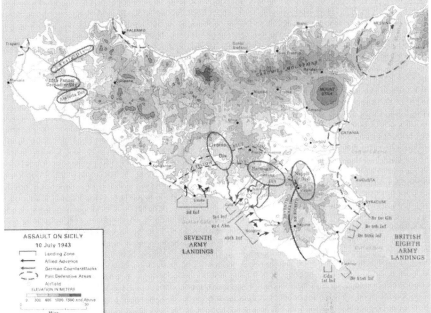

Italy may have been out of the war, but the Germans still had a strong defensive hold over the Italian peninsula in 1943. Although the Axis' attempts to resist the Allies' invasion on Sicily were badly outmanned and outgunned, leading to an evacuation of the island within a month, the Germans maintained defenses across the mainland for the rest of the year.

Nevertheless, with Allied forces now possessing a foothold in Italy, Churchill and Roosevelt began to plot an even greater invasion that would finally liberate Europe. In December 1943, President Roosevelt appointed General Dwight Eisenhower Supreme Allied Commander for the upcoming invasion, with General Montgomery as the top British commander to coordinate with Eisenhower.

Eisenhower
During the first half of 1944, the Americans and British began a massive buildup of men and resources in England, while the military leaders devised an enormous and complex amphibious invasion of Western Europe. Though the Allies theoretically had several different staging grounds for an attack on different sides of the continent, the most obvious place for an invasion was just across the English Channel from Britain into France. And though the Allies used misinformation to deceive the Germans, Hitler's men built an extensive network of coastal fortifications throughout France to protect against just such an invasion. Largely under the supervision of Rommel, the Germans constructed the "Atlantic Wall", across which reinforced concrete pillboxes for German defenders were built close to the beaches for infantry to use machine guns and anti-tank artillery. Large obstacles were placed along the beaches to effectively block tanks on the ground, while mines and underwater obstacles were planted to stop landing craft from getting close enough.

Rommel

Atlantic Wall 1942-1944

The Green Line marks the Atlantic Wall

A pillbox

The Atlantic Wall necessitated an elaborate and complex invasion plan that would ensure the men who landed wouldn't be fish in a barrel. Thus, the Allies began drawing up an elaborate battle plan that would include naval and air bombardment, paratroopers, and even inflatable tanks that would be able to fire on fortifications from the coastline, all while landing over 150,000 men across 50 miles of French beaches. And that was just the beginning; the Allies intended to create a beachhead that could support an artificially constructed dock, after which nearly 1 million men would be ferried to France for the final push of the war.

To say the Allies faced a daunting task would be an understatement. On the morning of June 6, 1944, General Eisenhower was carrying a letter in his coat that apologized for the failure of the operation. Found years after D-Day, Eisenhower's letter read, *"Our landings in the Cherbourg-Havre area have failed to gain a satisfactory foothold and I have withdrawn the troops. My decision to attack at this time and place was based on the best information available. The troops, the air and the Navy did all that bravery and devotion to duty could do. If any blame or fault attaches to the attempt, it is mine alone."*

By early 1944, the war at sea had turned distinctly in the Allies' favor. By that year, the German Navy, which had terrorized allied shipping since the outbreak of war, was severely hamstrung by Allied efforts and forced to remain within the confines of friendly harbors. Similarly, the once powerful U-boat fleet had been effectively and systematically hunted down by Allied naval and air forces. By the time the invasion of Normandy was underway and the Germans understood the extent of the invasion, the only naval resistance Germany could muster was raids by its fast and maneuverable E-boats, with some support from a dwindling U-boat fleet.

Any effective support for the German Army from its air force, the Luftwaffe, was equally unlikely. The Luftwaffe, which had smashed its way through Europe from 1939-1940, had been bloodied in the Battle of Britain and was in decline from 1943 onwards. By 1944, it was clear the Luftwaffe had lost the air war. Inferior airframes and training, the attrition of skilled pilots and the increased manpower and air assets of the Allies due to America's commitment in Western Europe made this clear. When the Allied invasion arrived, the Luftwaffe could only hope to provide limited cover and support to Germany's ground troops. The blistering joint air and land operations of the early part of the war were no longer a possibility.

Despite Allied naval and air superiority over Normandy, one significant impediment remained for the planned invasion: the German Army. Severely weakened and limited by the Versailles Treaty, from 1933-1939 under Hitler, the German Army established itself as Europe's leading military power. By the outbreak of hostilities in 1939, the German war machine was able to dominate the battlefield. By 1941, the German Army had an undefeated record, obliterating all that stood before it with a string of victories in Poland, France, the Low Countries, Scandinavia and Yugoslavia. Despite the devastation at Stalingrad, the German Army still posed a fearsome threat to the Western Allies.

Professor Samuel J Newland, in his introduction to 'The D-Day Companion', identifies Britain and the United States' greatest asset in their fight to bring about the defeat of Nazi Germany: a strong alliance and a clear goal from which the two nations never wavered. The importance of a strong alliance was quickly realized by both Franklin D. Roosevelt and Winston S. Churchill. As soon as Churchill came to power in 1940 he knew the defeat of Germany would require the entire might of the English speaking world, that being the British Empire and what Churchill called "the great Republic across the seas." Roosevelt, an admirer and supporter of Britain, was gravely concerned with the German domination of Europe in 1939, and he made preparations for the United States to enter the war on the Allied side even before Pearl Harbor.

The relationship was cemented at the A.B.C. Talks (American-British Conversations) between January and March 1941. At these talks Britain and the United States formalized the alliance which would hold through the darkest days of German domination in Europe through to the destruction of Nazi Germany. Although the British and American alliance was unwavering, the strategy to best ensure the defeat of Germany had yet to be determined. Bringing about the destruction of the Nazi state quickly was important and recognized by both leaders. Due to the fact that both Britain and the U.S. were democracies, a form of government which does not allow for drawn out strategies, the rapid defeat of Nazi Germany was paramount. The Allies were forced to seek as rapid a defeat of the enemy as possible before an election can bring about the replacement of the leader and his strategy for victory.

As a result, it became abundantly clear to the Americans that an amphibious invasion of Europe was a necessity. Upon the successful amphibious invasion of Europe, Allied forces would have to relentlessly drive back the German Army from France.

President Roosevelt and Prime Minister Churchill
The biggest problem facing the leaders of the Allied nations was exactly when and where such an invasion of Europe should take place. At conferences in Casablanca and Tehran, 'The Big Three', Roosevelt, Churchill and Stalin, discussed the problem at length. It was clear to all that the Allies would have to force their way in to Europe to have any hope of bring about the invasion of Germany. Up until 1943, the German defenders gave little thought to the potential for an allied landing of troops in Western Europe. At the same time, however, construction of Hitler's 'Atlantic Wall' continued, stretching from Norway in Northern Europe to France.

At that time, the German Army was more concerned with escaping its impending doom at the hands of the Russians in Stalingrad. This, coupled with the Allied invasion of Sicily and Italy, had still not woken Hitler to the prospect of a large scale invasion of France. Germany's apathy to the prospect of invasion is clear from the fact that German units were woefully underprepared for the upcoming Allied invasion. However, as Allied power grew through 1944, the Germans were forced to recognize that an invasion would be soon attempted. Under the command of Erwin Rommel, the German defenders of the French coast began serious efforts to shore up defenses in the areas around Pas de Calais and Normandy. Pillbox and bunker construction accelerated rapidly, millions of mines were laid and anti-landing devices were planted on the beaches of the region.

Entering 1944, France, once a lightly defended area, used largely for the recuperation of German soldiers from the Eastern front, was now the focus of Allied and German attention, with feverish plans made for the region on both sides. Reinforcements flooded into Northern France while tacticians planned for the impending invasion and counter-attack. The speed with which Germany had reinforced and strengthened the region meant that the Allies were less than certain of the success of the invasion. Britain, weary of amphibious landings after the disastrous Expeditionary Force campaign of 1940 came perilously close complete obliteration, was more than anxious. Allied military fortunes had been, at best, mixed. Professor Newton points out Britain, together with its continental allies, had lost its foothold in Europe but had managed to bloody the nose of Germany in the Battle of Britain in the summer of 1940. The Allies had lost Crete, yet stopped the Afrika Corps at El Alamein. With its American allies, Britain had successfully invaded Italy before becoming entangled in the costly German defense of the country. Britain, as a small island nation, lacked the manpower and supplies needed to singlehandedly defeat the German military. In comparison, the United States, an industrial colossus, had ample men and materials. Like Britain, American fortunes in the European theater were mixed, ranging from the successful landings in North Africa to the debacle of Kasserine Pass.

Given the skill of German infantry and past results, Allied leaders had plenty to worry about, especially when considering that an amphibious invasion is one of the most hazardous operations a military force can undertake. Russell Wigley, in his book, *Eisenhower's Lieutenants,* explained, "An amphibious assault is a frontal attack, with all the perils thereby implied. The assaulting troops have no room for maneuver. They cannot fall back. They have only limited ability to outflank strong points. They cannot do anything subtle." The painfully costly defeats of previous Allied amphibious landings at Dieppe and Gallipoli were all too well known to Allied planners.

A sense of fear and foreboding marred the weeks and months in the build up to the invasion. Churchill was aghast at Eisenhower's bombing plan to accompany the landings, which would have resulted in the deaths of between 80,000 and 150,000 French civilians. It would have been an outrageous number of civilian casualties, and more French citizens killed by Allied bombing than had lost their lives in four years of German occupation. Churchill felt it was better to continue the bombing of Germany rather than inflict terrible casualties upon their French allies in support of what may be a doomed invasion. Just months before the planned invasion of France, Allied forces had landed at Anzio, just south of Rome. Almost immediately, the Allied landing force was halted and almost driven back into the sea. Churchill himself had been a leading player in the invasion of Gallipoli in 1915, a debacle which almost cost him his career. The idea of landing on the heavily defended Normandy coast filled Churchill with fear. On one occasion, just weeks before the launch of *Overlord,* the Prime Minister was heard to say, ""Why are we doing this? Why do we not land instead in a friendly territory, the territory of our oldest ally? Why do we not land in Portugal?"

Churchill was not alone. Many of the British military planners had felt a cross channel invasion "smacked of a seaborne Somme". Churchill had, however, persuaded the U.S. to give priority to the war in Europe, a position which caused many difficulties for Roosevelt. Pearl Harbor had outraged America and inflamed popular opinion against Japan, yet American attitudes towards Germany and Italy were far more ambivalent, due to the large proportion of American citizens with German or Italian heritage. However, at the somewhat bizarre Rattle Conference, described as a combination of intensive study and a 1920s themed house party, organized by Lord Louis Mountbatten, the assembled company settled upon Normandy as the invasion destination. Although further from Germany, it offered the Allies the chance to capture two major ports, Cherbourg and Le Harve.

Facing these obstacles, it is perhaps best to consider what the alliance of millions of soldiers and support personnel were able to accomplish. On June 5, 1944, an armada of some 7,000 ships crossed the Channel towards the Normandy peninsula. Above it, 1,400 troop transports and 11,590 military aircraft of various types (along with 3,700 fighters) supported the landings. The following day, 175,000 soldiers were landed. The men who successfully invaded on D-Day earn all the credit they've since been given, but it was made possible by the enormous effort displayed in the planning and organization of the invasion.

Initial American views of British infrastructure were less than positive. British ports were charming visually, but antiquated, with unionized workers and British work-practices that maximized workload and minimized efficiency. As a result of conscription, the average age of Britain's 100,000 dockers was 52. To counteract this, American labor battalions were deployed under the command of General John C. H. Lee, commander of the U.S. Army Service of Supply (S.O.S.). Lee was a fervently religious man who believed his position as Commander of the S.O.S. was part of a divine plan, yet Lee lived lavishly in Britain, with a lifestyle that outpaced even Montgomery and Eisenhower.

Unfortunately for the Allies, Lee's command, despite his high opinion of himself, was marked by corruption and incompetence. Lee managed to survive attempts to force his resignation, as well as a severe dressing down from Eisenhower in 1942, and he went on to ensure the transformation of allied supply in Britain for the better by 1944. Under his supervision, enormous efforts were made by the Americans to ensure the forthcoming invasion had sufficient supplies for a successful landing and determined drive inland. Immediately prior to the invasion of Europe, nearly six and a half million square feet of storage and shop space had been built, with a further 13,500,000 square feet requisitioned. Lee had managed to acquire 43,500,000 square feet of storage and facilities to store 450,000 tons of ammunition, 175,000 tons of petrol, oil and lubricants and storage for over 50,000 vehicles. When Eisenhower was appointed Supreme Allied Commander in December of 1943, the invasion was half a year away, but much work was yet to be done.

General Lee

Britain, due to its limited size and manpower, had relied upon deception as a force multiplier. Churchill particularly understood the importance of deception, when at the "Big Three" Conference he said, "In wartime, truth is so precious that she should always be attended by a bodyguard of lies." The resulting *Operation Bodyguard* was the deception plan created for use with the Normandy invasion. The plan was to trick the Germans into thinking the expected invasion would come in late summer 1944, and would be accompanied by an invasion in Norway, Greece and elsewhere in Europe. The goal was to trick the Germans into defending areas away from the invasion, thus posing less threat to the success of *Overlord.* On an operational level it hoped to disguise the strength, timing and objectives of the invasion.

A further element of *Bodyguard* was *Operation Fortitude*. *Fortitude* marked one of the most ambitious, successful deception plans in the history of warfare. *Fortitude* was divided into two parts, North and South. Both parts involved the creation of fake armies, one based in Edinburgh in the north and one on the south east coast of England which threatened Pas de Calais, the most obvious area of France for invasion. The Allies went to remarkable lengths to ensure the success of the operation. A fictional U.S. Army group under George Patton was created in the south. Every effort was made to ensure operational security while also allowing the Germans to see the dummy war material and supporting infrastructure to add weight to the ruse. Dummy invasion craft were constructed at ports, inflatable trucks and tanks lined the roads in Scotland and around Patton's fictional army group. Luftwaffe aircraft were allowed fly over the inflatable army while being kept far from the actual invasion preparations. The deception was reinforced by frantic radio signals emanating from *Fortitude* north and south to the amount expected from a large size invasion group.

Inflatable British tank as part of *Operation Bodyguard*

A crucial factor to the success of Allied deception was the use of double agents. Successful espionage by Mi-5 had turned all German agents in Britain to the Allied side by the launch of *Overlord*. By the beginning of 1944, Mi-5 had 15 agents feeding false information to the Germans, with just enough reliable information to maintain their credibility. The most celebrated was 'Garbo', a Spanish agent who created a fictitious network of 24 spies while working as a double agent for the British. The benefits of having such a fictitious network of sub agents was Garbo could create an identity for his sub agents to best fit the information given to the Germans.

British Double Agent Garbo
Ensuring the Germans took the bait was a far more difficult prospect than creating the misinformation in the first instance. By 1944, the Allies had a massive advantage in terms of intelligence with the cracking of German enigma codes. Allied deciphering of German codes was so successful by 1944 that those responsible literally could not keep up with the overflow of information. What the intelligence was showing was that the Germans, in the days preceding the invasion of Europe, still had no real idea when or where the invasion was to take place. To complement the allied deception effort, the Royal Air Force dropped twice as many bombs on the Pas de Calais than it did in Normandy in preparation for the invasion. The operation's success can be seen in the length of time it took the Germans to realize it was deception, even after the landings of June 6. It was not until mid-July that the German High Command realized Patton's threat to Calais from southern England was over. Without *Fortitude*, the Germans would have had free reign to maximize its forces at the point of attack in Normandy and with it, it is unclear whether the Allied invasion would have succeeded. Against such a formidable foe, however, the Allies needed to rely on every trick in the book.

From 1941-1944, the Germans were preoccupied with Russia, which ensured that their efforts in Western Europe had a defensive focus. From late 1941, Hitler ordered the construction of a vast line of defenses along the Atlantic coast. As Hitler's plan to kick down Russia's front door died in the bloodbath of Stalingrad, France became a recuperation zone for wounded and exhausted German soldiers from the East. The overwhelming majority of German soldiers who were capable of fighting were transferred eastwards, while the French garrison was comprised of the wounded, exhausted, elderly and invalid, coupled with battalions of Russian prisoners of war, forced to fight for Germany or face death in German camps.

By mid-1943, Hitler's Atlantic Wall looked formidable, with trenches, ditches, machine-gun nests, minefields, fortified artillery placements and bunkers. Over 8,000 such installations were operational, and 2,300 anti-tank guns and 2,700 guns larger than 75 mm were in place. However, Field-Marshall Gerd von Rundstedt, commander of the German forces in France, was still less than convinced of the strength of the Atlantic wall. He, along with many commanders in France, felt that the notion of an impenetrable Atlantic Wall was more of a figment of Hitler's imagination than a reality on the ground. Von Rundstedt argued that a static line defense such as the Atlantic Wall was only of use if there was defensible depth in the form of fall-back positions. Hitler, at the behest of von Rundstedt to reinforce France, sent Rommel to the area to shore up

German defenses. Rommel oversaw the laying of millions of mines and underwater obstacles on the most likely landing beaches of the region, which was designed to keep the Allies from successfully landing ashore and driving the invasion force back into the sea. He wanted as much defenses as possible on the beaches, with infantry divisions as close as possible to landing sites and panzer divisions nearby to immediately strike at the landing forces.

Field Marshal Gerd von Rundstedt

A picture of German fortifications on D-Day. The countless small holes show the extent, and limited effect, of Allied shelling.

Even as the Atlantic Wall was strengthened, *Operation Fortitude* tricked Hitler into keeping 13 divisions in Norway rather than reinforcing the Normandy peninsula. It had also tricked German High Command into believing that 89 Allied divisions were preparing to land, with enough landing craft to bring 20 divisions ashore. In actuality, the figures were 47 and 6 respectively. Overreliance on intelligence crippled German defensive efforts in Normandy; it would not have taken a genius commander to realize that an exhausted Britain and a U.S. Army fighting a multi-theater war in the Pacific, Africa, Western Europe and Italy could not have fielded 87 divisions to attack Europe. Instead the Germans swallowed Allied misinformation hook, line and sinker. Statistics show the extent to which the German High Command was tricked by Allied deception plans. The Fifteenth Army, based at Pas de Calais, grew to a strength of 18 infantry and two panzer divisions. The Seventh Army, based in Normandy, had just 14 infantry and one panzer divisions. To make matters more complicated for the smaller force defending Normandy, the size of their theater of operations stretched for 995 miles of coastline. Rommel and von Rundstedt were both reminded of Frederick II's maxim, "He who defends everything, defends nothing."

At the outbreak of World War II, none of the belligerents could have expected to make an opposed amphibious invasion on the large scale of *Operation Neptune*, the codename for the Normandy landings on D-Day. Yet, with the early stages of the war going badly for both sides, amphibious landings became a crucial strategy. The prospect of a large scale invasion came only after the Allies were forcibly ejected from the European continent. Dr. Andrew Gordon, in his article *'The greatest military armada ever launched'*, reminded readers of the analogy Napoleon used to characterize the European powers as elephants, while describing Britain as a whale. The metaphor stood true in 1940, as Britain was able to slink back into the sea and live to fight another day, while the German war machine was left standing on the shores of France.

Germany dominated the land, while Britain was safe across the Channel so long as it could dominate the air above Britain and the seas around it. Eventually, either of the powers would have to learn how to enter and dominate the other power's theater of influence. Upon American entry into the war, U.S. planners pushed for a landing in Europe and determined push towards Germany, ideally in 1943. The British viewed such a proposal as premature, but they established a planning staff in July 1943 under the command of Admiral Bertram Ramsay, to lay the groundwork for invasion.

Ramsay

Under Ramsay, the areas of the Normandy coast between the rivers Vire and Orne were chosen as the landing zone, and it was under Ramsay that the ideas behind the MULBERRY harbors and the ingenious pipeline-under-the-ocean (PLUTO) were conceived. Churchill claims to have thought of MULBERRY harbors first, however, the most likely inventor is Commodore John Hughes-Hallet, known to have stated: "if we can't capture a port, we must take one with us." The problem was as huge in scale as it was simple in principle: the Allies needed to prefabricate a harbor the size of Dover in England, then tow it across the Channel and install it at the invasion beaches. What was needed was a sheltered, deep-water anchorage within which large ships could speedily unload supplies and reinforcements.

The solution was the MULBERRY harbors. Ground-breaking and complex, the harbors were comprised of 146 concrete caissons, to be sunk along an outer perimeter to act as breakwaters and ensure calm seas within the harbors. Prior to the creation of the MULBERRY harbors, any invasion which failed to secure a major port almost immediately would be doomed to failure, thus the reason the Germans had chosen ports as the location of their heaviest defenses. For a defending army the options were simple, hold all major ports until the unsupported invaders are repelled, exhausted, destroyed or run out of ammo, or destroy all major ports beyond short term repair. The MULBERRYS made German holding or destruction of French ports more of a nuisance than a disaster.

Ambulances coming ashore from the Mulberry harbors

Upon his appointment as Supreme Allied Commander in January 1944, Eisenhower wasted little time in demanding the scale of the landings be increased from three divisions to five. This step had far reaching ramifications in terms of resources and transport. Extra landing craft, support vessels, mine sweepers and bombardment vessels would be needed in a hurry to match the expansion of the invasion plans. Luckily, the U.S. forces were able to muster the extra ships needed.

In the early spring of 1944, the final stages of *Neptune* took shape. Landings would occur at five separate beaches in divisional strength. Prior to this, Beach Reconnaissance Parties were covertly landed at the five sites on dark nights to ascertain the nature, defenses and gradients of the beaches. The day before the invasion, D-Day -1, Allied minesweepers would have to be visible to the German defenses in order to complete their duties successfully. Either due to bad weather, German withdrawals or poor patrolling, the minesweepers were not detected. It was at Ramsay's headquarters that Eisenhower and the other senior commanders spent the final days and hours before the decision to go was given.

In the early hours of the morning of June 4, the decision was made upon the advice of meteorologists. In the days before the decision to launch, the weather approaching the Normandy beaches had been the worst for years, so bad that a landing would be all but impossible. Landings could be undertaken for just 10 days per month due to the tides and the need for a full moon to aid navigation. Delaying the landings in the early part of June would have meant that another attempt could not have been made for at least two weeks, and with well over 150,000 troops already on their ships waiting to go, that situation was not acceptable. Luckily for the Allies, chief meteorologist, Captain Stagg, with the aid of a meteorological station on the west coast of Ireland, was able to inform the assembled commanders that a brief clearing in the weather for a number of hours looked likely.

Ramsay, head of Naval affairs, informed Eisenhower that the Royal Navy would do whatever was asked of it, Montgomery, commander of the ground forces favored immediate action, while Leigh-Mallory, commander of the air-fleet was hesitant, worried that the bad weather would limit the support his air force could give to the landing troops. After a brief pause of no more than a few seconds, Eisenhower simply said "Let's go". With that, the largest invasion fleet ever assembled began its journey towards the Normandy coast.

From the very beginning of June 6, 1944, events did not go as the Allies had planned. In the first operations of the day, a cloud of Allied aircraft flew overhead, targeting German troop concentrations, infrastructure and fortifications throughout the Normandy countryside. On D-Day alone, Allied air forces flew over 14,000 sorties, compared to just 100 for the Luftwaffe, a clear sign of the total superiority the Allies enjoyed.

The Allied airborne assault in the early morning hours of June 6, 1944 proved to be as full of complexity, drama, heroism, confusion, loss and effort as the beach landings that followed. However, despite the heroism, the airborne assaults did not go to plan. The final plan for the Allied airborne invasion called on the 82nd Airborne to drop its regiments on either side of the Merderet River. The paratroopers would control the plateau west of the river and two major roads north of the Douve River before it joined the Merderet. East of the river, the division's theater of operations included the town of Ste-Mere-Eglise, five roads, a rail road and two small towns. The 101st Airborne's theatre covered about 400 square miles east of Ste-Mere-Eglise-Carentan Road. The 101st was charged with opening the route for the 4th Division of Utah to come off the beach. The fortunes of the 101st and 4th divisions were complementary. The 4th relied on the paratroopers to clear as much German artillery as possibly to allow the successful invasion of Utah, while the 101st needed the 4th's armor to come ashore to add weight to its attacking prowess.

On the British side, the 5th Parachute Brigade prevented German use of Pegasus Bridge, while the 3rd Parachute Brigade were charged with seizing four other bridges. The 6th Airlanding Brigade came in by glider to provide light vehicles, heavy machine guns and artillery. In one of the most famous and spectacular missions of the whole campaign, D Company, 2nd Battalion, the Oxfordshire and Buckinghamshire Light infantry, took Pegasus bridge after the most magnificent piece of piloting of the war, in which their glider pilots managed to guide them within yards of their target bridge. The attackers poured out of their battered gliders, completely surprising the German defenders, and took the bridges within 10 minutes. It was in this action where the first Allied casualty of D-Day was suffered and also where the first house to be liberated in France was situated.

At the top left of the image is Pegasus Bridge. It's clear how remarkably close the glider pilots managed to land.

Cafe Gondree at Pegasus Bridge claims to be the first house to be liberated in France.
However, while the weather was good enough to carry out the attacks on June 6, the early morning hours had low cloud-cover, making it hard for the Allied aircraft to locate and hit their targets. The Allies' planes mostly missed German fortifications on their bombing runs, and tens of thousands of paratroopers who were to land directly behind German lines were dropped out of place due to poor visibility. The only true advantage the paratrooper drops had for the Allies was that the scattered nature of the paratroopers confused the German defenders.

The contribution of Allied air power to the success of the invasion did not end with the actions of D-Day. Allied air power smashed the remaining Luftwaffe in France as it moved forward to meet the landings, and it also targeted roads, infrastructure and German supply lines. Coupled with Allied deciphering of German codes, the air forces were able to inflict terrible damage. On June 9, the Allies deciphered German communications that revealed the exact location of Panzer Group West. The following day, the Allies destroyed the panzer group's communications entirely, killing 17 staff officers, including the Chief of Staff. Without this supremacy in the skies, the landings might have faced stiff opposition from the Luftwaffe, which would have been devastating.

The span of the landings covered an area of 55 miles, a length large enough for the Allies to ensure a funnel of resupply could be held. As previously mentioned, amphibious landings are one of the most difficult aspects of warfare, no more so than during the Second World War, where technological advances, such as the machine gun, mortars and other portable weapons capable of inflicting terrible losses, allowed a relatively small number of defenders to inflict horrific casualties upon a landing force.

The U.S. 4th Division was assigned Utah Beach, while further inland the 82nd and 101st Airborne divisions were landed to ensure German reserves could not hinder the landing troops' progress. Omaha beach was assigned to the 1st Infantry Division, with half of the 29th landing there also. The British were assigned beaches codenamed Gold and Sword, where they expected to face a stern German counterattack. The Canadians were to take the fifth and final beach, codenamed Juno.

Luckily for the Allies, German defenses were bewildered and disorganized due to the confusion and power vacuum created by the imposition of Rommel on Van Rundstedt's territory. The 21st Panzer Division, for example, was widely dispersed, making a combined-arms counterattack virtually impossible. Another example of poor German organization can be seen at the landings on Omaha. Despite Rommel's order that the 352nd Infantry Division be moved closer to the beach, its commander, Dietrick Kraiss refused. This insubordination was to prove a lifeline for the soldiers on Omaha who would, most likely, have been obliterated had an entire division been waiting for them as they landed.

The British had been eyeing up France's coastline and had prepared ingenious armored vehicles to assist the landings. Under the command of Major-General Percy Hobart, flame-throwing tanks, flail tanks to clear mines and bridging equipment, mockingly known as Hobart's "funnies", proved to be a monumental success on the British landing beaches. Omar Bradley, the U.S. commander of ground forces was, unfortunately for his troops, uninterested in such machines. American troops were forced to cross the killing zones and minefields unaided by the new inventions.

Due to the reinforced German positions and heavy artillery pieces with which the Allies faced, the British laid on a two hour bombardment before attempting a landing. Unfortunately for the U.S. forces, particularly on Omaha, Bradley felt a 20 minute bombardment would be sufficient, relying on the Army Air Force to launch a massive attack. But such an attack had been made impossible for the Air Force due to the low cloud cover that had resulted in bombers entirely missing the German positions below. Bradley further compounded the impending misery and torment for his ground troops by completely disregarding the advice of Major-General Pete Corlett, a veteran of successful Pacific amphibious landings. Bradley's attitude was far from open minded and dismissed Corlett's advice by saying "anything that happened in the Pacific was strictly bush-league stuff." Bradley's decision not to employ adequate naval bombardment robbed his troops of crucial support. For example, a Brooklyn type cruiser, as was available to Bradley on D-Day, could fire 1,500 five inch shells in ten minutes, and when directed by spotter aircraft, its fire was deadly accurate. Yet Bradley, with his deep suspicion and prejudices against the U.S. Navy, remained ignorant. Nevertheless, and to the relief of the U.S. troops at Omaha, when it became obvious the landings there were teetering on failure, a number of destroyer skippers moved their vessels so close to the shore that they risked beaching to support the hard-pressed troops.

Landing at Utah Beach

In the narrative of D-Day, Omaha Beach has become the best known part of the attacks among Americans, due to the various difficulties the Americans faced there before managing to succeed. But it's essential to remember that each of the 5 beaches were their own story, and largely forgotten is the remarkable success of the American landings at Utah Beach, which were easier in comparison to the other four landing zones.

The 82nd and 101st Airborne, dropped the night before the landings, had ensured little German resistance remained. In one of the finest and most famous pieces of soldiering of the day, 101st Airborne Lieutenant Richard Winters, of Band of Brothers fame, almost single-handedly took out a German battery. On the beaches, despite an abnormally strong tidal current which swept forces 2,000 yards further south than planned, the landings at Utah encountered little opposition. From the outset, everything went right for the Americans. 28 out of the 32 amphibious tanks made it ashore, with the only major obstacle facing them being the sand dunes and flooded fields of Normandy. Even by noon, the 4th Infantry was able to advance from the beaches and expand their theater of command into the Normandy countryside. The 4th's casualty rate illustrates the success of Utah: 197 casualties out of a total landing force of 23,000 men.

Aerial view of Omaha Beach on D-Day
If the landings at Utah could be described as easy, those at Omaha were chronically bad. Due
to the aforementioned failure to reinforce Omaha Beach, despite Rommel's insistence, the U.S.
Army encountered just two battalions, rather than the ten which should have been in position.
Those two divisions, however, were more than enough to guarantee the U.S. Army one of its
worst days in history.

Despite the fact the Germans had just two battalions in position, the landings at Omaha were a
disaster. Some military operations are dogged by bad luck, and Omaha is certainly one of those.
To begin with, the initial air bombardment completely missed its intended target, and the naval
bombardment of just 20 minutes hardly damaged any German defenses. General Bradley had
told his men, "You men should consider yourself lucky. You are going to have ringside seats for
the greatest show on earth." However, Rear Admiral John L. Hall, in reference to the lack of
naval bombardment, countered, "It's a crime to send me on the biggest amphibious attack in
history with such inadequate naval gunfire support.

Bradley

Things went wrong even before troops hit Omaha Beach, but inadequacies in naval and air bombardment weren't the only problems. The invasion called for deploying inflatable tanks on the water that could provide cover for the infantry, but the officer in charge of releasing the amphibious tanks panicked and sent them into the deep swells of the Channel, causing 29 of the 34 tanks immediately sinking to the bottom. Finally, since the landing came at low tide, the troops were forced to move across 300 yards of water, followed by 100 yards of beach, steep dunes, and finally swamp, minefield and barbed wire. If a soldier had managed to run the gauntlet and survive, he then faced a climb up the cliffs to the high ground.

The result was, unsurprisingly, a slaughter. Much of the first wave of troops was gunned down before they could get out of the water. Machine gun and rifle fire pinned down those landing craft not destroyed by underwater mines, while those pinned down in the dunes, many gravely injured, were in no position to return any meaningful fire. After these first landing vehicles kept landing along a narrow strip unsheltered against the German defenders, similar landings were suspended during the morning hours of the operation.

Only the ingenuity of the on-looking destroyer captains, who risked beaching their craft to aid the unfortunate troops, provided some relief. Before sun had set on June 6, over 2,500 U.S. troops were dead, with some units incurring up to 95% casualties. Only thanks to the efforts of low ranking officers and NCOs did the U.S. avoid complete annihilation on Omaha. Pressing through the unimaginable fire, a few managed to begin clearing German defenses.

Omaha Beach on the afternoon of D-Day

Recovering the dead at Omaha

By the end of D-Day, troops on Omaha had only managed to grab two small beachheads, isolated from each other no less, making it the least successful landing spot among the five beaches. It would take a few more days for the Allies to firmly consolidate its hold on Omaha Beach and begin to push inland, after which a MULBERRY harbor was placed there. Somewhat fittingly, the harbor experienced the worst storms in the area in decades, and three days of storms irreparably wrecked the harbor on June 22.

Nevertheless, the preciously bought beach became the main supply zone for the invasion of France. Over the next three months, the Allies used Omaha Beach to land a million tons of supplies, 100,000 vehicles, and 600,000 men, while evacuating nearly 100,000 casualties.

Using Omaha Beach after D-Day

Landing on Gold Beach

The aims of the British landings at Gold were to establish a link between the British and the U.S. forces at Omaha. Due in part to the heavy naval bombardment of Gold Beach, the British forces were able to overrun the German defenses in most places, although they suffered heavy losses in attacks on German strong points such as Le Hamel. For the British it was a success, but certainly not a smooth, unopposed ride as the following quote shows: "We hit two mines going in…They didn't stop us, although the ramp was damaged and an officer standing on it was killed. The first man off was a commando sergeant in full kit. He disappeared like a stone into six feet of water. The beach was strewn with wreckage, a blazing tank, bundles of blankets and kit, bodies and bits of bodies. One bloke near me was blown in half and his lower half collapsed in a bloody heap on the sand."

Like other sectors, Gold Beach did not go entirely according to plan, mostly because the tidal waters that day left the water levels higher than planned. Engineers who were meant to remove some of the obstacles found that British ships were passing over them, which was helpful in some ways and harmful in others. As a contingency, the amphibious tanks had to be landed on the beach, providing necessary cover for the infantry.

After about 3 hours, the British had successfully established a beachhead on Gold Beach. The British division was able to advance through the suburbs of the town of Bayeux after penetrating the German defenses, one of the few Norman cities to fall without a fight. Of the 25,000 men who landed on Gold Beach, only about 400 became casualties. "Hobart's Funnies", which had been the subject of ridicule, proved invaluable at Gold Beach, with the different modified tanks clearing minefields, bridging ditches, and creating trackways across the sands to facilitate movement on and off the beaches.

By the end of D-Day, the British soldiers who landed on Gold Beach were about 6 miles inland, allowing them to link up with the Canadians on Juno Beach. Moreover, the success at Gold was crucial to the embattled U.S. Army on Omaha, because it drew German fighters away from the struggling Americans.

Landing on Juno Beach

The 3rd Canadian Division landing at Juno Beach experienced much of the same success as the British, albeit with higher casualties. Due to the Canadians arriving late on the beach, the tide was high, ensuring Rommel's underwater mines were able to inflict as much damage as possible. No fewer than 20 of the 24 lead landing craft were damaged or destroyed. The German army also managed to put up stern defenses around Juno.

Like the British however, the Canadians had the foresight to land their amphibious tanks on the beach when circumstances required it. With the help of these tanks providing cover, the Canadians were able to flank the German defenders, breaching the strong outer layer of German defenses relatively quickly in the northern section of the beach.

The Canadian soldiers landing in the south had it worse. As the 8th Brigade's reserve battalion, Le Régiment de la Chaudière, headed to shore, mines badly damaged their landing crafts, and the soldiers lost almost all of their supplies swimming to shore. With Canadian units pinned down in the south, reserves that landed less than an hour after the initial attacks found to their horror that the German strongholds defending their sector had not been reduced. The 400 man No. 48 (Royal Marine) Commando lost nearly 200 men within seconds of landing.

Despite suffering a total of about 1,000 casualties, the Canadians were able to pour through and push inland. German forces were unable to mount a counterattack until the brutal, murderous Waffen SS Hitlerjugend arrived the following day. By then, the Canadians were well positioned enough to absorb and survive the vicious counterattack. While they received heavy casualties, killed, wounded and captured, with many of the captured brutally murdered by the SS, the

Canadians held their ground and pressed on towards the main provincial town of Caen.

Coming ashore on Sword Beach

The Sword landings were, in comparison to those at Juno, quite easy. Generally, the heavy naval bombardment quelled German resistance, except the heavily defended stronghold of La Breche, which held on for up to three hours. The men on Sword Beach were the only ones to face a determined German counterattack, which came from the 21st Panzer division. But air superiority and effective defenses ensured that the German counterattack almost entirely fizzled out, and the Germans that made progress were eventually compelled to retreat by the end of the day anyway.

Still, two main problems confronted the British attackers. As British forces piled onto the beach, those at the front struggled to break through some German lines, creating a backlog on the beach that left some of the British wide open to indiscriminate German artillery, which inflicted significant loss of life and panic. The 3rd British Division, after landing on Sword, was tasked with meeting up with the British Airborne, which had taken the strategically important Pegasus Bridge in one of the few airborne operations that was successful on D-Day. From there, the British units were to move south towards Caen, eventually linking up with the British and Canadians landing on Gold and Juno Beaches.

However, with British forces massing outside Caen, the plan began to go wrong. Due to the congestion on Sword Beach, the supporting armor was unable to reach the infantry further south.

Further compounding the British problem, the heavily defended Hillman fortress stood directly in their path. A particularly bloody and drawn out battle ensued which lasted for most of the afternoon. As British troops pushed towards Caen they encountered elements of the 21st Panzer Division, ensuring Caen would not fall until the middle of July. Considering the varying degrees of success on all the landing beaches, it is perhaps a blessing in disguise that the taking of Caen was delayed, as it allowed Allied forces to better coordinate their attack against the well defended city.

By the end of D-Day, the Allies had managed to successfully land 170,000 men: over 75,000 on the British and Canadian beaches, 57,000 on the American beaches, and over 24,000 airborne troops. Thanks to Allied deception, the German army had failed to react to prevent the Allies from making the most of their landings. Just one division, the Hitlerjugend, would arrive the following day. Despite a fearsome and bloody day, the majority of the Allied forces had held their nerve, and most importantly, achieved their objectives. This ensured *Operation Overlord* was ultimately successful, and victory in Europe would be achieved within less than a year.

24 hours after the landings on June 6, 1944, however, the Allies still had plenty of work to do, and when the Allied High Command assessed the situation on the ground, it was clear that on no front had all of the objectives been achieved. The British and Canadians were ashore on Gold, Juno and Sword, yet Caen lay firmly in German hands. And in most cases, the various invasion forces lay clustered in isolated bands.

The Allies were left with a number of difficult tasks, most importantly capturing the critical port of Cherbourg and ensuring Allied forces were able to successfully link up before a push further east was made. Taking the town of Carentan was also of critical importance to the Allies, as the town was situated between the U.S. flanks. So important was the town that General Bradley was quite prepared to destroy every square inch of it if necessary.

Adding to the difficulties of taking the town was the fact that the German Army had blown up a bridge approaching the town. Engineers had moved material to repair the bridge but had failed to do so. The devout German 6th Parachute Regiment, which consisted of teenagers, held the territory immediately north of the town, which the U.S. intelligence thought had been abandoned. The 101st attack on the town began at 12.15 a.m. on June 11, with the 3rd Battalion of the 502nd Parachute Infantry leading the way. The soldiers dashed toward the bridge only to find that it had been unrepaired. Thus, the soldiers were forced to cross the river in a small boat, three at a time, until they reached an iron Belgian gate which the Germans had blocked the road with. As the gate would open just 18 inches, it forced the soldiers to squeeze through one by one. 50 yards past the gate lay the German paratroopers who poured machine gun fire and mortar rounds into the trapped Americans. Compounding the threat, two Luftwaffe fighters strafed and pounded the men, with I Company taking 25% casualties.

As the remaining Allied soldiers poured forward, with no chance of retreat, the situation seemed bleak. The remaining German paratroopers were embedded in a large farmhouse awaiting the U.S. assault. What they had not expected was for Colonel Robert Cole to, in a Medal of Honor winning assault, order his men to fix bayonets and charge the farmhouse. Due to the stress of battle, noise, fear or confusion, as Cole charged and turned to see his men, just 70 of his 250 men had followed his lead. Undeterred, Cole and his 70 men stormed the farmhouse, with the remainder of his troops frantically trying make up for their initial failings. Despite a fierce German resistance, Carentan fell to the Americans on June 12 and thus, Utah and Omaha were connected.

Even in its wildest dreams the German Army could not have inflicted the damage which was done to the allies on June 18. The worst storm to hit the area in 40 years crashed into Allied shipping and the MULBERRY harbors. Over 800 craft were sunk, and the crucial MULBERRY harbors bore the brunt of it. The harbor at Omaha was completely destroyed, with the harbor at Arromanches severely damaged. The effect of the great losses was that now the capture of the port of Cherbourg became of even more immediate importance. After a strong Allied attack and siege, the port fell on June 27, with 22,000 American dead and wounded. German casualties are not known, but over 39,000 prisoners surrendered. Unfortunately for the Allies, however, the Germans had completely destroyed the port. "Beyond a doubt the most complete, intensive, and best-planned demolition job in history" as one U.S. engineer put it.

Churchill was not overstating the achievements of *Operation Overlord* when he described the plan "the greatest thing we have ever attempted". The greatest armada the world had ever seen had landed 170,000 soldiers on the heavily defended beaches of Normandy in just 24 hours. More remarkable was the fact that the operation was a success on every major level. Deception, tactical surprise and overwhelming force had contributed to the establishment of an adequate beachhead. Confusion and dissent had stopped the Germans massing for any great counterattack. The Atlantic Wall which Hitler had placed so much faith in had been breached, and the race to Paris was on.

Operation Overlord aimed to have the Allies reach the Seine River within 3 months of D-Day, and it's a testament to the men who fought and served on D-Day that the goal was reached early. To do so, the Allies overcame firm resistance from the Germans, atrocious weather that limited resupply for the Allies, and the difficult terrain of Normandy, which included endless hedgerows providing hidden cover. And the Allies reached their objective ahead of time despite the fact the objectives of D-Day were not entirely met; the Allies had not captured Caen, St-lo or Bayeux on the first day.

Nevertheless, the landings were clearly a resounding success. Casualties were significantly smaller than those expected by commanders, and the significance of D-Day to the morale of the Western world, much of it under German domination, cannot be underestimated. For France, Poland, Czechoslovakia, Belgium, Holland and more, who had suffered over four years of occupation, the great democracies were finally coming to their rescue. American, British, Canadian, Polish, Commonwealth, Greek, Belgian, Dutch and Norwegian soldiers, sailors, and airmen all participated in the Battle for Normandy, which saw the Allies on the banks of the Seine River just 80 days after D-Day.

The Battle of the Bulge

While the Battle of the Bulge is often characterized as a last ditch attempt by the Germans in Europe, that was not at all what Hitler had in mind when he conjured up the offensive. In fact, Hitler truly believed he could pry apart the Allied armies, and his philosophy was seemingly dictated by a peculiar point of view pertaining to America itself. As a youth, Hitler was fascinated by Karl May's novels about Native Americans, and he was equally interested in the movie *Grapes of Wrath*, which he saw several times and came to believe represented America at large. One political scientist noted that as a country with a social structure, Hitler saw nothing when he looked at the United States: "The astounding narrowness of his horizon is also evidenced by the fact that Hitler hardly noticed a world power of the United States." Only incidental references to the U.S. exist within his notorious book *Mein Kampf*, but later on, with so many American cars on German roads, he became rapt with America's industrial structure. He needed to fit it into his universal view of racial superiority, leading to his conclusion that since the U.S. had such a mongrel culture, it had to have been the Nordics who made it so successful.

Historian Stephen Sears, consultant to General S.L.A. Marshall, summarized this mistaken view: "Without their air power [grounded by weather], the Americans had no stomach for fighting, Hitler insisted; once through the front-line positions, the German assault forces would find nothing to oppose them but hapless cooks and mechanics, led by bank clerks trying to be officers."

Hitler

Hitler's underestimation of the United States as a military power came from its post-World War I condition. According to historian Harold Winton, "In 1939, the United States had no army capable of fighting on European battlefields…the American Army's capacity to transform itself during the next few years was as impressive an achievement as any in military history." Of course, the U.S. had proven several times in North Africa, Italy, and the Pacific that the nation, when fully mobilized, was no paper tiger, but Hitler apparently disregarded American successes elsewhere, including on D-Day a few months earlier. Hitler may have been the only one fooling himself; it has been a prevailing conclusion for the last 69 years that the offensive was an enormous gamble on Hitler's part and not by any means a guaranteed recipe for success. Germany was nearing exhaustion by 1944, and many of its best soldiers had been killed or captured. It had no allies in Europe and could no longer dominate in the air, all while facing Russian forces to the east. Some of his officers tried to talk Hitler out of the proposed offensive, but he refused to listen.

For Hitler's plan to succeed, the Germans needed to destabilize and starve the Allies of supplies, which meant the large port of Antwerp had to be taken. This mission would be left to the Sixth Panzer Division under the command of Sepp Dietrich. In a corresponding phase, the Fifth Panzers, under the command of Hasso von Manteuffel, was to attack the center of American forces and capture the roadways and rails of St. Vith on their way to Brussels. The Seventh Army, under the command of General Erich Brandenberger was to attack the southern Allied flank and prevent American reinforcements from mounting any significant action against Manteuffel's Fifth by creating a buffer zone. The Fifteenth Army was held back to neutralize any counterattack. All told, the Germans still had more than a quarter of a million soldiers in the region to use during the offensive, and as Hitler had hoped in delaying an offensive until the end of 1944, the weather would somewhat neutralize the Allies' airpower advantage due to low cloud cover.

Dietrich

Manteuffel

In planning the offensive, Hitler had a number of issues to consider. First was the advance of the Soviet army on the Eastern Front. The Soviet army's summer offensive had overrun the German Army Group Center, and they had also advanced through Ukraine, Romania, and Bulgaria, and had made their way onto the Hungarian Plain. Hitler understood that an offensive against the massive Soviet army on the Eastern Front would do little more than delay their advance. Meanwhile, the Allies on the Western Front were vulnerable because the movement of their supplies was dependent on the shipping capacity of several port cities, with Antwerp being the most important. By concentrating his forces in the west and then breaking through the weak, American-held area of the Allied front line in the Ardennes, Hitler believed the Germans could retake Antwerp, isolate most of the British-Canadian 21st Army Group, and seize this important Allied logistical center. Hitler also targeted the Ardennes because he believed the Americans were less capable soldiers than the British, and that they would not put up much of a fight against a large-scale German offensive. As Hitler reportedly put it, "The purpose of these attacks will mainly be to eliminate the Americans south of our entry point – to destroy them bit by bit, to eliminate them division by division."

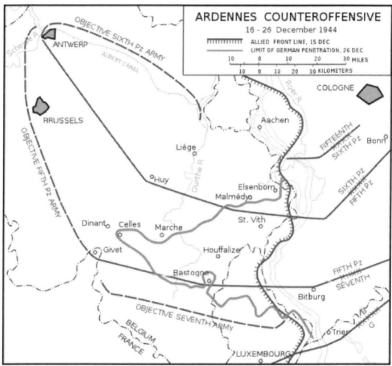

The Germans' best case scenario, with their advancing routes in red toward Antwerp

If successful, Hitler calculated that the offensive would buy the German army three or four months in which it could focus on the Soviets. Hitler hoped that creating such a window, in which the Germans could concentrate on only one front, would allow them to bog down the Soviet advance and compel the Allies into a negotiated peace. In terms of the best case scenario, the offensive could split the British and Americans along the Western Front, fracture their alliance, and reduce the war into a one-front war by early spring of 1945.

One thing the Germans had going in their favor were the Allied armies' dispositions in late 1944. The Allies, fresh off the Normandy landing, and in a constant state of movement, suffered from insufficient intelligence concerning this offensive, and were indeed caught off-guard. The recent liberation of Paris was accomplished with the benefit of superior French intelligence, but those resources withered as the Allies neared Germany. This alone supports Robert Merrian's claim that America "received two great surprises during World War II. The first was Pearl Harbor, and the second was the Battle of the Bulge." He further suggests that the latter was, in a sense, even more inexplicable than the first. By the time the fighting started, Americans were situated to the north and south of the Ardennes, and even today, debate persists over why General Dwight D. Eisenhower left the center so lightly defended. The most obvious point is that the terrain in the middle was unsuitable for open warfare, but some have claimed that Eisenhower hoped to bait Hitler into attacking through this region and that he was alerted to the planned German offensive before it started. However, Jerry D. Morelock, in his review of Charles Whiting's text on the Battle of the Bulge, suggests that responsibility for the lightly defended center lay with "those who decided that the United States could fight a major war on two fronts by mobilizing only ninety divisions, for therein lies the actual root of Eisenhower's dilemma – and Hitler's opportunity." When the fighting started, 200,000 Germans would be launching attacks against less than 100,000 Americans.

Eisenhower

The Allied response was further complicated by the presence of English-speaking Germans dressed as American soldiers spreading misinformation behind the lines, cutting communication lines and changing road signs ("Operation Greif"). Some parachuted in, while others drove in captured American jeeps and trucks wearing the dog tags of killed American soldiers. The tactic is said to have caused such confusion that American soldiers reacted by attempting to confirm their own with questions about America that presumably only a real American could answer. One anecdote was that even General Omar Bradley, commander of the 12th Army, was interviewed three times with questions about football and other items of Americana. The subterfuge did enough damage that those who were caught were quickly court-martialed and executed.

Beginning in the Fall of 1944, Allied intelligence intercepts revealed that many German armored formations were being withdrawn from the front lines in order to be rebuilt. Most notably, these armored formations included the elite SS Panzers. But just what these movements indicated caused a great deal of debate among Allied intelligence officers. Some, like Col. Benjamin Dickson of the American First Army and Col. Oscar Koch of the American Third Army, believed that the Germans were planning an offensive; in fact, Dickson believed that the Ardennes was a likely site of attack, while Koch, in a special intelligence briefing to Third Army Commander George Patton, suggested that the units in the Ardennes were vulnerable to German attack. Such an attack could expose the Third Army's northern flank to any German forces breaking through the Ardennes.

By late November, Patton was beginning to suspect the possibility of a large-scale German counterattack to the north of the Third Army's sector, and though it was still more of an intelligence hunch than anything definite, his worries were exacerbated by General Bradley's decision to use that area to rest the battered VIII corps and to introduce green units fresh from the U.S. But there were all sorts of issues facing new troops, as one of them, Donald Chumley, later explained, "I arrived with very low morale -- I was 19, just out of high school -- a farm boy with little experience in anything. I had 17 weeks basic training at Fort McClellan, Alabama and shipped over not knowing and very fearful of what the future would be like. There was snow on the ground. I spent the first night sleeping in a stable on some straw with about two hours of guard duty standing outside in the cold." Of course, the new soldiers were positioned where they were precisely because it was seen as a safe backwater, which was why in Patton's view it was dangerous, and he noted as much in his diary. Mindful that the Third Army would likely be sucked into any such battle, he had his planners study and map the road network to the north.

Patton

In early December, British Maj. General Kenneth Strong submitted a new intelligence report that suggested the German reserve being created via the withdrawal of the German armored units was strong enough to be utilized to break the Allied lines. Like Dickson and Koch, he reported that a possible German objective could be to attack the overstretched Allied units in the Ardennes. General Eisenhower, the Supreme Allied Commander of American and British forces in Western Europe, found this report compelling enough that he sent Strong to Luxembourg to brief General Bradley, but Bradley and his staff did not seem to take Strong's report seriously, For example, Brig. Gen. Edwin Sibert of the 12th Army Group wrote, "It is now certain that attrition is steadily sapping the strength of German forces on the Western Front and that the crust of defense is thinner, more brittle, and more vulnerable than it appears on our G-2 maps, or to the troops in the line...The enemy divisions....have been cut by at least fifty percent...The [German] breaking point may develop suddenly and without warning." Meanwhile, Bradley echoed Sibert's beliefs, telling Strong that he was "aware of the danger" presented by a possible German offensive and had "earmarked certain divisions to move into the Ardennes should the enemy attack there." Just prior to dismissing Strong, Bradley nonchalantly demonstrated his belief that the Germans were too weak to attack by remarking, "Let them come!"

Bradley

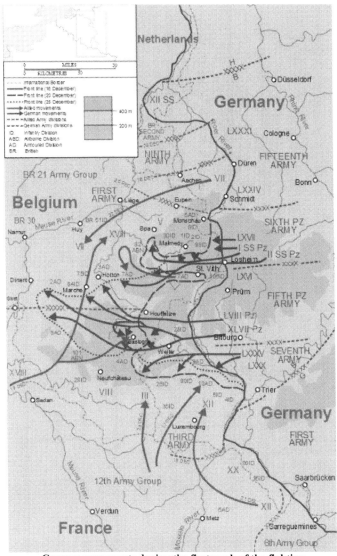

German movements during the first week of the fighting

The Germans would come soon enough. In the early morning hours of December 16, Operation Mist began with approximately 90 minutes of artillery barrage coming from over 1,600 field pieces. As Hitler himself had commanded, "There must not be one gun barrel that does not join in this artillery preparation." At the same time, the artillery barrage alone did not demonstrate the gravity of the coming German advance. As German forces coalesced, General Troy Middleton, leader of the VIII Corps, called up the 168th Engineer Combat Battalion, but that unit was at half-strength and had received no weapons training with bazookas or machine guns.

Middleton

The immediate targets were the U.S. V and VII corps of the First Army, under the command of General Courtney Hodges, and the XXI corps, commanded by General Bradley. Although much of the fire was ineffective, the volume of fire from these artillery pieces was a major surprise to American units stationed in the area, and the American lines were breached on the first day as surprised soldiers fell back, doing what they could to slow the action. According to the memoirs of Sergeant John Kline, a 19 year old machine gun squad leader, "It was the coldest and snowiest weather 'in memory.' Other firsthand accounts note that "men, tanks and trucks stormed over the border…tank turrets sprayed the area…fired into houses and outbuildings…swept fire across streets…hit whatever American soldiers they could."

On December 16, the town of Monschau, along the northern portion of the Ardennes front, was held by the American 38th Cavalry Squadron, led by Lt. Col. Robert E. O'Brien Jr. Key to the defense of Monschau was high ground to the north, east, and south, and between the three hills were two entry points to approach the town. The initial artillery fire from the Germans knocked out wire communications throughout the sector held by the 38th Cavalry, and the initial German attack occurred into the center of the squadron's defenses at Monschau. Because of the deployment of tanks in strong defensive positions near the town, the German assault was quickly stopped, and German troops proved particularly vulnerable to the 38-mm "canister" antipersonnel rounds that the Americans utilized. During the rest of the day, sporadic German patrols probed the areas around Monschau as they looked for weak points in the American defense, but these were met by American troops and turned back. By the night of December 16th, it had become obvious to the leaders of the 38th Cavalry that the attack that day was part of a massive German offensive, so that night, reinforcements arrived in the form of six machine gun crews as well as Company A of the 146th Engineer Battalion.

At Höfen, another town along the northern part of the front, the 3rd Battalion, 395th Infantry faced a German attack that began just before 6:00 a.m. on the 16th and focused on five points along the battalion's front. Like Monschau, the initial artillery fire had cut wire communications, which meant the 395th was unable to coordinate with the 196th Field Artillery until a few hours into the attack. Without the 196th Field Artillery launching counter-artillery fire, the brunt of the attack had to be turned back by infantry troops using rifles, machine guns, and mortars. The 395th was able to hold off the attack, and by 7:45 a.m., the Germans had withdrawn except for one penetration at the center of the battalion position. Within an hour, this small group of German troops was engaged by soldiers pulling back from the front, and German losses at Monschau and Höfen amounted to 204 killed and 19 prisoners captured. For the Americans, only 4 soldiers had been killed, with 7 wounded and 4 missing.

The battle at St. Vith began to unfold on December 16th and would follow on the heels of a military tragedy in the Schnee Eifel. St. Vith, like Bastogne a short distance away, was a small village of approximately 2,000 civilians, and although not situated on major strategic lines, it did have an important purpose for the German advance toward Antwerp. Reinforcements would flow over these roads, isolate the enemy in the Schnee Eifel, and protect supply lines. In this forested region along the Belgian border, the American 422nd and 423rd, upwards of 9,000 men, were encircled by two German movements, and found themselves in a situation where it was too late to escape or resist. Finally receiving updated news, the two units learned of the decision of General Alan Walter Jones in St. Vith not to withdraw them, so they moved in parallel but were not in contact. At one point, they mistakenly fired on each other. Also severed from the rest of the line were several artillery, engineer, automatic anti-aircraft, reconnaissance and tank destroyer units. Eventually, about 6,000 of these men surrendered to the Germans on the 19th.

As the German attack moved forward toward St. Vith on the 16th, General Jones had reached the conclusion that all the late arrivals and lack of coordination rendered a daylight attack possible, so he postponed it until the morning of the 17th. However, on the German side, with five hours of daylight remaining, elements of the advance guard moved to within two miles of St. Vith, progressing several miles almost entirely uncontested, with the bulk of the German units arriving by evening. Still not realizing the full measure of the German advance at St. Vith, only one combat command was offered to reinforce the 106th Division, and a second would stand ready if needed, but under no circumstances was a third to be brought up. Furthermore, General Jones could not formulate accurate timetables for the arrival of the various units, especially with the mass of equipment being moved, nor did the incoming units suspect the magnitude of the coming invasion or the precarious position of those already in St. Vith.

American soldiers at St. Vith marching past a wrecked tank.

Reinforcements led by General Hasbrouk would arrive early on the 17th, but due to the poor conditions, the armored columns that were supposed immediately to his rear did not materialize at the proper time. Traffic jams ensued, and traveling the 14 miles from Vielsalm took several hours. Still oblivious to the German presence, the first arriving tank corps dismounted their vehicles without care for the environment, and two were hit quickly, with a third retreating. Some have asserted that German planes might have seen American movement on the ground, but regardless, American communication was sporadic and their intelligence was poor.

General Bruce Cooper Clarke of the 7th Armored Division arrived to inform Jones that his troops would not be there until the afternoon, meaning that with German tank divisions a short distance away and approaching rapidly, reinforcements would not come in time. A disillusioned Jones turned his command over to Clarke, who was able to arrange a three-sided defense within a few hours. The traffic jams that plagued the Americans were doing no better for the Germans on the other side of the town, but in the end, superior German armor overmatched what the Americans were able to bring up. St. Vith would fall to the Germans by December 21.

As Patton had suspected, the Germans had attacked in the Ardennes and punched through the thinly held sector directly to the north of the Third Army, but the Third Army, unaware of the German attack in the morning, had continued normal operations along the Saar River to the south, which is what would allow the "bulge" in the line to start growing. At the same time, the same poor winter weather that grounded Allied aircraft hampered German movements, particularly their armored units, which disrupted the advance.

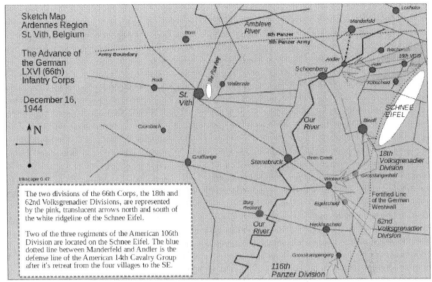

German advances on the 16th in the northern part of the Ardennes

Eventually, the "bulge" from this outbreak would grow to a dimension of 60 miles deep and 50 miles wide, but upon receiving news of the German attack, Patton would prepare to turn his army around. Early on the 17th, Patton ordered General John Milliken's III Corps to prepare to switch axis and move 50 miles north, and when he met General Bradley on the 18th, Bradley endorsed the plan. Those two senior generals then presented Patton's plan to Eisenhower and the British on the 19th at a meeting in Verdun.

German soldiers in the Ardennes

On December 17, the second day of the offensive, the German advance matched and exceeded the first in terms of raw brutality. At Monschau-Höfen, the Germans renewed their attack, and even though the main German assault was repulsed, the units of B Troop were stretched thin and were in danger of being overrun by the German battalion along the northern flank at Mutzenich Hill. The situation was only restored around noon, when B Troop was reinforced by A Company of the 47th Armored Infantry Battalion, 5th Armored Division. When those reinforcements arrived on the scene, the American forces were able to push out against the Germans. In the afternoon, German forces attempted to mass for a new assault, but American artillery observers sent fire into that area. By the end of the fighting in this sector on December 17th, another 200 German soldiers had been killed, with 26 captured. American casualties were again light, with only 2 soldiers killed and one wounded.

While German units to the north had been unable to penetrate American defenses at Monschau and Höfen, the story was quite different to the south. Near the town of Büllingen, E Company was able to hold off units from Kampfgruppe Peiper, but further south, the Germans had broken through the 99th Division on their right and had penetrated into the Losheim Gap. Later, it was relayed to Allied Command that the 99th Division had been overrun by German armored and infantry divisions. This forced the Allies to begin a withdrawal from the area, but the 39th Infantry faced numerous problems during their retreat. For the 1st Battalion of the 39th, the position that they were supposed to retreat towards was already occupied by the Germans, so they had to move southeast, where they came under heavy artillery fire that created heavy casualties for the two companies toward the back of the retreating column. The 2nd Battalion was also attacked during its retreat but was able to get to its designated position with few casualties. Once they reached this position, however, they encountered a series of German attacks that began when three tanks made their way through the defense perimeter to the east without being fired upon. For the soldiers of the 2nd Battalion, it was unclear whether the tanks were American or German, and by the time they realized they were indeed German, the tanks were on top of the soldiers' position. Firing at that point would have only given away their position and allowed the German tanks to fire their big guns at close range, so the 2nd Battalion let the tanks pass through, where they would encounter fire from the 2nd Division's artillery. One tank was knocked out, and the other two opened fire, at which point four more tanks appeared. Two of the tanks were destroyed by mines, and the other two were disabled by bazooka teams.

Shortly after that encounter, more German tanks arrived from the main body of Kampfgruppe Müller, and while the 2nd Battalion was able to take out four more tanks, units of the Kampfgruppe were able to sneak through the American lines. At about 11:00 p.m. on the 17th, units from the 38th Infantry were attacked, most likely by the portions of Kampfgruppe Müller that had slipped past the 2nd Battalion. Five tanks and 80 infantrymen attacked the 3rd Battalion of the 38th, but the Americans were able to stop the attack, and by midnight, most of the fighting on the battlefield had ceased.

December 17 also witnessed of the Nazis' most naked atrocities committed against military troops during the entire war. During the 17th, an American truck convoy, Battery B of the 285th Artillery Observation Battalion, collided with the First Panzer Division under the command of General Joachim Peiper, whose troops were known by reputation as the "Blowtorch Battalion." They had, by many accounts, crossed Russia burning everything in their path, and they had massacred a great number of citizens in villages along the way. Being entirely out-gunned, the American company, consisting of about 80 men, left their vehicles and surrendered, only to be taken to an open field and shot with machine-gun and pistol fire. Following the group execution, English-speaking officers walked among the bodies and asked any if they needed assistance. Those who answered were shot again. It was the single largest atrocity committed against American soldiers in Europe during the war, and Americans were not able to reach the site until January. After the bodies were located, it was discovered that 41 had been shot in the head.

A picture of American soldiers taken prisoner by Peiper's men

Pictures of the murdered Americans

Ultimately, retribution for the Malmedy Massacre would come with 74 members of the SS being tried in a Dachau courthouse, and it was there that German officers explained that Hitler had ordered them to be as brutal as possible to intimidate the enemy. Peiper himself had ordered his men to show no quarter and thus take no prisoners. As a result of the trials, 43 received death sentences, including General Peiper, while 22 received sentences of life imprisonment, including General Dietrich. They were taken to Landsberg Prison, where Hitler had written his *Mein Kamp* after the Beer Hall Rebellion, but political difficulties ensued following the sentencing. The Soviets were encroaching from the east, and the German outcry against Americans holding war trials left the Allies worried that the trials would drive the Germans into the Soviet camp. There were accusations as well that the prosecutor was Jewish. Under these and other political pressures, the death sentences were commuted to life imprisonment. Peiper was the final prisoner released in 1976. He settled in France, but his home was set ablaze shortly thereafter and he died in the fire. It was later found that the fire brigade's water hoses had been cut.

Peiper

Members of the 101st Airborne watch supplies being airdropped into Bastogne

December 17 had confirmed the rumors of a major German offensive that had spread around the American line during the previous day, and it was a harsh dose of reality for many American soldiers who had grown optimistic about the progress of the war and believed they could see the light at the end of the tunnel. When the fighting started, the 101st Airborne, stationed at Mourmelon, France, was receiving some much needed rest and relaxation, including furloughs, and officers were planning Christmas celebrations. Letters home reflected the surprise of hearing the news from the previous day, such as this one by one of the men: "Things are really getting hot today – sounds like there's 'beaucoup' trouble northeast of here…"

Nearly half of the American front in the Ardennes at the beginning of Germany's offensive was defended by just one division: the 28th Infantry Division. The line that the 28th was supposed to hold stretched along a highway leading south from St. Vith through the villages of Heinerscheid, Fischbach, Hosingen, Hoschied, and Diekirch. The highway ran along a ridge that reminded troops of Skyline Drive in the Shenandoah Valley of Virginia, so they nicknamed it "Skyline Drive." The man in charge of the 28th Infantry Division, Maj. Gen. Norman Cota, deployed all three of his infantry divisions in a north-south line paralleling the highway and was thus left with only one battalion in reserve. Because of the thinness of the defenses that General Cota was forced to deploy, if the Germans broke through at any point along the line protected by the 28th, there would be no way to plug the holes and stop the ensuing German advance.

The pressure of the German forces, especially through the center of the American defenses, had already put a strain on units of the 28th division during December 16th, and by December 18th, the 116th Panzer Division began a push forward through the center and the 2nd Panzer pushed forward to the south, which began to break down the 28th Infantry's defenses in that area. The 2nd Panzer advanced more than 5 miles in this southern section before becoming entangled in logistical problems related to the narrow and muddy road conditions. However, even with these logistical problems, the division's reconnaissance battalion was able to make it to Magaret, a town roughly 2.5 miles away from Bastogne, and by the night of the 18th, the German division's headquarters had made their way to that location as well.

Bastogne would become a legendary linchpin in the defense against the Ardennes Offensive, in part for its strategic importance but also because of the almost superhuman effort made to protect it. Seven important roads converged with the town of Bastogne, and the Germans, on their way to Antwerp, recognized its importance as a hub, but with the weather obscuring the military map and intelligence at an unusually low rate of abundance or reliability, no Americans on the ground, from private to general, knew precisely what was about to happen, or in what way it would manifest itself. Three officers, Colonel S.L.A. Marshall, Captain John G. Westover and Lieutenant A. Joseph Webber, collaborated to put it quite succinctly in the Washington Infantry Journal when they described Bastogne as "a series of small, dramatic military actions related more by circumstances beyond the control of the defensive forces involved than by the design of a single commander…"

On December 18, as more paratroopers began to arrive in Bastogne, and at a greater rate, German General Fritz Bayerlein reasonably interpreted it as the beginnings of a counter-offensive. However, he would make the mistake of hesitating rather than proceeding into what was at the time a weakly defended Bastogne, buying the Allies more time to reinforce and prepare. That evening, General Middleton's one standing order to GeneralAnthony McAuliffe was, "Hold Bastogne." Once the necessary leadership was in place, three distinct blocking actions were taken. William Desobry took his troops to Noville in the north, Lt. Colonel Henry T. Cherry dug in at Longville to the northeast, and Lt. Colonel James O'Hara took Wardin to the east. Moving along provincial roads at night to reach the Bastogne area, lights were doused or dimmed to avoid aerial attacks, and as one soldier put it, "Hell of a long ride without lights after dark – say, there's lots of Jerries around here."

Allied armored units were already fighting a few miles to the east on the 18th when Colonel Julian Ewell, whose regiment would meet the Germans first, received his instructions. He was given discretionary command over the 501st Parachute Infantry, but it was fervently hoped that the roadblocks a few miles out in each direction, would be sufficient to hold back the German advance. In fact, the paratroopers were given orders to "take it easy", so that they would avoid over-commitment and being surrounded. At the time, Ewell did not realize that armored elements were already retreating toward the town and taking heavy punishment from Panzers on the roads. Those on the Allerborn-Bastogne Road had been badly compromised, and an armored unit ambushed on the road to Magaret lost all of its vehicles.

Ewell

After that, the Germans began to believe their advance to Bastogne would be largely unimpeded. Their intelligence asserted that two American airborne divisions were closing in to enter the battle at Bastogne, but that most Americans converging on the position were moving by truck. Thus, the German command estimated that there would be no sizeable American presence until the 19th. However, German General Meinrad von Lauchert's Panzer Division lost a day pursuing and mopping up American resistance off of the roads, and the Panzer Lehr and the 26th Volks Grenadieren Division circled through two other villages to enter Bastogne from the north. To this point, the only disadvantage experienced by the Germans, other than fuel concerns, was that they had advanced so rapidly to keep pace with one another that they didn't actually have time to coordinate the siege. Further, rain and fog complicated movement and awareness on both sides.

In the face of the Panzers, the American defenders brought out everything they could find, including light armor from repair, and the roads were mined in the middle of the night as Panzers approached. Ewell left the road to secure high ground at Bizory and Hill 510, joined by the 158th Engineer Combat Battalion. One Panzer division turned aside to meet the Americans in the Noville area, which served as one of the three blockades to the German advance, and while the fog still hung low over the region, Americans and Germans lobbed grenades at one another until German artillery established an advantage. When the fog lifted, the imposing German tank presence could be seen in its various locations, but as they moved on the town, some of the vehicles that had gone off-road bogged down and others were attacked by American Sherman tanks. The Germans retreated for the moment, deciding that the ground was deficient, but even still, 20-30 of artillery continued to fall on Noville each minute. The outlying American infantry counterattacked Germans on the high ground, but they inadvertently collided with the 2nd Panzer. More Americans entered the fray, optimistically expecting sizeable and fresh reinforcements in a short time, but they were unaware that some units in the surrounding area had already become crippled. After these counterattacks fizzled out, Bastogne was eventually encircled and all roads were cut, resulting in a complete siege. Assuming their work was done, one of the Panzer divisions actually departed the area.

In fact, the fight was far from over. From that point forward, American forces pulled together everything and everyone available, including tank crews of destroyed vehicles, infantrymen broken off from their units, and all manner of stragglers. This ragtag defense became known as "Team Snafu." The 333rd, a black battalion comprised entirely of African-American soldiers led by white officers, was brought into the Bastogne siege as well, having held the line out on the roadways as long as they could. Considering the racism and belief that African-Americans lacked the intelligence and will to fight, the order to have the 333rd reinforce Bastogne showed just how desperate Bastogne's situation was. They were given carbines and told to protect the city, and in the end, held their sector through valorous actions, resulting in a unit award for the 333rd: the Presidential Unit Citation.

After he had heard about the German offensive, Patton was keen to sever the burgeoning bulge at its base from behind, but he was instead ordered to aim instead for the trapped troops at Bastogne. When Eisenhower asked him how long it would take to relieve the 101st Airborne at Bastogne, Patton told him, "As soon as you're through with me." In fact, Patton had already devised operations for his Third Army that he believed could have three of his divisions attacking the Germans in two days (on December 21), which astounded the unbelieving Eisenhower. Eisenhower told him, "Don't be fatuous, George. If you try to go that early you won't have all three divisions ready and you'll go piecemeal." Eisenhower insisted that he play it safe by delaying any counterattack until the 22nd, after which Patton walked over to a telephone and contacted his command center with the order, "Play ball."

In an astonishing feat of planning, logistics and discipline, Patton's army redirected 133,000 vehicles, 62,000 tons of supplies, and the vehicles and men covered a combined distance of 1.5 million miles. To his superiors' amazement, Patton was poised to reach Bastogne and attack the Germans on December 22, and on December 21, he told Bradley, "Brad, this time the Kraut's stuck his head in the meat grinder, and I've got hold of the handle."

Of course, for Patton's Third Army to relieve the siege, the men had to hold out a few days, which they were able to do because supplies were parachuted in and the Germans eschewed frontal assaults. The defenders were faced with dwindling resources, ammunition and food, but their morale stayed high due to news of imminent reinforcements arriving. Furthermore, letters and journals written by defenders in Bastogne also took note of British broadcasters reporting, "Americans hold out in Bastogne." All in all, around 2,000 supply sorties were launched by the Allies once the skies cleared, and supplies for the encircled troops in Bastogne were dropped, increasing the difficulty for the Germans to maintain the siege. At the same time, Allied planes attacked German vehicles and troop positions with impunity, with one bomber reporting, "The boys shot up some big convoy coming toward this way with tanks and troops. Darned good thing the weather changed…Capt. Parker who joined us on the 19th was controller…what a 'phony' too, you'd think he won the war by himself."

.Despite the fact the siege was increasingly hard to maintain, the Germans remained so confident that elements of the 5th German Panzer Division bypassed the town to the west and northwest in a move to further encircle Bastogne. On the 22nd, the Germans sent an ultimatum to General McAuliffe, the acting commander for General Maxwell Taylor (who was on leave). Four Germans approached under a white flag and delivered a request for surrender within a two-hour window:

> "To the U.S.A. Commander of the encircled town of Bastogne.
>
> The fortune of war is changing. This time the U.S.A. forces in and near Bastogne have been encircled by strong German armored units. More German armored units have crossed the river Our near Ortheuville, have taken Marche and reached St. Hubert by passing through Hompre-Sibret-Tillet. Libramont is in German hands.
>
> There is only one possibility to save the encircled U.S.A. troops from total annihilation: that is the honorable surrender of the encircled town. In order to think it over a term of two hours will be granted beginning with the presentation of this note.
>
> If this proposal should be rejected one German Artillery Corps and six heavy A. A. Battalions are ready to annihilate the U.S.A. troops in and near Bastogne. The order for firing will be given immediately after this two hours' term.
>
> All the serious civilian losses caused by this artillery fire would not correspond with the well known American humanity.
>
> The German Commander."

To this point, the Americans had held Bastogne "at all costs", and McAuliffe had already been buoyed by news that the 4th Armored Division was on its way to relieve the 101st. One American officer, Lt. General Harry W. O. Kinnard, later recalled McAuliffe's reaction to reading the ultimatum:

> "McAuliffe realized that some sort of reply was in order. He pondered for a few minutes and then told the staff, 'Well I don't know what to tell them.' He then asked the staff what they thought, and I spoke up, saying, 'That first remark of yours would be hard to beat.' McAuliffe said, "What do you mean?" I answered, 'Sir, you said Nuts.' All members of the staff enthusiastically agreed, and McAuliffe decided to send that one word, 'Nuts!' back to the Germans. McAuliffe then wrote down: 'To the German Commander, Nuts! The American Commander.'"

McAuliffe

As it turned out, the threat of a massive artillery barrage was unfounded and never took place. The Luftwaffe bombed the city, but the Americans hung on until reinforcements began to arrive. On December 22, elements from Patton's Third Army arrived to lift the siege, and Milliken's corps punctured the German positions despite stubborn resistance and truly appalling weather. Patton's Army had reached Bastogne within four days, and as always, Patton led from the front, urging his men onwards, leaping out of his jeep in the snow to help shove a stranded lorry, and deliberately exposing himself to fire. For once, even he used superlatives to describe the action at Bastogne, calling it "the most brilliant operation we have thus far performed, and it is in my opinion the outstanding achievement of the war. This is my biggest battle."

Patton's jeep at Bastogne

When units from the 4th Army arrived on the 26th, the siege of Bastogne was truly lifted, and little German resistance remained to the north. To the northeast was but a single regiment, the Grenadier 78. The southern regiments, 901 and 39, were badly battered, and the 15th Panzer and Regiment 77 were in disarray. The 2nd Panzer and Panzer Lehr were still a ways removed from the town and in a deteriorating condition. The American defenders lost 3,000 men during the siege, a majority of which came from the 101st Airborne, a unit dubbed out of admiration, "The Battered Bastards of Bastogne." Some members of that defense were so proud of the victory that they claimed Patton's eventual intervention was unnecessary. Meanwhile, McAuliffe's reply to the German ultimatum is still celebrated in the town of Bastogne, where the famous "Nuts" Museum stands.

By the 20th of December, British General Bernard Montgomery had been given command over all American forces to the north, and the American leadership hoped to attack toward Malmedy to stop the German movement, but when that proved impractical, units that had been in St. Vith retreated before the Panzers until they could join other units and arrange a defense elsewhere. On the morning of the 21st, five days after the German offensive in the Ardennes commenced, the 84th Division transferred from their positions in the Siegfried Line to move to the northwest corner of the Bulge around Marche-en-femenne, Belgium. Their mission was to hold the Marche-Hotten Line at all costs and prevent the German Panzer columns from crossing the Meuse River and moving towards Antwerp.

Montgomery

A British Sherman tank positioned near the Meuse River
The Meuse River was a natural Belgian roadblock to military action and thus represented a strategic prize. Allied leadership was unsure of the Germans' intentions, but despite its "vagueness", in the words of Montgomery, the British general made sure that he could defend the major crossings even though British responsibility did not go so far as the bridge at Liège. General Ewart C. Clark reported with alarm that the various Meuse crossings (Liège, Huy, Namur, and Givet) were so lightly-guarded that it approached "absurdity", and the defenders could not possibly deter a German crossing, which later turned out to be the case. However, given Montgomery's provisions for flanking any approaching unit to the river, the American military officers were increasingly confident that the river could be held.

Despite individual heroics across the American line, by the 23rd, the Germans had advanced so far that German General Gerd von Rundstedt sent a request to Hitler asking that the advance be halted due to stretched supply lines and exposed flanks. Naturally, Hitler refused, and on Christmas Eve, while Allied forces did what they could to prevent the bulge from growing larger, the outside world heard that members of the Sicherheitsdienst carried out reprisals against the Belgian resistance by murdering almost all the young men in the village of Bande, from which just one escaped. Furthermore, 800 American troops lost their lives in a torpedoed troop transport, sunk by a German U-boat in the English Channel.

Murdered Belgian civilians

Meanwhile, the fighting continued elsewhere. Journals written by soldiers around the Malmedy area mentioned the use of tank destroyers to attempt to stem the German advance, which gained ground yard by yard. The weather was clear and cold, and according to a journalist attached to the 3rd Armored Division, they saw American bombers: "Fortresses and Liberators, in tight formation like shoals of tiny silver fish coursed over the blue, inverted bowl of the sky." Nevertheless, German planes were still able to attack American positions as well. Jack Jagodinski explained how his unit reached the front on December 24 and was quickly subjected to strafing: "During one of our firing positions, the 88's zeroed in on our gun position. One shell hit the cooks' tent, which was just to the rear of our gun, causing a death and injuries to our cooks. As the shells were zooming in, a fellow crewman by the name of Private Friel suggested we dash out to our howitzer and return the unfired shells into a nearby dugout. Hurriedly, the two of us moved the shells under cover. The 88 shells were dropping around our guns. Fortunately, no further hits on us. Orders came through to pack up and move to another position. During the snow storms, our prime mover with howitzer attached was not winterized for snow travel, and in traveling up or down hills, we were forced to take our winch, pull it to the top of the hill, tie it around a tree, and pull up our vehicles."

Meanwhile, the Germans were advancing elsewhere, which touched off fighting around Heiderscheid. American soldier William McKenzie described the initial German assault on the morning of the 24th:

> "The morning of December 24, about daylight, something woke me. I looked out the second story window and saw men, camouflaged in white, sneaking along the road in back of the house. Since I knew our men had no reason to be infiltrating, I opened fire. The shot woke everyone else in town. ...The shooting went on for

about ten minutes, and we pinned down the Germans, which must have been the scouting element for the tanks, because lo and behold a column of 29 German tanks and half-tanks, loaded with men, came up out of the draw in back of the town and surrounded it. I figured this was the end of me, because we had already heard about the massacre at Malmedy. I figured I might as well keep shooting until the end.

The Germans never got off the half-tracks to attack. Using some bazookas and rifle grenades and the help of a couple of TD's and AT guns, we set 11 tanks and half-tracks on fire and many Germans burned to death in their seats. These were Hitler's elite SS troops. The other 18 tanks and half-tracks returned to the draw and continued on their way. Thus ended the 'Battle of Heiderscheid.'"

On Christmas Day, the 2nd Panzer Division reached the 60 mile mark in the offensive, where it would spearhead the advance of the Fifth Panzer Army. The 2nd Panzer had been delayed by fighting north of Bastogne around Noville on December 19th and 20th, and it also had its advance stalled due to a lack of fuel. It was not until December 22 that they were able to recommence their advance westward toward the Meuse. To oppose their advance, the 84th Division deployed road blocks, in addition to placing guard units at the major Meuse bridges. Additionally, the 84th was reinforced by six battalions of French light infantry.

The leading elements of the 84th Division made contact with the 2nd Panzer Division, and the American units were quickly pushed back by the Panzer advance, losing the town of Hargimont but holding the Namur-Marche road. Behind the 2nd Panzer Division, the Panzer Lehr Division also made its way into the area, where they battled against American units for control of the town of Rochefort, which was located southwest of Hargimont. The American units in the area, made up of the 3rd Battalion of the 335th Infantry, initially held off repeated attacks by the Panzer Lehr Division thanks to their strong defensive position, but they had low levels of ammunition and were also outnumbered by the Germans. The troops were also so closely engaged with German units that when the call came for a retreat out of the area, they were unable to do so. Thankfully, when they finally managed to disengage and retreat, they were not pursued by the Panzer Division, which had just undergone a 10 hour march followed by at least 20 hours of combat.

Meanwhile, the lull in fighting there allowed British units to arrive and reinforce the Americans. British forces included the 3rd Royal Tank Regiment and the 23rd Hussars of the British 29th Armoured Brigade, the 43rd Infantry Division, 53rd Infantry Division, as well as the 51st Infantry Division and 6th Airborne Division. These British units turned the tide of the fighting near the Meuse, and over the next few days the Germans would have to shift from attack to survival.

Furthermore, on the 26th, the British Bomber Command attacked St. Vith with 294 aircraft, including 146 Lancasters, 136 Halifaxes and 12 Mosquitos. Through bombing campaigns and counterattacks, the Allies captured over 13,000 Germans, but the Germans claimed to have captured 30,000 Allied troops and several hundred tanks as well. However, Hitler was informed on the 26th that the Antwerp objective was no longer a possibility, and Rundstedt is said to have described the day as "Stalingrad number two."

A picture of American POWs taken on December 22

By December 27, the German offensive had ground to a halt, and from that point forward, the movement began to be reversed. The German drive to the Meuse River was halted, and much of the armor was stalled, making them easy prey for air attacks. The 2nd Panzer Division had been surrounded for two days, and the artillery and air strikes, combined with problems getting ammunition and fuel, had all created massive problems. Some units had become isolated, and as losses mounted, the 2nd Panzer withdrew back toward Rochefort. By the time they reached Rochefort, the 2nd Panzer Division had lost about half of its transport, a quarter of its personnel, nearly all of its reconnaissance battalion, and almost two-thirds of the 75 tanks and 45 assault guns that they possessed prior to the start of the offensive.

Northeast of the 2nd Panzer Division's location, the 116th Panzer Division was also dealing with problems as they engaged the positions held by the American 84th Infantry Division. When the Führer Begleit Brigade withdrew from its positions to redeploy around Bastogne, the nearby 116th Panzers had to stop their engagement and expand its line to cover the withdrawal. At this point, logistical considerations forced the 116th Panzers to cease any offensive movements and instead focus on defending the territory they had gained over the past few days.

As the German panzer attack stalled, the American units facing the 2nd and 116th Panzer Divisions, especially the 2nd Armored Division, began to exploit the German's stalled momentum and pushed forward. Meanwhile, the U.S. 84th broke the German enclave between Verdenne and Bourdon, and while the Third Army moved forward from Bastogne, the 7th Air Force attacked road intersections, railways and communications. The Sauer River was crossed by the Allies in Luxembourg, and the 5th Infantry captured Berdorf. In the Alsace region of France, near the border with Germany, the U.S. 7th took up defensive positions.

With the writing on the wall, Hitler finally ordered a halt to the advance on the 28th, but he would still not permit retreat. This only managed to leave exhausted German forces vulnerable to air attacks and reinforced and rejuvenated Allied ground forces. However, just as the Germans had to go through during their advance, the advancing Allies had to deal with tough weather conditions, as platoon leader Lou Novotny explained:

> "It was around December 28, 1944, in the vicinity of the town of Humain, Belgium. The morning was bitterly cold and foggy and the snow was about two feet deep with the fir trees covered with snow. Our platoon was the point as we reconnoitered through the dense forest towards our objective, the high ground overlooking a snow and fog covered valley. The enemy lines being about 400 yards to our front. We dug our fox holes securing our position until the orders came to attack the enemy. The fog was heavy, visibility was only about 20 yards. Darkness began to set when the platoon leader met me. He was about to place concertina barbed wire in front of our defense positions. The platoon leader was to make contact with the platoon on our left flank. I was to contact the platoon on the right flank. We separated, with the fog getting dense and darkness falling rapidly. I thought I had walked more than far enough to contact the platoon on the right flank, so we could start setting up the barbed wire in front of our defensive position. Getting near, I started to walk more slowly. I did not want to startle anyone as I came upon them out of the fog, thinking I was the enemy and be shot at. Wondering when I would make contact, I slowed down considerably, walking in the wrong direction. Approaching enemy lines, I heard German voices. Visibility in the thick fog was about six feet. From the sounds I heard, I calculated that I was twenty yards from an enemy machine gun position."

Also beginning on December 28 and continuing into January, the Allies employed jamming techniques from the air over Belgium with three B24 Liberators, which made communications between German tanks difficult. The Germans had experienced little difficulty with ground communications to this point, but they seemed unable to speak between one another after the jamming action, called JACKAL, was deployed.

By New Year's Day 1945, Nazi Germany was in the throes of a desperate fuel shortage, which affected the nation as a whole and the Battle of the Bulge. In an attempt to save the deteriorating situation, two new operations were launched on the ground and in the air, each in support of the other. The new mission of the Luftwaffe, called Operation Bodenplatte, was an attempt to regain air superiority during a lull in the Battle of the Bulge by mounting major raids on air bases in Belgium, France and the Netherlands. This was intended to support a new ground action called Operation Nordwind, which obviously relied on the reestablishment of air dominance. Every viable aircraft was redeployed for the mission, which would encompass attacks on 16 bases.

Ultimately, almost half of the entire Luftwaffe arsenal was lost during the operation, and neither operation approached success. Hampered by the same weather that had stalled Allied planes, once the German pilots were in the air, their flight plans sent them across areas heavily guarded by their own anti-aircraft units. Many were shot down by friendly fire, since communication to the ground sites had been sparse and inaccurate. Making matters worse, the operation was relying on new pilots, many of whom were brought up with poor accuracy skills and little flying experience. A lot of the novices were shot down because they were flying at vulnerable speeds and altitudes. Even those who knew what they were doing had to deal with incomplete maps and instructions out of fear that those maps and instructions would fall into Allied hands, but this meant many of the pilots did not understand exactly what they were supposed to do. Perhaps the most notable aspect of the air campaign was that the launching of at least one V-2 missile was reported during this time.

Meanwhile, the Germans on the ground reacted to American attacks by initiating a series of counterattacks in which Panzer Lehr Division and Führer Begleit Brigade engaged the American 87th Division. These two German divisions forced the 87th Division back a few miles and forced the Americans to commit all of their reserve infantry to stop the German advance, but neither the Panzer Lehr Division nor the Führer Begleit Brigade were able to break through the 87th Division's front line. Although the battle in this sector saw fierce fighting, the Germans were unable to achieve their goals, and the Americans held them off before General Patton would begin a general offensive on January 8th. Bodenplatte and Nordwind would be the final Nazi offensives of the war.

On January 2, Operation Autumn Mist was initiated by the Germans, who had formed a line stretching from Grumelscheid, Luxembourg to Lutebois, Belgium after their retreat from Bastogne, St. Vith and other points toward Antwerp. The operation was conceived as an alternative to the initial advance, and it aimed to have German forces turn north and encircle Allied forces in Belgium and the Netherlands.

Once again, this operation was wishful thinking, because by the time the operation was ready, a lack of resources made success impossible. Instead, the next few days would be marked by British operations against the town of Bure, the farthest point of German penetration, in an effort to literally pierce and reduce the "bulge." Other villages and towns, such as Grupont, Rochfort and Dinant, were included in the clean-up assigned to the British 6th Airborne. Some of the British troops had to endure the season's worst conditions; some soldiers were forced to camp on Chapel Hill at a height of 1,000 feet without good shelter and vulnerable to the snow. Three tanks were lost within the town and another in a flanking maneuver, but many civilians had remained, and Allied tank crews were given food and wine by an order of nuns that had decided to remain.

On January 3, German Panzer divisions attacked Reharmont, Fosse, and the high ground around Abrefontaine, where they halted and waited for supplies after sustaining greater casualties than at any other time in the Battle of the Bulge. However, the American 505th Parachute Division initiated a counteroffensive in extremely cold weather, and with the support of the 628th Tank Destroyer Battalion, they successfully took Goronne, Belgium and captured 100 prisoners.

With the Germans falling back, Patton's Third Army began an offensive along the southern portion of the Ardennes. The 90th Division would be the spearhead for the offensive, and their attack came as a complete surprise to Germany's Rothkirch LIII Corps and the 5th Parachute Division. The attack split the 5th Parachute from the positions of the 104th Panzergrenadier Regiment of the 15th Panzergrenadier Division, which allowed the 90th to take the town of Berle and advance several miles. At the same time, the American 26th Division made its way forward and took the town of Bavigne, as well as the high ground northwest of it, and to the south, the 137th Infantry attacked the town of Villers-la-Bonne-Eau, driving back the Germans with sustained mortar and artillery fire. The Germans were outnumbered and outgunned as they were forced to fall back; for example, the 5th Parachute faced two American divisions with artillery and tank support, and they were outnumbered by roughly 4-1 and outgunned by an even greater margin. Meanwhile, the 14th Parachute attempted to disengage and regroup with the 5th Parachute, but their route took them into the line of fire of the 90th Infantry Division, which forced heavy losses on the Germans. At the end of two days of fighting, the Americans had suffered casualties of 72 killed, 182 wounded and 12 missing, while the Germans suffered casualties of 100 killed, 320 wounded, and 130 captured or missing.

Donald Chumley, a raw recruit whose unit was in Luxembourg and first saw action on January 6, described the fighting the Americans encountered in that sector: "I hesitate to tell of my own experiences those first few days. Many who were not there would think I fabricated the details. Believe me, it happened. Advancing through a wooded area, we were hit with small-arms fire and mortar fire. I was carrying the M-1 and four extra bandoliers of ammunition over my shoulder. All of a sudden two of the bandoliers dropped to the ground in the snow. I picked them up and found the band was cut through either by shrapnel or by a bullet. About the same time a piece of shrapnel hit my wrist and made a very small flesh wound. This would have resulted in a Purple Heart but it was not reported. I was thankful to still have my arm and to still be alive and in one piece. We immediately dug in to hold our positions and to get protection. While digging, I had my gloves up on the mound of dirt from the hole. Suddenly, one glove moved. I picked it up and saw the thumb had been torn away by shrapnel or small-arms fire. I need not say I was glad my hand was not in the glove."

On January 7, General Montgomery gave a press conference at Zonhoven, and some asserted that in his account of the Battle of the Bulge to that point, he was actually paying tribute to the American soldier in support of Eisenhower to protect him from the British Press. However, to most American ears, it sounded like self-promotion, as though he had liberated Bastogne himself and had led the lion's share of fighting in the overall offensive. In one of the most notorious quotes, Montgomery claimed, "As soon as I saw what was happening, I took certain steps myself to ensure that if the Germans got to the Meuse they would certainly not get over the river." As historian Alex Kershaw characterized the speech in *The Longest Winter*, "The picture Montgomery gave of the battle was of massive American blundering: only when he had been brought in to command the armies holding the northern shoulder had catastrophe been averted."

Naturally, the press conference outraged American military officers, or as historian Max Hastings put it in *Armageddon*, Montgomery "opened a petrol can on to Anglo-American tensions, then used the personal pronoun to ignite it...Even after sixty years, it remains astonishing that a highly intelligent man who had reached the summit of command could be capable of such vainglorious folly." Bradley and Patton felt so belittled by the speech that they threatened to resign. For his part, Bradley offered a highly public and unauthorized rebuttal, and Patton complained that far from saving the Allies at the Battle of the Bulge, Montgomery's caution had prevented them from bagging "the whole German Army...War requires the taking of risks and he won't take them."

Eisenhower was eventually forced to sack Montgomery, but he was persuaded to allow him room to apologize. Montgomery outwardly regretted giving the speech, and Eisenhower's memoirs later noted, "I doubt if Montgomery ever came to realize how resentful some American commanders were. They believed that he had belittled them – and they were not slow to voice reciprocal scorn and content." Montgomery later tried to walk back his comments, but he still insisted that the Bulge was an "unnecessary battle" brought about because the Allies hadn't moved forward fast enough after D-Day.

On January 8, Hitler finally agreed to pull back his forces, with 600 tanks and 1,600 aircraft already lost. However, German artillery still posed a problem for the advancing Allies, as graphically explained by soldier Ronald McArthur:

"We set our guns up on the high ground on each side of a trail in the woods. There were several tanks with us in the attack. It was all quiet nearly all afternoon, only a few small arms fired at us during the day. Then, all of a sudden at about four o' clock, we were hit with a terrific artillery barrage. The shells were coming in hitting the trees and exploding. We were exposed to vicious tree burst shrapnel coming down on us.

After some time, I told my assistant gunner to man the gun as I was going out to cut some large branch logs that had been knocked down from the shelling. This was afternoon, January 11, 1945. The logs were to be placed over our foxhole to protect from further shell bursts. I left the gun and went about 100 yards toward the lead tank that had been knocked out during the battle. I got about four logs cut when WHAM, I was shot through the face by a German sniper. He had been left behind as we drove Germans off the hill. He was out in front of the knocked out tank.

I fell flat on my face in about 15" of snow. My only thought was, 'When will he let me have it again?' The bullet must have been a soft-nosed one as X-rays later revealed that I had pieces of shrapnel in my cheek and the roof of my mouth. The bullet had gone through my left cheek just below the jaw bone and exited out my right cheek, taking nearly all of upper teeth and gums as well as most of the lowers. I remember feeling numbness in my mouth. I thought my tongue was gone. I put my hand in the opening and was relieved to find it intact. The opening of the right cheek was up to under my eye and back nearly to my right ear."

Throughout the next week, the Germans began withdrawing behind the Siegfried Line, with fierce fighting at Vianden and Hoscheid in Luxembourg. On the 13th, in the bitter cold, the First Platoon G Company of the 119th Infantry, 30th Infantry Division approached Malmedy. It was this platoon that first found the American soldiers massacred on the 19th by Peiper's Germans, and the platoon noted that the dead soldiers had their hands tied by wire behind their back, clear evidence that they had been executed. A Panzer was found that had been altered to resemble an American tank, and the platoon destroyed it. Other members of the platoon noted that younger reinforcements had already swelled their ranks; as one letter put it, "Old timers like us welcomed the new men that filled our ranks, some of them eighteen years old, and scared to death. We were all scared, and as the saying goes, 'had seen the elephant.'"

On January 14, the Allies recaptured Honvalez and Bovigny in Belgium, and the two towns were so close together that the 329th Infantry B Company was unsure of which town served as the objective, so they measured the area with artillery fire. The plan was to enter the center of the city and work to the outside, and the first stage of that plan received little resistance. The road to Bovigny was cut, and 30 prisoners captured, but an 8 man German patrol dressed as soldiers from the B Company 36th Division approached temporary headquarters and shot the guard. Two tank destroyers and one light tank were lost.

On January 16, the U.S. First and Third Armies met in Houffalize, Luxembourg, and shortly afterward, Patton and Montgomery met there. The 52nd Lowland Division, First Command Brigade crossed into Germany from Holland, attacking at Heinsberg in "Operation Blackcock." Houffalize was a strategic crossroads on the banks of the Meuse River, and was fiercely defended by the Germans. The town was virtually destroyed in the battle, and 200 citizens lost their lives in the fighting.

From January 19-20, the 7th Armored Division prepared for the retaking of St. Vith by moving first to Waimes. The plan was to occupy about 10,000 yards of high ground to the north of the town and as far east as Ambleme. The attack began on the 20th, and Diedenburg was occupied by mid-morning, but the next phase was postponed for 90 minutes because reconnaissance patrols had difficulty returning. Once under way, troops encountered mines, and the terrain was impassable. Companies B and C met heavy small-arms fire, and the battle continued into the night with heavy artillery bombardment until about midnight. 115 prisoners were captured from the 118th Volksgrenadier and 3rd Parachute Division.

The fighting was so tough that one medical officer wrote home on the 20th, "I don't want to give you a word picture of the circumstances under which I am writing – but they aren't good. Most of the fellows have just quit writing until circumstances and the situation changes." Nevertheless, the Allies ultimately recaptured St. Vith on the 23rd, more than a month after St. Vith became one of the first strategic spots to fall at the beginning of the German advance. As the German commander von Manteuffel later said of the fighting for St. Vith, "It is the war of the small men, the outpost commanders, the section commanders, the company commanders; those were the decisive people here, who were responsible for success or failure, victory or defeat. We depended upon their courage; they could not afford to get confused, and had to act according to their own decisions, until the higher command was again in a position to take over. I believe I can say, and I have the right to make this judgment, that the Germans did this admirably well, at the same time however, I am also convinced this was the case with the American forces, who after all succeeded in upsetting the entire time schedule, not only of the attacking unit in St. Vith, but also of the 5th and 6th Panzer Armies. That is a fact which cannot be denied."

Over the next week, the last of the German forces in Luxembourg surrendered on January 21, and American forces advanced from St. Vith. The French First took bridges over the River Ill in Alsace, the U.S. Third Army reached the Clerf River, and the British 2nd entered Heinsberg, west of the Ruhr River. On the 27th, Patton's Third Army took Oberhausen, and with that, Germany's gains in the Battle of the Bulge had been all but eliminated. By the time the campaign was over, there were at least 82,000 German casualties and 77,000 American casualties. Later reports claimed over 100,000 German casualties and over 100,000 American casualties as well. As Churchill summed it up, "The Germans have made a violent and costly sortie which has been repulsed with heavy slaughter, and have expended in the endeavour forces which they cannot replace, against an enemy who has already more than replaced every loss he has slaughtered." After the war, one German officer dryly told Hitler, "Berlin will be the most practical as our headquarters. We'll soon be able to take the streetcar from the eastern to the western front." Hitler allegedly laughed at the dark humor.

Stephen E. Ambrose, in his article, "Eisenhower and the Intelligence community in World War II," asked why, considering the endless thread of British intelligence victories over the Germans, the Allies didn't win the war sooner. He goes on to answer that they actually did. When Eisenhower took over command in North Africa in 1942, his command was many times larger than anything he had ever conceived of, and his knowledge of intelligence was almost nil. By the end of 1944, however, quite the opposite was true. Eisenhower had become an intelligence sophisticate, and he was appalled at the primitive nature of American information-gathering. The British, on the other hand, were brilliant at it - "...the entire British intelligence establishment was at Eisenhower's disposal, and it made a crucial contribution." Up to the Battle of the Bulge, including the Normandy invasion and the liberation of Paris, Eisenhower could depend on British intelligence.

However, as Allied troops moved away from the beaches and major cities toward Belgium and Luxembourg, and as Hitler became increasingly irrational, this great asset was diminished. Ambrose explained, "Eisenhower had almost as good a grasp on the German order of battle as did Hitler...Hitler lived in a fantasy world, creating divisions at the snap of a finger, restoring destroyed units with a wave of his hand. Ironically, that was a chief reason why Hitler was able to surprise Eisenhower at the Battle of the Bulge."

Another nagging question asked by some scholars goes back to Montgomery's claim that the Battle of the Bulge was an unnecessary battle, and it is still debated whether the Allies could have capitalized on their earlier successes in the summer of 1944 to end the war by the Fall, which would have precluded the necessity of such a large-scale battle in difficult terrain and winter weather. Was the Battle of Bulge a result of earlier failings, lack of coordination and Allied disunity? There is still no consensus answer, and it would be impossible to determine what alternate casualties might have occurred in a direct invasion thrust at the heart of Germany, or whether such a decision would have even been successful at all without German losses at the Battle of the Bulge. Given what happened at the end of 1944, what is clear is that the Battle of the Bulge was essential for the ultimate defeat of Germany in Western Europe.

The End of the War in Europe

It would be impossible to identify any one event in a vacuum, but many historians consider the Battle of Kursk in the summer of 1943 as the beginning of the end for Berlin. Sometimes considered the greatest tank battle ever fought, at Kursk, Hitler's planned offensive failed, and two large Soviet counterattacks drove the German forces into retreat. As in so many other battles, Soviet soldiers were ordered into frontal assaults on the German armies, causing them to take extremely high casualties, especially in comparison to the German losses, but even as early as 1943, Germany could not afford the losses they were taking. Thus, Russian general Georgy Zhukov saw Kursk as an opportunity to "wear the enemy out in defensive action, destroy his tanks, and then ... by going over to an all-out offensive...finish off the enemy's main grouping."[80]

---

[80] Henrik Bering, "Zhukov: The Soviet General," Policy Review 176 (2012), https://www.questia.com/read/1G1-312292093.

Zhukov

Tony Le Tissier, author of several books about the Battle for Berlin and the end of the war, writes that after the decisive battle of Kursk, the Soviets encouraged one another with the call "On to the Reichstag!" Stalin, with what he felt was almost certain knowledge of the outcome of the war at this point, worked to secure his position as the unquestioned ruler of the Soviet Union in the aftermath of the war, and in order to ensure a lack of challenge by one of his two great generals, Georgy Zhukov and Ivan Konev, he allowed them to compete for the prize of reaching Berlin first.

Konev

The Soviet armies would pay dearly for the advances they made on Germany after Hitler's invasion of Russia ended in failure: "According to the Soviet Union's estimates, the Red Army's losses in the war totaled more than 11 million troops, over 100,000 aircraft, more than 300,000 artillery pieces, and 100,000 tanks and self-propelled guns".[81] Such losses, coupled with the extreme suffering that the Soviet soldiers had experienced in the years before the attack on Berlin, ensured that the thirst for revenge would be high upon arrival. Moreover, as the Soviet armies moved through Eastern Europe, they were the first to discover concentration camps and death camps, furthering their anger. The comparison of Germany's standard of living with their own was another cause of outrage, all of which encouraged the men to show no mercy: "We will take revenge…revenge for all our sufferings…It's obvious from everything we see that Hitler robbed the whole of Europe to please his Fritzies…Their shops are piled high with goods from all the shops and factories of Europe. We hate Germany and the Germans deeply. You can often see civilians lying dead in the street…But the Germans deserve the atrocities that they

---

[81] Evans, Richard. *The Third Reich at War*. 707.

unleashed."[82]

Despite their heavy losses, after the Soviet victory at Kursk, the long drive to Berlin could begin in earnest. Germany's losses were mounting, and the Soviet armies were on the rebound, with an advantage of almost 5:1 over Germany in manpower, as well as superiority in tanks, aircraft, and artillery. Even with these major advantages, however, the race to Berlin would inflict a heavier toll on Soviet armies than they had yet seen, and with Berlin itself heavily defended by 30 mile deep defenses in multiple directions, the Soviets would eventually suffer over 100,000 lives just taking the city, along with 350,000 other casualties.

In the months leading up to the final battle, there was a strange division amongst the German people regarding their fate. While Hitler called for the remainder of Berlin's population to take up arms and the most loyal responded to the call, many in Berlin were resigned to a seemingly inevitable defeat. In his study of Berlin in 1945, historian Antony Beevor described a city in which a grim humor had come to replace once hopeful and proud demeanors. Though humor was certainly an attempt at levity in the face of serious concerns, Germans nevertheless joked about the soon-to-arrive Russians, referring to LSR (Luftschutzraum air-raid shelters) as actually standing for "Lernt scnhell Russich" ("Learn Russian quickly").[83] In the air raid shelters, Berliners regularly found themselves in crowded conditions, waiting out the bombing raids that were taking place on a regular basis in 1944. In a city of 3 million, Beevor explained how a tightly-packed and unsanitary atmosphere became an expected part of life in Berlin. By the year's end, much of the city's beauty and a great deal of its functionality had been destroyed.

[82] Ibid., 708.
[83] Beevor, Antony. *The Fall of Berlin 1945*. New York: Penguin Books, 2003.

A picture of damage done to Berlin during a 1944 air raid

In the wake of the Battle of the Bulge, "The Basic Order for the Preparations to Defend the Capital" was issued on March 9, 1945, not because Hitler expected an attack on Berlin imminently but merely to inspire the people's defenses in case of an emergency and to make the point to potential attackers that "Berlin would be defended block by block".[84] It read in part:

"To defend capital to the last person and to the last cartridge:
Proceeding from quantity of forces, available for direct defense of capital, struggle for Berlin will be conducted not in open battle, and basically to have character of street fights.

This struggle of an army should conduct with fanaticism, imagination, with application of all means of introduction of the opponent in error, military cunning, with insidiousness, with use in advance prepared, and also caused by difficulties of the moment of every possible improvised means on the earth, in air and under the earth...

...the precondition for successful defense of Berlin is deduction by all means each quarter, each house, a floor, each fence, each funnel from a shell!

In struggle in back of the opponent the problem consists in using all means of military cunning and insidiousness and to do to the opponent the maximum harm and a loss..."[85]

---

[84] Simons, Gerald. Victory in Europe. Alexandria, Va.: Time-Life Books, 1982.34.
[85] Ibid. 35.

Joseph Goebbels awarding a medal to Hitler Youth on March 9, 1945
By April 1945, the end of the European war was near, but as historian Richard Bessel explains in his book on the final year of the war that "the regime was still able to function, albeit with increasing difficulty".[86] This difficulty is most credited to the Allied bombing raids, which were destroying large parts of the city. For example, the morning bombing raid on April 9 followed 313 previous ones that had destroyed major parts of the city, and these raids were carried out with extreme regularity at the end of the war, with the United States carrying out bombing during the daylight and the British bombing at night. However, despite the destruction and death that these raids resulted in, Cornelius Ryan noted that the city still attempted to maintain some semblance of normalcy: "Postman delivered the mail; newspapers still came out daily; telephone and telegraphic services continued; Garbage was collected. Some cinemas, theaters, and even a part of the wrecked zoo were open. The Berlin Philharmonic was finishing its season. Department stores ran special sales. Food and bakery shops opened each morning..."
At this point, Hitler had already survived an assassination attempt and was now living underground in a bunker beneath the Reich Chancellery. Meanwhile, his closest advisers were making personal decisions regarding whether to remain loyal to the Fuhrer until the bitter end, seek ways to save themselves personally, or determine a way that would let Germany end the war with some measure of dignity through dialogue with the enemy.

[86] Bessel, Richard. *Germany 1945: From War to Peace.* New York: Harper, 2009, 93.

Picture of the rear entrance to Hitler's bunker

Though Hitler believed initially that the city of Berlin would never need defending, it was clear that the people would benefit from safety measures both emotionally and, if necessary, physically. For the safety of the city, Hitler and his Nazi war leaders ordered the construction of barricades and water-filled ditches to place obstacles in front of oncoming forces and tanks, and as things grew increasingly desperate, Hitler also decided to introduce some combat roles for women, children, and the elderly. Not only would they "undoubtedly fight fanatically", but it increased the chance of German fighting men staying in the fight if the person behind him was a woman or child.[87] For these, the *Panzerfaust*, a shoulder-carried grenade launcher, was the most common weapon, and though more advanced versions were in existence by 1945, most of the *Panzerfaust* in use by elderly, female, or even very young Berliners were single use weapons with a range of only 100 feet.

---

[87] Ibid.42.

Bundesarchiv, Bild 183-H28160
Foto: o.Ang. | Februar 1945

German soldiers holding the grenade launchers

Of course, Hitler was hardly the only leader planning out end-of-war scenarios in April 1945. With the race toward Berlin in full throttle, General Dwight D. Eisenhower's Allied armies were within 200 miles of the city, but his biggest battles now took place among his allies, as he now had to deal diplomatically with Churchill, Montgomery, and French war hero Charles de Gaulle. After crossing the Rhine River, General George Patton advised Eisenhower to make haste for Berlin, and British General Bernard Montgomery was confident that they could reach Berlin before the Soviets, but Eisenhower did not think it "worth the trouble".[88] Eisenhower's forces went on to capture 400,000 prisoners on April 1st in the Ruhr, but despite his success there, not everyone agreed with Eisenhower's decision, especially Winston Churchill. In Churchill's thinking, the decision to leave the taking of Berlin to the Soviets would leave lasting trouble on the European continent, a more pressing concern for the British than for Americans an ocean away. In tension-filled exchanges, Churchill made his position clear, but President Roosevelt was ill and had no stomach for angering the Soviets. For his part, Eisenhower saw his role as a purely military one, so he refused to "trespass" into political arenas that he was under the impression had been worked out at the Tehran and Yalta conferences. In fact, Roosevelt had promised Stalin that he could enter Berlin despite the obvious threat to postwar security for the European countries, and Eisenhower wanted to avoid being a pawn in the political maneuverings of the three leaders. As a result, his major concern was to avoid as many casualties as possible in the coming weeks of the war, and if the Russians were prepared to attack and had the better opportunity to do so, it would save lives of American soldiers who would otherwise have to fight their way in from the west.[89] Eisenhower did not share his peers' (Patton and Montgomery, specifically) concerns of "arriving victorious in Berlin on top of a tank."[90]

Eventually, Eisenhower made the fateful choice not to move the American forces toward Berlin but to "hold a firm front on the Elbe" instead. In making this decision, Eisenhower left Berlin's capture to the Soviet army, and his decisions have been the cause of much debate ever since. The Allied armies in the west would thus concentrate on encircling the Ruhr Valley, the center of Germany's industry, instead of competing with the Soviets for control of the city.

---

[88] World War II: A 50th Anniversary History. New York: Holt, 1989.288.
[89] Humes, James C. Eisenhower and Churchill: The Partnership that Saved the World. Crown Publishing Group, 2010.
[90] Ibid.

Eisenhower

There were many concerns about the Soviet Union reaching Berlin, and all of them were understandable. Most people, especially the Germans, expected far worse treatment from Soviet conquerors than the British or Americans, especially since Hitler's attack on the Soviet Union (Operation Barbarossa) had been so unexpected that it stunned even Stalin into temporary inaction. Hitler and the Germans were going to pay dearly for the treatment that the Russians, both civilians and soldiers, had received at the hands of the German armies. Furthermore, the fear of a Soviet strategic advantage in Europe, anchored by a Soviet-controlled Berlin, loomed over both eastern and western European nations. Lastly, even if Stalin kept his word about the division of post-war Germany, allowing him unchallenged control was viewed as dangerous to a world with a weakened Britain and a United States looking to return to the isolation the Atlantic Ocean had previously provided.

Churchill and Roosevelt had always disagreed on Stalin's real motivations and limits, and Churchill needed to maintain strong ties to the Americans as the war came to a close. During one of the meetings between the three, Stalin suggested that once the German armies had been defeated, 50,000 soldiers should be executed by the conquering armies in vengeance for the losses Germany had inflicted on Europe. That suggestion horrified Churchill, who stormed out of the meeting, but Stalin followed to assure Churchill that all that had been said was in jest. Churchill had very little choice but to take Stalin at his word, but he was always far more cautious than Roosevelt when it came to trust in Stalin's judgment or word. In any case, he wrote a letter to Roosevelt after his exchange with Eisenhower in March in which he said, "I wish to place on record the complete confidence felt by His Majesty's government in General Eisenhower and our pleasure that our armies are serving under his command and our admiration of his great and shining quality, character, and personality".[91] In a note he added to Eisenhower's copy of the letter, he expressed it would grieve him to know he had pained Eisenhower with his comments but still suggested that "we should shake hands with the Russians as far east as possible."[92]

By April 17, in a meeting between Eisenhower and Churchill, the fact that the Soviet army was positioned just over 30 miles from Berlin with overpowering men, artillery, and tanks convinced Churchill that the decision to allow the Soviets to lead the attack on the city was necessary. It is important to keep in perspective that Roosevelt's death just 5 days earlier likely played a role in Churchill's willingness to give in. Churchill had spent several years negotiating with both Stalin and Roosevelt, and he may have felt that time would not allow for further discussion on the matter. Eisenhower also was under pressure to end the war in Europe as soon as possible so that American forces and attention could be directed toward the fight against Japan. The campaign in Okinawa had just started and would last until June, and the extent of the carnage there made clear that Japan had no intention of surrendering anytime soon.

Bundesarchiv, Bild 146-1995-081-13A
Foto: o.Ang. | März 1945

In the weeks that led to the fall of Berlin, many in the city seemed resigned to the fact that the war was over, and what had once been a gleaming vision of Germany's greatness provoked

---

[91] Ibid.
[92] Ibid.

either bitterness or cynicism from the people. Historians often refer to the "gallows humor" that was heard around the city, often in response to the latest "encouraging" news from the party propaganda machine, but while some of these Germans greatly feared the Soviet arrival, others believed wholeheartedly that the Americans would arrive first. One historian recounts German women preparing their homes to receive American soldiers and speculating over which city might suit the Americans' taste the best. Even upon the news of Hitler's death, observers were surprised that many Berliners betrayed no remorse or sadness, only a resignation to the fate that now awaited them.

On the other end of the spectrum lay the Nazi faithful. These men and women, and even some children, took very seriously Hitler's call to remain loyal to the Reich to the very last drop of blood. They would be the holdouts who continued to defend their city even as it stood battered and broken while the Soviet banner was waving from the top of the Reichstag. These were the final defenders of the German capital, and they were able to inflict heavy damages on a Soviet army that was out for revenge and outnumbered them heavily while moving into the city with tanks and artillery.

Berliners were not only outnumbered but nearly out of supplies by the time the Russians surrounded the city on April 21. Hitler, in his bunker beneath the city, was alternately hopeful and depressed. Albert Kesselring, Hitler's field marshal who had seen him last on April 12, was later convinced that Hitler's optimism at the time was real: "Looking back, I am inclined to think that he was literally obsessed with the idea of some miraculous salvation, that he clung to it like a drowning man to a straw."[93] He seemed to truly believe that Berlin could be saved by some last minute changes, whether it was based on his confidence in a favored SS general, a last-minute break of relations between the British and the Soviets, or the extraordinary will of the German faithful.

In this last hope, Hitler might have had some actual reason for confidence, considering the feats accomplished by the people of Berlin in the days before the surrender. Berliners defended the city to the bitter end, despite the bleak outlook, and while suicide or physical escape from the city was the choice for many, there remained 75,000 troops and 1,750,000 residents ready to fight for the city or at least to attempt a stand off until the Americans arrived. With that in the back of Germans' minds, the thought of surrender became less horrific.

In reality, while the residents of Berlin had a military defense, the commander of the defenders, Helmuth Reymann, only had 41,253 men at his disposal, and fewer than 15,000 of them were trained soldiers; the rest consisted of 1,713 policemen, 1,252 Hitler Youth and Labor Service boys and men, and 24,000 Volksstrum troops that were mostly old men and/or those who had previously been deemed too sick or weak to fight. Arming them was also an issue, as only 42,095 rifles, 773 sub-machine guns, 1,953 light machine guns, 263 heavy machine guns, and a small stock of mortars, field guns, and Panzerfaust were available for these defenders."[94]

Considering these numbers, the resistance put up by the Germans was quite astounding. Tales of the difficulty of taking Berlin, even after the Soviets had gained access to the city, were told not only by Germans but by their enemy. The Russians themselves put the number of shells they fired on the city at 1.8million, more than one for every resident, yet the taking of official buildings was a painstaking process that required Soviet soldiers to fight from room to room and floor to floor.[95] At least part of this fierce commitment was based on the threats their leaders

[93] Kershaw, 919.
[94] Chen, Peter C. Battle of Berlin 16 Apr 1945 - 2 May 1945. World War II Database. n.d.
[95] Simons, 112.

were receiving from the party to fight to the last breath or be shot, but the power of the Nazi propaganda and tales of Soviet soldiers also surely kept them in the fight.

Some historians have remarked that Hitler was able to glorify death by painting it as the ultimate sacrifice to the Reich, a show of loyalty that could never be questioned since it was the final word, and the German concept of *Volk* had been one of the first to capture the hearts and imaginations of German Nazis throughout Europe. The idea of a commonality existing amongst all Germans as a special race of people with superior values and abilities was powerful, and the *Volk* were seen as the secret weapon of Germany. They eschewed weakness and personal privilege, concerned only with the nation's glory and the restoration of Germany to its rightful position as one of the world's great powers. In the early days of the Nazis' rise, *Volkish* newspapers and other cultural markers helped to spread the ideals of "Germanness".

When discussing the role of ordinary Germans in the war, it should be remembered that some Germans did not know the extent of what had taken place in the concentration camps outside of their city. While they had to be aware of the arrests and deportations of the thousands of Jews from Berlin even as late as 1944, some assumed (as the Jews themselves often did) that they were being transported to Poland or other places in Eastern Europe. When the British 4th armored division reached a death camp at Ohrdurf, the soldiers forced the mayor and his wife of the nearest town to walk through the camp, after which they returned home and hanged themselves.[96]

It is true that any discussion of the extent of knowledge the average Berliner had of the scope of Nazi atrocities can sound like a defense of apathy, but it's necessary to know what the *Volksstrum* believed they were fighting for to have a correct understanding of their loyalty to the bitter end. Germans had been told that in order for Germany to rise again, the conspirators that had held them back must be eliminated. Painting Germany as a glorious underdog whose greatness was about to be displayed for the whole world to see had the German public literally at Hitler's beck and call. Much has been written about the amount of knowledge the average German had, whether or not they were regular informants of the Gestapo, and their willingness to submit to Nazi rhetoric and even bring Hitler to power through political means. Historians still debate the nature of the average German and what he believed he was fighting for by supporting the Nazi party and Hitler. For the Fuhrer himself, there was no question; in his last will and testament, he made it clear that he had only Germany's interests at heart and that all blame should go to the "international statesman who were either of Jewish descent or worked for Jewish interests". He predicted, "Centuries will pass away, but out of the ruins of our towns and cultural monuments the hatred will ever renew itself against those ultimately responsible whom we have to thank for everything: international Jewry...After six years of war, which in spite of all setbacks will go down one day in history as the most glorious and valiant demonstration of a nation's life purpose, I cannot forsake the city which is the capital of this Reich. As the forces are too small to make any further stand against the enemy attack at this place, and our resistance is gradually being weakened by men who are as deluded as they are lacking in initiative, I should like, by remaining in this town, to share my fate with those, the millions of others, who have also taken upon themselves to do so. Moreover I do not wish to fall into the hands of an enemy who requires a new spectacle organized by the Jews for the amusement of their hysterical masses. I have decided therefore to remain in Berlin and there of my own free will to choose death at the moment when I believe the position of the Fuehrer and Chancellor itself can no longer be held. I die with a happy heart, aware of the immeasurable deeds and achievements of our soldiers at the

---

[96] World War II: A 50th Anniversary History. 290.

front, our women at home, the achievements of our farmers and workers and the work, unique in history, of our youth who bear my name."[97]
Who were the members of the *Volksstrum*? They were an army made up of men ages 16-60 who were not already serving in the German military. The organization of the *Volksstrum* in 1944 was meant to aid the dwindling military might of the Reich, but historians speculate it also kept civilian men watching the destruction of their cities from entertaining thoughts of uprisings.[98]
There were those who resisted the fight, if not always for ideological reasons. The Volksstrum, due to limits in military weapons, were divided into two groups, those who had arms and those who would serve as replacements, picking up the arms of a fallen comrade. One *Volksstrum* leader, ordered to take his men into combat without uniforms, with limited weapons, and with no ammunition recalled, "I told the party leader I could not accept the responsibility of leading men into battle without uniforms…Although my men were quite ready to help their country, they refused to go into battle without uniforms and without training. What could a Volksstrum man do with a rifle without ammunition? The men went home. That was the only thing we could do."[99]
In *Penalty Strike*, the memoir of Soviet soldier Alexander V. Pyl'cyn, he remembered being invited to see the Reichstag after it had fallen into Soviet hands. Upon entering Berlin, he saw white surrender flags waving in blown out windows, women, children, and the elderly hiding in their houses (which, he remarked, was "like in all countries"), and men and boys separated from their defeated Volksstrum and Hitler Youth units wandering without purpose. "They had been hoping", he said, "to defend their Reich to the edge of destruction. Many of them sacrificed their lives, just for the sake of the crazy ideas of their insane Fuhrer, while some tried to hide in basements, change their uniforms for civilian clothes, and hide in the mass of civilians."[100]
The Werewolf organization could best be described as a group of German vigilantes dedicated to guerilla actions in the final months of Nazi Germany. They sometime worked in conjunction with the Volksstrum, but some authors discount the group's effectiveness, seeing the Werewolf more as wishful thinking and rebellion than as a serious threat to foreign occupiers within Germany. The words of at least one intelligence report seem to indicate that the allies took the Werewolf threat seriously: "The Werewolf organization is not a myth…In every important city, the Werewolf organization is directed by an officer of the SD…Membership…is made up of persons of all ages and of both sexes, with a high proportion of fewer than twenty years of age…The present cadres of the Werewolves are estimated to number more than 2,000."
The last time Hitler was ever seen in public was on his 56th birthday, April 20th 1945. That morning, he met with some members of the Hitler Youth who had gathered in the gardens of the Reich Chancellery to wish the Fuhrer a happy birthday. Hitler seemed to go through the motions of greeting these young boys, aged 14 or 15, patting a few on the head or cheek before heading back to his bunker for more listless "celebrations" by loyal staff and advisors. Dorothea von Schwanenfluegel, a 29 year old woman in Berlin at the time, recalled, "Friday, April 20, was Hitler's fifty-sixth birthday, and the Soviets sent him a birthday present in the form of an artillery barrage right into the heart of the city, while the Western Allies joined in with a massive air raid.

[97] The Private And Political Testaments Of Hitler, April 29, 1945 [United States, Office of United States Chief of Counsel for Prosecution of Axis Criminality, Nazi Conspiracy and Aggression, 8 vols. and 2 suppl. vols. (Government Printing Office, Washington, 1946-1948), VI, 259-263, Doc. No. 3569-PS.]
[98] Carruthers, Bob, and Willhelm Willemar. Götterdämmerung: The Last Days of the Wehrmacht in the East. Barnsley: Pen & Sword Military, 2012.
[99] Le Tissier, Race for the Reichstag. 22.
[100] Alexander V. Pyl'cyn. Penalty Strike: The Memoirs of a Red Army Penal Company Commander, 1943-45. 168.

The radio announced that Hitler had come out of his safe bomb-proof bunker to talk with the fourteen to sixteen year old boys who had 'volunteered' for the 'honor' to be accepted into the SS and to die for their Fuhrer in the defense of Berlin. What a cruel lie! These boys did not volunteer, but had no choice, because boys who were found hiding were hanged as traitors by the SS as a warning that, 'he who was not brave enough to fight had to die.' When trees were not available, people were strung up on lamp posts. They were hanging everywhere, military and civilian, men and women, ordinary citizens who had been executed by a small group of fanatics. It appeared that the Nazis did not want the people to survive because a lost war, by their rationale, was obviously the fault of all of us. We had not sacrificed enough and therefore, we had forfeited our right to live, as only the government was without guilt. The Volkssturm was called up again, and this time, all boys age thirteen and up, had to report as our army was reduced now to little more than children filling the ranks as soldiers."

As her account suggests, in the last days of the war in Europe, the Hitler Youth organization was more than just a publicity front, because these young boys would actually be called upon to protect a city whose able-bodied men had long since been called to give their lives for the Reich. With the other males still in the city being under the age of 8 or over the age of 80, the Hitler Youth were not simply living in the city but were essentially charged with its defense.

Gerard Rempel calls the plan to charge these young men with their country's defense "a children's crusade to shore up crumbling defenses and offer thousands of teenagers as a final sacrifice to the god of war".[101] Though their purpose was initially to become indoctrinated with Nazi rhetoric and be the face of Germany's next generational leaders, Nazi leadership showed almost no inhibition about sending these boys into battle when times became desperate. During the last months of the war, many Hitler Youth boys were put into 10-15 member tank-destroying units, armed only with three machine guns and a bazooka. Artur Axmann, a 32 year old youth leader, led the Hitler Youth military efforts in Berlin, and in a Hitler Youth meeting in March 1945, Axmann had rallied young boys with this call: "There is only victory or annihilation. Know no bounds in your love of your people; equally know no bounds in your hatred of the enemy. It is your duty to watch when others tire, to stand when others weaken. Your greatest honour is your unshakeable fidelity to Adolf Hitler."[102] Axmann received a harsh response from General Karl Weidling when he announced his intentions to use the boys to defend the rear of Weidling's Panzer Corps: "You cannot sacrifice these children for a cause that is already lost. . . . I will not use them and I demand that the order . . . be rescinded".[103]

---

[101] Gerhard Rempel, Hitler's Children: The Hitler Youth and the SS (Chapel Hill, NC: University of North Carolina Press, 1989).
[102] Le Tissier, Race of the Reichstag, 23.
[103] Ibid, 239.

Axmann
However, it was too late for the boys that Axmann led. They were already being killed and crushed by Russian tanks, fleeing if possible and waking up in a bunker to find that most of their friends were dead. During the last few months of the war, the number of available Hitler Youth meant that boys as young as 12 were actually being led into military situations and were expected to defend their city against the vengeful Soviet troops.

Picture of a German teenager receiving a medal

As if that wasn't enough, young girls under the auspices of the BDM (the League of German Girls or the Band of German maidens) were expected to play their part to save Germany. They were asked to set up hospitals, care for the wounded and refugees, and keep order in public transportation stations, among other tasks. Melita Maschmann carried out Axmann's orders with the girls in her care, and she had this to say about the experience: "I shall never forget my encounters with the youngest of them, still half children, who did what they believed to be their duty until they were literally ready to drop. They had been fed on legends of heroism for as long as they could remember. For them the call to the 'ultimate sacrifice' was no empty phrase. It went straight to their hearts and they felt that now their hour had come, the moment when they really counted and were no longer dismissed because they were still too young...If there is anything that forces us to examine the principles on which we operated as leaders in the Hitler Youth and in the Labor Service, it is this senseless sacrifice of young people."[104]

---

[104] Rempel, 241.

The top leader of Hitler Youth was Baldur Benedikt von Schirach. He claimed that he had no desire for the boys to fight, and that he used his power to prevent it, but he was demoted for criticizing the plans to keep the boys out of harm's way. In addition to challenges to this claim, there remains the fact that Von Shirach's purpose was to indoctrinate the youngest of Germans to remain loyal to Hitler and his cause. He later admitted that while he had opposed the idea of the youth taking part in the fight, his educational programs had caused the youth to desire to do exactly that.[105]

[105] Ibid.

Von Schirach (right) with Hitler and Hermann Göring
Of the 5,000 Hitler Youth defending Berlin, only 500 survived, but Axmann abandoned his boys and hid in the mountains with another Hitler Youth group until after the war. The fervor of the boys and girls was a result of a hard-line education that included lessons, songs, and poems, as well as a system of rewards and recognitions. The official song of the Hitler Youth can be loosely translated "The Rotten Bones are Trembling" and shows the type of indoctrination that the youth heard in the organization:

"The rotten bones are trembling,
Of the World before the Great War
We have smashed this terror,
For us a great victory.
And if there lies in ruins from battle
The whole world,
therefore the devil may care;
We build it up again
And the elders may chide,
So just let them scream and cry,
And if the World decides to fight us,
We will still be the victors.
They don't want to understand this song,
They think of slavery and war.
Meanwhile our acres ripen,
Flag of freedom, fly!
We will continue to march,

Even if everything shatters;
Because today Germany hears us,
And tomorrow the whole World."

Of course, for all the indoctrination and the pomp and circumstance, calling upon mere children to stand as a line of defense was beyond desperate. One Berlin resident described seeing one of the youngsters instructed to defend Berlin: "In honor of Hitler's birthday, we received an eight-day ration allowance, plus one tiny can of vegetables, a few ounces of sugar and a half-ounce of real coffee. No one could afford to miss rations of this type and we stood in long lines at the grocery store patiently waiting to receive them. While standing there, we noticed a sad looking young boy across the street standing behind some bushes in a self-dug shallow trench. I went over to him and found a mere child in a uniform many sizes too large for him, with an anti-tank grenade lying beside him. Tears were running down his face, and he was obviously very frightened of everyone. I very softly asked him what he was doing there. He lost his distrust and told me that he had been ordered to lie in wait here, and when a Soviet tank approached he was to run under it and explode the grenade. I asked how that would work, but he didn't know. In fact, this frail child didn't even look capable of carrying such a grenade. It looked to me like a useless suicide assignment because the Soviets would shoot him on sight before he ever reached the tank. By now, he was sobbing and muttering something, probably calling for his mother in despair, and there was nothing that I could do to help him. He was a picture of distress, created by our inhuman government. If I encouraged him to run away, he would be caught and hung by the SS, and if I gave him refuge in my home, everyone in the house would be shot by the SS. So, all we could do was to give him something to eat and drink from our rations. When I looked for him early next morning he was gone and so was the grenade. Hopefully, his mother found him and would keep him in hiding during these last days of a lost war.'"

Soviet rocket launchers aimed at Berlin in April 1945

"The Soviets battled the German soldiers and drafted civilians street by street until we could hear explosions and rifle fire right in our immediate vicinity. As the noise got closer, we could even hear the horrible guttural screaming of the Soviet soldiers which sounded to us like enraged animals. Shots shattered our windows and shells exploded in our garden, and suddenly the Soviets were on our street. Shaken by the battle around us and numb with fear, we watched from behind the small cellar windows facing the street as the tanks and an endless convoy of troops rolled by...It was a terrifying sight as they sat high upon their tanks with their rifles cocked, aiming at houses as they passed. The screaming, gun-wielding women were the worst. Half of the troops had only rags and tatters around their feet while others wore SS boots that had been looted from a conquered SS barrack in Lichterfelde. Several fleeing people had told us earlier that they kept watching different boots pass by their cellar windows." – A Berlin resident's description of the advancing Soviets

Encouraged by the choices of the Americans, and perhaps fearing they might change strategy, Stalin summoned his commanders to make plans to arrive in Berlin first, and no later than April 16th at that.[106] Conditions in Berlin had reached the point of crisis well before the Soviets arrived. As one German officer wrote, "Traffic had ceased almost entirely. On the streets there was scarcely a person left to be seen. In the main arterial roads barricades had been built out of rails which had been ripped up and tramcars had been pushed over. The streets were partially dug up to erect positions for defensive weapons. The city of millions...prepared itself for a defense that was taken very seriously by large sections of the population, especially by the adolescent youth, while every soldier who assessed the situation soberly if only be convinced of its senselessness."[107]

In the fighting that led to the Battle for Berlin, even with the German armies greatly outnumbered and fighting with fewer resources and reserves, the Soviets had the same casualty ratios against the Germans that they had experienced throughout the war: 4 Soviet soldiers lost for every 1 German. However, much like Grant, Sherman, and Lincoln agreed on strategy during the American Civil War, Stalin and Zhukov both accepted that the objective of the Russian armies was to win, not protect the lives of the troops. As Zhukov once said, "If we come to a minefield, our infantry attacks exactly as it were not there." The tendency to move men forward in almost any situation meant that these men would suffer a great number of deaths, and many of them seemed senseless before their arrival in Berlin, but the Soviet Union, desperate for recruits to push back the German armies that had invaded their lands, used prisoners, criminals, and all other kinds of elements in their infantry divisions.

Hitler, refusing to admit defeat and (as always) ready to put the responsibility for the situation on the German people and his own military officers, issued his final "Order of the Day":

"Soldiers of the German-Eastern Front! For the last time the Jewish-Bolshevik arch-enemy has lined up his masses for attack. He is trying to smash Germany and exterminate our people. You soldiers from the east yourselves already know to a great extent what fate threatens German women, girls, and children most of all. While the old men and children will be murdered, the women and girls will be reduced to becoming barracks whores. The rest will march to Siberia. We have been planning for this threat and since January of this year, everything has been done to build up a strong front. A powerful artillery is greeting the enemy. The losses of our infantry have been replenished by countless new units. Alarm units, reactivated units, and the Volkstruum are reinforcing the front. This time the

---

[106] Bessel, 94.
[107] Bessel, 102.

Bolshevist will experience the old fate of Asia i.e. he must and will bleed to death in front of the capital of the German Reich. Whoever does not do his duty at this moment is a traitor to our people. The regiment or division that abandons their position is behaving so disgracefully that they will have to be ashamed in front of the women and children who endure the bombing terror in our cities…Whoever gives you orders to retreat without your knowing him well is to be arrested immediately, and if necessary to be bumped off straight away — no matter what rank he holds. If every soldier on the eastern front does his duty in the coming days and weeks, the last onslaught of Asia will break apart, just as despite everything the breakthrough of our opponents in the west also will fail in the end. Berlin remains German, Vienna will be German again, and Europe will ever be Russian. From a blood brotherhood, not for the defense of an empty notion of father land, but for the defense of your *Heimat*, your wives, your children, and thereby of our future. At this hour the entire German people look to you, my eastern fighters, and hope that only our steadfastness, your fanaticism, through your weapons and under your leadership, the Bolshevik onslaught suffocates in a bloodbath."

Those who had personal contact with Hitler during the days of the Soviet approach to the city described him as physically weak but still fully committed mentally to having German forces fight to the death. General Gotthard Heinrici, commander of army group Vistula, was to defend the line against the Soviets poised to strike at Berlin, but one of Heinrici's operations officers described the German army as "a rabbit, watching spellbound for a snake to strike and devour it".[108] Nonetheless, Hitler remained convinced that all that was needed was a stronger commitment by the fighting men and the following of his orders by his officers; if the Reich fell, it could only be because of traitors inside of Germany's government making deals with the allied powers. The mentality was similar to that harbored by the Nazis and other Germans in the wake of World War I, and the refusal to believe loyal Germans could have been in any way responsible for the defeat in the previous helped pave the way for the next.

---

[108] Simons.

Heinrici

Another factor that kept Hitler in denial until the bitter end was his abiding hope that the Allies would begin to bicker among each other as they approached Berlin, allowing the Germans to sue for a separate peace. Hitler and especially his propaganda leader, Joseph Goebbels, had high hopes of this after the death of Roosevelt in early April, but while the Soviets and other Allies didn't always see eye-to-eye, they all remained determined to finish the war to the point of unconditional surrender.

On April 16th, Zhukov launched his attack from the bridgehead at Kustrin (to the east of Berlin) and planned to take the heights of Seelow in the first day of the offensive. He was under a tight timetable imposed by Stalin, who was worried that the Americans and British intended to beat him to Berlin, but both Zhukov and Stalin proved wrong in their instincts on these two matters. The Americans would not compete to liberate the city, and Zhukov would be delayed by two full days before he could take the Seelow Heights. Zhukov's forces were met with incredible resistance from Germans desperate to defend the largely female and child population of the city, and the German commander had pulled back his forces to the Seelow Heights, where the explosions of Zhukov's artillery fire helped the German forces see the Soviet positions.

A map of the lines at the start of the war and the Soviet encirclement of Berlin

The Germans attempted to counterattack with a panzer unit on the 18th, but that attack failed, and the German fronts along the Oder and Niesse River began to crumble.[109] Zhukov finally took the Seelow heights, but it cost his army 30,000 soldiers. Zhukov's armies faced other problems and heavy fighting that caused delays, but his fellow general to the south, Konev, was making great progress. Stalin gave Konev permission to turn his armies toward Berlin, thus signaling the start of a race between the two Russian officers for the capture of the city, and Hitler's refusals to allow Heinrici to reinforce his army with soldiers defending nearby fortress cities, despite the general's repeated requests, meant that the Soviets were within 20 miles of Berlin by Hitler's 56th birthday, April 20. On April 21, the Soviets reached the cities of Zossen, Erkner, and Hopegarten, making major progress toward the goal of surrounding the city on all sides.

With Hitler more and more disconnected from reality and occasionally giving orders to divisions that no longer existed, the proximity of the Soviet armies was unthinkable to him. As the Soviets began to shell the city, Hitler was "puzzled," to the extent that he wondered aloud whether the Russians had built a railroad bridge over the Oder River and were firing a railroad

[109] Carruthers, Bob, and Willhelm Willemar. Götterdämmerung: The Last Days of the Wehrmacht in the East. Barnsley: Pen & Sword Military, 2012. 14.

siege gun that had a range of 50 miles. When a Luftwaffe officer replied that there was no bridge of that sort in the area and the truth dawned, "Hitler fell silent."[110]

For his part, Heinrici was understandably frustrated, and he eventually sent a message to Hitler that he would resign from his position and fight the rest of the war with the *Volksstrum*, but Hitler replied by saying the 9th army would continue to fight. On April 22, Hitler relieved Heinrici's Vistula of the command of Berlin and took personal command of the city's defense, but the panzer corps that Hitler summoned to Berlin ignored his order and moved further south.

Hitler believed that one of his favorite SS generals, Felix Steiner, could work a miracle by gathering men from various units and the Volksstrum to reform a line of defense at the Oder River. However, when this impossible task went unfulfilled, Hitler lost all emotional control, screaming and crying in front of the Nazi leadership, and it was at this point that his staff first heard the Fuhrer admit that the war was lost and that he would remain in Berlin and commit suicide. As other Nazi leaders decided whether to stay with Hitler and face the prospect of suicide, try to escape from Berlin without detection, or to attempt a negotiation with the enemy in order to reach a deal, Hitler was more and more isolated and less convinced each day that the battle tide could be turned back.

---

[110] Ibid.

Steiner

Moreover, Hitler made a somewhat off–handed comment that Hermann Göring, the World War I ace who led the Luftwaffe in World War II, would have to do the negotiating "since there was not much fighting left to be done." This led to a mistaken message being delivered to Göring, who was subsequently informed that Hitler would step down and allow Göring to negotiate a peace for Germany. When Göring telegraphed the Fuhrer to confirm the news and promise to "act for the best interests of our country and our people," Hitler was convinced by Martin Bormann, a Göring enemy, that Göring was actually trying to wrest leadership from the Fuhrer, and Hitler ordered Göring's arrest as a result. [111]

---

[111]Ibid.,76-78.

Göring

Though General Konev and the general protecting the flanks of both armies, Konstantin Rokossovsky were both important to the Soviet advance on Berlin, it is Zhukov who gets the most credit for the taking of the city. Much has now been written of Zhukov's legacy as a commander, but while his rise to power from a peasant background inspired the admiration of any of his own peasant troops, his ruthlessness on the battlefield at the expense of their very lives compelled many to describe him as an untalented brute. Still, for many Russians, both today and in his own time, Zhukov's bravery and willingness to fight made him a hero of the Soviet cause, and another member of the high command on which Zhukov served said of the general: "In the constellation of Soviet Generals who so conclusively defeated the armies of Nazi Germany, he was the most brilliant of all. At all stages of the war, in strategic, tactical, and organizational matters, Zhukov was always clear-headed and sharp, bold in his decisions, skilled in finding his bearings, in anticipating developments and picking the right instant for a decisive stroke. Making the most of fateful decisions, he was astoundingly cool and level-headed. He was a man of extraordinary courage and self-possession. I have never seen him flustered or depressed not even at critical moments."

Rokossovsky

Zhukov's reputation as a winner on the battlefield is unquestionable, but he remains a controversial figure. After the war, he fell out and then back into favor, and based on political machinations, Stalin almost immediately accused him of corruption and taking credit for the victory. However, later Soviet leaders reinstated Zhukov to positions of power, and after several more cycles of criticism and rehabilitation, he is seen today as one of the Soviet Union's greatest war heroes. At the same time, others put a large share of the blame on Zhukov for the incredibly high casualty rates suffered by the Soviet armies as they advanced on the eastern front. Zhukov once explained to Eisenhower that his method of clearing minefields was to order his soldiers to run through them, and his orders upon being placed as the general in charge of defending Leningrad from German capture read as a threat: "All commanders, political workers, and soldiers who abandon the indicated line without written order from the front or military council will be shot immediately."

Writing of the conditions that Zhukov faced in his own armies, Geoffrey Roberts argues that the Soviet army was composed largely of poor Russians who had been forced into military service and had witnessed the effects of Stalin's collectivization programs at home. The soldiers of the Soviet armies were thus unconvinced that they were fighting for some great cause or great leaders. This, Robert explains, is the reason why it remains "difficult to envisage how such an army could have been held together in the terrifying conditions of the ferocious fighting that obtained during the Soviet German war except by a regime of harsh discipline and exemplary punishment." Roberts estimated that the Soviet armies Zhukov presided over saw the shooting of at least 158,000 of their own men, a measure which Zhukov saw as necessary to maintain discipline. According to Roberts, "There is no hint that Zhukov ever regretted or even had second thoughts about any of the harsh measures he authorized." Of course, Zhukov's ruthlessness in battle benefited him individually at the least, as it would be soldiers from his army, not from Konev's, who would raise the Soviet flag over the Reichstag. It would also be Zhukov who accepted the surrender from the Germans generals the day after V-E Day.

Soviet generals and their men also understood that the taking of the city would come at a high cost. In early April, Soviet generals met to discuss their plan of attack, and by using maps of the city's defenses that had been gathered from aerial photographs and the testimony of German prisoners, the generals concluded that tanks would be of little use in the battle for Berlin. Instead, as Soviet General Mikhail Katukov said, "With dogged, persistent fighting we would only be able to advance step by step and would have to bite our way through the enemy defenses with bloody fighting. However, the victories of our troops in previous battles had given us much confidence. No one doubted that we would sweep aside the whole of the enemy fortifications on the approaches to Berlin".

The Soviet armies moved quickly after April 16, but now that Berlin was in sight, the progress slowed considerably. General Konev explained, "The closer to Berlin, the denser the enemy defenses became, and the enemy infantry were supported by more and more artillery, tanks, and Panzerfaust."[112] If anything, this only provided additional time for Soviet soldiers looking for ways to right the wrongs they believed had been committed by the Germans in Russia. Many historians wrote of the amazement Russian soldiers felt when they saw the sheer amount of foods, consumer goods, and even the condition of the bodies of German women, most of whom had not suffered from hunger in the war like their Russian counterparts. Thus, countless Russian soldiers spent their time destroying rail lines and other infrastructure and sending the materials back home for use in building the Soviet war machine, and capturing Germany's cultural trophies, including art masterpieces that were hidden throughout the Reich, became a way of seeking revenge on the Germans for what they had destroyed.[113] The plunder of Germany was so great that the number of parcels being received in the Soviet Union from soldiers in the Reich had increased by 1,000 times since January 1945. In addition to large amounts of food, "Officers took rare books, paintings, hunting rifles typewriters, bicycles, bedding, clothes, shoes, musical instruments, and especially radios…"[114]

On April 23, Stalin gave the order that Zhukov's armies will be the ones to take Berlin first by declaring a boundary line on the west side of the Reichstag, and though they suffered a setback on April 24, they were able to close off Berlin from the west by the end of the day. On April 25,

---

[112] Simons,78.
[113] Evans, 708.
[114] Ibid., 709.

the Soviets made their first contact with the Americans near Torgau, Germany.

Picture of an American soldier and Red Army soldier embracing in front of a sign that reads "East Meets West" at Torgau

On April 26, Zhukov and Konev launched an attack against the propaganda ministry building, taking sniper fire, counterattacks, and ambushes from the cover of rubble left across the city by British and American air power. Nonetheless, the Soviets gained control of both airfields, ending German flights out of Berlin from that point forward, and the following day, the Soviets reached the Postdammerstrasse Bridge. The following morning, they began an attack on Berlin's zoo, the Tiergarten, where many Germans had taken refuge.

A flak tower manned outside of Berlin's zoo

A tower located at the zoo

By April 28th, the Soviets issued an order for occupation of Berlin which placed all political and administrative powers of the city in Soviet hands. The surrounding of Berlin meant, to the Soviets, that it was only a matter of time before the city would be completely in their hands.[115] The next day, Hitler learned that Göring believed he had been named Hitler's successor and that

---

[115] Windsor, Philip. City on Leave: *A History of Berlin, 1945-1962*(London: Chatto and Windus), 1963. 32.

Himmler has been negotiating with the Allies through the Swiss. Later that day, he dictated his last will and testament to Tradl Junge, one of his personal secretaries.[116]

In the meantime, the Soviets were advancing towards the heart of Berlin, and on April 30, the Soviets seized several government buildings while sustaining heavy losses. Three failed assaults on the Reichstag meant more losses, but the Soviets were able to establish a path for their tanks to be put to use beyond an anti-tank dam that had guarded the building, as well as establish defenses behind their armies to prevent an attack from the rear. At about 2:30 in the afternoon, a rumor circulated that the Soviet flag had been raised over the Reichstag, and with many units eager to be the ones to hoist their colors over the city, the report was assumed to be true, so Zhukov cabled a declaration to headquarters. Later, as the armies arrived in the Konigsberg Plaza, they came to a realization that no flag had been raised and that the plaza was only halfway under Soviet control. It was then absolutely necessary to take the Reichstag or face the wrath of General Stalin, but it would take another 10 hours of fierce hand-to-hand combat throughout the Reichstag building that the Soviet banner unit found their way up a back staircase and wedged the banner's flag into a crevice of a statue found on the roof. That evening, the Soviet flag finally flew over the city, and Alexander V. Pyl'cyn, a Soviet soldier, recalled seeing the Soviet-held Reichstag upon entering the city: "Smoke was still streaming from some of the windows of the large, dark building. It did not look magnificent at all! The red banner, our Soviet banner, was flying high over the skeleton of the former glass dome! That was not a mere flag. That was a banner of victory!"[117]

Picture of a soldier holding a Soviet flag atop the Reichstag

[116] Kershaw, Ian. *Hitler: A Biography.* New York: W.W. Norton and Company. 948.
[117] Alexander V. Pyl'cyn. *Penalty Strike: The Memoirs of a Red Army Penal Company Commander, 1943-45.* 168.

The Reichstag after the fighting

Of course, the most memorable event that took place on April 30 didn't involve combat. Instead, that is the day Hitler committed one of the most infamous suicides in history, shooting himself in his underground bunker some time after coming to the realization that Germany had no hope of winning the war. Suicide had become such an accepted idea in the underground bunker that all of Hitler's associates had been issued capsules of prussic acid with which to end their lives when the time came. Over the previous week, Hitler had come to speak openly of his plan to kill himself, blaming the "traitors" who proved unable to defend the city of Berlin and the German people for their lack of will in the fight. To die for the German cause was honorable, he believed, and his loyalty to the Berliners he had chosen to stay with until the end would become part of his legacy. He asked those who pressured him to leave and govern from elsewhere in Germany, "How am I to call on the troops to undertake the battle for Berlin if at the same moment I withdraw myself to safety?"[118]

Having tested an arsenic pill on his dog the day before, Hitler arranged for himself and his new wife, Eva Braun, to spend their last minutes alone. Braun, reclining on a couch, took her own life with a poison capsule, while Hitler was found with a gunshot to his head. Hitler had given orders that their bodies be thoroughly consumed lest the Soviets seek to desecrate the memory of the Fuhrer, and some witnesses remembered that he became adamant on this point after seeing the treatment of Mussolini's body by Italian leftists.

Hitler and Braun

Many who had been with Hitler in the last days of the war chose a similar fate. The next most infamous deaths were those of Hitler's propaganda minister, Joseph Goebbels, his wife Magda, and their 6 children, aged 4-12. Their deaths took place on May 1, 1945. The children, put to sleep with morphine and subsequently poisoned with cyanide, were immediately followed to their deaths by their parents, who were shot in the Chancellery gardens. In a letter to her son in an African POW camp, Magda Goebbels wrote of her decision: "We have been in the Fuhrerbunker for six days already— daddy, your six little siblings and I, for the sake of giving our national socialistic lives the only possible honourable end...You know your mother— we have the same blood, for me there was no wavering. Our glorious idea is ruined and with it everything beautiful and marvelous that I have known in my life. The world that comes after the Fuhrer and National Socialism is not any longer worth living in and therefore I took the children with me, for they are too good for the life that would follow, and a merciful God will understand me when I will give them the salvation...May God help that I have the strength to perform the

[118] Marshall Cavendish, History of World War II, vol. 3 (New York: Marshall Cavendish, 2005), 768, https://www.questia.com/read/120564463.

last and the hardest. We have only one goal left - loyalty to the Fuhrer even in death."[119]

The Goebbels family (with the picture altered to include the oldest son)
David Beisel, professor of Social Sciences at the State College of New York, discussed the concept of suicide in Berlin particularly and in the greater Reich. Several reasons for what Beisel called a European "preoccupation" with suicide exist. First, some desired to simply follow Hitler to his death, as seen in Magda Goebbels's desire to be "faithful" to the Fuhrer even after his own self-inflicted death. Some could not face the disillusionment that came with the German defeat, which "had shown the notion of Aryan superiority to be a sham: how could a superior race have been defeated by 'inferior Russians?'"[120] Still others believed that a world without Hitler's ideals could not be faced, and that any world without the ideas of National Socialism was not worth living in. Lastly, some committed suicide in a response to their own emotions of fear and failure.

Whether they took their own lives (and in many cases the lives of their own wives and children in the process) in fear of what would happen when the Russians came, or in the shadow of the "failure" to being about Hitler' plans for domination over all of Europe (and the fear of retribution), those that died at their own hands were many, and Beisel contends that the phenomenon has been overlooked by historians. [121]

---

[119] Knopp, Guido. Hitler's Women. Psychology Press, 2003. 101.
[120] Beisel David R. "The German Suicide, 1945." The Journal of Psychohistory. Spring, 2007. 34.
[121] Ibid.

Picture of a street in Berlin with heavy damage

In October 1944, the Russians had taken their first German village, Nemmersdorf in East Prussia, and though they would not hold the village for long, the taking of it proved particularly brutal. The extreme violence and mutilation that the Soviet soldiers wreaked there helped to spread the already-present fear of Soviet troops and the worry about having to surrender to the Soviet army throughout Germany. Stalin's thoughts on the behavior of his armies helped to perpetuate their behavior; in defending the actions of his soldiers to a Yugoslavian freedom fighter who had criticized them for violence and rape, Stalin replied, "Yes, you have, of course, read Dostoevsky? Do you see what a complicated thing is man's soul, man's psyche? Well then, imagine a man who had fought from Stalingrad to Belgrade--over thousands of kilometers of his own devastated land, across the dead bodies of comrades and dearest ones! How can such a man react normally? And what is so awful in his having fun with a woman, after such horrors? . . . We opened up our penitentiaries and stuck everybody in the army. The Red Army is not ideal. The important thing is that it fights Germans--and it is fighting them well, while the rest doesn't matter."[122]

German military estimates put the total population at the outbreak of the Battle of Berlin at 2.7 million people, but 2 million of them were women. With the young and able-bodied men already fighting on the battlefield and the able and active now serving in citizen defense groups, males in the city were largely children or the elderly. For this and other reasons, Berliners greatly feared that a Russian attack on Berlin would result in a widespread rape of the city's inhabitants, and while this fear was certainly reinforced by Nazi propaganda intent on painting the Soviets as inhuman, it was also based in reality. Reports had already come in from refugees who had experienced the Soviet treatment firsthand and doctors who were witnesses to the results of such attacks. Cornelius Ryan wrote of one female gynecologist who started carrying a cyanide pill as a result, a practice that was mirrored by many residents of the city; the means to end one's own life was considered by many a necessity unless, it could be hoped, the Americans or British reached Berlin first.[123]

In plenty of cases, suicide would have unquestionably been a more palatable option. Evans charges that though "women and girls were subjected to serial rape wherever they were encountered", in Berlin it was often done in front of male family members, who would likely be killed if they attempted to intervene.[124] Victims of rape were often, though not always, shot after the soldiers had had their way, and estimates of the numbers of women raped in Berlin itself were "at least 100,000", according to hospital estimates.[125] To avoid such a fate, many German women attempted to dirty themselves, dress as children (it was believed the brutal Soviet soldiers would treat smaller children with kindness), or hide in garbage cans, under mattresses, and anywhere else they could think of that might keep them from attack. One Berlin woman described their plight: "The next morning, we women proceeded to make ourselves look as unattractive as possible to the Soviets by smearing our faces with coal dust and covering our heads with old rags, our make-up for the Ivan. We huddled together in the central part of the basement, shaking with fear, while some peeked through the low basement windows to see what was happening on the Soviet-controlled street. We felt paralyzed by the sight of these husky Mongolians, looking wild and frightening. At the ruin across the street from us the first Soviet orders were posted, including a curfew. Suddenly there was a shattering noise outside. Horrified, we watched the Soviets demolish the corner grocery store and throw its contents, shelving and furniture out into the street. Urgently needed bags of flour, sugar and rice were split open and spilled their contents on the bare pavement, while Soviet soldiers stood guard with their rifles so that no one would dare to pick up any of the urgently needed food. This was just unbelievable. At night, a few desperate people tried to salvage some of the spilled food from the gutter. Hunger now became a major concern because our ration cards were worthless with no hope of any supplies. Shortly thereafter, there was another commotion outside, even worse than before, and we rushed to our lookout to see that the Soviets had broken into the bank and were looting it. They came out yelling gleefully with their hands full of German bank notes and jewelry from safe deposit boxes that had been pried open. Thank God we had withdrawn money already and had it at home."

Discussion on the atrocities committed by the advancing Soviet armies has been a subject of discussion amongst historians since the end of the war. Some have proposed the theory that the

---

[122] Djilas qtd. in Martin K. Sorge, The Other Price of Hitler's War: German Military and Civilian Losses Resulting from World War II (New York: Greenwood Press, 1986), 118, https://www.questia.com/read/26184632.
[123] Ibid, 31.
[124] Evans, 701-711.
[125] Ibid.

actions of the Soviet troops were a result of great chaos as the war came to a close. According to this view, Soviet soldiers were growing restless and disorderly, and as their commanders lost control, the German people suffered the brunt of it as the Soviets advanced. However, others think differently. Richard Evans, author of *The Third Reich at War*, argued, "The atrocities they committed were a symptom not of the breakdown of discipline and morale, but of the group cohesion and collective mentality forged in the heat of battle…The Germans had plundered and destroyed, so why should they not do the same?"[126]

In fact, several sources record that Soviet officers, upon entering a city, would occasionally warn the German women about the Russian soldiers behind them. As one Soviet officer recorded in his journal, "The rape of girls--it is not justifiable…The soldiers have done a lot. But this behavior is now being countered. Yet enough has been done to have the Germans cross themselves a hundred years from now in memory of the winter of 44/45." As this makes clear, there was knowledge of the situation amongst the Russian leadership, and even an acknowledgement that it was wrong. It was not unheard of for a Russian officer to awake the morning after an alcohol-fueled attack on a local woman and send her a package of food and supplies by way of apology, penance, or to assuage guilt.

Certainly, the average Russian soldier was motivated by a mixture of revenge, anger, bravado, and alcohol, but many of them claimed their violent treatment of other Germans was nothing more than payback for what Germans had done during their invasion of Russia. Most historical records do not record the German armies taking part in any type of widespread sexual assaults in their invasion of the Soviet Union, but their notoriously shocking treatment and ruthless killing of Russian men, women, and children (including babies) is documented. Far from being above using rape because of their moral standards, rape as a weapon of war would likely have been looked upon with horror by a German army indoctrinated with messages about German hygiene and the subhuman nature of the Slavic people.

Regardless, the soviets believed Germans could only learn through the harshest of treatment. Since Germany had entered Russia with ferocity and aggression, it became "absolutely clear that if we [the Soviets] don't really scare them now, there will be no way of avoiding another war in the future".[127]

---

[126] Evans, 709.
[127] Ibid., 710.

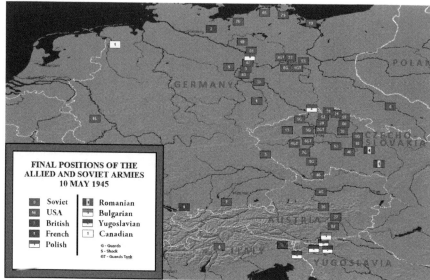

The lines at the end of World War II

The Battle of Berlin ended with an inevitable Soviet triumph, but by the time Germany officially surrendered, the Soviets had suffered over 350,000 casualties and had lost thousands of artillery batteries and armored vehicles. The Germans had suffered upwards of 100,000 dead and over 200,000 wounded, not to mention the horrors visited upon the civilian population in the wake of the battle.

With the fighting mostly coming to an end on May 2, the chain of German surrenders in the field outside of Berlin took off like dominoes. Field Marshal Wilhelm Keitel signed Germany's unconditional surrender on May 7, and news of the final surrender of the Germans was celebrated as Victory in Europe (V-E) day on May 8, 1945. Churchill delivered the following remarks to cheering crowds:

"My dear friends, this is your hour. This is not victory of a party or of any class. It's a victory of the great British nation as a whole. We were the first, in this ancient island, to draw the sword against tyranny. After a while we were left all alone against the most tremendous military power that has been seen. We were all alone for a whole year.

There we stood, alone. Did anyone want to give in? Were we down-hearted? The lights went out and the bombs came down. But every man, woman and child in the country had no thought of quitting the struggle. London can take it. So we came back after long months from the jaws of death, out of the mouth of hell, while all the world wondered. When shall the reputation and faith of this generation of English men and women fail? I say that in the long years to come not only will the people of this island but of the world, wherever the bird of freedom chirps in human hearts, look back to what we've done and they will say 'do not despair, do not yield to violence and tyranny, march straightforward and die if need be-unconquered.'"

Pictures of the Germans' unconditional surrender on May 7

Of course, the announcement of surrender was met with a far different emotion among the Germans, as one Berliner remembered: "The next day, General Wilding, the commander of the German troops in Berlin, finally surrendered the entire city to the Soviet army. There was no radio or newspaper, so vans with loudspeakers drove through the streets ordering us to cease all resistance. Suddenly, the shooting and bombing stopped and the unreal silence meant that one ordeal was over for us and another was about to begin. Our nightmare had become a reality. The entire three hundred square miles of what was left of Berlin were now completely under control of the Red Army. The last days of savage house to house fighting and street battles had been a human slaughter, with no prisoners being taken on either side. These final days were hell. Our last remaining and exhausted troops, primarily children and old men, stumbled into imprisonment. We were a city in ruins; almost no house remained intact."

The controversy over Eisenhower's decision not to press for Berlin remains, but any debate over whether the Allied armies were in a position to take Berlin must acknowledge the fact that the most significant American forces were over 200 miles from Berlin in mid-April. Nonetheless, others point to smaller American forces that were within 50 miles of the city before being told to move in the opposite direction.

The strongest critiques of Eisenhower's decisions portray him as naïve about the consequences, or as an unwitting tool of the Soviets, but his defenders call his decision "dead on".[128] Soviet

---

[128] Kevin Baker, "General Discontent: Blaming Powell-And Eisenhower-For Not Having Pushed Through. (in the

casualties in taking the city rivaled those lost by the Allies at the Battle of the Bulge, and considering the earlier agreements with Stalin, General Omar Bradley believed that the Americans would have to pay "a pretty stiff price to pay for a prestige objective, especially when we've got to fall back and let the other fellow take over."[129]

Eisenhower vigorously defended himself against criticism upon his return from the war, pointing out that those who criticized his position on the issue were not the ones who would have been forced to comfort the grieving mothers of soldiers killed in an unnecessary fight to take Berlin. During his 1952 presidential campaign, he faced further criticism, and in response, he emphasized his warnings about the danger of the Soviet threat to Europe rather than discuss his decision to stay away from Berlin. Historian Stephen Ambrose saw this attempt at self-salvation by Eisenhower as wishful thinking, and that there was no evidence of Eisenhower warning against the Soviet threat to Europe during his time as general: "The truth was that he may have wished by 1952 that he had taken a hard line with the Russians in 1945, but he had not".[130]

Controversies aside, generations continue to look back at World War II as the most important event of the 20th century. Much has been written about the leaders, the armies, the causes, and the battles, but the city of Berlin, representing for the world Hitler's stronghold and control, had to be taken in order for the war to come to an end. Berlin would be given no quarter in the weeks and months to come, and when it was divided by the Allies, Berlin became the center of a proxy war between the two great superpowers that emerged from the war.

Online Resources

Other World War II titles by Charles River Editors

Bibliography

Addington, Scott. *The Third Reich: A Layman's Guide.* Online/Amazon, 2014.

Brown, Timothy S. *Weimar Radicals: Nazis and Communists Between Authenticity and Performance.* New York City, 2009.

Evans, Richard J. *The Coming of the Third Reich.* New York, 2005. (Reprint.)

Evans, Richard J. *The Third Reich in Power.* New York City, 2006.

Gilbert, Martin and Richard Gott. *The Appeasers: the Decline of Democracy from Hitler's Rise to Chamberlain's Downfall.* Boston, 1963.

Hughes, R. Gerald. "The Ghosts of Appeasement: Britain and the Legacy of the Munich Agreement." Journal of Contemporary History, Volume 48, Number 4, pp. 688–716, 2013.

Jurga, Tadeusz. *Bzura 1939.* Warsaw, 1984.

Kershaw, Ian. *Hitler: A Biography.* London, 2008.

Kurowski, Franz. *The Brandenburger Commandos: Germany's Elite Warrior Spies in World War II.* Mechanicsburg, 1997.

Leibovitz, Clement, and Alvin Finkel. *In Our Time: The Chamberlain-Hitler Collusion.* New York, 1997.

Manchester, William. *The Last Lion: Winston Spencer Churchill Alone, 1932 – 1940.* London, 1988.

McDonough, Frank. *Neville Chamberlain, Appeasement, and the British Road to War.* Manchester, 1998.

Parssinen, Terry. *The Oster Conspiracy of 1938.* New York, 2003.

Prazmowska, Anita J. *Britain and Poland, 1939-1943: The Betrayed Ally.* Cambridge, 1995.

News)," American Heritage, November-December 2002, https://www.questia.com/read/1G1-93611493.
[129] Ibid.
[130] Ibid.

Shirer, William L. *Berlin Diary: The Journal of a Foreign Correspondent, 1934-1941,* New York, 1942.

Shirer, William L., and Rosenbaum, Ron. *The Rise and Fall of the Third Reich: A History of Nazi Germany.* (Electronic edition.) New York City, 2011.

Snyder, Timothy. *Bloodlands: Europe Between Hitler and Stalin.* New York, 2010.

Stewart, Graham. *Burying Caesar: the Churchill-Chamberlain Rivalry.* Woodstock, 2001.

Williamson, David G. *Poland Betrayed: The Nazi-Soviet Invasions of 1939.* Barnsley, 2009.

Zaloga, Steven J. *Poland 1939: The Birth of Blitzkrieg.* Oxford, 2002.

Free Books by Charles River Editors

We have brand new titles available for free most days of the week. To see which of our titles are currently free, click on this link.

Discounted Books by Charles River Editors

We have titles at a discount price of just 99 cents everyday. To see which of our titles are currently 99 cents, click on this link.

77293972R10424